A Handbook of
Integrative Psychotherapies for
Children and Adolescents

A Handbook of Integrative Psychotherapies for Children and Adolescents

Sebastiano Santostefano

Dear Patty,

With appreciation of
your dedication to the
mission of ICAD and
to your invaluable
contributions. Who would have
thought that from our
first days in the classroom
at BC we would be traveling
the same journey

JASON ARONSON INC.
Northvale, New Jersey
London

Seb
3-18-98

Director of Editorial Production: Robert D. Hack

This book was set in 10 pt. Adobe Caslon by Alpha Graphics of Pittsfield, NH and printed and bound by Book-mart Press, Inc. of North Bergen, NJ.

Library of Congress Cataloging-in-Publication Data

Santostefano, Sebastiano, 1929-
    A handbook of integrative psychotherapies for children and adolescents / Sebastiano Santostefano.
        p. cm.
    Includes bibliographical references and index.
    ISBN 0-7657-0083-2 (alk. paper)
    1. Child psychotherapy—Philosophy.   2. Adolescent psychotherapy—Philosophy.   3. Eclectic psychotherapy.   4. Child psychotherapy—Case studies.   5. Adolescent psychotherapy—Case studies.
    I. Title.
    RJ504.S25   1998
    618.92'8914—DC21   97-10315

Printed in the United States of America on acid-free paper. For information and catalog write to Jason Aronson Inc., 230 Livingston Street, Northvale, New Jersey 07647-1726. Or visit our website: http://www.aronson.com

Contents

To Susan, our cave, and its treasures
that continue to grow within
in spite of storms without:
Damon, Natalie, Stephanie, Jessica, and Cristiano.
And to our Sebbie whose brilliant flight
continues in another world.

Preface

According to Schnider (1990), psychology is at a critical crossroads. One of the forces the discipline faces, which I believe applies equally to child psychotherapy, is a centrifugal trend that results in disunity, divisiveness, and self-limiting specialization. Paraphrasing a quote from his illuminating discussion, child therapists read only what they must to help them in their own specialty. The specialties in child therapy are well known, each segregated from the other: psychodynamic therapy, cognitive therapy, behavioral therapy, and cognitive-behavioral therapy. And most therapists have been trained to conceptualize their work in one of these frameworks (Schacht 1984). Three clinical reports that appeared nearly a century ago could be viewed as forecasting this segregation.

In 1905 Shephard Ivory Franz described his efforts to train a patient, who had a paralytic stroke, to speak. His goal was to teach the patient the name of familiar colors, numerical digits, four lines from a written text, and the German word for pen, a piece of information the patient did not have as part of his past. In his attempt to achieve this goal, Franz designed techniques that reflect present day principles of cognitive therapy. First, he selected a finite amount of information for the patient to master—6 colors, 9 numerical digits, and 1 line of a text. Moreover, he presented the patient with information in a step-wise fashion, starting with simple patterns of information and gradually shifting to more complex ones. Further, he presented a given piece of information repeatedly, a few minutes each day, over many days. In carefully prescribing the complexity of information, and in repeatedly asking the patient to manage it, Franz suggested that a cognitive "habit" or function was being structured.

In 1909 Freud reported the treatment of a five-year-old boy, conducted by his father and supervised by Freud. This case set the stage for the emphasis given in psychodynamic child psychotherapy to the use of interpretation as the main tool that brings unconscious motives to conscious awareness, thereby resolving conflict and relieving the problem behavior. The boy was afraid that horses would bite him, a fear that generalized to other large animals. Freud stated his broad treatment plan clearly, "I arranged with Hans' father that he should tell the boy that all this business about horses was a piece of nonsense and nothing more. The truth was, his father was to say, that he was fond of his mother and wanted to be taken into her bed. The reason he was afraid of horses now was that he had taken so much interest in their widdlers as well as his own" (p. 28). And so, over many months, father delivered interpretations to his son that would gradually "enlighten him" of the notion that his oedipal longings for mother resulted in the fear that he would lose his widdler at the bite of horses—e.g., Hans, "Don't put your finger to the white horse; it'll bite you." Father responded, "I say, it strikes me that it isn't the horse you mean, but a widdler, that one mustn't put one's hand to" (p. 29).

In 1924 Mary Cover Jones described her attempts to help Peter overcome his fear of rabbits and furry objects, using a technique that forecast the emergence of behavioral therapies. She extinguished the fear by pairing the noxious stimulus (a caged rabbit) with pleasurable stimuli and responses (eating food). Initially, while the child ate at a table, the caged rabbit was placed at some distance. Over a number of meals, as the child showed no signs of fear, the cage was moved closer, step by step. In the last phase, the rabbit was released at the table while the child ate happily.

After these first clinical reports representing the beginnings of different approaches, segregation in psychotherapy was, and is, tenaciously maintained. However, during the past several years, interest in psychotherapy integration has been growing (Garfield 1994). This interest is reflected by the formation of the Society for the Exploration of Psychotherapy Integration (SEPI), the journal this society launched in 1991, and by the appearance of two handbooks (Norcross and Goldfried 1992, Stricker and Gold 1993). Interest in integration is also reflected by paradigm shifts that have been occurring in each camp of psychotherapy. Cognitive and behavioral therapists are becoming interested in learning about clients from the inside (their meanings and fantasies) as well as from overt behaviors and conscious thoughts, while psychodynamic therapists are becoming interested in learning about clients from the outside (aspects of relationships that are corrective) as well as from inferred unconscious motives and meanings (Messer and Winokur 1984). Stimulated by these developments, debates among segregated camps of adult psychotherapy are ongoing (Mahoney 1993, Wachtel 1994).

However, it is my impression that mainstream child psychotherapy remains severely segregated and that, relative to the field of adult psychotherapy, little or no attention is being paid to integration. This impression is derived from my teaching courses and presenting at programs, over the years, that have been attended by graduate students in clinical, school, counseling and social work programs, psychiatric residents, and trainees in child psychoanalysis. This volume is intended to contribute to the desegregation of child psychotherapy, provide one model of integration, and stimulate interest in integration. Therefore, the reader will not find cookbook recipes that define how one should conduct psychotherapy with children and adolescents who have been assigned to one or another diagnostic category, although such volumes are available (Reinecke and Dattilio 1996). Instead the reader will find a therapeutic model with technical guidelines, framed within a developmental-dialectical perspective, resulting from integrating child psychotherapies that can be applied to all or most children, whatever their diagnoses. The model and methods I present to stimulate interest in integrating child psychotherapies evolved over the past three decades, influenced by the continuous interpenetration of my research activities and clinical experiences.

My interest in integration has roots in childhood experiences which I have discussed elsewhere (Santostefano, in press). But beginning with the adolescence of my professional development, after military service as a medic, I enrolled in the University of Connecticut and decided to switch from a pre-med major to psychology, discovering that I was fascinated by philosophy and the mind. However, at the time and in that program, behaviorism and animal research were emphasized, leaving me with the nagging feeling that the dilemmas of life were not being addressed. Yet, I was fascinated by the animal experiments of Gestalt psychology which were not part of the ethos of behaviorism. Familiar to some, one classic experiment went something like this: a monkey was placed in a cage, along with a stick and chair. A banana hung out of reach on a string from the ceiling. Leaping, the monkey reached for the banana but to no avail. Then the monkey took the stick and swung at the banana, or stood on the chair reaching upwards, repeatedly trying each solution and still failing to retrieve the banana. After many efforts, the "sacred moment" of insight came. The monkey stood on the chair, stick in hand, reached up and easily obtained the banana. Experiments such as these aroused in me what were then vague notions about the relation between action and insight, and the importance of integrating action and their meanings with cognitive activity, notions that would surface in graduate school and eventually find their way into my views concerning psychotherapy with children.

While attending graduate school, we were assigned undergraduates who had applied for treatment. One of my cases, a member of the varsity wrestling team, from time to time asked to walk around outside or sit on the steps. I noticed that the thoughts and feelings which he experienced when walking about were different from those he experienced when sitting in the office. And I noticed that particular memories about his mother occurred to him when he repeatedly rubbed the palm of his hand against the cement steps. My supervisor, William Snyder, representing one prevailing view (still maintained in some quarters) that therapy should take place in an office, advised me to explore within myself why I went outside. But he did listen to my wondering whether there was more to what happens in therapy than reflections and interpretations by the therapist. Influenced by such questions, I conducted research for my doctoral dissertation on the topic of actions as measures of personality (Santostefano 1960, 1962) which later continued as a program of studies on the relations among action, fantasy, and language as modes of expression (Santostefano 1965a,b, 1968a,b, 1977).

After receiving my doctorate, I enrolled in a two-year post doctoral program in clinical child psychology at the University of Colorado Medical Center where I was supervised by psychoanalytically oriented psychologists and psychoanalysts to whom I am indebted (John Conger, John Benjamin, Gaston Blom, and others).

After completing my post doctoral, I continued on the staff of the University of Colorado Medical Center and, with the benefit of an NIMH Career Teacher Award, spent time with George Klein and David Rapaport, two psychologists-psychoanalysts. These tutorials sparked my interest in understanding cognitive functioning within personality and development, an interest which also lead to a series of initial studies (Santostefano 1964a,b). In addition, while continuing clinical work, I participated in several research projects which provided me with the opportunity to continue my interest in studying the meanings of actions and gestures. As one example, in a study of monozygotic twin children, I asked each twin (with the other absent) to stand on one of two wooden boxes which were identical with the exception that one box was half the height of the other. The actions the twins took predicted which child was dominant and which deferent in their relationship as determined later by treatment sessions.

Throughout this time I was receiving intensive supervision in child psychotherapy. However, my studies of the relations among action, cognition, meaning, and development continually impacted what I did in treatment sessions. As one example, I began twice-weekly sessions with "Albert" in the best way I knew at the time and within the psychoanalytic tradition to which I had made a commitment. I entered each session sustained by the conviction that if I could help this boy successfully resolve his unconscious conflicts, he would loosen his constriction and inhibition and perform better at home and school. However, as treatment progressed, I noticed behaviors which suggested to me that whatever else troubled this boy, he simply was not experiencing stimulation around him, stimulation *I* took for granted *he* was taking for granted. For example, when touching surfaces of different textures, he did not spontaneously show signs that he was aware of differences. And when we entered the playroom one day, he did not react to the fact that furniture and play material had been completely rearranged by housekeeping staff since our last session. I wondered whether what I was observing was related to the fact that his mother was hospitalized for six months before he reached his second birthday. At that time in the psychoanalytic camp, little attention was paid to the significance for psychotherapy of the first two years of life, since the focus was on the years beyond the age of three-four and how a child resolved her/his Oedipal conflict.

Now and then I interrupted my nondirected format, which emphasized dialogue Albert and I exchanged while we "played," and asked him to join me in various activities. For example, we went outside to have a "feeling contest." I closed my eyes and Albert placed my fingers on one of the bricks that made up the wall surrounding the clinic. Then he lifted my hand away and again placed my fingers on a brick. My job was to decide whether I was feeling the same or a different brick. Then Albert took a turn. And whenever Albert stepped out of his robotic mode, I took him outside and set up a series of contests, each requiring a different degree of assertiveness and delay (e.g., hurling tennis balls at a tree trunk and lobbing them into a wastebasket). When I reviewed these sessions with one supervisor, an excellent clinical psychoanalyst who, however, was not into research, he became puzzled and annoyed. I will never forget one of his comments: "I don't know what you're doing; but I *do* know that what you're doing is not psychotherapy." I had not yet learned, nor had my supervisor, about London's (1964) book which appeared at this time. Discovered much later by me, London analyzed "insight" and "action" therapies and argued that therapy which attempts to integrate action and insight might be more effective for a wider range of problems than one that emphasizes only one of these approaches.

In the early adulthood of my professional career, I left Colorado and joined the faculty at Clark University, the home of Heinz Werner and organismic-developmental psychology, where I learned more about relations among body perceptions, cognitive functioning, and development from Seymour Wapner and other colleagues. A few years later I joined the faculty of the Boston University School of Medicine where, stimulated by discussions with Louis Sander and Gerald Stechler, psychoanalytically oriented, infant researchers, I became interested in how observations of infants provide a way of understanding how experiences that occur in the first two years of life contribute to later development. During my tenure at Clark University and Boston University School of Medicine, I completed training in adult and child psychoanalysis.

These early research and clinical experiences, and exposure to the organismic-developmental viewpoint and psychoanalytically oriented infant research, along with my own training in psychoanalysis, converged into research conducted with populations of clinical and public school children that concerned cognitive functioning and the relations among action, fantasy, and language as modalities of expression (e.g., Santostefano 1977, 1978, 1986). This work influenced my initial proposal concerning the treatment of children, that: clinicians should move beyond nosology and diagnose from the viewpoint of development (Santostefano 1971); principles of infant development could be a useful guide in conducting psychotherapy with children (Santostefano and Berkowitz 1976); and therapists should address cognitive functioning within personality and interrelate what a child does, imagines, and says (Santostefano 1980b).

I next assumed a position as director of the department of child and adolescent psychology, McLean Hospital/Harvard Medical School where I continued my clinical work and research for twenty-years, a phase I consider the middle age of my professional career. I continued studies of the relations among action, cognition, meanings, and emotion (Santostefano 1978, 1985, Santostefano and Moncata 1989, Santostefano and Rieder 1984), and at the same time focused on constructing an integrative approach to psychotherapy with children. With my first attempt, I described treatment guidelines that integrated cognitive development and psychodynamic psychotherapy, on the one hand, (Santostefano 1978, 1995a) and, on the other, guidelines that integrated what a child does, imagines, and says within psychodynamic psychotherapy (1986b, 1988b). I elaborated this integration (Santostefano and Calicchia 1992), emphasizing the importance of the first two years of life, and the relationship and enactments between child and therapist rather than interpretation and self talk. I also reported a series of studies (Santostefano 1995b) that illustrated the heuristic value for psychotherapy of integrating embodied meanings, overt behaviors, cognition, and emotion.

◧ ◧ ◧

This volume integrates, elaborates, and extends these earlier reports. Chapter 1 discusses the need for integration in child psychotherapy, some of the obstacles to integration, and why the field should be desegregated before integration can be considered. Chapter 2 articulates segregation that has persisted in psychology, between objective and subjective knowledge, body and mind, and cognition and emotion, while Chapter 3 considers how the practice of segregation has influenced child psychotherapy. If boundaries are removed, and segregation dissolved, issues emerge, outlined in Chapter 4, that should be considered when integrating child psychotherapies. Chapters 5 and 6 describe an integrative model, the glue for which relies upon developmental and dialectical principles. These principles, which derive from observations of infants during the first two years of life, are extended into childhood and adolescence, emphasizing how cognitive functioning is embedded in personality functioning and adaptation, and how what a child does, imagines, and says become interrelated. Relying on this developmental-dialectical model, Chapter 7 outlines guidelines for conducting a form of integrative psychotherapy consisting of a continuum of structured and unstructured interactions, discusses assessments the model indicates are necessary to plan treatment, details how change is conceptualized and the catalysts that promote change, considers where therapy could take place, and considers what the emphasis should be during the first sessions child and therapist share. Case illustrations of structured interactions are described in Chapter 8 and of unstructured interactions in Chapter 9. Diagnosis from the viewpoint of the proposed developmental-dialectical model, versus the viewpoint of nosology, is considered in Chapter 10, as well as a series of research studies that illustrate the types of questions raised, and the methods devised to answer them when the proposed model is followed. The final chapter condenses several major themes developed throughout.

This volume is intended for students learning about psychotherapy with children and adolescents who may not have yet become hardened psychodynamic, or cognitive, or behavioral therapists, and therefore may be more open to integration. This volume is also intended for their teachers and supervisors in the hope that they may become interested in the heuristic value of integration. I am sure that some of my psychodynamic colleagues, when considering this text, will conclude that I have omitted one or another consideration at the heart of their approach, and that some of my cognitive-behavioral colleagues will come to the same conclusion. I very likely have. But my intention was to present enough of each approach to set the stage for a discussion of integration. Therefore, while I present one model of integration, my main interest is in stimulating as much interest in the topic of integration among child psychotherapists as there appears to be among adult psychotherapists.

I conclude with expressions of gratitude and appreciation to my wife, Susan, who has gathered much experience and knowledge from her five "in-vivo internships," each involving her raising our five children—experience and knowledge which she astutely applies in her clinical work and brings to our discussions. I am also grateful to the many colleagues from whom I have learned as I have tried to contribute to their training and development, notably Dr. Scott Creighton, Dr. Patricia Burke, and Dr. Michael Robbins.

1

The Need to Desegregate Child Psychotherapy and Obstacles to Integration

CONTENTS

In this volume I articulate issues that I propose should be considered by those interested in integrating concepts and methods from two or more of the following schools of psychotherapy and theory: psychodynamic, behavioral, cognitive, and developmental. In addition, I present a conceptual model and therapeutic techniques for conducting psychotherapy with children and adolescents that integrate views from each of these schools.

At first glance the reader may exclaim, "Another type of psychotherapy! Aren't there enough of them?" The exclamation is warranted: according to one survey (Kazdin 1988), there are 230 forms of therapy in use with children. But my main interest is not to present "another type" of psychotherapy as such and convince the reader to embrace it. My goal is more ambitious and difficult. It is my hope that the integrative model and rationale described here will stimulate the reader to step out of the present-day, segregated world of psychotherapy and into a world of psychotherapy that has no boundaries. If I am successful in assisting the reader with this task, then he/she, whether a beginning or experienced therapist, should be in a position to search for other forms of integration. To pursue this goal, I take the reader, in this and the next three chapters, on several journeys, which cover landscape not ordinarily traveled by textbooks on child psychotherapy.

There are several reasons why these preliminary journeys are necessary. Although there are 230 forms of therapy in use with children, only three broad approaches are dominant at this time: cognitive, behavioral, and psychodynamic. Moreover, these schools remain segregated for the most part, each holding to its beliefs, while ignoring or rejecting those of the others. Therefore, it is necessary that we first desegregate the world of child psychotherapy. But this is not a simple task, if we consider proverbs quoted by Colby and Stoller (1988): "Each sect has its truth, and every truth has its sect," and "Out of all delusions we select one, one which matches us best and we proclaim it the truth" (p. 28). These proverbs converge with an opinion George Kelly (1965) expressed over thirty years ago: once a clinician selects a point of view, this truth hardens, a condition he called "hardening of the categories." The experienced child therapist, then, is likely to have hardened his/her commitment to psychodynamic views, or cognitive views, or behavioral views. And the beginning therapist, whether in a graduate course or participating in an internship, is likely to have been "imprinted" by one of these views as presented by mentors.

Therefore, the several journeys we will take are intended to soften the categories the reader has already accepted as true. These journeys will travel through questions such as: Does segregation really exist in psychotherapy? What types of segregation has psychology practiced for more than 100 years, and how have they impacted on the practice of psychotherapy? Is it so that disciplines providing psychotherapy (e.g., clinical psychology, psychiatry, social work, psychoanalysis) inherit a segregated world and practice segregation? Are most therapists trained to peer through only one lens, and therefore see either the skin and muscles of behavior near the "surface," or vascular and skeletal systems that are "deep"? And how can the field of psychotherapy be desegregated?

While interest in desegregating and integrating psychotherapy has been expressed since the 1930s, it is only in the past twenty years that a growing number of practitioners, researchers, and theorists have expended increasing effort to establish "equal rights" for all schools of thought (see Garfield 1994, for a historical review of interest in psychotherapy integration). These efforts have led to the formation of the Society for the Exploration of Psychotherapy Integration, which began publishing its *Journal of Psychotherapy Integration* in 1991. That interest in psychotherapy integration is growing and receiving recognition is also reflected by the fact that Arkowitz (1992) was invited to write a chapter on "Integrative Theories of Therapy" for the volume (Freedkeim 1992), published to honor the centennial of the American Psychological Association. As someone with a long-standing interest in psychotherapy integration, beginning with attempts to integrate cognitive and behavioral psychology and psychoanalysis (e.g., Santostefano 1967, 1969a,b, 1978, 1994, 1995a), I was excited to see the formation of this society and the publication of its journal. However, as someone who has also had a long-standing interest in child psychotherapy, I have noticed that psychotherapy integration as it relates to children is relatively neglected, not only in issues of this journal but also as reflected by two recently released handbooks on psychotherapy integration. In one (Norcross and Goldfried 1992), none of the eighteen chapters is devoted exclusively to integration in child psychotherapy. And in the other (Stricker and Gold 1993), only one of thirty-seven contributions is devoted to integration in child psychotherapy. In this chapter and those to follow, I hope to stimulate interest in the need for psychotherapy integration with children.

THE NEED FOR INTEGRATION IN CHILD PSYCHOTHERAPY

The need to continue searching for models and methods of psychotherapy seems clear. In any given year, a minimum of about 7.5 million children in the United States need help with significant mental health problems, and only a fourth of these receive some form of treatment (Weisz and Weiss 1993). Moreover, given the increasing reluctance on the part of mental health workers to use inpatient treatment programs that remove children from their families, schools, and communities, the treatment of children takes place increasingly in outpatient settings.

What treatment approaches are being used to help children? While over 200 forms of therapy have been reported, one survey (Kazdin et al. 1990b) suggested that only a few approaches are favored by clinicians. Over a thousand child therapists were asked to rate which treatment approaches they found useful for children. Psychologists reported they found an eclectic approach most useful, followed by behavior modification and cognitive approaches. In contrast, psychiatrists reported they found a psychodynamic approach most useful, followed by eclectic and psychoanalytic approaches. There are two other angles from which we could view this survey. First, if we hold to one side those psychologists and psychiatrists who favored an eclectic approach, we see a clear indication that professional disciplines have biases about child psychotherapy. Psychologists favored behavior modification and cognitive methods, while psychiatrists did not. In contrast, psychiatrists favored psychodynamic and psychoanalytic methods, but psychologists did not. Second, if we now focus on the number of respondents who rated an eclectic approach as useful, we come upon an impressive observation. Although psychologists and psychiatrists differed in their views of the effectiveness of behavior modification, cognitive, and psychodynamic methods, they were in strong agreement about an eclectic approach: 72 percent of the psychologists reported that they found an eclectic approach to be useful; 74 percent of the psychiatrists also reported they found an eclectic approach to be useful.

That therapists prefer an eclectic approach has a long history. Garfield (1994) reported that E. Lowell Kelly, in his 1960 presidential address to members of the Division of Clinical Psychology, American Psychological Association, described the results of a survey he had conducted: of more than 1,000 clinical psychologists, almost 40 percent declared themselves to be eclectics falling just short of the 41 percent who declared themselves to be psychoanalytic or psychodynamic. Garfield also summarized 10 surveys conducted between 1976 and 1990 showing a steady increase in therapists preferring an eclectic approach. In the most recent survey, 68 percent of psychiatrists, clinical psychologists, and social workers surveyed expressed a preference for eclecticism, reflecting that an eclectic approach apparently has established roots in social work and continues to grow in clinical psychology and psychiatry.

Should the experienced therapist, or the therapist-in-training, sometimes approach children they treat using a behavioral technique, sometimes a cognitive technique, and sometimes a psychodynamic technique? From the viewpoint of integrative psychotherapy, the answer to this question is No. The following clinical vignette illustrates the need for integrating approaches in child psychotherapy.

How Should Sally Be Helped: A Clinical Vignette

One winter day, on her way to school, Sally, 9 years old, spotted a square opening in a metal pole of a street light. The plate that usually covered the opening was not there. Pushed by curiosity, she thrust her left hand into the opening and received an electric shock that hurled her back more than 10 feet, leaving her unconscious and her glove and sleeve scorched. Emergency room personnel agreed that the voltage should have killed her, but miraculously did not. Neurological and pediatric examinations conducted after the trauma, and again months later, produced no evidence of neurological or physical damage.

During the next school year, Sally began to display a number of behaviors that concerned parents and teachers. From academic performance that previously had been adequate, her performance now slipped below grade expectation. More than this, while she had always been a child with an animated, exuberant style, she had become hyperactive and inattentive, which resulted in the school psychologist's diagnosing her as afflicted by attention deficit hyperactivity disorder. There was still another area of concern. When standing among a group of children in the playground, she frequently reached out and, with a pincerlike motion of her thumb and forefinger, snapped at the ears and buttocks of peers. One behavior in particular made everyone quite anxious and triggered a request for an evaluation outside of the school system. On several occasions children witnessed Sally urinating on the floor of the school bathroom and ran to the teacher to report the disaster. Scurrying to the bathroom, the teacher found Sally squatting over a pool of urine.

For the present purpose I select only a few elements of the evaluation. Sally was surely hyperactive and restless. She constantly moved about the playroom as she coped with cognitive, intellectual, and projective tests, and play materials. During the evaluation, she shared that she was frightened by fantasies when she was lying in bed waiting to fall asleep, and when she was sitting over "the hole of the toilet." One fantasy involved "a giant lobster, it tears you all up with humongous claws!" The other fantasy involved, "a monster, it spits on you and covers you all over with hot spit!" Another major theme of Sally's evaluation concerned her conviction that boys were smarter than she and that other girls were prettier and favored by the teacher. These complaints were followed by associations to her father, who frequently yelled at her, while favoring her brother.

With this vignette before us, a number of questions emerge when we consider how a therapist could help Sally. Should a therapist treat the hyperactivity by training Sally to use self-instruction as a way of regulating her restlessness and so that she can become more attentive and successful with academics? Or should a therapist treat the frightening fantasies of a giant lobster and monster with the technique of systematic desensitization by training her to relax and imagine less frightening scenes and gradually more frightening scenes? Or should a therapist help Sally gain insight into the unconscious dynamic that the giant with its hot spit is a symbol of the pole with its electrical current, as well as a symbol of father punishing her for being a bad girl? Or should the therapist sometimes use a behavioral technique, at other times a cognitive technique, and at other times a psychodynamic technique? Integrative psychotherapy urges a therapist to address the whole child rather than select as the target of treatment either irrational thoughts, hyperactive behavior, or unconscious fantasies. At this point it seems appropriate to raise the question, What is integrative psychotherapy?

WHAT IS INTEGRATIVE PSYCHOTHERAPY?

What is the viewpoint of integrative psychotherapy and what is psychotherapy integration? To introduce an initial response to this question, I turn to those who have grappled with the topic. Wachtel (1984) noted that "integration is not just a hodge podge of eclecticism, a salad with a little of this and a little of that tossed in. The goal, rather, is the development of a new, coherent structure, an internally consistent approach both to technical intervention and to construction of theory" (p. 45). Stricker (1994) reminded us that the various targets of psychotherapy (emotion, behavior, cognition, relationships, conscious, unconscious) exist within the same person. Thus he pointed out, "I hope [therapists] will not reach the point where they will treat behavior or cognition much as physicians treat livers or knees, without regard for the person who houses the liver, the knee, the behavior, and the cognition" (p. 35). Integration, then, attempts "to make whole," to unify a body of knowledge in a systematic way that is coherent and heuristic (Sechrest and Smith 1994). As concepts from different theoretical models are integrated into a theory, techniques are forged that are guided by the conceptual integration (Stricker 1994).

Although interest in psychotherapy integration is increasing, a careful look at the comments just quoted illustrate why agreement has not emerged as to what constitutes integration (Garfield 1994). For example, Wachtel (1994) and Sechrest and Smith (1994) bring our attention to the notion that integration involves weaving together concepts and theories in a new way. Stricker's comment could be construed to mean that integration involves selecting cognitive therapy techniques to treat cognition, behavioral techniques to treat behavior, and psychodynamic techniques to treat unconscious issues. While Arkowitz (1992) characterized integration as containing three main directions (theoretical integration, identifying common factors among therapies, and technical eclecticism), Garfield (1994) noted "technical eclecticism is viewed [by many authors] as eclecticism rather than psychotherapy integration since [the] focus is on selecting appropriate procedures and techniques to fit individual clients and not the integration of specific theories" (p. 129). Later I will have more to say about technical eclecticism, which I view as an obstacle to integration.

The model and treatment strategies presented here, in integrating concepts and methods from four schools of thought, represent one form of integration that I believe provides an approach to child psychotherapy that is more heuristic than that of any one of the four approaches when each stands alone. The main elements of the model include (1) developmental processes involved in symbolizing, representing, and giving meaning to experiences, especially embodied activity; (2) developmental processes involved in sharing these symbols and meanings with others; (3) developmental processes that link together what a child does (actions), imagines (fantasizes), and says (language and thought); (4) developmental processes involved in translating unconscious, embodied symbols and meanings into conscious forms; (5) developmental relations between cognition and emotion on the one hand and, on the other, between the unity of cognition/emotion and the behavioral modes of action, fantasy, and language; (6) how symbols and metaphors, representing experiences in the past, guide thoughts, emotions, and actions in the present; (7) how symbols and metaphors that represent past experiences, and guide present behaviors, undergo change and why some remain impervious to change.

THE NEED TO DISSOLVE SEGREGATION
BEFORE CONSTRUCTING AN INTEGRATIVE VIEW

As noted earlier, experienced child psychotherapists who were surveyed favored either a behavioral, cognitive, or psychodynamic approach. When conducting psychotherapy, these psychotherapists peer through a lens that permits him/her to see only behavioral concepts and methods, or cognitive concepts and methods, or psychodynamic concepts and methods. And the concepts and methods the therapist sees are held as true and the others as less worthy. But some psychotherapists favored two approaches. When conducting therapy, these therapists peer through "bifocals" that bring into view, for example, cognitive and behavioral concepts and methods, or behavioral and psychodynamic concepts and methods. We also learned that a significant number found an eclectic approach useful. When conducting psychotherapy, these individuals peer through a lens that brings into view three viewpoints, which they employ flexibly, at one moment borrowing cognitive techniques, at another psychodynamic techniques, and at another behavioral approaches. These therapists use a "trifocal lens," so to speak. The critical point is that if a therapist peers faithfully through one lens, then the contributions from other viewpoints are segregated and pushed out of view. Moreover, whether a therapist peers through a bifocal lens or a trifocal lens, what he/she sees are polarized and segregated concepts and methods. And while each treatment approach is acknowledged, only one is viewed at any one moment as true or correct and the others neglected.

Eclecticism: A Source of Segregation
and a Potent Obstacle to Integration

Because the majority of clinicians surveyed favored an eclectic approach, I discuss an article by Arnold Lazarus (1995) that, although addressing adult psychotherapy, serves to illustrate how eclecticism results in segregation. Still another reason for my selecting this article is that it helps to set the stage for my position (proposed by a number of theorists we consider later) that an integration of concepts and theories is necessary to devise integrated therapy methods.

Thirty years ago, long before integrative psychotherapy became a movement, Lazarus (1967) espoused technical eclecticism. With technical eclecticism, a therapist borrows methods and techniques from any school of therapy as long as it meets some particular need of the patient. Since that time, and the publication of "Multimodal Behavior Therapy" (Lazarus 1976), he has elaborated this position in numerous reports. His recent (1995) article serves my purpose because it provides a succinct summary of this position with clinical examples.

Here Lazarus sketches three psychotherapy patients. The appointment with the first patient began at 2 P.M., and Lazarus characterizes his approach as follows, "I say very little. He dwells on childhood memories and I listen attentively. Occasionally, I may ask a question . . . now and then, I may make a comment or share an observation . . ." (p. 35). At 3 P.M. he is engaged in a therapy session with another patient. "By contrast . . . I am very active, disputational, energetically parsing dysfunctional beliefs, and often resorting to a form of Socratic questioning" (p. 36). At 4 P.M. Lazarus was busy using role-playing and social skills training techniques to help another patient rehearse two important upcoming events: the remarks she will make at a ceremony when she receives her firm's annual award, and how to approach her mother assertively, rather than timidly or aggressively, about an unresolved issue.

Following these clinical sketches, Lazarus states:

> The point I wish to make here is that I was not practicing psychodynamic therapy at 2 P.M., cognitive therapy at 3 P.M., and behavioral therapy at 4. Rather, I was employing listening and reflecting techniques at 2, cognitive restructuring techniques at 3, and behavioral rehearsal techniques at 4. *The techniques I selected were in keeping with my perceptions of the clients' specific needs and expectancies.* . . . [p. 36; italics mine]

At first glance this statement provides a sound argument. But if we focus on the sentence I italicized, several issues at the heart of an integrative approach come into view, which I introduce here and elaborate in the next chapter. Lazarus selected techniques in keeping with *his* perception of the clients' needs. But what guides these perceptions? Isn't Lazarus, at 2 P.M., peering through a psychodynamic lens in order to see and select the technique of listening and reflecting, and at 3 P.M. through a cognitive lens in order to see and select cognitive restructuring techniques, and at 4 P.M. through a behavioral lens in order to see and select rehearsal techniques?

Lazarus's reply is No. He is firm in his opinion that he is not peering through theoretical lenses. For example, he states, "As a technical eclectic, I can use operant techniques or psychodynamic techniques without subscribing to the theories that gave rise to the methods I employ" (p. 36). Lazarus not only argues that he is borrowing techniques without considering the theories out of which they emerged, but he also argues against the integration of theories. "I have emphasized for many years that a blend of different theories is likely to result only in profound confusion" (p. 36). He is even more blunt in rejecting the notion, proposed by a number of others cited earlier (e.g., Wachtel, Stricker, Sechrest), that integrating concepts from different theoretical viewpoints is a necessary condition to technical integration. "I strongly favor technical eclecticism and regard theoretical integration with considerable suspicion if not disdain" (p. 37).

In fact, other clinical examples Lazarus describes in this article to support his theoretical position illustrate that from patient to patient he is subscribing to one or another theoretical lens that brings into focus what he perceives. For example, he describes an intensely anxious patient who negotiated a business merger that significantly compromised his partner. Lazarus states, "He denied having feelings of guilt and proceeded to rationalize that, because of his partner's alleged hostility to him, he had done nothing improper" (p. 33). In the course of treatment this patient learned that his business partner reminded him of his bullying and intimidating older brother. He also learned that the business merger that compromised his partner may well have been a way of "getting back" at his brother. Lazarus follows this clinical sketch with,

> The foregoing . . . alludes to several psychotherapeutic processes that served to elicit information of which the patient was unaware and that enabled him to make some seemingly important connections between past and present feelings. He got past certain *rationalizations* and *denials* and *gained insight* into possible motives behind his behavior. Was I administering psychodynamic therapy? In my opinion, I was not. I was using, for want of a better term, applied psychology. [p. 33; italics mine]

Again, I bring the reader's attention to the words I italicize. When Lazarus uses "rationalization," he is referring to the observation that the patient justified cheating his partner by explaining and believing that his partner had always been antagonistic and hostile toward him (the patient). But where do rationalizations come from? Did the patient invent this behavior? He certainly did not. Rationalization, as a behavior, appears before us only when we look at behavior through a psychodynamic lens that conceptualizes the mind as using a variety of strategies (mechanisms of defense). To avoid painful anxiety, these mechanisms relocate (away from the self) the feelings, motives, and impulses that are experienced by a person as wrong or bad. In spite of Lazarus's disavowing the influence of theory, he would not have perceived and understood this behavior on the patient's part as a "rationalization" if he did not have available a particular theoretical lens that brought this behavior into view. Along the same line, we could ask how Lazarus came to perceive and understand behaviors he termed *denials* and *insight*.

The point I am emphasizing is that whether Lazarus was selecting techniques in keeping with his "perception" of the needs of his 2 P.M., 3 P.M., and 4 P.M. clients, he was peering through different theoretical lenses that brought particular phenomena into view: a cognitive lens, a behavioral lens, and a psychodynamic lens.

Lazarus disagrees with my position. "Technical eclecticism" he states, "permits me to select techniques from any discipline without necessarily endorsing any of the theories that spawn them. The trap lies in equating observations with theories" (p. 31). Lazarus must also disagree with Kuhn's (1962, 1977) now famous thesis that, at every level of science and observation, paradigms or points of view that already exist in the mind of the scientist or therapist influence what is observed. Lazarus would argue that if you perceive that a patient needs a wheel, you borrow a wheel and use it. Kuhn would argue that unless you have seen a stone rolling down a hillside many, many times, and then from these experiences evolve the concept of objects capable of circular motion, you would not see a wheel even when it is before your very eyes.

Next I turn to Lazarus's case of Ms. W, which he used "to illustrate the virtues of technical eclecticism and to epitomize several of the traps of theoretical integration" (p. 30). I use the case to illustrate that what appear to be virtues of eclecticism are in fact obstacles to integration, and to forecast a key concept that guides an integrative approach, namely, holism. Ms. W complained to Lazarus that during the past year she had experienced overwhelming panic when venturing away from home unless accompanied by her husband. An inventory she had completed for Lazarus revealed several additional difficulties: marital discord, tension with an older brother, resentment toward her parents, poor self-esteem, and difficulty with being assertive. Lazarus noted that "the first error that many therapists make is to assume that Ms. W's other problems are necessarily connected to her agoraphobia" (p. 30).

The integrative approach would not view possible connections between Ms. W's agoraphobia and her "other problems" as an error. Rather, from a holistic view, the question would be raised whether and how her agoraphobia, marital discord, tension with an older brother, resentment toward parents, and difficulty with being assertive form a pattern of actions, fantasies, and thoughts. In addition to serving as a reminder of holism, the treatment methods Lazarus used to help Ms. W also relate to questions raised by the integrative approach I propose.

At the start of treatment, Lazarus taught Ms. W relaxation and breathing techniques. The model we will consider would ask what meanings, conscious or unconscious, Ms. W gave to these body experiences. While practicing a breathing technique, for example, did she think of a child she saw in a shopping mall who was choking on some refreshment while the mother stood by seemingly indifferent? Following the relaxation phase, Lazarus introduced "in vivo" desensitization techniques. He and Ms. W took short walks, followed by automobile rides. Again, the integrative model described in a later chapter would ask what meanings these body experiences, shared directly with the therapist, held for Ms. W, and what thoughts and fantasies she experienced while walking and riding. Lazarus provides some information that responds to these questions. He reports that "during and after" several of these excursions, Ms. W related disturbing flashbacks "to real or imagined memories." For example, she recalled being censored by parents and being humiliated and rejected by peers. And she described experiencing a sense of abandonment that she connected to living with foster parents for several weeks at the age of 4 while her mother was undergoing surgery. Again, Lazarus stresses that "these additional problems may or may not have had a bearing on her agoraphobia" (p. 30).

In contrast, my integrative-holistic perspective would form an organization of the following ingredients: taking walks and automobile rides with the therapist, experiencing a sense of abandonment during these walks and rides, experiencing memories when she was scolded by her parents, experiencing memories when she was humiliated and rejected by peers, experiencing memories of being forced to live with strangers when mother was in the hospital. From this organization of actions, fantasies, and thoughts, a holistic perspective would raise several questions. Why did Ms. W experience these disturbing flashbacks during and after taking walks with the therapist and not at other times (e.g., during relaxation training)? Were there other activities that could have been included during or after the walks that would have facilitated elaborating these particular memories and fantasies, with their emotions, and facilitated constructing others? Could these reconstructed memories be connected to actions she does take and might take in her present environment in order to facilitate change? Is there a process that links these cognitions, emotions, and actions so that each defines and is defined by the other?

Throughout the article, and in discussing Ms. W, Lazarus seems to take extra pains to support the position that he is not making use of psychodynamic concepts. He notes, for example, "My theoretical understanding of [Ms. W's] process did not invoke oedipal issues, the nuances of object relations, drive/structural or ego psychology models . . ." (p. 31). But how could Lazarus know that his understanding of Ms. W did not include oedipal issues unless he looked through a psychodynamic lens that brings oedipal behaviors into view? At another point he notes, "I may observe that someone is displacing anger or denying his or her rage, but to do so does not mean that I am thereby endorsing any psychodynamic theories vis-à-vis defense mechanisms" (p. 31). How could he observe someone "displacing anger" unless he is looking through a lens that brings such behaviors into view? And why does he exert such effort to disavow that he is using psychodynamic concepts?

Rigid Psychotherapy Kaleidoscopes:
Further Obstacles to Integration

These questions relate to why different camps of psychotherapy exist, why these camps have remained segregated from one another, and why some therapists pledge allegiance to one camp and renounce others. Or, as illustrated by Lazarus' article, why some therapists borrow techniques from all camps while disavowing the theories that gave rise to the techniques. As we discuss in more detail in Chapter 2, psychotherapists, following the trend in general psychology, have adopted a Western philosophical view of human behavior that has dominated for centuries; namely, dividing knowledge into sects or camps, maintaining them as segregated domains, and seeing one as more privileged or true than others. What the segregationist lens obscures is the possible ways the segregated domains could be unified as one, an integration that might be heuristically valuable to therapists.

In addition to the tradition of segregating knowledge that typifies Western thinking, there is another factor that makes the task of grinding an integrative lens difficult. This factor, as noted earlier, was characterized by Kelly (1965) as "hardening of the categories." Once a therapist embraces a category, or a point of view, once a therapist grinds a lens that brings into view either cognitive, behavioral, or psychodynamic considerations, the lens hardens, obscuring other considerations.

How do we regrind a lens so that, as we look through it, what comes into focus is an integration of ideas that is different from what we perceived before? To address this, I would like to use a kaleidoscope as a metaphor. The reader has probably already embraced an approach to child psychotherapy so that, when "looking" at psychotherapy, he/she peers through a kaleidoscope that already holds a particular design. Referring to our earlier discussion, if the reader is a psychologist, it is likely that his/her kaleidoscope contains the designs of cognitive and behavioral methods. If the reader is a psychiatrist, it is likely that his/her kaleidoscope holds the designs of psychodynamic methods. Counseling psychologists, school psychologists, and social workers have most likely been introduced to one or another kaleidoscope by virtue of the particular school of therapy that dominated the setting in which he/she was trained. And many readers may have been introduced to the merits of an eclectic approach, using different methods for different children, as illustrated by our discussion of Lazarus's article. Moreover, it is likely that once the reader has declared citizenship in one of these schools of thought, the culture and views of the other schools are likely to be ignored or viewed as less effective.

In other words, the therapist, experienced or novice, already has constructed a "psychotherapy kaleidoscope" that holds a relatively fixed design. What I have observed is that when therapists look at the same child through their preferred psychotherapy kaleidoscope, they frequently see different problems and the need for different techniques. I am sure, for example, that when a psychodynamic therapist peers through his/her kaleidoscope at Lazarus's 4 P.M. appointment, he/she would see needs and techniques different from the behavioral rehearsal Lazarus used to help this patient. The psychodynamic therapist would likely see a person who is anxious and fearful about having to stand up before a crowd and make a speech in connection with her receiving an award; a person who is anxious and fearful about approaching her mother assertively; and a person who experiences anxiety, guilt, and conflict over aggressing and winning, whether in transactions with parents or others. From this view the psychodynamic therapist would not engage this person in rehearsing a speech she will give at the awards ceremony, as a behavioral therapist would, but would attempt to resolve "the underlying conflict" by making conscious particular feelings and attitudes that are rooted in early experiences with mother. Is one therapist more correct than the other? Is there something we can learn from both approaches if we integrate them?

I am stressing the opinion that to learn from different approaches the reader needs first to recognize the particular psychotherapy kaleidoscope he or she tends to peer through. Referring to the philosophical quotes I mentioned at the start, the pattern you see has become familiar and gives you the illusion that it matches you best and is very likely "the truth." To construct a new design for your kaleidoscope, we should first shake it and disrupt the existing, familiar pattern. To do this, we will take several steps.

DISRUPTING THE PATTERN ONE TYPICALLY SEES WHEN PEERING INTO A PSYCHOTHERAPY KALEIDOSCOPE

In an effort to begin to shake up the reader's psychotherapy kaleidoscope, with its familiar patterns, I ask the reader to accompany me on two detours. One considers how psychotherapy has been defined and some of the general issues raised about psychotherapy with children. The second detour takes us to an imaginary clinic where a cognitive therapist, a behavior therapist, a psychodynamic therapist, an integrative therapist, and a developmental consultant have been asked to observe a child and make recommendations.

What Is Psychotherapy? The First Detour

Since psychotherapy has been defined in many different ways, I have selected responses by therapists from different persuasions to illustrate that a given definition may make total sense to one therapist looking through a particular kaleidoscope and make no sense at all to a therapist looking through a different kaleidoscope. Reisman, a psychologist, (1973) defined psychotherapy as "the communication of person-related understanding, respect, and a wish to be of help" (p. 10). Coppolillo (1987), a child psychiatrist and psychoanalyst, stated that "psychotherapy is an art . . . and the practitioner of this art must work with the discipline all art requires" (p. 207). Coppolillo also defined therapy according to the location required to meet the child's needs. Inpatient treatment is indicated when the child presents a psychosis that might endanger his/her welfare. Day treatment is indicated when a child requires milieu therapy and remedial education. Individual therapy is indicated when the child needs the opportunity to do "his healing" where it needs to be done: "in his daily world and not just in the office of his therapist" (p. 201). Family therapy is indicated when the "interdigitation" of pathology among family members keeps the child's difficulties alive.

Others have defined psychotherapy by emphasizing goals. Hammer and Kaplan (1967), taking a psychoanalytic perspective, defined psychotherapy in terms of helping the child advance through psychosexual stages (from oral, to anal, to genital, to oedipal), relinquish the pleasure principle for the reality principle, and develop the ability to subordinate the need for immediate gratification and accept delayed gratification. Coppolillo (1987), who we noted is a psychoanalyst, makes no mention of helping a child move through psychosexual stages, but sees the goal of therapy as enabling the child to use self-knowledge and awareness in the service of achieving self-regulation. For Spiegel (1989), who embraces an interpersonal-psychodynamic view of child psychotherapy, the goal of treatment is to enhance the child's self-esteem, help the child view him- or herself and others in more realistic ways, and become aware of his/her feelings. Kendall and Braswell (1985), who combine cognitive and behavioral techniques, stated that the aim of their approach "is to teach children to slow down and cognitively examine their behavioral alternatives before acting" (p. 1) and to "teach thinking processes" (p. 4).

Strupp (1973), who has made important contributions to research in psychotherapy, states that "psychotherapy is an interpersonal process designed to bring about modification of feelings, cognitions, attitudes, and behaviors which have proven troublesome to the person seeking help from a trained professional" (p. 3). Later (1986a,b) he gave more stress to the significance of the relationship between patient and therapist in defining psychotherapy as "the systematic use of a human relationship to effect enduring changes in a person's cognition, feelings, and behavior" (1986a, p. 513).

Providing a similar definition, Corsini and Wedding (1989), in their review of several forms of psychotherapy, point out that all therapies are methods of learning and all intend to change how people think, feel, and act. Others have given similarly inclusive definitions. Weisz and his colleagues (Weisz et al. 1987b) defined child psychotherapy as "any intervention designed to ameliorate psychological distress, reduce maladaptive behavior or enhance adaptive behavior through counseling, structured or unstructured interventions, training programs, or predetermined treatment plans" (p. 543). The definition of child psychotherapy offered by Kazdin and his colleagues (Kazdin et al. 1990a) is similar: "an intervention designed to decrease distress, symptoms, maladaptive behavior and/or improve adaptive prosocial functioning" (p. 730).

Shirk (1988) provided a much more differentiated, and in my view particularly useful, definition of child psychotherapy. First, he discussed the ways in which child psychotherapy differs from adult psychotherapy (e.g., children rarely refer themselves; adults present their concerns verbally while children use symbolic play, repetitive activities, and fragmented stories). He also discussed the ways in which child and adult therapy are similar (e.g., each involves a process of expressing thematic material, and learning or unlearning, within a supportive relationship). Of relevance to my thesis, Shirk distinguished between psychotherapy that is concerned on the one hand with changing the meaning of behavior, viewing overt behavior as a form of representation, and on the other with changing behavior itself, viewing overt behaviors as cognitive-behavioral skills. Last, Shirk defined child psychotherapy in terms of three dimensions: (1) structure—the degree to which the activity is directed by the therapist or by the child; (2) medium—a continuum of exchanges between child and therapist from conversation to play; and (3) communicative functions—a continuum of communications by the therapist ranging from interpretations that analyze the meaning of a child's behavior to communications that provide a corrective emotional experience in a supportive environment. I return to the heuristic value of Shirk's definition in future chapters.

What Does a Psychotherapist Do?

These various definitions leave us with several questions. What form should person-related communication take? Is respect and the wish to help enough? Exactly what is involved in practicing the art of psychotherapy? What does a therapist do to help a child advance through psychosexual stages and to become free to use self-knowledge and self-awareness in achieving self-regulation? And what does a therapist do to decrease a child's distress, modify how the child feels, thinks, and behaves, and improve the child's adaptive prosocial functioning? The child therapist raising these questions has available different recommendations. Discussed in more detail later, I mention two at this point. Psychotherapists representing the psychodynamic approach (e.g., Coppolillo 1987, Spiegel 1989) propose that the child should be allowed to engage in whatever play activity and discussions he/she chooses. Psychotherapists representing cognitive and behavioral perspectives (e.g., Hoffman 1984, Hughes 1988, Kendall and Braswell 1985, Meyers and Craighead 1984) propose that the child should be engaged in various tasks designed and directed by the therapist. Whether the child is free to play and discuss, or required to work on a task, the aim is to change how the child thinks, feels, and behaves. Which approach should the child therapist choose? As we grapple with this question, we soon realize that we should not make a choice until we address still another question. How does free play and discussion, or working with tasks, change the way a child feels, thinks, and behaves?

The Psychodynamic View

This view holds that a child changes as the child gains insight into mental conflicts that are outside of awareness (that is, that are unconscious). The child is expected to learn that his thoughts, feelings, and actions are generated from within his personal world rather than activated by persons and stimulation in his environment. This learning is brought about as the therapist employs several tools. I summarize these following Coppolillo (1987, p. 213).

1. *Inquiry*—an attitude the therapist maintains and which the child eventually imitates and assumes when beginning to question her/his own motives.

2. *Empathy*—enables the therapist to know what the child is experiencing.
3. *Introspection*—the therapist teaches the child to look at his/her own private thoughts and fantasies.
4. *Associations*—the therapist uses the child's associations to decode unconscious motives.
5. *Help the child understand why he/she is in therapy*—initially the therapist learns about the child's difficulties by asking questions about issues raised by parents and teachers. Then the reason for therapy is explained.

   You already told me that sometimes you have sad thoughts and scary feelings. During our meetings we will try to find out the reasons why these thoughts and feelings keep coming back. Sometimes the person who worries doesn't even know the reasons for the worries. That is what you and I will work on together. If you can find out the cause of the worries, we can then see how we can make them go away. [p. 123]

6. *Help the child understand that there is an unconscious*—eventually, the child is taught that there are thoughts and wishes outside of awareness which need to be uncovered.

   You know, sometimes people's minds play tricks on them. A thought or a feeling at the back of your mind, that you hardly know is there, can cause you to be afraid or act in a certain way. When you find out what your thought or feeling is, it's not scary or bossy anymore. [p. 250]

7. *Countertransference*—the therapist uses his/her own thoughts and feelings, activated by the child's behavior, as a source of data about the child's difficulties.
8. *Interpretation and pressing the child to express his/her thoughts, feelings, fantasies, and conflicts in words*—for many psychodynamic therapists making an interpretation is the "sacred moment" that promotes change. The therapist provides a verbal interpretation of some wish, fantasy, or motive that to that point had been outside of the child's awareness. "All of what the therapist thinks about and does is organized around the intention of getting the child to express his conflict in verbal terms. . . . The psychodynamic therapist has a powerful tool in tackling the task of inducing the child to express conflicts in verbal terms" (Coppolillo 1987, p. 299).
9. *Understanding (analyzing) the transference*—as interpretations are integrated, the child learns that feelings, thoughts, fantasies which she/he had been directing toward the person of the therapist in fact stem from, and are related to, other significant persons in the child's life.

The Cognitive-Behavioral View

This view holds that a child changes as he/she learns how to use self-talk to regulate some aspect of behavior identified as inappropriate and maladaptive, and/or as the child is trained to develop social skills and to solve problems using behavioral strategies. The child is expected to use these acquired cognitive and behavioral skills to achieve successful adaptation in particular social contexts (e.g., classroom, playground, falling asleep, coping with the fear of darkness). This learning is brought about as the therapist employs several tools.

1. *Help the child define and understand his/her problem.* Following Meichenbaum (1977), the therapist could begin by saying, "As I understand it, you came here because you are having trouble [Here the therapist notes the referral problem; e.g., doing schoolwork; teachers and parents think that you move around too much]. I would like you to tell me more about this. What is the problem as you see it?" (p. 250).

   From this beginning the therapist asks other questions
   - To learn about the severity of the problem ("How serious a problem is this as far as you are concerned?")
   - To learn about the generality and determinants of the problem ("When does the problem come up? Are there certain places in school or home where you think you have the most trouble?")
   - To learn whether any conditions alleviate the problem ("Think about the times when your problem is better. What sorts of things are going on then?")
   - To learn about the child's perception of the origin of the problem ("What do you think is making you have trouble doing schoolwork and sitting still?")
   - To learn whether the child sees the problem as producing consequences ("When you had trouble doing your math, what did the teacher do? What did your parents do?")

   In addition, the cognitive-behavioral approach uses methods to learn about the content of the child's internal dialogue while finishing schoolwork. For example, the therapist could show the child a picture of a child seated at a school desk, pencil in hand and facing a worksheet, and ask the child to describe what the child in the picture is thinking and feeling and what the child could do to handle the situation. Relying on the child's responses to questions and stimuli such as pictures, the therapist devises tasks that involve some combination of techniques, a few of which are sketched here.

2. *Self-instructional training.* The child is taught the skill of instructing himself/herself while coping with any problematic situation, following a sequence of procedures: (a) the child observes the therapist perform a task while speaking aloud several guiding comments; (b) imitating the therapist, the child performs the task instructing himself/herself aloud; (c) the therapist performs a task while whispering self-instructions, and the child imitates this performance; (d) the therapist performs a task using covert self-instructions (e.g., pauses, strokes her/his chin); (e) the child performs a task using similar covert self-instructions.

3. *Behavioral contingencies*. Rewards are provided to reinforce the desired behavior; for example, (a) self-reward—the child comments to himself/herself, "I did a good job"; (b) social reward—the therapist smiles and makes comments such as "fine, good"; (c) response-cost—the child is given tokens as rewards and loses some number for behaving in ways that contribute to the problem; (d) self-evaluation—the child is asked to complete charts at home that evaluate how he/she managed performing some target behavior.
4. *Homework assignments*. The child performs self-instructional training at home or school.
5. *Modeling*. The child observes a demonstration of the behavior to be learned. The modeling could be provided by the therapist or by film.
6. *Affective education*. The child is trained to recognize and label his/her emotions, and those of others, associated with various facial expressions, body postures, and interpersonal situations.
7. *Role-playing*. The child is engaged in playing roles in imagined situations, which initially make use of hypothetical contexts and later contexts that replicate aspects of the child's environment.
8. *Training tasks*. The child is asked to complete a series of psychoeducational problem-solving tasks that initially consist of simple, impersonal cognitive games and gradually consist of more complex, interpersonal, emotionally evocative cognitive games.

Comparing the Kaleidoscopes of Psychodynamic and Cognitive-Behavioral Psychotherapies

Comparing what we see when we look through the kaleidoscopes of psychodynamic and cognitive-behavioral therapies, several elements are common to both: (1) psychotherapy is a method of learning designed to decrease distress and maladaptive behavior and to improve adaptive functioning; (2) self-knowledge and self-awareness is necessary for self-regulation; and (3) a child needs to become aware of, and label, his/her emotional experiences.

Other elements are shared, if not in content, at least in form. For example, a psychodynamic therapist models constantly, although he/she may not present the modeling as a formal, circumscribed interaction as does the cognitive-behavioral therapist. The psychodynamic therapist models an attitude of inquiry and introspection concerning private thoughts, feelings, motives, and fantasies. Similarly, the psychodynamic therapist is likely to reward the child with smiles, facial expressions of approval, and comments such as "that's great!"—although not in an organized, formally circumscribed way.

Each approach shares one more element, namely, the central position given to verbalizing. I spotlight this element because the question of whether and when verbalizing is emphasized is a core component of my integrative treatment model.

We noted that psychodynamic psychotherapy, including forms influenced by the "interpersonal school," emphasizes helping the child verbalize his/her motives, emotions, and fantasies, and also emphasizes the therapist's verbal interpretation of these behaviors. Self-instruction and self-talk, and the role of words in the regulation of behaviors, are also emphasized by cognitive-behavioral therapy. As I discuss in detail in later chapters, the model and methods I propose recommend that the therapist should not emphasize engaging the child in discussions of the presenting problem and should not press the child to verbalize his/her fantasies/wishes. But more about this later.

A comparison of the kaleidoscopes of each approach also brings into view patterns of shapes and colors that are quite different. The cognitive-behavioral kaleidoscope brings into view some unit of behavior that is the target complaint (e.g., irrational thoughts, restlessness, fears), which is seen as rooted in particular environments. The problem behavior becomes the direct target of therapeutic intervention (e.g., irrational thoughts are replaced by more realistic ones; the child is trained to be less restless by performing a graded series of tasks while using self-talk). In contrast, the psychodynamic kaleidoscope looks beyond the child's problem behavior and brings into focus some presumed, unconscious, mental conflict (e.g., between the wish to be aggressive and internalized prohibitions against the wish). This conflict, with its anxiety and guilt, is seen as the cause of the child's difficulties and becomes the target of numerous interpretations until the conflict becomes part of the child's conscious awareness. These interpretations include fantasies and feelings the child experiences toward the therapist, experiences that are essentially ignored by mainstream cognitive and behavioral therapies.

Shaking up the Cognitive-Behavioral and Psychodynamic Kaleidoscopes with Questions about Child Psychotherapy

With these kaleidoscopic patterns in our view, I begin to shake them up with the following questions. What if an aggressive-impulsive child tries to act upon the person of the therapist by winding a rope around her/him? Should the psychodynamic therapist interpret this action in terms of some presumed, unconscious fantasy? For example, "Is this the way you would like to stop your mother from picking on you?" Should the cognitive-behavioral therapist explain to the child that the rope is not part of the steps in self-instructional training? In response to this issue, Reisman (1973) states, "It would be absurd for the therapist to allow himself to be bound and gagged while playing cowboys and Indians with a client" (p. 47). And what if a child sits silently and sullenly in the playroom, ignores the therapist, and makes clear he wants to go outside? Should the psychodynamic therapist interpret to the child that he/she is resisting and wants to run away from the problems they are trying to solve? Should the cognitive-behavioral therapist focus on the silent behavior and introduce a program of self-assertion? Coppolillo (1987) seems firm in the opinion that psychotherapy appropriately takes place behind closed doors. Similarly, Spiegel (1989) takes the view that allowing a child to go outside the treatment room for therapy raises ethical and therapeutic questions.

During treatment children display other behaviors that shake up the cognitive-behavioral and psychodynamic kaleidoscopes. For example, what if a child takes home all the materials that are being used in some task the therapist introduced, and then does not return them? What if a child brings some item from home to the treatment room and insists on using it instead of the skills-training material the therapist has been using? Would self-talk training, or interpretations, be appropriate techniques in treating an impulsive, distractible 4- or 5-year-old?

To shake up the kaleidoscopic patterns further, I ask the reader to consider the behaviors of several children whom I observed in my practice. I am sure the same behaviors have been observed by other therapists, and I am equally certain that these behaviors will eventually be encountered by the therapist-in-training.

When I entered the waiting room to greet a 10-year-old boy for an initial appointment, he was not there. I found him standing at the entrance to the building. His jacket was pulled over his head and zipped up so I could not see his face, nor could he see mine. Father, who was kneeling by the boy, was trying to coax him with soft, reassuring comments to remove his jacket. The boy did not budge.

On another occasion I greeted a 5-year-old girl and her mother in the waiting room for an initial consultation. After introducing myself and chatting with them for a minute, I invited the child to accompany me to the playroom. In response, she anxiously grabbed mother's body. The more mother urged her to go along, the more mother reassured her that she would "have fun," the more the child clutched her mother in fear and desperation.

In my third example I greeted a 7-year-old boy who was sitting by his mother in the waiting room, happily sharing pictures of a magazine with her. A second after I introduced myself and invited the boy to join me, he leaped up and rushed into the treatment room. There, in a matter of a minute or two, he darted about, handling at least a dozen items located on shelves. Then he began tossing several of them across the room, sometimes clearly aiming at a window.

In my last example a high school female slouched in a chair located on one side of the waiting room, as far away from father as the room size permitted. She returned my greeting with a long stare. I noticed her army jacket and boots, as well as the four earrings on her left ear and three on her right. When I invited her to join me, she grunted that she would not go "in the office to talk" but would go outside to talk.

When responding to each of these behaviors, which are quite typical in one's work with children and adolescents, what does the therapist do? Should the therapist say anything, and if so, what? In my view, the recommendations outlined above by psychodynamic and cognitive-behavioral approaches do not seem appropriate. These children would not have been receptive to the relatively extensive, verbal commentaries recommended by Coppolillo (1987) and Kendall and Braswell (1985) that we considered earlier (i.e., "You sometimes have scary feelings. We will try to find out the reasons why" or "As I understand it, you came here because you are having trouble . . ."). I will return to these examples in later chapters to illustrate how the proposed integrative model addresses these issues.

Four Child Therapists and a Developmentalist Provide Consultation to Help a Child: The Second Detour

To further soften the conceptual categories the reader is accustomed to seeing when looking at child psychotherapy, and to further shake up the patterns unique to psychodynamic and cognitive-behavioral kaleidoscopes, let us take our second detour. With this detour I hope to illustrate how the problem behaviors a child presents are "seen" very differently when cognitive, behavioral, and psychodynamic kaleidoscopes are used to "look" and decide what to do.

Imagine the following. Five professionals have been asked to observe interviews with children and their parents from behind a one-way vision mirror. They understand that after each observation they will share opinions on how the child should be helped. Four of these consultants are practicing child psychotherapists: one a cognitive therapist, another a behavioral therapist, the third a psychodynamic therapist, and the fourth an integrative psychotherapist. The fifth, a developmental researcher, is not practicing psychotherapy. She has conducted a number of studies on cognitive and emotional development and maintains a strong interest in how children develop and change.

Eager to get started, our five consultants are walking about the observation room. To help them feel at home, the room has been furnished with various items, each holding significance for one or another of them. On one wall are portraits of Pavlov, Watson, Skinner, and Wolpe, which the behavioral therapist, feeling a surge of pride, carefully studies. The cognitive therapist is surprised to find, on a nearby wall, portraits of the soviet psychologist Vygotsky and his student Luria, who proposed that internalizing verbal commands is the crucial process by which a child establishes voluntary control over behavior. Someone must have been aware, the cognitive therapist whispers to himself with pride, that the technique of self-instruction training was based upon Luria's theory. And next to these, the cognitive therapist finds portraits of Albert Ellis and Samuel Beck, leaders of the cognitive therapy movement in the United States.

The psychodynamic therapist immediately spots the portraits of Sigmund Freud; his daughter, Anna Freud; Harry Stack Sullivan; and David Rapaport. She notices that these portraits have been hung on a wall opposite the one on which are displayed the portraits of behaviorists and cognitive therapists. "Very interesting," she mutters, and wonders if the persons who arranged the room were aware that they were reflecting their view that cognitive-behavioral and psychodynamic schools stand on opposite sides. This possible interpretation quickly leaves her attention when she notices, with excitement, a copy of the photograph taken in 1909 of a group of psychoanalysts who, along with G. Stanley Hall, a founding father of psychology in the United States and then president of Clark University, are sitting around Freud during his only visit to the United States.

The developmental researcher is proud to see portraits of leading figures in her domain: James Mark Baldwin, who formulated a developmental psychology in 1895; Jean Piaget, whose developmental studies of the reasoning of children turned American academic psychology on its ear in the 1950s; and Heinz Werner, who launched a developmental theory, similar in some ways to that of Piaget, but that articulated principles that created more of a bridge from developmental psychology to clinical practice.

Conspicuously, there are no portraits for the integrative psychotherapist to examine. A sign on the wall simply notes, "Exhibit to Be Completed." Although disappointed, the integrative psychotherapist understands. Psychotherapists have yet to feel the full impact of a movement for psychotherapy integration that is gaining momentum. But still, she reflected, there are a number of persons whose portraits could have been included if their hosts had taken a harder look at history. For example, Thomas French and Franz Alexander in the 1930s attempted to relate psychoanalytic concepts to Pavlov's concepts of conditioning. John Dollard and Neil Miller authored a book, *Personality and Psychotherapy*, published in 1950, that attempted to integrate concepts of psychoanalysis with learning theories of the time and that stimulated much research. And then there was Paul Wachtel, whose 1977 volume, *Psychoanalysis and Behavior Therapy*, proved to be one main force stimulating others to think about integrating different approaches to psychotherapy. And then there was . . . many other names tumbled into the mind of the integrative psychotherapist. But she stopped her ruminating when she acknowledged to herself that interest in integrating different approaches to psychotherapy is not yet integrated enough into the thinking of most therapists to be seen as a point of view.

In addition to the portraits, various items have been carefully located in each corner of the room. In one is a couch and puppets used by psychoanalysts. In another corner is a replica of the rabbit cage used by Mary Cover Jones to treat a 3-year-old boy who was afraid of rabbits. Next to it is a replica of another cage used by Skinner to train his pigeons. In a third corner are diaries and checklists used by cognitive therapists. In the last corner, arrayed on a table, are balls of clay and colored disks used in Piaget's conservation tasks.

As the cognitive, behavioral, and psychodynamic therapists interact, their identities seem clear. They chat amicably, each reflecting confidence that comes from practicing a type of psychotherapy for many years. From their casual conversations one gets several impressions. Each knows the others; each has a clear notion about what the others believe and do in their therapy with children. Each disagrees with the others' position, as they see it, but each is polite and accepting, given the context of the consultation.

The developmental researcher is puzzled about why she was invited. Yet she certainly is very pleased to be present. She has been frustrated for years by the degree to which child developmental research and theory has been segregated for the most part from the practice of psychotherapy with children and, for that matter, also with adults. At conferences and conventions there have been many panels and symposia on psychodynamic therapy, cognitive therapy, behavioral therapy, and especially on cognitive-behavioral therapy. But there have been no conferences suggesting that developmental concepts have become central in helping children. If such symposia have taken place, they do not seem to have had a very big impact on how psychotherapy is practiced. She reminds herself that developmentalists hold their conferences primarily to discuss research findings, while psychotherapists hold their conferences to discuss clinical techniques that promote change in children. In spite of this segregation, the developmental researcher notices that the therapists relate to her with warmth, at times glance in her direction, and even occasionally pose a comment. The developmentalist thinks to herself, "It's about time they invited me; maybe they *are* interested in developmental issues."

The integrative therapist seems to be a stranger to the group. She has been sitting among them for some time, but no one has looked in her direction, let alone addressed her. While the others have not conveyed any overt dislike of her, she feels uncomfortable, something like a recent immigrant. It seems as if the cognitive, behavioral, and psychodynamic therapists have heard of her recent arrival to the world of child psychotherapy. But they do not have a clear sense of who she is or what she stands for. What makes it even worse, they do not know what language to use when speaking to her.

At this point the first set of parents enters the office. The five professionals immediately become quiet, crowd in front of the one-way mirror, and attentively peer at a young couple. These parents are obviously distraught as they describe difficulties they have experienced with their son, Harry, who is 5 years old. When he started preschool, several months ago, he had extreme difficulty coping with classroom demands. In a recent school conference, the teacher complained to them that Harry was very hyperactive. He constantly ran about the classroom and was able to sit with other children for only a minute or two, whether a story was being read or the class was engaged in a coloring task.

But the problems Harry presented from the start of preschool had recently become even more troublesome. On several occasions he suddenly spit at and slapped classmates and teachers without provocation. And on three occasions he bit a classmate on the forearm. Harry's teachers struggled to help him. When they observed that he was beginning to escalate, they asked him to sit in the "quiet corner" and look at picture books. At the suggestion of a consulting psychologist, they rewarded him with stickers of "smiley faces" whenever he remained in the quiet corner for the designated period of time. At the suggestion of another consulting psychologist, they tried the technique of showing him, at the start of the day, five Hershey's chocolate kisses (which he loved). They explained that he could eat them at the end of the day, but each time he slapped or bit anyone, he would lose a candy.

In spite of these various strategies, Harry's inappropriate behavior continued. A few weeks ago the parents of the other children held a meeting with the director of the school and insisted that Harry be removed from the classroom. As a result, Harry was expelled. Although this decision devastated Harry's parents, they understood why it was necessary. They acknowledged that before entering school Harry displayed the same behaviors at home. There, without provocation, he occasionally hit, bit, or spit at his parents, his younger sister, and his grandparents. The parents had hoped that when Harry entered school, he would settle down and gradually get over his hyperactivity and aggressiveness.

As the parents conclude their interview, Harry darts into the adjoining playroom. A handsome, robust-looking boy, his dark eyes dart about as if he is frantically sizing up the situation. But these visual sweeps do not include looking at the examiner, whom he seems to ignore. He quickly moves to a table, takes a crayon, and rapidly draws some sort of abstract design on a sheet of paper. Then his eyes catch a jar of play dough. He takes out the play dough and busily makes small balls, each about the size of a marble, and lines them up across the tabletop. On several occasions he licks the clay or holds it to his nose, apparently to smell it.

Suddenly he hurls a clay ball against the wall, and then another. The examiner reminds Harry that he should not throw clay against the wall and sets a wastebasket near him. Harry flings a ball of clay in the direction of the wastebasket but misses it by a good distance. Then, without hesitation, he hurls another ball of clay against the wall, followed quickly by another. Now he walks over to the window. For some seconds he stands still and stares outside, seemingly lost in private thought. Suddenly he begins to yank on the curtain with vigor. The examiner puts his arms around Harry, gently reminds him that he cannot hurt anything in the room, and urges him to try the game of flinging the clay balls into a box. But Harry continues pulling on the curtain. A few minutes later the examiner comments that their meeting is finished. When the examiner opens the door, Harry races toward the waiting room and his parents.

At this point our consultants are asked to express their thoughts about Harry's difficulties and how he could be helped. The behavioral therapist immediately speaks up and notes that it seems clear that Harry is very hyperactive and impulsive, shows a very short attention span, and seems to fit the diagnosis of attention deficit hyperactivity disorder. The behavioral therapist is about to continue when the cognitive therapist enthusiastically joins in. He points out that in order to understand Harry's lack of control and hyperactivity, and how he could be helped, it is necessary to consider a point of view that derives from the Soviet psychologist Luria. At this moment he gestures to the portrait on the wall as if to affirm the importance of what he is about to suggest. Luria, he reminds everyone, proposed that by internalizing verbal commands, the child establishes voluntary control over his/her behavior. Initially, a child's behavior is controlled by the verbal commands of others, usually adults, and thus the control of behavior is external and located within others. Then the child's own, overt verbalizations, what the child says out loud, direct and guide his behavior. The control is still external but performed by the child. Finally, by the age of 5 or 6, the child's behavior is controlled by his own covert self-verbalizations. Now the control is internal and executed by the child. From these opening comments the cognitive therapist concludes that Harry shows that he does not have available self-verbalizations that guide and regulate his behavior. Moreover, he shows that the verbalizations of others seem to have no influence on his actions. He needs to be taught to slow down before taking action. He needs to learn to cognitively examine the alternative ways he can behave.

The behavioral therapist immediately agrees and becomes very involved with the cognitive therapist in an animated discussion of how Harry could be taught to think before taking action so that his thoughts control and regulate actions. The two therapists clearly understand each other. Harry, they begin, should be given a course in self-instruction training. They explain that as Harry and his therapist work together on a task, his therapist models each of several important steps intended to train Harry to internalize verbal commands that would eventually serve him in regulating his own behavior. First his therapist models pausing for a moment in order to identify the requirements of the task at hand and to select an approach to the problem. Next his therapist copes with the task by verbalizing comments that guide particular responses. Last his therapist reinforces himself by saying, "I did really good with that one." They quickly add that Harry's therapist could also model making an error. Here his therapist illustrates how the child could make use of coping statements in the face of failure by saying, "Oops, I made a mistake; next time I'll try to go slower and concentrate more."

At this point the psychodynamic therapist, puzzled and somewhat irritated, interrupts this animated discussion, saying, "I don't get it. You mean Harry's treatment would involve having him watch the therapist work on a task?"

The cognitive and behavioral therapists respond. "That's only the first phase of treatment. After his therapist shows him each step of self-instruction, Harry performs a task imitating the therapist. Harry goes through each step and makes the same statements out loud that his therapist did."

Still skeptical, the psychodynamic therapist says, "Give me an example of what the therapist works on to demonstrate these steps."

The cognitive therapist explains that there are various tasks cognitive and behavioral therapists have found useful with young, aggressive children. With one, you give the child a sheet of paper on which are printed rows of different geometric shapes. Then the therapist says (Camp and Ray 1984):

> I am going to show you a new way of working on problems with the Copy Cat game. You have to say what I say and do what I do. I call it thinking out loud because we say out loud what our brain is thinking. We'll start with an easy problem. You probably would not think of it as a problem. But we are going to pretend it is like a problem we have to solve. Later on we'll do lots harder problems and then this thinking out loud will really help. On your sheet of paper and my sheet of paper are a lot of designs. The problem we have to work on is coloring in only the circles without going outside the line. You pick a crayon and I'll pick one. Let's learn to think out loud to help us do this paper. You be a copy cat. You must copy what I say and do (*therapist holds a crayon high in the air*). I am going to think out loud. What is my problem? I am supposed to color the circle. How can I do it? I'll go slowly. I'll be careful. I'll outline the circle first. Then, I can go faster in the middle. That's my plan. Here I go (*therapist begins coloring*). [p. 326]

"That's it? Harry watches the therapist color!" exclaims the psychodynamic therapist, who is struggling to control her anger and disbelief. "Do you think Harry would sit long enough to listen to that speech?" Sensing that an argument is about to explode, the developmental consultant, who seems to be less emotional, interrupts by asking, "What comes next?"

The cognitive and behavioral therapists again speak in unison. They go on to explain that there are several other important phases in self-instructional training. After Harry shows he understands and can perform each of the steps while working on a task, his therapist models by working on another task, but now the therapist whispers the statements to himself. Again Harry takes a turn working on a task, now whispering the statements to himself. In the next phase his therapist works on another task but now uses a variety of behaviors and gestures that convey that he is thinking the statements that previously were spoken out loud and whispered.

"Like what?" asks the psychodynamic therapist, who is now beginning to gain some control over her irritation.

"Well, like rubbing his chin, looking hard at the task, and pausing to convey that he is concentrating on each step," chorus the cognitive and behavioral therapists.

"Then Harry imitates the therapist's gestures?" asks the psychodynamic therapist.

"Yes," the cognitive and behavioral therapists respond. The behavioral therapist continues to emphasize that it is important that the training be repeated with tasks that are carefully constructed to form a graded series, increasing in difficulty and complexity. As one example, after the coloring task, the therapist could give

Harry a sheet of paper on which are printed rows of different geometric shapes. On the left side are problems and on the right side, possible answers. In the first row there would be a series of alternating circles and squares. At the end of the row is a circle. Harry would have to decide which shape comes next. On the right side would be three different shapes and he is to mark the one that comes next. Gradually, step by step, the tasks would contain stimuli that are more emotionally evocative and related to interpersonal issues. As an example, Harry learns to identify emotions by looking at pictures of children and adults interacting in different situations, and labeling the emotions the persons in the picture are showing. While examining other pictures, Harry is asked to describe what is going on, mention possible responses a key person in the scene could make to deal with the problem depicted, and discuss the consequences of each action. In this way Harry is taught to take another person's point of view and to learn how to engage in self-evaluation. In the last phase of treatment his therapist enacts the behavior depicted in a picture and Harry imitates this behavior. Then they reverse roles and Harry models some behavior and his therapist imitates him. This role-playing is done in various hypothetical situations designed to meet the unique needs of the child being treated.

"What would be one example for Harry?" asks the psychodynamic therapist, who now seems in complete control of her irritation.

In response, the behavioral therapist recalls that Harry's parents had illustrated his impulsiveness by describing an incident during which his brother took one of his toys from a box and Harry spit on him and slapped him. The behavioral therapist explains that Harry would be asked to play that he is using toys and his therapist would play the role of his brother and take a toy from a box. Harry would then use the self-instruction he learned to cope with this incident.

"Or," the cognitive therapist adds, "his therapist could play Harry listening to the teacher read a story, and Harry would play a classmate sitting next to him. His therapist, as Harry, gets the urge to hit him playing the classmate. To control his urge, his therapist models self-instructions he and Harry had already rehearsed. Then they would reverse roles, and Harry would play himself and his therapist would play the classmate."

Having outlined how they would help Harry, the cognitive and behavioral therapists turn to the psychodynamic therapist, clearly conveying that they now expect her to propose a formulation and treatment plan. Understanding the invitation, the psychodynamic therapist begins.

"I have a very different view of Harry and how therapy should help him. First I want to mention that therapy is a process shared by two people; therapy is a journey that the child takes you on, traveling through the child's personal world, a terrain that you have never seen before. If you begin with tasks, you run the risk of blocking Harry from taking you into his personal world. First he has to be provided with a relationship within which he can eventually discover and share the secrets that are causing his trouble. By secrets I mean unconscious fantasies and wishes. What I'm saying, then, is that it's important to learn what unconscious mental conflicts are responsible for Harry's spitting, biting, and hyperactivity. One guess I have is that he hasn't yet resolved his anger over being replaced by his younger sister. He could be crippled by intense sibling rivalry. When slapping, biting, and spitting on other kids, then, he is expressing rage toward his sister that he is displacing onto other kids. Moreover, this intense sibling rivalry is very likely also rooted in his relationships with his parents, and here is another possible source of his conflicts. His mother seems to pamper him and cling to him. Father seems distant from Harry and more invested in his daughter."

The integrative psychotherapist seems to understand what the psychodynamic therapist is saying. But the eyes of the cognitive and behavioral therapists take on a glassy stare and their attention drifts away. Noticing their expressions, but undaunted, the psychodynamic therapist continues without missing a beat, determined to get them to understand why the underlying dynamics of behavior are important.

"We would need to find out more about Harry's oedipal fantasies, the love and hate he feels unconsciously toward each parent. For example, is he struggling with the fact that while he initially won the queen, his mother, he also thinks that he subsequently lost her to his sister when she was born. Then there's the issue that his father, the king, appears to be a weak, passive figure. Father doesn't seem to represent attributes that Harry can idealize and internalize. For this reason Harry could be caught in a terrible bind that stirs up a great deal of anxiety. He does not have a strong authority figure whose standards he can identify with and internalize. He has not developed a good enough superego that could help him keep his impulses under control. Harry needs to gain insight into these various dynamics. He needs to become conscious of these issues so that he can discuss them. When he does, his biting, spitting, and slapping should diminish as well as his hyperactivity."

As the psychodynamic therapist completes her comment, the cognitive and behavioral therapists are still looking with blank stares. They have heard such formulations before, but do not understand what the psychodynamic therapist is talking about. While everyone sits in a moment of silence, the developmental consultant steps in. Because she is not a therapist, and still uncertain as to whether she belongs, she addresses the others in the third person, speaking in a didactic tone and comparing the positions discussed thus far.

"Both the cognitive and behavioral therapists, as well as the psychodynamic therapist, are saying that they are committed to promoting change in Harry's behavior and relieving him of his suffering. The cognitive and behavioral therapists believe it is important to choose a specific target behavior, as the cause of Harry's difficulties, and change that behavior. So they focus their interventions on Harry's aggressive and impulsive behavior. They set out to change that behavior by using tasks that will teach him how to use verbal statements to regulate himself, and they also use modeling. The psychodynamic therapist believes change will come about as Harry gains insight, as he becomes aware of the conflicted forces and meanings in his unconscious. These are two different views of change.

"While we grapple with this difference," the developmentalist continues, "I would also like to bring attention to the importance of trying to understand Harry's status in terms of different lines of development. These include his cognitive functioning, the relationship between his cognitive functioning and his emotional functioning, and the modes and modalities he uses to interact with others and give meaning to experiences. Shouldn't we be interested in how Harry constructs knowledge and what interpretation he gives to his experiences? The psychodynamic therapist has emphasized in her formulation the meanings Harry has given experiences. For example, she speculated that Harry is enraged with his sister because Harry construes that she has taken away his mother's favor, which had been Harry's until the sister arrived. And the psychodynamic therapist also speculated that Harry experiences his classmates as representations of his sister and experiences his father as a weak figure.

"But there is more one can say about the meanings Harry gives experiences. In recent years infant research has been teaching us a lot about how knowledge is constructed in the first two or three years of life, how experiences become represented and symbolized. Research stresses that from the first months of life action leads to representation and representation leads to action, so that sensorimotor or body-based experiences are the foundations from which higher functions emerge, such as fantasizing and thinking with words."

Beginning to feel the confidence that comes to her when she is lecturing to a class, the developmentalist continues. "Developmental research suggests that one way of conceptualizing change is in terms of the degree to which a stimulus or context results in a particular response based upon the child's history of stimulus–response contingencies. Another way of conceptualizing change is in terms of the degree of differentiation or articulation some behavior reflects. In this view, behaviors, whether actions, fantasies, or thoughts, progress from organizations that are global to organizations that are differentiated and articulated. Harry seems to show a narrow range of behavioral and emotional responses. His mode of responding and representing seem global, even for a 5-year-old, and he relies a great deal on action and very little on fantasy play and spoken words. At the same time, from the other view, it seems that all his environments—home, school, family members, teachers, and peers—are associated with aggressive-hyperactive responses."

"That's exactly the point!" interrupt the cognitive and behavioral therapists, seizing upon this last comment and ignoring the other suggestions by the developmentalist. "And the clinical goal is to provide him with words that control action."

The cognitive, behavioral, and psychodynamic therapists are about to engage in a debate, each having seized for support one or another of the developmentalist's remarks. However, recognizing that the exchange could become unpleasant, they turn to the integrative psychotherapist. Each hopes that this newcomer would lean the discussion more in her/his direction.

The integrative psychotherapist begins by saying, "You know, there's a Chinese proverb that goes something like this, 'Each sect has its truth and each truth has its sect.'" Uncertain as to how to elaborate this opening for everyone's benefit, she is relieved when at that moment the next set of parents is ushered into the interviewing room.

With that, the five consultants immediately turn and focus their attention on the interview that has already gotten under way. The parents are meticulously dressed. What is more striking, the mother is nearly 6 feet tall, and the father stands a head above her. They are discussing their 15-year-old daughter, Mary. She struggles to do her homework, recently spending an entire weekend to write a three-page paper for her English class. Mary has always been subdued and shy, having little to do with friends. Her social isolation has become more apparent since she entered high school. Moreover, while Mary has been exceptionally neat throughout childhood, she has become obsessively meticulous of late. She sometimes spends hours cleaning the kitchen and rearranging cupboards. Mother thinks Mary uses this activity to avoid doing her homework.

Speaking as if he is making a confession, father spontaneously discusses that Mary had extreme difficulty with toilet training. Many battles took place around the potty until Mary passed her third birthday. Then one day father screamed at her and angrily sat her on the potty. From that day on Mary accommodated. The reason for father's guilt now seemed apparent to each of the consultants. But there was something else. Mary did not want to use words and sentences, sometimes resorting to "baby babbling." After Mary began using the potty at age 3, and until the age of 5, she would slip into long phases of selective mutism. The pediatrician, when consulted, noted that Mary would eventually grow out of it. In middle childhood the habit of using baby talk faded away for the most part, and Mary only occasionally slipped into this style of speech.

At this point the parents leave the office and Mary enters. She is a tall girl for 15 years, attractive and very stylishly dressed, more so than what seems typical for teenagers these days. She holds herself very straight and walks rather stiffly. She sits and looks directly at the examiner but avoids eye contact, responding to questions with slow, soft, but steady comments. She reports that her biggest problem is her inability to get her schoolwork done. She offers that other girls are better than she in gym class and that she experiences excessive stress during French class, especially when the teacher calls on students to respond in French. She is convinced that her pronunciation of French is atrocious. She also acknowledges that she feels uncomfortable, even afraid, in strange situations. She is particularly afraid of the dark, and leaves the lights on in her bedroom throughout the night.

When Mary leaves, the behavioral therapist immediately initiates the discussion. "It seems clear," he notes, "that Mary could benefit from systematic desensitization. Let me explain," he adds, as he recognizes the look on the psychodynamic therapist's face, which suggests she is not in agreement. "The therapist would begin by helping Mary articulate the particular qualities in persons and situations that arouse anxiety and fear. Then the therapist would help Mary construct a list of situations that typically occur in her daily life, in which she experiences these qualities. The situations would be ranked from those that arouse the least anxiety and fear to those that arouse the most. Then Mary would be trained in the method of muscle relaxation. Following this, Mary would begin the process of systematic desensitization. With this technique, while imagining the least stressful situation, she would practice relaxing, taking as many trials as necessary until the situation she is imagining stirs up little or no anxiety and fear. Then she would move to the next most anxiety-provoking situation on her list. She would imagine this situation while practicing relaxation until that situation becomes relatively neutral. In this way, step by step, she would move to each situation on her list until the most feared situation in the hierarchy is tackled."

The cognitive therapist agrees and points out that in addition to anxiety and fear aroused by particular situations, Mary is also impaired by irrational beliefs, like her conviction that all girls in gym class are better than she is and that her pronunciation of French is atrocious. Self-talk instruction could also help replace these irrational beliefs with more rational ones. Moreover, "The technique of coping statements could help counter these irrational beliefs," elaborates the cognitive therapist.

"What is that technique?" the developmental researcher asks.

"Mary would prepare a self-talk dialogue that she would use when in a stressful situation. For example, when she enters the French class, Mary would say to herself, 'When I walk into French class I will probably be very nervous. But nothing has ever happened in French class that would give me cause to be afraid. The other kids are friendly and enjoy being there. I'm going to say hello to them and to the teacher. I can speak French as well as the other kids can. If I make a mistake, so what, all the other kids make mistakes, too. We are in the class to learn.'" The cognitive therapist elaborates, "In the treatment sessions Mary would rehearse this self-talk dialogue following the same steps we outlined when discussing Harry. First she would rehearse the statements aloud, expressing confidence and competence, then she would whisper the statements to herself, and eventually say them in her mind. Again the therapist would take turns and model these steps. Mary could also write the statements on a card and take the card with her to read just before she enters the class."

"I understand what you're trying to do," responds the psychodynamic therapist, "but aren't you leaving out a lot? I mean what if you help Mary to be less anxious in French class, won't the anxiety find another situation where it will express itself? What you're leaving out again are the unconscious conflicts that are the source of Mary's fear and inhibition. She seems to be a mixture of an obsessive and anxious personality. Her early trouble with toilet training and her refusing to talk suggest a major unconscious conflict that has to do with rage over being controlled and having to give in to authority. She cleans the kitchen and stays away from friends because it helps her control her unconscious rage and its anxiety. Her struggle with writing an English paper, putting her thoughts on paper, is an extension of her early struggle with putting feces in the potty. She must gain insight over these issues if she's to become freer emotionally and socially as well as academically."

The developmental researcher again launches reminders that sensorimotor experiences are the foundation of higher cognitive functioning, and that Mary's unique physical experiences, especially her encopresis at the age of 3, have to be addressed if higher cognitive functions are to be promoted. Moreover, symbolic functioning surges at the age of 2, when language begins to be the main mode with which symbols are constructed and shared with others. Mary's selective mutism suggests these developments were derailed. "We cannot presume we understand what she means by taking the words she uses at face value. And given recent research on mother–infant interaction, we need to learn more about Mary's unique experiences transacting with her mother in her first years of life." The developmentalist concludes by summarizing again how each of the therapists views the task of promoting change. The cognitive and behavioral therapists believe that therapy should focus on specific target behaviors that are causing suffering in Mary's current daily life—such as her fear of speaking in French class and her belief that all girls in the gym class are better than she. In contrast, the psychodynamic therapist does not believe one should focus on these symptoms. Rather, the symptomatic behaviors will change as Mary uncovers unconscious meanings and conflicts and works them through.

At this point, again as if to avoid a debate, the three therapists and the developmental researcher turn to the integrative psychotherapist who has been silent but attentive. She accepts the invitation and begins, "Let's ask whether and how each of the points of view you represent could be integrated. Let's ask ourselves, would we be better able to help Mary, would we come up with new techniques to help her, if we integrated cognitive, behavioral, psychodynamic, and developmental viewpoints?"

The three therapists and developmental consultant respond in unison, "Oh, you propose we take an eclectic position? We should take something from each approach, whatever would be of help to Mary. Maybe we should combine some psychodynamic therapy with systematic desensitization. We could help her uncover unconscious conflicts and rage while also providing her with tools that would help her become less afraid of gym and French classes."

"No," replies the integrative psychotherapist. "I do not mean take a little of this and a little of that. I mean integration that results in a new model of therapy that prescribes and guides new therapy techniques."

"We don't understand," respond the four.

At this point the integrative therapist again relies on a metaphor. "Well, I believe Nietzsche once said something like, 'Mankind has a bad ear for new music,' or maybe he said something like, 'Mankind seems not to be able to hear new music when it is first played.' I'm suggesting that the integrative psychotherapy I will describe for children and adolescents will at first sound strange to your ears. I believe some parts will sound familiar to the cognitive therapist, other parts to the behavioral therapist, other parts to the psychodynamic therapist, and still other parts to the developmental researcher. I hope each of you considers all of the parts and tries to integrate them. Then the whole of the approach should become clear."

CULTIVATING AN INTEGRATIVE VIEWPOINT
REQUIRES ADDITIONAL PREPARATION

At this point I will assume the voice of the integrative psychotherapist and devote the remainder of this volume to elaborating and discussing the particular form of integrative psychotherapy I propose for children. As I discuss my model and the methods it prescribes, I am sensitive to the possibility that it may not be seen as a totality by all readers. I believe there is merit to Nietzsche's caution, which the integrative psychotherapist reported in the imaginary consultation described above. We are not likely to hear music that is new, that is unfamiliar. The more we have listened to one type of music, and committed ourselves to it, the more we are likely not to hear, understand, and appreciate some very different musical form. Or, if we hear it, the sound is so alien that we screen it out, in some way dismiss it, or fit it into our already existing musical preference.

In a similar way, returning to our metaphor of "psychotherapy kaleidoscopes," therapists tend to become very accustomed to seeing one pattern of colors and shapes while looking at child psychotherapy. If the kaleidoscope is shaken and a very different pattern is presented, the danger is that the therapist will not see the totality of the new and different pattern but tend to see sections that contain shapes and colors that are familiar. I hope the discussion thus far has helped to soften to some degree the reader's existing categories about child psychotherapy and has begun to shake up the pattern held by the reader's psychotherapy kaleidoscope.

However, there is still more we can do to prepare ourselves for an integrative perspective if we ask, "Why do different viewpoints of psychotherapy exist that require integration?" If a therapist is familiar with and likes a particular pattern of colors and shapes, or prefers to listen to and dance to the music of one viewpoint, why is it so difficult to see a different pattern or to hear the music of another? Why is it that for more than a century psychological investigators and theorists have drawn boundaries that divide the discipline of human psychology into segregated sects, with each holding its truth and each truth surrounding a sect? These questions are addressed in the next chapter.

2

Segregation in Psychology: The Tendency to Construct Boundaries

CONTENTS

To address the questions I raised at the close of the previous chapter, I discuss here particular boundaries American psychology has drawn over the years, segregating the discipline into sects. These boundaries in turn have influenced the segregation of psychotherapy into cognitive, behavioral, and psychodynamic camps, with cognitive and behavioral sometimes joining forces. If we understand the reasons why we tend to separate human psychology into sects, and what is being segregated and polarized, we should be better able to go beyond segregation and engage in the process of integration. Referring to our earlier discussion, when looking through the kaleidoscope of child psychotherapy, the reader may see only cognitive psychotherapy, or behavioral psychotherapy, or psychodynamic psychotherapy, or some combination of cognitive and behavioral psychotherapy. With the discussion to follow, I hope to further disassemble the kaleidoscopic design the reader is accustomed to seeing and set the stage for us to see a different design that integrates parts of each of these main approaches.

THE AIM OF SEGREGATION: AVOIDING WHAT IS CONSTRUED AS UNPLEASANT/UNTRUE/INCORRECT

When asking over the years what we should observe and understand, which concepts we should hold as true and pursue, American psychology has drawn many boundaries—between, for example, clinical practice and research, normal and pathological, conscious and unconscious, behavioral and psychodynamic, verbal and nonverbal. Once a boundary is drawn, one member of the polarized pair is viewed as true and more worthy than the other. Why this tendency to divide domains of knowledge into poles and then focus on one while subordinating the other? To address this question, I find the writings of Ken Wilber (1977, 1979) very helpful. He convincingly argues that in Western thinking, when we attempt to understand and give meaning to an experience, knowingly or unknowingly, we immediately draw mental boundaries that cast the experience as one of a pair of opposites: for example, good versus evil, freedom versus restriction, beautiful versus ugly, success versus failure, appearance versus reality. To quote Wilber:

> So successful [is] this mapping of nature that . . . our lives are largely spent drawing boundaries. Every decision we make, our every action, our every word is based on the construction, conscious or unconscious, of boundaries. I am not now referring to just self-identity boundaries—important as that

certainly is—but to all boundaries in the broadest sense. To make a decision means to draw a boundary line between what to choose and what not
to choose. To desire something means to draw a boundary line between
pleasurable and painful things and then move toward the former. To maintain an idea means to draw a boundary line between concepts felt to be true
and concepts felt not to be true. . . . [1979, p. 17]

Wilber also discussed how the Eastern way of experiencing is characterized
more by a process of forging holistic meanings. To illustrate this process, consider
that the Chinese convey the meaning of *crisis* by combining two brushstrokes. One
conveys the meaning of *danger* (phonetic pronunciation WAY); the other, the
meaning of *opportunity* (phonetic pronunciation GEE). In combining the two
brushstrokes, the meaning of crisis unites being aware of danger and recognizing
opportunity.

Why is there the proclivity to draw boundaries in Western thinking? According
to Wilber, beginning with Greek philosophers, we have been oriented to construe
experiences as containing either pleasure or pain. The boundary the mind draws
serves to renounce the part that arouses pain, freeing us to pursue pleasure. In my
example then, instead of experiencing a crisis as unifying the pain of danger with
the excitement of opportunity, Western thinking splits off what is construed as
the cause of pain and pursues what is presumed to avoid the crisis.

In its early years, when the discipline of American psychology was taking shape,
the Western tradition of constructing boundaries was already exerting considerable influence. Investigators of the day were apparently busy dividing and segregating issues. But one of the founding fathers of psychology seemed to be unhappy
with this tendency. In perhaps the first discussion of personality assessment published more than a century ago, Sir Francis Galton (1884) had this to say as he
surveyed what students of human behavior of that day were doing: "There are two
sorts of [investigators] . . . those who habitually dwell on pleasanter circumstances
. . . and those who have an eye out for the unpleasing ones" (p. 180).

A few years later, Frederick Lyman Wells provided a more explicit example
of how investigators, who were shaping the infant field of psychology, were dwell-
ing on "pleasanter circumstances" in order to avoid "unpleasing ones." Wells (1911,
1912, 1914) had just published his extensive experiments with the "free-association
method." By the time he conducted his studies, the procedure was already very
familiar. The examiner spoke a word to which the subject was to reply with the
"first thing it makes you think of, the first word it suggests to you." Once the associations were obtained, the investigator studied the reaction time to each stimulus
word, as well as the content of the associations, in search of correlations that reveal
"mental and affective processes."

The free-association method had been reported in Europe in 1883 by its originator, Sir Francis Galton, as one way to study a person's "emotional life," and subsequently introduced into the United States in 1887 by James McKeen Cattell in

two classic publications (see Santostefano 1976c). During the next twenty years, following Cattell's work, numerous reports of the technique appeared, reflecting the extent to which the free-association test method had captured the interest and enthusiasm of students of behavior. When Wells reviewed these studies, he noticed a trend that disturbed him. He believed that too many investigators of his time had been avoiding the unpleasant goal of learning about a person's "emotional life" by "hiding themselves" in pleasanter studies of grammatical, lexical, and intellectual connections between the stimulus word and the associated response. The following comment by Wells (1912) reflects the extent to which he was concerned about this segregation.

> Such experiments [of word association] lay bare the mental and emotional life in a way that is startling and not always gratifying . . . so startling and so ungratifying, in fact, that workers with association experiments seem long to have been effectively blocked from any progress along this line . . . the psychology of today is very much a science of looking for the truth and hoping you won't find it. . . . [p. 436]

Since the work of Galton and Wells, American psychology has continued to draw boundaries dividing issues into opposing camps. Three of these boundaries have particular relevance for the model of integrative child psychotherapy outlined in this volume. The first boundary we consider segregates "real knowledge" and "subjective knowledge," resulting in opposing viewpoints, each with its assumptions and propositions. Within this segregation of knowledge, I nest two other boundaries: one segregates body and mind; the other, cognition and emotion, reflecting the influence exerted by the more basic division of "real" and "subjective."

THE BOUNDARY DIVIDING THE BASIS OF KNOWLEDGE: OBJECTIVE/REAL VS. SUBJECTIVE/APPEARANCE

At first glance the issues I raise in this section may seem misplaced in a volume concerning child psychotherapy. But there is one important reason why a discussion of the segregation of knowledge, as either real or subjective, is very relevant. If we accept the view, discussed in the previous chapter, that psychotherapy is a learning process in which patient and therapist gather knowledge in an effort to promote change, we are faced with several questions that should be addressed. What is knowledge? How is knowledge acquired? How does the child construct and continuously revise knowledge and his/her understanding of him-/herself, the world, and experiences? These questions require us to place one foot in philosophy and the other in human psychology so that we will not lose sight of our focus, namely, an integrative approach to child psychotherapy.

In philosophy and the history of science there have been two responses to the question, "What is knowledge and how is it acquired?" These responses reflect a boundary dividing two opposing camps that have engaged in revolutions and counterrevolutions for centuries (Overton 1994, 1997a, Overton and Horowitz 1991). One camp is usually referred to as "objectivism" or "realism" and the other as "interpretationism" or "rationalism." For convenience I will use the terms *objectivism* and *interpretationism* in my discussion. I will try to show why it is important for a therapist to be aware of whether he/she stands in one or the other of these camps, or whether the therapist sometimes stands in one and sometimes in the other. As we will soon discover, the position one takes about how knowledge is acquired eventually results in fundamentally different therapeutic concepts and methods. Moreover, an understanding of these opposing positions is necessary, I believe, in any effort to think about how to form an integrative approach to psychotherapy for children.

To discuss this issue, I borrow heavily from the illuminating writings of Overton (1994, 1997a,b; Overton and Horowitz 1991), which the reader is encouraged to review directly. While I rely on Overton for aspects of this discussion, I take responsibility, of course, for the way I present his ideas. To aid our discussion, I have inverted, and added to, Overton's schema (Overton and Horowitz 1991, p. 2) to construct Figure 2–1, which outlines the pathways and levels followed by objectivism and interpretationism.

Level I: What Is Knowledge and How Is It Acquired?

The starting point of each pathway involves epistemology, the study of knowledge and how it is acquired. The position of objectivism holds that knowledge exists independently of a person's cognitive and perceptual activity. In other words, the external world contains fully sufficient knowledge that already exists, and the person or knower is separate from this knowledge. Knowledge of the external world is acquired, or learned, by the person's perceptual, cognitive, and behavioral activity. In contrast, interpretationism holds that there is no knowledge as such in the environment existing independent of the knower. Therefore, a person and knowledge are not segregated. Knowledge is constructed when the person's perceptions, cognition, and actions engage the environment. As we can see from Figure 2–1, when taking one or the other of these starting points, we are led to very different strategies of knowing, assumptions about knowledge and the knower, clinical concepts, and views of how change in knowledge and behavior takes place.

Level II: Strategies of Knowing

Moving to the second level, we are now concerned with the ways in which we determine that what we know is scientific. What strategies would we accept as provid-

LEVELS	OBJECTIVISM	INTERPRETATIONISM
I **What Is Knowledge and How Is It Acquired?**	Knowledge exists independent of the knower.	Knowledge is constructed by activity of the knower.
II **Strategies of Knowing**	Neutral, controlled observations result in knowledge that is independent of the knower.	All knowledge is determined by the observer's assumptions and preformed concepts.
III **Metatheoretical Assumptions**	Boundaries can be set between: the observer and observed; the observed and environment; the real event and subjective experience.	Observer and observed are two poles on a continuum, each defining and defined by the other, and engaged in a dialectical process.
IV **Metaphors of Human Functioning**	Machine metaphor: person is a machine; inputs (stimuli) activate the machine to produce outputs (responses) that are mediated by internal stimuli and responses (cognitions).	Organic metaphor: person is a cell embedded in an organization of cells and engaged in an active dialectical exchange with them.
V **Change and Growth**	Growth results from accumulation of behaviors and representations that correspond with the real world or from elimination of behaviors and cognitions that are maladaptive.	Growth results from repetitive cycles of differentiation and integration of one's behavior and those of others participating in the relational matrix.
VI **Approaches to Psychotherapy**	Cognitive-behavioral therapies.	Psychodynamic-interpersonal-humanistic therapies.

FIGURE 2–1
The Pathway and Ladder of Objectivism and Interpretationism

ing scientific approaches to determining what is knowledge, how it is acquired, and how it changes? The rules that distinguish "science" from other types of knowing are called *demarcationist strategies*. These strategies demarcate, or distinguish, science from other types of knowing. Since objectivism holds that knowledge already exists in the environment independent of the observer (Level 1), objectivism accepts the strategy that neutral, direct, and well-controlled observations will eventually discover that knowledge, and emphasizes that these observations must be made before interpretations can be formulated.

One example of the objectivist position is found in the several editions of the *Diagnostic and Statistical Manual of Mental Disorders* that have gained dominance in clinical practice over the past thirty years, including the most recent, the *DSM-IV* (American Psychiatric Association 1994). These manuals are presented as free of any theory and based solely on empirical research findings. Clinicians are asked to collect "neutral" observations of a patient's presenting problems and history and then determine whether a required number of behaviors are reported/observed before deciding if a patient qualifies for a diagnostic label. For example, to qualify for the diagnosis of attention deficit hyperactivity disorder, predominantly inattentive type, the clinician must determine that six or more of the following behaviors have persisted for at least six months: (1) makes careless mistakes in schoolwork; (2) has difficulty sustaining attention in tasks; (3) does not seem to listen; (4) fails to finish schoolwork; (5) has difficulty organizing tasks; (6) avoids tasks that require sustained mental efforts; (7) loses task-related items such as pencils; (8) is easily distracted; (9) is often forgetful. In the camp of objectivism, then, distinctions are maintained between fact and interpretation, between description and explanation, and between data and theory. If these distinctions are maintained, relationships and sequences can be determined between stimuli and the effect they have on a person.

The demarcationist strategy followed by the camp of interpretationism is quite different. Since interpretationism holds that there is no knowledge as such in the environment (Level I), the interpretationist takes the position that all observations, including those controlled in some experimental way, are influenced by what the observer already thinks. The phenomena observed are shaped by the lens the investigator looks through, which consists of assumptions, concepts, and beliefs the observer already holds as true. Thus neutral, pristine observations as such are not possible. Given that the observer participates in, and in part determines, what is observed, how does one explain and understand what one observes? The investigator searches for patterns, or organizations, displayed by the phenomena being observed, rather than connections between cause and effect. Explanations or conceptualizations of phenomena, then, are based upon these patterns. Examples would be patterns of cognitive and/or behavioral activity that are interpreted as "mental schemas," "embodied schemas," "attachments," "cognitive style," and "representations of interactions generalized," all of which we will return to later. As can be seen, this type of explanation involves constructing a metaphor that symbolizes or represents the pattern observed. Metaphors, then, are accepted as scientific interpretations.

Applied to the diagnostic evaluation of presenting problems, the interpretationist would not look to see whether six of the nine predefined behaviors listed above exist. Rather, the interpretationist would look for patterns of behavior that reveal, for example, some aspect of a child's body image (e.g., when approached by a depressed parent, the child's body slumps and the head turns away), aspects of the child's cognitive activity (e.g., the child looks away each time the parent looks at the child, or the child turns to some solo activity each time the depressed parent attempts to ask the child to perform some task), and indications of how the child represents interactions with others and what the child expects from others (e.g., the child displays these behaviors when interacting with an adult who is not depressed).

Another example contrasts the demarcationist strategies of objectivism with those of interpretationism. There has been a debate in psychoanalysis between two positions. One, anchored in objectivism, assumes that certain events that occurred in the past, because they are traumatic, are repressed and forgotten along with emotions and meanings associated with them. When psychoanalytic treatment lifts the repression that has kept these events outside of awareness, a "historical truth" is uncovered. The memory and its meanings are seen as knowledge that existed independent of the person's mental activity and that is contained in the traumatic event. The other position in this debate is anchored in interpretationism. When participating in psychoanalytic treatment, a person does not construct "a historical truth" but "a narrative truth." That is, events that have occurred in the past are reconstructed and re-created by the person in the present in order to give meaning to them within the context of the unique relationship that is developing with the therapist.

Level III: Metatheoretical Assumptions

Strategies of knowing are based on particular metatheoretical assumptions, the third level depicted in Figure 2–1. Since objectivism accepts that well-controlled observations will uncover knowledge that already exists (Level II), objectivism also assumes that the observer can maintain several boundaries that enable him/her to gather knowledge that already exists. One boundary is set between the observer and the person being observed. Another boundary is set between the individual and the environment in order to observe how the individual responds when the environment stimulates him/her and how the environment responds when the individual acts upon the environment. A third boundary is set between the "real" (that is, some actual event or phenomenon) that the observer perceives on the one hand and, on the other, the "subjective" (what the person being observed reports). Further, the individual is assumed to be inherently passive and to respond whenever stimulation occurs. Last, to learn as much as possible about particular stimuli that lead to particular responses, both stimuli and responses are broken down into parts that can be added and subtracted.

In contrast, interpretationism assumes that two persons cannot be divided with one viewed as the observer and the other as the object of observation. Nor can subject and object be split, whether the subject and object are a person and some stimulus in the environment or a person and someone else. Rather, subject and object are viewed as two poles on a continuum, or two sides of a coin, forming a relational matrix. Each person is involved with the other in a continuous dialectical process within which each defines the other and each is defined by the other. In addition, when entering this dialectical process, each person comes with, and introduces, an organization of activity that transacts with the organization of activity presented by the other.

Level IV: Metaphors that Guide the Construction of Concepts, Questions, and Methods Used to Address Them

As metatheoretical assumptions become elaborated (Level III), they organize around a metaphor. The metaphor depicts fundamental images that guide the types of questions asked and the concepts and methods constructed to address these questions. For decades, the metaphor of "a machine" has been used to characterize the metatheoretical assumptions of objectivism, while an "organic" metaphor has been used to characterize the metatheoretical assumptions of interpretationism. Along with discussing each of these metaphors, we will consider how each constructs images of what happens between two or more persons (interpersonal issues), what happens within an individual (interpersonal or intrapsychic issues), and the meanings a person gives experiences.

The Person as a Machine: The Metaphor of Objectivism

The assumptions of objectivism have been represented by a metaphor that symbolizes a human as if he/she were a machine. The particular machine used as the referent for the metaphor has changed as various machines have taken turns dominating our culture (e.g., telegraph system, telephone switchboard, hydraulic pump, and most recently the digital computer). Whether one or another of these machines is used as the metaphor, the investigator is guided by the same set of fundamental images. These are: behaviors can be separated into parts; the parts can be added or subtracted in some fashion; the whole can be defined by adding the parts; behaviors are aroused by stimuli; the relationships between stimuli and responses are linear; the machine receives "inputs" defined either as "stimuli" or "information"; the machine delivers "outputs" defined either as "responses" or "behaviors."

How the machine metaphor images the space between inputs and outputs, that is, the inside of the machine or person, has changed over the years as the particular machine used has changed. Early on, in the 1920s, the work of John B. Watson, which led to the initial behavioral approaches to therapy, focused on inputs and outputs and paid no attention to the inside of the machine save for the position that it should be ignored. Watson rejected concepts such as consciousness, mind, and imagery, namely, the interior of the machine, and believed that given stimuli, responses could be predicted.

When B. F. Skinner introduced his work a few years later, a shift occurred in how the machine was viewed. Unlike Watson, Skinner conceptualized the organism as active, in that it exhibits behaviors, and the environment as selecting and reinforcing particular responses. In spite of this shift from the image of a passive to an active machine or person, it is important to note that Skinner's work, for the most part, continued Watson's position that the inside of the machine or person should be ignored because what one sees there is dangerous, at least to science. This view is poignantly reflected by a statement Allan Paivio (1975) made some years ago at a time when what Watson and Skinner believed about the inside of the machine or person was quite influential.

> Skinner warned us against the diversionary effects of fascination with the inner life. I agree that the possibility is ever present. Mentalistic ideas are so seductive that one is in danger of being led by them down the garden path of intraspectionism and mysticism forever. For that reason only a tough-minded behaviorist can afford to entertain the seductress. [p. 263]

Ignoring the inside of the machine, Skinner asserted, "A person does not act upon the world, the world acts upon him" (1971, p. 202). This statement frames his principles of operant learning, which exerted, and still exert, a significant influence on behavioral approaches to treatment. At the heart of operant theory is the principle that the individual's behavior is related to the consequences it produces in the environment. This position has been characterized as the A: B: C of behavioral theory, which relies on the metatheoretical assumption that a boundary can be set between the individual and environment. The "A" stands for the *antecedent*, environmental conditions, or stimuli, that evoke the person to produce some form of *behavior*—the "B" in the paradigm. The person's behavior in turn produces some *consequence* in the environment—the "C" in the equation.

The consequence determines, in two ways, whether and how often the particular behavior will occur in the future. If the consequence contains positive reinforcement (the behavior produces a rewarding outcome), the behavior will occur again in response to those particular antecedent stimuli. If the consequence contains negative reinforcement (the environment responds with some form of punishment), the behavior is not likely to occur again in response to the related antecedent stimuli and/or other behaviors will emerge that serve to avoid the undesirable, aversive consequence. From this view, then, if a behavior is maintained or increases in frequency, it is being reinforced by environmental consequences. If a behavior decreases in frequency or is eliminated, it is being punished by consequences. The A:B:C of behavioral theory is still influential, as illustrated by Hollin's (1990) application of the A:B:C model in assessing and treating young offenders: "The force of this position is that [since] the consequences of an individual's behavior are delivered by the environment in which the behavior occurs, then the causes or determinants of behavior are to be found *outside* of the person" (p. 8; italics mine).

Following Skinner, and recalling Paivio's comment, a behaviorist came along who apparently was tough-minded enough to look inside the machine and take on "mentalism, the seductress." With his "social learning theory," Bandura (1977) introduced two new images that attempted to define the interior of the machine or person. First, social learning theory introduced the image that between antecedent stimuli, and the behaviors they evoke (the "A" and "B"), there are "internal" stimuli, and responses connected to them, that mediate between and connect external stimuli with external behavior. Similarly, there are internal stimuli and responses that mediate between and connect behaviors and the consequences associated with them (the "B" and "C"). Moreover, the relations between internal stimuli and responses are constructed by the same learning principles of reinforcement that relate external stimuli with external responses. As this position developed, internal stimuli and responses came to be referred to as "symbols," "representations," "thoughts," and "cognitions." Since, as we shall see, the same terms came to be used by interpretationists, it is important to note that in the machine metaphor a cognitive mediator (i.e., a representation) is evaluated in terms of whether this internal cognition distorts or accurately represents some external event as it exists outside the person.

From the notion that internal cognitions mediate between external stimuli and responses, social learning theory introduced a second, new image of what the inside of the machine looks like. Accepting operant theory's position that behavior is acquired through reinforcement and punishment from the environment, social learning theory added that behavior could also be learned by observing the behavior of others who serve as "models." The process by which this learning occurs was conceptualized in stages and required additional images of the inside of the machine. In the first stage the image concerns the degree of attention a person pays to the model's behavior. Another image conceptualizes whether and how what is perceived is retained at a cognitive level. A third image concerns how the information retained, once a model has been observed, leads to the reenactment of the observed behavior.

The notions of learning by observing models, and of internal cognitive mediators, also elaborated how reinforcement and motivation are imaged within the person or machine. While external consequences could reinforce some behavior, as originally proposed by operant theory, now with modeling and internal cognitive mediators, vicarious reinforcement is also possible. That is, reinforcement can come from imitating some desirable behavior produced by a model. In the same way, self-reinforcement is also possible. With these images added to the inside of the machine, stimuli and responses contained in a person's private thoughts could also reinforce some behavior.

As cognitive research mushroomed in the '70s and '80s, the digital computer became the metaphor of the machine or person. With the image of a computer as the interior of the machine, the space between external stimuli and overt responses was viewed as "information" that is "processed." But previous images were retained. "Internal" information still consisted of symbols, representations, and thoughts viewed as internal responses to internal stimuli. And the processing of this internal information was still viewed in terms of whether external events, which are taken as objectively real, are being distorted in any way. The case of Mary, discussed in the previous chapter, provides an illustration. Mary's inhibited behavior, from the viewpoint of the cognitive and behavioral therapists, was determined by internal cognitive mediators such as her private conviction that "everyone in class is better than I am," a conviction that would be considered a distortion of the real world.

While retaining previous images introduced by social learning theory, when the computer became the machine metaphor of a person, new images were again introduced that elaborated the "inside." One image, for example, portrays several distinct stations within the machine, each station performing a particular step in processing information. To portray these stations, psychological models have been developed and referred to as "social information-processing models." These models emphasize the importance of determining whether or not an error occurs, or a deficiency exists, at one or another station. As an example, one model (Dodge 1986) proposes that there are five stations, arrayed in sequence, that process internal information. Each station plays a role in producing appropriate social behavior. Accordingly, an error or deficiency at any one of these stations results in problematic behavior. The five stations are (1) searching for and attending to a message, (2) interpreting the message using available mediational units, (3) searching for and listing possible responses, (4) deciding which response from the list generated is the most effective, and (5) enacting the response selected. This model has been offered to conceptualize childhood conduct disorders, particularly childhood aggression.

How the Machine Metaphor Images Interpersonal Relationships

How does the machine metaphor view happenings that occur between two persons? Each person is seen as exerting an independent, direct, causal influence on the other. Therefore, relationships are acquired and determined by some schedule of reinforcements provided by the external environment as well as by the availability of behaviors of others serving as models to be imitated. In addition, interpersonal difficulties are understood as being under the direct control of discrete environmental or neurobiological factors or some combination. Anxiety is understood as resulting from classical conditioning in response to a specific stimulus. This view of interpersonal processes has resulted in an emphasis on techniques such as training in relaxation, modeling, and imaging events that cause personal distress, techniques that we will return to later.

How the Machine Metaphor Images Intrapersonal/Intrapsychic Processes

In terms of what happens within an individual, the machine metaphor presents an image of the interior as containing discrete responses and stimuli that are snapped together in a linear fashion to form chains called "mediators." These chains, viewed as "representations" or "symbols," derive from direct learning and imitation and serve the purpose of expressing attitudes, feelings, and expectations. To capture this mechanical image, Foster and his colleagues (1988, cited in Overton and Horowitz 1991) refer to Bandura's writings on social learning theory as follows:

> "Although not disputing the powerful effects that external contingencies exert on behavior, Bandura has maintained that these effects are mediated by cognitive events and processes that are critical links in causal chains producing behavior. He has defined covert events broadly to include verbal mediators, imaginable mediators (images), and arousal mediators (reactions with physiological components). These can serve as stimuli and consequences for other covert and overt responses." [p. 21]

How the Machine Metaphor Images the Meanings a Person Gives Experiences

There are several interrelated ingredients in this image. First, experience is something that happens to a person. Experience is a particular piece of input or information that is acquired by the person. Once acquired, the experience is cast as a "cognitive representation." This representation or meaning is evaluated in terms of how well it fits the "real" event that was experienced. Given this linear view of an event and its meaning, cognitive representations are considered to be either distortions or accurate reflections of the "real." Therefore, problem behaviors are defined as "cognitive distortions" of what the environmental event really means.

In summary, cognitive, behavioral, and cognitive-behavioral therapies rely upon the machine metaphor and its images. In these therapeutic approaches, psychological problems are defined in terms of the absence or deficiency of cognitive skills (mediators) that are assumed to be necessary for adequate functioning. Psychological problems are also defined in terms of the role mediators play in distorting "real" external events. Treatment techniques are designed to provide the cognitive skill or mediator that is absent, and/or that adjust, correct, or modify the mediator distorting opportunities and limitations presented by the real world.

Kendall (1991, cited in Overton and Horowitz 1991) reflects the images of the machine metaphor.

> "The human organism responds primarily to cognitive representations of its environment rather than these environments per se . . . cognitive structures (cognitive representations), or templates, are an accumulation of experiences in memory and serve to filter/screen new experiences . . . anxiety and depression for example are typically linked to misconstruals or misperceptions of the social/interpersonal environment." [p. 23]

The Person as a Plant or Cell: The Organic Metaphor of Interpretationism

For decades, interpretationism has been guided by images that depict a person as a plant or cell. These images have been cast as an "organic" metaphor. While the particular growing organism used as a referent has varied (e.g., a plant, a cell, an embryo), the metaphor has retained particular images that are interrelated: (1) the cell (or person), along with other cells (persons) and the atmosphere (environment) that surrounds it, forms a totality, a holistic system (the image of holism). Accordingly, the cell and the surrounding cells and atmosphere are in a continuous, reciprocal, dialectical relationship (the image of dialectics); (2) the cell (person) is inherently active, self-organizing, and directional, continuously reorganizing and moving from one state or level of existence that is relatively global and undifferentiated to states and levels of being that are increasingly articulated, differentiated, and integrated (the image of dynamics and direction). As we consider each of these images of the organic metaphor, it is important to keep in mind that each aspect influences the other and is influenced by the other.

The image of holism.   Applied to a person and his/her experiences, holism presents the view that, from birth, behaviors are inherently and necessarily organized. This principle focuses attention on the pattern or organization formed by a person and others, including the environment. Whether infant and mother are being considered, or two other persons, the unit is viewed as emerging from an initially undifferentiated matrix. Erikson gave this principle a central position in his thinking: "It is well to remember the epigenetic principle which is derived from the growth of organisms in utero. Somewhat generalized, this principle states that anything that grows has a ground plan, and that out of that ground plan the parts arise . . . to form a functioning whole" (Erikson 1980, p. 53).

A number of investigators have been influenced by the perspective of holism, two of whom serve as illustrations. Reviewing their work with Down syndrome infants, Cicchetti and Schneider-Rosen (1984) concluded that "consistent with the organizational perspective of development, efforts should be made not toward cataloging specific capacities in the cognitive and affective domains, but rather toward obtaining a more holistic picture of the infant in which changing integration and organization of competences becomes a central objective" (p. 397). Similarly, Decarie (1978) commented, after noting that in the infant's experiences the mother can be sucked, smelled, touched, grasped, felt while being rocked, heard and not seen, seen and not heard, "[I]f we ever hope to be able to describe the infant . . . or child as a whole and not 'en pièces détachées,' we have to work toward an apparent contradictory goal by studying simultaneously the perceptual, mental and affective components of . . . phenomena" (pp. 199–200).

From the image of holism, then, the psychological property of some behavior is determined by the total context of which it is a part. Thus two behaviors that appear identical may be understood to be different; for example, a 6-year-old pushes a peer in the playground, and a 25-year-old pushes a colleague in the office. At the same time, two behaviors that are manifestly different may be understood to be identical; for example a 5-year-old injures the family's pet kitten and also breaks his baby brother's rattle. As far as holism is concerned, there is no division between the person and another, or between the person and the environment. There is no inside space or outside space as such. There is one totality that forms an organization.

The image of dialectics.   The view that a person is a part of an organized whole brings with it the image that a person is inherently and continuously engaged in a dialectical relationship with the other parts of the whole within which the person is functioning. Piaget (1952), among others, centered this dialectical image in his conceptualization of development: "Relationship is . . . a fundamental category, inasmuch as it is immanent in all psychic activity and combines with all the other concepts. This is because every totality is a system of relationships just as every relationship is a segment of a totality" (p. 10).

The notion of dialectics, which has its roots in the philosophy of Hegel, proposes that any entity inherently brings with it a contradiction or an antithesis. As the original thesis (or concept) and its antithesis (or paradox) differentiate, the space, or difference, between them is negotiated and becomes the ground on which a new concept is formed that integrates them. In this way a "relational matrix" is formed consisting of three parts: the original concept, its antithesis, and the unit formed when they are integrated. But the dialectical process is a continuous one. Once integration is accomplished, the unit that has been formed becomes a new concept that brings with it another paradox. The new concept and its antithesis again differentiate, the difference between them negotiated, resulting in another new concept with its antithesis, and so on. This cycle of differentiation and integration is repeated over and over again. Hegel used as one example the dialectic between master and slave. A *master* implicitly implies that someone else is constrained. A *slave* implicitly implies that someone else is free and in control. Thus the notion of master cannot be understood without the notion of a slave, and the notion of a slave cannot be understood without the notion of a master. Each notion implies the other, and in that sense they are identical. Yet at the same time the notion of master and slave is distinct. As these notions are articulated and differentiated they would eventually become integrated to form a new concept.

Along the same line, a person's thoughts, emotions, and actions are never perfectly matched with those of others, nor with the environment's opportunities and limitations, all of which form an organization of which the person is a part. From the image of dialectics, the person and another inherently define a contradiction or paradox. The thoughts, emotions, and actions of a person, as part of the organization, both define and are defined by the thoughts, emotions, and actions of another. As the two sets of thoughts, emotions, and actions are negotiated, each gradually differentiates, and together each moves toward an integration to form a new matrix or relationship. The dialectical process of differentiation and integration brings us to another main image produced by the organic metaphor: the dynamics and directiveness of behavior.

The image of dynamics and directiveness of behavior.   The organic image of the dynamics and directiveness of behavior emphasizes two issues. The image of dynamics emphasizes that when embedded in an organization that includes others, a person does not experience stimulation passively. Rather, from birth, he/she makes use of innately given behavioral organizations or modes of functioning, such as motoric rhythm patterns, sensory thresholds, and cognitive/emotional responses, that enable him/her to actively approach, avoid, select, and organize stimulation. The image of dynamics also emphasizes the notion that behavioral structures or organizations, and the functions these structures perform, are always two sides of the same coin. Organization is activity and activity is organization.

The image of directiveness of behavior emphasizes that, as behaviors within a person and between persons engage in a dialectical process, differentiate, and integrate, the totality formed by these behaviors moves from initial states that are global and undifferentiated to states of increasing differentiation and hierarchic integration. Of particular importance, as cycles of differentiation and integration are repeated, each previous, "old" behavior is not replaced by a new one but becomes integrated within the next level of organization.

The image of self and mutual regulation.   One more image emerges when the images of holism, dialectical process, dynamics, and directedness of behavior are combined. As an organization of behaviors within an individual, or between individuals, differentiates in a dialectical process, the organization becomes unstable. To reestablish a state of stability, the organization attempts to regulate itself by evolving new, more differentiated and integrated behaviors, either within an individual (self-regulation) or between individuals (mutual regulation).

How the Organic Metaphor Images Interpersonal Relationships

The image of the relationship between two or more persons should be apparent from the foregoing discussion. Each person is defined by and defines the other and each actively approaches, avoids, and selects stimulation from the other. Since the thoughts, emotions, and actions of one person are never perfectly matched with those of the other, the relationship inherently defines a paradox that is unstable. As the paradox between the two persons is negotiated, the two persons differentiate, and elements of each become integrated. With this integration the relationship moves to a new level of stability. At this new level another paradox is articulated and the process of differentiation and integration continues.

We could take the infant and mother as a paradigm. Initially, the infant and the mother form a unit. This psychological oneness is eventually differentiated into "twoness"—me and not me; infant and mother. While this notion is prevalent in various psychodynamic theories, Piaget (1967) also made use of it in his formulation of cognitive development.

> At the onset of mental evolution there is no definite differentiation between the self and the external world, i.e., impressions that are experienced and perceived are not attached to a personal consciousness sensed as a "self" nor to objects conceived as external to the self. These opposing poles will only gradually become differentiated. [p. 12]

Once differentiation has taken place, a dyad is formed, namely, the mother–infant relationship, which contemporary psychodynamic theorists term *attachment* and *object relations*. The infant creates the mother–infant relationship, but the mother also creates the mother–infant relationship. Each is waiting to be created or defined by the other in the service of undergoing cycles of differentiation and integration. Further, the infant (or mother) does not move toward either autonomy from the other or attachment to the other. Rather, infant and mother are always moving simultaneously toward both being autonomous from the other and attached to the other. A client and therapist who are engaged in meetings, or two persons who engage in various encounters, would be viewed in the same way.

How the Organic Metaphor Images Intrapsychic/Interpersonal Processes

The images used to portray developments within a person are the same as those used to portray interpersonal processes. As we noted in the preceding discussion, images of holism, dialectics, differentiation, and integration define and establish a person's sense of self and the relationship between that self and other persons (object relations). At the same time, through the same processes, a person's "internal object relations" are established and defined (Overton and Horowitz 1991, p. 15). Internal object relations are conceptualized as mental organizations that determine the ways we know, feel, and give meaning to the world and our experiences with others.

In Piaget's cognitive theory, these internal object relations are termed *schemas* and *operations*. These mental organizations represent actions a person has taken with things and persons, define what the person expects from interactions with things and persons, and guide actions the person takes in the present. In psychodynamic theory one or another aspect of intrapsychic processes is referred to as, for example, "psychic reality," "ego functions," "mechanisms of defense," "subjective self," "internal world." I will use an example that relates to a model elaborated in later chapters. A child's conscious thoughts (e.g., the child believes that "everyone in school is better than I am") form an antithesis with fantasies the child frequently entertains while daydreaming (e.g., being as powerful as Superman and a Power Ranger). The space between these thoughts and fantasies defines a paradox, an organization of internal relations that is unstable. As experiences with others are assimilated, involving both successes (e.g., winning a race) and failures (e.g., receiving a grade of D), the paradox is negotiated, and the thoughts and fantasies in question are integrated to form a new organization of relationships (self regulation). This new organization eventually differentiates again as other experiences are encountered. In this way the intrapsychic system is viewed as an open system involved in continuous and active exchanges with the environment and others.

How the Organic Metaphor Images the Meanings a Person Gives Experiences

The meanings a person gives experiences are at the heart of the organic metaphor. All activity, all experiences, involve the construction of meaning rather than the acquisition of information. Moreover, unlike the machine metaphor, meanings are not evaluated in terms of whether they correspond to the "real" meaning of an event. There is no real meaning outside the person as such. In keeping with the dialectical image, all meanings are coconstructed both by a person and another as each participates in reciprocal exchanges within their relational matrix. Meanings form the ground relied upon by various psychodynamic approaches to therapy. These approaches define psychological problems in terms of "conflict" between one meaning (e.g., a wish or desire) and another meaning opposing it (e.g., the wish is bad or wrong). Meanings in conflict can be assigned to the self and/or to others with whom the person is transacting within a relational matrix. Anxiety (distress) is seen as arising from conflict between meanings that are in opposition and/or from the loss of relationships. Anxiety also arises from the failure of mental strategies (mechanisms of defense) that participate in giving meaning to experiences and in regulating negative emotions.

Conflict between meanings also includes whether or not, and the degree to which, meanings operate inflexibly or rigidly within the relational matrix. Meanings are viewed as rigid when they have not differentiated within a dialectical process and/or the paradox between meanings has not resulted in a new organization that is equipped to handle new, more complex demands. Inflexible meanings are dysfunctional and therefore nonadaptive, since they fail to benefit from both interpersonal and novel intrapsychic challenges and experiences. Therefore, from the view of the organic metaphor, as Overton and Horowitz (1991) pointed out, "the aim of treatment is to facilitate the development of adaptive meanings that promote further growth (differentiation and integration); not to adjust 'inaccurate' representations in conformance with the 'real'" (p. 24).

Level V: Change and Growth

At the last level we consider how change and development are viewed by each camp. For objectivism, and its metaphor of a person as a machine, change and development take place as the person *adds* (accumulates) behaviors and representations of experiences (symbols, beliefs, meanings) that correspond with what the real world requires, and *subtracts* (eliminates or replaces) behaviors and representations that do not correspond to the real. In addition, change and growth are defined in terms of whether "mediators" become more efficient in processing representations at various points along a series of steps. Moreover, efficiency is defined in terms of behaviors that are required by others.

For interpretationism, with its organic metaphor, change and development take place as a person, participating in a dialectical process, revises and renders more flexible (differentiation-integration) meanings (cognitive/affective understanding) assigned to experiences that have been coconstructed with another. Earlier meanings are not replaced but are integrated within new meanings to form a new organization of cognitive/affective understanding. This cycle is repeated continuously as new salient experiences are assimilated. Revised meanings are not evaluated in terms of what is considered to be real or desirable according to others, but in terms of whether the meanings are coordinated and agreed upon within the particular relational matrix in which the person is participating.

The next boundary we consider, that between body and mind, reflects the strategies of knowing, assumptions, and metaphors of objectivism and interpretationism.

THE BOUNDARY BETWEEN BODY AND MIND

A boundary between the body and mind has been maintained in Western thinking from the writings of Greek philosophers to those of Sartre, Merleau-Ponty, and others of the twentieth century (e.g., Fisher 1990, Kagan 1978, Spicker 1970, Tiemersma 1989). All grappled with the dualism of soul (or mind) and body, which, as the source of passion and pain, was segregated as undesirable. Adopting this view, American psychology split off the body as a psychological concept and held it in the shadows until the 1980s (Cash and Pruzinsky 1990).

This was not the case, however, when two fledgling disciplines, neurology and psychoanalysis, were beginning to take shape at the turn of the century. The psychology of the body was not split off probably because the methods of these emerging clinical disciplines relied upon the patient's close scrutiny of experiences that inevitably revealed preoccupations and distortions pertaining to the body. Neurological reports appeared that described, for example, patients who felt their bodies had disappeared and who experienced a limb as present when it had been amputated. Within this climate, in 1926, the neurologist Henry Head proposed an unconscious "body schema" to conceptualize how body perceptions are integrated to form a picture of the body-self that becomes a frame of reference for orienting body movements and integrating body experiences (Fisher 1990). Although giving little attention to how body experiences are tied to personality, early neurologists legitimized the study of body image phenomena.

Paul Shilder is credited with being the first to construct a bridge connecting body and mind (personality). Combining observations of neurological and psychiatric patients, and concepts from neurology and psychoanalysis, he single-handedly upgraded the study of body experiences (Fisher 1990). In Shilder's major work, *The Image and Appearance of the Human Body* (1935/1950), he conceptualized body image as a construction that is cognitive, largely unconscious, and continuously changing. He emphasized that body image represents a synthesis of wishes, emotions, and interactions with others.

> [T]he image of the human body means the picture of our own body which we form in our mind, that is to say, the way in which the body appears to ourselves. [p. 11]

> The body contracts when we hate, it becomes firmer, and its outlines towards the world are more strongly marked. . . . We expand the body when we feel friendly and lovingly. We open our arms, we would like to enclose humanity in them. . . . We experiment with the [body]. . . . When even so the body is not sufficient for expression of the playful changes and destructive changes in the body, then we add clothes, masks, jewelry which again expand, contract, disfigure, or emphasize the body image and its particular parts. [pp. 210–211]

> Beyond that there is the immediate experience that there is a unity in the body. This unity is perceived, yet it is more than a perception. . . . We may call it body image. [p. 11]

Shilder, then, conceptualized body image as ever changing, gaining expression in everything from one's clothing to the ability to empathize or become angry, and as having relevance for experiences in everyday life as well as pathology. Following Freud (who proposed that a body ego is constructed first, forming the foundation of higher mental functions), Shilder attributed importance to early experiences with the body and its openings ("It is by these openings we come in closest contact with the world," 1935/1950, p. 124). He also viewed body parts that mimic body openings as symbolic equivalents (e.g., the eyes are symbolic openings through which the world "wonders into ourselves"). While he agreed with Freud on most points, he differed in placing more emphasis on body image as a changing, evolving entity. Of particular relevance to my thesis, he concluded that the unity of the body image, and its evolving changes, depends upon the unfolding of interactions and relationships with others (e.g., he suggested that in Freud's case of Dora, her hysterical coughing was not so much an expression of erotic sensations in the throat but of identification with attributes of her mother). Last, he anticipated the emergence of body therapies with his exploration of the effects of exercise and dance on body image (Fisher 1990, Kepner 1987, Pruzinsky 1990).

Following Shilder, several early psychoanalysts added formulations to the concept of body image. To mention a few, Alfred Adler emphasized that various forms of maladjustment compensate for a sense of body inferiority. Carl Jung noticed that persons experienced their bodies as protective enclosures within which they can find refuge and fend off attack. Theodore Reich hypothesized that in coping with certain mental conflicts, a person models his/her body after something with hard surfaces, symbolizing a defensive strategy.

More recently, psychoanalysts (e.g., Freedman 1977, Gottschald and Uliana 1977, Grand 1977) have focused on body experiences that occur during treatment sessions, demonstrating that hand movements and lip caressing, for example, are expressions of particular meanings and feelings and form the basis for their revisions. Mahl (1987) proposed that the process of repeating actions and gestures in the treatment situation transforms body meanings into fantasies and conscious thought. For example, he described an adult patient who, during psychoanalytic treatment sessions, repeatedly rubbed the back of her hand against a nearby roughly plastered wall. From these body experiences a memory emerged of her father regularly rubbing his beard against her face, leaving her tingling with excitement.

Wachtel (1987), in his lucid discussion of the relationship between action and insight, emphasized the importance of studying the body language of patients during psychotherapy, language that he proposed serves adaptive, expressive, and defensive purposes. Other psychoanalysts (Kramer and Akhtar 1992) have discussed how movements, postures, gestures, sweating, and other bodily expressions that occur during psychoanalytic treatment sessions are a part of the patient's communications, conveying symbolic meaning, and therefore important data for the therapist.

Other investigators have also addressed these same issues in ways that clearly converge with Shilder's holistic, dialectical concept of body image. Pruzinsky's (1990) discussion of "somatopsychic approaches" to psychotherapy and personal growth (e.g., dance therapy, psychomotor therapy) is one example. After proposing that, at the present time, most forms of psychotherapy portray the patient as a "disembodied entity," he articulated several basic assumptions regarding human change in psychotherapy. For example, the development of the sense of "self" is based on the experience of being embodied, and that all experiences take place in the context of bodily experience (e.g., touch, movement). Along the same line, Kruger (1990) integrated developmental and psychodynamic perspectives of body image change. He outlined how various body experiences in infancy promote or derail body image development, how these early experiences in turn give rise to particular representations of experiences, and, accordingly, why therapists should address nonverbal (e.g., postures, gestures) as well as verbal behaviors. I will have much more to say about the embodied basis of experience and the significance of embodied meanings for psychotherapy in later chapters.

I have proposed, on the basis of studies of children in the laboratory and participating in psychoanalytic treatment sessions (Santostefano 1977, 1988a, 1991b), that taking action with the body and body parts, fantasizing (imaging), and verbalizing are alternative systems of coding and expression that form a developmental hierarchy of integrated behavioral modes. These coding systems give meaning to experiences, and contribute to the form our physical, mental, and emotional responses take. Early in development, experiences are coded and given meaning via body/action symbols; with development these body-based meanings are translated into fantasy images/symbols and later into language symbols. I return to this proposal and its implications for child psychotherapy in later chapters.

In spite of this interest in body image within psychoanalysis, the topic received only isolated attention within mainstream psychology until cognitive research freed it from the bondage of behaviorism. At that point the body as a psychological construct entered through the doorway of cognition. For example, Wapner and Werner (1965) demonstrated that body attitudes influence perceptions of objects and judgments of one's position in space. Fisher and Cleveland (1958) illustrated that a person's body image boundaries correlate with types of pathology and personality traits. But after these programs peaked in the 1960s, interest in body image research declined (Tiemersma 1989). Of the exceptions, one deserves attention. Demick and Wapner (1987), extending Wapner's long-standing work with the psychology of the body, have amassed data on the role body experiences play in how individuals negotiate various life transitions (e.g., from home to nursery school; from community to psychiatric setting) and have proposed a developmental-holistic model of body experience.

More recently body image research has resurfaced, focusing mainly on eating disorders, weight problems, and the effects of plastic surgery (e.g., Cash and Pruzinsky 1990). However, the conceptualizations of a number of these investigators differ from that of Shilder's holistic, dialectical view, and reflect the zeitgeist of objectivism. The subjective body image of a person is viewed as separate from the observer and as reflecting distortions of the "real image" that exists independent of the knower. Freedman's (1990) discussion of cognitive-behavioral perspectives on body image change provides one example. Following a contingency model, he proposed, for example, that "First, A, an activating event (stepping on a scale), leads to B, a bridging thought and self-statement ("I'm too heavy") which triggers C, a conditioned emotional response (anxiety, disgust). . . . Behavioral disturbances may thus be both a cause and an effect of faulty thinking" (p. 273). Freedman also segregated "body-image percepts" (cognitive interpretations of external stimuli) from "body-image affect" (emotional responses generated by *conscious* thoughts about the body), from "body-image attitudes" (ideas and rules that organize one's view of the physical self). In a similar vein, Shontz (1990) proposed that body image be segregated into parts and distinctions made among "body schemas" (perception of one's body in space), "body concepts" (knowledge about the body expressed verbally), and "body values" (emotionally charged attitudes about the body).

The influence of the objectivist view that segregates knowledge from knower, and real from subjective, can also be seen in the methods employed in more recent studies of body image. Unlike earlier attempts, these methods do not engage the body in producing a response as a way to evaluate some aspect of body image, but segregate the body and mind. These studies rely for the most part on pencil and paper inventories and interviews that gather conscious knowledge about body image rather than unconscious symbolic representations of body image as emphasized by Shilder and psychodynamic investigators. For example, of the more than forty popular methods used by investigators (Thompson et al. 1990), nearly half ask a person to respond to questionnaires or to choose between statements such as, "I like my looks just the way they are" and "I am physically unattractive." The second most widely used method asks an individual to rate satisfaction with each of a series of silhouettes that vary in body size/weight. Sometimes the individual is guided during this rating by instructions to distinguish "how you *think* each [figure] looks, and how you *feel* each looks." Reviewing these methods, Thompson and colleagues noted, "In many cases (even with alterations in instructions), it is difficult to determine if the measure is tapping into an affective or cognitive component of body image" (p. 33).

Since Shilder's publication, then, a boundary has been maintained between body and mind, with the exception of some work in psychoanalysis and in cognitive research of the '60s and '70s. The more recent interest in body image issues implicated in weight problems and eating disorders reflects another form of body-mind segregation. The popularity of questionnaires as stimuli to measure body image, rather than using the body as a stimulus, suggests, I believe, an attempt to keep body experiences at a distance and segregated from conscious thoughts and beliefs. In addition, the conclusion by Thompson and his colleagues that research does not make clear what aspect of body image is cognitive and what aspect is emotional, and the proposals that segregate body concepts from body values (emotions), reflect the boundary between cognition and emotion that has also been maintained by American psychology.

THE BOUNDARY BETWEEN COGNITION AND EMOTION

A boundary line has also been persistently drawn in Western thought between cognition and emotion from the essays of early Greek philosophers to those of the nineteenth century (Kagan 1978). While some argued that thought and emotion should be unified, the boundary was successfully maintained in order to preserve thought as right and rational and to protect it from passion and the irrational (Bruner 1986).

If we take a closer look at this issue in the first decades of this century, we make a curious observation. Little or no attention was being paid to cognition and emotion. At that time, the ethos of orthodox behaviorism, with its taboos against mentalism, successfully drew a boundary between the mind (with its emotions) and overt behavior, renouncing the former and embracing the latter as the only legitimate topic for psychology. Behaviorism provided scientific justification for splitting mind and emotion and for segregating what Galton (1884) had earlier called the more pleasant and unpleasant things, as noted earlier.

John B. Watson, who is credited with declaring behaviorism a new movement in 1914, was clear about what this movement was segregating and renouncing as untrue. For Watson, psychology should be

"the [science of behavior] . . . never to use the terms consciousness, mental states, mind, content, will, imagery, and the like. . . . In a system of psychology completely worked out, given the responses, stimuli can be predicted; given the stimuli, the responses can be predicted." [Watson 1914, cited in Messer and Winokur 1984]

From the start, then, behaviorism, with roots in conditioning research of the Russian physiologist Ivan Pavlov, valued empiricism and objectivism. This behavioral orientation quickly held much appeal for psychology in the United States because of its commitment to laboratory research, studies of learning, and the importance of quantifying information, and because it eliminated subjective, private experiences that were difficult to describe. True, there were other positions at this time in addition to behaviorism: for example, Tolman's model of purposeful behavior, psychoanalytic concepts translated for American psychology by David Rapaport and others, and Gestalt psychology found most notably in the developmental model of Heinz Werner. But for American psychology at this time, the lens of behaviorism seemed too powerful to resist (Bearison and Zimiles 1986). As behaviorism gained prominence, a few voiced vigorous opposition. Henry Murray (1960), for example, had this to say about Watson and his behaviorism.

with this sword [behaviorism] he murdered, on his right, the meandering introspection's of Tichner, and on his left the nativistic drive theory of McDougall; ever since that triumph, Watsonian behaviorism has constituted the fixed image of American psychology—shallow, mechanistic, Philistine, soulless in the minds of a large number of Continental thinkers. [p. 250]

Then along came the studies and concepts of Jean Piaget, which legitimized the study of cognition and provided one way of understanding the forbidden mind. American psychologists quickly embraced this viewpoint, cast aside the boundary between the mind and behavior, and produced a flood of research, resulting in the rapid development of a sophisticated cognitive science (H. Gardner 1985). As cognition, "the mind's new science," grew to the size of a giant, the boundary between cognition and emotion, dormant during behaviorism's suppression of the mind, was established. Investigators began to locate themselves either on the side of cognition or on the side of emotion. As those who stood on the side of emotion peered over the boundary, they became quite upset at what they saw. The cognitive giant was growing too rapidly, and, worse, was neglecting emotion. As a result, those in the camp of emotion began to protest vigorously that emotions were being relegated to second class citizenship. And skirmishes between cognition and emotion were launched. A sketch of conferences that sprang up over a ten-year period illustrates the skirmishes that resulted from the boundary that had been located between cognition and emotion.

In 1975, the Social Science Research Council established a committee to address "the concern that an understanding of the development of emotion appeared meager when compared with the growing knowledge of cognitive growth" (Read 1984, p. ix). Shortly thereafter, another conference was convened by the Educational Testing Service because, "In the past two decades a plethora of studies on cognitive and perceptual development have appeared while affective development has been almost ignored" (Lewis and Rosenblum 1978, p. viii). A year later still another conference was sponsored jointly by Wheelock College and Bank Street College because, "It is becoming commonplace to express discomfort with the recent . . . narrow, even exclusive, focus on cognitive phenomena" (Shapiro and Weber 1981, p. vii). When social psychologists expressed their concerns about the segregation of emotion, the 1981 Annual Carnegie Symposium was devoted to the topic and responded: "[R]esearchers have lately focused on cognition to the exclusion of affect . . . what is the role of emotion in cognition? We leave it to the poet, playwright, the novelist. As people we delight in art and music. We fight, get angered, have joy, grief, happiness. But as students of mental events, we are ignorant of why and how" (Clark and Fiske 1982, p. ix). And in 1983, the Piaget Society decided to focus its annual conference on the issue of the segregation of thought and emotion (Bearison amd Zimiles 1986).

It is interesting to note that throughout these various conferences the boundary that had been constructed between cognition and emotion was not questioned. It seems to me that in the minds of most investigators presenting at these conferences this boundary was experienced as something "real" rather than as a conceptual convenience. Because the boundary was experienced as real, investigators raised an increasingly complex tangle of questions. Izard and colleagues (1984) provided examples: "Is a feeling state a special type of cognitive process? Do feelings become associated with and bonded with images and symbols and if so, how? What is the difference between cognition about emotion and cognition that is a component of emotion? And is cognition the result of emotion or the cause of emotion? Regardless of the theoretical interpretations investigators followed, they tended to define and measure emotional variables and cognitive variables separately" (pp. 3–6).

Curiously, Jean Piaget, who was credited with freeing American psychology from the ethos of orthodox behaviorism, was also held responsible for the division that developed between cognition and emotion and the emphasis given the former (Bearison and Zimiles 1986). Everyone agrees that Piaget conducted few data-based studies on emotional development in contrast to his many studies of reason and logic. But, unlike investigators who followed him, Piaget recognized that cognition and emotion were conceptual conveniences serving research and that the boundary between them was imaginary. More than that, he seemed clear about why he had chosen one over the other. When Decarie (1978) brought to Piaget's attention that in his seventy years of publishing he seldom referred to emotional processes, Piaget replied, in an often quoted personal communication to her, "Freud focused on emotion, I chose intelligence" (p. 183). In his autobiography (Campbell 1977) Piaget gave the reason. "I have always detested any departure from reality . . . preferring the study of normalcy and the workings of the intellect over that of the tricks of the unconscious" (p. 116). Moreover, he shared the reason for his choice. He preferred "the workings of the intellect" because his mother's poor mental health had a profound impact on him when he was a young child. Piaget, then, drew a boundary, still used by some, that equates "normalcy" with the "workings of intellect" and emotions with the "tricks of the unconscious." But in recognizing that the line between cognition (intellect) and emotion (tricky unconscious) is a conceptual convenience, Piaget was able to make significant contributions to our understanding of unconscious mental activity (Piaget 1973). I return to these contributions in chapters that follow.

Cognition and emotion will remain segregated, I believe, as long as investigators view the boundary as real and the domains as opposites, either independent of each other (e.g., Zajonc et al. 1982), parallel and interacting with one another (e.g., Leventhal 1982, Piaget 1981), or with one dominating the other (e.g., Izard 1982, Mandler 1982). The integrative model of psychotherapy discussed in later chapters attempts to forge cognition and emotion as one and illustrates the benefits of this union for child psychotherapy.

CONCLUDING COMMENT

In this chapter we considered that, from its earliest days, the study of human behavior has divided functioning into domains by establishing a variety of boundaries. We discussed three: a boundary dividing two views of how knowledge is acquired—objectivism and interpretationism; a boundary dividing body and mind; and another dividing cognition and emotion. Recall that Francis Galton felt that students of human behavior laid down boundaries in order to separate pleasant circumstances from unpleasant circumstances. I believe there is another possible reason, which is reflected by the images of objectivism and interpretationism. Who decides what is real, adaptive, normal, and expected? Who decides what is to be done to change things? When these two questions are woven together, they form a cord or question that is critical. Who is in control—investigator or subject? Therapist or child? This cord of control plays a part, I believe, in how we segregate, approach, and handle what is pleasant and unpleasant. If emotions and the tricky unconscious, as Piaget put it, are experienced by the investigator and clinician as very unpleasant, then they are more likely to shape concepts and methods that provide them with control over what they view as "real" and over what is to be done to promote change. If emotions and the tricky unconscious are not experienced as particularly unpleasant by clinicians and investigators, who, according to Galton, have no eye but for unpleasing circumstances, then these individuals are more likely to shape concepts and methods that encourage them to share the patient's "unpleasantness" and to share control. In the next chapter we will consider the approaches to psychotherapy that have emerged from the images of objectivism with its preference for the intellect, cognition, and unilateral control on the one hand and on the other approaches that have emerged from the images of interpretationism with its preference for body, emotion, and bilateral control.

3

How the Boundaries between Real/Subjective, Mind/Body, and Cognition/Emotion Influence Child Psychotherapy

CONTENTS

To illustrate how the practice of segregation described in the previous chapter has influenced approaches to psychotherapy with children, I have selected the two major, current approaches: cognitive-behavioral and psychodynamic. As we shall see, the former has been influenced more by the strategies of knowing, metatheoretical assumptions, and metaphors of human functioning of objectivism, while the latter by those of intepretationism.

OBJECTIVISM THE GROUND OF COGNITIVE-BEHAVIORAL THERAPY: THE BODY AS OVERT ACTIVITY AND COGNITION AS CONSCIOUS PRODUCTS

Several historical reviews describe the origin and development of behavioral therapy, and show how, in the 1970s, cognitive therapy emerged, exerting a significant influence on behavioral therapy (e.g., Arkowitz and Messer 1984, Corsini and Wedding 1989, Meyers and Craighead 1984, Stricker and Gold 1993, Wachtel 1977, 1987). As behavioral therapy and cognitive therapy interacted, each influenced the other, resulting in a growing interest in integrating the two approaches, which eventually shared a common set of propositions about child psychotherapy.

Whether the child to be treated is socially withdrawn, aggressive and hyperactive, suffering from a learning disability, experiencing a specific fear, suffering from generalized stress and anxiety, mentally retarded, or a juvenile delinquent, four broad propositions guide cognitive-behavioral therapies: (1) the child's problem behavior is the target of treatment, and should be carefully delineated; (2) the events/stimuli that trigger the problem behavior should be carefully determined; (3) mediators connecting these events/stimuli with the problem behavior should be established; (4) a treatment program should be designed that actively and directly addresses the targeted behavior so that maladaptive responses, with their mediators, are corrected or replaced.

Identifying and Evaluating the Behavior Targeted for Treatment

The first step the cognitive-behavioral approach emphasizes concerns identifying and assessing, in advance, the problem behavior that is to be the target of therapy. To illustrate how information is gathered about a child's problem behavior, I use Hollin's (1990) application of the cognitive-behavioral approach in assessing young offenders. Hollin employs a "functional analysis" (i.e., Skinner's A:B:C model), which is typically followed in clinical practice by mainstream cognitive-behavioral therapists (see previous chapter for a discussion of the A:B:C paradigm).

> As the name implies, a functional analysis is concerned with understanding what function, what payoffs, the behavior has for the individual concerned. The guiding framework for a functional analysis is the A:B:C sequence based on Skinner's three-term contingency. Thus, behavioral assessment is concerned with discovering as much as possible the antecedents of a particular behavior, the behavior itself, and the consequences it produces in order to suggest the exact nature of the relationship between antecedents, consequences and the behavior in question. [p. 26]

With the A:B:C model as a guide, Hollin paid close attention to the environmental events/stimuli that preceded the problem behavior (A); for example, whether an antecedent event/situation existed recently or long ago, involved a particular place (such as a classroom), a particular time of day (such as meal time), or particular words or actions by an individual or group of persons, and contained unique physical features (such as high or low temperatures). Hollin advises that careful attention also be given to articulating the behavior that is to be the target of therapy (B), and to determining whether this behavior is public (e.g., violating property) or private (e.g., personal thoughts, emotions), and the number of times the target behavior occurred within a given time interval. He also stressed the importance of detailing a child's history of consequences (C) associated with the target behavior, and whether consequences were "social" (e.g., praise from peers), or "physical" (e.g., vandalizing cars) or whether they occurred soon after, or long after, the target behavior.

> Proximal outcomes are the immediately observed outcomes following a specified behavior. Distal outcomes are those outcomes that will occur after a period of time. Whereas reasonably clear statements can be made about proximal outcomes, only probable statements can be made about distal outcomes. For example, it can be readily seen that successfully stealing a car will result in a quicker journey time than walking. In contrast, it can be suggested with some confidence, but not with certainty, that if enough cars are stolen on enough occasions, the person will be caught and legally punished. [p. 28]

Hollin's clinical use of Skinner's A:B:C model in evaluating a child's presenting problem reveals the influences of objectivism: (1) diagnostic data about the child's problem exist in the child's behavior and in the child's environment independent of the diagnostician (knower); the child does not collaborate with the diagnostician in constructing the data; (2) neutral, well-controlled observations by the diagnostician will produce the environmental conditions that evoked the problem behavior and how others in the environment responded to the behavior, either rewarding or punishing it; (3) to make neutral observations, boundaries are set separating the diagnostician and child on the one hand and on the other the child and his/her environment; (4) the child's problem behaviors (outputs) are understood as due to particular stimuli and reactions by the environment. Showing the influence of the machine metaphor, either the child acts upon the environment or the environment acts upon the child. Child and environment are seen as separate entities.

Hollin's discussion of assessment methods used to gather data required by the A:B:C paradigm is also influenced by the objectivist image that segregates what is real from what is subjective, with the former held as more true. Hollin distinguishes between "direct measures" and "indirect measures." Direct measures—measures of overt behavior—are the most desirable because "a person's motor behavior can be observed, recorded, and cross-checked by different observers" (1990, p. 31). In contrast, indirect measures, such as self-observation and interview, are not "authentic" since they cannot be as carefully recorded and cross-checked by different observers. "If a person is asked to report on his or her thoughts or feelings, it is impossible to determine the authenticity of the report" (p. 31). Hollin's discussion of interviewing, observation, cognitive tests, and rating scales is cast within the assumption that the "real" should be observed as much as possible, while the examiner keeps a wary eye on the subjective.

The image of objectivism can be seen again in still another way. After paying considerable attention to various issues involved in articulating the target behavior, as well as its antecedents and consequences, Hollin devotes only one paragraph to the diagnostician doing the observing. The focus is on the objectivist view that knowledge, which already exists, can be obtained if the observer makes use of well-controlled observations.

> Finally, the observer should not be neglected. Observers must be physically suited for the task, be able to record accurately and reliably, be trusted to complete the task properly, and respect confidentiality. It is undoubtedly beneficial to train observers and to keep them informed of progress during recording to counteract the phenomenon of observer drift as the individual gradually shifts his or her observational criteria . . . there should always be some check of inter-observer agreement, which may be a simple visual comparison of data or, if the data set is large and complex, involve the use of statistics. . . . [p. 35]

In summary, the cognitive-behavioral approach emphasizes that a child's problem behavior, along with its antecedents and consequences, must be delineated in as much detail as possible. The behavior targeted should be overt actions or conscious thoughts that lend themselves to objective assessment. Referring to the previous chapter, and forecasting our next chapter, the focus then is on the body as overt, conscious, physical activity, and on the mind as overt, conscious, mental activity, or what theorists refer to as "surface" behaviors and "cognitive products."

As a guide in gathering diagnostic data, the A:B:C paradigm makes a valuable contribution in reminding therapists of the importance of making careful observations upon which decisions about treatment are based. However, the A:B:C paradigm also raises a question when we look at this model through the issues raised at the close of the previous chapter. There I noted Francis Galton's century-old observation that some students of behavior separate "pleasant" from "unpleasant" circumstances in order to segregate what is viewed as real from subjective. I proposed that some students of behavior might separate real and subjective in order to maintain control as they approach and handle what is unpleasant. When a child's problem behavior is identified and evaluated following the A:B:C model, the child does not have control over defining what is a problem for him/her, and therefore does not have control over selecting the target of treatment. Nor does the child define whether a particular behavior has been followed by positive or negative consequences. Rather, a parent, teacher, school principal, cognitive-behavioral therapist, and other persons make these decisions. What is assumed to be behavior typically followed by negative consequences may not in fact be the case, resulting in treatment techniques that may miss the intended mark.

To illustrate this notion, consider the following anecdotes. Jimmy was referred by the State's Bureau of Children's Social Services because he had stolen a number of items from a drugstore, the most recent being a two-pound box of chocolates. Charlie was apprehended for stealing a baseball bat from a sports store. And once again Mary broke a classroom rule and was sent to the principal's office for the eighth time this term. From the view of the store owners, police, and therapist, following the A:B:C model, stealing a box of chocolates and a baseball bat were followed by negative consequences when Jimmy and Charlie were apprehended, and the behaviors should therefore be extinguished. Similarly, from the teacher's view, Mary's behavior was repeatedly followed by a negative consequence, namely, appearing before the principal, and her behavior should therefore be extinguished.

But when each child was included in constructing diagnostic information, rather than segregated by a boundary, and when each child participated in defining what is for him/her a positive and negative consequence, the therapist learned that what others had defined as negative, the child defined as positive. In Jimmy's case it was learned that with each act of stealing he anticipated with excitement his mother's delight when she received another "gift." Charlie felt more valued and admired by his gang members when he brought baseball equipment to the vacant lot where they played baseball. And for Mary, being sent to the principal's office was not a punishment at all but a reward. Her father had separated from her mother some time ago and then disappeared. Mary revealed that she enjoyed sitting in the principal's office, whether he urged her to try harder or sternly reprimanded her. The principal reminded her of her father, and she liked him very much.

With these examples I am emphasizing that if adults, rather than the child, decide what are negative or positive consequences, the therapist could design a treatment plan that misses the mark.

Designing a Treatment Program that Modifies the Target Behavior

Once the problem behavior is identified, with its antecedents and consequences carefully detailed, a wide variety of cognitive-behavioral techniques are available to help a child (see Brems 1993 for an excellent discussion of these methods). As several of these techniques are sketched, the reader should notice the influence of objectivist images. For example, each technique holds the assumption that a child's problem behavior can be corrected or replaced directly, by behaviors and words the therapist prescribes and the child enacts, or indirectly, by revising or replacing the child's cognitions (e.g., conscious thoughts, beliefs) that mediate between environmental stimuli and the resulting consequences. In addition, forecasting the next chapter, these techniques tend to separate the body and mind, centering on a child's overt activit[y] [an]d the words prescribed are "cognitive products" (conscious self-statements) th[at ... distinguis]hed from cognitive structures (unconscious meanings).

Each treatm[ent ...] [on]e of two broad categories. One relies on the principle [of reinforce]ment, the other on the principle of punishment. With th[e ...] [recei]ves rewards contingent upon his/her performing behavio[r ... by] the environment. As a result of reinforcement, the [... es]tablished part of the child's repertoire of behaviors. Rewa[rd ...] [r]aising the child, and providing the child with a model to imit[ate ...] [... d]esires. With the second category of techniques behavio[r ...] environmental expectations is suppressed or interfered with [...] [r]esult, the behavior is decreased and/or eliminated. For exa[mple ... se]ssion a child is given ten tokens that can be cashed in for [a ... a t]oken is taken away each time the child walks away from so[mething ...] [he/sh]e/sl and the therapist are working.

The pri[nciples of rei]nforcement and punishment show the influence of sever[al im]age[s ... fir]st, machine metaphor: that a boundary exists between the [chil]d and [envir]onment; that inputs stimulate the child to behave in a particu[lar wa]y, [... th]at growth results when problem behaviors are replaced by [...] environmental expectations. In addition, treatment tech[niques ...] inv[ol]ve activity the child and therapist coauthor but [...] a[nd th]e child, which relates to the assumption that a boundary can be set between the therapist and the child. Moreover, the relationship therapist and child construct receives relatively little attention, although the therapist encourages the child to ensure that she/he is comfortable. Most attention is paid to the behaviors required of the child by the particular technique being used. With this introduction as a backdrop, we consider several of the more commonly used cognitive-behavioral techniques.

Self-Instructional Training

This treatment technique, considered in the previous chapter, is one of the most popular among cognitive-behavioral therapists working with children. The therapist introduces a task that addresses the child's problem behavior, and performs the task while talking aloud and articulating several problem-solving skills. The therapist (1) defines the problem ("Let's see, what am I supposed to do?"); (2) focuses on the task and the response required ("I better concentrate and focus in, and think only of what I am doing right now"); (3) selects a response required by the task ("I think this is the right one"); (4) rewards himself/herself ("Not bad, I really did a good job"). The therapist repeats these steps with a similar task, now whispering these self-instructions, and then using gestures expressing the same comments in private thought.

Modeling

Self-instruction training is frequently integrated with the technique of modeling, another popular cognitive-behavioral treatment method. Modeling has been used to eliminate behavioral deficits, reduce excessive fears, and promote adaptive, social behavior. The child is exposed to behaviors to be learned, usually demonstrated by the therapist, but sometimes displayed by videos. After the therapist models some behavior, the child imitates the therapist, and then they reverse roles. By alternating with the child, task by task, the therapist demonstrates problem solving and the use of self-instructions. Frequently, when applying this technique, a distinction is made between modeling "mastery" behavior and modeling "coping" behavior. With the former, the therapist demonstrates some ideal behavior; for example, handling a series of math problems rapidly and correctly with a minimum of difficulty and frustration. In contrast, when the method is designed to display coping behaviors, the therapist occasionally makes mistakes and shares with the child any difficulties that are encountered while completing the task. Kendall and Braswell (1985) recommended that in early stages of treatment the therapist should model mastery and in later sessions coping behaviors.

Kendall and Braswell (1985) provided the transcript of a treatment case to illustrate modeling mastery behavior. After teaching the child the steps of self-instruction to solve math problems, the therapist said,

OK? . . . this [problem] is not the easiest but it is not the hardest either. 17 + 14 . . . I think I'll copy that onto my paper. . . . What am I supposed to do here? Well, I'm supposed to add. There's a plus sign here. I'm supposed to add these together. OK, that's what I am supposed to do. . . . Actually, what I'm supposed to do is figure out the correct answer, right? OK, and the second step is to look at all the possible things we could do with it. Remember when we do a math problem the step we are supposed to do is to look at the sign and see if it is adding or subtracting or multiplying or dividing. [p. 131]

In subsequent sessions the therapist combined self-instruction and modeling coping behavior. To begin, the therapist acknowledged that he was selecting a more complicated math problem.

Therapist: How about this one, 84 ÷ 7? What's the first thing we are going to do?

Child: Write it down on paper.

Therapist: OK, now what? Gee, it's been a long time since I've done this type of a problem. Some of the others have been so easy . . . now I really got to think.

Child: Write it down on paper.

Therapist: OK, but then what?

Child: Start the problem.

Therapist: Yeh, but I'm not sure exactly. Wait. OK, I think you do this one number at a time. If I take my time, I get it.

Child: The first one is 7.

Therapist: Let me think. OK, 7 goes into 8 once. Then 7 doesn't go into 4. That isn't right. Wait. There's no hurry; let me think more. What about the one I left over. That makes it 14. OK, then you do 7 goes into 14.

Using other tasks, the therapist continued blending self-instruction with modeling coping behaviors, demonstrating not only the use of self-instruction but also strategies the child could use to cope when solutions to problems are not readily available.

Before continuing, we should pause to articulate an understanding of how objectivist images influence the techniques of self-instruction and modeling. Both methods are viewed as something the therapist does to the child, emphasizing the boundary that exists between the two. With both methods, inputs by the therapist will result in outputs by the child that are required by the environment; what the child is making of the experience, as well as the relationship between child and therapist, does not receive special attention. These influences are reflected by the following clinical anecdote, which Kendall and Braswell offered to illustrate a different issue: namely, the therapist should find a way to model coping behaviors while managing a daily routine in order to demonstrate to the child that the skill he/she is learning can be applied in everyday living.

> *Therapist:*   How's your soccer team doing? (*therapist puts briefcase on top of desk*)
> *Child:*   Pretty good; we won our last game. I scored a goal, too.
> *Therapist:*   Great (*opens briefcase upside down and materials spill out onto the desk and floor*). Heck, why am I dumb? No, wait. I'm not dumb; I just didn't think.
> *Child:*   Huh?
> *Therapist:*   I didn't think. . . . I didn't remember which is the top and which is the bottom of the briefcase.
> *Child:*   Oh.
> *Therapist:*   Let's see; how can you tell which is the top? (*examines case; child watches*) Here, this little label is on only one side. It's on the top. If I can remember that this goes on the top, then I won't spill all these things next time (*pause*). The label goes on the top (*now the statement is whispered— introducing one of the steps from self-instruction training*). [pp. 131–134]

In this anecdote the therapist began by asking the child about his soccer game. The child responded, apparently with pride, that his team won and he scored a goal. The therapist ignored this material, opened his briefcase, and continued with his plan to model coping skills aided by self-instruction. The personal meanings and emotions the child brought to this moment, which related to winning and scoring a goal, were not included as part of the therapeutic relationship and coping skills training. The possible role these meanings and emotions were playing in the child's relationship with the therapist, and in the child's psychological development, were not given center stage. We will have more to say about this below in the section on psychodynamic therapy.

Modifying Cognitive Mediators

Modifying a child's cognitive mediators concerns revising a child's thinking and understanding after he/she experiences a situation or stimulus and before responding. This technique is frequently embedded within the technique of modeling. Kendall and Morison (1984) provided an illustration by comparing the treatment of two socially isolated children. In one vignette a group of children are involved in a vigorous game of soccer. The target child, who is physically capable but socially isolated, stands at the edge of the field and appears to glance at the activity. A therapeutic aide addresses the child and suggests joining the other children, "Come on, let's play too!" With this, the aide joined the game and kicked the ball. The child turned away, no longer paying attention to the activity.

The second vignette illustrates how a child's cognitive mediators were taken into account. This therapeutic aide also took interest in a child, and stood next to him. While watching the soccer players, the aide, thinking out loud, said, "Gee, they're really running around. Is it OK to do that? (*pause*) Oh, this is recess, I forgot, I guess it's OK to run around; but what if they break something? (*pause*) I guess that's not very likely. They play here all the time and haven't broken anything yet (*pause*). Maybe I'll play too (*pause*). No, they're better players than I am (*pause*). But look there! That wasn't such a good kick, I could do that. I could just run around even if I don't kick it much at all. Maybe I will play for a few minutes" (p. 281).

Discussing the implications of these vignettes, Kendall and Morison noted, "By directly attending to cognitive processing factors, the second (therapeutic) aide thinks through the process in a manner consistent with how the isolated child might interpret the situation. The model in the second case has produced a greater likelihood of the child's participating" (p. 281).

One phrase in this quote reflects the influence of objectivist images on the technique of modifying cognitive mediators, and distinguishes this technique from a similar one employed in psychodynamic therapy. The phrase I have in mind is ". . . the second aide thinks through the process in a manner consistent with how the isolated child might interpret the situation." In other words, in cognitive-behavioral therapy the meaning a child gives to an experience is determined by cognitive mediators that *the therapist* selects as "consistent" with how the child should interpret the experience. The approach is quite different in psychodynamic therapy, in which the child is left to author his/her meanings and the cognitions that mediate them.

Correspondence Training

The techniques of reward, punishment, self-instruction, modeling, and modifying cognitive mediators are sometimes embedded within other techniques. One such technique is termed *correspondence training*. Here, it is assumed, as with self-instruction, that it is possible to control nonverbal behavior by modifying verbal behavior. Correspondence training involves three different procedures. With one, the "say-do" technique, the child is asked to state what she/he is going to do. Then the child is rewarded if the behavior corresponds with the stated intention. With the "do-say" technique, the child describes what he/she has done previously, and the therapist rewards the child if the statement accurately describes the behavior. With the "show-do" technique, the therapist correctly performs some target behavior. Then the child is asked to show the therapist what the behavior would look like if enacted in a setting in which it should occur. Subsequently, the child is given the opportunity to perform the target behavior in the designated setting. If the child displays the correct behavior, he/she is rewarded. Usually with correspondence procedures, if the child incorrectly states that he/she performed the target behavior, the therapist points out the inaccuracy, helps the child describe the behavior more accurately, encourages the child to do better at the next opportunity, and does not provide a reward (Whitman et al. 1984).

Correspondence training reflects several objectivist assumptions: that the objective can be separated from the subjective; that the mind can be separated from the body; and that an experience or behavioral act can exist independent of the knower. With each procedure, the child is trained to construct thoughts and words that the therapist evaluates as corresponding to the target behavior. In other words, the child is trained to describe the target behavior as accurately as possible, but the therapist determines what is an accurate description. Correspondence training conveys to a child that there is some behavior "out there" that is desired by others and that can be discovered and accurately labeled.

Role-Playing

Role-playing is a cousin of the "show-do" correspondence technique. In addition to thinking through a problem situation, a child enacts behaviors that are judged by others to be adaptive. Usually, in the first sessions of role playing, the child is asked to enact dealing with hypothetical problem situations. In subsequent sessions the child is asked to enact behaviors that deal with a situation that simulates a real problem for the child. To begin, various situations are written on index cards. Examples include: "You are watching television, and your mother/sister changes the channel." "You tear your pants at recess and someone is making fun of you." "You are playing a new game and your friend starts to cheat" (Kendall and Braswell 1985, p. 136). After several situations are recorded, the child is asked to take each card and discuss the situation following several steps. First the child describes the problem. Then the child thinks of three or four alternative ways of coping with the situation. With the third step the child evaluates the consequences associated with each alternative. Then the child selects one of the alternatives as most desirable. With the fifth step the child is encouraged to use self-reinforcing statements to reward himself/herself for demonstrating good problem solving.

When the child understands what is involved in a role-playing task, a card is selected from the deck and child and therapist enact the scene. Kendall and Braswell (1985) provided a clinical example.

> *Therapist:* What does your card say?
> *Child:* It says you are watching television but your little brother keeps chang-
>   ing the channel.
> *Therapist:* So what is your problem? Or to use our "step-words," what are
>   you supposed to do?
> *Child:* Well, I guess I'm supposed to figure out how to handle that situation
>   with my brother.
> *Therapist:* Right. [p. 137]

The therapist then engaged the child in discussions that followed the steps noted above. This child described two alternative ways of coping: "telling mother" and "working out a deal with my brother." Then the therapist and the child enacted each situation.

Kendall and Morison (1984) noted that when therapist and child eventually engage in enacting the situation, some children may become quite excitable. While an increase in "emotional arousal" is desirable, they pointed out, this arousal may occasionally take the form of "silliness" that impedes the conduct of meaningful role-playing. At such times the therapist could hold up a "stop sign" or ask the child to "freeze as though he/she were a statue" (pp. 140–141). Their discussion of this possibility serves as another point of comparison between objectivism and interpretationism. Since role-playing is presumed to provide the child with adaptive behaviors that will replace or correct maladaptive behaviors, the therapist determines whether the child's emotions "impede" this treatment technique. By holding up a stop sign, the therapist segregates and subordinates the child's emotions so that the behavior the therapist prescribed can be enacted by the child free of emotional interference.

Systematic Desensitization with Children

The method of systematic desensitization is intended to reduce anxiety and fear by repeatedly exposing the child to anxiety-producing stimuli (whether physical objects or imagined scenes) without the child's experiencing the harm that he/she anticipates. The following broad steps define this technique: (1) stimuli that evoke anxiety are determined; (2) a hierarchy representing a continuum along which the child's fearfulness and anxiety vary from little to considerable is constructed of these stimuli; (3) the child is trained to relax; (4) while relaxed, the child is asked to manipulate some item, or to imagine some scene at the low-anxiety end of the continuum. When this encounter is accompanied by little or no anxiety, the child is exposed to the next item on the hierarchy until little or no anxiety is experienced. In this fashion the therapist exposes the child to each item in the hierarchy until the item that arouses the most anxiety/fear is engaged with little stress. To illustrate, Melamed and colleagues (1984) used this technique to help preschoolers prepare for dental procedures. Each child handled a hierarchy of anxiety-arousing items, from those presumably producing the least anxiety to those arousing the most (e.g., mirror and explorer, clamp, X-ray film, syringe, dental chair).

The method of systematic desensitization seems to me to have one foot in objectivism and the other in interpretationism. By asking the child to engage physical objects, pictures, or imagined scenes that the child has designated as anxiety-provoking, the therapist is entering the child's subjective world. In some instances, when applying systematic desensitization, a cognitive-behavioral therapist may not focus on learning the unique meaning a child is giving to some stimulus or situation. For example, one child revealed in treatment that she imagined an X-ray machine "leaves little holes inside your body." Another child was afraid of visiting the dentist because he felt he was being punished for not eating his vegetables, a crime mother frequently reminded him of committing. And another child was gripped with terror that the dentist would take "a part of my body." Yet, by exposing the child to stimuli known to arouse fear and anxiety, the therapist is addressing emotions that derive from the child's unique underlying fantasy and is providing the child with opportunities to cope with the fantasy and its emotions. To close these comments, I strongly recommend Wachtel's (1977) discussion of systematic desensitization as one ground on which cognitive-behavioral and psychodynamic therapies could be integrated.

Tasks Graded in Difficulty

Presenting a child with a series of graded tasks/stimuli is one of the hallmarks of cognitive-behavioral therapy with children. Whether the content of the intervention emphasizes self-instruction, modeling, correspondence training, systematic role-playing, or desensitization, cognitive-behavioral therapists typically administer a hierarchy of tasks beginning with stimuli that are less complex and emotionally neutral. Then, in a stepwise fashion, tasks that are gradually more complex and emotionally evocative are introduced.

The technique of graded tasks, it seems to me, is a cousin of systematic desensitization, but has two feet in interpretationism rather than one. Further, I believe the technique assumes a principle of change from the interpretationist position, which articulates a very different view from that implied by other cognitive-behavioral techniques we have considered. The method of graded tasks implies that change involves building upon previous behaviors; in contrast, the other techniques we have considered view change as resulting from replacing one behavior by another or by controlling behavior with words. As we discuss in more detail in Chapter 5, the notion that change involves building upon previous behaviors relates to the developmental principle that organizations of behavior that develop later do not replace earlier behaviors but assimilate and integrate the previous organization.

From this view, when a child initially engages a simple stimulus requiring a global organization of behavior, the cognitive-behavioral function required is organized and stabilized as the task is engaged over and over again. Then, when a related but more complex stimulus, requiring a more complex organization of behavior is presented, the child builds upon the previous behavior to cope with a new task.

Without this assumption guiding the technique, a therapist would present a variety of tasks in random order, some simple and some complex. By beginning with a simple task and then designing related tasks so that each is another step up a stairway of cognitive-behavioral growth, a child keeps one foot on the step just mastered, while raising the other foot to the next higher step, in her/his climb to a higher level of growth. In my view, the emphasis given to the technique of graded tasks is one of the most significant contributions of cognitive-behavioral psychotherapy with children. I will have much more to say about this topic in future chapters, and make major use of the concept of graded tasks in the integrative psychotherapy I propose.

A Recap

The assessment and treatment approaches that are typical in cognitive-behavioral therapy reflect the influence of objectivist images discussed in the previous chapter:

1. Knowledge about the child and what the child should do exists in the environment independent of the child, and neutral, well-controlled observation will reveal that knowledge.
2. To gain this knowledge, boundaries are set between therapist and child, between child and environment, and between what is considered to be real and desirable behavior on the one hand, and the child's subjective, maladaptive functioning on the other.
3. The child's behavior is defined as maladaptive by the environment, resulting in negative consequences.
4. To help the child achieve "real" or desirable behavior, the therapist trains the child in various cognitive and coping skills that manage or inhibit stimuli that evoke the problem behavior and/or that change the child's cognitive mediators that misrepresent environmental stimuli.
5. Change occurs when the child has accumulated the necessary coping and cognitive skills. An exception to this view of change is provided by the technique of graded tasks, which promotes psychological functioning that gradually becomes more differentiated and integrated as a child copes with more complex tasks.

INTERPRETATIONISM THE GROUND OF PSYCHODYNAMIC PSYCHOTHERAPY: THE BODY AND EMOTION IN THE MIND

Interpretationism, with its organic metaphor, has influenced psychodynamic approaches to psychotherapy beginning with the concepts and methods of its originator, Sigmund Freud, and those of his followers, who moved in new directions. Before setting out to consider illustrations of how present-day psychodynamic therapies are influenced by interpretationism, I believe it might be necessary, at least for some readers, if we pause to say a few words about what is meant by "psychodynamic."

What Does Psychodynamic Mean?

While it is generally recognized that the term *psychodynamic* derives from Freudian psychoanalysis, there is less awareness that the term has undergone continuous change. Wachtel (1987) provided a particularly useful discussion of this issue. Whenever the term *psychodynamic* is mentioned, he pointed out, what the author usually refers to, and what the reader conjures up, is some notion of Freudian psychoanalysis of the early 1900s. Little attention is paid to changes and developments introduced by Freud following his initial formulations, as well as to vast revisions in theory and technique contributed by numerous writers since Freud. Wachtel cited Bandura and Walters (1963) to illustrate:

> "The psychodynamic 'disease model' thus leads one to seek determinants of deviant behavior in terms of relatively autonomous internal agents and processes in the form of 'unconscious psychic forces,' 'dammed-up energies,' 'cathexes,' 'countercathexes,' 'defenses,' 'complexes,' and other hypothetical conditions or states having only a tenuous relationship to the social stimuli that precede them or even to the [behavioral symptoms] or symbols that they supposedly explain." [p. 215]

Wachtel pointed out that if Bandura and Walters had written this characterization of psychoanalysis in 1913 instead of fifty years later, they would have been raising cogent issues. I would add that more than twenty years after Bandura and Walters expressed their view of "psychodynamic," we still find statements that conjure up a notion of psychoanalytic concepts that dominated in the early 1900s. For example, comparing the notion of determinism in psychoanalysis and behaviorism, Mahoney (1984) pointed out that for psychoanalysis "[I]t is apparent that the primary dynamic is a transformation of energy" (p. 313) and that psychoanalysts prefer a "hydraulic model of energy exchange" viewing the individual as "pushed and pulled through a life-long sequence of hedonistic conflicts" (p. 314). The notion of transformation of energy, as well as other concepts, had already been discarded, or extensively revised, a number of years before Mahoney wrote this statement. Some readers, then, may still carry a definition of psychodynamics that is based upon "ancient" concepts. If the reader is to articulate an understanding of the influence interpretationist images exerted on psychodynamic concepts and treatment techniques and compare them with objectivist-based concepts and techniques, we should take a moment to sketch revisions that have taken place in psychodynamic theory. Because I mention only a few as illustrations, the interested reader is referred to comprehensive historical reviews available (e.g., Klein 1976, Lear 1990, Mitchell 1988, Wachtel 1977).

A Sketch of Revisions in Psychodynamic Concepts Influenced by Interpretationist Images

The reader who is not aware of the origin of psychodynamic thinking may find it interesting to learn that Freud was initially influenced more by objectivism since his first formulations relied upon a stimulus–response model. He observed that symptoms (responses) that patients brought to him disappeared only when they eventually remembered "real" childhood events (stimuli) that had actually occurred. To understand these observations, Freud and his colleague, Breuer (Breuer and Freud 1895), conceptualized these patients as suffering from "reminiscences." That is, because these events and their meanings were unacceptable to the person's conscious sense of himself/herself, the mind intentionally repressed them. In this repressed state the memories remained split off from the rest of the individual's personality and from everyday experiences, and therefore their meanings were never revised in response to feedback from the environment. As the reader might notice, this model is influenced by objectivist images of "real" environmental events as inputs activating particular outputs (behavioral symptoms).

But Freud soon revised this model. Now, instead of viewing a patient's reports of past disturbing events as "real," he conceptualized them as fantasies representing wishes and impulses (usually forbidden ones) that the person harbored during childhood, wanted to express in action, but did not. This reconceptualization broadened Freud's position from a traumatic memory theory to a more general theory of personality, shifting his model toward interpretationism. That is, he took the position that there is no environment "out there" as such; rather, environments, and experiences with them, are constructed by the mind. The term *psychodynamic* no longer meant that "actual" traumatic childhood events impacted the mind. Now *psychodynamic* meant that a wide range of wishes, constructed by the mind, influenced how childhood events were construed and experienced.

How do these wishes give meaning to experiences? Freud proposed that in the first years of life experiences with different body zones take turns in coding (symbolizing) experiences and form a developmental hierarchy: bodily experiences, with the mouth dominant first, followed by anal experiences, and then experiences with genital excitation. Freud's model also proposed that meanings given to experiences could become fixated in one of these zones and fail to move to the next level. While this model shifted toward the interpretationism view, it still retained some of the emphasis of the first model; namely, that meanings and wishes (inputs or stimuli) that caused the patient's difficulties (outputs or responses) are to be found in the patient's childhood history. Freud continued to give relatively little attention to the role of present-day, ongoing experiences with the environment.

In 1923 Freud reformulated his theory once again. Now he gave more attention to a person's dealings with the environment. In this formulation he proposed three psychic agencies termed *ego*, *id*, and *superego*. The ego was conceptualized as a system of psychological functions (e.g., perceiving, remembering, taking action, maintaining a view of oneself) that transacted with the environment while simultaneously dealing with and coordinating presses from the id or "libido." The id was conceptualized as containing impulses and wishes containing energy that paid no attention to environmental limitations and prohibitions, pressing for expression in action. The superego was conceptualized as rules and standards of authority figures and the environment with which the individual had identified and subsequently internalized. But the goal of psychoanalytic treatment remained the same as outlined by earlier models: to uncover, tame, and rechannel repressed impulses and wishes that give meaning to experiences, to bring into consciousness what is unconscious. However, this revision in theory added the treatment goal, "where id was, let ego be."

During the development of his second and third models, Freud seemed to be influenced by views of interpretationism in his search for ways of understanding how meaning is given to experiences. Yet it is interesting to note that even in these revisions he "crossed over" into objectivism. For example, he remained influenced by the demarcationist strategy of objectivism that all concepts must be reducible to a physical basis. And when he conceptualized the ego and id, he proposed that the system (ego) and the energy for that system (id) are separate, and that a person as a system is active only in response to stimulation (energy). Thus the ego (cognitions, conscious beliefs, conscious intentions) was conceptualized as a structure without energy, and the id (drives, impulses, wishes) was conceptualized as a source of motivating energy without structure.

But even during Freud's lifetime, major interpretationist concepts were added to the psychodynamic position. For example, Heinz Hartmann presented what was then a major shift in emphasis—the notion that adaptation to the environment was as critical as unconscious meanings, and person and environment each act upon, influence, and shape the other. This lecture was first published in 1939 and forecast, as well as influenced, the interest that surged in the 1940s and 1950s in interpersonal, person–environment relationships, and in what came to be called "object relations theory."

Harry Stack Sullivan, who was a major force during this surge, made an explicit commitment to interpretationism and its organic metaphor. To formulate his concepts, Sullivan (1953) borrowed three principles from biology: the principle of communal existence (relationships), the principle of functional activity, and the principle of organization. When the latter two principles are combined, a concept emerges that views organizations of behavior as activity and activity as organization. Sullivan's position was elaborated by W. R. D. Fairbairn, who emphasized that the system of activity we call the person is always directed toward evolving relationships with others; that is, the person is always "object seeking." Bowlby emphasized "attachment," and Winnicott the matrix formed by an ongoing relationship between persons (Masling and Bornstein 1994, Overton and Horowitz 1991).

These contributions, as well as many others, resulted in a "revolution" within psychoanalytic theory that gave central importance to relationships, and the dialectical process, as the foundation of personality development and personality difficulties. This revolution, summarized and elaborated by Mitchell (1988), influenced revisions in psychodynamic concepts such as transference and insight (Gill 1984). Related to our interest, this revolution revised the meaning of psychodynamic as involving cyclical events between person and environment (Wachtel 1987), revisions I return to in the following chapters.

To conclude this sketch of what psychodynamic means, we should notice that major revisions took place over a span of 100 years: from Freud's first models of repressed memories of real events and dammed-up unconscious energy to the focus on interpersonal relations and adaptation to environments. We should also notice that even with these revisions the meanings a person constructs and assigns to experiences, and the importance of unconscious mental processes, have remained at the center of the psychodynamic position. As we turn to consider psychodynamic approaches to therapy, then, and the influence the approach reveals of interpretationist images, the reader should be aware that I try to represent the psychodynamic approach more as it has been outlined in the last decade, not as characterized in the 1930s and 1940s.

Identifying a Child's Problems and Conducting Treatment

To begin, we can repeat the statement used earlier to introduce cognitive-behavioral therapy and the influence of the objectivist position. Whether the child to be treated is socially withdrawn, aggressive and hyperactive, suffering from a learning disability, experiencing a specific fear, or suffering from generalized stress and anxiety, or is a juvenile delinquent, three broad propositions guide approaches to psychodynamic therapy.

1. While mindful of the child's presenting difficulties, the therapist looks beyond these target behaviors, or symptoms, and helps the child uncover meanings that have been outside his/her awareness (unconscious) and that are in conflict and the cause of the child's problems.
2. To accomplish this, the therapist initially focuses on establishing a "working relationship" and "therapeutic alliance" with the child. Particular ingredients of the relationship formed by therapist and child are viewed as critical and necessary for therapy to take place—a position strongly influenced by the interpretationist image of dialectics.
3. The child's symptoms and behavioral problems are resolved when the conflict among unconscious meanings is clarified and resolved.

To illustrate these broad propositions, and the influence of interpretationism on psychodynamic technique with children, I have selected two volumes by psychodynamic therapists as references for techniques used in mainstream psycho-dynamic child psychotherapy. Coppolillo (1987) presents what I believe is typical of most current psychodynamic approaches to child psychotherapy. Spiegel's volume (1989) reflects the interest in emphasizing interpersonal issues.

Establishing a Therapeutic Alliance

Psychodynamic therapy initially emphasizes establishing a special relationship with the child, reflecting the influence of the interpretationist image of dialectics. This beginning differs sharply from that of cognitive-behavioral therapy, which emphasizes that initially the target (problem) behavior and its antecedents and consequences should be articulated. Clearly following the image of dialectics, Coppolillo begins his presentation of psychodynamic child therapy by pointing out that advances in our physical world and technology have pressured therapists to keep their gaze exclusively on what is "objective and real." Instead, he proposes that a therapist should keep in mind that everything that happens between therapist and child, and all contacts by a child and therapist with parents, teachers, and peers, is part of the child's "inner, personal world." Moreover, everything in the treatment room, from the rug on the floor to the books on a shelf, could become symbolic expressions of the child's inner world. A child and therapist will soon set out to discover and construct this inner world. But before doing so, a preliminary and critical need must be met. The focus at the start is not on a child's problem behaviors, but on child and therapist constructing a special therapeutic relationship. It may take three or twenty meetings to accomplish this critical prerequisite.

How does the therapist know that a good-enough dialectical (therapeutic) relationship has been constructed? Coppolillo proposes that this goal is met when six "achievements" have been reached:

1. The child attains a degree of comfort.
2. The child communicates as a matter of course.
3. The child and therapist achieve a working alliance, a mutually shared sense that they are allies in the relationship. The child allies him- or herself with the therapist and the task of observing and evaluating his/her own emotions, wishes, and thoughts.
4. The child becomes aware, to some degree, that some of his/her behaviors and thoughts are generated from within him- or herself rather than elicited by external circumstances (parents, peers, teachers).
5. Child and therapist begin to share in constructing and representing the child's inner, private fantasies and thoughts with words, images, and symbolic play.
6. The child is helped to grasp a preliminary sense of the notion that some wishes and feelings are unconscious.

Constructing and Sharing How the Child Represents (Symbolizes) His/Her Experiences

Once the child and therapist have developed a good-enough, dialectical, therapeutic relationship, they set out to construct and share various meanings the child uses to represent his/her inner, private world and experiences. Here, too, the influence of interpretationist images seems apparent: that all knowledge is constructed by the knower; and that the knower and observer are two poles on a continuum, each defining and defined by the other and together engaged in a dialectical process. With one example Coppolillo (1987, pp. 247–248) describes a 5-year-old enuretic boy who had been silent and listless for two sessions. Now he hands the therapist a doll and says, "Here, you be the Dad; I'll be the Mom."

> *Therapist (taking the father doll)*:   Okay, what are we going to do, Mom?
> *Child:*   We've got to take the baby to the doctor.
> *Therapist:*   Okay, Mom, let's go. You show me where the doctor's office is.
> *Child (walks to the desk, carrying the mother and baby doll)*:   What's wrong with my baby? (*Looks at the therapist for an answer, obviously now assigning him the role of the doctor.*)
> *Therapist (in a conspiratorial, off-stage whisper)*:   What does the doctor say?
> *Child (whispers back)*:   He's sad.
> *Therapist (pontificating)*:   He's sad. (*Whispers, asking*) Why is he sad?
> *Child (whispering)*:   Because they whip him when he wets the bed.

To construct and share meanings or representations that influence a child's experiences, many different materials are used (e.g., puppets, costumes, sand, water, finger paints; see, for example, Schaefer and Cangelosi 1993). These items are used in various formats (e.g., fantasy play, storytelling, role-playing. See, for example, Kottman and Schaefer 1993). In addition, the process of constructing and sharing meanings that shape the child's experiences occurs simultaneously with, or is an integral part of, attempts by the therapist to discover and uncover those meanings that represent unconscious wishes and fantasies that are viewed as the source of the child's difficulties.

Discovering and Uncovering Unconscious Meanings/Wishes/Fantasies

Once the child has developed a good-enough alliance with the therapist and has begun constructing and sharing meanings/fantasies, the therapist makes use of particular tools in a phase of treatment that could involve one, two, or three sessions a week for a period of one to three years. This phase of treatment pursues a twofold goal that reflects the influence of interpretationist images: (1) uncovering the child's unconscious wishes, feelings, and meanings that define his/her personal world and influence his/her behavior, meanings viewed as the cause of the child's emotional conflicts and problems; and (2) labeling these meanings with words (interpretations) so that they can be understood and regulated at a conscious level. All of the play, activity, and talk in which the child and the therapist engage is focused on this twofold goal. All of what the therapist thinks about and does is organized around the intention of getting the child to express in verbal terms inner, unconscious meanings.

To begin cultivating the sense that some wishes and feelings are unconscious, Coppolillo found the following comment useful: "You know, sometimes people's minds play tricks on them. A thought or a feeling at the back of your mind, that you hardly know is there, can cause you to be afraid or to act in a certain way. When you find out what your thought or feeling is, it is not scary or bossy any more" (1987, p. 250).

How are these unconscious meanings discovered? Reflecting the demarcationist strategy of interpretationism that accepts patterns of phenomena as scientific information, Coppolillo points out that the therapist continually examines his/her interactions and play with the child, as well as the child's descriptions of events in his/her daily life, in search of patterns that convey a particular unconscious meaning. Once a pattern is identified, the therapist interprets the underlying meaning, wish, or motive. To illustrate the interpretationist strategy of discerning patterns, one of Coppolillo's examples should be useful (1987, pp. 221–222).

Teddy, an 8-year-old boy, was being treated for aggressive, unruly behavior that started after the sudden death of his father with whom Teddy shared a close relationship and "mutual admiration." Coppolillo notes that Teddy had not been able to discuss or mourn his father, and speculates that his aggressive behavior was very likely a manifestation of unconscious pain over the loss that had not yet been expressed consciously.

In one particular session, Teddy complained about a teacher whom he felt was mediocre, and added, "He ain't no Harmon Killebrew." (For the reader who is not familiar with baseball history, Harmon Killebrew was once a superb, professional baseball player.) The therapist knew that Teddy and his father were great baseball fans and surmised that Killebrew was one of their heroes. To help Teddy elaborate the possible unconscious meaning of this conscious association to a mediocre teacher, the therapist said that he wasn't sure what Teddy meant. "You know," Teddy answered, "not the greatest, like . . . he just ain't no Oscar Mayer."

Sensing the beginning of a pattern, and mindful that father was a butcher, the therapist continued to reflect his confusion in the hope of elaborating the pattern. The therapist asked, "Oscar Mayer?"

Teddy replied, " Yeah, the greatest. My father used to tell me that Oscar Mayer was the greatest. The best hot dogs . . . he [the teacher] ain't no Harmon Caballero."

With this, Teddy introduced still another ingredient in the emerging pattern. Coppolillo points out that when this session took place, Carmen Cavallero (whom the child called "Harmon Caballero") was a very popular pianist. It seems likely, I think, that the therapist also noted to himself that Harmon Killebrew's first name was similar to, and linked phonetically to, the pianist's first name.

At this point, relying on the pattern of associations Teddy had constructed, the therapist inferred the possible unconscious meaning of the mediocre teacher Teddy complained about at the start of this exchange. The pattern included Harmon Killebrew, the baseball hero; Oscar Mayer, the best hot dogs as declared by father; and Carmen Cavallero, the great pianist. To begin to lift this pattern and its meaning into Teddy's awareness, the therapist said, "Teddy, is that the way that these three people are alike? They're the greatest?"

Teddy responded, "Yeah! They are the best. My father used to say that."

Then the therapist made an interpretation. "Teddy, I think you're saying that your father was the greatest and, since he died, you just don't see how anyone can be as great as he was for you." At this, Teddy began crying softly.

In later sessions Teddy elaborated this pattern of associations, and its meaning, by acknowledging that for him the therapist's name (Henry Coppolillo) sounded more and more like the fictitious name "Harmon Cabarello," which he had introduced earlier. This experience on Teddy's part was considered a "transference experience." That is, Teddy unconsciously synthesized the names Harmon Killebrew, Carmen Cavallero, and Henry Coppolillo to form the name "Harmon Cabarello," thus experiencing the therapist as the greatest. As the pattern and its meaning became elaborated, Teddy revealed his conflict around wanting to love and be loved by someone like his father, but feeling guilty about this wish.

This therapeutic anecdote also illustrates other tools used by psychodynamic therapists to discern patterns of behavior, discover their unconscious meanings, and label them at the conscious level. Coppolillo provided a detailed description of each of the following tools.

1. *Inquiry and empathy.* The therapist maintains an attitude of inquiry and empathy in order to experience what the child is experiencing.
2. *Introspection.* The therapist teaches the child introspection. For example, at an appropriate moment, the therapist could say, "You know, when you told me that, a picture of another boy I knew came into my head."
3. *Verbalizing experiences.* The therapist helps the child put into words experiences that he/she had but may not have been able to describe. For example, "Have you noticed when you think of your little sister you get a picture in your head? That picture has parts in it like where she is and what she's doing or who is with her. Look at the picture inside your head and tell me about it."
4. *Searching for patterns in the child's symbols.* The therapist carefully tracks the child's associations in search of patterns.
5. *Countertransference.* The feelings and thoughts a therapist experiences in response to the child's behavior are examined by the therapist for clues about

possible patterns that might reveal unconscious meanings. Here the therapist is obligated to be aware of his/her personal, cultural convictions and
prejudices and whether and how they differ from those of the child.

6. *Play.* Unstructured play enables the child to reveal hidden wishes and
   fantasies.

7. *Constructing a common language with the child.* This tool derives from the
   heart of the dialectical image and requires that child and therapist develop
   and share a "private language." Here a system of symbols and signs invented
   by child and therapist serves as a vehicle of communication and makes the
   therapeutic relationship a unique experience for both child and therapist.

Interpreting (Labeling) Unconscious Meanings and Wishes

Since central importance is given to uncovering unconscious meanings and lifting
them into awareness with the tool of interpretation, it is not surprising that considerable attention is given by psychodynamic writers to the topic of how and when
the therapist constructs an interpretation that is offered to the child.

Coppolillo's discussion is particularly clear and recommended to the reader
interested in learning more about the process of interpretation. Here I summarize
his main points. He notes that many therapists err in thinking that most comments
the therapist makes to a child are interpretations. In fact, most comments are
explanations, clarifications, directives, admonitions, invitations, or trial balloons,
and these various comments prepare the ground for an interpretation. At the moment an interpretation is made, "both therapist and patient are ready to exchange
something of great conceptual importance" (Coppolillo 1987, p. 290). The importance of this exchange for psychodynamic therapists is dramatically conveyed
by Winnicott (1971), who described the interaction around an interpretation as a
"sacred moment" (pp. 4–5). It is at this moment, with this particular type of interaction, that the therapist hopes to promote change.

What happens that makes this moment sacred for psychodynamic therapists?
One of the child's neurotic conflicts, namely, unconscious conflicted meanings, is
dismantled and rendered powerless in prescribing maladaptive behaviors and emotions. Before we describe what is meant by dismantling a conflict, we need to remind ourselves of the concept of neurotic conflict held by the psychodynamic approach. The child unconsciously harbors a wish, plan, conviction, or fantasy that,
if carried out, or *recognized consciously*, would produce intense, painful anxiety.
Teddy, discussed earlier, provided an example. He harbored an unconscious wish
to love and be loved by someone like his father. But this wish collided with his
allegiance to his father, a collision that resulted in considerable guilt and anxiety.
To avoid, or in some way manage, this anxiety, the mind (ego) constructs defenses
that in some way displace or disguise the unconscious wish or motive that causes
the anxiety/guilt. In Teddy's case we found that he was being critical of a "medio-

cre" teacher as a way of defending against the guilt and anxiety generated by the love and admiration he felt for the teacher. In the jargon of defense mechanisms, his ego was using "reaction formation," that is, his love for the teacher was disguised by inverting it into critical, demeaning emotions directed toward him.

With these reminders as a backdrop, interpretation for the psychodynamic therapist is not a single act but a long process. Much like a chess game, interpretation involves many steps leading to the "sacred moment." At that moment, after many preliminary moves have been made, the conscious mind captures and gains victory over the unconscious wish and the conflict/anxiety it arouses. The many steps involved in making an interpretation can be summarized as follows:

1. First, the therapist helps the child identify and clarify patterns of behaving that appear in the child's interactions with the therapist, and with others, and that are considered to be symbolic expressions of the child's unconscious conflict.
2. Once the pattern of behaviors is articulated, the therapist helps the child recognize the defense being used to ward off anxiety that arises from the wish, impulse, or fantasy implicated in the child's conflict.
3. As the defense loses its power, the child consciously begins to experience the anxiety, usually as "scary feelings." Then the therapist focuses on labeling these feelings and on helping the child understand how he/she had been using particular behaviors to avoid these scary feelings.
4. The concluding interpretation, "the sacred moment," integrates and summarizes the previous interpretations and explanations. A summary interpretation is made only after there is behavioral evidence that the defense mechanism the child previously used to manage the conflict has now been removed (interrupted), and the emotions that emerged after the defense was removed have been labeled.

In one of Coppolillo's (1987) examples of a summary interpretation, he describes first the anxiety, and the obsessive defense used to manage it, and finally he labeled the impulse.

> We didn't know what we were scared of when you first came to see me. We figured out that having to count up to 1,000 before you went to school was a way of trying to get rid of scary feelings. Now we know that you were scared because you were furious at your teacher when she didn't treat you special. [p. 296]

The sessions following the construction of a core interpretation are typically viewed as "a phase of working through." Now the therapist uses play, activity, and discussions with the child in ways that apply the interpretation they have shared to other situations. How does a therapist judge whether an interpretation has been effective? Coppolillo discusses several criteria: for example, the child's anxiety level lessens; the child introduces another conflict indicating readiness to go further; one of the child's symptoms may disappear; with a burst of enthusiasm, the child begins a new activity that sets the stage for a new theme.

Terminating the Relationship

The interpretationist position, with its emphasis on the dialectical relationship between therapist and child, also influences the care psychodynamic therapy takes in deciding when and how this special relationship is concluded.

Reflecting the importance of this topic, Coppolillo devoted a chapter to termination. Criteria for termination include, for example, that the child shows he/she is free from internal oppression, relates productively with others, responds to the environment in more flexible ways, and is free of symptoms. Again reflecting the centrality of the dialectical image in psychodynamic psychotherapy, Coppolillo also gave special attention to developments *within the therapist* that signal the therapeutic relationship can now be gradually terminated. For example (1987, p. 322):

> "1. The child has become more interesting to the therapist. This is because the sphere of the child's own interest has expanded, he (the child) is no longer so preoccupied with his anxiety or the avoidance of it that he ignores the rest of the world."
>
> "2. The therapist feels better liked than before because, having resolved ambivalence, the child's affections spring more spontaneously from attachment rather than loneliness or fear."
>
> "3. The therapist feels less need to support. This is because the child is more secure, since his trust has not been betrayed and he has been respected."
>
> "4. The therapist feels less responsible for carrying the relationship because the child is more spontaneous. Neither trust nor affection have been demanded of him, but have been earned by the therapist . . ."

Psychodynamic Treatment from an Interpersonal Perspective

At this point I ask the reader to recall our earlier discussion that in recent years the psychodynamic approach has been increasingly influenced by theories concerning relationships (Mitchell 1988). What do we see if we look at child psychotherapy once the psychodynamic lens is adjusted to zoom in on, and magnify, the dialectical image of interpretationism? Do we see anything that was not as readily visible when we looked through Coppolillo's lens of present-day, traditional psychodynamic therapy? To address this question, I use Speigel's (1989) volume, which he presented as a description of child therapy from an interpersonal point of view.

Several considerations come into sharper focus when we look through Spiegel's lens, issues that are not as articulated when looking through Coppolillo's. With one, for example, Spiegel pointed out that if a therapist has an office in some way connected to his/her home, the therapist's home and family become factors in the child's therapeutic relationship with the therapist. We can readily see that an interpersonal point of view would notice this issue. Spiegel's lens magnifies still another issue, namely, limit setting, to which he devoted an entire chapter. How much freedom a therapist permits and what limits a therapist imposes are carefully discussed. This issue includes how the therapist reacts when a limit is imposed by a child. As one example, Spiegel cites a case by another therapist. A child was asked to clean up water he intentionally spilled. The child responded by asking what if he did not clean up the water—what would the therapist do? The therapist responded he would do nothing. Spiegel disagrees with this therapist. He proposes instead, that it would be more natural and appropriate if the therapist expressed his anger and stuck with the limit that was set.

In addition to considering issues such as the therapist's office and limit setting, the interpersonal view brings two more issues into focus. One concerns the relevance for child psychotherapy of research and concepts concerning early childhood development. The interpersonal position emphasizes that personality structures and dynamics result from interpersonal interactions during early childhood. Accordingly, special attention is given to interactions between infant and mother in the first years of life as a major source of data for the therapist. The second issue also stems from the emphasis given mother–child interactions and concerns challenging the importance of verbal interpretation, which is the heart of psychodynamic therapy. The interpersonal viewpoint proposes that, instead of verbal discussions and interpretations, psychotherapy should provide the child with interpersonal experiences commensurate with the child's stage of development. The following statements by Spiegel (1989) illustrate this shift away from verbalizing and interpreting.

> Infants do not begin development with a spoken language . . . treatment of children should be in the lexicon of the patient. The patient should not be forced to use the lexicon of the therapist. [p. 29] Unlike many child therapists, I do not see the aim of good therapy with children by getting them to talk about their concerns and problems in a straightforward manner . . . but to affect their concept of themselves and others . . . all of this need not be accompanied by insight about the origin and dynamics of their disorder. . . . [p. 28] The traditional psychoanalytic approach places strong emphasis on highly intellectualized verbal interpretations which I feel is inappropriate for children. [p. 31]

For Spiegel then, instead of emphasizing verbal interpretation, therapy should emphasize providing the child "a microcosm of life experiences," (p. 31) with opportunities to work out new ways of dealing with problems of living. But if therapy is to provide the child with a microcosm of life experiences, while avoiding verbal interpretations, what about the long-standing, psychodynamic commitment to make conscious what is unconscious? Here Spiegel proposes that interpreting through metaphors is the tool the therapist should use instead of "highly intellec-tualized verbal interpretations" (p. 31) that make a statement about some hidden fantasy in a straightforward manner.

One of Spiegel's case examples illustrates his use of symbolic actions (the lexi-con of the young child), embedded in fantasy play, as metaphoric interpretation in treatment. A 3½-year-old girl, whom he had already seen in about fifteen sessions, arrived in tears, clutching her mother and refusing to enter the playroom. Spiegel removed the child from her mother and took her to the playroom where she con-tinued to cry. There the child demanded, "Get out of here." Spiegel asked what would she do if he left, and she responded that she would continue crying and that when time was up, he was to knock on the door and she would let him in. Spiegel told her that he could not leave the room, but he would go into the "hiding closet." Then, he said, since he would be lonely there, he would like to take a couple of puppets to keep him company. She reluctantly agreed. While the child continued to cry in the playroom, Spiegel, situated in the closet, began a conversation be-tween the puppets loud enough for her to hear. The puppets argued whether the child was crying because she was mad or sad about leaving her mother. Finally, the puppets knocked on the door and stated they had a question for the child. One puppet declared the child was sad because she left mother, and the other that she was mad at mother for leaving her. Both puppets wondered, "Which is it?" The child answered, "It's like they are both mixed in together" (p. 42).

While using symbolic play to make interpretations in this anecdote, and in other anecdotes throughout his volume, Spiegel sometimes relies on expressing thoughts literally. Forecasting a position I develop in later chapters, I propose that when communicating to a child, a therapist should, as much as possible, use ac-tion symbols ("the child's lexicon") with verbal symbols elaborating these actions at least early in treatment.

A Recap

If we reflect on the psychodynamic treatment approach that is typically practiced at this time, including elaborations introduced by the interpersonal perspective, we should see the influence of interpretationist images: (1) the child's knowledge about his/her world of experiences does not exist outside of the child (out there) but is constructed by the child; (2) in order to gather this knowledge, the therapist estab-lishes a particular relationship with the child, and in this way enters the child's personal world; (3) as the child experiences trust and an alliance with the therapist, the child begins to share motives, fantasies, and wishes that are unconscious and in conflict with one another, and the cause of the child's difficulties; (4) the therapist uses fantasy play and discourse to help the child uncover these unconscious motives and fantasies and to resolve conflict by consciously understanding the issues involved; (5) change results when the child integrates elements of his/her personal, unconscious world of motives and wishes with other, already conscious, motives and wishes.

CONCLUDING COMMENT

In this chapter we considered some of the ways in which the cognitive-behavioral approach to treatment has been influenced by the objectivist position (discussed in the previous chapter) while the psychodynamic approach to treatment has been influenced by the interpretationist position. We saw that in the cognitive-behavioral approach a child's problem behavior is targeted for treatment. This behavior is viewed on the one hand, as determined by particular environments, or antecedent conditions, and on the other by consequences that occur in the environment in response to the behavior. Here we see the objectivist influence in that a boundary is drawn between child and environment, and between "real" events and the child's subjective experience. To help the child, the therapist administers various tasks the child is asked to perform. These tasks are designed to change the problem behavior directly, or to change the environment (antecedent conditions) by correcting the way in which the child's cognition is misrepresenting the environment. The child gains control over the problem behavior by accumulating skills. The child's subjective experience—both in and out of awareness—and the child's relationship with the therapist are ignored for the most part.

We also saw that the psychodynamic approach is so influenced by the interpretationist position as to virtually ignore the child's overt, behavioral problem and the environment in which the problem behaviors occur. Psychodynamic therapy is almost exclusively preoccupied with the child's subjective experience, that is, the meanings, motives, and fantasies, both in and out of awareness, that characterize the child's unique personal world. Whatever the child's problem, the therapist uses fantasy play and discourse to enable the child to reveal and share these personal motives and fantasies. Discovering unconscious meanings and motives is important because the child's problem and distress are viewed as determined by conflict that exists among these meanings and motives. Growth and change result when the child integrates these problematic, unconscious motives and wishes into his/her conscious thoughts and fantasies.

The two approaches to treatment, one from the view of objectivism and the other from the view of interpretationism, are very different. Yet our goal is to integrate these approaches. The reader might wonder with me, why can't we just erase the boundary between objectivism and interpretationism and use tasks like self-instruction and coping skills training along with fantasy play? But if we keep in mind the images of objectivism and interpretationism, which bring very different considerations into view, and then lift the boundary between them, we would immediately be flooded with questions. Should the behavior selected for treatment be on the outside and the surface (i.e., manifest/overt) or inside and deep (i.e., a meaning that is seemingly invisible)? How can we join what a person says with what a person imagines and does? And what is cognition? Does it involve surface or deep behaviors? And how should we view the relationship between cognition and emotion? What should we make of the role that meanings play in a person's daily life? Are unconscious processes more important than conscious processes, or vice versa? And what about the significance of environments and situations? What is the role of psychological conflict in a child's problem behaviors? What should a therapist do to help a child? Administer tasks, play, talk, or interpret the child's motives? And perhaps most provoking of all the questions, what about the relationship between patient and therapist? Do we ignore it? If we do not, does the relationship play a particular role in how a child changes?

In the next chapter we lift the boundaries we have articulated between objectivistism and interpretationism, body and mind, and cognition and emotion, and attempt to address these questions.

4

Dissolving Boundaries: Issues to Consider When Integrating Approaches to Child Psychotherapy

CONTENTS

Up to this point we have considered boundaries that have divided the real and subjective, body and mind, and cognition and emotion. We have also considered some of the ways in which the assumptions of objectivism and interpretationism have influenced the treatment approaches of cognitive-behavioral and psychodynamic therapies. As we continue our discussion, we should remind ourselves that nature does not produce a real world, omitting a subjective world, or produce a subjective world, omitting a real world. And nature does not produce individuals who have a mind and no body or a body and no mind. Nor does nature produce individuals who feel and do not think or who think and do not feel. To integrate these domains, it is first necessary to remove the boundaries between them, "to desegregate the field." This position was recommended by the 1986 workshop on psychotherapy integration sponsored by the National Institute of Mental Health (Mahoney 1993).

But how do we remove boundaries to begin the process of desegregation? Boundaries dissolve when we accept the proposition that what appear to be opposites share a fundamental unity. The notion that opposites share an identity, while prominent in Eastern thought, has also been advanced in Western writings. For example, Alfred North Whitehead's philosophy proposes that events usually considered irreconcilable are actually like the crest and trough of a single wave. The unity of opposites found its way into physiology in the writings of Ludwig von Bertalanffy, the theoretical biologist, who proposed an "organismic" viewpoint in 1928 (1928/1962). In the 1930s and '40s the organismic viewpoint in turn became a central feature of Gestalt psychology, which emphasized that the literal and the figurative, the real and the subjective, are two poles of a field that is inherently relational. For example, while a curved line divides space so that we perceive space on one side of the line as concave and on the other as convex, the line also simultaneously unites the two perceptions of space since neither exists without the other. As another example, we can take the familiar ambiguous figure of the vase–person that appears regularly, or did so at one time, in elementary psychology textbooks (Figure 4–1). From one point of view we experience two faces turned toward each other; from another, a vase. While lines define both faces and a vase, each does not exist without the other. Moreover, either the faces or the vase could be the focus of study. Yet both are parts of a single whole that is present (Overton and Horowitz 1991).

This organismic, "gestalt" perspective was extended by Heinz Werner (1948) into a developmental psychology. He proposed that the study of organizations of behavior, which develop toward increasing differentiation and integration, should be preferred over the study of segregated elements. This proposal has been echoed by many investigators and clinicians influenced by the organismic prospective. For

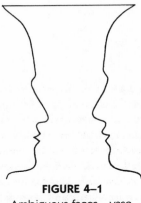

FIGURE 4–1
Ambiguous faces—vase.

example, observing that investigators tend to define and measure emotion and cognition separately, Izard and colleagues (1984) concluded, "We think it may be useful to hold open the possibility that there may be one ultimate integrating system that . . . may fruitfully conceptualize human activities as a function of an integration of perceptual, cognitive, motor, and emotional processes" (p. 8).

But if the body and mind, cognition and emotion, and the images of objectivism and interpretationism are to be taken as an organized whole rather than detached pieces, what fundamental unity do they share? If cognition is the trough, for example, and emotion the crest, what is the wave? If the body is the trough and the mind is the crest, what is the wave? And if the objective is the trough and the subjective the crest, what is the wave? An approach to these questions is provided by Schacht's (1984) cogent discussion of six models that have been followed by investigators interested in the question of integrating different therapies. A sketch of these models should serve the reader in thinking about desegregating psychotherapy and in evaluating the integration proposed in the next chapters.

SIX MODELS TO GUIDE INTEGRATION IN PSYCHOTHERAPY

With Schacht's first model, therapists take the position that two or more approaches to therapy are fundamentally incompatible, and usually one is valued as unique. When this model is followed, discussions are replete with metaphors of conflict; for example, "behavior therapy versus dynamic therapy," "rival systems of belief whose relative value is a matter of moral judgment." The article by Lazarus (1995), which we considered in Chapter 1, provided one illustration of a position that renounced the use of psychodynamic terms as unnecessary. Referring to our earlier discussion of American psychology's tendency to draw boundaries, Schacht's Model I converges with Wilber's (1979) reminder of what happens when a boundary separates two concepts as fundamentally incompatible. "A boundary line, as any military expert will tell us, marks off the territories of two opposing and potentially warring camps" (p. 10).

Another point Wilber makes typifies what happens if Schacht's second model is followed to integrate therapies. "And when the opposites engage in conflict a typical way of solving the problem is to attempt to diminish one, or to reduce it to the other" (p. 20). Investigators who follow Schacht's (1984) Model II translate the language of one therapeutic approach into that of another that is viewed as primary, "a sort of mother tongue that can wholly encompass the ideas and observations of the other's treatment" (p. 115). Many illustrations of this model were first introduced in the 1930s. Franz Alexander translated psychoanalytic concepts into the language of Pavlovian conditioning. Decades later Dollard and Miller (1950) translated psychoanalytic concepts into the language of learning theory. (For more recent examples, see Arkowitz and Messer 1984, Marmor and Woods 1980.) Unfortunately, during these translations one approach is declared as primary, resulting in the very divisiveness that Wilbur pointed out. Consider, for example, Eysenck's (1960) statement (cited in Marmor and Woods 1980) that psychodynamic psychotherapy, "when shorn of its inessential and irrelevant parts, can usefully be considered a minor part of behavior therapy" (p. 295).

When therapists follow Schacht's Model III, two therapies are viewed as complementary and suitable for dealing with separate problems in the same patient. Two therapists work with the same patient on different issues using different approaches. Or the same therapist works with a patient using one therapeutic approach during one phase (e.g., exploratory psychoanalytic psychotherapy to uncover past conflicted experiences with parents) and a different therapeutic approach in another phase (e.g., assertiveness training to cope with anxiety over competing in gym class). With this model the patient is viewed as doing the integrating. Various therapies are seen as "options" that the therapist selects, depending upon the specific clinical problem and treatment goal. In a discussion of "when the patient does the integrating" (p. 133), Gold (1994) described a series of cases in which more than one approach was used at different stages of treatment.

When Model IV is followed, the therapist uses two or more different therapies with a patient with the intention that the methods will interact within the patient to produce a result superior to that obtainable with either therapy alone. The main difference between this model and the previous one is that here different treatment methods are not introduced to handle separate problems. Rather, two or more methods address the same problem, but each retains its identity.

With the fifth model, integration takes place within therapeutic techniques. In contrast to Model IV, in which the techniques of each therapy remain unchanged and integration lies within their effects on the patient, therapeutic techniques here represent some hybrid of two approaches. Schacht cited the "psychodynamic behavior therapy" developed by Feather and Rhoads (1972a,b) as an example. These authors integrated the behavioral procedure of systematic desensitization and the psychodynamic technique of uncovering unconscious impulses and fantasies. The result is a therapeutic method that desensitizes adult patients to underlying impulses and fantasies, rather than simply desensitizing them to overt symptoms. I (1995) described a treatment method for children with attention deficit disorders that consists of structured tasks that gradually become stimuli a child uses to symbolize, represent, and work through meanings given to experiences.

The last strategy, Model VI, presents "the most formidable intellectual challenge" (Schacht 1984, p. 119). Here the goal is to integrate propositions and concepts in an effort to construct a model of human functioning that is heuristically valuable in psychotherapy. These models are often expressed in terms of a key metaphor. Schacht offered as one example the model of "man as an information-processing machine" (p. 120), a metaphor we have already considered in some detail. Writers who are pessimistic about integration focus their arguments at this level. They take the position that behavioral and psychodynamic therapies, for example, are fundamentally incompatible because the conceptualization of human functioning and/or reality of each approach is fundamentally different.

While Schacht suggests that Model VI represents one kind of integration among several and "is not necessarily superordinate to the others but is simply more abstract" (p. 120), he seems to see the value and need for integrating concepts.

> The particular units of analysis selected by a proponent of therapeutic integration do not spontaneously coalesce into a seamless whole . . . any choice of elements must be arranged and organized and must be embedded in a framework of conceptual relationships. These relationships . . . constitute the infrastructure of any given discussion of therapeutic integration. . . . [p. 114]

Ten years later, Stricker (1994) supported this position. "There is a powerful argument for the maintenance of an internally consistent theoretical structure within which techniques from other approaches can be incorporated with the need to appreciate the reverberations throughout the theory of technical innovations . . . this is what is meant by assimilative integration . . ." (p. 33). Mahoney (1993) also agreed. He reviewed technical eclectics, who proposed that treatment techniques can be selected without considering the theory on which they rest, and integrationists, who argued that since theory and techniques are inseparable, concepts from different viewpoints should be integrated. From this review he took a stand: "[M]y own evolving position on this matter leans towards the integrationists' arguments" (p. 6).

Agreeing with Stricker and Mahoney, I have attempted to follow Schacht's sixth model in my effort to construct a conceptual scaffold for child psychotherapy that attempts to dissolve the boundaries between objectivism and interpretationism, body and mind, and cognition and emotion. The model of human functioning that I believe is heuristically valuable for an integrative child psychotherapy centers on a synthesis of particular developmental concepts. The key metaphors that express the model are agricultural ones, such as a growing plant and its surrounds. In preparing for my integrative model, when I attempted to dissolve the boundaries we have considered, a number of interlocking issues came to my attention. Many of these issues had already been debated in the literature on adult psychotherapy. But when I turned to the literature on child psychotherapy, I found relatively little assistance. More than ten years ago, Arkowitz (1984) pointed out that interest in integration has neglected child psychotherapy. Discussions since then have continued to focus on the pros and cons of integrating adult psychotherapies. One dramatic illustration of how little attention has been paid thus far to integration in child psychotherapy is provided by the observation that only one of thirty-five chapters in a recent handbook on psychotherapy integration (Stricker and Gold 1993) is devoted to child psychotherapy, and only one to adolescent psychotherapy. In another handbook (Norcross and Goldfried 1992) none of the eighteen chapters is devoted to child psychotherapy.

The issues that I believe should be considered by any integrative model of child psychotherapy emerged over the years from my own research and experience as a child therapist and from reviewing the discussions by others interested in integrating approaches to adult psychotherapy. The reader is encouraged to examine the integrative model I propose, as well as those proposed by others, through the lens provided by these issues. In my mind the issues are related hierarchically (see Table 4–1). The first one we consider in the discussion to follow, surface versus deep

TABLE 4–1.   A Hierarchy of Issues that Should Be Considered by Models of Psychotherapy Integration for Children

ISSUE	
I	Are behaviors to be treated outside and on the surface or inside and deep?
II	The need to relate what a person does with what a person imagines, thinks, and says
III	The relation between cognition and emotion
IV	The meanings a person gives experiences
V	Conscious and unconscious processes
VI	Contexts, environments, and situations
VII	Psychological conflict
VIII	The relationship between patient and therapist
IX	What should the therapist do to help? Reconsidering the importance given to verbal labeling and interpretation
X	Developmental principles: The glue for integration

behaviors, influences the shape of, and is influenced by, the second issue (the relations among what a person does, imagines, thinks, and says). This issue in turn influences and is influenced by the others we consider: the relation between cognition and emotion, the role of meaning in experiences, the notion of conscious and unconscious mental processes, the context in which experiences occur, and conflict in human functioning. These issues converge on the relationship that evolves between child and therapist and on the question of what can a therapist do, in addition to talking, to help a child. The issues also point to a series of needs that should be addressed by any integrative approach to child psychotherapy. Therefore, after we review each issue, I conclude the chapter with a discussion of these needs. The reader will wonder how these needs can be met. In the next two chapters I outline a particular developmental-dialectical model that I propose has considerable heuristic value in accomplishing this task.

ISSUES TO CONSIDER IN CONSTRUCTING AN INTEGRATIVE MODEL

Issue I: Are Behaviors to Be Treated Outside and on the Surface or Inside and Deep?

Debates over whether the determinants of human behavior are located "outside" (e.g., overt actions, verbalized conscious thoughts and beliefs) or "inside" (e.g., unconscious wishes, impulses, fantasies) have been going on since the time of Greek philosophers and continue to the present (e.g., Jacobson 1994, Mahoney 1984, 1993, Wachtel 1987). More recently, the positions of objectivism and interpretationism have resulted in two views that have filtered into approaches to psychotherapy: that behaviors to be treated are either "outside and on the surface" or "inside and deep." As we discussed earlier, cognitive-behavioral therapy, rooted in the machine metaphor of objectivism, has tended to focus on what are considered surface, observable behaviors (e.g., speaking overtly or covertly as in self-instruction training, modeling the actions of others, rewarding some overt behavior). In contrast, psychodynamic therapy, rooted in interpretationism, has tended to emphasize inferred behaviors viewed as "inside and deep" (e.g., a wish to be fed is inferred when a child waters a plant).

One example of the debate over whether therapy should address outside or inside behaviors is provided by Messer and Winokur (1984). They discussed behavioral and psychoanalytic therapies in terms of the concepts of "visions of reality" and "ways of knowing." The former concerns the assumptions one holds about the nature and content of reality. The latter refers to the means one uses to learn about that reality. As the reader may notice, these concepts converge with our discussion, in Chapter 2, of how objectivism and interpretationism assume what knowledge is and how it is acquired. Messer and Winokur argued that behavioral therapy operates primarily within a vision of reality that sees only the "outside" of a person—observable aspects of a person and situations that can be controlled and

predicted. Moreover, this vision sees conflicts a person experiences as surface behaviors that can be corrected by the therapist with manipulative actions. While
embracing this vision, the ways in which a cognitive-behavioral therapist reasons and knows are "discursive," "scientific," and "demonstrative." Information
is known by observing from a distance, by experiencing it as something outside
of oneself and already existing as true. This way of knowing assumes that the
therapist can be separated from the patient in order to determine what is true in
an absolute sense (e.g., Jacobson 1994), and has stimulated a proposal that a
patient can be trained to be a "scientist" and learn how to obtain "true" knowledge (e.g., Mahoney 1974).

That cognitive-behavioral therapies focus on outside behaviors is poignantly
illustrated by Kohlenberg and Tsai's (1994) discussion of "radical behaviorism."
They pointed out, for example, "[I]t is impossible to devise treatment methods that
focus on non-behavioral entities . . . that cannot be directly contacted or observed
by the therapist" (pp. 194–195). In a related article, Jacobson (1994) noted, "For
pragmatic reasons, radical behaviorists call events external to the organism that
influence behavior 'causes' because they can be directly manipulated by therapist
and client . . . *we have direct access only to events external to the client* or subject; thus
we can directly observe their effects on the behavior of interest" (pp. 109–110; italics
mine).

On the other hand, psychodynamic therapies, Messer and Winokur (1984)
argued, operate within a vision of reality that focuses on the "inside" of a person;
that is, a patient's introspections and subjectivity, expressing inferred wishes and
fantasies that oppose each other. These opposing forces cannot be corrected but
only confronted with the hope of gaining some mastery over them. While embracing
this vision, the ways in which a psychodynamic therapist reasons and knows are
"intuitive," "poetic," "empathetic," and "dialectical." By "poetically" fusing and transacting with the patient in a dialectical discourse, the therapist forms a union with
the patient. The following comment by Mitchell (1988) dramatizes how the psychoanalyst's poetic-dialectical way of knowing hopes to capture a vision of the inside
of a person.

> Unless the analyst effectively enters the patient's relational matrix or, rather,
> discovers himself within it—unless the analyst is in some sense charmed by
> the patient's entreaties, shaped by the patient's projections, antagonized and
> frustrated by the patient's defenses—the patient is never fully engaged and
> a certain depth within the analytic experience is lost. [p. 293]

To recap the issue of outside versus inside, I paraphrase Winokur and Messer
(1984). Cognitive-behavioral therapies, with their objectivist emphasis on outside/
surface behaviors, circle around the outside of the patient. In contrast, psychodynamic therapies, with their interpretationist emphasis on inside/deep behaviors,
enter inside the patient.

In terms of work with children, one example of the outside/inside dichotomy can be seen in one popular approach to categorizing the problems of children and adolescents. Problems are viewed as either "externalized" or "internalized"—in other words, as either outside or inside (Weisz and Weiss 1993). Externalized problems include, for example, fighting, vandalism, and stealing. Internalized problems include, for example, fearfulness, withdrawal, complaints of headaches, stomachaches, and other bodily pains. It seems that in the United States there is a focus on "outside problems," since externalized behaviors are the most frequent reasons why children are referred to clinics (Weisz and Weiss 1993). But this vision of reality is not maintained in all countries. In Thailand the most common referral problems tend to be those that are viewed as "inside or internalized" (Weisz et al. 1987a).

Concluding Comment

As we can see, visions of reality as either outside or inside leave us with perplexing questions. For example, why are behaviors such as "fighting" viewed as external and on the surface, while behaviors such as "feeling inadequate" viewed as internal and deep? Is stealing necessarily more visible than feeling inadequate?

From another angle, could surface and deep behaviors such as fighting and feeling inadequate be related in some way? Imagine a child standing timidly on the edge of a playground, watching others racing about in a baseball game. For a few moments the child spontaneously engages in a vivid fantasy in which he vigorously beats upon a boy who has hit a home run. Since the same child is standing timidly, and simultaneously fantasizing fighting someone who hit a home run, could the behaviors be related in some way? Is it possible to remove the boundary between surface and deep behaviors and search for relationships that integrate them as one? These questions converge with one Mahoney (1993) posed. Noting the ongoing debates over the merits and mechanisms of "surface structures" versus "deep structures," he asked, "[H]ow do changes at one level reflect and reciprocally influence changes at the other?" (p. 6). These reflections relate to the next issue: the need to integrate what a person does with what a person imagines and says.

Issue II: The Need to Relate What a Person Does (Action) with What a Person Imagines (Fantasy), Thinks, and Says (Language)

In the previous chapter we noted that while cognitive-behavioral and psychodynamic therapies are interested in action, fantasy, and language behaviors, each focuses on one of these modes, namely, what a person thinks and says.

Cognitive-behavioral therapies rely on the notion that if the right words and thoughts are expressed overtly or covertly, as in self-instruction training, these words and thoughts can regulate and control actions. Reflecting this assumed connection between verbalizing and interacting, Kendall and Braswell (1985) stated that "improving the child's ability to accurately recognize and label his/her emotional experiences, as well as the emotions of others, may be a necessary step for improved interpersonal problem solving" (p. 135). These therapists also rely on the notion that if verbalized cognitive mediators represent a situation correctly, a person would function within that situation with appropriate behaviors. Recall from Chapter 3 the shy boy described by Kendall and Morison (1984), who because he was uneasy about participating in a soccer game was provided with verbalized statements intended to modify how his cognitive mediators viewed the situation.

The emphasis given to language is illustrated by Knell (1995), who proposes an integration of cognitive-behavioral methods and play to treat children. Although noting that "therapy must be more experiential than verbal" and "the child should be allowed to interact without the need for complicated language skills" (p. 28), the author clearly emphasized the importance of language, as reflected by the following.

> One opportunity for therapeutic intervention is in encouraging and facilitating the child's language to describe experiences and emotions. [p. 28] They [children] may also benefit from efforts to . . . learn to express certain maladaptive behaviors in more adaptive language-based ways . . . teaching youngsters to understand that they are angry, what it means to be angry, and how to say it in words instead of behavior may be a beginning in helping them deal with their feelings. . . . Using language rather than aggressive behaviors may provide some of this sense of mastery and control. . . . While the child is acting out his anger by kicking the play carriage, a punching bag, or a puppet representation of his sister, the therapist can help the child label his feelings. Merely acting aggressively in therapy does not teach the child that there are alternatives. Labeling the aggression . . . can offer the child some other, more adaptive way of dealing with his frustration and anger. [p. 29]

If we turn to psychodynamic therapies, we find the same influence: that spoken words have power to regulate actions, fantasies, and emotions. Early in his writings, Sigmund Freud set the stage for the focus on verbalizing. In his work with adults he viewed everything a patient did, all actions, as resisting the task of lifting repression and revealing, with spoken words, some forbidden, unconscious fantasy and wish (Mitchell 1994). It is interesting to note that when the psychoanalytic approach gave rise to the treatment of children, the emphasis on encouraging the child to express his/her concerns in words dominated, in spite of the use of play activity. For example, Erikson (1964) noted that "children . . . need to be induced by systematic interpretation to reconsider, on a more verbal level, the constellations that have overwhelmed them in the past . . ." (p. 265). Anna Freud (1965) held that the child "gains its victories and advances whenever [conflicts] are grasped

and put into thoughts or words" (p. 32). Kennedy (1979) emphasized the importance of providing a child with a language-conceptual framework.

This emphasis on verbalizing continues to the present, whether the author
describes a "traditional" psychodynamic approach to child therapy (e.g., Coppolillo
1987) or an "interpersonal" approach (e.g., Spiegel 1989). For example, echoing
earlier writers, Coppolillo (1987) noted, "The therapist has a powerful tool in tackling the task of inducing the child to express conflicts in verbal terms" (p. 245).

While emphasizing the importance of verbal labeling, both cognitive-
behavioral and psychodynamic therapies do not provide us with a conceptualization
that sufficiently articulates how verbalizing one's concerns is connected to the actions one takes and why it is so important to induce a child to cast thought and
feelings in verbal terms. Nor is much attention paid to the observation that actions
vary in form. For example, a boy may kick the door to his brother's bedroom and
on another occasion kick his brother. In a similar vein, little attention is paid to the
observation that fantasies vary in form. For example, a child may fantasize herself,
sword in hand, galloping through the playground on a horse, in pursuit of a gigan-
tic dragon. Or the same child may fantasize herself standing with hands on her
hips, challenging a playground bully. Spoken words also take different forms. A
child may shout, "I'll smash your face!" or "I'll beat you in a race any day!" Is there
a way to relate different forms of action, fantasy, and language behaviors, as well as
to relate expressions in one mode with expressions in another?

For cognitive-behavioral therapies, verbalizing seems necessary because conscious thoughts are viewed as having the power to control overt actions. For psychodynamic therapies, verbalizing seems necessary because, by verbally expressing a
fantasy or feeling, the issue shifts from an unconscious to a conscious level. Given
the emphasis on verbalizing, and given the tendency to equate verbalizing and self-
talk with cognition, a related question emerges. What is cognition, and is cognition a surface or deep behavior?

What Is Cognition? Is It Surface or Deep Behavior?
Two Cognitive Revolutions and Two Views of Cognition

The term cognition is used in many different ways and appears to have no generally accepted referent. This seems to be all the more surprising since a "cognitive
revolution" has been occurring in psychology for the past several decades (Dember
1974, Gardner 1985). Actually, there have been two revolutions. A sketch of the
history of each will enable us to evaluate how cognition is viewed at the present
time and applied in therapy.

It is hard to imagine that there was once a time when cognition was essentially ignored by both investigators and clinicians. But this was the case in the decades prior to the 1950s. Why was there little interest in cognition during this early
period? One reason was the rise of behaviorism with its "glorification of the skin"
(Gruber et al. 1957, p. 203). Another was the preoccupation by psychoanalysis with

unconscious motivation, feelings, and psychic conflict. But the situation soon changed. Three symposia, convened between 1948 and 1955, sparked the first cognitive revolution that became known as the "New Look" (Santostefano 1991a). What was it that was new? Investigators abandoned the search for universal laws that explained cognitive activity as a self-contained entity and set out to integrate cognitive functioning and personality. Cognition was considered in terms of perceptual activity, and investigators tried to connect the "surface activity" of perception with the "deeper" structures of personality.

The stage for the first cognitive revolution was set by Heinz Werner's (1949) introduction to a symposium on "Interrelations between Perception and Personality" held at the 1948 convention of the American Psychological Association. Studies of perception as cognition were flourishing, but separate from the growing interest in personality. Werner emphasized that although psychology had begun to recognize "that the perceived world pattern mirrors the organized need pattern within" (p. 2), psychology had done little to that date to integrate a psychology of perception with a psychology of personality.

Responding to this need, Werner and Wapner (1949) offered their "sensoritonic-field theory of perception." With this, they forecast the importance of locating perception within the individual and the individual within the environment. "The theory cannot be fully understood unless we relinquish the traditional notion of perception as a self-contained unit and replace it by a field concept which defines the relationship between organism and object" (p. 92). Others also responded to Werner's call for testable hypotheses linking perception and personality. For example, Klein and Schlesinger (1949) conceptualized "perceptual attitudes" that coordinate information from the environment and from "the personal world of the perceiver" (a concept I discuss in more detail in the next chapter). Witkin (1949) conceptualized the importance of individual differences in the body's perception of the upright, and McCleary and Lazarus (1949) discussed perception without awareness.

These issues received further attention the following year, reflecting the rapid momentum of the New Look approach. A second conference convened at the University of Texas in 1949 was guided by the view that "the study of perceptual activity provides a basic approach to an understanding of personality and interpersonal relations. Perceptual activity supplies the material from which the individual constructs his own personally meaningful environment" (Blake and Ramsey 1951, p. iii). Discussing his studies of learning and perception, Hilgard (1951) pointed out, "We are trying to discover how perception may be influenced by the realities outside and by the realities within ourselves" (p. 95) and proposed that the individual attempts to maintain a state of "*dynamic* equilibrium" between these influences.

For Frenkl-Brunswick (1951) the best way to capture a person's dynamic equilibrium is to study the person in his "natural cultural habitat," echoing the field theory Werner and Wapner presented the previous year. Klein (1951) also elaborated his concept of perceptual attitudes that he presented the previous year. He viewed cognition as actively constructing states of dynamic equilibrium between an individual's personal, subjective world and the environment, and he emphasized individual differences. "The concept of equilibrium is useful only if we wholeheartedly recognize that the kind of balance, and the means for reaching it, are different for different people. One man's equilibrium is another man's discomfiture" (p. 330).

Agreeing with the need for hypotheses that link perception and personality, and forecasting an integration of cognition and personality, Bruner (1951) urged investigators to define concepts that forge cognition and personality as one.

> For there cannot be one way of thinking about perception when one is interested in personality and another way of thinking about it when one is interested in size constancy. The two approaches must inevitably converge. At that happy point of convergence, doubtless, personality theory and perceptual theory will themselves merge into a common theory of behavior. [p. 122]

From this second conference, then, there came a call for new concepts that forged perceptual activity and personality as one process, and that defined how an individual's cognition equilibrates environmental stimuli with those from the personal world of need, emotion, and motivation. But there was another theme that received prominent attention at this conference, namely, unconscious processes and cognitive functioning. Recognizing the dominance of behaviorism at the time, Bronfenbrenner (1951) attempted to desensitize the aversion of this country's psychologists to the concept of the unconscious. He gently pointed out that what we call unconscious is any mental process of which we are not directly aware. Miller (1951) was more blunt. He asked psychologists to devote attention to what he called "the psychology of ignorance," or mental activity outside awareness. He used the following anecdote to help his message. After Sergeant York had captured 132 Germans single-handedly, he was asked how he did it. He replied, "It was simple. I just surrounded them." For Miller, York's comments simply, yet cogently, hinted at the meaning this experience shaped in York's unconscious.

The issue of unconscious, cognitive processes became the focus of the third symposium that served to launch the New Look movement. Convened at the University of Colorado in 1955 (Gruber et al. 1957), behaviorists and psychoanalytically oriented researchers and clinicians articulated three motifs: (1) cognition is at the center of a person's adaptations to environments; (2) the environments to which a person adapts are cognitive representations or symbols rather than actual things as they are; and (3) unconscious cognitive structures code or determine what pictures a person takes, so to speak, of a specific environment.

The thrust of the New Look revolution, then, was influenced in a major way by the interpretationist position we discussed in Chapter 2. Cognition was defined as unconscious structures that equilibrate environmental stimuli with stimuli from the personal, subjective world of emotion and motivation in the service of adaptation. Referring to our previous discussion, the reader may notice that this concept views cognition as "deep" behavioral structures. Moreover, the notion of cognition equilibrating environmental and personal stimulation (e.g., fantasies) in the service of adaptation (action) provides one way of establishing connections between cognition, fantasy, and action. Research influenced by this view flourished in the 1960s and '70s (see Santostefano 1978 for a review) but was then eclipsed by a second revolution (H. Gardner 1985).

In sharp contrast to the interpretationist view of the first revolution, the second revolution was influenced by the objectivist position. Now research shifted the focus from cognition as unconscious "meaning" to cognition as "information." And research also shifted the focus *away* from cognition as coordinating meanings, assigned both to environmental stimulation and personal feelings and motives, and *toward* cognition as involving the "processing of information." Recalling his participation in the first revolution, and reviewing developments in the second, Bruner (1990, 1992) argued that the introduction of the computer as the ruling metaphor was responsible for this shift. Further, he urged that cognitive science return to the original New Look emphasis on unconscious meaning. At this point we turn to consider how these two cognitive revolutions influenced psychotherapy.

Cognition in Psychodynamic Therapy

As the New Look elaborated its concepts and observations, Robert Holt (1964) informed psychoanalysts, some ten years after the Colorado symposium, that cognition was emerging as a powerful point of view and urged them to consider how this view of cognition could influence their clinical work. Apparently, his suggestion was not followed by many. John Benjamin (1961) pointed out that the field of cognition was a stepchild in clinical practice. Soon after, Arieti (1970) commented that cognition was the "Cinderella" of psychoanalysis and consistently neglected by clinicians. The neglect, however, was not total. Yet it is interesting to note that those psychodynamic therapists who did address cognition relied upon Piaget's cognitive psychology rather than the concepts of the New Look (Anthony 1956, Decarie 1965, Lewis 1977, Wolff 1960).

Since these early writings, volumes have appeared that address cognition and psychodynamics (e.g., Horowitz 1988) and cognitive science and psychoanalysis (Colby and Stoller 1988). In addition, a few writers have described forms of cognitively oriented psychodynamic psychotherapy for adults (e.g., Feather and Rhoads 1972a,b, Wachtel 1977, Weiner 1985) and children (Santostefano 1995a). Unlike earlier clinicians who relied on Piaget, these attempts to integrate cognitive considerations into psychodynamic therapy by and large maintained the motifs of the New Look approach; namely, that cognition is at the center of a person's adaptations to the environment, and that the environments to which a person adapts are unconscious, cognitive representations.

Yet in spite of these contributions, cognition continues to receive relatively little attention in the psychodynamic camp. For example, two volumes devoted to psychodynamic psychotherapy with children (Coppolillo 1987, Spiegel 1989), considered in previous chapters, do not list cognition in the index. In a handbook of child psychoanalysis (Wolman 1972), cognition is given spotty attention and in relatively general terms. For example, the reader is reminded that the thinking of the latency child, in contrast to that of an adolescent, is relatively realistic, concrete, and associated with action; that in preadolescence there is a proliferation of prelogical thinking and magical beliefs; and the male and female may find his/her thinking impaired because of sexual preoccupation.

Cognition in Cognitive-Behavioral Therapy

The picture is quite different in cognitive-behavioral therapy, where considerable attention has been, and is, given to cognition. However, what is considered to be cognition appears not to have been influenced by the first cognitive revolution. Rather, many different behaviors were proposed as cognitions to be treated and changed. One volume (Emery et al. 1981) provided illustrations. Here cognition was defined as "sleeping cognition" (p. 288), "dream content" (p. 231), "helplessness . . . anxiety" (p. 231), "discussing perceptions of an event" (p. 57), "a person's tendency to drift from topic to topic" (p. 88), and "distortions" of one's physical appearances (p. 71). Some authors (e.g., Cacioppo and Petty 1981) proposed a broad definition of cognitive behavior to be addressed in therapy—"those thoughts that pass through a person's mind" (p. 310)—while others (Bedrosian and Beck 1980) proposed a more circumscribed one—"dysfunctional ideation" (p. 128).

To make matters more confusing, still other behaviors were proposed as cognition in cognitive-behavioral therapy: *attributional styles*—the inferences a person draws across different situations to explain why a particular event occurred (e.g., John was picked for the baseball team because "taller people are better"); *role-taking* (or perspective-taking)—the degree to which a person assumes the point of view (thoughts, perceptions, and emotions) of another person; *cognitive problem-solving*—whether and how a person thinks of alternative solutions to a problem (e.g., Joe wants to play with a toy that Harry has; think of different ways he could get it). In addition, cognitive therapies defined cognition as belief systems and thought patterns (e.g., I am not very good at what I try). And, as we discussed in previous chapters, cognitive-behavioral therapy considers cognition as verbalized statements and self-instruction, which refer to the thoughts a person says to himself/herself while dealing with situations and performing tasks.

The confusion caused by the many ways in which the term *cognition* is used was clarified, to some degree, more than a decade ago by Arnkoff and Glass (1982) with their excellent critique that still serves us today. First they pointed out that there is an "overwhelmingly narrow focus in the literature on self-statements and beliefs" (p. 9). Then they articulated several problems that arise from the emphasis given self-statements and beliefs by cognitive and behavioral therapies. Highlighting a few of the points they made provides a bridge to the next issue we will discuss, namely, the meaning given to experiences.

1. A belief or self-statement, such as "I am a failure," may have several meanings, and several different statements may convey a single meaning (e.g., "I hate life; I like the color gray"). Connecting with our earlier discussion of outside and inside behaviors, and of the first cognitive revolution, Arnkoff and Glass suggested that what a person says may be the "tip of the iceberg," and therefore there is a need to consider "surface and deep" cognitive structures in order to learn the meaning underlying a particular verbalized statement.

2. The literature tends to dichotomize self-statements and beliefs as irrational versus rational, unrealistic versus realistic, and task irrelevant versus relevant. Not only are these bipolar distinctions used interchangeably, but underlying these classifications is the inherent assumption that it is better to be rational, realistic, and task relevant than it is to be irrational, unrealistic, and task irrelevant. Because of these assumptions, self-statement therapies set out to help the client identify "bad thoughts" and replace them with "good ones." Arnkoff and Glass proposed that an "irrational" thought could sometimes be adaptive, while a rational thought, maladaptive, depending upon the meaning the thought holds for the individual and the function it serves.

3. Some experiences may be less amenable to self-report because of their inaccessibility to language. A belief could have been formed prior to the full development of language.

Two years after Arnkoff and Glass's critique, Hollon and Kriss (1984) attempted to clarify the concept of cognition by proposing two types: cognitive products and cognitive structures. *Cognitive products* are conscious behaviors, such as beliefs, self-statements, and automatic thoughts that one can directly access and observe. This definition of cognition is employed in all cognitive-behavioral therapies in which the therapist tries to change or replace irrational thoughts and beliefs or tries to train the patient to use self-talk to guide actions. Cognition defined as products also applies to psychodynamic therapy and its emphasis on inducing patients to state in verbal terms the wishes and fantasies that occupy them.

Cognitive structures, on the other hand, are defined as "underlying unconscious organizations" that shape the organization given to information, converging with the emphasis of the first cognitive revolution. Since cognitive structures operate at an unconscious level, their content cannot be observed directly and must be inferred from cognitive products (Kohlenberg and Tsai 1994, p. 195). Examples would include Piaget's concept of schemas, and the psychoanalytic concept of mental mechanisms of defense, which we discuss in more detail later. As the reader may notice, the distinction between products and structures converges with Arnkoff and Glass's proposal that both "surface and deep" cognitive structures need to be considered.

Concluding Comment

If we combine the critiques by Arnkoff and Glass, and Hollon and Kriss, and the motifs of the symposia that launched the first cognitive revolution in the 1950s, several questions emerge that an integrated model should address:

1. How can we connect the meanings and fantasies a person assigns to experiences, the unconscious pictures a person takes of events (deep cognitive structures), with overt behaviors, conscious thoughts, and verbalizations (surface, cognitive products)?
2. How can we operationalize the notion that unconscious cognitive structures equilibrate environmental stimuli, as construed by a person, with stimulation from a person's subjective world of emotions and fantasies?
3. How can we operationalize and relate the different expressions that occur within each of the different behavioral modes (action, fantasy, and language), and how can we relate expressions in one mode with expressions in another?
4. What is the cotter pin that links actions to fantasies, and fantasies to words, so that if one mode moves or turns so do the others?

At this point it should be helpful if we consider illustrations of how some therapists have addressed these questions. R. A. Gardner (1993), in describing a psychodynamic approach to child therapy, chose to segregate verbalizing, fantasizing, feeling, and doing and offered no connection between these modes. "Human behavior lends itself well to being divided into thoughts, feelings and actions . . . Furthermore, the sequence here is also important. Thoughts generally precede feelings and feelings precede actions" (p. 165). From this assumption he devised the "Talking, Feeling, Doing Game," presented as a formboard game, that plays a central role in his therapy. The child selects cards from one of three stacks; each card poses a question the child is to address. The "talking cards" encourage the child "to speak about his/her opinions on a wide variety of subjects related to life problems all children confront" (e.g., "What sport are you worst at?"). The "feeling cards" encourage the child to verbalize feelings (e.g., "What do you think happens to people after a person dies? What can you say that would make a person feel good?"). The "doing cards" involve physical activity performed by the child (e.g., "What is the most selfish thing you ever did? Make believe you're doing that thing now"). Significantly, although including play activity, Gardner emphasized the use of language. "I use doing cards as a point of departure for direct discussion" (p. 188).

In contrast, others (Horowitz 1988) linked fantasy to action by conceptualizing fantasy as a plan for action. Knapp (1988) has elaborated this notion, which I consider in more detail in my integrated model. He conceptualized that fantasies are embedded in, and emerge from, preverbal, sensorimotor, bodily experiences fused with developing emotions and motives. These fantasies contribute to the organization of actions and eventually could be expressed in thoughts and language. Knapp's conceptualization of fantasy activity contains the following ingredients: (1) fantasies are rooted in Piaget's sensorimotor stage before symbolic thought and language emerge; therefore, fantasies are embodied; (2) fantasies are linked to core emotions and motives, and thus organize urges and guide their expression in action, thought, and language; (3) fantasies tend to be repetitive; that is, they continually gain expression in evolving cycles.

The questions I raised above, and the different responses provided by Gardner and Knapp, bring us to related issues that also deserve our attention: the relationship between cognition and emotion, the experience of meaning, conscious and unconscious processes, the role of the environment, and human conflict. We consider each of these in turn.

Issue III: The Relation between Cognition and Emotion

In Chapter 2 we noted that a boundary has been maintained between cognition and emotion and that considerable attention has been devoted to how the two are interrelated (e.g., Bearison and Zimiles 1986). This issue continues to capture considerable interest, as illustrated by the appearance of a journal devoted to the topic (*Cognition and Emotion*). While some writers have proposed that cognition and emotion are independent of each other, others have proposed that although separate, cognition and emotion interact. When embracing the latter view, investigators are cornered into taking the position that, during this interaction, either cognition or emotion is dominant (e.g., Arnold 1960, Bower and Cohen 1982, Mowrer 1960). Moreover, as Izard (1977) and Bruner (1990) pointed out, when cognition is viewed as dominant, thinking and reasoning are considered "good" and emotion as "bad" and in need of control.

Sidestepping whether cognition is good and emotion bad, several authors have attempted to relate cognition and emotion in some way. For example, Royce (1973) joined cognition and emotion with the concept of "style linkages." He conceptualized cognitive activity involved in scanning information as a "cognitive style," the degree to which one responds to stimuli either impulsively or with reflection as an "affective style," and how one articulates a field of information in terms of what is relevant and irrelevant as a "cognitive-affective" style. Of particular importance to my discussion, these styles are conceptualized as stable, inflexible traits. In a similar way, Izard (1978) conceptualized affective-cognitive structures as traitlike characteristics that form stable, enduring personality orientations. These orientations result in, for example, a person tending to be either passive, hyperactive, or anxious. In another attempt, Mandler (1982) focused on how a person "appraises" stimulation and conceptualized "descriptive cognitions" and "evaluative cognitions." Descriptive cognitions are judgments and thinking based upon stimuli that are "out there." Evaluative cognitions involve judgments and thinking that do not necessarily depend on stimuli in the environment, as, for example, when a person experiences that his/her self-esteem is threatened. Relying on our previous discussions, descriptive cognitions are surface behaviors, or cognitive products, while evaluative cognitions are deep behaviors or cognitive structures.

Whether the connection between cognition and emotion is conceptualized in terms of Royce's style linkages, Izard's affective-cognitive structures, or Mandler's descriptive-evaluative cognitions, these formulations leave unattended an issue that is central to child psychotherapy. Cognition is not operationalized as mobile functions, or organizations, that shift and change in response to changes in stimulation. Mandler acknowledged that his notion of appraisal failed to address this issue when he pointed out that a horse could be judged as beautiful at one time and ugly another, when the person has had no experiences with horses that could account for this change in appraisal. But psychodynamic child therapists are very familiar with the questions raised by this issue. How should we understand that in one session a child may experience and express disgust and unpleasure while shaping "long BM's" of clay, and in the same or another session experience and express pride and pleasure while shaping "a rocket" from clay?

In a related issue, Izard (1982) expressed a view that appears opposite to that of Mandler's; namely, that no appraising or symbolic process is required "for sensing pain or sexual pleasure." But here, too, clinicians have long held as a dictum that what is pain for one is pleasure for another and vice versa, and what is pain for a person at one moment may be experienced as pleasure at another. Referring to our previous example, the child may experience and express disgust and unpleasure while shaping long BM's of clay, and at another time experience and express considerable pride and pleasure when forming the same shapes with clay.

If we peer at cognitive-behavioral therapy and psychodynamic therapy, adjusting our lens so that the issue of cognition and emotion comes into focus, it seems to me that how therapists consider cognition and emotion is not influenced to any appreciable degree by these investigators. Rather, the positions taken by both cognitive-behavioral and psychodynamic therapists are influenced more by the concepts of Piaget and Freud. To illustrate this opinion, I begin by sketching the views proposed by Freud and Piaget on the relationship between cognition and emotion.

Freud's View of the Relation between Cognition and Emotion

Freud's initial view of the relation between cognition and emotion is perhaps most vividly represented by his famous metaphor (1923) that represented emotion (the id) as a galloping horse and cognition (the ego) as a rider struggling to maintain control over galloping emotions: "[The ego] in its relation to the id . . . is like a man on horseback who has to hold in check the superior strength of the horse . . ." (p. 25).

Three years after proposing his famous rider–horse metaphor, Freud (1926) made clear that he had *changed his mind* about his view depicting the ego (cognition) a weak victim of stronger drives (emotions). Now Freud took the position that cognition had more power.

> At this point it is relevant to ask how I can reconcile this acknowledgment of the might of the ego with the description of its position which I gave in *The Ego and the Id*. In that book I drew the picture of the dependent relationship to the id and to the superego, and revealed how powerless and apprehensive it (the ego) was in regard to both and with what an effort it maintains its show of superiority. This view has been widely echoed in psychoanalytic literature. Many writers have laid much stress on the weakness of the ego in relation to the id and of our rational elements in the face of demonic forces within us; and they display a strong tendency to make what I have said into a cornerstone of a psychoanalytic Weltanschaung. Yet surely the psychoanalyst should, of all people, be restrained from adopting such an extreme and one-sided view. [p. 95]

Freud delivered this gentle scolding in the context of a discussion about his revised view: that the ego (cognition) exerts power and control in dealing both with the environment and with representations of drives. "Just as the ego controls the path to action in regard to the external world, so it controls access to consciousness . . . it exercises power in both directions, acting in the one manner upon the instinctual impulse itself and in the other, upon the representative of the impulse" (Freud 1926, p. 95). The reader may note that comments such as these anticipated the concept, articulated in the New Look cognitive revolution described earlier, that cognition controls and coordinates information and emotion. As discussed in the next chapter, for my integrative model I rely upon research I have conducted within the New Look framework, which operationalizes cognition as coordinating stimulation and emotion.

Piaget's View of the Relation between Cognition and Emotion

Piaget (1981) proposed two hypotheses about the relationship between cognition and emotion. With one, cognitive and emotional aspects of behavior are always present simultaneously in all situations, and one does not result from or cause the other. With the second hypothesis, cognition and emotion are functionally parallel, each domain following its own developmental course.

Hesse and Cicchetti (1982) discussed how Piaget's two, parallel, developmental pathways relate to one another, one concerning cognition, the other emotion.

Briefly, in the sensorimotor period (0–2 years) the infant engages in reflexes and "circular reactions" that coordinate and integrate visual, auditory, and bodily experiences that form the first mental schemas of experience. This period is paralleled by the first stage of emotional development, in which "affective reflexes" occur, as when the infant loses balance, and "elementary feelings" such as pleasure and unpleasure, which are linked to the infant's own activity, are experienced.

In the preoperational period of cognitive development (2–7 years) symbolic thinking gradually emerges. Information is engaged increasingly through the manipulation of symbols of objects, rather than objects themselves. But in this stage children cannot yet reason logically or deductively. Judgments are strongly influenced by perception so that, for example, two events appear related because they occur together in time and not because of a cause–effect relationship. This stage is paralleled by a phase in emotional development when emotions, such as sympathy, superiority, obedience, defiance, are guided by schemas deriving from reactions to objects and persons. As with cognitive stimuli, the child can attend to only one emotion at a time and cannot deal with two emotions that appear contradictory.

This changes during the next period of concrete operations (7–11 years). Although the child's cognition is still oriented toward organizing concrete things and events, now the child can conserve information and deal simultaneously with two pieces of information that may appear contradictory. Conservation is a cognitive process by which concrete information, and actions on that information, are transformed and conserved as images. As a result of conserving actions as images, the child experiences images and language as autonomous from actions and immediate perceptions. The child becomes freer to think about his thinking and his representational world. With the benefit of conservation, the child understands that although an object may be transformed, certain properties do not change (e.g., the child knows that the amount of water doesn't change when poured into a differently shaped vessel). The next stage of emotional development parallels these achievements. The child can now conserve two emotions (e.g., the parent loves me and is angry at me, but remains the same parent). During this phase, moral values are conserved, resulting in, for example, feelings of justice, honesty, and cowardice.

In the final stage of cognitive development (11–15 years), information is gathered not only from existing reality but, in particular, from the realm of possibilities, abstractions, and propositions. This cognitive stage is paralleled in emotional development by the emergence of ideological emotions that concern, for example, social ideals, freedom, charity, and justice.

With this sketch of Freud's and Piaget's views of the relation between cognition and emotion, I now turn to illustrate my opinion that these two views, for the most part, are relied upon by both cognitive-behavioral and psychodynamic therapies.

Psychodynamic Therapy and the Relation between Cognition and Emotion

Psychodynamic therapists have relied almost exclusively on Freud's revised view of the relation between cognition and emotion. They have also elaborated how cognition attempts to regulate emotions activated both by the environment and by the subjective world of unconscious wishes, fantasies, and urges. The basic principle that guides these elaborations concerns how cognition prevents painful emotions from entering conscious awareness.

Horowitz's (1988) edited volume, which the reader is encouraged to examine firsthand, is one source providing excellent discussions of these elaborations. For Horowitz, when considering the relation between cognition and emotion, the starting point is defined by what he termed a "psychodynamic configuration." A configuration consists of at least three factors: (1) wishes, (2) anxieties and fears associated with the threat of consequences if wishes are expressed, and (3) mental mechanisms of defense. A configuration concerns how the self wants to relate to others, what the self wants to obtain from or give to others, the wishes and fears associated with what one wants from and gives to others, the emotions associated with what one imagines are the aims of others toward the self, and the cognitive mechanisms used to manage these emotions and information. This configuration of wishes, emotions, and mental defenses is presumed to operate outside of awareness. Referring to our earlier discussion, a "psychodynamic configuration" is a "deep," unconscious cognitive structure. Moreover, these unconscious mental structures are viewed as being in a "dynamic" relationship. That is, when a conflict exists between opposing wishes/urges, the disturbing ideas, and the emotions associated with them, are warded off in some way from being represented and experienced directly in one's awareness.

What are the ways in which cognition regulates this configuration so that a person's awareness is protected from emotions that would otherwise be very disturbing? Here cognition is conceptualized as making use of a series of "mental mechanisms of defense." While the notion of mental defenses is not well represented in many theories of cognitive science (Horowitz 1988), it is one cornerstone of psychodynamic theory. Mental defenses are believed to be activated and intensified by high emotions, stress, and conflict. Moreover, defenses are unconscious structures, since defenses are not consciously experienced by a person, nor observed by another. Rather, defenses are inferred from aspects of a person's behavior and the context in which they occur. (Referring to our earlier discussion, defenses are inferred from surface behaviors and cognitive products.) While psychodynamic theorists have not agreed upon an "official" list of defense mechanisms that regulate emotion, Knapp (1988) described those most commonly mentioned.

One mechanism involves selective inattention. Here, cognition excludes a disturbing idea and its emotions by focusing elsewhere. When efficient, this cognitive activity constitutes *repression*. Usually repression is viewed as a primary or basic defense, and all other cognitive maneuvers are understood as supporting repression in one way or another. When repression is complete, the person denies or avoids some emotion. As one example, a child sat calmly, with a blank facial expression, upon hearing that his mother had died.

With another defense mechanism, an idea with its emotion is admitted into conscious awareness but in a symbolically disguised form. For example, a child may represent an urge to be angry and attack someone by symbolically playing that a thunderstorm appears and lightning strikes a doll figure. When this process is efficient, it is understood as *sublimation*. Note that with sublimation the emotion/urge is experienced in consciousness albeit in a disguised form.

With another defense mechanism, the emotion is detached from the wish or urge to which it belongs. Only the idea enters conscious awareness, with the disturbing emotion "isolated" or repressed. For example, a child who entered treatment because he enjoyed torturing the family pet kitten eventually became interested in learning about torture methods used during the Spanish Inquisition. As he gathered information in a calm, detached manner, he constructed "a book," complete with figures. When this cognitive mechanism is efficient, it is termed *intellectualization*. Here potentially disturbing ideas are engaged with well-rationalized and dispassionate thinking and curiosity.

With the cognitive mechanism termed *reaction formation*, a disturbing feeling is replaced in conscious awareness by an equally strong or stronger feeling that is "safe" and "acceptable." For example, a 6-year-old girl expressed "love" for her newborn sib in ways that parents and relatives saw as exaggerated. She proclaimed her love dozens of times each day, was very active assisting mother in bathing and feeding the infant, and was preoccupied with the infant's safety. Here, anger and envy directed toward the infant were inverted and replaced by love and caring. However, at times, the mechanism of reaction formation slipped and became less efficient. For example, on one occasion, when mother turned away from the changing table on which the infant was secured with a strap, the girl emptied a can of powder on the infant, covering it from head to toe. "I was only trying to help!" she protested when scolded by mother.

With the last cognitive mechanism we consider, the person manages a disturbing feeling by splitting or segregating persons as either good or bad, and assigning the disturbing feeling to someone designated as bad. When efficient, this mechanism is referred to as *projection*. For example, a boy who harbored intense hate toward a sib became preoccupied with his belief that a classmate bully hated him.

Psychodynamic configurations of anxiety/fear/guilt and mechanisms of defense, associated with disturbing emotions/urges, are not viewed as static over time. Rather, a person's day-to-day living, and encounters with different persons and contexts, are influenced by several psychodynamic configurations that shift and change continuously as the person copes with each situation. Horowitz (1988) has conceptualized these shifts, each with its unique configuration of consciously experienced emotions and unconscious mechanisms of defense, as "states of mind." He demonstrated the heuristic value of the concept with a clinical case of a 24-year-old woman who sought help after her father's death. Horowitz artfully traces when, how, and why various states of mind influenced the woman's subjective emotional experiences. At times, for example, she denied that father was dead, repeatedly suggesting to friends he was still alive. She also experienced guilt over the thought that she could have saved him from death if she had taken better care of him. In another state of mind she experienced his death as another example of how he frequently abandoned her when she needed him.

In addition to the concept of psychodynamic configurations, some psychodynamic therapists have also relied on Piaget's model; for example, Lewis (1977) gave Piaget's concept of conservation a major role in his view of psychodynamic child psychotherapy. Lewis proposed that in order to resolve ambivalent feelings (hate and love of each parent), the child needs to have developed sufficient conservation. With the benefit of this cognitive achievement, the child becomes free to employ language as a tool to describe and conceptualize experiences, however contradictory and emotionally laden. Lewis urged psychoanalysts to be mindful that before the age of 7, a child has not yet achieved sufficient conservation to think about his/her thinking, and to talk about feelings, without experiencing them. He also reminded psychoanalysts that a child older than 9 years could conserve information inadequately and therefore experience difficulty achieving appropriate distance from events.

In a discussion of emotional understanding and child psychotherapy, Nannis (1988) described a perspective that also relies upon Piaget's notions, especially the concept of conservation. For example, she pointed out,

> My own clinical experience suggests that when children are trying to deal with more than one feeling state, either the ability to feel simultaneous feelings, or the ability to create changes from one emotional state to another, the children in therapy . . . differ from their nonclinical peers . . . they seem to have greater difficulties allowing that they could feel two conflicting feelings about a similar situation [p. 94] . . . at the very least, we need to acknowledge the relation between cognitive skills and emotional understanding . . . a young child whose reasoning is perceptually bound would believe that feelings are present only if the physical manifestation [is] present . . . therefore, if Dad is not smiling, he is not happy with you [and the child] would believe that you can only feel two feelings at once if you can make two faces. Therefore, it may be difficult for the young child to know that Mom still loves you when she is yelling at you. [p. 101]

While some authors rely on Piaget's theory, the conceptualization of psychodynamic configurations typically dominates psychodynamic therapy, which aims to modify unconscious mechanisms of defense a person uses. As we leave the view

of cognition and emotion held in psychodynamic therapy, we should remind ourselves that here cognition involves mental activity outside of awareness (cognitive
structures), conceptualized as a mobile system that equilibrates emotions aroused
both by the environment, as symbolized by a person, and by a person's subjective
world of wishes and fantasies.

Cognitive-Behavioral Therapy and the Relation between Cognition and Emotion

It seems to me that the cognitive-behavioral view of the relation between cognition and emotion implied by the interventions of many therapists relates to Freud's
initial formulation of cognition (the rider) struggling to control stronger emotions
(the horse). These therapists emphasize strengthening conscious cognition, or
cognitive products (discussed earlier), so that cognition has the power to control
or stop emotions and urges. Consider Kendall and Braswell (1985), who characterized their presentation as follows. "Simply stated, this book is about teaching
children to slow down and cognitively examine their behavioral alternatives before
acting" (p. 1). Their "affective education training program" was designed to provide the child with "an opportunity to practice self-instructional skills while grappling with problematic situations that pull for a more impulsive, emotional type of
responding" (p. 135). A look at one of their clinical vignettes illustrates a therapist
trying to help a boy's cognition become strong enough to control his galloping horse
of emotions. Participating in self-instruction and coping skills training (see Chapter 3), the boy selected as his problem situation that when watching television his
little brother keeps changing the channel.

> *Therapist:* So what is your problem? Or to use our "step-words," what are
> you supposed to do?
> *Child:* Well, I guess I'm supposed to figure out how to handle that situa-
> tion with my brother.
> *T:* Right, now that you know what the problem is, what are some things
> you can do about it?
> *C:* I could hit my brother, but then my mom would really be mad.
> *T:* We will think about which things would be best to do in just a mo-
> ment. One possibility you thought of would be to hit your brother.
> What would be another thing you could do? Let's see if you can think
> of at least two more possibilities.

Here, it seems to me, the therapist sidestepped the child's first response, that
he would "hit his brother" and pursued a course that would inhibit this response.

> *C:* Uh, . . . I could tell my mom!
> *T:* Yes, you could tell your mom. What's another idea?

C: I could try to work out a deal with my brother, but I don't know about that one . . .

T: Good. That's three different possibilities. You could hit your brother or you could tell your mom, or you could try to work out a deal with your brother. . . . Now, let's think hard about each one. What would happen if you decided to hit your little brother?

C: Well, he'd get mad and start crying. Then he'd probably go tell mom and I'd get in trouble.

T: Would hitting your brother mean you would get to watch your TV program?

C: No, I'd probably get sent to my room.

T: How would everyone feel after you hit your brother?

C: Well, my brother and mother would be mad. It might feel good to hit my brother (*pause*), but it wouldn't feel good to have to go to my room.

T: Let's think about the next choice—telling your mom. What would happen if you did that? [pp. 137–139]

Hitting the brother was the child's first solution to the problem, and he made it clear that it would "feel good" to do so. But the boy is urged to consider other options (thinking, problem solving) in order to strengthen the ability of cognition (the rider) to block the galloping horse of emotion and impulse.

Other examples are provided by Hughes (1988) in a volume describing cognitive-behavioral therapy with children in schools. In a discussion of hyperactivity, this author noted that self-controlled children have the skills needed "to inhibit inappropriate responding and to instigate appropriate action" (p. 140). In other words, self-controlled children are blessed with a rider (cognition) that can control the horse (emotion). Accordingly, training in self-instruction, embedded in problem-solving training and role-playing, is among the major techniques used to help children who do not have self-control. With one technique the child is trained to verbalize a set of self-directives or commands before responding to a task; for example, "I must listen to directions," "I must look and think before I answer." With these self-statements, cognition holds the horse still, if only for a moment.

Similarly, other cognitive-behavioral techniques proposed for children (e.g., systematic desensitization, coping skill training, stress inoculation, and self-control; Meyers and Craighead 1984), while not discussed explicitly in terms of cognition and emotion, could be viewed as strengthening cognition in its struggle with emotion. For example, children who were afraid of the dark were taught to vocalize self-instructions such as, "I am a brave boy," and "I can handle myself in the dark." O'Connor (1993), in outlining structured group play therapy for children, segregated a "cognitive component" that cultivates problem-solving strategies, which in turn are relied on in an "emotional component"—guided discussions designed to help children make connections between emotions and behavior.

Some cognitive behavioral therapists rely upon Piaget's model. Knell (1995) provided one illustration.

> In the same way that children have difficulty understanding that the quantity of liquid does not change when it is poured from a tall, thin container to a short, fat one, so will they have difficulty focusing on two affective dimensions . . . without conservation of affect, the child may be greatly influenced by single environmental events . . . for example, when the popular young boy does not get picked by peers for a ball game one day, he may believe he is always unliked. Or when the bright young girl does poorly on a test, she may believe that she is always stupid. [pp. 26–27]

In discussing the clinical implications of this view, Knell emphasized the power that spoken words and labeling (cognitive products) have in controlling emotion, an emphasis that seems to keep one foot in Piaget's model and the other in Freud's initial model of a horse and rider. "One opportunity for therapeutic intervention is in encouraging and facilitating the child's language to describe experiences and emotion" (p. 28). As one example, she mentioned a child who is angry about the birth of a new sibling, so he tries to kick the baby carriage "and thus hurt his new sister." With another, a child is angry and tries to break a toy because his parents are going out for the evening, leaving him with a baby-sitter. To help these children control their emotions, Knell believed that "teaching these youngsters to understand they are angry, what it means to be angry, and how to say it in words instead of behavior may be a beginning to helping them deal with (control) their feelings" (p. 29). Knell also discussed how cognitive-behavioral play therapy helps children manage their emotions in the midst of a variety of problems—elimination problems, divorce of parents, diffuse fears. The techniques used in each instance focus for the most part on helping the children develop cognitive products (conscious thoughts) to control emotions—identifying and changing irrational beliefs, rehearsing positive self-statements, and rephrasing and shaping socially appropriate expressions of feelings (e.g., the child says, "I want to punch the bear's face," and the therapist says, "You're mad because . . .").

Concluding Comment

The reader may notice that our discussion of the relation between cognition and emotion elaborates the questions we raised when we considered the relation between what a person does, fantasizes, and says. On the one hand we have Freud's initial view that conscious cognition (cognitive products) struggles to control emotional surges from gaining expression in action. This notion seems to be represented in cognitive-behavioral techniques designed to strengthen cognition's ability to block, control, or otherwise steer emotions so that the child does not act before thinking. On the other hand we have Freud's revised model that unconscious cognitive mechanisms (cognitive structures) operate to disguise emotions in some fashion so that painful anxiety and guilt do not enter conscious awareness, and so that emotional urges do not gain direct expression in action. This view dominates technique in psychodynamic therapy. We also have the Piagetian notion, used by both cognitive-behavioral and psychodynamic therapists, that how emotions are conserved in images is important, enabling the child to experience emotions as autonomous from the actions they require and to acknowledge that two opposite emotions (love and anger) could be felt toward the same person. Is there a way to integrate these notions heuristically, providing child therapists with guidelines that define when, and with which techniques, a child can be helped to improve how he/she regulates what he/she does, fantasizes, and says? Furth (1983) proposed that much could be learned about cognition and emotion if we examine where the concepts of Piaget and Freud meet.

Issue IV: The Meanings a Person Gives to Experiences

To begin, I should make clear what I mean by "meanings a person gives to experiences." When assigning "meaning" to some experience, a person is involved in constructing a symbol that represents the experience in some way. It is generally accepted that when a symbol or metaphor is constructed (as well as its close relatives, simile and analogy), something is described or expressed in terms of properties that belong to something else (Santostefano 1988b). For example, consider a 3-year-old, walking along with his parent, who spotted a jogger. The young lad immediately leaned his body forward, and with each exuberant "Choo! Choo!" vigorously thrust his right arm forward and back. Our 3-year-old provides us with an example of a symbol consisting of actions, fantasies, and language. In exclaiming, "Choo! Choo!" and in thrusting his arm forward and back, while apparently fantasizing a train, he is saying, "The man is a powerful train engine!" At an older age, with language more fully developed, this same child could make use of a simile ("That man is running like a powerful engine!") and an analogy ("That man runs as if he is a powerful engine!").

How is meaning transferred from one thing to something else? There are two views, one referred to as comparison/substitution and the other as interaction. With the first, the referent and its substitute are classified together and compared on the basis of a similarity or shared attribute. In our example, the attribute of power is the basis of comparison between the referent (jogger) and its substitute (train engine). The interaction view takes the position that while a symbol compares objects, and substitutes one for the other, a symbol also achieves a new meaning, a new totality, that goes beyond the objects compared and substituted and that synthesizes present and past experiences with them. Considering our example from this vantage point, the jogger is experienced by the toddler in terms of a new meaning that transcends particular properties of both the jogger and a train engine, and within which both are no longer what they once were.

Meaning and Psychodynamic Therapy

As we discussed previously, the meaning given to experiences became one main cornerstone of Freud's psychoanalytic theory and treatment. And the meaning given to experiences has continued to hold a central position in the various extensions of psychodynamic therapy and to preoccupy psychodynamic theorists.

When Freud learned that many of the memories patients presented proved to be, from his point of view, fantasies expressing wishes, he was faced with the problem of explaining the origin of these fantasies. To account for this phenomenon, he introduced the concept of "instinctual drives." With this concept he gave up the view that environmental factors determine behavior in a major way and ushered in the importance of personal meanings as causes of behavior. To conceptualize the process of how meaning is constructed, Freud coined the term *psychic reality*, a notion that to that point had not been articulated by continental philosophy (Barratt 1984). For Freud, psychic reality included wishes, memories, and fantasies, accompanied by emotions, that a person injects, usually without awareness, into day-to-day stimulation and experiences. Psychic reality defined the self and the world as it is understood and experienced by the individual.

However, writers following Freud modified this concept so that psychic reality became synonymous with distorting reality and with psychopathology. For example, if a child feared dirt or school, the child was viewed as dominated by psychic reality, and when free of this fear, functioning in "objective reality." This dichotomized concept led to a twofold view of the process of constructing meaning: one as "real" and therefore normal, and the other as a distortion of the real, or as "imagined," and therefore abnormal. The reader should notice that this modification shifted away from Freud's interpretationist position and toward the position of objectivism (see Chapter 2), which sets a boundary between the real and the subjective. One consequence of this split was the view that different symbols are used to construct meanings: images are used to construct psychic reality and words are used to construct objective reality. I return to this consequence below (Issue IX) when I discuss the importance given to verbal labeling and verbal interpretations in psychodynamic therapy.

However, psychoanalytic investigators, especially those influenced by observations of infants (see Chapter 5), have advocated more recently that the original, more heuristic concept of psychic reality be retained (Barratt 1984). From this view the reality with which a child negotiates is constructed by the child's representational activity and consists of all that the child experiences and understands, whether or not this fits with the conventions of family/community. Thus the environment and psychic reality become one, integrating the child's cognitive, emotional, and physical activity. Accordingly, the same concepts are applied whether a child is judging a sausage-shaped piece of clay as the same or longer than another, or whether the same child is pretending to eat the clay as a hotdog or flee from it as a snake. What the child knows, does, and feels is what the child represents.

One more aspect to Freud's concept of psychic reality (meanings given to instinctual drives) deserves our attention. For Freud, his theory of instinctual drives joined the body and mind as one, conceptualizing a connection between "psychical representation," that is, cognitive meanings representing experiences, and actual bodily experiences. With this theory he forecast the emergence years later of embodiment theory, to which I return in the next chapter. It is also important to remind ourselves that investigators who take states of hunger and thirst, or other metabolic needs, as paradigms of instinctual drives, are in error, as Rapaport (1960) pointed out. In these cases drives are treated as somatic conditions rather than as mental representations of those conditions, which was Freud's intention.

The following statement illustrates the close connection Freud saw between body experiences and meaning.

> An instinct appears to be a concept on the frontier between the mental and the somatic, as the psychical representative of stimuli originating from within the organism and reaching the mind, as a measure of the demand made upon the mind for work in consequence of its connection with the body. [1915, pp. 121–122]

Our previous discussions of psychodynamic therapy for children make clear that the meanings a child gives experiences, and changes in these meanings, continue to be the hallmark of psychodynamic therapies. In comparing psychodynamic therapies with behavioral therapies, Gill (1984) used the issue of meaning as the distinguishing feature. Psychodynamic therapies, he argued, examine and attempt to change the meaning of behavior, while cognitive-behavioral therapies attempt to alter the behavior directly and ignore its meaning.

In a similar vein, Shirk (1988), in his informative volume on cognitive development and child psychotherapy, points out that the psychodynamic therapist considers overt behavior important because of the meaning it reveals, rather than because of its contingencies. But he also argued that the tendency of cognitive-behavioral therapy to conceptualize both cognition and behavior as skills suggests that the significance of meaning is far less prominent. As we turn to the view of meaning in cognitive-behavioral therapy, we will find that the picture has changed to some degree from that portrayed by Gill and Shirk.

Meaning and Cognitive-Behavioral Therapy

Initially, cognitive-behavioral therapy ignored the issue of meaning. However, as cognitive theory and therapy grew, along with cognitive-behavioral therapy, the meanings a person gives experiences gradually received some attention. For example, in the early days of cognitive-behavioral therapy, Thompson (1981), in a provocative article that asked the question, "Will it hurt less if I can control it?" took the position that therapy should focus on changing the meanings a person gives experiences. "[T]he challenge now is to discover the types of meanings that can be used (by a person) and to explore how to help individuals develop the ability to assign meanings that will be most beneficial to them" (p. 99). Arnkoff (1980), in a discussion of psychotherapy from the perspective of cognitive therapy, proposed that the meaning given to an experience is the " ultimate issue" that needs to be considered in treatment.

While not considering meaning to be the ultimate issue, Kendall and Morison (1984), in their discussion of cognitive-behavioral therapy with children, seemed to approach meaning through the concept of "cognitive mediators" and "cognitive processing." They pointed out that in addition to the type of reward used to reinforce behavior, it is also important to take into account "how each child thinks about events and event outcomes . . . an adult may provide social praise, but the child's cognitive processing of that experience may render the praise nonrewarding" (p. 280). In this statement, while they do not use the terms *unconscious* and *meaning*, they do seem to be saying that the meaning the child gives to praise that an adult verbalizes may render the adult's statements as having meaning other than praise.

And in a volume on cognition and psychotherapy, Mahoney (1985) questioned the emphasis on techniques that replace maladaptive thoughts with realistic ones and employ self-instruction. He noted, "I do not believe that the simple cueing, recitation or reinforcement of positive self statements, or the rationalistic reconstruction of explicit beliefs, are optimal or sufficient approaches for facilitating significant and enduring personal development" (p. 14). Echoing Thompson (see above), who noted that therapists need to discover a patient's meanings, Mahoney also proposed that "one major task for therapist and theorist lies in the realm of identifying the structures and processes through which our clients construct and construe their everyday existence" (p. 18) . . . "the heart of change is found in how meanings change" (p. 26).

More recently, Bohart (1993) elaborated the issue of meaning in terms of the issue of "experiencing and knowing."

> Experiencing is a way of knowing that is immediate, embodied, holistic and contextual. It is a way of apprehending patterns in one's life space that includes a nonconceptual, nonverbal level as well as "ordinary" thinking and feeling and "higher" levels of processing. For instance, one can have the experience of oneself as thinking; one can also have the experience of oneself as experiencing. [p. 52]

Bohart drew attention to several aspects of experiencing meaning that will be useful when we turn to integrating body and mind and cognition and emotion. He pointed out that experiencing meaning is immediate, relying more on direct perception and recognition and less on thinking and conceptualizing. Converging with Freud's instinct theory, and the positions of Lakoff (1987) and Johnson (1987), he also pointed out that experiencing meaning is bodily, involving perceptions, sensations, and actions that form the foundation for thoughts and concepts that later label the experience. And experiencing meaning is holistic and contextual, integrating patterns of sights, sounds, smells, actions, and touch perceptions as well as spoken words, all embodied in contexts that include relationships with others.

Of particular relevance to the thesis I present in this volume, Bohart proposed that experiencing meaning occurs at various levels from embodied, nonverbal to conceptual, verbal experiences. Converging with our earlier discussion of the tendency for cognition to be defined as spoken words, he also argued that cognition is most typically equated with "conscious cognition (i.e., thinking) and therefore does not adequately capture the nature of experiencing" (p. 56). Moreover, since cognitive-behavioral therapies focus on changing beliefs, how a person experiences, Bohart suggested, tends to be neglected. Because experiencing meaning is neglected, he contended that "rational conceptual knowing by itself does not appear to be therapeutic" (p. 61), a view, Bohart reminded us, that was first noted by Freud and, as we pointed out earlier, was also expressed by Mahoney.

Concluding Comment

Psychodynamic therapy has always viewed meanings given to experiences as the main focus of treatment. But meaning has been inferred primarily from the words spoken by the patient. Cognitive-behavioral therapy, while initially ignoring the issue of meaning, has in recent years gradually paid more attention to it, although the essence of meaning is still found in spoken words. If we accept Freud's view, echoed by Bohart, that experiencing meaning is holistic and contextual, involving sights, smells, sounds, and actions as well as spoken words, as a person interacts with others, the importance of interactions between patient and therapist comes into view as they together construct meaning. We return to this issue after discussing others that are related.

Issue V: Conscious and Unconscious Processes

As the reader may have noticed, the concept that mental and behavioral activity takes place both within a person's subjective awareness (conscious processes) and outside a person's subjective awareness (unconscious processes) was embedded in each of the topics considered thus far. Yet the issue of conscious and unconscious processes appears to continue to divide mainstream cognitive-behavioral and psychodynamic therapies. Because the concept divides the two approaches, and because I ascribe to the proposal by some (e.g., Arkowitz 1984) that it is important to include unconscious factors in any effort to integrate psychotherapies, I pause to devote some attention to the issue.

That unconscious processes exist and are of central importance is taken for granted by psychodynamic therapy and is perhaps the most essential, distinguishing feature of its approach (Horowitz 1988, Wachtel 1984; see Knapp 1988, for a useful discussion of the psychodynamic view of the unconscious). The importance of unconscious processes predated Freud by several centuries, but it took Freud to drive it home (Colby and Stoller 1988). Freud consistently maintained the view that we are not aware of many of the motives, wishes, and attitudes that guide our behavior and that we actively keep these motives and attitudes outside of awareness to spare ourselves the anxiety they generate. This assumption, as we discussed, monopolizes what psychodynamic therapy views as its goal, namely, bringing unconscious motives, wishes, and attitudes into awareness. And, as noted earlier, unconscious processes dominated research of the first cognitive revolution with its focus on the relationship between perception and personality. While most psychodynamic therapists take unconscious processes for granted, some writers have paused to articulate their view of its importance. For example, in a volume (Colby and Stoller 1988) devoted to the interface between cognitive science and psychoanalysis, Stoller had this to say when he reviewed several reasons why he "appreciated" psychoanalysis.

> No other field had tried so hard to find the form, dynamics, purposes, origins, and effects of unconscious forces—both those that can, with more or less work, become conscious and those that, never conscious, can be at best only dimly made out by an observer. And no other field has had the enthusiasm, nerve, arrogance, and at times, courage to try to systematize these unconscious aspects of subjectivity. [p. 35]

In contrast to this positive view, the notion of unconscious processes has continued to be invisible within cognitive-behavioral therapy, or at best at the edge of its stage. This is not surprising since, as we considered earlier, the heritage of cognitive-behavioral therapy initially eliminated feelings and mental activity and anything else that seemed subjective. There was nothing in the "black box." Therefore we are not surprised to find the concept of unconscious mental processes conspicuously absent from descriptions of cognitive-behavioral therapy prior to 1980 (e.g., Bedrosian 1981, DiGiuseppe 1981, Feuerstein 1980, Kendall and Hollon 1979, Meichenbaum 1977).

But beginning in 1980, in my view, this initial position gradually changed as several developments within cognitive-behavioral therapy exerted an influence. As cognitive-behavioral researchers attempted to identify aspects of stimulation that accounted for positive or negative reinforcement of some behavior, and to use these findings to devise treatment techniques, they noticed that some outcomes or responses could not be attributed to the direct effect of the technical procedure used. To account for this, theorists began to formulate what were conceptualized as "nonspecific effects." Examples included what a person expected of some stimulation or treatment, and suggestions, advice, and encouragement provided by the therapist or investigator. In a related development, the notion of cognitive mediators brought attention to mental activity that occurred after a person perceived a stimulus and before the person enacted a response. Mendelsohn and Silverman (1984) argued convincingly that phenomena that cognitive-behavioral therapists conceptualized as nonspecific effects and cognitive mediators refer to many of the same phenomena that psychodynamic therapists conceptualize as unconscious fantasies.

Another turning point that influenced the view cognitive-behavioral therapy held of the unconscious was reached, I believe, when two critiques of cognition appeared, which we discussed earlier. Arnkoff and Glass (1982) criticized the "overwhelmingly" main focus on conscious self-statements and beliefs. They also drew attention to the possibility that a conscious thought may be the tip of the iceberg, below which were cognitive processes outside awareness. In the other critique, Hollon and Kriss (1984) conceptualized the tip of the iceberg as cognitive products (conscious beliefs, self-statements, private behaviors) and the rest of the iceberg as cognitive structures (unconscious organizations that shape the organization and meaning given to information).

In part because of these influences, the notion of unconscious processes has been slowly easing itself in front of the windshield of cognitive-behavioral therapy and has come into view at least for some cognitive-behavioral therapists. One example is provided by "radical behaviorism" and its "functional analytic psychotherapy" (Jacobson 1994, Kohlenberg and Tsai 1994). In this approach the therapist behaves in ways that reinforce some particular behavior the patient displays within the relationship with the therapist, behaviors that relate to ways in which the patient can overcome difficulties in everyday life. These radical behaviorists are quite open in their acceptance of the notion of an unconscious. As Kohlenberg and Tsai (1994) put it:

> Reinforcement is ubiquitous in our daily lives and in psychotherapy—it almost always occurs naturally and is rarely the result of someone "trying" to reinforce another. The strengthening occurs at an unconscious level—that is, awareness or feelings are not required. [p. 178]

In spite of these developments, the importance of unconscious processes appears not to have found its way yet into mainstream cognitive-behavioral treatment of children. The subject of the unconscious is still noticeably absent, failing to appear in the index of many volumes (e.g., Hughes 1988, Knell 1995, Matson and Ollendick 1988).

Concluding Comment

If we accept the importance of including unconscious processes in an integrative model of psychotherapy for children, how should we conceptualize the unconscious? Consider, for example, an encopretic boy who modeled sausagelike shapes and small balls of clay, showing no evidence that he was conscious of the possible meaning of his activity. Then at one point he added water and made soupy clay. As he oozed the clay between his fingers, he grinned with pleasure and excitement, mumbling, "A BM," suggesting that he was becoming aware of his equation between clay and feces. Still later he took small sections of clay and angrily "exploded" them against the wall. Although this activity made clear that he was experiencing clay as bombs exploding, he was not yet conscious of the possible equation between defecation and destruction. Is the unconscious some dark cave into which we push thoughts and fantasies that have been previously formed? If we shine a light into the cave, will we discover these preformed thoughts and fantasies? How can we operationalize unconscious processes in a way that serves the treatment of children? The integrative model I propose attempts to address these questions.

Issue VI: Contexts, Environments, and Situations

The psychology of the environment and situations received a surge of interest in the early 1980s (Magnusson 1981, Shapiro and Weber 1981, Zimmerman 1983), emphasizing that behavior is dependent upon the context in which it occurs. In addition, situations and events were viewed as holistic phenomena experienced as unified wholes rather than as discrete stimuli.

The importance of the environment was ushered into psychodynamic theory by Heinz Hartmann in 1939 with his essay "Ego Psychology and the Problem of Adaptation" (published in English in 1958). He introduced "autoplasticity and alloplasticity" to conceptualize the reciprocal relationship between the individual and the environment in which a person both changes and is changed by the environment. He also conceptualized environments in terms of whether the stimulation was usual or unusual, given a person's history. I (e.g., 1978, 1986) made central use of these concepts in my studies of cognition and emotion both in molar environments (e.g., adults preparing for a parachute jump and children preparing for surgery) and in molecular environments (e.g., test stimuli designed to evoke fantasies and emotions). We consider these studies in Chapter 6.

Wachtel (1984, 1987) has perhaps been the most active psychodynamic theorist concerned with reciprocal influences between person and environment. He formulated his concept of "cyclical psychodynamics" in order to "describe people's difficulties in terms of vicious cycles in which neither impulse nor defense and neither internal state nor external situation is primary; they are continually determining each other in a series of repeated transactions" (Wachtel 1984, p. 48). For

Wachtel, whose discussions concern adult psychopathology, while a person's behavior is influenced by some unconscious meaning (e.g., he discusses a young man who was anxious about being swallowed up by his girlfriend), a person also seeks current relationships in situations that converge with that meaning (e.g., the young man chose female companions who dominate him). In spite of contributions by several investigators since Hartmann's early emphasis on the environment, psychodynamic therapists still pay less attention to the environment than they do to a person's inner world of unconscious fantasies and motives.

The picture is quite different in cognitive-behavioral therapy, which from its inception has maintained a primary focus on the environment, viewing a person's behavior as determined by discrete stimuli and situations. Then Bandura (1977) introduced his social learning theory with the concept of "reciprocal determinism." According to Hughes (1988), with this concept "Bandura turned Watson's brand of behaviorism on its head. Rejecting a unidirectional view of the effects of the environment on the individual, Bandura viewed the person–environment relationship as a reciprocal influential process" (p. 6). Reciprocal determinism acknowledged that while a situation or stimulus acts upon a person, the person also acts upon the stimulus or situation.

While similar to Hartmann's concepts of auto- and alloplasticity, and Wachtel's concept of cyclical psychodynamics, the concept of reciprocal determinism maintained a boundary between the person and the environment, influenced by the machine metaphor (see Chapter 2). Either the person constructs the environment and acts accordingly, or the environment constructs the person and acts accordingly, defining a linear relationship (Overton and Horowitz 1991). In this linear view of person-environment relationships, therapeutic efforts are directed at resolving or eliminating the paradox by changing either how the person acts on the environment or how the environment acts on the person.

Knell's (1995) application of cognitive-behavioral play therapy provided illustrations. Techniques are presented for problems that are framed within discrete environments: for example, the toilet, parents who are divorced, and environments that have sexually abused a child. Using one of Knell's illustrations, an encopretic boy is treated with the behavioral technique of shaping. The child is encouraged to play with a toy bear near the toilet. Then the therapist has the bear approach the toilet, sit on it, and make a bowel movement. With the behavioral technique of positive reinforcement, as the bear keeps his pants clean and uses the toilet, the therapist gives the bear praise and stickers. Following the technique of positive self-statements, the therapist speaks for the bear, "I feel good when I use the toilet" (p. 135). In these examples the child–environment relationship is linear and the direction of the influence is from the child to the environment (i.e., the child, through the bear, acts upon the toilet in various ways). From the viewpoint of Wachtel's cyclical psychodynamics, what is missing is the meaning the toilet holds for the child and how this meaning guides the child to seek particular experiences with a toilet that act upon him in some particular way.

An example of a linear model that depicts the direction of influence from the environment to the person is provided by Matson and Ollendick (1988) . In describing cognitive-behavioral training procedures designed to enhance children's social skills, they state, "The degree of social skills is directly related to the number and type of prosocial acts performed by others toward the person evincing social behaviors" (p. 1).

Another illustration of how the objectivist viewpoint sets a boundary between the person and the environment comes from Hollin's (1990) cognitive-behavioral therapy with young offenders. Hollin cautions that when the therapists choose some antisocial behavior as the target of therapy, they should be alert to the possibility that a youth may invent or exaggerate some offense. To cope with this, he recommends comparing the youth's self-report with police records. The report by police is then taken as the "truth." A psychodynamic therapist, influenced by the interpretationist position, would explore the cyclical interplay between two dynamics: (1) the meaning for the youth of exaggerating or inventing antisocial behavior, and the role of this meaning in guiding the child to seek the police and act on them in particular ways; and (2) the ways in which the police construe and act upon the child.

Concluding Comment

Both cognitive-behavioral and psychodynamic therapies acknowledge the importance of the person–environment relationship. But if we are committed to including the previous issues (e.g., surface and deep behaviors, unconscious cognitive structures and conscious cognitive products, and meaning), then the relation between the child and environment (including the environment of a therapeutic situation) should be conceptualized along the line of Wachtel's concept of cyclical psychodynamics: that a person responds to environments but also seeks particular environments and stimulation that fits with, or satisfies, unconscious configurations of fantasies, wishes, and defenses. The linear concept that the therapist changes either the behavior the child imposes on the environment or the way environment act upon the child seems less heuristic.

Issue VII: Psychological Conflict

Cognitive-behavioral and psychodynamic therapies are interested in stresses, anxieties, and difficulties a person experiences that define conflict. Psychological conflict implies that some behavior, idea, or emotion is opposed by another behavior, idea, or emotion. How do cognitive-behavioral and psychodynamic therapies typically view these opposing forces? As we might guess, the view each therapeutic approach holds is related to the position each assumes in terms of the issues of surface versus deep behavior, the relation between cognition and emotion, the significance of conscious or unconscious mental processes, and the role of the environment.

Although concerned with relieving a person's stress, cognitive-behavioral therapy has not emphasized the importance of conceptualizing conflict. As Wachtel (1987) pointed out, Bandura's influential volume (1969) does not contain any references to "conflict." And I noticed that two other early influential volumes do not list conflict in the index: Meichenbaum's (1977) on cognitive-behavioral modification and Beck's (1976) on cognitive therapy. Moreover, in later volumes on cognitive therapy and cognitive-behavioral therapy, the topic of conflict is absent (e.g., Emery et al. 1981, Guidano and Liotti 1983, Kendall and Hollon 1979, McMullin 1986). And the topic of conflict is also conspicuously absent from volumes that focus on cognitive-behavioral therapy with children (e.g., Knell 1995, Meyers and Craighead 1984).

Yet several cognitive-behavioral therapists have given some attention to the concept of conflict. When presenting the foundations of cognitive therapy, Hoffman (1984) addressed the issue of conflict in terms of Piaget's concept of equilibration, which we considered earlier. For Hoffman, a conflict concerns the degree to which the organization of a particular schema (cognitive structure) is too discrepant with behaviors and information that are available for assimilation. If this discrepancy continues over time to be too great, "frustration will be accumulated as the cognitive structure tries to relate to these particular situations" and "will be loaded with negative feelings" (p. 32). He described the hypothetical example of a toddler who learns that his needs are met in numerous and varied situations by the actions of others. This child's cognitive structures would then be discrepant in any future environment that does not present the same degree of nurturing activity.

Other authors (Arkowitz and Messer 1984, Wachtel 1987) conceptualized conflict from the viewpoint of cognitive-behavioral therapy as involving competition among different thoughts and/or behavioral responses that have been reinforced in different ways by the environment on the one hand and as involving opposition by the environment to particular thoughts or behaviors on the other. From a cognitive-behavioral viewpoint, conflict is determined for the most part by the environment, and can be eliminated by either replacing or controlling conscious thoughts and actions with techniques such as self-instruction training, modeling, and social skills training. Conflict can also be eliminated with techniques that modify environments that oppose a person's thoughts or behaviors; for example, modifying parents who are too demanding, or modifying a classroom that is unstructured.

The picture is quite different in psychodynamic therapy. A person is seen as inherently locked in a struggle that consists of "inner forces" opposing each other (wishes/urges, internal prohibitions, mechanisms of defense). These forces are not on the "surface" but deep and unconscious, and are inferred from the constellation of a person's psychological activity (see earlier section in this chapter on "Psychodynamic Therapy and the Relation Between Cognition and Emotion"). Unconscious wishes and urges are viewed as opposed by moral standards that the person has assimilated from parental figures (superego) as well as by conscious thoughts and actions (ego) a person uses to adapt to changing environments.

As discussed earlier, the psychodynamic notion of conflict also includes whether or not unconscious mental mechanisms of defense—those cognitive maneuvers used to manage a conflicted configuration so that painful emotions are blocked from entering conscious awareness and so that unconscious wishes do not result in maladaptive action—are efficient. In this view, since conflict is inherent in human functioning, it cannot be eliminated but can only be alleviated. To relieve a person's conflicts, treatment focuses on bringing wishes and fantasies into awareness and on restructuring mechanisms of defense that are not operating efficiently. For example, as a person becomes aware that he/she is angry at a parent for some reason, the person also changes the degree to which he/she projects the anger onto authority figures, such as a teacher, which previously resulted in the stress of experiencing the teacher as angry at him/her.

Concluding Comment

In considering conflict, cognitive-behavioral therapy has focused on conscious thoughts and cognitive skills (cognitive products), while psychodynamic therapists have focused on unconscious wishes, moral prohibitions, and mechanisms of defense (cognitive structures). Is there anything else that can be said about conflict that could suggest a link between these positions? Interestingly, suggestions have been made by psychodynamic therapists. Lewis (1977) provided one example by integrating Piaget's theory of cognitive development into his psychodynamic therapy for children. He pointed out that psychoanalysis usually considers anxiety and stress as stemming from intrapsychic conflicts noted above; that is, between wish and superego prohibition. In addition, he argued, anxiety and stress could also stem from a mismatch between a child's cognitive organization, or stage of cognitive development, and the complexity of information the child is attempting to master. The reader may notice this position is the same as that proposed by Hoffman (1984). For example, consider a 9-year-old child who has not yet developed the capacity to conserve information. Because of this maturational lag, the child may experience states of anxiety because he/she has difficulty taking appropriate distance from events and feelings. The importance of a child's cognitive development, especially whether the child's cognition efficiently equilibrates emotions, wishes, and environmental demands, plays an important role in several of the techniques proposed in later chapters.

Issue VIII: The Relationship between Patient and Therapist

The relationship between patient and therapist has not been assigned the same degree of importance by cognitive-behavioral and psychodynamic therapies. This is not surprising if we remind ourselves of the viewpoints of objectivism and inter-pretationism that have influenced each of these approaches. Recall that if the position of objectivism is taken, a boundary is set between the therapist and patient, subordinating the importance of the relationship between the two. On the other hand, if one assumes the interpretationist position, the therapist joins the patient in a dialectical process to construct knowledge and therefore the relationship is considered crucial.

By comparing the views of the patient–therapist relationship that have evolved within cognitive-behavioral and psychodynamic therapies, several issues become articulated that I believe are essential to an integrative approach to child psychotherapy.

The Patient–Therapist Relationship in Psychodynamic Therapy

In his first writings on psychodynamic psychotherapy, Freud (1904, 1905, 1912, 1913, 1914) assigned a central position to the patient–therapist relationship with the concepts of "alliance" and "transference and resistance." He used the term *alliance* to conceptualize a particular quality of the relationship between patient and therapist that concerned their mutual commitment to engage in the task of resolving conflict. He used the term *transference* to conceptualize another quality of the relationship. Freud noticed that when a patient interacted with him in treatment sessions, the person gradually relived and repeated behaviors he/she had already developed to conduct his/her emotional and cognitive life, behaviors that had grown from past experiences with significant caregivers. He also proposed that the individual cannot escape repeating (transferring) his/her unique behaviors in the treatment situation, acting them out in the relationship with the therapist instead of remembering their origin.

For example, in the beginning of treatment, one of Freud's patients did not remember being defiant and critical toward his parents as a child, but instead behaved in this way with the therapist. Another patient did not remember being ashamed as a child of certain activities and afraid of being found out by his parents. Rather, the patient expressed shame over being in therapy and was preoccupied with keeping it a secret from friends. Freud assumed that because a patient did not remember, or was not aware of these issues, her/his way of knowing or remembering was to repeat the behaviors in the relationship.

Freud also conceptualized that the compulsion to repeat an action, instead of knowing and remembering, related to the view that transference behaviors served as resistance to change. He raised a question that must also occur to us. Why are transference behaviors so ideally suited as a means of expressing resistance to change? Freud answered from his interest in the role that repressed impulses play in the formation of neurotic symptoms. He assumed that if a patient is transferring feelings and perceptions onto the therapist—as if the therapist, for example, were mother or father—it would follow that the patient would find it very difficult to admit knowing of a wish or impulse, since in doing so the impulse would have to be revealed to the very person to whom it relates.

For Freud, as the patient relived and worked through his/her resistance to change in the treatment situation, the patient's unsuccessful behaviors were re-formed. One of his early statements illustrates the importance he gave to the relationship, and to in vivo experiences, as a means of resolving resistance.

> We must (eventually) treat his illness not as an event of the past, but as a present day force. This state of illness is brought, piece by piece, within the field and range of operation of the treatment, and *while the patient experiences it as something real and contemporary (in interactions with the therapist)*, we have to do our therapeutic work on it. . . . [1914, vol. 12, p. 151; italics mine]

While the nature of the patient–therapist relationship remained at the center of psychodynamic therapy, almost immediately after Freud developed his position psychoanalysts began to debate the question: What is the proper stance a therapist should take in the therapeutic relationship? (for a review see Messer and Winokur 1984). For example, some therapists, emphasizing one of Freud's notions, argued that the therapist should remain a "blank screen" and "neutral" so that the patient could more readily experience the therapist as someone else, and repeat behaviors that cause difficulties in everyday life. These episodes of transference behaviors, then, would more likely be "distortions of reality" from which the patient could learn about the sources of his/her difficulties.

From this classical viewpoint, the essence of therapy was to reconstruct a patient's history from transference behaviors and to interpret how that history of unconscious, infantile motives "distorted" the patient's views of, and experiences with, the therapist and therefore others (Gill 1984). In the process of reconstructing a patient's history, the therapist stood outside the patient's relational matrix, "looked in, pointed a finger at behaviors from the past, and enjoined the patient to renounce them" (Mitchell 1988, p. 292).

On the other side of the debate, as interpersonal concepts received increasing attention within psychodynamic theory, other therapists emphasized the importance of the therapist' s humanness. Rather than viewing the relationship in terms of how the patient distorts reality, distortions that the therapist pointed out and interpreted, these therapists argued that the "real relationship" between patient and therapist was more important. Here, transference behaviors were viewed not as symbols of the past but as experiences occurring within here-and-now transactions between patient and therapist. While the patient construed the therapist, the therapist also construed the patient, each participating within the other's relational world. From this position the concept of transference was revised.

For example, Weimer (1980) proposed that the interactions between therapist and patient "taking place over time will create and change the meaning of events and actions for both client and therapist. The result will be a client whose behavior and perspective have been changed as much by his or her own activity as by the intervention of the therapist" (p. 389). A few years later, Gill and Hoffman (1982) stated, "We believe that the therapist's actual behavior strongly affects the patient's actual experience, including what are usually designated as the transferential aspects of that experience. . . . We differ, therefore, from those who emphasize distortion of reality as the hallmark of transference" (p. 139). Gill (1984) elaborated this position in his proposed revision of psychodynamic psychotherapy and transference. While the patient, in the here and now, repeats ways of behaving that originated from past experiences, the behaviors of the therapist exert an influence on how the patient behaves and, "in this sense, co-determines the transference" (p. 169).

In addition to the debate over whether the therapist should view himself/herself as a "blank screen" versus as a participant in a relationship, considerable attention has been given to how the therapist should "listen with the third ear" and to concepts such as empathy. Here, some writers attempted to integrate the concept of the therapist as a "blank screen" with that of "participant." Greenson (1977), addressing adult psychotherapy, discussed this integration.

> [The therapist] listens consciously, intellectually and detachedly, [and] at the same time from the inside as a participant. This kind of listening requires that the analyst have the capacity to shift from participant to observer, from introspection to empathy, from intuition to problem solving thinking, from a more involved to a more detached position. It is necessary for him to oscillate, make transitions, and blendings of these different positions . . . the essential mechanism in empathy is a partial and temporary identification with the patient. In order to accomplish this, it is necessary to regress from the position of the detached, intellectual observer, to a more primitive kind of relationship in which the analyst becomes one with the person he is listening to. . . . [pp. 100–101]

I will have more to say in future chapters about the issues of a "co-determined transference" and the therapist as both an observer and participant, since these concepts of the patient–therapist relationship play a central role in my integrative model for children.

The Patient–Therapist Relationship in Cognitive-Behavioral Therapy

The attention paid to the patient–therapist relationship has been quite different in cognitive-behavioral therapy. As we noted earlier, the heritage of behavioral therapy and its younger sib, cognitive-behavioral therapy, was initially rooted in the animal laboratories of Pavlov, Watson, and Skinner and their objectivist position. As part of this heritage, cognitive-behavioral therapy focused on environmental causes of the patient's difficulties and on techniques that replace or correct behaviors and thoughts. Given this focus, the relationship between patient and therapist received little or no attention (Arkowitz 1984). The relationship was typically viewed only in terms of the rapport and cooperation required on the part of the patient for him/her to engage in and perform the various cognitive-behavioral tasks introduced by the therapist.

Even when Bandura's (1969) volume appeared, introducing concepts of modeling and cognitive mediators, the relationship was not given particular attention. Bandura viewed the patient–therapist relationship as a friendship, or as a substitution for some lack in the patient's life, and discounted the importance psychodynamic therapy gave to the relationship and to "transference." As Rhoads (1984) pointed out several years later, "In behavior therapy the focus is less on the patient's fantasy life and very little, if at all, on his or her relationship with the therapist—unless something in the relationship interferes with the therapy" (p. 198).

However, more recently, there has been a shift in the attention paid to the patient–therapist relationship, at least among those who represent an approach called "functional analytic psychotherapy," which emerged from "radical behaviorism" (Jacobson 1994, Kohlenberg and Tsai 1994). This approach views the patient–therapist relationship in a way that resembles that of psychodynamic therapy. Kohlenberg and Tsai proposed that when following the "core guideline" of radical behavior therapy, the therapist should "watch for clinically relevant behaviors (CRBs)" (p. 185). CRBs are defined in much the same way that Freud defined transference behaviors eighty years earlier. CRBs are behaviors that occur within the treatment session that represent and repeat behaviors that "clients complain about in outside relationships" (p. 185). However, this approach departs from traditional psychodynamic therapy in proposing that in addition to watching for CRBs, the therapist should "evoke" these behaviors during the session.

Whether these clinically relevant behaviors are generated totally by the patient or evoked intentionally by something the therapist says or does, the therapist then provides the patient with opportunities to develop behaviors that correct or improve the CRB. For example, the authors referred to a patient who complained that he withdraws and feels worthless when "people don't pay attention" to him during conversation. If this client showed similar withdrawal behaviors when interrupted by the therapist, the therapist engaged the client to be "assertive" and to direct the therapist back to what the client was saying. In so doing, the therapist reinforced the desired behavior. Maintaining an allegiance to behaviorism and objectivism, reinforcement is paramount for these authors. "Contingencies are the primary means of change" (p. 185). Here again the approach departs from that of psychodynamic therapy, which focuses on helping the patient become aware of the meaning of transference behavior rather than directing the patient to behave in some particular way.

Functional analytic psychotherapy also relies on the concept of "shaping." The patient typically displays a large pool of clinically relevant behaviors. The therapist carefully selects from this pool some behavior to reinforce. Here, Kohlenberg and Tsai caution that the therapist should be alert to the possibility that a particular behavior may be a problem for one patient but represent improvement for another. For example, they described a patient who pounds on the armrest of a chair and yells at the therapist, "You just don't understand me!" If this behavior came from a client who has difficulty expressing feelings, it would be viewed as improvement and behavior that the therapist should reinforce. If the outburst is typical, the therapist would suggest an alternative way to express feelings "that do not involve aggressive, physical demonstration" (p. 186). Echoing Freud, they urged therapists to learn to observe clinically relevant behaviors (or what Freud called "transference reactions"). Unlike Freud, who focused on exploring the meaning and origin of these behaviors, they proposed that if the therapist recognizes CRBs beforehand, he/she is "more likely to naturally reinforce, punish and extinguish these behaviors in ways that foster the development of behavior useful in daily life" (p. 186).

A Panel Discussion of the Therapeutic Relationship as Viewed from Different Theoretical Orientations

Over a decade ago, Rhoads (1984) believed that the major difference between cognitive-behavioral and psychodynamic therapies hinged on the relationship between patient and therapist, with the former approach ignoring the relationship for the most part, and the latter assigning the relationship a central position. Has this difference changed in any appreciable way during the past decade? The proceedings of a panel discussion (Gaston et al. 1995) suggested that the difference Rhoads articulated still exists.

Therapists from each of three persuasions—psychodynamic, cognitive-behavioral, and experiential-humanistic—were invited to discuss the patient–therapist relationship. I will mention only highlights of this informative panel discussion, which the reader is urged to read in the original.

The psychodynamic panelist presented a view that emerged from Freud and that we discussed earlier.

> Usually in dynamic therapy, we talk more about the alliance and transference; the alliance refers to the collaborative and realistic aspects of the relationship, and transference and countertransference to the more distorted reactions from both the patient and the therapist. . . . If you don't have a good alliance with your therapist and you develop negative transference reactions, you will leave your therapist. The same thing with very positive transferences. If you have a weak alliance with your therapist, and you develop a very strong, positive transference, there is a danger you are going to be frustrated . . . in long term therapy, the therapist makes sure that

the transference neurosis develops so that the therapist can access the patient's inner world of transactions with others in distorted views of the world. [p. 8]

Referring to elaborations of Freud's original formulation, this panelist also pointed out that the patient develops an attachment to, and identification with, the therapist much as a child attaches to and identifies with a "good enough mother."

The cognitive-behavioral therapists noted that the concept of alliance "simply does not exist or has not until recent years" (p. 4). They pointed out that the emphasis has been on technique rather than on the relationship. But as behavioral therapists started to apply techniques in clinical practice, the importance of the relationship became clear. "More and more, behavior therapists have now recognized this" (p. 4). When viewed from the behavioral vantage point, the alliance serves several different functions, most of which are preparatory to working on cognitive-behavioral tasks.

[T]he alliance functions to facilitate between-session risk taking; encourage clients to carry out various forms of homework; increase the positive reinforcement value of therapists so that they can encourage any changes that occur; facilitate any modeling that may occur by virtue of therapeutic self-disclosure in a good therapeutic relationship; keep up the client's hope and positive expectancies during the at times uneven road to therapeutic improvement; and overcome any resistance or noncompliance that may exist. [p. 4]

While these panelists indicated that cognitive-behavioral therapists have come to recognize the importance of the relationship, the comment above suggests that the emphasis is still on techniques and tasks, with the relationship viewed as important only in terms of what the therapist plans to do to the patient. Unlike the psychodynamic view of the relationship as a dialectical give and take, the next quote dramatically reflects the objectivist position that a boundary separates patient and therapist and that the therapist has "procedures" that must be performed on the person of the patient. Here the cognitive-behavioral panelists cast the relationship within a metaphor of surgery and anesthesia.

When we conceptualize the alliance from within a cognitive-behavioral point of view, we think of it as akin to the anesthesia that occurs during major surgery. Somebody goes into the hospital for surgery because there are certain procedures that need to be implemented. In order for these procedures to take place, the person must be under anesthesia; the anesthesia facilitates what is really important (i.e., the procedures). However, if anything goes wrong with the anesthesia during the surgery, then that becomes the priority. Similarly, within a cognitive-behavioral point of view, a good alliance is necessary and often crucial. Without it, you just can't proceed. . . . [p. 5]

In contrast, the experiential panelists pointed out that the relationship is the core vehicle for change, converging with the psychodynamic panelist and with therapists such as Gill, Weimer, and Mitchell, who, as noted earlier, advocated that patient–therapist interactions promote change. The relationship is necessary to achieve the goal of experiential treatment, namely, experiencing meanings, a goal that converges with Bohart's discussion of meaning and experience considered earlier. Accordingly, emphasis is given to how the therapist conveys empathic attunement and genuine caring to the patient. These components of the bond between patient and therapist enable the patient to experience and symbolize "felt-meanings" that occur during a treatment session. For the experiential therapist, change does not result from resolving transference nor from modifying behavior or cognition, but rather from evoking internal experiences and symbolizing them. Thus the relationship as a "safe working environment" is necessary if the patient is to engage in the task of experiencing. The alliance is not just anesthesia that allows operations to occur and the patient to tolerate pain. Rather, the alliance is necessary if the patient is to engage in the main task of therapy; namely, "experiencing" problem behaviors, discovering the meanings of these behaviors, and increasing "the capacity to symbolize these felt-meanings in order to strengthen the self" (p. 6).

Concluding Comment

In our consideration of the patient–therapist relationship, a number of ingredients came into view that should be considered in constructing an integrative model for child psychotherapy. Decades ago, Freud proposed that when interacting with a therapist, the patient repeats behaviors that cause problems in everyday living, and the therapist must address these very behaviors within the relationship to effect change. This proposal is also held important by those following radical behaviorism, while given little attention by mainstream cognitive-behaviorists.

In addition, psychodynamic therapists who have revised Freud's original position bring attention to the notion that within the therapeutic relationship the patient identifies with and attaches to the therapist in much the same way that a child identifies with and attaches to his/her caregiver. They also bring attention to behaviors and attitudes the therapist contributes within the relationship and emphasize a dialectical position: that while the patient construes the therapist in some personal way, the therapist also construes the patient, so that together they construct a relationship that is unique to them. These revisionists propose that transactions that occur within this unique relationship promote change as much as, or perhaps more than, what the therapist says (interpretations). This view is also held by radical behaviorists who propose that how the therapist interacts and responds to "clinically relevant behaviors" determines whether the patient will evolve more adaptive ways of behaving. Experiential therapy emphasizes that when reliving some issue within the therapeutic relationship, what is most important is that the patient discover and experience the meaning of what is being relived and then cast the experience in some symbolic form. Can we integrate these conceptual ingredients and then translate them into therapeutic techniques suitable for work with children? The integrative model outlined in the next chapter addresses this question.

Issue IX: What Should the Therapist Do to Help? Reconsidering the Importance Given to Verbal Labeling and Interpretation

We considered that cognitive-behavioral therapy emphasizes helping a child improve his/her ability to verbally describe experiences and label emotions, even when this approach is joined with play therapy. Similarly, psychodynamic therapy focuses on words spoken by the child and interpretations by the therapist. We should be surprised to find this emphasis on verbalizing, given that play and activity have been a major therapeutic tool nearly from the beginning when psychoanalytic concepts were applied to treating children. As Shirk (1988) pointed out in his historical review of this issue, Anna Freud, one of the founders of psychodynamic child therapy, took the position that play, drawing, painting, or staging fantasy games are not valid substitutes for verbal, free associating, and "talking about" emotional and interpersonal worries. From this heritage, psychodynamic therapists tended to view play as the object of interpretation, rather than having some other value. Both cognitive-behavioral and psychodynamic therapies, then, seem to deify and sanctify the spoken word.

Yet Bohart reminded us that meaning fuels the process of experiencing and that "conscious cognition" (i.e., self-statements, verbalizing, interpreting) does not adequately capture the nature of experiencing. This reminder relates to a surge of interest in revising the view that the spoken word has ultimate power in promoting change. The surge comes from an unlikely source, given that psychoanalysis, from its inception, viewed verbalizing as the "holy grail" of treatment. This interest actually started in the 1940s and '50s when a few psychodynamically oriented therapists began to express the opinion that interpretation (the spoken word) should be dethroned (for a review, see Shirk 1988). For example, in the area of adult therapy, Alexander and French proposed that instead of analyzing (interpreting) the meaning of a patient's communications, they should provide a "corrective emotional experience." In the area of child psychotherapy, Axline deemphasized verbal interactions and emphasized helping the child express emotions, attitudes, and thoughts through play. And Winnicott held that the purpose of the therapist's communications is to create a supportive "holding" environment for the child.

In recent years Mitchell (1994), a psychoanalyst, has become one major voice calling for the need to reconceptualize the role of language behavior in treatment. In a discussion of new developments in psychoanalytic theorizing, he reminded the reader that in the traditional psychodynamic treatment situation "the patient is expected to stop acting and instead speak about his conflictual feelings and thoughts . . ." and the analyst is expected to stop acting and instead use his/her experience "to fashion appropriate interpretations" (p. 98). Although Mitchell is discussing adult psychodynamic therapy, his comments apply to child therapy.

Of the problems Mitchell considered that stem from a focus on verbalizations and interpretations, I select one because it will feature prominently in my integrative model for children. Mitchell pointed out that, in spite of the therapist's best intentions and preparation, the patient could experience an interpretation, and other verbal comments by the therapist, as "assaults," presenting the therapist with "a dilemma." From my observations treating children in psychotherapy and psychoanalysis, and influenced by studies of the relations among what a child does, imagines, and says, I propose that a child could also experience an interpretation as an assault, and may do so more often than an adult does, and more often than the therapist might realize. I mention only one line of reasoning related to this proposal. First, a child therapist typically uses verbal labeling and interpretations when experiencing and expressing meaning, probably because his/her language mode is well developed and practiced. Talking is the usual way the therapist attempts to engage another. In addition, perhaps an equally strong influence comes from the therapist's training. The psychodynamic therapist typically has ascribed to guidelines, such as the one we noted by Anna Freud, that a child overcomes conflicts whenever they are put into thoughts and words. The cognitive-behavioral therapist typically has ascribed to the assumption that self-talk guides actions, and that the child benefits from expressing maladaptive behavior in "language-based ways" (Knell 1995).

But if we look at the mode of "talking" from the viewpoint of a child, the meaning a verbal statement captures—while perhaps correct and suited for the adult—may not be available to the child. Or talking may not be the mode the child prefers because he/she is experiencing meaning primarily in the modes of fantasy and action. Therefore, the primary mode a therapist typically uses to make meaning, namely, verbalizing, may not be the same as that dominating the child's functioning, whatever his/her age. Because of this mismatch, verbal statements and interpretations are often experienced by children as "assaults."

To illustrate this point I will turn first to a clinical vignette Coppolillo (1987) described in his text on psychodynamic therapy for children. For a number of sessions "Jeff" had been "guarded, reluctant to reveal anything about himself and showed little inclination to explore the significance of anything he said" (p. 215). In other words, the boy wasn't experiencing and expressing himself in the language mode that Coppolillo apparently preferred. In one particular session Jeff began to play a game of solitaire with a deck of cards he had brought with him. The therapist interpreted this behavior with the verbal statement, "Do you suppose that by playing solitaire, you're showing me how it feels to be ignored? [Jeff, picking up cards, replied] No solitaire. Just sit here and talk to this old shithead, son-of-a-bitch. With this, he walked off to pick up some items, handling them in a disinterested way" (p. 245). The boy's response to the interpretation seems to make clear that he experienced the therapist's verbal statement as an assault. The boy responded by verbally attacking the therapist and then walking away, placing the therapist in a dilemma.

How can we understand this moment in treatment and find a solution to the dilemma? Here I introduce Mitchell's (1994) discussion of "enactments." The boy's playing solitaire, verbally attacking the therapist, and walking away are examples of enactments. Mitchell noted that because of recent changes in the psychoanalytic viewpoint, some therapists see these enactments different from the way Freud did. Freud stressed that the patient should stop acting and verbalize his feelings and fantasies. (This is the same position held by cognitive-behavioral therapy, as discussed in Issue III.) Apparently ascribing to Freud's view, Coppolillo experienced the boy as guarded and showing little inclination to explore (i.e., talk about) the significance of anything he said. The notion of enactments takes a different position about doing and talking. Mitchell argued that enactments "are not departures from psychodynamic process, but the very stuff of analyzing" (p. 99). Rather than conceptualizing/verbalizing and action as inversely related, Mitchell viewed these modes of experiencing as "continuously interpenetrating each other" (p. 99). This position, the reader may notice, converges with our interest in interrelating what a child does, imagines, and says.

At this point I return to the clinical vignette and consider it from the view of enactments. When the boy began playing solitaire with cards, could Coppolillo have responded in some way other than verbally interpreting the behavior? What if Coppolillo took out a deck of cards, sat at the far end of the room, and preoccupied himself in a game of solitaire? Would he then be speaking to the child in the child's mode of the moment, namely, the action mode? Would Coppolillo say, in action symbols rather than in words, "I know what it feels like to be ignored"? Would the child then have produced other enactments to elaborate the meaning with which he was grappling without anything being said yet? The integrative model I propose relies heavily on concepts that guide the mode, including enactments, that a therapist selects to speak to a child.

To stimulate further discussion I turn to Spiegel's volume (1989). Since he elaborated an interpersonal approach to psychodynamic child therapy, we might anticipate that he would have much to say about the issue of why labeling and interpreting by the therapist should be reconsidered as the main activity. And we are not disappointed. His theoretical position is very related to the integrative model we will be considering. For example, he pointed out that the traditional psychoanalytic approach "places a strong emphasis on highly intellectualized, verbal inter-pretations, which I feel is inappropriate for children . . . from an interpersonal perspective, the adult model of verbally searching for the basis and modification of pathology must be modified for child therapy" (p. 3). Further, Spiegel disagreed with psychodynamic and cognitive-behavior therapy, both of which emphasize verbalizing and labeling feelings and conflicts. He stated, "I do not see the aim of good therapy with children as getting them to talk about concerns and problems in a straightforward manner" (p. 28). Spiegel proposed that instead of language, com-munication in therapy should make use of tone and volume of vocal expressions, facial expressions, gestures, body postures, and other nonverbal cues.

If the therapist is to avoid verbal labeling and interpretations, what should he/she do? Spiegel proposed that the therapist should speak through metaphor, expressing thoughts, ideas, and feelings symbolically so that "the child may be able to accept the meaning of the interpretation with little, if any, damage to his self-esteem" (p. 28). With this proposal Spiegel is agreeing with my concern, that an interpretation should be delivered in a form and mode that minimizes the possi-bility the child will experience the communication as an assault. Yet in spite of his theoretical position, I was disappointed to find that in many of his clinical examples Spiegel relied upon the spoken word, and *verbalized* metaphors.

To illustrate, I will sketch one of his anecdotes. Daniel, a 10-year-old, en-tered treatment because of encopresis. One day, when he walked into the play-room, Spiegel smelled feces. Spiegel had this to say about what he thought he should do at the time. "Feeling that any mention of it would be an accusation . . . but also believing that it could not be ignored, *I worded my comment about the odor in a way that I thought would help maintain his self-esteem*. I said, 'It smells like you had an accident in school today'" (p. 32; italics mine). Daniel replied that he did not have an accident and that accidents don't happen anymore. Spiegel let the matter drop.

At this point I pause to bring attention to the fact that Spiegel was concerned about whether his intervention would be experienced as an assault ("accusation"). Therefore he responded to the odor by carefully selecting his words. Unlike Coppolillo's anecdote, Spiegel's words apparently were not experienced by Daniel as an assault, very likely because the meaning of the words was denied by Daniel ("No, it doesn't happen anymore"). That Daniel did not experience Spiegel's com-ment as an assault is also supported by the fact that Daniel did not attack the thera-pist and walk away, as did Coppolillo's patient. Rather, he continued to play with a car he had constructed the previous session that was designed to be propelled by an inflated balloon expelling air.

During this play, Daniel was extremely careful to ensure that the car was well balanced and stable, using balls of clay as ballast. Spiegel thought to himself that "at some level, the propulsion by air from the balloon could have represented flatu-lence or the expelling of feces" (p. 33). In the course of constructing the car, Daniel took a small chunk of clay which he had been using to balance the car and placed the clay on the end of his nose. At this moment a particular metaphor occurred to

Spiegel: ". . . on a hunch and with no danger of injury to his self-esteem [Spiegel said to Daniel], 'You look like Pinocchio! Pinocchio lied to Gepetto about school. Sometimes telling the truth is just too difficult and embarrassing' (p. 33). Here Spiegel is using a verbal metaphor; that is, Pinocchio lied to Gepetto as Daniel must be lying to Spiegel. When Daniel ignored this comment and continued to play, Spiegel thought to himself, "I pursued the matter no further; my job was done. The important point was my expression of acceptance of his lying. . . . I do not know for certain that when Daniel placed clay on his nose, he consciously or even unconsciously was aware of his wish to convey to me that he had, in fact, lied. I assumed so because he acknowledged that he looked like Pinocchio, but it is conceivable that his behavior had another meaning" (pp. 33–34).

This vignette provides me with an opportunity to forecast aspects of my integrative model which views this moment in therapy very differently from the way Spiegel did. When Daniel placed clay on the end of his nose, Spiegel assumed that Daniel looked like Pinocchio. From this assumption Spiegel concluded that since Pinocchio lied to Gepetto about school, Daniel was expressing the meaning that he, too, had lied to Spiegel about not having an accident at school. Further, rather than responding in the mode Daniel was using (an action symbol), Spiegel used a verbal or linguistic metaphor, namely, Pinocchio, to express the meaning he gave to Daniel's behavior.

The integrative model I propose would argue that by placing clay on the end of his nose Daniel was expressing any one of several meanings, and the therapist needed to set out with Daniel to discover and construct which meaning Daniel was experiencing and expressing at the moment. To mention only a few possibilities, the clay could have symbolized feces on the end of the therapist's nose. In other words, the behavior could have been a retaliation toward the therapist ("Take that!") for commenting about the odor in the first place, or commenting that he had lied. Or the clay could have symbolized the child's recognizing that he smells. Or the clay could have symbolized that Daniel believes the therapist thinks he (Daniel) stinks.

What could Spiegel have done other than verbalizing a metaphor? From the view of my integrative model, Spiegel could have responded with some action symbol, thus matching the child's mode of experiencing meaning, in order to help the child continue elaborating the meaning. In this way the therapist would have been more certain about what Daniel was saying. For example, Spiegel could have become very involved with Daniel in locating pieces of clay in the car to ensure that it was "perfectly balanced." Or Spiegel could have placed a piece of clay on the end of his own nose by way of saying, within the action mode, " I hear you, tell me more."

As these comments suggest, my integrative model proposes that the therapist should refrain during the greater part of treatment from making verbal statements that "literally" describe what the therapist assumes are a child's feelings, thoughts, or wishes. To quote Spiegel again, I do not believe we should try "to get the child to talk about concerns and problems in a straightforward manner" (p. 28). The therapist should refrain from making verbal interpretations, at least while a meaning is being constructed and elaborated by the child. If the therapist is to refrain from verbally labeling thoughts, emotions, fantasies, and wishes, then what is he/she to do? The therapist should speak as much as possible through action metaphors. That action metaphors should be the focus of therapy with children agrees with the opinions of a growing number of psychodynamic therapists who have criticized the emphasis on verbal interpretation, urging that we pay more attention to action and interaction. Joining Mitchell, for example, Valenstein (1983) proposed that understanding and insight are driven home by persistent action and interaction as patient and therapist engage in a prolonged, repetitive process of testing and learning. Similarly, for Gill (1984), the main sources of change come from persistent interactions between patient and therapist and from new experiences and meanings the patient encounters and constructs with the therapist.

But my proposal, which is in accord with Mitchell's, that the therapist use enactments as well as words is fraught with problems we consider in future chapters. Many children, if permitted to be themselves in a treatment situation, continually express a wide range of actions (e.g., in one session, a child could run about the playroom, take out a formboard game and invite the therapist to join in competitive play, interrupt the game, take out a toy Jeep and slowly roll it over the floor completely preoccupied with private thoughts, ask for a piece of candy, scribble on a piece of paper with a crayon, and take out a pump gun and shoot Ping-Pong balls at the wall and then at puppets). Should the therapist respond with action symbols to each of these behaviors? If not, which behavior should the therapist select to engage in what Valenstein called a "repetitive process of testing and learning" and in what Gill called "new experience"?

And there is still another important question. Should enactments include introducing a task that the child is required to engage in? Beginning with Freud's (1912) position that "it is wrong to set a task before the patient" (p. 119), many writers (e.g., Messer and Winokur 1984) have cautioned therapists not to ask the patient to perform some task because to do so decreases opportunities to explore the patient's inner conflicts and resolve them through interpretation of transference behaviors. Yet cognitive-behavioral therapists do not hesitate to introduce tasks the child is expected to manage. How could we benefit from integrating the psychodynamic view of enactments and the cognitive-behavioral view of introducing problem-solving tasks?

Issue X: Developmental Principles: The Glue for Integration

With the nine issues we have discussed thus far before us, and recalling our discussion of the boundary that divides objectivism and interpretationism, a therapist is typically committed more to one side or the other of the several dimensions we considered: overt/surface behaviors versus inside/deep behaviors with their fantasies and meanings; conscious cognition with its cognitive products versus unconscious cognitive structures with their emotions; conscious versus unconscious processes; external environments versus internal representations of environments; conflict between a person's behaviors/thoughts and the environment versus conflict between a person's unconscious urges and the internal standards opposing them; the therapeutic relationship as anesthesia necessary for the therapist to introduce tasks and perform surgery versus the therapeutic relationship as containing interactions that form the basis for change; and the use of labeling with words versus labeling with symbolic enactments.

When making a commitment to one of these positions instead of its counterpart, a therapist probably feels he/she is standing on solid ground. Moreover, a therapist probably experiences anxiety when asked to step over the boundary to the other side, because the other side appears to be quicksand. Therefore, asking the therapist to think about integrating these polarities places him/her in a dilemma. If the cognitive-behavioral therapist decides to step over the boundary, keeping one foot on the solid ground of objectivism while avoiding the quicksand of interpretationism, where does he/she plant the other foot? And if the psychodynamic therapist decides to step over the boundary, keeping one foot on the solid ground of interpretationism while avoiding the quicksand of objectivism, where does he/she plant the other foot?

I propose that in each case, if the therapist places both feet on a platform constructed of particular developmental principles, he/she will discover that there is solid ground in both the cognitive-behavioral and psychodynamic approaches to child therapy. To set the stage for this proposal, which is elaborated in the next chapters, I turn to discuss how development is viewed in cognitive-behavioral and psychodynamic therapies with children.

Developmental Principles in Cognitive-Behavioral Therapy

Traditionally, developmental considerations have not been of central importance in cognitive-behavioral therapy. The topic is neglected by some volumes devoted to this approach. For example, the term *development* does not appear in the index of Meichenbaum's (1977) early, influential volume, and is also absent from the indexes of more recent volumes (e.g., Hollin 1990, Hughes 1988).

However, other cognitive-behavioral therapists have given attention to developmental considerations. In discussing the technique of providing the child with cognitive processes (mediators) associated with behavior the child is expected to model, Kendall and Morison (1984) noted the importance of taking into account the child's "developmental level." They pointed out that before the age of 5 or 6 self-instruction training may not be a desirable addition to treatment. Instead, these children should get a "heavy dose" of adult praise and coping models. For these authors, development equals chronological age. "Developmental level (or simply age) is an important consideration that is directly implicated in the proper execution of the training procedure" (p. 286). The view that development is synonymous with age is expressed again by Kendall and Braswell (1985), who noted that since a given cognitive-behavioral intervention (e.g., self-instruction, problem solving, replacing irrational beliefs) "require certain prerequisite skills" (p. 5), the age of the child should be considered. This recommendation is echoed by a number of contributors to an edited volume on cognitive-behavioral therapy with children (Meyers and Craighead 1984).

When cognitive-behavioral techniques are used to enhance children's social skills (Matson and Ollendick 1988), the position again is that children below the age of 6 may profit less from self-instructional training "since attending to both self-instruction and task performance is distracting and confusing to the child [and] self-instructional training and other cognitive based procedures are better suited for children who possess efficient cognitive skills to benefit from their use" (p. 56). The same view is held when cognitive-behavioral techniques are used in a group therapy format (O'Connor 1993).

Other cognitive-behavioral therapists have elaborated the notion of development by defining it in terms of Piaget's theory of cognitive stages. The relevance for clinical practice of Piaget's model has been discussed by several writers (e.g., Cohen and Schleser 1984, Sollod and Wachtel 1980) and elaborated by others (Shirk 1988) who have extended Piaget's views into various clinical domains that concern cognitive development and child psychotherapy. At the base of these discussions are Piaget's sequentially invariant stages of cognitive development.

Discussed in detail elsewhere (see Issues II and III), the concept of schema is the foundation of Piaget's model of development. A schema is a cognitive or mental structure by which a person intellectually (cognitively) represents, adapts to, and organizes experiences with things and the environment. In the first sensorimotor stage (0–2 years), schemas are formed by the infant's reflexes (e.g., sucking), representing actions and physical experiences (touch, taste, sound). During the preoperational stage (2–7 years), the child begins to develop symbolic representations of things but is unable to take different perspectives in a given situation, either perceptually or socially. During the stage of concrete operations (7–11 years), the child develops the capacity to conserve properties of experiences that are invariant despite transformations of information (e.g., the volume of water is perceived as not changing when poured into a differently shaped container). In the stage of formal operations (11 years and older), the child is increasingly able to think in terms of abstractions, hypothetical situations, and deductive reasoning.

Piaget's theory of schemas undergoing intrinsic change through a sequence of stages is supplemented by his concept of two processes that are developmentally invariant: organization and adaptation. The concept of organization assumes that cognitive structures are organized into a totality, and interrelated, so that a change in one part produces changes throughout the entire cognitive system. The concept of adaptation assumes that each experience provides the opportunity for change in the person's cognitive organization. In this adaptive process, aspects of a new experience are assimilated into, and become a part of, already existing cognitive structures. Thus a new experience is given meaning in terms of a person's existing schemas. In addition, as new experiences are encountered, the existing schemas reorganize, accommodating to the properties and demands unique to the new experience.

The relationship between assimilation and accommodation, within the process of adaptation, defines what Piaget termed *equilibration* and determines growth. When assimilation and accommodation are in a state of balance, equilibrium exists, and when in a state of imbalance, disequilibrium exists. Piaget proposed that human cognitive functioning inherently strives to reduce states of disequilibrium. In this way cognition is motivated to achieve states of equilibrium. States of moderate disequilibrium are optimal conditions for cognitive growth; that is, experiences and encounters with stimulation are moderately mismatched with what the existing cognitive structures can understand.

A number of cognitive-behavioral therapists have made use of one or another aspect of Piaget's theory of stages of schema development and the concepts of organization and adaptation when planning treatment programs for children (e.g., Guidano and Liotti 1985, Knell 1995, McMullin 1986, Seiler 1984).

Developmental Principles in Psychodynamic Child Therapy

Almost from its beginning, psychoanalytic theory and therapy, from which psychodynamic child therapy derived, was formulated by Freud as a developmental theory. However, unlike Piaget, the focus of Freud's theory was on the development and cognitive regulation of representations of drives rather than on cognitive activity involving encounters with external stimulation. In general, Freud's theory concerns what is referred to as "libido" development and psychosexual stages of development. Many revisions of this theory were introduced by Freud and others over a span of fifty years. Because a detailed review of these revisions falls outside the scope of our purpose, I mention here only those particular concepts that have relevance for my thesis. The reader is referred to presentations available in the literature (e.g., Kay 1972, Rapaport 1960, Wolman 1972).

As discussed earlier, Freud's initial theory was devoid of developmental considerations, conceptualizing behavior in terms of a stimulus–response model. A patient's symptoms were understood as the outcome of earlier traumatic experiences and unconscious memories and dammed-up emotions related to them. Freud switched to a developmental prospective in 1897 when he conceptualized that reports by his patients did not refer to real experiences as such but to childhood fantasies representing wishes that gratified instinctual drives (urges, emotions). These unconscious representations followed an inherent developmental course and determined conscious experiences and behavior as much as stimulation from reality.

Freud considered inherently maturating, instinctual drives as "constitutional factors," and environmental stimulation as "accidental factors." Moreover, he proposed a relationship between these two factors.

> [T]he constitutional factor must await experience before it can make itself felt; the accidental factor must have a constitutional basis in order to come into operation. To cover the majority of cases we can picture . . . "a complemental series" in which the diminishing intensity of one factor is balanced by the increasing intensity of the other. [1905, pp. 239–240]

As the reader may notice, Freud's conception of development at this time seems to be similar to that which Piaget formulated some years later. Freud's concept of representations of instinctual drives maturating intrinsically (independent of prior experience) is similar to Piaget's concept of cognitive schemas maturating intrinsically. And Freud's notion of a "complemental series" between constitutional and environmental factors is similar to Piaget's notion of cognitive assimilation and accommodation involved in a process of equilibration or balance.

While Freud (1923, 1930, 1932) thought that a number of relatively independent instincts derived from various bodily sources, he eventually settled on two major instincts. One concerned the notion of "libido," or love and construction (usually referred to as the sexual instinct). When he could not explain why people sometimes wish to destroy others and inflict or receive pain, he postulated a second major instinct, aggression or destruction.

He drew an analogy between the sexual instinct, sometimes referred to as *Eros*, and the physiological process of anabolism. The aim of the sexual instinct is to create and preserve life, to bind elements of life together, "by bringing about a more and more far-reaching combination [a more complex-differentiated organization] of the particles into which living substance is dispersed" (1923, p. 40). Similarly, he drew an analogy between the aggressive instinct, sometimes referred to as the *Death Instinct*, and the physiological process of catabolism. The aim of the aggressive instinct is to destroy things by undoing connections of the particles into which living substance is dispersed.

The sexual instinct, or Eros, became the focus of the first major elaboration of Freud's developmental theory. He conceptualized that the maturation (development) of the sexual instinct (libido) moves through several invariant stages during the first five years of life. These stages are typically referred to as "psychosexual stages." Freud defined each stage in terms of experiences with a particular body zone that dominates as the vehicle symbolizing the self and interactions with others. From birth to about the age of 18 to 24 months (the "oral stage"), experiences such as eating, sucking, and body/tactile sensations shape the first symbols of self and others. By the end of the first year of life, as teeth erupt, experiences with biting contribute to the construction of other meanings viewed as oral-aggressive in nature. Primary identification, or the wish to be like another person, is viewed as an early emotional attitude that emerges at this time. The infant swallows what it loves and loves what it swallows.

After the age of 2 (the anal stage), experiences with a different body zone dominate the construction of symbols. The anus expels and retains, and these experiences involve pleasure with urinating and defecating. In addition, the toddler now is required to accommodate to the environment's opposition to these pleasures, which prescribes when and where the toddler is to relieve his/her bladder and bowels. Now meanings such as rebelling, defying, and submitting are organized. Feces could take on the meaning of a gift to parents or a part of one's body that one does not want to give up. In the phallic stage of development (3–5 years) experiences with genital organs dominate in producing symbols now emphasizing power, ascendance, and anxiety over losing power.

The Oedipus complex emerges from the phallic stage. While the child loves both parents, erotic/sexual fantasies are experienced involving the parent of the opposite sex (e.g., the 4-year-old boy who tells his mother he wants to marry her and the 4-year-old girl who asks father to take her with him on a trip, noting that mother is too old and may die). When these fantasies are experienced, of course, they are accompanied by other fantasies that represent the parent of the opposite sex as competition, a threat, and as someone to hate—emotions that conflict with the love the child already has evolved. For Freud, how this oedipal complex is resolved by a child plays a pivotal role in whether and what type of behavioral symptoms and conflicts emerge later.

Following the phallic stage, with its Oedipus complex, psychological development enters the "latency phase" (6–11 years). During this time, sexual tensions (negotiated previously) are sublimated and eventually subside, and a sense of self-identity is stabilized. Then, in adolescence, with its biological changes, the same dynamics involving receiving, giving, resisting, submitting, ascending, and so forth erupt again and are renegotiated with parents, sibs, peers, and teachers. Freud believed, however, that developments during the first five years of life were decisive in determining the foundation of an individual's personality.

Freud's view of development included another closely related concept: that representations of instinctual drives, as they mature, are restrained and regulated by other intrinsic factors. While, as we noted earlier, aspects of Freud's developmental theory resemble Piaget's, the emphasis Freud gave to factors that restrain and regulate representations (schemas) is one major feature that distinguishes psychoanalytic and Piagetian developmental theories.

What are these factors that restrain and regulate representations or schemas? Freud conceptualized these restraining factors as the "ego," a concept he introduced in 1915 and revised during the next twenty-five years. The ego consists of various cognitive processes such as perception, thinking, memory. The task of the ego is to distinguish between, manage, and coordinate stimuli from the id (representations of instincts) and the environment. In addition to performing these "executive functions," ego processes also are involved in restraining the push for action that emerges from representation of instinctual urges.

How do ego processes delay the expression of drives in action? Freud conceptualized one restraining factor as involving a shift in cognitive functioning from what he called "primary process" thinking to "secondary process" thinking. Recall that the id was conceptualized as the seat of representations of all desires and seething urges that pushed for immediate expression and pleasure. Primary process thinking, which ignores logic, is guided by the wish for pleasure (Freud's "principle of lust," usually translated as the pleasure principle) and by the need for immediate satisfaction in action. Secondary process thinking is guided by the requirements of efficient adaptation (Freud's "reality principle"), and as taking into account the consequences of actions and reality prohibitions and opportunities. Freud postulated that in shifting from primary to secondary process thinking, mental structures inhibit and delay the expression of drive representations in actions. In delaying actions, in postponing physical encounters with persons and things, a "hallucinatory" (mental) image is constructed that replaces the need-satisfying object or event. The notion that images of persons, events, and experiences substitute for actual things forecast Piaget's concept of "internalized imitation" and Stern's concepts of "representations of interaction" and "evoked companion," which we discuss in Chapter 5.

Freud proposed another factor that restrained and delayed the expression of id impulses in action when he elaborated his theory of development further with the concept of "superego." Conceptualized as the child's conscience, the superego begins to develop during the anal phase and continues developing through the other stages. Motivated by the fear of punishment and the need for affection, a child gradually "internalizes" (assimilates) the demands, expectations, and rules of parents and eventually constructs a mental representation (superego) that considers these rules as his/her own. The superego gradually differentiates as a mental agency, consisting of representations of the values and attitudes of parents, "moral restrictions," and "strivings toward perfection." In general, the superego functions as a self-observer, a conscience, and this organization of internalized standards confronts the ego with its own demands.

Freud also elaborated his developmental theory with the concept of an "ego ideal," which also plays a role in taming and restraining the id. He conceptualized an aspect of the superego (parental values) as an ego ideal to give special attention to the phenomenon that a child idealizes particular attributes of the parents. Some of these attributes have a "social side," for example, in the national or ethnic heritage of parents. Since these attributes are idealized, they are represented as more powerful and glorious than they may be in reality. The representations that make up the ego ideal are used by the ego as a standard to measure itself. The ego ideal, then, is the source of "self love" (or what other theorists refer to as self-esteem) when a standard has been met successfully. If the ego ideal is not fulfilled, a sense of guilt (social anxiety) derived from a fear of parental punishment (loss of love) is experienced. I hope to illustrate in later chapters that the concept of an ego ideal is particularly useful in understanding aspects of a child's behavior during therapy and in planning how a therapist should respond.

Various aspects of Freud's developmental theory were elaborated by others. For example, Anna Freud (1946) detailed mechanisms of defense the ego uses to distinguish between and coordinate stimuli stemming from representations of instinctual urges on the one hand and prohibitions and expectations of the environment on the other. We discussed these mechanisms in the section on cognition and emotion (see Issue III). Heinz Hartmann (1939) elaborated a psychology of the ego in terms of the issue of adaptation. Erikson (1950) proposed stages of psychosocial development elaborating Freud's psychosexual stages. Moreover, these writers and others contended that, unlike Freud's initial proposal, ego functions (cognition) do not differentiate from the id (representations of drives) when reality requirements oppose drives. Rather, they proposed that ego functions (cognition) are organized from birth "outside of conflict," and as independent agents serve to moderate, as instruments of adaptation, between drives and environmental permissions and prohibitions.

It is interesting to note that in the past two decades psychoanalytic researchers have also focused on infant development. In contrast to Freud's position that the Oedipus complex at around 5 years shapes a child's personality, these investigators have elaborated how experiences in the first two years of life contribute significantly to the formation of personality (e.g., Lichtenberg 1983, Mahler 1979, Sander 1969, 1975, Stern 1985). The observations of these investigators have focused on how the infant develops the capacity for independent functioning (separation-individuation), constructs a sense of self and other, and negotiates various "developmental" issues and tasks with caregivers during the process of individuation. We consider infant research in the next chapter.

Freud's theory of libidinal drives, psychosexual stages, and the structures of ego, id, and superego were used by Anna Freud to formulate a developmental profile to aid in organizing diagnostic data about a child's "total personality organization including both strengths and weaknesses" (see also Boland and Sandler 1965, Silverman 1978, p. 110). In addition to the reasons for referral and data about family background, the profile emphasizes assessing the developmental level of drives (libido and aggression), and the ego and superego, using data from interviews with parents, family members, and teachers, direct observations of the child, and psychological tests. Assessment of libido development pays particular attention to whether a child has progressed to the phallic level or whether there has been significant regression to an earlier stage. With regard to aggressive drives, "since much less is known about the stages of development" (Silverman 1978, p. 113), aggression is considered according to its expression (covert and overt) rather than in terms of developmental sequencing, and in terms of whether aggressive expressions correspond with a child's level of libidinal development. Particular attention is also paid to variations in developmental sequencing. For example, a child may show, before the expected age, phallic-dominant behavior. Or a child may show a regression, revealing phase-specific conflicts that belong to an earlier age. In other cases, oral-anal manifestations may coexist with phallic, oedipal conflicts, with no one particular form of representation dominating a child's behavior.

The concepts of psychosexual stages and of mental structures (id, ego, and superego) have played a major role for years in how psychodynamic therapy is planned and conducted in treating children (e.g., Cangelosi 1993, Coppolillo 1987, Faust 1993, Hammer and Kaplan 1967, Pearson 1968, Wolman 1972). Moreover, the developmental concept of regression and progression in functioning is considered critical. As Gill (1984) pointed out, a major goal of psychodynamic therapy is to facilitate the emergence of developmentally early forms of behaviors transferred from early caregivers to the therapist. If these early forms of behavior are expressed by the patient, the therapist has access to disturbances in the person's development that contribute to his/her present problems.

We should note, however, that some psychodynamically oriented therapists make little mention of these concepts (e.g., Spiegel 1989). Others explicitly reject their utility, as illustrated by R. A. Gardner (1993). In outlining his "psychoanalytically oriented" approach to child psychotherapy, Gardner stated that his method

> is not based on Freud's theory of childhood psychosexual development. In fact, it is not based on any single, particular theory of development. Rather, it is based on specific developmental issues that are appropriate to that particular child at that time . . . there might be children who are having trouble with toilet training and others who are masturbating excessively . . . difficulties in adjusting to new situations, separation fears and so on; and each of these is dealt with some understanding of the developmental norm but without any need to fit the behavioral manifestation into a particular developmental theory. . . . [pp. 250–251]

But Gardner does not provide the reader with a clear picture of how the therapist would consider these various problems in terms of "specific developmental issues," and how each child is dealt with in terms of "some understanding of the developmental norm." While I agree with a number of the points Gardner makes, I do not agree with his conclusion that the child therapist need not fit a child into a particular developmental theory.

Concluding Comment

We have available various developmental concepts that could be useful to a child therapist in considering the wide range of problems that come to his/her attention. Cognitive-behavioral therapists have considered skills that a child must already have to engage in self-instruction training, correspondence training, or some other cognitive-behavioral intervention. Other cognitive-behavioral therapists have turned to Piaget's concept of development, especially the intrinsic unfolding of mental schemas representing cognitive actions on things and people. Psychodynamic therapists have turned to Freud's psychosexual stages, the development of agencies termed *ego*, *id*, *superego*, and *ego ideal*, and the notion that therapy should permit developmentally early forms of behaving to emerge (both overt actions and internal wishes and fantasies) so that disturbances in development can be addressed.

At the start of this discussion I proposed that if a therapist is interested in integrating approaches from both the objectivist and interpretationist positions, a developmental platform would permit him/her from stepping into the quicksand of either approach and would provide the glue for integration. If a child therapist agrees to join me in using a developmental theory as a guide for integrating, where would we find such a theory? Here we seem to reach an impasse. Choosing a developmental theory is complicated, given that the concept of development is a protean one (Kaplan 1959, Nagel 1957, Reese and Overton 1970, Wohlwil 1973). Development is variously taken to refer to growth, achievement of a new response, attainment of an ideal, end state, change occurring over time, or any observation employing children, especially of different ages.

No single, generally accepted theory of psychological development exists. Rather, several schools of development have been stimulating many studies. Each school emphasizes particular questions and classes of behavior, and each offers various concepts to account for observations made. Among these schools are social learning theory; the developmental theory of psychoanalysis; the cognitive-developmental theories of Jean Piaget, Heinz Werner, and Jerome Bruner; the field theory of Kurt Lewin; and the biological systems theory of Ludwig von Bertalanffy.

The child psychotherapist, then, finds that developmental issues, concepts, and research findings do not live in a single house but in many, varied houses. Two houses may claim that an area of development, such as cognition, lives inside, but one is a three-story, rambling structure; the other, a single-story, efficient, ranch-style structure. Although each of these houses claims to be the place in which psychological development lives, when we look inside one we find thinking and cognition, with emotion absent. When we look inside another, we find social learning with unconscious fantasies absent; in still another, we find interpersonal transactions, with cognition and emotion absent. In addition, houses of developmental psychology have also been constructed in terms of chronological age, with the discipline of infant development residing in one, childhood development in another, and adolescent development in another. The field of life-span developmental psychology has emerged during the past decades to counter this compartmentalizing and to emphasize that the same developmental principles can serve the study of behavior from birth to old age (e.g., Baltes and Schaie 1973, Goulet and Baltes 1970).

Because of this state of affairs and, in my view, because an integrative approach to child psychotherapy needs a single model of development, I found it necessary to construct a conceptual scaffold. But which planks, of the many offered by developmental theories in vogue, should go into the scaffold? Which scaffold would address the various issues we have considered and define what a therapist should do to help a child? The framework I have constructed derives from three of the schools mentioned earlier: the developmental theory of psychoanalysis, the cognitive-developmental theory of Piaget, and the organismic-developmental theory of Heinz Werner. In addition, the framework relies on concepts that have emerged from infant research. The next two chapters outline this framework and set the stage for me to illustrate how developmental principles can serve as the glue integrating objectivist and interpretationist concepts and psychodynamic and cognitive-behavioral approaches to child psychotherapy.

Before concluding this chapter and turning to the proposed developmental model, I consider needs that emerge from the issues we have discussed. As I commented at the start of this chapter, I believe these needs should be addressed by any approach to child psychotherapy that attempts to integrate concepts and techniques from multiple viewpoints.

NEEDS TO BE MET BY INTEGRATIVE APPROACHES TO CHILD PSYCHOTHERAPY: A SUMMARY

When the boundaries we considered in Chapter 3 were dissolved, issues emerged, ten of which I selected for discussion in this chapter. These issues in turn give rise to a number of needs that I propose should be addressed by any integrative model of child psychotherapy.

1. *The need for a conceptual model, expressed in terms of a key metaphor, that synthesizes therapeutic concepts and their operational definitions*

When including therapeutic concepts and methods that stem from (sometimes opposing) treatment approaches, the model should take into account how each concept, and the therapeutic technique it defines, affects and is affected by other concepts and techniques included in the model. The model should also be guided by a core metaphor. I have proposed a developmental-dialectical model framed by an embodied-organic metaphor as the glue for integration and as a possible way of addressing the following needs.

2. *The need to include as targets of therapy both outside/surface and inside/deep behaviors*

Outside behaviors include what a person does; for example, a child is hyperactive, hits other children, destroys property, remains withdrawn and shy, shouts epithets at teachers, or repeatedly tells parents he/she is the "worst kid" on the soccer field or the "dumbest" in math. Inside behaviors include what a person imagines; for example, every morning a child shakes her shoes because she is afraid that spiders might be in them; a child regularly fantasizes that he is an astronaut and a member of the Star Trek crew; a child is swamped with anxiety each time he looks at mashed potatoes because the image comes to mind of a squirrel he saw some time ago that had been flattened on the road by a car.

Relying on Figure 4–1, sometimes outside behaviors are the figure and the focus in treatment while inside behaviors are the ground. Sometimes inside behaviors are the figure and the focus of treatment and outside behaviors the ground. While at any moment or phase in treatment either outside or inside behaviors could be the focus of intervention or understanding by the therapist, one does not exist without the other. Outside/surface and inside/deep behaviors should be integrated to form one organization.

To illustrate the need to integrate outside and inside behaviors, consider the following examples. The outside behavior of the hyperactive child noted earlier (hitting other children) should be configured with this child's inside behavior. For example, he revealed in treatment that he anxiously avoided stepping on ants and always left a light on in his closet because of the persistent fantasy that the light prevented a monster from entering his room. Similarly, the inside behavior of the child who feared every morning that spiders might be in her shoes should be configured with her outside behaviors. For example, she acknowledged in treatment that she typically speaks to her mother with a biting tone, enjoys doing so, and realizes it is "something I need to stop, but can't."

3. *The need to design treatment techniques that connect outside/surface with inside/deep behaviors and that interrelate a person's actions, fantasies, and verbalizations*

Treatment techniques should be designed to focus on the manner in which a child regulates his/her body tempos and takes action (surface behaviors) and the meanings given to these experiences (inside behaviors). In other words, therapeutic techniques should be designed to guide the therapist in circling around the outside of the child while other techniques should guide the therapist in entering inside the child. Each technique should include a bridge from outside to inside behaviors, and vice versa, so that the child is engaged holistically rather than in detached pieces. The need for techniques that connect outside and inside behaviors brings with it other related needs.

A. The need to define the relations among different modes of behaving and experiencing and the role these modalities play as a child copes with and adapts to the opportunities, limitations, and prohibitions of changing environments

Concepts and techniques should relate what a child does (overt actions) with what a child imagines (fantasies) and says (overt and covert spoken language).

B. The need to define the relations among various forms of behaving and experiencing within a modality

Concepts and techniques should relate different forms of actions a child might take, different forms of fantasies in which a child might engage, and different forms of verbal expressions a child might speak overtly or covertly.

4. *The need to embed cognition within personality, to operationalize cognition and emotion, and cognitive products and structures, as integrated within one organization that serves a child when coping with changing environments*

Cognitive products are conscious beliefs, verbalized statements, and cognitive activities required in solving cognitive tasks. Cognitive structures are cognitive activities that occur outside of awareness that approach, select, and avoid stimulation, and that organize and give meaning to stimulation. The role that cognitive products and structures play when a child copes with and adapts to changing environments leads to other needs.

A. The need to operationalize how cognition equilibrates (coordinates) stimulation from the environment as construed by the child and from a child's subjective world of emotions, meanings, and fantasies (both in and outside of awareness)

B. The need to operationalize cognition as mobile functions that shift back and forth during the process of equilibrating from organizations that are undifferentiated and less flexible to organizations that are differentiated, integrated, and more flexible

C. The need to define how cognitive activity is motivation and how motivation is cognitive activity, and to operationalize the relation between cognition and emotion so that the equilibrating function of cognition results in a level of emotion that serves adaptation

D. The need to relate the concept of cognitive schemas of information about things and the concept of cognitive representations of motives, emotions, and interactions with others

E. The need to define how cognitive functions (both products and structures) serve to restrain motives and emotions from gaining immediate, direct expression in action

F. The need to define the relation between cognition and mental mechanisms of defense

G. The need to define the connection between cognition (thought) and action

5. *The need to operationalize how meanings are given to experiences and how meanings of early experiences contribute to the construction of meanings assigned to later experiences*

When a child constructs a meaning he/she experiences of some event or interaction, this construction involves an integration of body and mind, of cognition and emotion. Experiencing meaning is holistic and contextual, integrating patterns of sights, sounds, smells, and touch and kinesthetic perceptions, actions, and interactions.

A. The need to define how early bodily experiences result in the first non-verbal meanings, and whether and how these early bodily experiences form the foundation on which later meanings are constructed

B. The need to define how the construction of meaning is embedded in, and requires, interpersonal interaction

C. The need to define how the meanings a child experiences are related to the child's expressions in actions, fantasies, and verbalizations

D. The need to define how experiencing meaning occurs at several levels from embodied nonverbal to conceptual-verbal

6. *The need to operationalize conscious and unconscious processes*

A child may or may not be aware of some activity (e.g., action, thought) he/she is experiencing, nor of the meaning the activity holds for him/her.

A. The need to define whether meanings outside of awareness are already formed, or whether they are constructed in the present

B. The need to define how meanings that are outside of awareness are transferred into awareness

7. *The need to operationalize the environment in terms of a dialectic between child and therapist*

The child and his/her environment should be conceptualized as involved in a dialectical process with each negotiating its expectations from the other. Each influences and is influenced by the other, and each seeks particular stimulation from the other.

A. The need to operationalize how cycles of interaction between the child and others contribute to how a child's behavioral modalities become organized as instruments of adaptation and self-regulation

B. The need to operationalize how cycles of interaction between child and others contribute to how the child and others negotiate ways in which they regulate each other

8. *The need to operationalize psychological conflict as occurring both within the child's subjective world and between the child's subject world and his/her environments*

A child could experience stress, anxiety, and guilt because an action the child wishes to take, or has taken, is opposed by rules the child has internalized and believes he/she should follow. The rules may operate within or outside of awareness. Also, a child could experience stress, anxiety, and guilt because the organization of stimulation with which he/she is coping is not matched with the organization of the child's cognitive-behavioral functions that are attempting to coordinate stimulation with his/her subjective expectations or preferences.

A. The need to define how changes in the intrapsychic and interpersonal domains are related

B. The need to define how conflict can be alleviated by reorganizing and rendering more flexible the child's behavioral modes and modalities

C. The need to define how conflict can be alleviated by reorganizing and rendering more flexible the cognitive functions a child employs when regulating himself/herself

D. The need to define how conflict can be alleviated by reorganizing how a child regulates himself/herself in interactions with others

9. *The need to operationalize how interactions between child and therapist relate to interactions the child has experienced since infancy and how the child–therapist relationship plays a role in the treatment process*

A child interacts with a therapist with behaviors he/she has used, and uses, with others. And a child experiences the therapist both as he/she is and also as the child construes the therapist to be. A therapist interacts with a child with behaviors he/she has used, and uses, with others. The therapist experiences the child both as he/she is, and as the therapist construes the child to be. Child and therapist develop an attachment to each other and together construct a relationship and style of interacting unique to them. The relationship between child and therapist, and their interactions, should be designed to promote change.

A. The need to define and operationalize how the child–therapist relationship enables a child to experience problem behaviors, discover the meanings of these behaviors, and increase the capacity to symbolize these meanings

B. Given the view that the relationship between child and therapist has many of the ingredients that make up the relationship between infant/child and caregiver, the need to operationalize whether and how experiences that a child had as an infant, interacting with others, are related to experiences a child has interacting with others in the present, including the therapist

C. The need to define how child and therapist each construes the other and how they form a relationship that is unique to them

D. The need to define whether the interactions between child and therapist involve something a therapist does to a child or involve constructing a matrix of interpersonal experiences within which child and therapist do something to each other

10. *The need to operationalize what the therapist should do to help a child in addition to verbal labeling and interpretation*

A child verbalizes concerns or comments about his/her daily life, and cognitive-behavioral and psychodynamic therapists typically introduce either forms of training in verbalizing one's thoughts and feelings or verbal interpretations and explanations. But a child also expresses meanings and concerns and communicates about his/her daily life in action and fantasy. In addition to verbalizing, the therapist should make use of enactments.

A. The need to define how the therapist determines the dominant mode the child is using to communicate

B. The need to define whether and when the therapist should verbally interpret meanings or motives a child is presumed to be experiencing, teach a child labels that identify emotions, and teach a child statements a child could use to guide actions

C. The need to define whether and when the therapist should use actions, enactments, and fantasies to promote change

D. The need to define whether and when a therapist should introduce tasks a child is asked to perform, and when a child is permitted to determine and structure activity

E. The need to define whether and how enactments by a therapist in response to the child's enactments are similar to structured tasks

F. The need to define how a therapist determines whether an intervention he/she introduces is experienced by a child as an assault, disrupting the relationship

G. The need to define how disruptions in the relationship are repaired

11. *The need for developmental principles in constructing an integrative approach to child psychotherapy*

The need to define a developmental model that addresses each of the needs outlined above

The next two chapters outline the particular developmental-dialectical model I have constructed to meet the needs outlined above. Following this, I describe treatment cases that illustrate how developmental principles serve as the glue integrating objectivist and interpretationist concepts and psychodynamic and cognitive-behavioral approaches to child psychotherapy.

5

A Developmental Framework for Integrating Child Psychotherapy: The First Two Years of Life

CONTENTS

INTRODUCTION

In Chapter 4 I proposed that developmental principles could address the issues and needs that emerge when boundaries that segregate objectivism/interpretationism, body/mind, and cognition/emotion are dissolved. In this and the next chapter I discuss the developmental model I have constructed to guide concepts and techniques that make up the integrative child psychotherapy proposed in this volume. To introduce the model, I begin with the proposition that psychotherapy is one form of the general process of psychological development. The processes that take place between a child and therapist are fundamentally the same as those that take place between an infant or child and his/her caregiver. This position has been expressed directly by some (e.g., Blatt and Behrends 1987, Kruger 1990) and implied by others (Mahoney 1980, Orlinsky and Howard 1987, Sechrest and Smith 1994, Schneider 1990). In typical development a child and caregiver define a two-person field within which both coauthor a relationship and negotiate whether the child is left free to do whatever he/she chooses, or is asked by the caregiver to manage a task or meet some demand. So, too, in therapy, child and therapist define a two-person matrix within which both coauthor a relationship and negotiate whether the child is left free to wander about the playroom or asked to engage in a task.

Because I view the processes of child therapy the same as those that define child–caregiver experiences, I do not ask, "What knowledge should the therapist provide to a child to help him/her resolve problems and grow psychologically?"— whether that knowledge is self-instruction, social skills training, or insight through explanation and interpretation. Rather, I ask, "How should a troubled child construct knowledge with another person, and continually revise that knowledge, in order to promote psychological growth?" (See Lear 1990 for a similar position.) My response to this question is that, during therapy, child and therapist should engage in a process of dialectical, interactive enactments, following the same principles that define how a child and caregiver interact. Translating this broad proposal into techniques for child psychotherapy, the developmental-dialectical model on which these techniques rely should be discussed first. To facilitate discussion, I have cast the model within a metaphor of a three-story "developmental house," outlined in Table 5–1.

The foundation of this "developmental house" is formed by integrating concepts from three schools of thought: (1) the theory of emotional and ego development that has evolved within the psychodynamic school beginning with Sigmund Freud's formulations, (2) the cognitive-developmental theory of Jean Piaget (e.g.,

TABLE 5–1. A Developmental House: Principles to Guide Integration in Child and Adolescent Psychotherapy

Third Floor	• Guidelines for therapeutic techniques that define how child and therapist negotiate and enact the demands of each other; construct knowledge about the self, each other, and others; and facilitate psychological growth
Second Floor	• Three models of development from age 3 to adolescence: (1) life metaphors that represent past negotiations with developmental issues, construe and give meaning to present stimulation, and prescribe actions; (2) cognitive-behavioral regulators that equilibrate demands from life metaphors and environments; (3) action, fantasy, and language behaviors used to negotiate developmental issues with others in adaptations
Stairway to the Second Floor	• Embodiment-enactment theory: experiences during infancy extend into and influence what a person does, imagines, and says during childhood and adolescence
First Floor	• Principles of development during the first three years of life from the models of Piaget, Stern, Sander, and Beebe and Lachmann
Foundation	• An integration of propositions from the developmental theories of Freud, Piaget, and Werner

Flavell 1963), and (3) the organismic-developmental theory of Heinz Werner (1957, 1964, Werner and Kaplan 1963).

On this foundation rests the first floor, which contains principles that concern psychological development during the first three years of life in three selected areas: (1) how a relational matrix is formed within which a child develops; (2) how infant–caregiver interactions contribute to the infant's knowledge about the self and others, and to meanings an infant gives experiences; and (3) how infant–caregiver interactions contribute to the structuring and organization of an infant's cognitive-behavioral modalities, which serve the infant in regulating himself/herself and in participating in mutual regulations with others. To reach the second floor, we climb a stairway that contains principles of "embodiment-enactment theory" that synthesize several issues contained in the foundation and first floor and introduce concepts we encounter on the second floor.

The second floor, outlined in Chapter 6, contains principles that define how knowledge and meanings, initially constructed during the first two years of life, are extended throughout childhood in what the child does (action mode), imagines (fantasy mode), and says (language mode) when interacting with others and when coping with environmental demands, opportunities, and limitations. The second floor also contains principles that define how a particular set of cognitive functions that regulate and coordinate the demands of stimulation from a child's personal world of wishes, meanings, and motives with those of the environment as construed by the child. With both sets of principles, we consider multidirectional links between intrapsychic and interpersonal development, connecting a child's behaviors and cognitive functioning, with issues we discussed in Chapter 4: surface and deep behaviors, cognition and emotion, conscious and unconscious processes, meaning, conflict, and environment.

The third floor, discussed in Chapter 7, relies on the foundation and the first two floors. Here we find a set of guidelines for therapeutic techniques that define how child and therapist negotiate and enact the demands of the other; construct knowledge about the self, each other, and others; and facilitate psychological growth. In subsequent chapters these guidelines are translated into specific therapeutic techniques illustrated by clinical cases.

From this outline I turn in this chapter to discuss the foundation and first floor, which make up the developmental house I propose for child psychotherapy.

THE FOUNDATION: DEVELOPMENTAL PRINCIPLES INTEGRATING THE CONCEPTS OF SIGMUND FREUD, JEAN PIAGET, AND HEINZ WERNER

As noted in Chapter 4, no single, generally accepted theory of psychological development exists at this time. Therefore, for the foundation of my conceptual model, I have integrated assumptions from the developmental theories of Sigmund Freud, Jean Piaget, and Heinz Werner. Why did I select these particular theories, omitting, for example, social learning theory? More than three decades ago two leading developmental researchers and theorists, D. B. Harris (1957) and A. L. Baldwin (1967), critically evaluated major developmental theories. On the basis of their critiques, they recommended that any developmental model should contain the following ingredients.

1. Conceptualize individuals as active systems, maintaining some degree of integrity, stability, and self-regulation.
2. View change as involving a transition from behaviors that display simple, undifferentiated organizations to behaviors that display more complex, differentiated organizations; these transitions in organization should involve psychological functioning at several levels.
3. Include notions of intrinsic development (i.e., maturation) as well as change due to external stimulation.
4. Account for how new behaviors are acquired for the first time.
5. Include, as equally relevant, overt behavioral acts, thoughts, feelings, fantasies, drives, inhibiting or restraining behaviors, and peremptory as well as voluntary behaviors.

An integration of assumptions from the theories of Freud, Piaget, and Werner produces a set of developmental principles that in my view satisfy these recommendations and serve as a foundation for a developmental model of child psychotherapy. As we review these principles, the reader should notice that each builds upon and elaborates the others, and that together they form a foundation for psychological development. The reader is referred elsewhere (Santostefano 1978, Santostefano and Baker 1972) for a more detailed presentation of these principles and a review of research findings that support them.

The Principle of Holism

Holism requires that the meaning and psychological properties of any behavior (whether a perception, an action, a fantasy, a social interaction, or a spoken statement) should be determined by the total psychological context of which it is a part. From this view, then, two behaviors that are similar in form may be psychologically different if they are embedded in different contexts; for example, a 5-year-old hurls a wooden block while playing in his backyard and another while in his kindergarten classroom. At the same time, two behaviors that are different in form could be psychologically the same if embedded in similar contexts; for example, a 5-year-old kicks the family's pet kitten and also breaks his baby brother's rattle.

The Principle of Psychological Givens and Directiveness of Behavior

This principle brings to our attention that an individual does not experience and react to stimulation passively. Rather, from birth, an individual makes use of innately given behavioral structures or modes of functioning, such as motoric rhythm patterns, sensory thresholds, and emotional and cognitive response styles. These behavioral structures and modes of functioning enable the individual to actively approach, avoid, select, and organize stimulation, and to take action to accomplish some intention and/or to effect change in his/her relationship with the environment.

A fit, or synchrony, is usually guaranteed between a person's innately given behavioral structures and the type, pace, and intensity of stimulation from persons and things. When there is a good fit between a person's innately given behavioral structures and stimulation from others, the person's experiences provide psychological nourishment for the growth of his/her behavioral modes. When stimulation and a person's innately given behavioral structures are inadequately matched, the person's experiences become obstacles to the growth. In an effort to maintain synchrony between self and other, the individual regulates his/her behavioral responses at a pace that ensures coordination and mutuality between his/her evolving psychological structures and ever-changing environmental stimulation. In this way, even in the face of highly variable internal and external conditions, the individual maintains his/her integrity.

The individual's attempt to maintain integrity in the midst of changing stimulation is related to his/her tendency to develop toward relatively mature states under the widest range of conditions. Whenever development occurs, it proceeds in a particular direction: behaviors undergo change from organizations that are relatively global and undifferentiated to organizations that are differentiated, articulated, and hierarchically integrated.

The Principles of Stages of Development, Multiple Behavioral Modes and Goals, and Consistent Individual Differences

The assumption of an inherent course of change, from global to differentiated organizations of behaviors, leads to the proposition that each behavioral mode or system can be ordered along two interrelated continua that define stages of maturity. One continuum concerns the various behavioral modes the individual uses to function. The other continuum concerns the relations between the individual's behavioral modes and the environment.

When functioning at a developmentally early stage, the individual responds using one behavioral mode, and the individual's responses are immediate, requiring physical contact with the environment. Gradually the individual differentiates from the environment and functions with several differentiated modes that are capable of operating in contact with, or in the absence of, related environmental stimulation.

Piaget's model (discussed in previous chapters) provides one illustration. The infant initially gathers information about the texture of an object by mouthing and touching it (sensorimotor mode, defining a sensory motor stage). With development, the infant constructs mental schemas representing these physical actions and experiences. Now the child can determine the texture of some object by surveying it from a distance (perceptual mode, defining a perceptual stage) as well as by touching it.

As another illustration, I have proposed a developmental model of modes of expression that is discussed in detail in the next chapter. A young child may express aggressive feelings by kicking the pet kitten (action mode, defining an action stage). With development, the child constructs mental schemas representing such actions (fantasy mode, defining a fantasy stage). Now the child expresses aggression either directly with the action mode (e.g., engages a class bully in a fight) or less directly within the fantasy mode (e.g., entertains the fantasy of beating on the class bully in a fight). Still later, the child shouts at a class bully (language mode, defining a language stage). But in particular circumstances, this older child could also make use of actions and fantasies, having available multiple modes and alternative means to express aggressive intentions.

Progressing from one stage in a sequence to the next one results in the individual's having available multiple means to achieve the same goal. A child may either imagine his/her baby brother being frightened by a monster or perform some action to frighten the infant. Similarly, progressing from one stage to another results in multiple goals that can be used to serve the same mode of behaving. For example, when frustrated by mother, a child may use the fantasy mode and imagine retaliating against an older sister who is construed as a substitute for mother; when lonely in mother's absence, a child could use the fantasy mode to imagine receiving affection from a teacher. The availability of multiple modes and alternative goals frees the individual from the demands of the immediate situation so that behaviors may be expressed in more delayed, planned, indirect, organized, stage-appropriate ways. In addition, a child is able to discover alternative ways of behaving that acknowledge opportunities and limitations in the environment while permitting successful adaptation.

The developmental status of a stage of functioning (early versus advanced) is assessed in terms of several interrelated factors: (1) whether the organization of the behavior in question is global or differentiated; (2) the range of behavioral levels available to the individual, whether as a consequence of his/her developmental history or the context or situation currently influencing his psychological state; and (3) environmental circumstances, limits, opportunities, and expectations. For example, a 10-year-old child who has been confined for several years to a hospital bed has had limited opportunity to engage in, cultivate, and differentiate the action mode. Therefore, this child could exhibit a range of action behaviors that is narrower and more global than that exhibited by a 5-year-old. In another example, a 5-year-old who exhibits a narrow range of global fantasies typical of young children does not reflect a developmental lag, or regression, in terms of the development of the fantasy mode. But an adolescent who exhibits the same organization of global fantasies would be viewed as displaying a lag in the development of the fantasy mode, or a regression to an earlier stage.

The principle of differentiating behavioral modes, when combined with the principle of psychological givens and holism, defines the proposition that individuals display consistent differences from birth throughout the life span. For example, as a group, infants of one age sustain attention longer than a younger comparison group on a sixty-four-square checkerboard. But if we examine the attention span of each infant in the older group, we find individual differences, with one infant sustaining attention longer than another. As the behavioral mode of visual attention differentiates, the initial difference between the two infants persists. This difference has relevance not only for the rate of development of attention, but also for the relationship between attending and other behavioral modes.

Last, the principles of differentiating behavioral modes and goals, and stages of development, carry the assumption that early forms of functioning are not replaced by new, differentiated behaviors. Rather, early behaviors become subordinated by later developing forms and hierarchically integrated within them. Although subordinated, these early forms of behaving remain potentially active. For example, for many weeks a fifth grader had been appropriately controlled in the classroom and focused on academic tasks. Then his teacher, with whom he had a strong attachment, became ill, and a substitute teacher replaced her. In this context the boy became hyperactive and defiant, behaviors he had not shown since the first grade.

The Principle of Mobility of Behavioral Functions and of Developmental Stages

That subordinated behaviors have the potential to become active relates to the principle of mobility of behavioral functions and stages; that is, regression and progression of behavioral systems. As noted above, at any given stage of development the individual typically has available a range of behaviors representing different levels of some hierarchy. When operating at a developmentally early stage, the individual is characterized by a narrow, less flexible hierarchy of behaviors. The individual does not shift easily from one behavior or level in the hierarchy to another in response to changes in stimulation, opportunities, and limitations.

In contrast, the individual operating at a developmentally later stage is characterized by a broader, more flexible hierarchy of behaviors. Now the individual's functioning shifts easily, sometimes operating at a level characteristic of earlier development (regressing) and at other times operating at a more advanced level in response to changes in stimulation, opportunities, and limitations.

From this viewpoint, when a fourth grader gets up from his seat, interrupts his/her desk work, leaves the classroom, and enters the playground during recess, he/she "regresses" to the action mode, running, pushing, and wrestling in a vigorous game of King of the Mountain. Upon returning to the classroom, the same child shifts "progressively" to modes of functioning characteristic of higher levels of development. Now motility and expressions in action are delayed and subordinated, and thinking and fantasizing dominate as he/she completes a page in a workbook.

Progressive or regressive shifts from one level to another are presumed to result in a good fit between the individual's adaptive intentions and needs (both emotional and cognitive) on the one hand and the opportunities, limitations, and expectations presented by the environment on the other. Shifting among levels of functioning in order to maintain a good fit with environmental changes is presumed to foster development and ensure adaptive success.

The Principle of Motivating Forces and Regulating Structures

Long-range and short-range motivating forces stimulate the individual to make use of innately given, motoric, perceptual, cognitive, and emotional functions. These forces are goal directed and require particular qualities, types, tempos, and degrees of stimulation.

Long-range forces correspond to representations of instinctual drives or embodied experiences. The reader is referred to the previous chapter for a discussion of the concept of instinctual drives as representations of interactions that are experienced either as connecting (bonding) or disconnecting (aggression) with others and things. Two characteristics of long-range motivating forces should be underlined. With one, drive representations continually push for immediate expression in action. With the other, drive representations are inherently coordinated with and directed toward particular persons, objects, and interactions. As behavioral modes maturate and as the child accumulates experiences (with maturation and experience influencing each other), the ways in which long-range forces are expressed behaviorally are gradually shaped and modified.

As behavioral modes maturate and as experience is accumulated, psychological structures that regulate and restrain long-range forces also develop. Here the reader is referred to the previous chapter for a discussion of various mental mechanisms that restrain and regulate representations of love and aggression that push for immediate action. Long-range forces are usually regulated by substituting one goal for another and by making use of alternative modes of behaving whenever the sought-for object or preferred mode of expression is prohibited or unavailable because of intrapsychic or environmental circumstances.

Consider, for example, a 3-year-old longing to be cuddled by mother, who is away on a trip. This toddler may cuddle mother's wool sweater, which mother gave him/her upon her departure. The sweater is an alternative goal that substitutes for mother's body, permitting the toddler to continue expressing, in the action mode, the representation of the instinctual drive of affection. At age 6 years, with the fantasy mode more differentiated, the child does not resort to action, but mentally constructs and entertains a scene, imagining mother's return and caress. Regulating mechanisms, then, block, delay, modify, or redirect the representations of long-range forces, enabling the individual to coordinate various forms of behavioral expression with changes created by the environment.

Short-range motivating forces include, for example, curiosity and the need for change and complexity. These forces emerge when the individual's cognition undergoes differentiation as new experiences are assimilated. The psychodynamic concept of stimulus nutriment (Rapaport, cited in Gill 1967) and Piaget's concept of alimentation (Flavell 1963, Wolff 1960) are examples of short-range motivating forces. The concept of alimentation proposes that the individual must "nourish" his/her cognitive schemas or structures by repeatedly assimilating environmental "nutriments" that sustain them. As we discussed previously, Piaget conceptualized that cognition becomes increasingly structured and differentiated whenever existing schemas are in a state of moderate disequilibrium with existing stimulation because the complexity of the stimulation is slightly greater than that of the schema. This state of disequilibrium motivates cognition, so to speak, to repeatedly assimilate the more complex information and gradually accommodate (reorganize) the schema to fit the complexity of the stimulation. This whole process is repeated when the restructured schema again reaches for information that is more complex. In normal cognitive development, then, cognitive structures are motivated to seek a level of complexity of information that is only slightly greater than the complexity of the organization of existing schemas. To address abnormal or derailed cognitive development that patients typically present, Rappaport elaborated Piaget's concept of "alimentation." He proposed that cognitive structures may remain fixed in their organization, or may lag in assimilating and differentiating, when they become part of an organized mental defense or coping strategy. In these cases the "nourishment" a cognitive structure seeks concerns avoiding or minimizing stress and therefore the cognitive structure avoids particular stimulation rather than assimilating it.

Unlike long-range forces, short-term forces, then, are not inherently coordinated with particular interactions with persons or things. Rather, short-term forces are coordinated with organizations of information in the environment and in a person's subjective world. Short-term forces seek and avoid particular organizations, qualities, degrees, and tempos of stimulation, and are motivated to maintain a state of equilibration between cognitive structures and information contained in the environment and a person's subjective world.

The principles we have considered thus far converge on the adaptive process.

The Principle of Adaptation

The adaptive process involves a reciprocal-dialectical relationship between the individual and his/her environment (e.g., parent, teacher, peer). Each defines the other and each is defined by the other as poles on a continuum that inherently forms a paradox, or difference, concerning the intentions of each. To deal with this paradox, the person and the environment negotiate with and attempt to influence the other in continuous cycles of interaction in order to achieve a mutually agreed upon degree of coordination. The individual acts upon the environment, making use of an evolving series of average and expectable behavioral organizations (perceptions, cognitions, actions, fantasies, spoken words) that more or less match environmental expectations and opportunities. At the same time, the environment acts upon the individual through a continuous, evolving series of average-expectable organizations of stimulation and demands that more or less fit the behavioral modes available to the individual. In this dialectic, then, the individual has available behavioral modes that are preadapted to handle confrontations from the environment, while the environment usually provides opportunities and makes demands that suit the individual's stage of development.

Demands and stimulation from the individual and the environment are never perfectly matched, however. In adapting to these mismatches, the individual shifts from a more recently acquired level of responding to earlier levels, or evolves a new differentiated mode, such as thought in place of action (the principle of mobility of functions). Consider, for example, a 4-year-old who enters a preschool class-room for the first time, an environment that requires him to share and wait more than he does at home. At first the child responds to this change, and the frustra-tion it arouses, by regressing to a form of behavior he used earlier, withdrawing to a corner of the room. Gradually, as the child negotiates with the teacher, learning her limits and expectations, he transforms his withdrawn behavior into helping the teacher distribute crayons.

Although the adaptive process occurs continuously, at certain critical periods within the life span particular behavioral systems are especially ready to deal with and assimilate particular classes of stimulation. If the critical experience is not made available, the behavioral system assumes a deviant line of growth. Considering the 4-year-old again, if the teacher is not active and creative in engaging the child to join the group, the child's use of detaching and withdrawing may persist as a way to manage any demand or prohibition.

Last, the individual and the environment, in their dialectical process, deter-mine which behaviors and stimulation are adaptive. One individual may experi-ence a particular context as average and expectable; for example, an inner-city child and a rural child each playing in his/her community. But if the inner-city child is suddenly transferred to a rural street and the suburban child to an inner-city street, each would experience stimulation that is not average and expectable for him/her, and the behavior each child displays could be viewed as a developmental failure. Thus behavior viewed as adaptive in one situation may be viewed as a develop-mental failure when resorted to by the same individual in other contexts.

Comment

These principles that make up the foundation of the developmental house I pro-pose do not play a significant role in current approaches to treatment with chil-dren except for psychodynamic therapies in which one or another principle could be found. There are exceptions, and one is represented by Brems's (1993) volume. I compare the proposed foundation of development with this volume for two rea-sons. Brems also outlined an integrative approach to psychotherapy with children, and the author gave special attention to the importance of development. However, a comparison helps articulate what I mean by development and dialectics as a guide for child psychotherapy.

In terms of her commitment to integration, Brems noted, "The book's most outstanding feature is its diversity in presenting techniques. It represents an attempt at integrating interpersonal, systemic-psychodynamic case conceptualization with numerous techniques, including behavioral strategies, art, storytelling and parent education" (p. xii).

Brems's goal, then, is very much the same as the intention of this volume: integrating psychodynamic and cognitive-behavioral concepts and methods. In addition to this similarity, Brems devoted a chapter to "a developmental context for child psychotherapy," pointing out that "no discussion of children can be complete without giving some thought to development" (p. 45). Acknowledging that "there are several models of development," Brems selected one that she termed "dialectic." "Only one [model] is comprehensive in its look at the interaction between the individual and the environment . . . development occurs and is not only guided by physical or biological factors that occur within the individual, but also impacted by psychological, cultural, and external factors" (p. 46). To illustrate, Brems pointed out that a 3-year-old child, referred because of aggressive behavior, may not be displaying a "normal" struggle with autonomy. Rather, the child may be displaying aggressive behavior because of the death of a parent (psychological factor), frequent severe headaches (biological factor), or having survived a recent earthquake (outer physical factors) (p. 46).

Although this view of development is termed "dialectic" by Brems, her definition does not correspond with that offered in this volume and by others (e.g., Overton 1994). In the example provided by Brems, the environment (an earthquake, death of a parent) or biology (headaches) act upon the child. If we call upon our discussion of the adaptive process, a number of issues are missing in Brems's example: the meaning the child gives to these happenings, how these events define the child, and how the child and these environmental factors negotiate the paradox that exists between them. Referring to other principles in our foundation, if the child was referred because a parent died, for example, attention would be given to the content and organization of the child's fantasies about the death, statements about the death, and aggressive behavior; how these modalities approach, avoid, and select stimulation from this event; and whether the child's aggressive behavior remains inflexible, appearing in all contexts, or shifts flexibly, appearing at his/her home but not at the home of relatives. Of particular importance, these principles would pay attention to how the remaining parent and relatives define the child in terms of the loss, and what expectations they present to the child and how the child defines the remaining parent and relatives in terms of the loss and what expectations he/she presents to them.

Brems's discussion provides me with another opportunity to emphasize an aspect of my developmental model that forms a bridge to the next floor, namely, the relation between the first three years of life and childhood. In a section titled "Development Made Relevant to the Child Therapist," Brems provided excellent summaries of several models of infant and childhood development, and proposed that "to be able to appreciate the developmental needs and milestones of the children he/she treats, the responsible child therapist must have familiarity with all these developmental models . . ." (p. 48). However, Brems does not offer an integration of these models that could guide what a therapist should do. Moreover, she does not connect developments during the first years of life with those that occur later that have relevance for psychotherapy integration. Instead, segueing from a discussion of infant development, she discusses development in 4- and 5-year-old children and children in middle childhood (6–10 years old) as a separate topic, apparently because psychotherapists typically do not treat infants and toddlers. "Infants are never, and toddlers are rarely, seen in psychotherapy. Hence, while infants and toddlers are fascinating human beings, here descriptions will be provided only for healthy 4- and 5-year-olds" (p. 57).

I take a very different approach. In the next section, I describe principles of development during the first two years of life that derive from the foundation we have just considered. In addition, in Chapter 6, I take these principles of infant development and extend them into childhood. In Chapter 7 an integration of developments during infancy and childhood is translated into guidelines for treatment. With this integration I hope to illustrate the proposition offered earlier, that processes that take place between infant and caregiver are the same as those that take place between a child and therapist, and that what an infant experiences influences what that individual does, imagines, and says later in childhood. To illustrate the latter, the present chapter closes with a discussion of a 16-year-old boy whose presenting difficulties originated in the first two years of life.

At this point we leave the foundation and climb to the first floor where we begin at the beginning and consider how knowledge is constructed about the self, others, and experiences during the first two years of life.

THE FIRST FLOOR: HOW KNOWLEDGE ABOUT SELF, OTHERS, AND EXPERIENCES IS CONSTRUCTED DURING THE FIRST TWO YEARS OF LIFE AND HOW COGNITIVE-BEHAVIORAL MODALITIES ARE FIRST ORGANIZED

Following the pioneering research of Piaget, investigators of infant behavior and infant–caregiver interactions—many influenced by psychodynamic views —gathered observations and formulated concepts that articulate how an infant constructs knowledge about himself/herself and others and gives meaning to experiences with things and other persons, whether the infant is touching and experiencing the fringe of a pillow or mother's hair. These investigators have taken the position that knowledge an infant constructs and the reality with which the infant negotiates are shaped by the infant's representational activity so that an infant's subjective world and her/his environment become one, integrating the infant's cognitive, emotional, and physical activity. What the child knows, does, and feels is what the child represents. This position is in agreement with Bohart's (1993) proposal, discussed in the previous chapter, that the construction of knowledge and meaning is embedded within all experiencing and knowing, and occurs at various levels from embodied nonverbal to conceptual verbal experiences.

With these introductory remarks we come to a question of central importance to child therapy. How are knowledge and meanings constructed in the first two years of life? If we accept the principle located in the foundation of our model, that early behaviors are not replaced by later behaviors but become integrated within them, then the ways in which a child constructs knowledge and meanings during treatment have their roots in the first years of life. Since a child therapist typically works with children between the ages of about 4 years to adolescence, we need to conceptualize how meanings constructed in the first years of life are extended and assimilated into meanings and behaviors that emerge after the age of 3 years.

To address this need, I draw upon formulations of five infant investigators. Each brings into focus a particular set of considerations that, when integrated, provide a view that is particularly useful in designing the process of child psychotherapy from an integrative perspective: (1) Piaget's stages of cognitive development that define how knowledge about things is constructed; (2) Stern's (1985) concepts that build upon and extend Piaget's, focusing on the construction of knowledge and meaning about the self and other persons; (3) Sander's (e.g., 1962, 1964, 1976, 1987, 1989) model of interpersonal issues caregiver and infant "negotiate"; and (4) Beebe and Lachmann's (1994) proposals that provide a way of integrating Piaget, Stern, and Sander. As each of these models is discussed, the reader may find Table 5–2 helpful in relating the contributions of each with those of the others.

Piaget's Model of the First Two Years of Life

Piaget's studies of cognitive development focused for the most part on how knowledge about things is acquired and how an infant and child construct and reconstruct his/her understanding of the environment. As discussed in previous chapters, he proposed that cognitive development follows four stages from birth through adolescence: the sensorimotor stage (0–2 years), the preoperational stage (2–7 years), the stage of concrete operations (7–11 years), and the stage of formal operations (11–15 years). Here we take a closer look at the sensorimotor period.

Piaget proposed that the processes involved in constructing knowledge at the dawn of human life define six interrelated stages. In Stage I (0–1 months) the infant experiences a variety of bodily sensations (e.g., sucking, tongue movements, tactile perceptions, gross body movements, sounds) when contacting his/her own body and the environment. Although these experiences are uncoordinated, they gradually shift from being mere reflexes to becoming "acquired adaptations." As

TABLE 5–2. Models of Development in the First Two Years of Life

PIAGET		STERN		SANDER	
Months	Cognitive Development	Months	Self-Development	Months	Infant (I)–Mother (M) Negotiations
(0–1)	Acquired adaptation	(0–2)	Emergent self: relate diverse experiences (emotions, bodily events) in interactions with caregiver and things	(0–3)	Initial adaptation: I's cues and M's activity become coordinated
				(3–6)	Reciprocal exchange: organizing crescendos of emotion/behavioral exchanges
(2–4)	Primary circular reactions: rhythmic cycles of activity coordinating schemas (experiences) with different modalities	(2–7)	Core self: construct first representations of interaction that summarize and conserve repeated experiences with others including constellations of actions, sensations, and emotions	(6–9)	Early directed activity: I actively controls stimulation and anticipates some response; M accommodates by remaining passive and/or responding to direction
(4–8)	Secondary circular reactions: provoking responses from the environment and making interesting sights last			(9–15)	Focalization: I's directions to M more differentiated in having needs met, including protection from danger; I explores unknown; M unconditionally available
(8–12)	Coordinate secondary circular reactions: imitate action of others			(12–20)	Self-assertion: with newly formed autonomy, I asserts self in opposition to M; M gives permission and sets limits
(12–18)	Tertiary circular reactions: discovering new ways of accomplishing goals, performing actions that become play rituals	(7–14)	Subjective self: sense and understand motives and intentions of others that lie behind and guide physical actions	(18–24)	Testing aggression: I's assertions become explicitly aggressive behaviors; I attempts to "make up"; M punishes, permits, and provides alternatives
(18–24)	Experimenting with mental representations of things: imitate persons that are absent—deferred imitation	(15–24)	Verbal self: symbols shared in language as well as actions, facilitated by deferred imitation	(12–24)	Inventing symbolic behaviors that are shared: in sharing and inventing symbols, I and M increase their understanding of other's intentions and of alternatives available for mutual regulation
				(0–24)	Consolidate body image

these acquired adaptations are repeated, they result in the beginnings of mental schemas, or mental representations of bodily experiences.

In Stage II (1–4 months) reflexes that occurred during the first month of life are elaborated in what Piaget termed "primary circular reactions." Now the infant engages in activity that coordinates schemas representing experiences with different modalities (e.g., vision and touch, sound and touch, vision and sound, one body sensation and another). The infant sucks his/her thumb, not because of chance contact, but through coordinating hand and mouth, a coordination that relies upon schemas that derived from previous experiences with each of these body parts. The infant repeats a given activity over and over again in rhythmic cycles, hence the term "primary circular reactions."

During Stage III (4–8 months), in contrast to primary circular reactions of the previous stage, which involve the infant's own bodily activity, the infant engages in secondary circular reactions and is concerned with consequences in the environment that result from his/her activity. Secondary circular reactions involve behaviors the infant repeats in order, as Piaget put it, to "make interesting sights last." The infant repeats behaviors in order to sustain contact with an environment that in some way, or for some reason, has appeal for the infant. As these repetitive behaviors are attempts to maintain interesting contacts with the environment, the infant begins to be oriented outward, that is, beyond the self. For example, the infant deliberately imitates a sound or movement performed by another so that the other person will continue to make the sound or movement, participating in a cycle of interactions. It is during this stage that the infant begins to show that he/she experiences "intentions."

In Stage IV (8–12 months) secondary circular reactions and the mental schemas that result from them, are coordinated to form a new totality that deals with new situations. For example, the infant sets aside an obstacle (e.g., a sheet of cardboard) in order to reach a desired object (e.g., a rattle) and does so repeatedly, frequently with laughter. Moreover, because the schemas of secondary circular reactions are now coordinated, when in the previous stage they operated independently, the infant is able to imitate actions of others with behaviors that are structurally analogous rather than identical. For example, when Piaget opened and closed his eyes, the infant first opened and closed his hands, and then his mouth.

In Stage V (12–18 months) two particularly significant developments occur. First, secondary circular reactions of Stage IV give rise to "tertiary circular reactions." With this term Piaget distinguished repetitive behaviors the infant uses to experiment actively with the environment in order to discover new ways of accomplishing goals. For example, to obtain a toy placed under a blanket, the infant repeatedly explores different ways to pull the blanket away. In the second significant development of this stage, as new adaptations are discovered through trial and error exploration, the infant transforms the behavior of a tertiary circular reaction into a play ritual. Piaget described his infant daughter who one day pressed her nose against her mother's cheek, forcing the infant to breathe much more loudly.

"This phenomenon at once interested her . . . she drew her nose back . . . sniffed and breathed very hard (as if she was blowing her nose) then again thrust her nose against her mother's cheek, laughing heartily" (Piaget, cited in Flavell 1963, p. 128). Piaget reported that the infant repeated these actions at least once a day for more than a month "as a ritual."

In the last (VI) phase (18–24 months) the infant continues to discover and invent new ways of accomplishing things. Unlike the previous stage, however, the infant relies more on mental experimentations rather than on trial and error actions. Therefore, the infant is now able to acquire new knowledge prior to taking action. For example, a carriage is set against the wall. Instead of tugging and pushing in trial and error experimentation, the toddler looks over the situation, walks to the other side, and pushes the carriage away from the wall. As schemas are combined mentally, without being accompanied by experimental actions, another important development occurs that distinguishes this stage. The infant shows the capacity for what Piaget termed "deferred imitation." Here, when an important person or thing is absent, the toddler reproduces the person or thing in some way and shows that he/she is capable of true pretending or make-believe. In other words, as discussed in the previous chapter (see section on Meaning), the child is now symbolizing by transferring properties from one object to another. For example, upon observing mother put on a hat and leave the room, the toddler places a napkin on his/her head, pretending it is a hat.

Stern's Model of the First Two Years of Life

Stern's model elaborates and extends Piaget's because the concepts he introduced emphasize the role of emotions and interpersonal interactions in the construction of knowledge and meaning and how an infant develops a sense of self. Stern began with the principle of holism, which makes up part of our foundation. The infant's experiences with things and persons are unified wholes that include sensations, perceptions, actions, cognitions, "categorical emotions" (such as anger and joy), and "vitality affects" (such as surging, exploding, and fading). For Stern there are no perceptions, cognitions, or actions without accompanying emotions, and emotions do not occur without a context of perceptions, cognition, and actions.

Of particular importance to my topic, Stern also proposed that all knowledge and meanings are constructed within subjective experiences that always involve other persons and may involve inanimate things. Instead of using one of Stern's examples to illustrate this proposal, it might be interesting to consider one of Piaget's observations of his 2-month-old child, which he offered to illustrate the characteristics of primary circular reactions (see above).

"[The infant] scratches and tries to grasp, lets go, scratches and grasps again . . . this can only be observed during feeding time when the infant gently scratches his mother's bare shoulder. [Then, a few days later] the behavior becomes marked in the cradle itself. [The infant] scratches the sheet; then grasps it and holds it a moment, then lets it go, scratches it again, and repeats the cycle without interruption. This play lasts a quarter of an hour at a time, several times during the day. [Now Piaget places his fist against the palm of the infant's right hand.] . . . [The infant] scratches and grasps my fist. He even succeeds in discriminating my bent middle finger, grasping it separately and holding it a few moments. . . . [In the next few days] I note how definitely the spontaneous grasping of the sheet reveals the characteristics of circular reaction—groping at first, then regular rhythmical activity, scratching, grasping, holding and letting go, and finally progressive loss of interest." [Piaget, cited in Flavell 1963, pp. 93–94]

In this observation Piaget focused on the infant's rhythmic grasping, holding, and letting go of a bed sheet. Stern would focus on the infant's rhythmic scratching of mother's shoulder and the rhythmic grasping of father's fist and finger as well as the rhythmic scratching and grasping of the bed sheet. Stern would also emphasize the emotions involved during these moments; for example, that the infant's interest and emotions surged as he grasped the shoulder and sheet, and then faded when he let go.

As these elements are repeatedly experienced, they give rise to knowledge and meaning about the self and others as well as about the texture of things. At the center of Stern's model, then, is the proposition that all knowledge is constructed within an interpersonal context, resulting in a sense of self and others. Applying this proposition to Piaget's observation, as the infant constructed knowledge about the bed sheet he also constructed knowledge about himself and others as he engaged mother's shoulder and father's fist and finger, and as he experienced the *emotional tones* accompanying the availability of these body parts. It is interesting to note that in a publication later in his career, Piaget (1973) suggested he had come to the same point of view; namely, that early cognitive development is embedded in interpersonal experiences. "I also suggested . . . that the first object endowed with permanence was another person, and not an indifferent inanimate object" (p. 260).

As experiences with persons and things are repeated, how are their elements integrated and conserved over the course of many self–other transactions? Here Stern introduced the concept of "Representations of Interactions [that have] Generalized" (RIGs). Whenever the infant repeatedly experiences constellations of sensations, perceptions, emotions, and actions that differ in only minor ways, the infant gradually constructs a generalized memory, an abstraction or prototype, of these many experiences. Any given generalized memory prescribes what the infant expects and how the infant performs. The construction of RIGs, then, is the process by which the self who acts upon the self and others, the self who experiences emotions, and the self who perceives one's body and actions all become integrated during the first two years of life. Stern noted that the process of constructing RIGs elaborates the psychoanalytic notion of body-ego. Also, the concept of RIGs includes, but involves more than, the process Piaget conceptualized in the construction of sensorimotor schemas, because with the construction of RIGs, emotions and interpersonal experiences are an integral part of each representation or schema.

What happens when an experience occurs that is similar but not identical to previously repeated experiences? In this case, elements of the ongoing experience activate an already established RIG, that is, a memory that Stern terms *evoked companion*. Evoked companions operate during transactions with another. As an example of the former, consider a mother who plays peek-a-boo in a different way because she is now depressed. In response, the infant uses the evoked companion from an already established RIG, representing previous peek-a-boo episodes with mother, as a standard against which to check whether mother's current emotional tone is a variation of the past or an entirely new type of self–other experience. If this new type of self–other experience is repeated and endures, a new RIG is constructed by the infant.

Evoked companions also operate when the infant is alone. As an example, consider a toddler who, while alone, stacks one block on another, bursting with exuberance. The child's exuberance is due not only to experiencing success with objects, but also relates to the evoked memory of stacking blocks while an enthusiastic caregiver cheered. As the reader may notice, the concept of evoked companion is similar to Piaget's concept of "deferred imitation." However, Piaget proposed that deferred imitation emerges at about 18 months. Stern has argued that the process unfolds beginning at 3 months, when infants show the capacity to use evoked recalls to evaluate experiences.

Last, the phenomena of RIGs and evoked companions are seen as the major processes that result in the emergence of four "senses of self" during the first two years of life. Stern proposed that each of the following senses of self builds on the previous one, and organizes experiences in a new way.

Emergent self (0–2 months). The sense of an emergent self develops during the first two months of life. The infant relates diverse experiences in interaction with caregivers and things that result in emotions, sensorimotor events, and the first global meanings.

Core self. From 2 to 7 months a core self emerges as the infant constructs the first RIGs. RIGs, mental schemas that summarize and conserve repeated experiences with persons and things, include constellations of sensations, sensorimotor actions, and emotional tones. The infant is now more equipped to anticipate what should be expected in interactions with others and whether a given experience is the same or different from previous ones. Furthermore, the infant begins to sense that he/she and the caregiver are separate physically, are different agents, and have different emotional experiences.

Subjective self. From 7 to 14 months a subjective self emerges. Now, for the infant, self and others are defined by more than the physical presence of infant and caregiver, each sharing actions and emotions. This new sense of self includes subjective mental states. That is, the infant senses and understands the motives and intentions that lie behind and guide physical happenings.

Verbal self. Beginning at about 15 months a sense of verbal self emerges. Now interactions between infant and caregiver are organized by the perspective that each of them contains personal knowledge that, in addition to action symbols, is expressed and shared in language symbols.

Sander's Model of Mother–Infant Negotiations during the First Two Years of Life

Sander's model elaborates the contributions of Piaget and Stern by the interactions that take place between infant and caregiver. On the basis of longitudinal observations of mother–infant interactions, Sander proposed that infant and mother are involved in a continuous and active process of give and take, with each attempting to influence and accommodate to the other in mutual adaptations. He conceptualized this process of give and take as mother and infant "negotiating" particular "issues." These negotiations contribute to the organization and development of the infant's cognition, motility style, expressions of emotions, and style of seeking, engaging, and avoiding caregivers. Mother and infant negotiate nine issues, each overlapping the previous one, and the degree of success in negotiating one issue influences the success with which the next issue is negotiated. Parenthetically, while Sander defined these negotiations in terms of infant and mother, other persons (e.g., father, aunt, grandmother, nanny) who are significantly involved in the infant's care would of course be viewed as partners in these negotiations.

Issue #1: 0–3 Months—Period of Initial Adaptation

During the first stage, mother and infant fit (coordinate) mothering activities with cues the baby gives of his/her states, indicating what is necessary for him/her to thrive. The infant presents behaviors—states of alert inactivity, various cries, smiling, fussing, being content. The mother also presents behaviors—accuracy in reading the baby's cues, type and timing of stimulation she provides (rapid, delayed, consistent) when feeding and bathing the infant. The infant's behaviors influence and also assimilate and accommodate to mother's behaviors. Likewise, the mother's behaviors influence and also assimilate and accommodate to the baby's behaviors.

Whether infant and mother successfully negotiate this first issue is reflected by the degree to which the infant has developed a predictable, organized rhythm of feeding, eliminating, sleeping, and wakefulness. In addition, the infant begins to respond to mother in a discriminating way, quieting for her more readily than for others. In terms of mother's behavior, success with this first issue is reflected by her developing the subjective sense that she is intimately aware of her baby's behavior and feels she "knows" her child. Of particular importance, success with this issue depends upon the balance mother can maintain between her empathy with the infant's needs and her objectivity. Success also depends upon whether mother can view her infant as an individual apart from projections of her own needs.

Issue #2: 3–6 Months—Period of Establishing Reciprocal Exchange

The issue negotiated in the second stage concerns the extent to which interactions between mother and infant include back-and-forth, active-passive alternations of behaviors exchanged between them. Sander gave special importance to exchanges that take place around the infant's rapidly developing smiling response. Mother smiles and then pauses, allowing the baby to respond. Then mother moves her smiling face closer to the baby and pauses again, waiting for the infant to react. Then mother makes another presentation, now with a new stimulus added, a touch, a vocalization. Throughout this back-and-forth process the infant gradually elaborates his/her response, beginning with a localized smile, then including arms, legs, trunk, and voice in exuberant, wiggling, infectious, joyful play. The quality, crescendo, and organization occurring during this reciprocal activity is crucial. Similar reciprocal exchanges occur during feeding, changing, and other childcare activities. An important related issue is the extent to which mother can allow the child to play or to pursue some solo activity.

Issue #3: 6–9 Months—Period of Early Directed Behavior

To this point the interactions between mother and infant are largely due to mother's initiative. During this period, the baby begins to use smiling to initiate and direct social contact with mother. The manner in which mother responds to the baby's initiative forms the basis for the negotiation of the third issue. Several behavioral dimensions now become important. The infant experiences qualities of intention and anticipation. The infant intends to engage a person and some form of stimulation, and anticipates in turn some response and stimulation. Further, in initiating and directing, the baby begins to show preferences for stimulation, attempting to actively control or avoid stimulation that is approaching as well as stimulation that is disappearing. In the realm of social activity, these qualities are seen in the well-known stranger anxiety that appears during this stage. In crying and fussing when a stranger appears, the baby is attempting to control and direct stimulation.

At the same time, the infant is directing and selecting behaviors when engaging inanimate objects. The infant is now more active in reaching out to manipulate and avoid physical objects around him/her. The major accommodation required of mother during this period is that she remain more passive than was required of her during the first two periods. Mother should honor the infant's directions and preferences for particular social exchanges and for objects that she removes or brings within the infant's reach.

Issue #4: 9–15 Months—Period of Focalization

During this period, the infant's directed activity becomes increasingly more differentiated so that more explicit cues are sent to mother for responses. Now the baby focuses mother on his/her person as someone who can fulfill needs. The infant is now negotiating unconditional availability of mother, one of the important ingredients in the infant's developing autonomy.

As the child becomes physically more mobile, exploring larger space, he/she also sends more differentiated cues to mother that concern the need to be protected from stressful stimulation and danger as well as the need to enter the unknown. Mother's responses may require that she physically contact the child or that she give only her attention and awareness. Above all, mother should maintain her own integrity as she permits and enjoys her infant possessing her. If mother can provide this degree of focalization while still maintaining the reciprocity negotiated earlier, she makes available a stable base from which the child can move away from her and explore increasingly larger geographies with competence and curiosity. Sander proposed that the infant needs to successfully negotiate focalization, and needs to be guaranteed the total availability of mother as a base of operation, so as to begin asserting himself/herself against mother and the larger environment, a process that takes place in the next period.

Issue #5: 12–20 Months—Period of Self-Assertion

As the child experiences her newly formed autonomy, the extent to which she may assert herself in opposition to mother now becomes the focus of their negotiations. With curiosity and motor skills growing, with a secure feeling that she can separate from mother yet have her available, the child begins to show more negativism ("No!"), possessiveness ("Mine!"), temper outbursts, and exhibitionism (e.g., when naked, the toddler dashes into the livingroom filled with company). In response, mother sets limits and gives permission both physically and with emotional reactions. Toilet training introduced at this time becomes one arena in which these negotiations take place. Other arenas include, for example, getting dressed, meal time, and asking the child to return a toy to a playmate. Mother's responses could vary in terms of consistency, ambivalence, and guilt and also in terms of the imagination she uses in suggesting alternatives. For example, if the child insists on exploring a potentially dangerous kitchen utensil, the mother could offer another that is relatively safe. If the child refuses a particular food, the mother could offer a suitable alternative.

To negotiate self-assertion successfully, and to make further gains in autonomy, the child must sense that his/her victories in being self-assertive are accepted by mother. If mother's behaviors are severely limiting, the child could surrender the push for self-assertion. As a result, the child's explorations of the environment, and

interactions with others, become inhibited. If mother and child successfully negotiate the child's bids for self-assertion, they are prepared to enter the next two phases
in which they will shape the role aggressive tensions play in the child's manage-
ment of relationships, information, and environments.

Issue #6: 18–24 Months—Period of Initial Testing of Destructive Aggression

The child's assertive behaviors gradually give rise to explicitly aggressive behaviors
toward persons and things. The child's aggressive intentions vary; for example, to
destroy some object, to scatter materials, to injure another child. During this phase,
the child is often aggressive toward some household item that is especially valued
by mother. ("He knew that was my favorite vase! I told him not to touch it!") And
the child shows a sense of triumph and achievement in performing acts of aggression. ("Yeah!") The child may attempt to "make up" with mother by initiating an
activity that pleases her or by undoing the aggressive act (e.g., sticking Scotch tape
on pieces of a broken vase).

Several dimensions of mother's behaviors are especially important if she is to
contribute to the successful negotiation of this issue. Mother should distinguish
among various destructive intentions displayed by the child (e.g., biting in play versus
in anger). And her responses (severe limits, physical punishment, threats of loss of
love) should be coordinated in terms of the intentions she infers. A related consideration involves the extent to which mother allows aggressive behaviors that the
child could employ as alternatives. For example, if the toddler is banging a toy
hammer against the refrigerator, does mother set an old pan beside it and invite
the child to hammer it instead? Last, the mother could initiate a making-up process (e.g., provide the child with the opportunity to repair, or witness the repairing
of, some damaged object). Responses such as these begin the task of negotiating
the modification of aggression that takes place during the next period. If aggression is effectively modified, the child does not surrender ambition, assertiveness,
and pleasure in achieving goals that serve development generally and, in particular, that facilitate future explorations of information and relationships.

Issue #7: 24–36 Months—Period of Modification of Aggressive Intentions

The child's aggressive behavior gradually becomes modified as the child accommodates to and internalizes the standards of caregivers and develops multiple modes
and alternative goals for expressing assertiveness (e.g., shifts from pounding a souvenir ashtray valued by mother to pounding wooden pegs into a formboard). The
child also begins to show socially acceptable aggressive play and to substitute flexible play for stereotyped play. It is important that mother provide a flexible range
of opportunities for aggressing. The successful negotiation of this issue is associated with several outcomes. The child: (1) shapes expressions of aggression that fit

household standards; (2) modifies, and renders more realistic, his/her sense of omnipotence; (3) internalizes parental standards for asserting and aggressing; and (4) begins to test these standards with other persons and environments.

Issue #8: 12–36 Months—Shared Play and Symbolic Behaviors Invented during Interactions

Throughout the second and third year, negotiations with earlier issues contribute to the child's elaborating various ways of communicating. The issue emphasized here is whether and how play and verbal behaviors, which child and caregiver share, solidify their relationship. What is the mother's ability to understand, respond to, and stimulate the child's symbolic and verbal behaviors? And to what extent does the child internalize symbolic communication invented in the process of interacting with mother? In solidifying their relationships through symbols, mother and child increase their understanding of the other's intentions and of the alternatives available for mutual exchange. It should be noted that the negotiation of shared, symbolic behaviors, including verbal behaviors, takes place at the same time as three other issues are being negotiated: self assertion, initial testing of aggression, and modifying aggressive intentions.

Issue #9: 0–36 Months—Consolidation of Body Image

Throughout the first three years the child negotiates and constructs a body image and sexual identification. The child expresses curiosity in his/her body and the bodies of parents and sibs through exhibitionistic, seductive, and autostimulating behaviors. Parents respond with interest, stimulation, and prohibitions, and parents and child communicate about the body and body parts. Throughout these many transactions the child develops perceptions and sensations of body tensions, cognitive schemas of body parts, and a sense of body self or body image (see Chapter 2).

Beebe and Lachmann's Three Developmental Principles

Reviewing a wide spectrum of infant research, Beebe and Lachmann (1994) have proposed three developmental principles to conceptualize how interactions in the first year of life become the foundation for how an infant gives meanings to experiences. While these principles overlap conceptualizations proposed by Piaget, Stern, and Sander, they also integrate their concepts in ways that are particularly useful in articulating techniques for child psychotherapy. The three principles are (1) ongoing regulations, (2) disruption and repair of regulations, and (3) heightened affective moments. Emphasizing the interrelations among these principles, Beebe and Lachmann pointed out that ongoing patterns of regulation must exist between infant and caregiver before either one can perceive a disruption in a pattern of interaction. And a moment of interaction that is charged with intense emotion can either disrupt or repair established patterns of interaction.

The Principle of Ongoing Regulations: The Dialectic between Self-Regulation and Mutual Regulation

Ongoing regulations consist of two interrelated systems: self-regulation by the infant, and mutual regulation by infant and caregiver. With self-regulation the infant gradually recognizes what he/she can expect in his/her interactions with a caregiver and the patterns these interactions form. As these patterns of interactions are repeated, the infant constructs mental schemas that represent them. Stern's concept of "representations of interactions generalized" (RIGs), which we considered earlier, is an example.

With mutual regulation, the infant and caregiver gradually develop a system of shared rules that regulate the actions of each. Here both infant and caregiver develop expectations that each is affected by the other, and each affects the other in predictable ways. These expectations are also represented with schemas. Sander's concept of issues that infant and caregiver negotiate, discussed above, is an example of mutual regulation.

Ongoing regulation involves a dialectic between self-regulation and mutual regulation. To illustrate, I sketch one of the studies reviewed by Beebe and Lachmann (1994). During face-to-face social play between infants (2–6 months) and their mothers, the investigators recorded when the infant looked away. "Looking away is one of the infant's major methods of dosing the level of stimulation and regulating arousal" (p. 139). The investigators also measured the infant's heart rate during a period of five seconds just before the infant looked away. They observed that at this moment the infant's heart rate increased sharply, suggesting that the infant was stressed by the level of stimulation and interaction that was taking place. The investigators also measured heart rate during the five seconds just after the infant looked away. Here they observed a sharp decrease. Taken together, both observations suggested that looking away was successful in avoiding stimulation and was a major way the infants engaged in self-regulation.

Sometimes a mother responded to the infant's looking away by lowering her stimulation, following which the infant typically looked back at mother. In these cases the child's looking away served mutual regulation. On the other hand, if the mother "chased" the infant when he/she looked away by continuing or increasing the level of stimulation, the infant looked away for a longer period of time and withdrew more severely. In these instances both self-regulation and mutual regulation were disrupted. As the authors pointed out, "The very same behaviors through which the infant regulates [his/her] arousal (e.g., looking away) function at the same time as interactive regulators" (p. 140).

In addition to demonstrating the interrelationship between self and mutual regulation, this study illustrated another point made by Beebe and Lachmann: that the success with which the infant establishes self-regulation is dependent on whether infant and caregiver are successful in establishing mutual regulation. This viewpoint is illustrated by another study the authors reviewed. In this study mothers were asked to look at their infants, but to remain completely immobile and unresponsive. This experimental condition, termed *still face*, usually creates stress in infants. Those infants who had previously shown adequate mutual regulation with their mothers continued to signal mother when dealing with her still face, rather than withdrawing or displaying disorganized scanning.

With their first principle, then, Beebe and Lachmann emphasized that the construction of knowledge and representations of experiences require a dialectic between mutual regulation and self-regulation. If the construction of knowledge and representations is viewed only in terms of the infant's self-regulations, pretty much as Freud and Piaget did, then the contribution of dyadic interactions is omitted. Or if the construction of knowledge and representations is viewed only in terms of dyadic interactions, pretty much as social learning theory does, in which the environment molds the child or the child molds the environment, then the contribution of self-regulation is omitted. Knowledge about experiences and meanings given to experiences are constructed by both self-regulation and mutual regulation occurring at the same time.

But everyday observation, as well as laboratory studies, remind us that ongoing regulations can go awry. What happens when infants and caregivers are not synchronized during their mutual regulations? This question leads to the next principle proposed by Beebe and Lachmann.

The Principle of Disruption and Repair

Inevitably, some interactions violate what the infant expects from mother, and also violate the system of rules infant and mother have shared to regulate their actions with each other. How often are expectations of ongoing regulations violated? Apparently, quite often. Studies show that as early as the second and third month of life infants and mothers, whether interacting in typical, real-life situations or in experimentally designed conditions, match their behaviors (such as facial expressions, body movements, and smiling), only about 30 percent of the time. However, this situation is not as bad as it appears at first glance. Studies also show that when mothers and infants are not synchronized, or enter a state of disruption, they return to a matched state of mutual regulation within two seconds about 70 percent of the time. Infants as young as 2 months of age have been observed trying to repair disruptions created by a nonresponsive mother.

The still-face condition noted earlier, in violating what the infant expects, has been used to study disruption and repair of ongoing regulation. In these studies, for example, if mother continues staring with a nonresponsive, immobile face, the infant initially attempts to elicit the interest he/she expects by greeting the mother with a smile. As mother continues to be unresponsive, the infant repeatedly looks at mother with a smile and then looks away. If the mother does not respond after a sequence of these singling behaviors, the infant withdraws, turning his/her body and head away from mother, often slumping and losing postural tonus. The infant, then, uses a variety of behaviors to cope with disruptions of what he/she expects from interactions with caregivers. Some of these coping strategies are adaptive: the infant continues to signal mother, focuses on something other than the mother, engages in self-comforting behavior. Other strategies are maladaptive: the infant withdraws, gives up postural control, displays a disorganized state. Investigators have proposed that these maladaptive behaviors suggest that the infant has given up.

What will prove to be of particular value when we construct guidelines for therapy are findings that relate an infant's experiences with repairing disruptions and aspects of an infant's cognitive/emotional development. For example, the more experience an infant has repairing disruptions, the more he/she is likely to use adaptive coping strategies to deal with disruptions (e.g., the infant focuses on something other than mother or engages in self-comforting behaviors). Gradually, repairing disruptions becomes an interactive skill, and the infant constructs a schema that represents the view that repairing interpersonal disruptions is possible. In addition to enhancing the use of adaptive coping strategies and cultivating the expectation that making up is possible, successful experiences with repairing disruptions contribute to the infant's developing a sense of hope, a sense of being effective, and a more secure attachment with others. In one study infants 4 to 6 months of age, who had more experiences repairing disruptions, tended to use the more adaptive coping strategies we noted above. Moreover, by 6 months these infants showed stable individual differences. In other words, they tended to rely on the same behavior to repair an interruption (e.g., engaging in self-comforting behaviors). At one year of age these same infants showed more secure attachments to their mothers than did infants who did not have as many opportunities to repair disruptions.

If repeatedly experiencing success in repairing disruptions results in schemas that represent hope and competence in "making up with others," it follows that repeatedly experiencing failure in repairing disruptions also results in the expectation that there is no hope and that one is incompetent in making up.

One major source of data about chronic, major disruptions comes from studies of depressed mothers and their infants. Infants of depressed mothers have been observed to be regularly disengaged. Moreover, these infants expect disruptions to occur and expect that they cannot be repaired, expectations that become organized as enduring schemas. Even when engaged by a responsive adult, these infants still respond by remaining disengaged or by protesting. Last, given that between depressed mothers and their infants there are numerous disruptions without repair, the balance between self-regulation and mutual regulation is disturbed. These infants become preoccupied with self-regulation and with managing negative emotions. As a result, they fail to develop adequate interpersonal coping strategies and an adequate sense of hope and self-competence.

The Principle of Heightened Affective Moments

Powerful emotional moments also contribute to the construction of schemas and representations of interactions of what is to be expected. Researchers have documented that in the first weeks of life infants experience a range of emotions (e.g., interest, joy, distress, surprise, sadness). In addition to these "categorical affects," emotions surge and fade, varying in intensity. While emotions accompany ongoing regulations as well as disruptions and repair of regulations, Beebe and Lachmann argued that intense emotional experiences play a sufficiently unique role in the construction of representations to justify their being considered as a separate principle of organization.

Some supercharged moments that occur during the daily rhythm of interactions between infant and caregiver exert an influence on the representation of a particular exchange that is greater than what could be attributed to timing; examples include when caregiver and infant coo back and forth, echoing their tones, and when the infant falls asleep at mother's breast. Another example is found in Sander's observation that infants and mothers exchange a crescendo of emotions when negotiating reciprocal exchange. "The organizing power of affectively supercharged moments thus derives from both the infant's capacity to categorize and expect similar experiences, as well as from the impact of the heightened affect itself" (Beebe and Lachmann 1994, p. 148). It is important to note that heightened affective moments, when positive, contribute to the repair of disruptions.

Other highly emotional moments occur only once or a few times, which relates to the issue of trauma. Here Beebe and Lachmann reviewed clinical data as well as research findings. In one example an adult patient became preoccupied with having been burned at 11 months. This traumatic event became a major organizing theme in this person's psychotherapeutic analysis. Another adult patient remembered a physical sensation that he termed a "stick in the tushie." Later it was learned that this sensation referred to a lumbar puncture the person experienced at the age of 6 months. Another therapist described a child who had experienced multiple invasive medical procedures as an infant. During treatment this child expressed the wish to be hurt. As one way of looking at single, heightened moments, Beebe and Lachmann referred to Stern, who proposed that while RIGs are formed by averaging a repeated pattern of interactions, sometimes one experience can exert unusual influence and give shape to a salient representation because it cannot be averaged with other similar experiences. When disruptions are sufficiently severe, they typically lead to heightened negative affective moments that may traumatically disrupt self-regulation.

The Three Principles and Bodily Experiences

Beebe and Lachmann (1994) point out that the three principles provide a more differentiated way of conceptualizing how bodily experiences are organized. In accord with Sander's proposal that body image is negotiated throughout the first years of life (see also Shilder, Chapter 2), these authors note that the body is involved in all interactions, since perceptions, cognitions, emotions, and arousals are all bodily experiences. "Does the infant expect the comfort of clinging, or handling that is rough and constraining? Does the mother have postural, facial, and vocal responses of aversion, disgust, and withdrawal? What will be organized is the expectation that compelling bodily needs will or will not be adequately regulated, with particular affect and arousal patterns" (p. 153). Further, the crucial role of bodily experiences is self-evident in the principle of heightened affective moments, because research has shown that heightened emotions are simultaneously heightened bodily states. That individuals form unique representations of bodily states can be inferred from the treatment of children and adults, examples of which were noted above. For example, in the case of the child who experienced invasive medical procedures as an infant, this experience was organized and represented as a heightened negative bodily state. Accordingly, upon entering psychotherapy, the child engaged the therapist in a process of ongoing regulation guided by the expectation that repetitive, painful bodily events would and should occur.

The Three Principles and Internalization

As our discussion to this point should make clear, the main thrust of Beebe and Lachmann's critique is to show how observations of infant researchers support the view that during the first years of life transactions between infant and caregivers become located within the infant's mind as organized expectations or schemas; that is, they become "internalized." The process of internalization has been of central interest to psychodynamic theorists since Freud. Beebe and Lachmann offered the definition of internalization by Roy Schafer, a psychoanalyst who has written a great deal about this topic: "All those processes by which the subject transforms real or imagined regulatory interactions with his environment, and real or imagined characteristics of his environment, into inner regulations and characteristics" (p. 154).

While psychodynamic theorists have focused for decades on how an individual "transforms real or imagined . . . interactions with the environment . . . into inner regulations," it took the observations of infant researchers, beginning with Piaget, to demonstrate that the process begins in the first year of life. Infant researchers, Beebe and Lachmann argue, made two particularly significant contributions to the concept of internalization. In the first year of life the interactions that are internalized depend upon the actual presence, actions, and emotional tones of other persons with whom the infant is transacting. This view is amply demonstrated by the observations of Piaget, Stern, and Sander discussed earlier. Second, and of special importance to us, there is continuity between interactions that are represented and internalized in the first year of life and interactions that are represented later in life. "The presymbolically represented experiences of the first year bias the developmental trajectory in transformational ways . . . when these experiences are later encoded symbolically, they retain the impact of the first year" (Beebe and Lachmann 1994, p. 155). This position converges with that of a number of authors who have articulated embodiment theory, a set of concepts to which we turn next.

CONCEPTS FROM EMBODIMENT-ENACTMENT THEORY: A STAIRWAY TO THE SECOND FLOOR

At this point we find ourselves at a stairway that concerns what is sometimes termed *embodiment theory* and sometimes *enactment theory*. My thesis is served by preserving both terms. There are several reasons why I consider embodiment-enactment theory an effective stairway leading from the foundation and first floor to the second floor, where we consider development from the age of 3 years and beyond. Embodiment-enactment theory provides (1) a bridge connecting the meanings given to experiences that occur during the first two years of life with those occurring later, (2) a way of conceptualizing psychological change that applies to infancy and childhood, and (3) principles that bring us closer to articulating how we can translate concepts of development into techniques of use to child therapists.

For this discussion I rely upon Overton's (1994) statement and my discussion of it (Santostefano 1994). Embodiment-enactment theory has emerged in recent years influenced by the contributions of psychoanalytic theory, Piaget's cognitive-developmental theory, and Heinz Werner's organismic-developmental theory as well as the conceptualizations of others (e.g., Johnson 1987, Lakoff 1987). The early roots of embodiment-enactment theory, Overton proposed, have their origin in the principle of embodiment outlined by the philosopher Hegel, who proposed that a person and all of his/her functions are embodied in two dimensions: in one the person is a thinking being; in the other this thinking being operates in a medium of expressions and interactions with others.

Embodiment-enactment theory conceptualizes the mind as a relational concept and includes both a person's body-self experiences (which relates to our earlier discussion of self-regulation) and a person's experiences with other persons (which relates to our earlier discussion of mutual regulation). Also from this view, "The mind emerges out of embodied practices that both construct and are constructed by the phenomenological world" (Overton 1994, p. 231). Karl Stern (1965) proposed that knowledge originates in the early mother–child relationship. The notion that the mind emerges out of embodied practices is reflected by several models we have already considered. Freud proposed that the first ego (that is, the first mind) is a "body ego." Piaget (1977) proposed that "action is primary" in the development of the mind, and that during the first two years of life the infant's actions on things give rise to mental schemas that represent these actions. We also discussed Stern's concept that the infant's interactions with others produce mental representations of those interactions; Sander's notion of infant–mother negotiations that structure and organize the infant's mind and behavior; and Beebe and Lachmann's three principles of interaction that define how a child's mind is organized in the first year of life, setting the stage for mental representations.

If the mind is relational, involving the body-self and the behaviors/emotions of another, which should become the focus of observation, the self or the other? Here it may be helpful to recall our previous discussion of the need to dissolve boundaries. We noted that if we look at a figure (Figure 4–1, Chapter 4) containing two lines, we see two faces from one point of view and a vase from another point of view. We also noted that although there is only one set of lines, both the faces and the vase—that is, both points of view—are legitimate topics for study. Embodiment-enactment theory addresses how the individual's embodied mind develops *while* interacting with others and the environment. By way of contrast, a sociological theory could focus on how the environment develops while interacting with individuals.

A View of Psychological Change

Embodiment-enactment theory offers several basic propositions that set the stage for a view of how a person's psychological functioning changes. Dovetailing with a principle that contributed to the foundation of our developmental model, human activity is conceptualized as inherently organized. How does an organization of activity change? Change occurs, as Overton (1994) put it, when the activity of a person "bumps into" the activity of others that opposes or resists the person's activity. Thus restrictions to one's activity, or a mismatch between the organization of one's activity and that of another, is one necessary condition for change and defines "failures." Another condition for change occurs when the organized behaviors of others affirm and match the organization of the person's activity, a condition providing "successes." Overton's notions are related to Piaget's concept of equilibration discussed in the previous chapter.

Change, then, always occurs through partial successes and failures, and affirmations and resistances by others in response to an individual's activity are not separate processes but rather complementary ones. The reader may notice that these two conditions for change embrace concepts we discussed earlier; for example, Freud's notion of factors that inhibit the expression of representations of drive in response to environmental prohibitions; Piaget's concept of the accommodation of mental schemas in response to mismatches with environmental stimulation; and Beebe and Lachmann's notion of disruption and repair.

As the individual (or body-self) engages in continuous cycles of activity with others, cycles that both affirm and resist the individual's organized activity, the whole self–other system moves toward greater complexity (the principle of directiveness of behavior in our foundation). For embodiment-enactment theory, complexity means that the organization of activity within the individual, and between the individual and others, increases in terms of the number of elements in the activity that are differentiated, the degree to which these elements are integrated, and the degree to which the resulting integration is flexible—that is, differentiation, integration, and flexibility.

It can be seen, then, that cycles of change occur simultaneously in two interrelated domains. In one domain a person's mind gradually differentiates from that of others, forming organizations of interaction with others that are more and more integrated and complex. Simultaneously, and converging with the principle of multiple modes and goals considered in our foundation, differentiation and integration also occur within the individual, resulting in multiple behavioral modalities that become interrelated and flexible, and that are involved in representing actions and experiences. As Overton (1994) noted, a representation involves re-presenting, that is, presenting again, some activity in one or another modality. For example, activity could be represented with another activity, as in deferred imitation. Or activity could be represented by an image or fantasy. Or activity could be represented by spoken words. As the individual develops different modes of expression, embodiment-enactment theory proposes that optimal functioning requires the flexible interplay among these spheres of expression as well as among levels within a sphere. To conceptualize change as viewed by embodiment-enactment theory, Overton used the notion of a spiraling "arrow of time." As the body-self-mind of an individual engages in continuous cycles of activity with others, the system spirals toward greater complexity, resulting in new patterns of activity that integrate new, more flexible properties.

As we complete our climb up the stairway of embodiment-enactment theory, I would like to take a moment to underline Johnson's (1987) contribution to this viewpoint because it spotlights a part of my thesis that we discussed in previous chapters; namely, most approaches to child therapy make use of spoken language as an independent, isolated system, rather than as having connections with embodied experiences. Johnson convincingly argued that years after infancy "the body is in the mind," and that meanings verbalized by a child or adult are not independently contained in sentences but are forever influenced by early body experiences (see also Lakoff 1987). Converging with the formulations of others discussed earlier, Johnson proposed the concept of "embodied image schemas" to conceptualize how, during the first years of life, patterns of bodily movements and interpersonal interactions give rise to organized meanings. But Johnson took a further step, connecting meanings constructed early in life to those constructed later. Initial body-based schemas continue to develop during subsequent experiences because they are "metaphorically projected" into higher levels of functioning that develop. These initial, body-based schemas, then, serve as principles around which meanings are organized later in life.

With this proposal Johnson emphasized an issue that holds particular signifi-cance for my approach. The original body-interpersonal experiences not only shape the original embodied image schemas but also constrain subsequent, more abstract, metaphorical forms these schema take. For example, Johnson noted that all chil-dren and adults develop the metaphorical understanding of "more is up," reflected in statements such as "Turn up the heat," and "I feel up." But, he argued, this metaphorical understanding of the word "up" is not an accident. Rather, the meta-phorical understanding results from the constraints expressed by thousands of bodily experiences during infancy that gave shape to the meaning that "moving up verti-cally" means "more." We can readily imagine how many times a toddler adds liq-uid to a container, or blocks to a tower, observing that as the level goes up there is more.

Johnson emphasized, then, that embodied enactments in the first years of life are not replaced by modes of symbolizing and expression that emerge later. Rather, the actions and interactions experienced during infancy, and the meanings they represent, become extended into modalities that develop later (e.g., taking action, fantasizing, verbalizing), contributing to the unique form an action or fantasy or verbal expression might take. In other words, what one experiences in the first two years of life spirals into what one does, imagines, and says later in life. To illustrate this proposition, and the various concepts we considered in this chapter, I turn to a clinical case.

EXPERIENCES IN THE FIRST TWO YEARS OF LIFE SPIRAL INTO WHAT ONE DOES, IMAGINES, AND SAYS LATER IN LIFE: A CASE ILLUSTRATION

In this chapter I set out to discuss a developmental model that I proposed would guide the construction of an integrative psychotherapy for children. The founda-tion of this model, or developmental house, as I called it, included developmental principles that derive from the theories of Freud, Piaget, and Werner that satisfied criteria for a developmental theory outlined by Harris and Baldwin; i.e., holism, directiveness of behavior, multiple behavioral modes and goals, mobility of behav-ioral modes, motivating forces, regulating and restraining behavioral structures, and an adaptive process conceived as a dialectic between a person and others.

From the principles of Freud, Piaget, and Werner we then discussed devel-opment during the first two years of life as conceptualized by infant researchers. The concepts of Piaget and Stern articulated how an infant engages in self-regulation. While encountering things and persons, the infant develops mental schemas that represent experiences with things and that become increasingly ela-borated; the infant also develops psychological modalities and a sense of self and others. The concepts of Sander articulated how an infant engages in mutual regu-lation, negotiating various issues with caregivers that also contribute to the organization and structuring of the infant's behavioral modes. The concepts of Beebe and Lachmann articulated how self- and mutual regulation are two sides of the same coin, each influencing the other. These authors also articulated that disruptions of what the infant and caregiver expect from each other, and interactions that occur in the context of intense emotions, also play a critical role in shaping the infant's behavior in the present and in future interactions.

Last, embodiment-enactment theory introduced a concept that is critical for psychotherapy with children and adolescents. All of what these investigators formulated does not disappear at the close of the second year of life. Rather, experiences during infancy, and the meaning an infant gives to these experiences, are conserved as mental schemas. These schemas are then extended into experiences encountered later in life, giving unique shape to their meanings and guiding what a person understands and does. From the view of embodiment-enactment theory, what one experiences during the first two years of life spirals into what one does, imagines, and says later in life.

John's Presenting Problems

While numerous research reports support the various developmental concepts discussed in this chapter, I forecast the value they hold for child psychotherapy with a clinical case involving an adolescent (Santostefano 1991b). The cause of his suffering and the reason he sought a consultation provide us with an opportunity to explore how experiences during the first two years of life spiral into, and influence, the meanings given to later experiences. The case is particularly suited to our interests because this boy first pulled his hair at the age of 20 months, and continued to do so throughout childhood and adolescence, in spite of the fact that he was functioning relatively well until he sought help. As we shall see, the concepts we have considered in this chapter provide us with a way of understanding the origin of his hair pulling and why this behavior seemed impervious to change. After presenting the clinical material pretty much as it evolved in the office, I organize the data in terms of the concepts we have discussed.

John was 16 and in the tenth grade when he first came to see me. He was a handsome, neatly dressed boy, slender yet athletic. I began by commenting that although his parents telephoned me, I wanted to learn from him why he had asked for a consultation and how he thought I could be of help. Initially tense, he soon expressed himself quite well, maintained eye contact, and showed a good capacity to interact and experience various emotions, from laughter to tears.

John talked first about his accomplishments as a gymnast (he had already won several awards). He had always been an excellent student except for the past two terms when, much to his confusion, his grades dropped dramatically. His social life with both male and female friends had been going OK, although he recently stopped seeing a girlfriend because of difficulties he did not specify. And of late he had lost his enthusiasm for gymnastics and guitar lessons. With embarrassed laughter he finally introduced one of his problems as he saw it: daily fights between him and his sister, 17 months younger. For example, she wore one of his sweaters without permission, and on another occasion borrowed his bike and dented the fender, happenings that inevitably led to "real fights." Sometimes he started the fights, as when he poured water on her bed. What infuriated John the most was the fact that his parents, especially father, did not interfere or referee.

During the last minutes of this first interview, John introduced the problem that the parents had already described with much concern when they telephoned for an appointment. Now struggling to express himself, he said he has been pulling out hair from the top of his head "for a long time." He pushed aside his wavy hair to reveal an area, about 2 inches square just above the hairline, totally devoid of hair.

John agreed to return, and over several weeks gradually developed sufficient trust to share personal details about his hair pulling. It was a ritual. Each day he went into the bathroom, carefully felt the bald area with his fingertips, and if he detected a hair stub, he plucked it out. He was aware of a sense of compulsion, of "having to do it" and acknowledged that the pinch of pain "felt good and exciting." He had not been particularly troubled by his habit during grade school, but recently some of the kids who noticed the bald area had begun to call him "skinhead." He could not remember the first time he pulled his hair, but he believed he started during kindergarten, because he remembers his teacher continually bugged him to stop "twirling" his hair.

In one attempt to learn about the meanings unique to John's personal world, I asked him to discuss the greatest person he had read about. John discussed Abraham Lincoln, giving particular attention, I thought, to his bushy hair and beard. From this he associated to a recent habit he had developed. While doing his homework, he fondled the furry head of a toy lion from his childhood days. Visibly anxious and embarrassed, he puzzled both about why he had begun to do this and why the activity excited him.

During a following meeting, John announced there was something that troubled him more than the hair pulling and that in fact was the main reason why he had asked his parents if he could see someone. With much difficulty he described the confused combination of excitement and anger he experienced when interacting with a science teacher and when taking showers with classmates after gymnastics. Bursting into tears, he wondered whether he was "becoming gay." After he collected himself, I acknowledged his pain and noted it would help me help him if he would discuss the teacher and classmates further. As he did, I noticed that he centered on particular details: the teacher in question maintained a beard, and John was most aroused when taking a shower in the presence of a particular classmate who had already developed considerable body hair.

At this point I would like to underline one observation that gradually impressed me during these initial interviews and that later proved to carry special significance. I noticed that whenever John talked about his hair pulling, the science teacher, the classmate with body hair, or the toy lion, he would arch his shoulders back so that his abdomen curved out. At first this body posture was almost imperceptible. But over time it occurred with such regularity that I eventually became convinced that the posturing held some importance in the ensemble of John's psychology. As John and I continued our sessions, I obtained his permission to meet his parents. He understood I would maintain confidentiality and that information about his early childhood and his parents, combined with his own views and the results of psychological testing I had requested, would help me advise him whether, in his own words, he was "mental" and what he could do about his concerns.

John's parents, an articulate, very invested couple, made clear that their main concern about John had always been his hair pulling. Although they did not understand why he had asked to see someone at this point in time, they were relieved and hoped the consultation would lead to John's mastering the habit. Both agreed on how and when the hair pulling began. John was 20 months old and his sister a few months old. John had already shown difficulty accepting his sister, frequently poking her, sticking her with diaper pins, and on one occasion covering her from head to toe with baby powder. As a result, mother, who at the time was experiencing a post-partum depression, frequently scolded John and felt overwhelmed by her inability to contain her anger toward him. One day, while changing sister's diaper, mother turned away for a moment. When she returned, she found John poking at his sister. Mother screamed angrily and slapped him. John immediately crawled under the bed and refused to come out. A short time later father arrived, finding mother very upset over her failure, once again, to be patient with John and to divide her attention between John and the new baby. Father coaxed John from under the bed. At that moment both parents noticed hair strands in John's fist. An examination of his scalp quickly revealed he had pulled hair from the top of his head.

In the months that followed they observed that an area at the front of his scalp remained sparse and, with their pediatrician, concluded John was still pulling out his hair, although no one observed him doing this. From this beginning the parents carried the belief that mother's scream and angry slap caused the symptom. During John's nursery school years, the parents were advised to wait and see whether John would grow out of his hair-pulling habit.

When he did not, John was brought to mental health professionals, initially when he was 5 and on three other occasions to the age of 13 years. Each time, behavior modification programs were implemented, successfully eliminating the hair pulling for periods of up to several months. But each time the habit returned.

Reviewing John's development, the parents could not identify any major difficulty except for the hair pulling, the bickering between him and his sister which they considered typical sibling rivalry, and his tendency to be less cooperative and more irritable with mother while being "daddy's boy." Further, their overall assessment concurred with John's: he had always performed well academically and enjoyed friends; as he grew older he took guitar lessons and engaged in sports, focusing during the past two years on gymnastics, showing exceptional ability. The parents were confused, as was John, by his recent sudden poor school performance and loss of interest in his girlfriend, gymnastics, and guitar.

Still searching to understand John's hair pulling, and guided by hypotheses suggested by John's interviews and projective testing, I asked during one meeting whether father had ever maintained a beard. Although initially surprised by the question, both parents readily responded. Father maintained a beard before John was born and during his first years. Almost from John's birth, father enjoyed nuzzling his beard into John's body. Mother added that she also enjoyed bobbing her head back and forth so that her shoulder-length hair caressed John's body. Both parents laughed and guessed they were "ticklers."

Mother terminated her tickling when John was about one year old, very likely because she began to center on her new pregnancy. Father, on the other hand, tickled John daily, resulting in a series of "tickling" rituals. For example, when father changed John's diaper, and playfully rubbed his beard over John's belly, John wiggled and cooed with glee. Later, when father approached John, he would arch his back, sticking his belly upward, clearly inviting father to tickle him, much to father's delight. I will return to these play rituals and others that emerged during the first two years of John's life (described by the parents with the aid of a baby book), because these rituals illustrate how experiences in the first two years of life contribute to what one does, imagines, and says years later.

As both parents added pieces to these recollections, mother spontaneously asked father an intriguing question. "Remember what happened when you shaved your beard off?" Father had decided to shave off his beard sometime after sister was born. Minus his beard, father walked into John's bedroom, with mother following, both parents wondering what his reaction would be. John glared at father and quickly crawled to the corner of the crib, burying his face in the blankets. Father remembered John as obviously "stressed," whereas mother recalled he seemed "terrified." When mother picked up John, he burst into tears, refusing to go into father's arms. Both parents tried to reassure him, "Look! It's daddy! See, it's daddy!" as they placed John's hands over father's shaven face. Following this episode, John avoided father for a number of days, maybe weeks—they could not remember for sure. The parents were sure, however, that father had shaved his beard before the incident when mother slapped John.

The unique elements of John's case raise several questions related to my topic. How did John's ongoing regulations, and evolving sense of self and others, contribute to the moment when he first pulled his hair? Were there major disruptions of his ongoing regulations, and heightened emotional moments, that contributed to the onset of his hair pulling? What was its original meaning, and did this meaning undergo change? How and why did hair pulling persist uninterrupted from the age of 20 months to early adolescence in a boy who had until recently functioned adequately along several major lines: His capacity to work in school, to engage in peer relationships, and to enjoy interests? And how do we understand that at the age of 16 John felt pressed to talk to someone about his main worry which, as it turned out, did not concern his hair pulling but the surges of excitement and anger he experienced when in the presence of a teacher and a male friend, experiences that for John carried the meaning that he was becoming gay?

A Reconstruction of John's Psychic Reality and Early Self

I now attempt to illustrate how the concepts we have considered provide us with a way of reconstructing the beginnings of John's psychic reality, especially as it relates to our understanding of his hair pulling. In the discussion to follow, I relate available data about John's earliest experiences to phases during his infancy. In framing each phase, I integrate the models of Piaget, Stern, Sander, and Beebe and Lachmann for heuristic purposes. As we proceed, the reader may find it useful to refer again to Table 5–2.

Primary Circular Reactions, the Emergent Self, and Negotiating Initial Adaptation

A phase from 0–4 months. Recall that in Piaget's Stages I and II, primary circular reactions enable the infant to repeat experiences, such as hand sucking, not because of chance contact but through the coordination of schemas from various perceptual modes. At the same time, a self emerges that relates diverse experiences (emotions, bodily events, interactions with caregivers). During this time, the infant and caregiver are negotiating initial adaptation during which the infant develops predictable organized behaviors and the caregiver begins to know the infant independent from his/her projections.

It seems safe to assume that John fared well during this time, coordinating schemas from various sensory modalities during diverse experiences with both parents (there were no other caregivers present) and with things. While these experiences very likely included various emotional tones, one set of experiences could be viewed as a collection of heightened affective moments. Both mother and father enjoyed tickling and caressing John's body: mother with her hair and father with his beard. We can only speculate whether and how these recurring experiences might have joined with others involving inanimate things, such as fringes on a pillow. But we can argue convincingly that these recurring bodily experiences formed the beginning roots of a RIG involving intense bodily sensations in response to soft bristles from the persons of others and the emotional tone of surging excitement. We could also argue that, with this behavior, both parents were not developing an adequate sense of "knowing" John's uniqueness. Rather, each parent seemed to be projecting his/her own needs onto John, since each initiated and enjoyed caressing John with hair.

Secondary Circular Reactions, the Core Self, and Negotiating Reciprocal Exchange and Early Directed Activity

A phase from 4–12 months. During this phase the infant engages in repetitive behaviors in order to make "interesting sights last." At the same time, the core self emerges as the infant constructs the first RIGs that summarize and conserve repeated experiences with persons and things, including sensations and emotional tones. The infant is now more equipped to anticipate what should be expected and whether a given experience is the same or different from others. In addition, infant and caregiver negotiate being active and passive as they share a crescendo of emotions, as well as the infant's directing the caregiver's behaviors so that his/her needs are met.

We have several relevant observations from this period. When placed on the changing table, John began to arch his back, offering his belly to father and mother for tickling, a body posture that directed their behavior in order to make the interesting hair-brushing experience last. He also began to tighten his legs, making it difficult for a parent to change the diaper. This behavior seemed to be another attempt to direct the parents and ensure that tickling would come first, because he relaxed his legs once he was tickled. Still later, he rolled his head back and forth, imitating mother when she swished her hair across his body. During the intake interview, father had shown excitement when he recalled the way John arched his belly. "It was fantastic; he made it clear he wanted me to tickle him!" It seems appropriate to speculate that John was constructing a RIG we could call "hair-tickling–explosive excitement" that gradually became a part of his core self and extended into his subjective self.

Tertiary Circular Reactions, the Subjective Self,
and Negotiating Self-Assertion

A phase from 12–18 months. During this phase the infant is discovering new ways
of accomplishing goals that become play rituals. At the same time, self and other
are defined by subjective mental states, in addition to shared actions and emotions,
as the infant develops an understanding of the motives of others that guide physical happenings. During this time the infant negotiates mother's unconditional
availability. With the autonomy her availability brings, the infant begins to experiment with expressing aggressive intentions.

Given the emotional intensity of ongoing regulations that took place between
mother and John to this point in his development, we could easily argue that two
factors emerged during this phase that contributed to a major disruption in their
relationship: mother became depressed and preoccupied with her new pregnancy.
And mother stopped participating in hair-tickling play rituals.

Father and John continued hair tickling, however, in an evolving series of
highly ritualized play activities during which they discovered new ways of engaging each other in these heightened emotional moments. These play rituals took
place daily, continued until sister was born (John was 17 months old), and inter-
mittently thereafter for at least three months. For example, when in the high chair
John arched his back, which regularly resulted in father nuzzling him with his beard
several times during one meal. After dinner, father took to playing with John on a
fur rug, sometimes pretending he was an animal as the two crawled about, and
sometimes entertaining John with toys. In the midst of these play activities, John
would flip on his back, arch his belly upward, and roll his head back and forth. The
head rolling suggested that deferred imitation was operating since mother had been
rolling her head in tickling rituals until recently. In response, father nuzzled him.
Then John introduced a new ingredient. He would reach up, clutch father's beard,
and hang on while father swung his head back and forth, singing, "See-saw, Marjory
Daw," the two exploding with obvious delight.

During this time, mother, as already noted, became increasingly preoccupied
with her new pregnancy and steadily withdrew from John. It is important to note
that not only did she sharply decrease the pleasurable stimulation she had provided
John, but also, more often than not, she related to him with irritation.

Deferred Imitation, the Verbal Self, and Negotiating Aggressive Intentions

A phase from 18–24 months. During this phase, deferred imitation sharply increases
and becomes a critical part of the process of sharing meanings. The verbal self
emerges, which includes the self and others as storehouses of personal knowledge
expressed as meanings to be shared in language as well as actions. At the same time,
the infant continues negotiating self-assertion, experiments with expressing aggressive intentions toward things and other persons, and attempts to "make up."

During this phase John invented new meanings, further elaborating the ritualized play between him and father. When father entered the house, John scampered behind furniture. With considerable fanfare, father searched for John in
different locations exclaiming, "Where are you?" "Here I come!" When father discovered John, both screamed with delight as father carried John to the fur rug where
they engaged in nuzzling and beard-swinging games. Sometimes when father discovered John, he would be holding a piece of cloth over his mouth and chin clearly
representing a beard.

At this point, when John was 17 months old, sister arrived. Both parents
acknowledged that in the weeks following the birth of sister, mother's depression
increased as did her expressions of impatience and anger toward John. Significantly,
father gradually decreased participating in beard-nuzzling rituals with John, and
shifted some of the same activity and attention to sister. Here again John experienced a major disruption in his ongoing regulations with father.

In responding to these developments, John's behavior suggested that he
struggled in various ways to cope with the appearance of sister and mother's angry
outbursts as well as with preserving his special and exciting relationship with father. For example, in what could be interpreted as an attempt to make up with
mother, John on several occasions covered his sister with a blanket of baby powder
when mother was changing her diaper. And in what could be interpreted as testing aggressive intentions, on several occasions John stuck his infant sister with a
pin, saying, "Bum," the word he was already using when defecating in the potty.
And if father nuzzled sister with his beard, John attempted to interrupt this activity
by pulling at father's leg or flopping on the floor and arching his back, or by hiding
behind furniture, each an attempt to direct father to initiate their play rituals.
Whenever mother snapped at John, father interfered and protected him, encouraging mother to be more patient. Moreover, if scolded by mother, John immediately
ran to father and initiated a beard-nuzzling ritual using one of his prompts. This
ensemble of elements continued within John's developing self for about three
months, when father elected to shave his beard. This action on father's part proved
to be another major disruption for John, which I propose was a key ingredient in
why he began to pull his hair.

The Origin and Initial Meaning of John's Hair Pulling

We are now in a position to speculate with some confidence about elements of John's
psychic reality that formed the initial meaning of his hair pulling and that defined
why he pulled his hair for the first time at age 20 months. To begin, we need to
consider two of the RIGs John constructed within his core and subjective selves
before father shaved his beard. One RIG condensed, represented, and conserved
experiences with mother, the other with father.

The RIG involving mother initially included John's surging excitement and
tingling body sensations as mother's long hair slid across his body, and percep-

tions of mother's surging excitement as she rolled her head back and forth. But this RIG was disrupted and revised when mother became irritable, depressed, and withdrew from John. Still later, the "mother" RIG was revised again, now including mother cooing at and caressing sister and father shielding him from mother whenever her anger exploded.

The RIG involving father included John's body sensations accompanied by explosive excitement when father's beard rubbed against John's belly, neck, and cheeks; perceptions of father's surging excitement; John's sense of being at one with father and as separate from him (e.g., when hiding behind furniture); perceptions of father as protector from mother's depression and angry moods; father as security and well-being; and father as someone to pull away when he expressed affection toward sister. This RIG was disrupted and revised when father decreased his participation in hair-tickling games with John and engaged baby sister in beard nuzzling.

However, when father shaved his beard, the "father" RIG within John's subjective self was disrupted to a major degree, representing a particularly traumatic, heightened affective moment. This inference is supported by John's marked stress reaction upon seeing father without his beard. Recall that John seemed terrified, burst into tears, buried his face in a blanket, and avoided father for a number of weeks. The intensity of John's reaction is not surprising given the central position father's beard held in most of John's transactions with him, and in many of the key meanings that formed his subjective self: well-being, excitement, security, protection, separation-individuation, autonomy. When father shaved his beard, John was faced with a major task; namely, revising the "father" RIG to include father without a beard, while preserving these positive meanings. However, before John could accomplish this task, father had begun to decrease his participation in their play rituals, representing another disruption, and preventing John from engaging in interactions with father that could revise the "father" RIG.

And then mother, who had been withdrawn from him for some time, angrily slapped him while father was absent, representing a heightened, affective traumatic moment. Since John had not yet had the opportunity to revise the father RIG, he coped with this assault on the integrity of his self by calling upon the still well-established RIG of "bearded father" as an evoked companion. However, because the evoked father disagreed with the father who now was without beard, John, capable of deferred imitation, pulled hair from his head (as father had shaved hair from his face) in order to experience and preserve the already established meanings of well-being and security within his subjective self. In addition, the hair pulling could be viewed as an attempt by John to modify aggressive intention. That is, he pulled his hair instead of sticking pins in sister or mother in response to mother's slap.

To recapitulate, the origin of John's hair pulling is found in several interrelated factors:

1. Intensely stimulating play rituals of mother's hair caressing his body resulted in a RIG in John's emergent and core selves that conserved and

prescribed ongoing regulations with mother as affectionate and physically stimulating. This RIG was disrupted and not repaired.

2. Intensely stimulating, protracted play rituals centering on father's beard resulted in a key RIG within John's subjective self that gave singular importance to the beard as a symbol of well-being and security. This RIG was disrupted in a major way when father shaved his beard.

3. When mother slapped John, he had not yet constructed a revised RIG of a beardless father that preserved the embodied meanings represented by the beard. The slap was a traumatic, heightened affective moment.

4. John had reached a point in development where deferred imitation is a major device used in negotiating self and others and in sharing meanings and when negotiating aggressive intention becomes a major issue. To handle the assault to his subjective self, body integrity, and body image, John used deferred imitation to call upon his companion by pulling his hair as father had "pulled" his. The hair pulling also contained an attempt to modifying aggressive intention. Instead of aggressing toward mother, father, and sister, he aggressed toward himself.

If we now repeat the question, What was the original meaning of the hair pulling? my reply would be, Evoking well-being, security, and pleasure within the subjective self to cope with rejection by others and with aggressive tensions these rejections produced.

Why John's Hair Pulling Remained Impervious to Change from Age 20 Months to Adolescence

From this formulation of the original meaning of John's hair pulling, we can address other questions. Why did the hair pulling continue throughout development as a circumscribed activity, whereas other lines of psychological development proceeded relatively unimpeded? Did this original meaning undergo change? And why until the age of 16 did John experience almost no private thoughts or fantasies about his hair pulling except for a global sense of excitement and a sense of "having to do it"?

If we approach these questions from the psychodynamic model of intrapsychic conflict, we are required to consider the onset and continuation of the hair pulling as a compromised solution (i.e., a neurotic symptom) of conflict between, for example, superego dictates and unconscious wishes, a conflict that persisted unchanged throughout John's childhood. However, this model leads us into a major pitfall: neurotic symptoms occur only after symbolic thinking is fully developed. Viewing the hair pulling as a neurotic symptom runs counter to the data that support the proposal that the foundation of this behavior was constructed during the first 17 months of John's life. Therefore, the foundation consisted of hundreds of *nonverbal* physical, cognitive, and emotional experiences that took place before the superego as a mental organization of standards is expected to emerge and before he could possibly have developed elaborate unconscious fantasies.

I proposed above that instead of resulting from intrapsychic conflict, John's hair pulling was a coping device, born out of RIGs already well established prior to the age of 20 months, that relied on the processes of deferred imitation and modifying aggressive intentions. This position is in line with Stern's (1985) cogent argument that when an infant presents problems, these "are not symptoms of intrapsychic conflict within the infant [but] the accurate reflection of an ongoing interactive reality, manifestations of a problematic interpersonal exchange, not psychopathology of a psychodynamic nature" (p. 202).

However if we grant that John's hair pulling began as a coping device, why was the hair pulling (and related meanings) not transformed into a neurotic symptom and into symbols (fantasies) and words that John could share, once he developed the capacity for symbolic thinking? Recall that when plucking hair from his head during adolescence, John did not experience related fantasies, nor could he express the meaning of this activity in words. He was aware only of surges of excitement he experienced when pulling out a hair, and a sense of "having to do it." To address the question of why John's hair pulling was not translated into symbols, again I turn to Stern and Piaget for assistance.

Stern proposed that the verbal self, with its shared meanings, gradually builds upon nonverbal, unconscious core and subjective selves as the tool of language develops after the second year of life and symbolic thinking surges. Of particular importance to us, he also proposed that although some experiences contained within nonverbal RIGs are eventually translated into words as shared meanings, others are not. Stern noted that "some global experiences at the level of core and intersubjective relatedness do not permit language sufficient entry to separate out a piece for linguistic transformation. Such experiences, then, continue underground, nonverbalized, to lead an unnamed (and, to that extent only, unknown) but nonetheless very real existence" (p. 175).

Piaget (1973) took a step further and conceptualized that whether or not nonverbal experiences from the first two years of life are translated into symbolic forms during childhood relates to the "functional utility" the translation would serve. Paralleling the psychoanalytic notion of repression, he offered that sensorimotor schemas (and here I would include RIGs) are not translated into symbolic form (and therefore remain unnamed and unconscious, yet also operational) whenever the schemas are incompatible with, or "in conflict with," conscious ideas already constructed and accepted, and therefore existing at a cognitive level higher than sensorimotor schemas or RIGs. Because of this conflict, body-nonverbal schemas are actively held in the unconscious.

Applying these notions to John, after father shaved his beard, John constructed conscious ideas of father without a beard, but these ideas conflicted with a well-established RIG of the preferred, intersubjective bearded partner who defined John's core self as secure and valued. Because John did not have the opportunity to revise this RIG, there was clearly no functional utility in translating the initial sensorimotor abstraction of a bearded father into some symbolic/verbal form. However, there was functional utility in his preserving meanings from his original sensorimotor, nonverbal RIG of a bearded father. These meanings enabled him to cope with father's withdrawal from their stimulating games and mother's angry rejection of him in preference for sister. For these reasons the original unconscious sensorimotor meanings of the hair pulling remained impervious to change during his toddler years. In applying Stern's and Piaget's formulations to John's case, I am suggesting an additional consideration.

If major disruptions accompanied by heightened traumatic emotions are not adequately repaired, a nonverbal RIG is not translated into symbolic form even as childhood and adolescence unfold with their cognitive and behavioral maturation. Rather, the RIG remains unconscious, unnamed but active, without interfering with a child's social and academic functioning.

How does the untranslated RIG remain active without interfering with aspects of subsequent development? Some sensorimotor and emotional components of the original representation continue to gain expression in the behaviors of the child or adolescent, without the youth's having a conscious sense of "knowing" what the behavior means or being able to share its meaning with others in play or discussions. Moreover, the child typically does not experience conscious conflict/anxiety as such in connection with the behavior but only moments of bewilderment or embarrassment whenever the behavior is confronted by the environment.

John provides us with an example of this proposal. Recall that when I first met John, a particular action element and emotion of the original father-RIG could still be observed. In terms of the action element, he arched his shoulders back and protruded his stomach ever so subtly but noticeably when discussing his bearded teacher, the classmate with body hair, Abraham Lincoln, and his furry toy lion, which he had begun to fondle while doing homework. This body posture was clearly an expression of one aspect of the sensorimotor, embodied father-RIG constructed during infancy. During the hundreds of play rituals with father, John gradually articulated the body posture of thrusting his belly forward in order to initiate beard-snuggling rituals. In terms of the emotional element of the original RIG, John experienced a sudden surge of excitement when, for example, engaging the teacher, perceiving the hairy classmate, or plucking a hair from his head, emotions that clearly derived from the exhilarating excitement he experienced during play rituals and that became conserved as part of the nonverbal sensorimotor RIG. Last, we should notice that throughout childhood and into adolescence, while the bearded-father RIG remained underground and unnamed but active, this bearded father-

RIG continued to preserve the original embodied sense of security, esteem, and integrity; thus John functioned well academically and socially. During childhood and into adolescence, he did not experience intense anxiety or conflict but only moments of confusion and embarrassment when, for example, classmates called him "skinhead," or when he puzzled as to why he began fondling the toy lion. But then the efficiency of John's psychological functioning suddenly collapsed. Why?

John's Adaptive Success Collapsed When His Bearded-Father RIG Was Translated into Words

John's school grades plunged, and he lost interest in athletics, music, and friends. This collapse in his functioning seems to have occurred when the bearded-father RIG collapsed, no longer prescribing security, esteem, and competence. The bearded-father RIG collapsed when it became translated from an unnamed unconscious form to a named conscious form that, it turned out, did not serve adaptation. In John's case his unique psychology translated the bearded-father RIG into a particular symbolic form consisting of language and fantasy symbols represented by his anxiously wondering whether he was "becoming gay." John experienced this translation and the knowledge and knowing that he brought to it as an "assault" to his embodied, core-self that produced intense anxiety and turmoil, intrapsychic conflict (in contrast to interpersonal conflict) that contributed to his academic and social decline.

We can speculate why John's psychology constructed this particular verbal/fantasy symbolic translation. Here it is important to remind ourselves of embodiment-enactment theory and Johnson's concept of the "body in the mind," which proposed that verbalized meanings constructed later in life are not independently contained in sentences. Rather, verbal meanings are forever shaped and constrained by early nonverbal body experiences. Applied to John, we could ask, "What were some of the beliefs and self-references that maturations in adolescence now required him to construct?" He had entered puberty and was experiencing heightened biological changes and surges of genital/bodily excitement. Along with other adolescents, he was faced with the task of negotiating his psychosexual identification and preferences. Moreover, along with his peers, he overheard and participated in discussions and jokes about sexuality. As John coped with the impact of these biological and social experiences, his "mind" began to assign verbal meanings to these experiences. But, as we noted, "the body in the mind" participates in the shape given to these meanings. The "body" in John's mind was unique in containing a core nonverbal representation that included unnatural, protracted, and excessive body stimulation in play rituals with father, including excessively heightened explosions of excitement. When this "body" became injected into the process of constructing verbal meanings of John's biological and social experiences regarding psychosexual identity, John's mind propelled a translation in the form of a particular linguistic symbol: "I'm gay!" From this view, John's verbalized belief that he was gay was not randomly determined, then, but shaped by the unique developmental interferences he experienced in the first two years of life. And given John's tense anxiety and stress over wondering if he was "gay," we could speculate that this translation was not synchronous with other aspects of his personality, but in conflict with them.

Concluding Comment

John's case provides us with an illustration of how experiences in the first two years of life influence what a child does, imagines, and says later in life. This case also draws other issues to our attention: that some experiences from the first two years of life are translated into shared symbols (fantasies, verbalized meanings) that serve a "functional utility," that other embodied, nonverbal experiences are not translated but remain underground and unnamed but ever active, and selected action and emotional elements from the original representation could gain expression.

John's case reveals another issue that is critical in formulating integrative psychotherapy. If we accept that early experiences influence what a child does, imagines, and says in the present, and if some embodied nonverbal experiences are not fully translated into shared symbols, should the therapist emphasize translations in the form of verbalized meanings? We have discussed on several occasions that both cognitive-behavioral and psychodynamic therapies seem to prefer translations in the form of verbalized self-instructions, explanations, and interpretations. John's case provokes our thinking about this issue. His bearded-father RIG was initially translated into a nonverbal action symbol that was nearly identical to its referent, namely, plucking hair from his head. Later, in adolescence, the next translation again consisted of an action symbol (feeling fur of a toy lion). We should notice that while these translations involved action symbols, the conscious emotional experience was usually excitement that did not interfere with adaptations. Then the translation took a turn into another modality. John began to experience diffuse fantasies about a teacher and peer, this translation producing primarily excitement and a moderate degree of anxiety. When the translations took the form of a self-statement, "I am gay," conscious conflict and anxiety became intense, and John's adaptive functioning collapsed.

These observations raise several issues we have noted earlier about the conduct of child psychotherapy. Should embodied nonverbal representations be translated into words, and if so, when? If embodied nonverbal representations are translated only in the "language" of action and fantasy, is this sufficient to promote a child's psychological development? I emphasize these questions here and in future chapters when discussing clinical cases because I believe whether, when, and how embodied, nonverbal representations are translated into language, fantasy, action symbols is an issue frequently ignored and yet critical in conducting successful psychotherapy with children and adolescents.

The several issues stimulated by John's case form a bridge to the next chapter. There we continue our discussion of the developmental model I propose for integrative child psychotherapy and outline aspects of development that take place after the age of 2 years that have relevance to treatment.

6

A Developmental Framework for Integrating Child Psychotherapy (*continued*): From Age 3 Years to Adolescence

CONTENTS

In the previous chapter we discussed the foundation and first floor of the "developmental house" I propose as a guide for integrating child psychotherapy. Building on this foundation of principles that derive from the theories of Freud, Piaget, and Werner, the first floor elaborated how the construction of knowledge and meaning and the structuring of an infant's mental and behavioral modalities take place during the first two years of life. To reach this chapter from the first floor, we climbed the stairway of embodiment-enactment theory, which proposes that experiences and their meanings taking place during infancy are extended into and influence the shape of experiences and meanings from the third year of life and beyond. We concluded with a clinical case that illustrated how a boy's experiences during infancy influenced what he did, imagined, and said during a particular phase in his adolescence.

We now need to elaborate how the processes of self- and mutual regulation, disruption and repair of interactions, and heightened emotional experiences that occur during infancy continue to unfold beyond the third year of life. We also need to elaborate how interactions and negotiations with others and environments during childhood build upon meanings constructed during the first years of life, result in cognitive and behavioral modalities that gradually undergo differentiation and integration and become increasingly more flexible, serving the child's adaptations to ever-changing stimulation. Moreover, as we now tour the second floor of our developmental house, we should expect to find elaborations that provide a way of integrating what a child does, imagines, and says at both surface and deep levels. Of particular importance to our interest in child psychotherapy, these elaborations should also define the implications for adaptive functioning when the processes of self- and mutual cognitive regulation are derailed, when behavioral modalities remain inflexible, failing to differentiate, and when what a child does, imagines, and says are segregated experiences.

To address these needs, and relying upon laboratory and clinical studies, I have constructed a developmental framework that consists of three interrelated models (see Figure 6–1). The first model, which arches over the others, relies upon the concept of "life metaphors" to conceptualize a child's continuously evolving, subjective world. This concept defines how nonverbal representations of interactions, constructed during the first two years of life, form the ground out of which emerge organizations of representations of key developmental issues that a child continues to negotiate with others from the third year of life to adolescence. Life metaphors guide how a child construes present stimulation and prescribe which actions a child should take when negotiating developmental issues with others and situations.

The actions a child takes, as prescribed by life metaphors, are conceptualized as involving two processes, each framed by a model. With one, a set of cognitive-

I. Life Metaphors

- Represent past experiences negotiating key developmental issues
- Construe present stimulation
- Prescribe plans of action to negotiate developmental issues in present environments

II. Cognitive-Behavioral Regulators in Self- and Mutual Regulation

- Hierarchy of cognitive functions: from body regulation to conceptual thinking
- Coordinate and equilibrate demands of life metaphors and persons/environments as construed

III. Behavioral Modalities of Action, Fantasy, and Language

- Hierarchy of behavioral modes from action to fantasy to language
- Respond to demands for action from life metaphors and environments as coordinated by cognition

IV. Persons/Environments

- Prescribe/expect various forms of behavior
- Ever changing
- Usual/expected and unusual/unexpected

FIGURE 6–1

A Developmental Framework: Age 3 Years to Adolesence

behavioral functions that participate in self- and mutual regulations actively approach, avoid, select, and coordinate stimulation both from life metaphors and from changing environments in the service of adaptation (Model II). With the other, the behavioral modalities of action, fantasy, and language are conceptualized as the means by which the child engages and acts upon changing environments (Model III). An integration of these models forms a developmental framework that provides three doorways through which a child therapist could enter to facilitate change.

MODEL I: LIFE METAPHORS: FROM EMBODIED REPRESENTATIONS IN INFANCY TO METAPHORS IN CHILDHOOD

To bridge the previous chapter with the discussion to follow, I consider Piaget's sensorimotor schemas, Johnson's embodied image schemas, Stern's representations of interactions generalized, and Sander's negotiated issues as contributing significant elements to the "first nonverbal editions" of life metaphors. Two vignettes should be helpful in introducing the model (see also Santostefano 1986, 1988b, 1991b, 1995). One concerns a child behaving in his neighborhood, the other a child behaving in the treatment situation.

First vignette. Spotting a jogger, a 3-year-old leaned his body forward, and with each exuberant "Choo-Choo!" vigorously thrust his right arm forward and back as he playfully ran alongside the jogger for a few moments. Later he spotted the same jogger. This time the toddler scampered behind a tree and crouched low, his facial expression and body posture clearly suggesting he was experiencing something to be feared. It seems clear that the child is assigning different meanings to the jogger during each encounter and taking action accordingly. But we are left with questions. Why was the jogger assigned one meaning at one time (the jogger is a powerful train engine) and a very different one at another (the jogger is a monster)?

Second vignette. In the professional playroom, a child marched with sober, measured steps, holding a stick overhead and posturing strength and determination. When asked what she was playing, she did not reply. In another session she sat on the floor and nudged a pig hand-puppet against a doll while narrating an elaborate fantasy about a giant animal swallowing a person. In still another session, slouched in a chair, she laughed as she described a birthday present her brother received. "His cork gun was a plop." This vignette articulates the issue of multiple modes involved in constructing and expressing meaning. How can we understand the significance of why at one moment the child enacted being a confident, powerful figure without speaking a word; at another moment she engaged in miniature actions while elaborating a vivid fantasy of one figure engulfing another; and at another she verbally described the memory of a gift without taking action or engaging in a fantasy?

These questions bring us to the realm of metaphor construction, which we discussed briefly in previous chapters. However, since the formulation of life metaphor I propose here departs from typical ways in which metaphor has been conceptualized, it is necessary that we take a slight detour and consider a sketch of metaphor as presented in the psychological literature.

Typical Views of Metaphor

It is generally accepted that metaphor (along with its close relatives, simile and analogy) involves the transfer of meaning. That is, something is described in terms of properties that belong to something else. There are two views of how this transfer takes place. With one, the "comparison/substitution" view, a referent and the item taken as its substitute are classified together and compared on the basis of a shared attribute. In our first vignette, the attribute of power is the basis on which the toddler compared the referent (jogger) and its substitute (train engine). With the "interaction" view, a metaphor results in a new meaning that goes beyond the objects compared and substituted and synthesizes present and past experiences with them. As one example, in our second vignette the girl's brother, as she construed him, interacted with a cork gun and defecation, producing the linguistic metaphor of a "plop," and expressing the meaning that her brother is feces, a meaning that synthesized past and present experiences with him.

What functions are served by metaphor? Many have been proposed, beginning with Aristotle's view that metaphor is ornamental and useful in rendering discourse less dull. Later writers agreed with Aristotle, but proposed that these ornaments of language distort meaning, since language should convey only facts, or at best serve only to coin terms and new concepts. In sharp contrast, Ortony (1979) proposed that metaphors are "necessary" rather than "nice" and serve several important functions. For example, metaphors condense many facts, depict events that by their nature are not easily described with words, reconstruct experiences, and are vivid, lying much closer to a person's experiences than words do.

The purpose served by metaphor relates to key problems articulated by reviewers of this literature (e.g., Billow 1977, Ortony 1979, Ortony et al. 1978). They point out that most workers assume a word, or sentence, is the exclusive locus of a metaphor, a position still seen in writings on the use of metaphor in psychotherapy (e.g., Witzum et al. 1988). These reviewers proposed that metaphor construction also involves pretending and imaging, and that a broader definition should be adopted. For example, Billow (1977) underscored the need to study the relationships between metaphor and the process of play and imaging, and wondered if metaphor is an example of imaged thinking and not simply spoken language. Along the same line, Verbrugge and McCarrel (1977) proposed that metaphors invite pretending and imaging, as well as reasoning by analogy, and "may be basic to all growth and understanding, whether in the playroom, the psychotherapeutic setting, the scientific laboratory, or the theater" (p. 495).

The need to integrate spoken words, imaging, and pretending in metaphor construction is illustrated by our vignettes. In our first vignette the toddler was surely imaging a train engine as he verbalized "Choo-Choo." But he also leaned forward and thrust his arm vigorously back and forth. Later he was surely imaging and enacting when he spotted the same jogger, and without speaking a word crouched behind a tree displaying a facial expression of fear. And in our second vignette the child was very likely expressing metaphoric meaning when she marched with sober, measured steps about the playroom, holding a stick overhead and posturing strength and determination. The reformulation proposed in the following concept of life metaphor frees the definition of metaphor from its traditional locus in words and expands it by integrating actions, imaging, language, emotions, and cognition in metaphor construction. In this way metaphor construction and the purpose of metaphor is given a more central role in personality development.

The Concept of Life Metaphor: A Child's World
of Experiencing and Knowing

The reformulation of metaphor I propose defines a process that produces all of the meanings that relate to what a child experiences and knows. Here the reader is reminded of our discussion in Chapter 4 of meaning, knowing, and experiencing. We noted there that experiencing is a way of knowing and of constructing meaning that is immediate, holistic, contextual, and embodied, integrating patterns of sights, sounds, smells, actions, and touch perceptions as well as spoken words. The concept of life metaphor conceptualizes this pattern of symbols as involved in negotiating key developmental issues with others. A life metaphor represents and condenses past negotiations with issues, construes present stimulation in terms of them, and prescribes a plan of action to continue negotiating.

A Definition of Life Metaphor: Representations as Plans for Action

Phenomenologically a life metaphor is a persistent, habitual organization (pattern) of behaviors that *simultaneously* (1) represents past experiences, (2) construes present persons and situations, and (3) prescribes various behaviors/emotions as responses. The vehicles used to construct and express the meanings of a life metaphor may include images, words, thoughts, emotions, postures, and physical actions. Each persistent pattern of behaviors serves to negotiate a *key developmental issue* vis-à-vis the self and others; for example, attachment-trust-love, loss-detachment, separation-individuation, controlling-being controlled, dependence-autonomy/independence, initiating-reciprocating, ambition-dominance, and assertiveness-aggressiveness-competitiveness.

To clarify the definition further, it should be helpful to compare the notion of life metaphor with the concept of symbol formation. As discussed in Chapter 4, with symbol formation something is experienced in terms of properties that belong to something else. When a 2-year-old places a napkin on her head after observing mother put on a hat and leave the room, the properties of the hat are synthesized with those of the napkin that the toddler now experiences as a hat. In forming a symbol, then, the meaning a person experiences, which is termed the *referent*, is dynamically fitted with the behavioral expression of that meaning, which is termed the *vehicle* (Smith 1979, Werner and Kaplan 1963). *However, constructing a life metaphor involves constructing a pattern of referents and vehicles, the organization of which prescribes how a core developmental issue has been and is to be negotiated with others.*

The Origins of Life Metaphors

The first edition of a life metaphor emerges when a nonverbal play ritual, organized from 8 to 18 months, serves the negotiation of a fundamental developmental issue. Here the observations of infants and their caregivers discussed in the previous chapter are relevant. For a play ritual to give rise to a life metaphor, the infant should have (1) reached Piaget's fifth stage of cognitive development during which tertiary circular reactions discover new ways of accomplishing goals and become play rituals; (2) constructed the beginnings of Stern's subjective self within which the infant understands the motives of others; and (3) negotiated Sander's early issues of reciprocal exchange and directed activity, and become involved in negotiating focalization—when the infant gives more differentiated directions to caregivers, especially concerning the need for protection from danger and permission to explore the unknown.

The first edition of a life metaphor, with its shared meaning, undergoes a series of revisions after the age of 2 years. With each revision the child negotiates the same developmental issue at higher levels, building upon previous ones. This process, consisting of a revolving series of interpersonal activity rituals spirals, throughout childhood as an "arrow of time," a concept we discussed in Chapter 5.

An Illustration of the Development of Life Metaphors

To illustrate the development of life metaphors and how each builds upon previous ones, consider the following observations. At 18 months a child repeated a play ritual for several weeks in which he sat on father's lap and gestured so that father buttoned and then unbuttoned his shirt around the boy's body. At this point the toddler slipped off father's lap and scampered away, and father looked for him. With this play ritual, enacted at the dawn of symbolic functioning, the first edition of a meaning was being constructed and negotiated: attachment (at one with father's body) and separation–individuation (running off with father looking for him). A few months later the child initiated another play ritual that differentiated the meaning of attachment/separation to include allegiance and identification. Now the child insisted he sit immediately next to father at mealtimes, gradually extending the seating arrangement to the family car, restaurants, and homes of relatives.

During the first months of his third year, the child introduced still another ritual and edition, now including the negotiation of self-assertion while retaining a positive identification with father. The child requested that during mealtimes he use a glass identical to father's and that the liquid poured into each be exactly the same height. After drinking, child and father placed the glasses side by side and carefully judged which glass contained "bigger" or "smaller" amounts. A few years later the child engaged father in playing checkers, now negotiating aggression and competing against the idealized parent (while relying upon the previously successfully negotiated issues of separation, individuation, and identification). Still later the child engaged father in debates over the relative merits of the Boston Celtics versus the Los Angeles Lakers.

This anecdote illustrates Overton's (1994) notion of change as "the arrow of time." Each cycle of activity did not return to the original starting point but eventually spiraled, moving the system of child and father toward greater complexity and resulting in new patterns that exhibited novel properties that reflected increased differentiation, integration, and flexibility. The series of cycles formed a spiral of interpersonal activity, initially negotiating separation-individuation and then other issues. Each negotiation built upon the previous one and differentiated the activity matrix into a progressive, integrated series of self–other relations from "I am in you and also separate from you," to "I am by your side," to "Who is bigger/smaller?" to "Who is the greatest?"

In addition to the view of change as a process of differentiation/integration that characterized the evolving relational matrix of this child and father, embodiment-enactment theory (see Chapter 5) directs our attention to another phenomenon. The child's interactions and negotiations with father also resulted in the child's mind differentiating into different modalities of experiencing and representing. Initially, the vehicles the child used to construct meaning involved primarily gestures and actions (the shirt game). Gradually, imagination (fantasy) differentiated as a mode that assimilated actions and gestures and dominated in constructing representations (the glasses were fantasized as the persons of child and father). Still later, language (linguistic metaphors) emerged as a system of expression that assimilated fantasy and action (the debate over the merits of two basketball teams, each representing one of them). This progression in modalities is viewed as an ontogenetic shift from concrete behavioral systems that symbolize and express direct/immediate contact with others to abstract behavioral systems that symbolize and express indirect/delayed contact with others.

This illustration highlights three aspects of the concept of life metaphor that will play a dominant role when we design techniques for child psychotherapy. One concerns the proposition that another person, whom the child idealizes and with whom the child is identified, must be available and willing to participate in continuous cycles of interactions as the child negotiates a life metaphor. The second concerns how new life metaphors are constructed. The third concerns how existing life metaphors are revised.

The Availability of Others Who Are Idealized: A Critical Ingredient in Constructing, Revising, and Negotiating Life Metaphors

One necessary prerequisite for constructing a new life metaphor or revising an existing one is the availability of other persons whom the child idealizes and with whom the child is identified. As discussed in Chapter 4, psychoanalytic developmental theory conceptualizes an "ego ideal" as consisting of an integration of representations of positive, loving, synchronous experiences with parents or parental substitutes as well as imagined events concerning religious and important cultural figures. This integration of representations results in a set of standards of goodness and excellence that the child comes to desire. These standards, then, do not represent what one ought to do but what one genuinely wants to be. To further clarify the concept, the ego ideal is distinguished from the concept of "superego," which is viewed as an integration of representations of punitive, stern, and forbidding behaviors of parents and other significant persons. The superego is concerned primarily with controlling impulses and preventing wishes from gaining expression in action, while the ego ideal is concerned primarily with stimulating a person to take idealized action that emulates an idealized figure. Further, core aspects of a child's superego are viewed as formed from the ages of 4 to 6 years. In contrast, the ego ideal could undergo continuous change as life experiences bring new persons into a child's life. And if experiences with these persons result in heightened, positive emotional exchanges, then the standards and expectations of these persons become woven into the child's developing ego ideal.

To recap, negotiating a life metaphor, with its developmental issue, requires cycles of interaction with idealized persons if the life metaphor is to undergo revision and set the stage for the next developmentally higher issue to be negotiated.

How New Life Metaphors Are Constructed and Existing Life Metaphors Are Revised

As life metaphors develop, they revolve continuously through a series of interpersonal cycles of negotiation. Two processes are involved. One defines how a new life metaphor is constructed. The other defines how an already constructed life metaphor is elaborated, differentiated, and revised. In keeping with our dialectical approach, these are not independent processes. Rather, each defines and is defined by the other, and each influences the other.

The Construction of New Life Metaphors: Maturation Dominates

The process of constructing a new life metaphor is represented by Overton's (1994) image of "the arrow of time." Here a pattern of symbols (actions, fantasies, words, emotions) that defines a particular life metaphor and the developmental issue the child is negotiating spirals from one developmental level to a higher one. What factors cause a life metaphor to spiral? New behavioral modalities that code (symbolize) experience emerge intrinsically as a function of maturation. For example, in Piaget's model, discussed in previous chapters, a maturational shift occurs at about 2 years when the mind relinquishes coding experiences with sensorimotor schemas and emphasizes coding experiences with mental schemas that copy and represent actions on things (the beginning of the preoperational stage). Psychoanalytic theory provides another example. Shifts occur in how experiences are coded when different body zones mature and accordingly dominate as references when a child gives meaning to experiences: from the mouth that emphasizes meanings of nurture, to the anus that emphasizes meanings of being controlled, withholding/giving, to the genitals that emphasize meanings of ascendance, competence, and achievement. As the reader may notice, when a life metaphor spirals from one level to another, influences from the environment play a nonspecific role relative to maturational influences.

The anecdote discussed above of the boy and his father provides an example of the process of constructing new life metaphors as modes of expression mature. The "shirt" game made predominant use of macroactions. With the "glass" game, microactions were involved within the fantasy mode, which began to dominate. With the discussions of basketball teams the language mode dominated, subordinating and integrating actions and fantasies. Another example is depicted in Figure 6–2.

Before leaving the process involved in constructing new metaphors, we should remind ourselves of a principle discussed in Chapter 5, that while an earlier version of some organization of behavior is subordinated by and integrated within a later version, the earlier version remains potentially active, and can be reactivated and influence behavior. This developmental principle also applies to life metaphors. In the following example a child experienced the same interaction through different life metaphors. One metaphor was constructed early in development and concerned nurture (oral stage), another was constructed later and concerned control (anal stage), and another was constructed still later and concerned competitiveness and triangular relationships (phallic and oedipal stages). In treatment a child re-

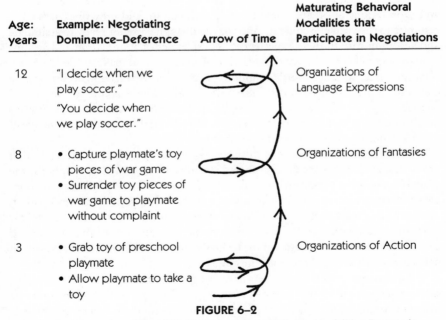

FIGURE 6–2

The Development of New Life Metaphors that Evolve as Modalities Emerge in Maturation: Spiraling Revolutions

vealed that while listening to mother read her a story, she construed the experience at one moment as mother giving her as much milk as her baby brother was receiving; at another time she construed the experience as mother controlling her since she had to go to bed after the story was read; at yet another she construed mother as jealous, reading to her as a way of keeping her away from daddy's lap and the "special times" she spends with him. As the reader may notice, the life metaphors and developmental issues revealed by these experiences are, respectively, reading is milk and being nurtured by mother, reading is you control what I do with my body, and reading is you keep me from the man I love because you want him for yourself.

How Life Metaphors Are Revised: Environmental Stimulation Dominates

The process involved in revising existing life metaphors is represented by the image of a continuous series of revolutions on a horizontal plane, a process that integrates Mounoud's (1982) model of revolutionary periods in development, Piaget's (1977) concept of equilibration, and the psychoanalytic concept of internalization. In revising existing life metaphors, the behaviors of others and environmental stimulation play a major role, while maturational influences play a nonspecific role. As illustrated in Figure 6–3, to negotiate a life metaphor, the child engages in a series of interactions and enactments with others. Throughout this series of experiences, the developmental issue the life metaphor represents "bumps into" the demands and expectations of others, construes this stimulation, and prescribes actions in response to the available context. And the life metaphor stands ready to assimilate and accommodate to these experiences. These cycles of assimilation and accommodation gradually revise the organization of elements that make up the life metaphor (gestures, fantasies, words, emotions) so that the organization becomes more elaborate (differentiated) and flexible (integrated). The example in Figure 6–3 depicts a 7-year-old boy who, in negotiating dominance and deference, "bumps into" the demands of a parent, teacher, sib, and peer, deferring to the demands of some and dominating over the demands of others.

Forecasting the relevance of this process for therapy, I emphasize again that one necessary prerequisite for revising an already constructed life metaphor is the availability of other persons whom the child idealizes and who participate without condition in a series of negotiations with the child. If a child idealizes a parent, aunt, uncle, or teacher early in development, and, later, sibs and peers, the child is more likely to identify with the permissions and prohibitions of that person and also internalize (accommodate to) the behaviors this idealized figure displays when participating in negotiations with the child.

To illustrate further the process of revising an existing life metaphor, we consider again the toddler who initiated a "shirt game" as a play ritual. Here it may be helpful to recall Sander's 8th issue (Chapter 5) when infant and caregiver construct and share an increasingly elaborated pool of shared symbols. As the shirt game cycled on a horizontal plane, the play rituals father and boy used were elaborated which,

Example: Negotiating Dominance-Deference
Age 7 years

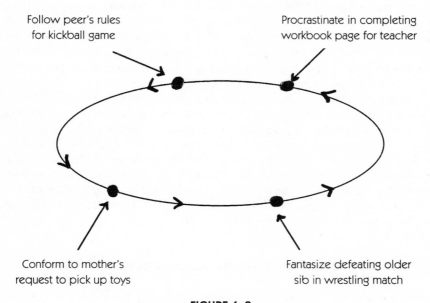

Follow peer's rules
for kickball game

Procrastinate in completing
workbook page for teacher

Conform to mother's
request to pick up toys

Fantasize defeating older
sib in wrestling match

FIGURE 6–3
Negotiating the Same Life Metaphor with Different Persons and Contexts:
Horizontal Revolutions

in turn, elaborated and differentiated the symbols they invented and shared to negotiate separation–individuation. The father, of course, wore different shirts from day to day, and on occasion a sweater, which resulted in the boy's crawling within it to engage in still another cycle. Also, as the ritual was repeated and the child ran off, the child hid behind different pieces of furniture and invented new, ingenious "hideouts," such as a cabinet. In the meantime, the father elaborated the techniques he used to search for his son. Initially he ran after him, spotting him seconds later behind a couch. As the boy elaborated his hiding techniques, the father elaborated his searching techniques. He used a small flashlight, and then a large one, as he aimed the beam under chairs and couches and in closets. Later he took one of the boy's favorite toys, an airplane, and "flew" it about, searching for him and calling out, "Where are you?"

I return to Figure 6–3 to highlight additional issues that concern revising existing life metaphors. Only four individuals and contexts are depicted. In daily living, of course, dozens of encounters with person and contexts could occur during a given week, which the child uses to negotiate an issue. Further, all three modalities (action, fantasy, and language) may be involved in a major way during any given negotiation, or only one or two modalities, depending upon a child's maturational level. In the example presented in Figure 6–3, the child is in a maturational stage during which action and fantasy behaviors play a major role (see Model III), therefore dominating or deferring to others with actions and fantasies. A younger child may utilize actions alone, while an older child may utilize an integration of actions, fantasies, and language expressions. Last, while every interaction in which the child engages does not necessarily involve negotiating and revising a life metaphor, interactions with idealized persons typically do.

Revolving continuously on a horizontal plane, then, life metaphors during normal development accommodate to experiences/environments and are ready to construe more complex stimulation and to require more complex interactions with others. As a life metaphor is cycled and recycled, with its constellation of symbols gradually elaborated, there are two outcomes that relate to psychotherapy: (1) the developmental issue being negotiated is framed within a differentiated, integrated, and flexible organization of behaviors; and (2) when the issue has been negotiated to a "good enough" point, the child is now equipped to begin the negotiation of another issue that builds upon the previous one.

The Issue of Past-Present, Conscious-Unconscious, and Dreams

Life metaphors may or may not be at work when an individual is experiencing some situation or reliving the past. For example, if a child describes a trip the family took last summer, revealing details that form a photocopy of the event, no metaphor is at work. But if the same child describes the trip while knocking hand puppets together, a metaphor of family conflict could be construing the event. Similarly, a dream does not automatically relate to a life metaphor. A child could describe a dream (e.g., a tall building) as she would a picture and not show evidence that a metaphor is construing the information. In contrast, while describing the dream, the same child could stack and topple blocks, suggesting one meaning imposed on the dream. Life metaphors are not necessarily synonymous with unconscious processes. A person could be aware or unaware of a metaphor at work. The boy who placed a piece of clay at the end of his nose, discussed in the previous chapter, was probably not aware of the metaphor he was negotiating with his therapist.

Criteria for the Successful Negotiation of Life Metaphors

Success is achieved when negotiations result in representations of developmental issues that are differentiated and integrated and that prescribe flexible cognitive and behavioral actions used to negotiate them. Success is a function of several interrelated factors:

1. A child's cognition is capable of perceiving opportunities and limitations of stimuli (persons and things) and recruiting them as vehicles to construct and express symbols (see Model II below).
2. A child is free to take action, fantasize, and verbalize what he/she means or intends (see Model III below).
3. A person with emotional responsiveness, whom the child idealizes, is available along with materials and opportunities for enacting play rituals.
4. The idealized person physically participates with the child in play rituals and negotiations, displaying a wide range of relevant emotions, for as long as the child prescribes.
5. The idealized person does not interfere with the child's revisions and does not introduce stimulation that is either excessive or too subdued, given the child's temperament.

From this discussion of life metaphor in normal development, we consider the concept when a child shows maladaptive behaviors that are likely to come to the attention of a therapist.

Life Metaphors and Maladaptive Functioning

When a child shows maladaptive functioning—for example, excessive fears, inappropriate aggression, hyperactivity, and inhibition in completing school work—the assumption is made that one or another life metaphor, and the developmental issue it represents, has remained fixed or rigid. More specifically, a life metaphor is maladaptive whenever:

1. The child's behaviors do not fit with developmental expectations in terms of cognitive and behavioral coding systems that should have emerged through the process of maturation.
2. The child's behaviors have failed over an extended period of time to assimilate and accommodate to available experiences that contain ingredients suitable for restructuring a life metaphor.
3. The child's behaviors are inappropriate for, and/or are rejected by, the child's usual environments, producing conflict with significant others (interpersonal conflict).
4. The child's behaviors meet the demands of his/her maladaptive metaphor but are at odds with the demands of standards of an idealized other that the child has already internalized, resulting in anxiety and guilt (intrapsychic conflict).

A brief example of each of these possibilities should be useful, although the clinical cases discussed in future chapters provide in-depth illustrations. In terms of developmental expectations, consider a 30-month-old who repeatedly smears the bathroom wall with play dough, finger paints, and sometimes feces. This behavior would not necessarily be viewed as prescribed by a pathological life metaphor because a child is at a stage in development dominated by a coding system that psychodynamic theory terms *anal*. The child is therefore negotiating the issues of testing and modifying aggressive intentions, and control versus relinquishing control, with organizations of behaviors that are influenced by this coding system. The responses of caregivers would influence the success with which the child negotiates these issues as cycles of interactions are repeated.

But if such behavior is displayed by an 8-year-old, it is likely that a pathological life metaphor is operating. In terms of the maturational development of coding systems, the 8-year-old would be expected to have other behavioral vehicles available to symbolize the issue of aggression and control, vehicles that reflect more indirectness and delay. For example, having been required against his strong protests to wear a particular pair of pants to a party, the child returns with mud splashed on one trouser leg. "It was an accident." The issue of modes of symbolizing and enacting that emerge with maturation receives more detailed discussion in the third developmental model discussed below.

In terms of a life metaphor failing to assimilate and accommodate to available experiences, consider an adopted third-grader. Since infancy she had not adequately negotiated reciprocity with her adoptive parents, who expressed considerable ambivalence over giving unconditionally and shifting flexibly between being active and passive. This child constructed a life metaphor that prescribed a sense of emptiness, excessive possessiveness, and envy. Now, while in treatment at the age of 10, she discussed various situations in which she experienced herself as an "empty basket" that others passed by, refusing to put something in it. During each of these experiences, she became sullen and withdrawn. For example, when in a restaurant with her family, she happened to be waited on last; when in the classroom, she was next to last in a line waiting to receive worksheets from the teacher; at a birthday party she happened to receive a balloon containing, she believed, less air than the balloons other children were given. Instead of assimilating other elements of these situations, the maladaptive metaphor dominated in shaping the same meaning and experience. She recalled later that in the restaurant father allowed her to have her favorite dessert (a large piece of chocolate cake), and in school, when she received her worksheets, the teacher complimented her on work she had previously turned in. In spite of numerous, similar experiences, her maladaptive metaphor did not accommodate, and was not revised.

In terms of behaviors rejected by the child's usual environments, consider a 12-year-old who is regularly lost in fantasy and quite content to spend endless hours at the computer playing interactive games involving battles between mythical figures. In the meantime, he is in conflict with his parents because he gives little or no time to homework, and because he is not cultivating relationships with peers.

While his excessive fantasy life is very likely meeting the demands of a life metaphor that involves asserting and aggressing, it is at odds with the demands of his environment (interpersonal conflict).

In terms of intrapsychic conflict, consider a 10-year-old who has failed to negotiate self-assertion, with its autonomy, in many negotiations with parents. Since his toddler years, his parents have consistently exercised control over what the child eats, plays, and wears. As a result, he organized a life metaphor that construes situations and prescribes behaviors that call for him to be passive and submissive. At the same time, since his toddler years, the child has had many interactions with an aunt and uncle who have been quite accommodating when the boy negotiated self-assertion. The boy internalized and conserved experiences with these idealized adults that resulted in a life metaphor that prescribed and permitted self-assertion and autonomy. Now, when assigned to a soccer team by the fifth-grade gym teacher, the boy is gripped with anxiety and conflict as the metaphor of passivity, born out of his negotiations with parents, collides with the metaphor of autonomy and self-assertion, born out of his negotiations with aunt and uncle.

COGNITION AND BEHAVIORAL MODALITIES IN NEGOTIATING LIFE METAPHORS: AN INTRODUCTION

The model of life metaphor interacts with and is elaborated by two others. One (Model II) defines cognition as involving "deep structures" (see Chapter 4) that determine which stimuli are selected and avoided by an individual and influence which meanings are given to experiences. This model pays particular attention to whether and when cognitive functions shift in organization as a life metaphor dominates, or a situation dominates in calling for action. The other model (III) concerns behavioral modes a child uses to express meanings prescribed by life metaphors and to negotiate developmental issues with others. This model gives special attention to whether a life metaphor is experienced and expressed in the action, fantasy, or language mode, or some combination, and therefore addresses the relations among what a child does, imagines, and says. As outlined in Figure 6–1, cognitive functions and behavioral modalities are conceptualized as mediating between the demands of life metaphors and those of environments as construed by the child.

Each model also defines how cognition and behavioral modes play a role in self- and mutual regulation. Recall the study, discussed in Chapter 5, illustrating that behaviors an infant used to regulate stimulation also served to regulate interactions. If the level of stimulation mother introduced was too high, the infant looked away, engaging in self-regulation to reduce the level of stimulation. If mother picked up the baby's cue and lowered her stimulation, the infant looked back at the mother and reestablished adequate mutual regulation. Looking away, then, served both self-regulation and mutual regulation.

The same relationship exists between self- and mutual regulation during a child's cognitive functioning while negotiating life metaphors with others. The model of cognitive functioning outlined below defines a set of unconscious cognitive processes that select, avoid, and organize stimulation so as to equilibrate the complexity of information and related emotions that impinge on a child's mind, therefore serving self-regulation. In selecting and avoiding stimulation, these same cognitive processes also contribute to the actions a child takes with others, therefore serving mutual regulation.

In a similar way, the model of behavioral modalities outlined below defines the expression of a meaning as serving self- and mutual regulation in terms of the degree of delay and directness that guide the expression. For example, while a child and peer walk home from school, the child may kick a trash can "in slow motion" instead of kicking the peer who is frustrating him. Shifting from an expression that is immediate and direct to one that is more delayed and indirect serves self-regulation. This shift also serves mutual regulation since child and peer can remain engaged and continue walking together.

Last, in keeping with the principle of holism, the models of cognitive functioning and behavioral modalities are embedded within personality and adaptation. In this way both cognition and emotion and what a child does, fantasizes, and says are integrated as one.

MODEL II: COGNITION IN SELF- AND MUTUAL REGULATION AND ADAPTATION

In formulating this model, I relied on my research conducted within the "New Look" that emerged in the 1950s (see Chapter 4). As noted earlier, investigators set out to correlate individual differences in cognitive and personality functioning, rather than search for universal laws that explain cognitive activity as a self-contained system (one characteristic of the Piagetian approach). In addition, cognitive activity was conceived as occurring largely outside of awareness, supplying material from which the individual constructed a personal world of meanings. The influence of the New Look approach on studies of cognition is illustrated by an investigation (Rosenwald et al. 1966) conducted over thirty years ago that unified cognition, emotion, and unconscious meanings. These authors asked adolescents to feel cut-outs that were immersed in water in one condition and in crankcase oil and flour ("fecal material") in another and to match each with one of several shapes. Speed and success were viewed as reflecting the adequacy with which a subject managed anal meanings and prevented related anxiety from interfering with cognitive activity. Subjects were also administered questionnaires assessing anal character traits (e.g., "I am a punctual person") and anal anxiety (e.g., "I get very upset when I waste time"). Rosenwald and colleagues found that subjects who performed more poorly in the oil–flour condition (versus the water condition) reported high anal anxiety; those who matched quickly and accurately in both conditions reported low anal anxiety.

George Klein's Model of Cognitive Controls

Of the investigators who pursued this New Look approach to cognition, the work of George Klein impressed me three decades ago as the most heuristic in integrating cognition, emotion, action, and meaning. In his research with adults (e.g., Klein 1951, 1954) he introduced a method that was relatively unique at the time. Most investigators, for example, were asking subjects to estimate the sizes of circles, or to locate a rod in the upright position while a frame surrounding the rod was tilted. In contrast, as did the researchers who used crankcase oil years later, Klein asked subjects to engage in various cognitive tasks that consisted of neutral stimuli and stimuli that evoked fantasies/emotions. For example, in his classic thirst study (Klein 1954) Klein asked subjects (half of whom had been served a thirst-inducing meal) to estimate the sizes of circles on which were placed various symbols, some thirst related and others thirst neutral. He observed that the fantasies and emotions of thirsty and nonthirsty subjects, evoked by the symbols attached to the circles, correlated with how these subjects differed in the ways they approached, avoided, and selected information. While other investigators of the time ignored individual differences in cognitive functioning as if they were "embarrassing bacteria" (Klein and Schlesinger 1949), Klein made central use of individual differences in conceptualizing an integration between cognition and emotion. For Klein these individual differences defined ego-cognitive strategies a person uses to remain in adaptive control of information. He labeled these strategies *cognitive controls* and conceptualized these processes as serving a coordinating, equilibrating function. That is, they coordinate environmental information and its requirements with the requirements of information from personal fantasies, emotions, and motives, all in the service of successful adaptation. As Klein (1951) stated, cognitive controls are cognitive mechanisms that "bring into harmony needs, impulses and wishes and buffer the turbulence from within against limitations from without, by selecting, avoiding, integrating and organizing information from the two worlds" (p. 36).

Klein conducted extensive research spanning more than twenty years. In one of his last published books (Klein 1970), he had much to say that relates to our interest in forging cognition and emotion as one, comments that are still quite useful.

> [T]o discuss drive as if it were a distinctive entity that "interacts" with a thought creates all sorts of mischief. It is only as structured affective-cognitive-motor events that drives our knowable as motivations and definable at all. Inasmuch as motivation involves knowledge, it is cognitive. It lends significance and meaning to what we see and do (assimilation, in

Piaget's terms), or it causes us to revise what we think we know (accommodation). Conversely, insofar as cognition has direction, it is motivated. A motive has consequences, and consequences involve ideational residues of actions, of affects, and of thoughts—all cognitive matters. Therefore, what is motivating about behavior and what is knowledgeful about motivation are one and the same. Motives in cognition are not motives "interacting" with cognition. [p. 360]

Motivation implies directions and intensity of activity. They are its core attributes. Motivation is not a matter of external stimulation or internal stimulation alone. To motivate behavior, rather than to simply arouse the organism, external stimuli must first become meaningful; the same is true of internal stimuli, or "drive." If drive is indeed unoriented, internally generated stimulation, it too becomes motivational only when it is cognitively represented, as in a wish, . . . without such a mediating process, external and internal stimulation have activating but not directional effects. [p. 364]

Klein was proposing that to integrate cognition and emotion/motives, we must grind a new lens. When looking through this lens, it may be helpful if a cognitive therapist, who may not usually pay attention to motivational issues, notices whether he/she can see a set of intersecting rectangles that form the galloping horse of motivation/emotion. A psychodynamic therapist, who may not usually attend to cognitive issues, should notice whether he/she can see a galloping horse of emotion/motivation as forming a set of intersecting rectangles. Each therapist should keep in mind that at the heart of Klein's formulation was the proposition that although the horse of emotion and the rectangles of cognition both exist, they are the same.

Santostefano's Concept of Cognitive-Behavioral Regulators in Children

Taking Klein's (1951) formulations as a starting point, I embarked on a program of research over three decades ago (Santostefano 1963, 1964a,b) to explore the concept of cognitive controls with both normal and pathological children as well as with adults. (For reviews of this research see Santostefano 1978, 1985, 1986, 1995b, Santostefano and Rieder 1984, Wertlieb 1979.) This program extended Klein's initial formulations along several lines: (1) cognitive control mechanisms were defined to include body image and activity, and body image was linked to cognitive activity at higher developmental levels that did not require the direct participation of the body; (2) cognitive control mechanisms were observed to operate in children as well as adults, from the age of 3 years through adolescence; (3) each cognitive control mechanism followed a particular developmental course; (4) various clinical groups of children showed particular deviations from these developmental lines; (5) assessments of cognitive controls predicted learning disabilities and adjustment problems; (6) regressive and progressive changes occurred in the organization of these cognitive mechanisms in response to changes in a person's environment and emotional state. Because my research supported a hierarchy of cognitive functions that integrate body and mental activity, and emphasized how cognitive functions regulate information from the environment and one's subjective world of fantasies, wishes, and emotions, I use here the term *cognitive-behavioral regulators* instead of Klein's term of *cognitive controls*.

Cognitive-Behavioral Regulators and Learning in the Treatment Situation

How does the concept of cognitive-behavioral regulators contribute to formulating an integrative approach to child psychotherapy? With one contribution, the concept provides a way of operationalizing how learning takes place in the treatment situation. Recalling our discussion in Chapter 3, we noted there that while schools of therapy differ on how therapy is conducted, they agree that psychotherapy is a learning process. If we begin with this consensus, we need a definition of learning that serves psychotherapy. Piaget (1977) provided a definition that I believe meets this need. "To know (to learn) . . . is to . . . reproduce the object [information] dynamically; but to reproduce, it is necessary to know how to produce (copy the information)" (p. 30). This definition of learning, then, articulates two steps: (1) copying and producing information, and (2) reproducing the information dynamically, that is, translating it into symbols. To illustrate what Piaget meant, and to set the stage for the cognitive concepts and techniques that are included in my integrative psychotherapy, I compare children during moments of psychotherapy.

The First Clinical Comparison

Case A. John, a 15-year-old, flopped into the chair he usually used. Suddenly he popped up, sat in another chair farther away from the therapist, and chuckled, "That [the chair he vacated] is hard on my back today." His right hand clenched his left; he glared at the therapist, looked away, and sighed, "Since we met last. . . ." He paused, handled an ashtray on the table next to him, glared at it, and seemed to be miles away. Shifting restlessly in his chair, he turned his attention to the bookshelves and wondered how many books they held, then recalled a vacation the family took this time last year. The books and vacation faded away as he commented, "Yesterday I was late for school. My father blasted me and made me put tools back in the garage. I felt like shit. I can't seem to do anything right. . . ." His attention shifted to a homework assignment. He ignored this thought, fingered the ashtray again, edged it toward the therapist, and said with a tone of irritation, "Your ash-tray is cracked like my father." Then he laughed anxiously.

During these moments, John regulated his body motility (e.g., he moved far-ther away from the therapist, shifted about in his chair, sat still) as he visually and tactually scanned and copied information from his external environment (e.g., books, ashtray) and from his subjective environment (e.g., a memory of a family vacation, anxiety over a homework assignment). As he coordinated information from these two environments, he organized a constellation of symbols that defined a theme, very likely without awareness: the office chair hard on his back; an inci-dent in which his father blasted him, causing him to feel demeaned and rejected; a cracked ashtray symbolizing father and therapist and associated with anger and anxiety. This theme, offered to the therapist for examination as a source for learn-ing (he pushed the ashtray toward the therapist), resulted from cognitive struc-tures that (1) copied and selected information from the environment and thoughts, fantasies, and emotions related to life metaphors; (2) coordinated and integrated these two pieces of information, transforming them into symbols that represented and expressed one of his conflicted life metaphors (i.e., authority is on his back, is cracked [flawed], and makes him feel impotent and angry); and (3) enabled John, while dealing with the issue, to pretend that the therapist is father and at the same time a source of assistance. During these moments, then, John's cognition was engaged in efficient learning as defined by Piaget, serving the process and goals of psychotherapy.

Case B. Tom, also 15 years old, sat relatively still, stared at the floor, and initiated no conversation, behaviors typical of him since the start of treatment six sessions ago. The therapist acknowledged Tom's difficulty being in treatment. Tom continued looking at the floor, carefully adjusted the creases of his trousers with thumb and forefinger of each hand, slowly picked at a piece of lint on his jersey, and stared out the window. After a long pause he commented that he was bored. Then, showing irritation, he pointed out that he was missing a special TV program because of his appointment. The therapist acknowledged, empa-thized with Tom's disappointment, and commented that he is trying to help Tom learn why he is failing school and has a difficult time relating to classmates. Tom glared at the therapist, looked away, and after a long pause said, "There are too many things racing through my mind." The therapist urged him to "catch one and share it." After another long pause Tom noted with irritation that he ". . . can't; they just go too fast; and if I could, why should I share it?" At this point he untied and tied his shoelaces, and then carefully repositioned a Kleenex box on the table.

Tom's behavior suggested that several cognitive dysfunctions were limiting the extent to which he could engage in a learning process as defined by Piaget. At one moment he was withdrawn and preoccupied with private thoughts; at another he was bound to external, isolated stimuli (e.g., creases of his trousers, lint on his shirt). As a result, he did not copy stimulation from personal experiences and life metaphors and then integrate them into shared symbols. While behaviors such as aligning the Kleenex box symbolized his need to keep order, such symbolic behaviors did not serve the process of learning. Rather, they served to control and restrict any input from the therapeutic relationship as well as from his private fantasies.

The Second Clinical Comparison

Case A. Mary, an 8-year-old, lived with her mother, who was separated from her father. Moments after entering the playroom, Mary placed a girl hand puppet on the table and then other doll figures, at first randomly, then gradually forming a ring around the girl puppet. She interrupted this activity to discuss that the father of a friend of hers had died. Then she continued locating other doll figures around the girl puppet. She interrupted this activity again to make an "exact" drawing of the home from which she had moved, taking much care to locate the correct number of windows and so on. Satisfied that she had made a good reproduction, Mary asked the therapist to draw "a mother" in the front yard while she busied herself drawing gravestones. Then she continued locating more dolls around the girl puppet, saying, "All of these are her mother and father," and then, with a burst of laughter, "That's impossible!"

Case B. Sally, a 10-year-old, sat passively before a game of checkers, an activity she had initiated each meeting since therapy started. When she did not engage the therapist in the game before them, she seemed submerged in private thought, dreamily tapping her fingers. As with past checker games, the therapist patiently waited for Sally to initiate conversation and play related to her occasional, unprovoked angry outbursts at home and her refusal to attend school. At one point the therapist commented, "Maybe it's hard to talk about what worries you, like school, because the thoughts scare you," and suggested they play a game with puppets. After a long silence Sally carefully moved a checker on the board and calmly mumbled, "Your move."

Case C. Harry, an 8-year-old, charged into the playroom and darted from toy to toy engaging each for seconds. He punctuated this frantic behavior with comments that seemed to bear no relation to the activity at hand; for example, "My father is the greatest!" (the therapist was aware that Harry's father is an alcoholic and sometimes abusive); "My teacher sucks! She said I stepped on chalk and squashed it, but Johnny did." As the session progressed, Harry's behavior escalated from restless, diffuse play to impulsive, destructive actions (e.g., he nearly tipped over a lamp). As with previous sessions, the therapist intervened by attempting to channel Harry's aggression into an organized game (shooting darts at a target), bringing attention to his difficulties—"You act like this in school, and it gets you in trouble"—and setting standards—"You can't hurt anything here." But, again, the therapist was forced to restrain Harry when he pounded his fist against the window, trying to lift it so he could throw out a toy.

In Case A, Mary's cognition efficiently copied and transformed information following Piaget's definition of learning. She selectively produced information from her external world and from personal metaphors as she shifted between pretend play (locating many "parents" around a girl doll), drawing an exact copy of her house, and recalling an event (the death of a close friend's father). As her cognition coordinated and symbolized this pattern information, a theme provided her with an opportunity to learn about the way she has construed the separation of her parents, which was probably one main reason why she refused to leave mother and attend school.

In contrast, Sally did not or could not copy information from current events, nor could she transform this information into symbolic form to reveal how she experienced her difficulty attending school. She maintained control over the therapist and over her fantasies by limiting her interactions to repetitive checker games. Harry, although very active, capable of engaging play material, and offering comments and complaints, was nonetheless unable to produce and transform information with contributions from personal metaphors in a way that would enable the therapist to help him work through his aggressiveness and school difficulties.

With these clinical examples before us, and the issues they bring to our attention, I turn to discuss the model of cognitive-behavioral regulators that has emerged from my program of research.

A Developmental Hierarchy of Cognitive-Behavioral Regulators that Copy and Transform Information

Cognitive-Behavioral Regulators: Definition and Process

When children and adolescents deal with various tasks, how many distinctively different processes account for the ways in which information is copied? Of the several cognitive functions identified, five have withstood the test of numerous experiments. Each follows a developmental course, from organizations of cognitive behaviors that are global, characterizing early development, to those more differentiated and integrated, characterizing later development. The five functions form a developmental hierarchy (see Figure 6–4, right-hand column).

1. *Body-image-tempo regulation.* This mechanism concerns the manner in which a person uses images/symbols to represent and regulate the body and body motility. The young child registers vague body perceptions represented in global images. In addition, body motility is poorly regulated. When asked to move fast and slow, the child produces nearly the same tempo and represents these with global images (e.g., a turtle walking, a rocket blasting off). With development, perceptions and representations of the body gradually become more articulated and differentiated (e.g., while

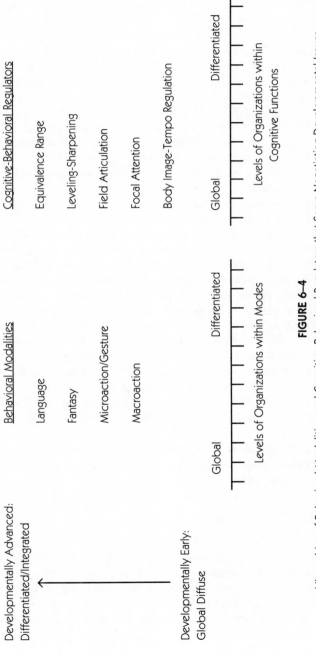

FIGURE 6-4

Hierarchies of Behavioral Modalities and Cognitive-Behavioral Regulators that Serve Negotiating Developmental Issues throughout Childhood and Adolescence

balancing on one leg, the child imagines a gymnast performing on parallel bars). And many tempos are refined and regulated, each distinguished from the other.

2. *Focal attention* concerns the manner in which a person surveys a field of information. The young child typically scans information slowly and directs attention only to narrow segments of the available field. With development, the child scans more actively and sweeps attention across larger segments of the field.

3. *Field articulation* defines the manner in which an individual deals with a field of information that contains elements both relevant and irrelevant to the task at hand. The young child attends equally to relevant and irrelevant information. With development, the child gradually directs attention toward what is relevant while withholding attention from what is irrelevant to the task at hand.

4. *Leveling-sharpening* concerns the manner in which a person constructs images of information that change or remain stable over time and compares these with present perceptions. The young child typically constructs fuzzy images of past information and fuses these with present perceptions so that subtle changes in information are not recognized. With development, the child constructs sharper, more differentiated images and distinguishes them from present perceptions so that subtle similarities and differences between past and present information are noticed.

5. *Equivalence range* concerns the manner in which information is grouped and categorized in terms of a concept or belief. The young child groups information in terms of a few narrow, concrete categories (e.g., "These go together because they are all round," "These are all happy"). With age, the child constructs increasingly broader categories, which are conceptualized in terms of more differentiated, abstract concepts (e.g., "These are tools," "These kids all break rules in school but not at home").

From the definition of each mechanism, we consider concepts that add to our understanding of how these mechanisms produce and transform information and serve learning and adaptation.

The Emergence of Cognitive-Behavioral Regulators and the Relationships among Them

These five functions become fully structured by the third year of life, although the cognitive activity of infants suggests that these functions begin to organize during the first years of life (Cohen and Salapatek 1975; see Santostefano 1978 for a review of selected studies). Moreover, the process of each remains the same throughout development, but the organization changes. For example, information is surveyed with the focal attention function whether the scanner is 3 or 13 years old. It is the organization of scanning that distinguishes these individuals. The 3-year-old scans with narrow-passive visual sweeps, a less differentiated organization, while the 12-year-old scans with broad-active, visual sweeps, a more differentiated organization. The growth of each of the other mechanisms is viewed in similar terms from less to more differentiated organizations.

These cognitive mechanisms are also viewed as interdependent and "nested one within the other," a view that has special relevance to the design of cognitive therapy techniques. When functioning adequately, the process of one mechanism is viewed as relying upon, and integrating, the processes of other mechanisms lower in the hierarchy. Consider as an example a child who was asked to look over and group various objects that share something in common. The child grouped a bottle of glue, a hammer, and a roll of Scotch tape because they are "things to fix with." While performing, the child regulated motility (body image-tempo regulation), scanned the available objects (focal attention), articulated the attributes of each (field articulation), compared perceptions of objects on the table with images of similar objects and past experiences with them (leveling-sharpening), and then united a particular cluster of objects in terms of a functional attribute they share (fixing). In constructing this group, the child's cognition subordinated other attributes of these objects as irrelevant to the category under construction (e.g., the bottle of glue was of white plastic, the Scotch tape holder red metal). In one of the clinical anecdotes described earlier, when John offered that the therapist's ashtray and his father "were both cracked," he constructed a category having scanned, articulated, and related a wide array of information.

Cognitive-Behavioral Regulators as Nonverbal and Verbal Activity: Connecting Deep and Surface Cognitive Structures

Referring to the discussion in Chapter 4 of surface and deep cognitive structures, the description of cognitive-behavioral regulators should make clear that words, thoughts, concepts, and beliefs are part of the process of only one mechanism, equivalence range. Moreover, since these cognitive regulators are nested one within the other, when a label (belief) is constructed to explain why a set of items belong together (e.g., "Most kids don't like me"), the verbal belief is nested within deeper *nonverbal*, sensorimotor cognitive activity (i.e., regulating body schemas and tempos, scanning, articulating information in terms of relevance, and comparing present information with images of past experiences). The notion that labeling relies on deeper, nonverbal cognitive structures suggests that, when indicated, a therapist should first rehabilitate deeper structures on which statements rely before treating beliefs or helping a child label feelings. To paraphrase the critique by Arnkoff and Glass (1982) (reviewed in Chapter 4), the therapist should first address the base of the iceberg rather than the tip.

Are Different Levels of Cognitive-Behavioral Regulators "Good" or "Bad"?

One of the most common errors made when considering levels of behavioral organizations is to view one level as "good" and another as "bad." As one example, cognitive therapies tend to view logical beliefs as good and illogical beliefs as bad (see Chapter 4).

In contrast with the framework proposed here, one function is conceptualized as developmentally higher (leveling-sharpening), or lower (field articulation), in a hierarchy, and one level within a function (e.g., narrow scanning) as developmentally less mature than another (e.g., broad scanning). These organizations of developmental levels do not define what is adaptively good or bad, however. Functioning with the focal attention process is not automatically "bad" while sharpening information is "good." Similarly functioning at the level of narrow scanning rather than broad scanning is not automatically "bad." Discussed in more detail later, any cognitive-behavioral regulator, and any level within it, could be adaptive or maladaptive depending upon the developmental status of the child, the environmental conditions and expectations, and the requirements of the child's life metaphors and their emotions.

Adaptive Intention and Cognitive-Behavioral Regulators

Since all cognitive-behavioral regulators are available for dealing with information from both the subjective world and environments, and since all mechanisms are theoretically both "good" and "bad," what determines which mechanism, or level within a mechanism, dominates a person's functioning at any given moment? Particular cognitive mechanisms, and levels within them, become operative depending upon an individual's "adaptive intention"; that is, the fit a person intends to negotiate, consciously or unconsciously, between the demands of the environment and those of his/her life metaphors.

For example, a teacher sends a child to the supply closet to obtain a particular workbook, "like this one." Guided by the intention to please the teacher, the child enters the closet, actively scans and compares perceptions of the attributes (e.g., color, size, lettering) of the workbooks on the shelf with an image of the book the teacher held up, and quickly selects the correct one. Another child, guided by the intention to deal with the requirements of a life metaphor that prescribes opposition, compares a fuzzy image of the workbook the teacher displayed with inefficient perceptions of the workbooks in the closet and returns with the wrong one.

Cognitive-Behavioral Regulators and the Issue
of Conscious/Unconscious Processes

The adaptive intentions that guide cognitive functioning are typically outside of awareness unless experiences, such as those made available in therapy, bring them into awareness. For example, a child about to undergo surgery may be conscious of coping with surrounding stimulation and his/her anxiety and fear. At the same time, the child may be guided by an unconscious intention to avoid information in the surrounding environment because it is construed as threatening, and to focus on private thoughts and fantasies. In a later section, research studies that illustrate the influence on cognitive functioning of unconscious intentions are discussed.

Cognitive-Behavioral Regulators and Mechanisms of Defense

Cognitive-behavioral regulators are viewed as mechanisms separate from, but functioning in concert with, mechanisms of defense. The effective functioning of mechanisms of defense requires the effective functioning of cognitive-behavioral regulators and vice versa. Each has a defensive purpose. Mechanisms of defense are organized to deal with conflict between representations of wishes/urges and the rules opposing them. (The reader is referred to Chapter 4 for a discussion of mechanisms of defense.) Cognitive-behavioral regulators are organized to deal with conflict between the demands of life metaphors and those of environmental stimulation as construed by the individual. Each has an adaptive purpose. Mechanisms of defense disguise and displace representations of wishes and urges. Cognitive-behavioral regulators seek and avoid information in order to maintain a level and pace of stimulation and emotion that serve learning and adaptation. When working in concert with mechanisms of defense, cognitive-behavioral regulators recruit particular information that contributes to actions a person will take, either toward or away from certain persons, objects, and events in the environment. We will return to these issues when we discuss the coordinating function of cognitive-behavioral regulators and how these mechanisms relate to the behavioral modalities a child employs when interacting with environments.

Cognitive-Behavioral Regulators, IQ, Academic Performance, Personality Dispositions, and Gender

Studies have demonstrated that the processes of each cognitive-behavioral regulator are unrelated to IQ, underlie performance with various academic tasks, predict learning disabilities, and accommodate to various personality dispositions and life experiences (e.g., Cotugno 1987, Rieder and Cicchetti 1989, Santostefano 1978, 1986, 1988a, 1995b, Wertlieb 1979). Last, while these mechanisms appear to operate independent of gender, they correlate with the degree of match or mismatch between psychosexual identity and gender. When psychosexual identity is discordant with gender, individuals tend to function at less mature levels of cognitive-behavioral regulators (Santostefano 1978, 1988a, Santostefano and Rieder 1984).

Comparing the Concept of Cognitive-Behavioral Regulators
and Piaget's Concept of Mental Schema

A comparison of the concept of cognitive-behavioral regulators with the more familiar concept of schema in Piaget's model may serve to articulate further the view of cognition proposed here. A cognitive-behavioral mechanism, like schema, is a behavioral analogue of structure in biology and conceptualizes a pattern of behaviors that include overt actions, perceptions, mental images, thoughts, and words. However, several important differences distinguish the two. As discussed in previous chapters, in Piaget's model the processes of schemas change throughout development from actions on objects (sensorimotor schemas) to mental imitations of these actions (cognitive schemas), to classifications (symbolic schemas) to logical-hypothetical thinking. A different schema process dominates each stage in development. In contrast, each cognitive-behavioral process, while undergoing differentiation from infancy through adolescence, maintains its essential organization and function. Further, all cognitive-behavioral regulators are viewed as operating simultaneously throughout development, although one may dominate the manner in which a person manages information in a particular situation. Finally, and of particular importance, cognitive-behavioral regulators, unlike Piaget's schemas, are conceptualized as assimilating and accommodating information both from contexts and from life metaphors, coordinating requirements of the two domains so that the associated emotions and representations are balanced to permit efficient functioning. The next section discusses the central position I give to this view of cognition: coordinating and equilibrating information from these two domains.

The Concept of Cognitive Orientation: The Coordinating Function of Cognitive-Behavioral Regulators

The role cognitive-behavioral regulators play in self- and mutual regulation is conceptualized as "cognitive orientation" and involves the coordinating function of cognitive-behavioral modalities. The concept of cognitive orientation brings attention to whether a person's cognition is oriented almost exclusively toward the calls for action from life metaphors or the calls for action from contexts as construed, or shifts flexibly between and coordinates the two. The concept also centers on the adaptive process that defines an individual and environment in dialectical interactions involving two sets of expectations. Diagrammed in Figure 6–5, the model conceptualizes five cognitive-behavioral regulators as dealing simultaneously with calls for action from life metaphors and from usual and unusual contexts. When coordinating and integrating calls for action from each domain, cognitive-behavioral regulators reorganize regressively or progressively (e.g., shift in organization from

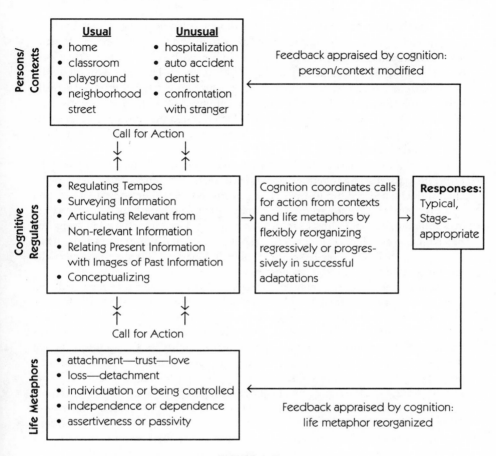

FIGURE 6–5

A Model of Cognitive-Behavioral Regulators Coordinating the Demands
of Life Metaphors and Contexts in Normal Development

leveling to increased sharpening or vice versa). Once some degree of coordination is achieved between the two calls for action, the person responds with a thought, belief, spoken statement, fantasy, or physical action or some combination thereof, always including emotions. After a response is rendered, cognitive-behavioral regulators perceive and assimilate the outcome of the response. This feedback contributes to changing the related life metaphor and its prescriptions and/or the situation/person with which the child is negotiating.

Examining an anecdote illustrates the model. A 6-year-old girl bounded happily through a neighborhood park, her father trailing a few steps behind. Passing a gentleman who greeted her warmly, she told him with excitement that they were on their way to fly a kite, quickly adding, "This is my bird kite that Uncle Charlie made with me. It can fly super high." At the same time her body leaped repeatedly, taking the form of a kite bobbing gracefully in mid-air. She abruptly said, "Let's go, Dad. This time the kite will go even higher." As they continued walking, she happily recalled flying a kite at the beach, and the "fantastic" kite exhibit they visited at the museum.

Chance would have it that when they set out again that same afternoon to fly kites, she passed another gentleman who also seemed magnetized by her exuberance and who greeted her warmly. The girl paused. Now her body slouched as if by heavy burdens. As she studied this man with a searching look, tears filled her eyes. She hurried on, failing to return his greeting. Her father asked her why she had begun to cry all of a sudden. Her response came in disjointed mumbles, "His blue eyes . . . white . . . really skinny . . . Uncle Charlie." But she made clear the issue was closed and asked to go home.

The father, of course, was puzzled. Uncle Charlie, a favorite of hers, had died just about a year ago, after a long bout with cancer. She mentioned Uncle Charlie during both episodes, yet why did she behave so differently? Reconstructing these experiences in terms of the concept of cognitive coordination provides one answer and illustrates cognitive functioning within personality and adaptation. When dealing with the first man, her cognitive-behavioral regulators perceived stimuli he presented: his robust physical appearance, warm greeting, and query, "What are you doing?" At the same time, her cognition perceived stimuli from a personal metaphor, which construed the man and the situation of the moment, in terms of representations of ambition/achievement/pride. This metaphor included condensations of many past experiences with Uncle Charlie, with whom she had constructed and flown many kites. The metaphor could be inferred, without much risk, from the repeated leaping and arching of her body, her exuberance, her spontaneous comment that Uncle Charlie made the kite, the height her "super" kite achieved, and the "fantastic" museum exhibit. Coordinating these two prescriptions, she responded with, "This time the kite will fly higher," and she proceeded to fly her kite.

When dealing with the second man, her cognitive-behavioral regulators centered on stimuli presented by him (his pale, thin physical appearance and blue eyes). However, these stimuli were construed by another metaphor that conserved her interactions with Uncle Charlie as he became pale and thin from chemotherapy treatment and concerned loss. In coordinating the prescriptions from this encounter, her cognitive regulators responded more to the metaphor and centered on the second man's skin color and thinness. Her cognition selected these details from many others and fused them with images of her uncle in the last months of his life. As a result of this coordination, her body slumped and she plodded home gripped with sadness. How this particular experience modified her metaphor of loss and separation is left to conjecture. In the year following her uncle's death, she experienced good-byes (by relatives visiting for a day, by her older brother returning to college) with tears, withdrawal, and constriction. But apparently the metaphor of loss/detachment gradually restructured since in later years such experiences were followed by more context-relevant behavior.

The model presented here, then, conceptualizes highly mobile cognitive structures as mediating between requirements, opportunities, and limitation of situations and those of life metaphors. When adequately developed, these cognitive structures enable a normal/neurotic child to continually develop a personal world yet deal simultaneously with environmental events in an organized process that fosters adaptation, personality development, and learning.

The Course of Cognitive Orientations in Normal Development

In normal development, do calls for action from life metaphors and contexts receive equal attention from cognitive-behavioral regulators from age 3 years to adolescence? My approach to this question relies on and elaborates aspects of Rapport's (Gill 1967) theory of ego (cognitive) autonomy. The assumption is made that in normal development cognitive functioning is autonomous both from fantasies/drives/motives and from environmental stimulation. Cognitive functions are guaranteed autonomy from the influence of fantasies by virtue of the fact that from birth these functions are inherently preadapted to and "fitted with" reality stimulation. Many studies illustrating that infants in the first days of life track moving targets and scan increasingly complex patterns, for example, could be viewed as illustrations of cognitive functioning inherently fitted to stimuli in reality. On the other hand, cognition's autonomy from the environment is guaranteed by the human's constitutionally given ability to transform stimuli into symbols and fantasies. As discussed in the previous chapter, infants in the first two years of life construct representations of interactions with persons and things. A person's capacity for representing (symbolizing), then, is viewed as protecting him/her from becoming stimulus-bound and a slave to environmental requirements.

What do we mean behaviorally when cognition is conceptualized as autonomous from both fantasy and reality? Consider the following behaviors of a 36-month-old toddler who shows he has emerged from the first three years of life with a solid capacity to exercise cognitive autonomy. He postures his body, extends his arms, and walks from a table to shelves across the room. There he surveys a large number of toys and then focuses on a 3-inch plastic figure of a space man. He rubs the head of the figure, saying, "helmet." He continues surveying, picking up and returning objects. Finally he takes a plastic spaceman, which now has a helmet, carries it back to his table, and sets it next to another identical figure.

At another time, the same child crouches on all fours, tosses his head, and opens his mouth wide. He crawls slowly across the floor, each forward movement of his arms and legs suggesting power and determination. He scans an array of toys and objects on the floor, crawls up to a short wooden stick, leaves it, goes to another, growls, picks up the stick with his teeth, and carries it back to his "house." There he drops the stick from his mouth next to a 6-inch wooden figure of a man (the stick and figure are the same length). He raises his head again, growls ferociously, and says, referring to the stick just dropped, "Me killed him, too."

Both vignettes would be viewed as moments of play. In the first, the play involves cognitive functioning that deals with information as it exists. In the second, the play involves cognitive functioning that deals with information as it is transformed or imagined. What is crucial for us is that *the same cognitive-behavioral regulators are operating in both episodes. In one they function relatively autonomous from fantasy; in the other, relatively autonomous from reality stimulation.*

Body image-tempo regulation is operating in the first episode when the boy extends his arms and walks across the room, and in the second when he crawls, tossing his head and posturing like a fierce animal. Focal attention is operating in the first episode when the boy surveys the toys on the shelf and in the second episode when he scans objects on the floor. Field articulation is operating in the first episode when the boy articulates relevant/irrelevant stimuli, selectively attending to a particular plastic figure, and in the second when he selectively attends to a particular stick. Leveling-sharpening is operating in the first episode when the boy compares the perception of the figure he picks up with an image (of a spaceman with a helmet), and in the second episode when he compares the perception of the stick with an image of a doll of a particular length. Equivalence range is operating in the first episode when the boy sets the spaceman figure next to one that is identical, and in the second when he lays the stick next to the wooden figure, each belonging to the same category ("Me killed him, too").

The vignettes illustrate that by the age of 3 years a normal child achieves the capacity to handle stimulation from reality and fantasy, using cognitive-behavioral regulators with autonomy.

Guided by these formulations, studies (Santostefano 1978) have suggested there are three phases in the developmental course of cognitive orientation. Before the age of 4 years, cognitive-behavioral regulators are oriented more toward information from life metaphors so that information in the environment is typically experienced in highly personal terms (e.g., a 3-year-old moves and uses a shoe box as if it were a truck). During the first half of latency (ages 5 to 9), tempo regulation, scanning, selecting relevant information, constructing memory images, and categorizing steadily and increasingly become more oriented toward information presented by contexts and persons. In this orientation, coordination provided by cognitive-behavioral regulators enables the child to keep a distance from, and regulate the interference of, emotionally laden fantasies and wishes. By emphasizing environmental information, cognitive regulators facilitate the growth of other personality functions (e.g., identifying with and internalizing the standards of parents and teachers and stabilizing mechanisms of defense).

During the second half of latency (age 9 to early adolescence), cognitive regulators shift to an orientation that is flexibly both outer- and inner-oriented. When registering body precepts, regulating motility, scanning, articulating relevant from nonrelevant, comparing images with present stimuli, and categorizing information, the older child now responds more flexibly both to the requirements of contexts and to life metaphors.

The Structuring of Cognitive-Behavioral Orientations in Long-Term Development

While these broad phases in cognitive orientation have been observed across various samples of children, unique differences have also been associated with different contexts/experiences that are sustained over long periods. During long-term dialectical exchanges between child and contexts, a child's cognitive orientation becomes organized and fitted to the complexity and pace of stimulation characteristic of the child's particular, usual environments. From this view, if a 5-year-old has been engaged for years in a dialectic with a caregiver whose pace of stimulation is rapid and emotionally intense, the orientation of this child's cognitive regulators would be different from that of a 5-year-old child who has been involved since birth in a dialectic with caregivers whose pace of stimulation is slow and emotionally low key. Along the same line, a cognitive orientation that becomes structured while a child is engaged in dialectics within a small inner-city apartment and street life would be different from that structured to manage stimulation typical of a rural community.

To illustrate how cognitive regulators are structured over time as the child engages in a dialectic with environments that for him/her are usual, I sketch two studies by others. (See Santostefano 1978 for a review.) In one, boys and girls were assigned a rating of socioeconomic status (SES) and administered tests that measured three of the cognitive regulators listed above: scanning, articulating relevant from irrelevant information, and holding images of information in memory over time. The results indicated that children who had been negotiating a lower socioeconomic environment showed cognitive functioning that was disrupted by the "distracting influence" of personal meanings and their emotions; that is, lower SES children showed a tendency to assume a cognitive orientation that centered on calls for action from life metaphors and to express these in action without adequately integrating expectations of contexts.

These results were similar to those of a second study that evaluated 120 African-American and Caucasian boys residing in a large, Midwestern city. Again, each child was assigned an SES rating, with thirty boys of each race falling within the low or high SES group. Again, all boys were administered tests that evaluated scanning, articulating relevant information, and holding images in memory over time. The test performance of the boys in the lower SES group, when compared to the high SES group, indicated that they characteristically scanned passively, attended more to personal meanings, and constructed global images of environmental information—all characteristics of a cognitive orientation that emphasized the prescriptions of life metaphors.

In this same study the investigator correlated scores the children obtained on tests of cognition with social deprivation as assessed by the Deprivation Index Scale. This aspect of the study provided a deeper look into the relation between stimulation with which the child negotiates over time and the structuring of cognitive orientation. With the Deprivation Index Scale, the investigator obtained information about several variables: (1) the degree to which the child's housing was dilapidated; (2) the number of children in the home under the age of 18; (3) the extent to which conversation took place at dinner time; and (4) the number of cultural experiences the child anticipated engaging in during the coming weekend. These variables were combined to produce a composite score. The Deprivation Index correlated significantly with test scores of the leveling-sharpening function. The direction of the relationship indicated that boys who tended to construct global, fluid images of environmental stimulation, and thus maintained a cognitive orientation that emphasized stimulation from life metaphors, experienced little social stimulation and interaction. Boys who constructed more differentiated, stable memory images (a cognitive orientation that included stimulation from environments) experienced a higher degree of social stimulation.

This configuration of results converges with discussions in Chapter 5 that pointed out that if a child is to construct stable representations of interactions, then interactions must be consistent in organization and repeated many times. We could speculate that if the physical makeup of a child's living quarters is shabby, then the arrangement and location of materials is fluid and unpredictable. And if there is little conversation at dinner time, the child does not experience consistent, predictable interactions with others, and does not experience calling up memories and giving them meaning in terms of the discussion at hand. How the orientation of cognitive-behavioral regulators is structured over a long period of time, then, is a function of whether stimulation provided by the environment is organized and consistent.

The Mobility of Cognitive-Behavioral Orientations in Short-Term Adaptations

While cognitive regulators and their orientation remain relatively stable from one usual situation to another, the organization and orientation could shift temporarily from the level maintained in long-term adaptation to a developmentally higher or lower level, and from one orientation to another, whenever the contexts and their meanings that the child is negotiating change the pace, intensity, and complexity of stimulation in ways that are unusual given the child's long-term experiences. In flexibly responding to these changes, cognition contributes to successful adaptations and learning. We considered an example from infant research in the previous chapter when infants were observed to look away if mother's stimulation was too intense. Examples of marked shifts in stimulation that could occur during childhood include mother becoming depressed upon learning that father lost his job, a child hospitalized for several months, the family moving to a very different community, type of housing, or school. These shifts in cognitive organization are referred to as the "mobility of cognitive-behavioral orientation."

Children differ in the flexibility with which cognition shifts to handle short-term changes in stimulation because of various factors; for example, the frequency, types, and timing of unusual changes in stimulation the child has experienced in the past, and developmental issues the child is negotiating at the time the change in stimulation occurs. In short-term adaptation, then, cognitive orientation reorganizes to equilibrate the requirements of stimulation as construed by the child and the requirements of the child's life metaphors and emotions (conscious and unconscious). If this equilibrating is successful, the child continues adequate self- and mutual regulation in the service of continued adaptation and learning.

Relating Long- and Short-Term Cognitive-Behavioral Orientation

To integrate long-term and short-term cognitive functioning, a child's cognitive functioning is represented both by a single level of a particular cognitive process and by a range of levels within that process and by a flexible orientation. The single level and orientation define a relatively stable cognitive organization that the child uses in self- and mutual regulations while dealing with a variety of environments that for him/her are *usual*. Here stimulation is modified slowly over the course of time. The range of levels within a given cognitive mechanism and shifts in orientation define a series of organizations through which a child's cognitive functioning temporarily shifts as the child engages in self- and mutual regulations while coping with short-term, *unusual* environments. When the environment returns to a state that is usual for the child, the new cognitive organization is relinquished and the child's cognitive functioning returns to the organization used in long-term adaptation.

To illustrate, consider a hypothetical situation involving an adolescent boy who has been brought into an emergency room and presented to the surgeon attending him. When at home and school, the adolescent flexibly and actively scanned both information in his environments and life metaphors. As he is brought into the emergency room, however, his scanning shifts, now limited to narrow pieces of the environment (e.g., a picture on the wall), and his cognition directs more attention at private thoughts and fantasies (e.g., he should have returned the blade guard on the mower as his father asked him to; it serves him right to get hurt since he failed his history exam, etc.). This shift in orientation toward subjective information serves to insulate the adolescent from an unusual situation over which he has no control, and serves to sort out personal meanings he has assigned to the accident. This shift is the outcome of short-term adaptation to an unusual environment since the boy has not been in an emergency room before.

For the surgeon, the emergency room is a usual environment. Approaching the boy, the surgeon scans actively and broadly and attends to information that is relevant to his intention of helping the adolescent (e.g., skin color, emotional state, location and type of wound). The surgeon withholds attention from personal stimulation that is irrelevant to his present intention (e.g., an earlier disagreement with a supervisor; his car would not start easily this morning). At the same time, the surgeon coordinates the information he registers with thoughts and memories that derive from his training in and past experience with injuries like the one before him. The surgeon's cognitive coordination is the outcome of long-term adaptation in many emergency room situations. Comparing these hypothetical experiences, we have an illustration of what George Klein (1951) meant when he discussed the equilibrating function of cognition. He noted that "One man's equilibrium is another man's discomfiture" (p. 330).

A Sketch of Studies of Cognitive-Behavioral Orientation in Long-Term and Short-Term Adaptation

A number of longitudinal studies have demonstrated the stability of a child's cognitive-behavioral regulators in long-term adaptation (see Santostefano 1978 for a comprehensive review). For example, in one study fifty-one kindergarten children attending the same public school were administered tests measuring the five cognitive-behavioral regulators listed earlier. The tests were then readministered when the children were attending first, second, fourth, and fifth grades. Correlations of test scores indicated moderate to strong stability of a child's cognitive functioning and orientation over this five-year period.

In another study kindergarten teachers were asked to rate children in their classrooms as either "typical" or "at risk" learners. The teachers judged 150 children to be typical learners and thirty-four to be at risk. All children were administered tests of cognitive-behavioral regulators. As a group, children rated as typical learners showed more stage-appropriate cognitive functioning than did children rated as at risk. However, when these test scores were analyzed by a discriminant function analysis, some typical learners showed developmentally immature cognitive functioning while some at-risk learners showed developmentally adequate cognitive functioning. Several years later, when these children were attending either the third or the fourth grade, thirty-three typical learners and twenty-seven at-risk learners were reevaluated. When kindergarten test scores were correlated with third- or fourth-grade test scores, the results indicated that a child's level of cognitive control functioning observed during kindergarten was sustained during subsequent years. Moreover, test performance obtained during kindergarten predicted academic difficulties these children experienced in the third and fourth grade more effectively than did teacher ratings.

Of the studies of short-term mobility in cognitive-behavioral orientation in response to changes in stimulation (Santostefano 1978, 1995b), a few are reviewed here to bridge cognitive therapy techniques I introduce in future chapters. This research responded to Hilgard, who, as discussed in Chapter 4, articulated the need for studies to discover how cognition is influenced by realities "outside" and "within" and how a person's cognition attempts to maintain a "dynamic equilibrium" between these realities. Several of these studies responded to Frenkl-Brunswick, who, as discussed in Chapter 4, proposed that the best way to capture how a person's cognition "dynamically equilibrates both realities is to study the person in his natural habitat." In this research (1) psychological tests were used that activate a particular cognitive-behavioral process; (2) following George Klein, each test consisted of two types of stimuli experienced as neutral, or as evoking conscious/unconscious meanings/emotions; therefore, the same cognitive control process was observed organizing and operating in response to each type of stimulus; (3) tests were administered when subjects were coping with a usual environment and again with an unusual environment that emphasized negotiating embodied meanings of safety/integrity; therefore, test results determined whether and to what degree cognition shifted in orientation in response to each context/experience.

In one study boys were administered two tests of the leveling-sharpening cognitive mechanism, and tests of personality, on three separate occasions: when at home, in a hospital bed before undergoing surgery for a hernia repair, and again at home thirty days after discharge. One test consisted of a scene depicting a doctor in a hospital room; the other a scene not related to hospitalization. Each scene was presented sixty-three times, five seconds for each display, with details eliminated accumulatively throughout the series. The child was asked to report any changes he noticed in the scene. Matched comparison groups consisted of boys evaluated at home, in a dentist's chair, and again at home, and boys evaluated only at home at three comparable points in time. When in the hospital (Time 2), relative to the home assessment (Time 1), the surgical group shifted most toward a cognitive orientation that attended to life metaphors, especially with the test scene of a hospital room. That is, they detected fewer changes.

A related finding moves closer to how mobility of a child's cognitive orientation plays a role in self- and mutual regulation as cognition attempts to equilibrate environmental stimulation, fantasies, and emotions. While all of the surgical boys shifted more toward leveling information in the environment from Time 1 to Time 2 than did the comparison groups, they differed in degree, showing individual differences in cognitive mobility. These individual differences correlated with a pattern of changes in personality functioning. Boys who shifted most toward leveling environmental stimulation when in the hospital produced fewer Rorschach images depicting barriers (indicating unconscious meanings were more available). With a thematic apperception test (TAT) they expressed more explicit fantasies depicting aggression and body injury (symbolizing the unconscious meaning assigned to the surgery). Further, the same boys were rated by their mothers as adjusting *best* postoperatively. In this instance, then, a shift in cognitive orientation away from contexts and toward fantasies was associated with successful adaptation. We interpreted these results as suggesting that when boys were in a hospital situation that limited the extent to which they could make active use of environmental stimuli, the leveling-sharpening process reorganized so that external stimuli were avoided while meanings from life metaphors related to the experience of surgery were attended to. This shift in equilibrating was associated with constructing differentiated fantasy representations that rehearsed imagined body injury/anxiety. These fantasized rehearsals in turn resulted in more adaptive mastery of the traumatic experience.

In contrast, another study illustrated how a temporary cognitive shift away from fantasies and toward environmental stimulation contributes to self-regulation and adaptive success. Young-adult novice parachutists were administered two tests: one depicted a parachutist in free fall, the other a parachutist descending with chute fully deployed. In each scene changes were introduced over sixty-three presentations that were relevant and nonrelevant for parachute jumping. The experimental group was administered the tests at home and again at the airport before executing a jump. The controls consisted of novice parachutists (from the same club) who were tested at home at two comparable points in time. A comparison of test scores from Time I to Time II resulted in significant differences. When at the airport, the experimental subjects detected significantly more parachute-relevant changes in the test scene, while controls showed no consistent shift. Moreover, the difference observed with the experimental subjects from Time I to Time II was more pronounced with the free-fall test scene than with the more benign scene of a slow descent. Given that none of the subjects had yet experienced a free-fall jump (the jumper opens the chute after falling some distance), we inferred that this scene evoked to a greater degree the meaning of danger to body safety. Accordingly, the leveling-sharpening process, when equilibrating in response to the free-fall scene, shifted in orientation to an even greater degree toward environmental, parachute-relevant information (information subjects used to ensure survival).

Cognitive-Behavioral Regulators and Orientation
in Clinical Populations

Children representing a wide range of "pathological difficulties" use the same cognitive-behavioral mechanisms as do "normals" to select, avoid, conserve, and organize information. They differ from each other, however, and from normals, in terms of the patterning of cognitive mechanisms. These differences in patterning can be interpreted as "organismic" attempts to employ a cognitive style that accommodates to and serves both the person's strengths and unique pathological vulnerabilities when coping with stimulation from the environment and from personal metaphors/emotions. For example, brain-damaged children (Santostefano 1978), viewed as vulnerable to and easily disrupted by stimulation from surges of fantasies/emotions, showed a cognitive style that combined narrow scanning with a hypermature organization of field articulation (an organization that excessively subordinates emotions/fantasies associated with stimuli). For the brain-damaged population this cognitive style served to limit the disruptive influence of fantasies/ emotions that contribute to the meaning of information. In this and other studies of clinical groups, we have observed patterns that reflect antagonistic relationships among cognitive functions (i.e., the operation of one process lessens or excessively enhances the operation of another) (See also Ottenson and Holtzman 1976, Santostefano 1964b, 1978, 1988a, 1995b, Santostefano and Rieder 1984, Wertlieb 1979).

The Course of Cognitive-Behavioral Orientation in Pathological Development

Do clinical populations show that cognitive orientation follows the same developmental course as that of normal children? A course opposite that of normals has been observed (Santostefano 1978). By the age of 9 years, cognitive mechanisms are either excessively occupied with information from fantasies, wishes, and impulses (inner-oriented), with external information inefficiently copied, or they are excessively occupied with external stimulation (outer-oriented), limiting the contribution of life metaphors and fantasies. Of equal importance, after the age of 9 years, cognitive mechanisms maintain these rigid orientations, failing to shift back and forth between contexts and metaphor in keeping with opportunities, limits, and demands. As a result, efforts to adapt usually are limited whether the task involves learning in school, in psychotherapy sessions, or from experience. How do these maladaptive cognitive orientations come about?

The Origins of Pathological Cognitive-Behavioral Orientations

Two types of mismatch between a person's unique cognitive makeup and his/her environments typically result in a pathological cognitive orientation. One concerns a mismatch between the child's developmental stage and "environmental accidents." The other concerns a long-term mismatch between the child's unique makeup/ temperament and physical/emotional characteristics of caregivers.

With the first type, an unusual environment that persists for some time interferes with a child's negotiating key developmental issues. For example, an

18-month-old requires a hip cast for over a year, limiting motility and physical experimentation with the environment, sensorimotor behaviors that are critical for further cognitive development. In another example a child is hospitalized for surgery at the age of 5, resulting in a cognitive shift that centers on the world of life metaphors at a time when the orientation of cognition is about to shift toward external information. In both instances the mismatch is a function primarily of the child's developmental stage and "environmental accidents."

In the second type of mismatch, the content of a child's interpersonal environment from infancy is uniquely ill-suited given the child's makeup. For example, the child's caregiver is regularly depressed, or ambivalent and inconsistent in responding to cues from the child (see Chapter 5). In another example, during the second year of life a child's testing of aggression, and physically experimenting with material, is sharply limited by caregivers who are conflicted about their own aggression. The child copes by solidifying a rigid, inner-cognitive orientation centered on an elaborate fantasy life of aggression leading to an obsession with computer war games. With another set of circumstances, if caregivers do not pretend, especially with humor, or if they are excessive in requiring the child to be orderly and clean, the child internalizes these standards and develops an orientation that centers on external stimulation as it is and avoids pretending what it could be. In these instances the mismatch is a function primarily of the state of the environment within which the child is required to negotiate life metaphors.

If atypical environments persist, the long-term adaptive process gradually takes hold. Cognitive mechanisms become organized to accommodate to the situation, fail to differentiate, and fail to develop the capacity to coordinate metaphors and contexts. Further, these dysfunctional cognitive mechanisms become autonomous and persist long after unusual environments disappear. For example, if, during the first two years of life, a child is continuously stimulated by a vigorous caregiving style that is excessive and ill-timed in terms of the child's unique makeup, the child could adapt by directing attention toward narrow segments of environmental stimulation, and focus attention on personal fantasies in order to attenuate the excessive stimulation. In this way a level of the focal attention process, characterized by passive, narrow scanning and an inner orientation, would be structured, becoming a slowly changing, habitual cognitive strategy. This strategy would then be employed years later in average environments (e.g., first grade) where it would fail to coordinate the requirements of the classroom.

Last, brain injury incurred in utero or in the first years of life could, of course, contribute to the formation of a pathological cognitive orientation. However, from the view of cognition proposed here, the same issues would apply; that is, how the child's cognitive functioning, now influenced by brain injury, becomes structured to coordinate external and internal information in terms of the child's capacity for complexity and change in information; the child's unique personal world; and the usual and unusual environments the child experiences.

Types of Maladaptive Cognitive Orientations

As diagrammed in Figure 6–6, various disruptions in ongoing regulations and traumatic, heightened emotional experiences could result in a child's managing these disruptions by organizing and stabilizing an inflexible cognitive orientation that does not adequately coordinate stimulation from contexts and life metaphors. Laboratory studies and clinical observations have identified three types of maladaptive cognitive orientations, each characterized by excessive inflexibility and each associated with maladaptations from the toddler years through adolescence.

Type I. Outer orientation. A pervasive, rigid, outer cognitive orientation that centers inflexibly on discrete, usually concrete, stimuli, permitting little or no contribution from metaphors and their calls for action. The clinical sketch of Tom described earlier provides an illustration.

Type II. Inner orientation. A pervasive, rigid, inner cognitive orientation that centers inflexibly on existing meanings from life metaphors, permitting little or no contribution from opportunities persons and situations provide for experimental actions. Clinical examples are provided in the next chapters.

Type III. Excessive shifts in cognitive orientation. When the calls for action of a life metaphor are perceived, cognition rapidly shifts to an outer orientation, centering on a reality detail *unrelated* to the metaphor as a way of avoiding its prescriptions. Similarly, when a reality detail and its requirements are perceived, cognition immediately shifts to an inner orientation, centering on a fantasy detail *unrelated* to the situation. By shifting excessively, cognition prevents/avoids integrating meanings and contexts. The clinical sketch of Harry, described earlier, provides an illustration.

Each of these pathological, cognitive orientations severely limits a child's ability to establish rituals of interaction with others that would otherwise permit the cycling and recycling of experiences as well as a child's ability to revise already established rituals. As a result, with each orientation modes of behaving fail to change, whether in everyday living or in the treatment situation.

In addition to laboratory and clinical studies (Santostefano 1978, 1988b, 1995b) that support the concept of rigid, pathological cognitive orientations, support also comes from a longitudinal study conducted by Wolf and Gardner (1979), who gathered their data without any discernible interest in psychotherapy. These investigators observed children in free play and dealing with structured tasks beginning at the age of 12 months. They concluded that between 12 and 24 months children develop one of two "styles" of activity that they termed "patterning" and "dramatizing." Patterners show a tendency to engage material in terms of external attributes and resist symbolizing (e.g., treating a toy block as if it were a cup). In contrast, dramatists take considerable liberties with external attributes of material and prefer symbolizing (e.g., using a toy block as a cup or a moving vehicle). These

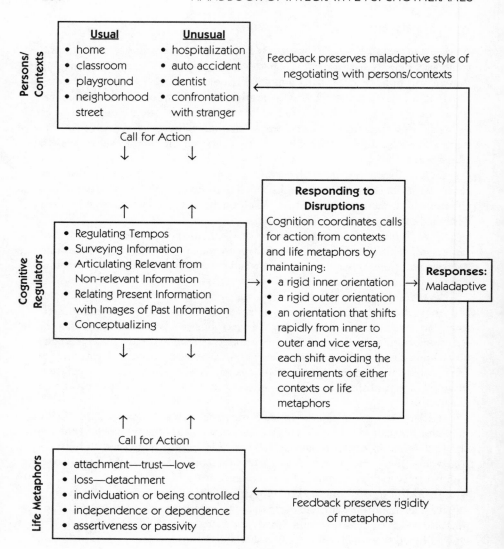

FIGURE 6–6

A Model of Cognitive-Behavioral Regulators Coordinating the Demands
of Life Metaphors and Contexts in Pathological Development

two styles of activity, as defined in this study, are identical to the outer and inner cognitive orientations described above.

Wolf and Gardner (1979) also concluded that from 24 to 36 months a child who is a patterner gradually integrates aspects of the dramatist style (and vice versa), resulting in a balance between patterning and dramatizing. Again, this conclusion is in accord with the proposal discussed above that by the age of 3 a normal child achieves flexible cognitive autonomy—at one moment transforming information in terms of highly personal metaphors and at another engaging information as it is.

Further, these investigators included observations that relate to cognitive pathology. They noted that while most individuals acquire skill in both styles, ". . . traces of these contrasting modes can still be observed. . . . For instance [in elementary school children] we find a significant minority who can still be characterized as strong patterners or strong dramatists. . . . It is possible that there exist individuals who remain throughout their lives capable of only one approach to material" (Wolf and Gardner 1979, pp. 134 and 137). These observations converge with mine. However, I take the position that rather than characterizing a minority of children, pathological cognitive orientations may be more pervasive than typically recognized, and implicated in various psychological difficulties. The clinical cases discussed in future chapters illustrate this position.

Another study of pretend behavior in the first years of life (Fein and Apsel 1979) also supported the concept of cognitive orientation. Paralleling Wolf and Gardner, these investigators found that by the age of 3 years normal children develop competence with a twofold process: engaging material as it is and engaging material in highly symbolic ways. Fein and Apsel referred to this development as an "apparent paradox." Rather than viewing these types of cognitive functioning as a paradox, the model proposed here views the capacities to pattern (copy) and dramatize (symbolize) information as basic tools in dialectical interactions that serve adaptation and learning throughout the life span.

Studies of Maladaptive Cognitive Orientations

If successful adaptation is associated with flexible cognitive orientation, equilibrating metaphors and environmental stimuli, it would follow that breakdowns in cognitive orientation would relate to maladaptations. Our studies of maladaptive cognitive orientation grew out of observations that when children were asked to look at a series of pictures presented in succession and to report anything that changed, sometimes they perceived changes that in fact did not occur. In other words, a balanced or equilibrated cognitive orientation was momentarily disrupted, shifting its orientation toward inner meanings. I conceptualize these errors as momentary losses of cognitive orientation, or as "slips of cognition." I use the term *slips* because results suggested that, as with slips of the tongue and other parapraxes, slips in cognitive orientation appear to be metaphoric extensions into cognition of the conflict a person experiences over whether or not to take physical action. In one study, for example (Santostefano and Rieder 1984), high-aggressive, hospitalized children produced significantly fewer errors, or slips of cognition, when detecting changes in an ongoing scene depicting interpersonal violence. In contrast, low-aggression children produced more slips. No group differences were observed with an aggressive-neutral scene. The meaning of this finding was clarified and elaborated by the following studies.

Another study (Santostefano and Moncata 1989) showed the same inverse relationship between behavioral violence and cognitive errors (slips in cognitive orientation). A series of pictures depicting two persons in a shoot-out was shown to a group of adolescents incarcerated because of violent behavior. They were asked to report any changes they observed in the scene. This group made the fewest errors, or produced the smallest number of slips in cognitive coordination. In contrast, an inpatient group produced more, an outpatient group even more, and a public school group the most. The performance of these groups did not differ with a test involving a nonviolent scene. These results suggested that, with children who were behaviorally aggressive, the meaning of interpersonal violence aroused by test stimuli depicting a shoot-out was in agreement with their representation (metaphor) of interpersonal interactions, resulting in little cognitive conflict and few slips in cognitive orientation (cognitive errors). On the other hand, with children who were less behaviorally aggressive, the meaning of interpersonal violence aroused by test stimuli depicting violence clashed with their representation of interpersonal interactions, resulting in more cognitive conflict and a greater number of slips in cognitive orientation.

This hypothesis was explored in a predictive study (Santostefano and Moncata 1989) with children hospitalized in a psychiatric facility and attending a hospital-based school. Children who on admission produced fewer cognitive errors (slips in coordination) with the shoot-out test scene displayed significantly more violent episodes in the hospital classroom per thirty hospital days than did children who produced more cognitive errors. Again, cognitive errors made with a nonviolent scene did not predict behavioral violence.

Concluding Comment

The conceptualization of cognition as a hierarchy of cognitive functions that coordinate opportunities, limitations, and demands for action presented by the environment on the one hand, and the demands for action presented by life metaphors on the other, provides a guide that specifies whether and when cognitive tasks are introduced in treating a child. The conceptualization also suggests cognitive interventions designed to reorganize a particular cognitive function and to render its cognitive orientation more flexible.

MODEL III: ACTION, FANTASY, AND LANGUAGE AS MODALITIES IN SELF- AND MUTUAL REGULATION

Introduction

I now turn to the third model that makes up the proposed developmental framework outlined in Figure 6–1. When a child negotiates life metaphors with others and environments, or with a therapist, he/she takes action, fantasizes, and verbalizes. As discussed in Chapter 4, psychotherapy is in need of a framework that conceptually and operationally defines the relationships among what a child does, imagines, and says as well as the relationships among different forms of acting, fantasizing, and verbalizing. Although receiving relatively little attention in recent years, interest in the relationships among behavioral modes has a long history in psychology. For example, over forty years ago, investigators were grappling with the observation that there seemed to be no consistent relationships among what a child expressed in fantasy (e.g., a story to a picture of the TAT), language (e.g., responses to a questionnaire), and action (e.g., behaviors in the playground) (see Crandall 1963, Hartup 1963, Lindzey 1952, Lindzey and Tejessy 1956, Megargee 1965, Rader 1957). Lindzey (1952) reminded psychologists that fantasy behavior does not always mirror overt behavior, while Brown (1958) noted, "We do not understand the relationships between modes of inner experiencing and overt behavior" (p. 66).

A number of years ago, in response to this need, I initiated a program of laboratory and clinical studies with colleagues to explore, as Brown put it, the relation between modes of inner experiencing and overt behavior (e.g., Blaisdell 1972, Eichler 1971, Santostefano 1960a, 1965a,b, 1968a,b, 1970, 1977, 1978, 1980a, 1995b, Santostefano and Wilson 1968). These studies supported developmental propositions that define the origins of and relations among what a child does, imagines, and says.

The Origin of Action, Fantasy, and Language Behaviors as Modalities of Experiencing and Expression

How does a child develop organizations of actions, fantasies, and language that become modalities that enable him/her to negotiate environmental expectations and those of life metaphors? With this question we form a bridge between development in the first two years of life (Chapter 5) and the emergence of modalities that participate as referents and vehicles in negotiating life metaphors throughout childhood. On one side of this bridge we noted that from birth an infant engages in continuous cycles of self- and mutual regulation and negotiations that become play rituals. These play rituals in turn become organized representations defining what the toddler expects from others.

On the other side of this bridge, beginning at age 3 years, Model I proposes that these ritualized activities and capacities, relying upon information gathered by cognitive regulators (Model II), are the ground out of which develop increasingly elaborate configurations of actions, images, emotions, and words that the toddler uses as referents and vehicles to continue negotiating more differentiated developmental issues or life metaphors, for example, attachment-love-detachment, separation-individuation, controlling-being controlled, dominating-submitting, identifying with the other, aggression-competition. As these negotiations continue, action, fantasy, and language behaviors, emerging through maturation, gradually become organized as modalities for experiencing and expressing life metaphors.

As in the case of infant–caregiver negotiations, how parents and other idealized persons respond to the child's modes of expression influence the form and organization these behaviors take. Parents, older sibs, and peers, relatives, teachers permit and oppose a child's modes of expression. As child and others engage in cycles of mutual regulation, they negotiate the paradox between them in a dialectical process. The child attempts to influence what the other permits and prohibits in terms of modes of expression, and others attempt to influence what the child prefers as modes of expression. During this process, if the child idealizes and identifies with these persons (see previous discussion of "ego ideal"), the child's modes of expression accommodate, gradually evolving organizations of actions, fantasies, and verbalizations that satisfy both the child and his/her relational world. Last, the timing and content of these permissions and prohibitions by idealized others, as well as the emotional tones that accompany their behaviors, are critical in the child's developing a flexible hierarchy of modalities.

An illustration should clarify this process. A 2-year-old child may express aggression and jealousy concerning his infant sib by thrashing on the floor (an undifferentiated response involving the action mode); by 3 he may poke the sib (a more differentiated, yet direct response). As restrictions and permissions are imposed by parents during many cycles of mutual regulation, the child might, at age 4, express his aggression by smashing the sib's toy (a less direct response). At age 6, as the child participates in cycles of negotiating, now including teachers, he may show greater delay and indirectness by kicking the toy wagon of a classmate in kindergarten hours after his sib aroused his anger that morning. By 7, with the emerging capacity to substitute action with fantasy, the child accommodates to the objections of others whenever he expresses aggression in action. Now the child's actions involve pointing his toy gun at his sib and "killing him" in a game of war, enacting macroaction and fantasy. By 10 he may "demolish" the toy troops of a neighborhood friend in a formboard game of civil war, now involving microaction and fantasy. And by 12, with the language mode differentiated and dominating, he may shout imprecations in the playground at a younger child who has recently joined the school.

In summary, the child's modes of expression "bump into" restrictions and expectations from others. And as the child's modalities accommodate to and assimilate each bump, as the child internalizes the standards of idealized adults, and as these standards become the child's "own rules of experiencing and behaving," the child's modalities reorganize to satisfy these standards. From this introduction I discuss aspects of the model and conclude with a sketch of selected studies that illustrate the support we have been able to muster.

Action, Fantasy, and Language as Hierarchically Ordered Modalities of Experiencing and Expression

Taking action, imaging (fantasizing), and verbalizing are alternative modalities that symbolize experiences (serve as referents) and express meanings (serve as vehicles) as the child engages in self- and mutual regulations negotiating life metaphors with others. For example, a child could experience a wooden cutout as a giant cookie by actually "munching" on the cutout. Or a child could image a giant cookie with no stimulus present, or could say, "I'm starving for a cookie."

The behaviors involved in these alternative modalities appear in a child's repertoire long before they are used as effective referents and vehicles. For example, an infant has the physical capacity to topple a tower of blocks years before she attends preschool where she performs an integrated, purposeful, symbolic act by toppling a structure of Lincoln Logs that a classmate constructed. Similarly, an infant constructs mental representations of interactions long before he fantasizes shooting down a peer with whom he is playing Star Wars in the backyard. And a toddler speaks words and verbalizes thoughts long before language becomes a differentiated, effective instrument of expression and experiencing.

Developmental Levels among Modalities

Although the three modalities are available throughout the life span, a developmental principle defines the interrelationships among them as well as the modality that dominates a child's experiences at particular phases in childhood. Younger children (from 2 to about 7 years) tend to represent and express experiences with actions and gestures. With development (from 8 to about 11 years) the action mode is subordinated by and assimilated into the fantasy mode, which dominates. Now images and fantasies are the vehicles used to express meaning and to rehearse actions before taking action physically. Still later (12 years and beyond), the action and fantasy modes are subordinated by and assimilated into the language mode, which dominates.

While subordinated, earlier modes of symbolizing and experiencing are not replaced by modalities that dominate later, but remain potentially active. When negotiating various life metaphors and contexts a child may shift from one mode to another. For example, at his classroom desk a 12-year-old looks at a friend and imagines himself "bigger" and more powerful; during recess this same child struggles past his friend to the top of a mount to become "king of the hill"; later, while walking down the corridor to the classroom, he turns and says to his friend, "I'm the greatest!"

The transition from action to fantasy to language modalities as alternative ways of experiencing and expressing meanings is determined by two simultaneously occurring and complementary processes. With one process the child articulates, differentiates, and distances himself/herself from persons, things, and events. With the other process the child delays or inhibits taking action. Both these processes are defined by the developmental principle of directness and delay (see Chapter 4). When taking action, the child is fused physically to some person, thing, or event, reflecting a high degree of directness (physical contact) between child and other. The child responds immediately, exercising little or no delay in taking action. When fantasizing, the child's experiencing is more distant from the physical environment (indirectness) since he/she "manipulates" an image rather than a person or thing as such. When fantasizing, the child delays taking action at least for the duration of the fantasy, and until the fantasy is enacted. When verbalizing, a child's experiencing is conceptualized as the least direct in terms of physical contact with persons and things. Words do not *physically* represent their referents, while a fantasy could, more or less, represent physical attributes of what is being experienced. For example, the spoken or written word *smash* bears no physical resemblance to an act or fantasy of smashing, nor do the words *New York* resemble the city physically. In addition, experiencing with words represents the greatest degree of delay from taking action.

How What a Child Does, Imagines, and Says Become Connected and Integrated

If actions dominate as referents and vehicles early in childhood, followed by fantasy and language, how are experiences in the action mode connected to experiences in the fantasy and language modes? As a child negotiates a life metaphor, his/her action experiences are never perfectly matched with his/her emerging fantasies, and language expressions that emerge are never perfectly matched with actions and fantasies. Relying on discussions in previous chapters of the dialectal process, self-regulation, and representation, the fact that modes of expression are never matched defines a paradox among them that is continuously negotiated.

Initially, as development proceeds, a child's actions are represented in fantasies (images) that initially do not fit, to some degree, the actions they are attempting to represent and express. During many cycles of interactions with others, the paradox between actions and fantasies is gradually negotiated so that fantasies increasingly provide more adequate representations of actions. Still later, these fantasy experiences initially are not adequately fitted to language expressions. Again, during many interactive cycles, the paradox between fantasies and verbalized statements is gradually negotiated so that language expressions increasingly provide a more adequate representation of fantasies. As these paradoxes are continuously negotiated, the experiences in one mode eventually establish representational roots in the others. Accordingly, a particular action could be represented by a fantasy; conversely, this fantasy could be represented by an action. Similarly, a language expression, with roots in representations of experiences in fantasies and actions, could substitute for fantasy or action expressions. If the paradox among modes has been negotiated successfully, the child is able to shift from one modality to another and back again, each mode carrying some representation of the life metaphor being negotiated. As the reader might guess, if the paradox among modes is not adequately negotiated, maladaptation results. I will have more to say about this later.

Developmental Levels within the Modalities of Action, Fantasy, and Language

Development within each modality follows the same transition, from expressions that are direct and immediate to expressions that are indirect and delayed. Consider a 5-year-old boy who pokes his younger sib, behavior reflecting directness and immediacy characteristic of the action mode. At another time the same boy could cover his sib with bath powder from head to foot. This behavior, while still within the action mode, is to some degree physically distant from the sib, since the powder and not the person of the child contacts the sib's body (i.e., it is less direct). This action conveys more delay in that it takes time to shake the powder from the can. Here, then, we have two expressions, or levels, within the action mode, one less direct and more delayed than the other.

Similarly, a 9-year-old who experiences the teacher favoring a peer could fantasize himself being hugged and complimented by the teacher, a fantasy that reflects directness and little delay since the teacher actually provides the love. In contrast, the same child could fantasize a TV character admiring a pet. This fantasy reflects less directness and more delay since the teacher is now symbolized by a TV character rather than literally, and since a pet (symbolizing the child) is receiving admiration rather than a hug.

In terms of levels within the language mode, consider as an illustration the clinical vignette reported by Coppolillo (1987) discussed in Chapter 4. The boy who avoided directly discussing the loss of his father, and preoccupied with criticizing a teacher, said, "He ain't no Oscar Mayer." We discussed how this verbalized meaning represented a less direct and more delayed expression of a sentiment this boy could not yet express in more direct language, namely, "There is no man who is as great as the father I lost."

Last, the same dialectical process that takes place among modes also takes place within a mode. Consider again a child who pokes at his infant sib. As this behavior "bumps into" the prohibitions of idealized adults, a dialectic takes place between this action and other possible actions the child might take (e.g., taking the infant's rattle, wanting a drink from the infant's bottle, covering the infant with powder). As the paradox is negotiated among these possible actions, a particular action emerges that enables the child to continue negotiating a life metaphor while also accommodating to the requirements of others. For example, the child could insist on sitting at the kitchen table between mother and the infant's high chair.

Action, Fantasy, and Language as Organized Modalities Expressing the Demands of Life Metaphors and Contexts

As diagrammed in Figure 6–7, the availability of action, fantasy, and language modes and the availability of degrees of directness and delay within each mode provide the child with multiple behavioral means and alternative goals to express the demands of life metaphors and contexts. In the developmentally mature individual, then, all three modalities are potentially available, along with many levels of expression within each modality that represent different degrees of directness and delay.

As we might expect, as a child negotiates a life metaphor, the persons and situations available to participate in these negotiations constantly change. The more a child has the capacity to delay, to engage in alternative modes of experiencing, and to engage alternative goals, the more the child can economically manage changes in the environment while at the same time meet the needs of the life metaphor he/she is negotiating. The child can successfully engage in mutual regulations with a range of persons (parents, sibs, relatives, teachers, peers) as well as situations (home, neighborhood, school, playground). And the child is spared the frustration of creating totally new opportunities to negotiate a life metaphor each time persons or situations change.

With the availability of multiple modes, a child is equipped to negotiate with persons and contexts that differ in terms of opportunities and prohibitions. For example, the parents of a 6-year-old may prohibit vigorous action expressions of a life metaphor because they are very low-key. But when continuing the negotiation of this same metaphor with a peer, the child may engage in vigorous action expressions because the peer has indicated that these expressions are acceptable.

A related issue concerns the mobility of action, fantasy, and language expressions in the process of adaptation. These behavioral modes, and levels within each, operate individually or integratively, depending upon the adaptive intention of the child and the requirements and opportunities contained within a situation. Changes in environmental conditions and/or shifts in the emotional-psychological state of the child could cause him/her to revert temporarily to a developmentally earlier modality or to an earlier level within a modality, representing a regressive shift. By the same token, changes in conditions and/or in the emotional-psychological state of the child could cause him/her to revert temporarily to a higher mode or level within a mode, representing a progressive shift. Developmentally early modalities are not replaced by later, developing ones but remain potentially active as means of experiencing.

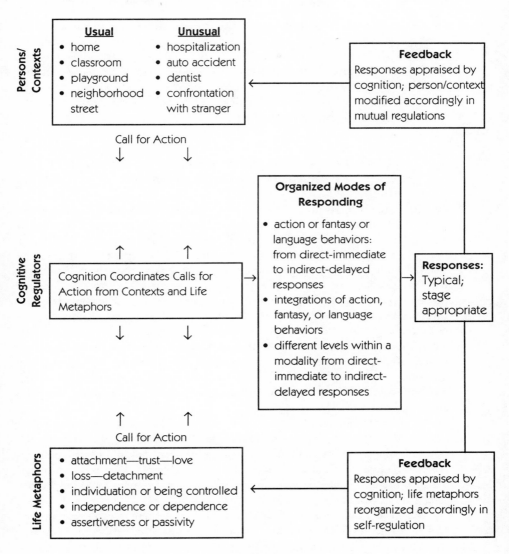

FIGURE 6–7
A Model of Action, Fantasy, and Language as Organized Modalities
Expressing the Demands of Life Metaphors and Contexts in Normal Development

As one illustration, a 12-year-old girl sitting in the classroom looks up from her desk work, peers at a friend, and engages the fantasy mode as she imagines herself to be more attractive and the favorite of a mutual male friend. At lunch in the cafeteria the same child now engages the action mode as she nudges past her female peer in order to sit next to the male friend. After lunch, while returning to the classroom, she exclaims to her female friend, "Don't you think my outfit is the greatest!" now engaging the language mode.

When the Modalities of Action, Fantasy, and Language Become Derailed in Development

As with cognitive regulators, significant, unrepaired disruptions of ongoing regulations with their traumatic, heightened emotions compromise the modalities of action, fantasy, and language as tools for negotiating. As diagrammed in Figure 6–8, when a significant disruption occurs, the child manages the disruption by calcifying a modality, so to speak, and segregating it from the others. When this happens, the paradox among modes fails to be negotiated. Therefore, as development unfolds, fantasies do not adequately represent actions, and/or verbal expressions do not adequately represent actions and fantasies. What a child does, then, is not integrated with and related to what the child imagines and says. As a result, when the child engages in negotiating developmental issues, he/she does not benefit from rehearsing actions in fantasy before taking action or verbalizing some meaning/issue that is housed in fantasy. In one sense, when negotiations among modalities are disrupted, one or more becomes an "independent" world of experience and expression.

The same types of mismatches between the child and environment that give rise to pathological cognitive orientations also derail the modalities of action, fantasy, and language. One concerns a mismatch between the child's developmental stage and "environmental accidents." The other concerns a long-term mismatch between the child's unique makeup/temperament and physical/emotional characteristics of caregivers.

As one example of the first, consider a child who entered treatment at the age of 9. When he was 5 years old, and in the "action phase" of development, he was standing at the edge of a field, watching his father operate a tractor. Suddenly the tractor tipped over and crushed the father. The boy was very attached to his father and had engaged in various interactive rituals with him. While he had been characteristically assertive and exuberant, after his father's accident he became increasingly inhibited, withdrawn, and frequently lost in solo fantasy play. He was finally referred for treatment when teachers became concerned because he would regularly stand at the edge of the playground "like a zombie." The traumatic disruption of his ongoing regulations with father, in terms of the issue we are considering, was managed by constricting and splitting off the action mode (within which he

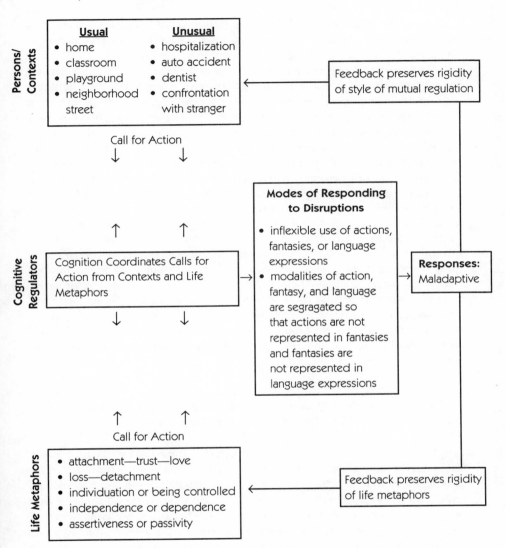

FIGURE 6–8
A Model of Action, Fantasy, and Language as Modalities Expressing
the Demands of Life Metaphors and Contexts in Pathological Development

had been actively involved) and conducting a private life in fantasy. For this boy, taking any form of action could result in disaster, and therefore taking action aroused intense stress. We discuss this boy's treatment in a future chapter.

In terms of a long-term mismatch between the child's innate temperament/ activity level and physical/emotional characteristics of caregivers, consider an example with nearly the same outcome. A toddler was appropriately active but her parents were excessively concerned with safety, orderliness, and giving direction. As this child, now capable of racing about, continued negotiating self-assertion, her parents regularly scolded her and gave her long "lectures" whenever she engaged in rituals that annoyed them. For example, she took out clothes different from those set out by mother, wandered next door ("Big kids live there; it's not safe!"), and repeatedly changed the seat assigned to her at the kitchen table. From these many cycles of interaction, intended to negotiate self-assertion and autonomy, by the age of 7 the action mode was constrained and the child had nearly completely retreated into fantasy. There was one exception. Having assimilated her parent's lectures, she began to make premature use of language, occasionally stepping out of her fantasy world and engaging her parents in "long arguments." Of course, the inverse could also hold. Consider parents who are guided by the notion that they want their child to be "tough" and "learn to stand on his own feet." Accordingly, they regularly encourage their child to engage in actions when negotiating issues long after the fantasy mode maturates. In this case the child could show inflexible use of action in situations such as the classroom where rehearsals of action in fantasy are expected.

A Sketch of Studies of Action, Fantasy, and Language as Modalities of Experiencing and Expression

To illustrate observations that support the proposed model, I summarize several laboratory studies. Observations of children in the treatment situation are considered in detail in future chapters. In each of the laboratory studies, psychological tests designed to assess a child's expressions in action, fantasy, and language were employed. Tests were also designed to assess whether a child preferred to express himself/herself in one modality rather than another (e.g., action versus fantasy versus language). Since these methods are discussed in detail elsewhere (e.g., Santostefano 1977, 1978) they are only summarized here.

The action mode was assessed by presenting a child with sets of objects (three objects in each set). The child was asked to perform, in any order he/she chose, each of three actions on objects as designated by the examiner. For example, with one set the child turned a screw into wood with a screwdriver, hammered a nail into wood, and smashed a light bulb. With another set the child cut one sheet of paper with scissors along a line, crumpled another sheet of paper, and tore up another. With another set the child drank from a bottle, gave a drink to a doll, and watered a plant. As these examples illustrate, each set called for actions that represented different degrees of delay and directness.

The fantasy mode was assessed with both unstructured and structured stimuli. With unstructured stimuli the child was asked to look at a picture and describe what was happening. One picture depicted an adult with hands near the neck of another adult; another depicted a child sitting alone at the doorway of a house. The stories a child developed were scored in terms of the degree to which a motive was expressed in direct/indirect and immediate/delayed forms. With structured stimuli the child was presented a series of pictures and asked to choose one of two expressions, stated by the examiner, that characterized what the person depicted in the picture was experiencing (e.g., Is she thinking about her mother at home or is she sucking on her pencil?).

The language mode was assessed by asking a child to speak aloud, for thirty seconds, "every word that comes to mind" after hearing a stimulus word spoken by the examiner. Stimulus words included both neutral and evocative words; for example, tree, knife, mouth, judge.

Preference for experiencing in the action versus fantasy was assessed by setting items behind two screens. The child was invited to perform an action or to look at a picture of someone performing the action and "imagine what's going on." For example, "You can knock down a building of blocks with a toy bulldozer, or you can look at a picture of someone knocking down a building with a bulldozer and imagine what's going on."

Preference for experiencing in action versus fantasy versus language was assessed by setting items behind three screens. Again the child was invited to perform an action, look at a picture of someone performing that action, or speak words describing that action. For example, behind one screen were located a watering can and a plant; behind another, a picture of someone watering a plant; and behind the third screen, a microphone into which the child verbalized, "The plant is hungry; I will feed it."

One study (Eichler 1971) examined age differences. The test procedures were administered to seventy-two boys, ages 6, 8, and 10, of average intelligence, from both high and low socioeconomic families, who had no history of psychological problems. A statistically significant age trend was observed with the test of the action mode. The 6-year-olds performed the most direct and immediate action first (e.g., they first broke the light bulb, then hammered the nail, and last turned the screw into wood with a screwdriver). The 10-year-olds more often performed the more indirect and delayed action first (e.g., they first turned the screw into wood and last smashed the light bulb). The 8-year-olds fell between. A similar statistically significant age trend was observed with the structured fantasy test. The 6- and 8-year-olds selected fantasy stories that depicted more direct and immediate expressions than did the 10-year-olds.

With the word association test, each age group verbalized about the same number of words to each stimulus word (tree and knife). However, the 6-year-olds verbalized the fewest number of aggressive words in response to the stimulus word, *knife*, the 10-year-olds the most. In addition, the words were assigned a ranking in terms of the degree of directness and delay conveyed. While the 6-year-olds associated fewer words to the stimulus word, the words they verbalized conveyed *more direct* and *immediate* expressions (e.g., "stab," "smash"). In contrast, the 10-year-olds, who associated the greatest number of words, verbalized more delayed, indirect expressions (e.g., "chip," "peel"). This age trend was also statistically significant. Taken together, these findings supported the proposition that the modalities of action, fantasy, and language are more direct and immediate in early development than later.

In another part of Eichler's (1971) study, these same boys were administered the test assessing preference for taking action versus fantasizing versus verbalizing. Statistically significant age trends were observed that support the model. Six-year-olds tended to take action, the 10-year-olds tended to verbalize experiences, and the 8-year-olds fell between.

In another study of normal adolescent boys and girls (Santostefano 1970), a significant, inverse relationship was found between ratings assigned to words associated in response to the stimulus word, and ratings assigned to fantasies produced in response to a picture. Adolescents who expressed aggression in fantasy ("It looks like this lady is choking the other one") tended not to express aggression in their verbal associations, while adolescents who expressed aggression in their verbal associations tended not to express aggression in their fantasies. For example, one boy associated to the stimulus word *knife* as follows: "Gun, shoot, kill, stab, wound, New York, men, children, streets, alleys, war, hate. . . ." In response to a picture, he described the scene in some detail before expressing the fantasy that one woman hurt herself when she fell down the stairs and the other woman is helping her up (a fantasy that reflects more delayed and indirect expressions of aggression).

Other studies have explored the modalities of action, fantasy, and language in various clinical populations such as institutionalized delinquents (Santostefano and Wilson 1968) and brain-damaged and orphan children (Santostefano 1965a). Differences in these clinical populations fit theoretical expectations. For example, orphaned children more often expressed nurture in direct and immediate actions. Another study (Santostefano 1970) compared expressions of aggression and nurture in the action mode by first graders and sixth graders judged by teachers as adjusting well, with expressions by a group of children from the second to the sixth grade (mean age 11 years 6 months) judged as immature and adjusting poorly. Both the well-adjusted first graders and the poorly adjusted group tended to perform the more direct immediate actions first, whether the action provided the experience of aggressing or nurturing.

Stoops (1974) reviewed fifty-five studies by other investigators who compared two or more modes of expression (action, fantasy, and language). While these studies employed a wide variety of assessment techniques, he concluded that thirty-five of the studies offered clear support for my developmental model of modalities, nine offered inconclusive support, and eleven reported findings contradicting the model. Indirect support is also provided by other reports. For example, Meyers and Craighead (1984) discussed a study that asked children to visually image ten scenes from least to most anxiety provoking. While the main purpose of this study is not relevant, one observation is. The investigators observed that one third of the children were unable to visualize the scenes. From the view of the model we are considering, these children showed that the fantasy mode had been constricted or blocked, very likely for reasons we will consider later.

I conclude this sketch of studies with the discussion of one particular investigation because it relates to the issue of self-regulation (i.e., progression and regression within modalities) as a function of experience, an issue that has direct implications for technique in child psychotherapy.

Blaisdell (1972) explored whether, following an aggressive experience, a progressive or regressive change occurs in the modality a child typically uses to experience and express aggression. He asked several interrelated questions. If a child preferred the action mode, what is the influence on the developmental organization of the child's action and fantasy modes if the child engages in aggressive actions? And if a child preferred the action mode but engages in aggressive fantasies, what is the influence on the organization of the child's action and fantasy modes? Similarly, if a child preferred experiences in the fantasy mode, what is the effect on the organization of the child's action and fantasy modes if this child engages in action versus fantasy experiences?

To select children who tended to prefer experiencing aggression in the action or fantasy modes, the Action versus Fantasy Test was administered to a large number of first and fifth graders (see above). The procedure consisted of five items. Boys who performed five actions, and therefore did not select any of the fantasy choices, were accepted as representing an "action-oriented" group. Boys who performed four or five of the fantasy choices, and none or only one action, were accepted as representing a "fantasy-oriented" group. Ten first graders and ten fifth graders were located to meet these criteria, resulting in a total sample of forty children: ten action-oriented and ten fantasy-oriented children at each of two grade levels.

About a week after the selection, each child was administered the Action Test to assess the degree of delay and directness the child expressed in the action mode (see above), and the Structured Fantasy Test to assess the degree of delay and directness the child expressed in the fantasy mode. Each child then participated individually in one of two experimental "treatment" conditions. Half of the action-oriented subjects and half of the fantasy-oriented subjects were randomly assigned to an "action" treatment condition and half of each group to a "fantasy" treatment condition.

In the action treatment condition the child was invited to perform aggressive acts on materials (e.g., punch a BoBo clown for one minute, break ten sticks, strike a sheet of unbreakable glass with a hammer ten times). With the fantasy treatment condition the child viewed a film of particularly aggressive moments of the Louis versus Schmelling 1930 boxing match and magazine pictures portraying violence. The children were asked to watch the film and then examine the pictures and to imagine what was going on. The duration of each treatment condition was about thirty minutes. Immediately following the experimental treatment each child was readministered the Action Test and the Fantasy Test.

Action-oriented boys, after experiencing the action treatment condition, showed a shift in the action mode toward more indirect and delayed action behaviors. For example, they turned the screw into wood first and smashed the light bulb last. At the same time, however, they showed a regressive shift in the fantasy mode, expressing more direct and impulsive aggressive fantasies. In contrast, fantasy-oriented boys, after experiencing the fantasy treatment condition, regressed in the action mode, expressing more direct and impulsive aggressive actions. For example, they chose to break the light bulb first and turn the screw into wood last. At the same time, they shifted progressively in the fantasy mode, expressing more indirect, delayed aggressive fantasies. In other words, when the treatment experience matched the child's preferred mode of experiencing, the children showed a progressive shift in the preferred mode and a regressive shift in the nonpreferred mode.

When the treatment was the opposite of the child's preferred mode, however, a child displayed indirect and delayed behaviors that suggested constriction of both action and fantasy modes.

These findings bring attention to the question, Which mode should the content of treatment emphasize for a child? Relying on this study, if a therapist engages the child's preferred mode, the organization of that mode is likely to shift toward more indirect and delayed behaviors. Yet other modalities are likely to shift regressively toward more direct and impulsive forms. If the therapist engages a mode opposite to the child's preferred mode, expressions in each mode are likely to make premature use of delay and indirectness. In future chapters I discuss therapeutic techniques that address this issue and the need to integrate modalities.

Integrating the Three Models to Guide Child and Adolescent Psychotherapy

The three models discussed above form the developmental framework that will serve as a guide for integrating child psychotherapy. To weave these models together, I rely upon concepts from infant research and embodiment theory discussed in the previous chapter: self- and mutual regulations, disruption and repair, heightened affective moments, and the embodiment of experiences, or the "body in the mind." The result is an approach to treatment that addresses the needs listed in Chapter 4: (1) surface and deep behaviors as targets of therapy integrating what a child does, imagines, and says; (2) cognitive products and structures, and cognition and emotion integrated as one; (3) how meanings of early experiences contribute to the construction of meanings assigned to later experiences; (4) cognitive and behavioral activity that occurs within and outside of awareness; (5) how a child and others engage in a dialectical process of negotiations; (6) conflict that occurs within a child's subjective world and between the child's cognition/behavior and environmental expectations; (7) how interactions between child and therapist promote change and what the therapist should do in addition to verbal labeling and interpreting. The approach that results from this integration is framed by several interrelated propositions.

• While negotiating one or another life metaphor, whenever a child experiences a significant disruption in self- and mutual regulation and related heightened traumatic emotions and the disruption is not adequately repaired, three domains of psychological functioning are compromised: life metaphors and their calls for action; cognitive regulators and the orientation these functions maintain; and the degree to which the modalities of action, fantasy, and language remain integrated so that what a child does, imagines, and says are interconnected.

• Unrepaired disruptions primarily compromise flexibility of functioning. A disruption leaves a child's negotiations with life metaphors incomplete so that they assign the same meanings to different experiences and prescribe the same maladaptive actions in different contexts. Further, to cope with a disruption, a child's cognitive orientation becomes excessively centered on external stimuli in order to avoid information from life metaphors, becomes excessively centered on fantasies in order to avoid information from environments, or shifts excessively between information from life metaphors and situations in order to avoid relating the two domains. And when impacted by a disruption, the modalities of action, fantasy, and language become segregated. The action mode is used excessively to avoid meanings contained in fantasy, the fantasy mode is used excessively to avoid taking action, or the language mode is used excessively in order to avoid taking action and fantasizing.

• The developmental stage during which unrepaired disruptions occur is a major factor in determining which life metaphors, cognitive regulators, and behavioral modalities are rendered less flexible.

• Unrepaired disruptions that occur once or over a relatively short period of time may have the same impact as those that are sustained over a long time. The unique meaning the disruption holds for the child—given the particular life metaphor the child is negotiating—and the child's cognitive and behavioral stage of development contribute to the degree to which life metaphors, cognitive regulators, and modalities are rendered less flexible. Short-term disruptions include, for example, a parent severely injured in an accident, a child witnessing beatings, or a car crash. Examples of long-term disruptions include mother in a prolonged postpartum depression or child contracting an infection and being absent from school for most of a school year.

• Unrepaired disruptions and traumatic, affective moments that are distal may have the same impact as those that are proximal. The unique meaning the disruption holds for the child—given the particular life metaphors he/she is negotiating—and the child's cognitive and behavioral stage of development contribute to the degree to which life metaphors, cognitive regulators, and modalities are compromised. Proximal disruptions involve the body of the child (e.g., the child is hospitalized, experiences excessive stimulation, witnesses a shooting). Less proximal disruptions involve the body of a loved one whom the child has idealized and with whom the child has developed a special attachment (e.g., an uncle dies of AIDS; an older brother is incarcerated). More distal disruptions involve happenings that occur in the child's neighborhood or elsewhere in the country (e.g., a neighborhood building burns down; the child watches TV reports of a building that was bombed in a distant city).

• All disruptions and their heightened emotional moments are represented in embodied, nonverbal schemas. Several factors determine whether an embodied, nonverbal representation is translated into shared symbols; for example, whether the disruption is proximal or distal, occurs during the first two years of life or later and over a short or long period of time, and contains traumatic stress as construed by the child.

• Whenever an interactive ritual and the developmental issue being negotiated are disrupted, some element of the nonverbal, embodied representation of this ritual may be translated into symbols, but an action/sensorimotor element, with its emotional tone, remains, unconscious yet active long after the disruption has dissipated, appearing in various derivative actions (e.g., tics, gestures, and other bodily forms of stress, noxious skin sensations, images/fantasies, repeated verbal expressions, and unexplainable aggressive actions). In these instances the embodied representation remains segregated from fantasy and language symbols, facilitated by a pathological cognitive orientation.

• If an embodied schema representing a traumatic disruption has been translated into symbols shared with others, a conflict exists between this representation and representations of what is expected or hoped for from interactions with others. The conflict is between a wish (representation) for some type of interaction and a symbolized representation of a disruption, that is, a prohibition of that wish. The person's cognitive regulators (as well as mechanisms of defense) and modalities of expression are organized to serve and perpetuate this conflict.

• Whenever an embodied schema representing a traumatic disruption has not been translated into shared symbols, the demands of this schema are not available to cognitive regulators and modes of expression in ways that serve growth.

• Throughout treatment, emphasis should be given to translating the action/sensory motor element of an embodied schema that had not been translated into shared symbols so that the nonverbal meaning represented becomes available to cognitive regulators and modes of expression and therefore benefits from cycles of dialectical negotiations with others.

The Importance of Translating Embodied Schemas
into Shared Symbols: A Forecast of Integrative Techniques

As the preceding discussion makes clear, the proposed model assigns a central role to unrepaired disruptions and to the importance of translating embodied representations of disruptions into symbols that can be shared with a therapist. Therefore, before closing this chapter, we take a moment to sketch examples of unrepaired disruptions observed in treatment as background for comments about the importance of translating embodied representations.

In the previous chapter we noted examples, provided by Beebe and Lachmann (1994), of unrepaired disruptions observed in treatment; for example, a child who continually enacted the wish to be hurt by the therapist expressed an embodied schema that derived from invasive medical procedures the child experienced as an infant. For other illustrations I turn to observations of three teenagers from my clinical practice to underscore the issue noted earlier—that all disruptions are represented in embodied, nonverbal schemas and that some aspects of these schemas are translated into symbols that a child shares while others are not. When describing stressful situations that required her to remain grounded and confident (e.g., taking an exam, going to a school dance), Sally typically gripped the arms of the chair in which she sat or paced the office squeezing some object. Gradually she repeated a statement as an organizing theme, "I seem to be losing my grip again." I learned in parent meetings that mother, who as a child had been traumatized when lost in the woods, had been excessively anxious about Sally's safety. At about age 2, Sally began to engage in a play ritual of running away from mother whenever they went shopping. Mother usually responded by scolding Sally and slapping her hands. "Don't let go of my hand!" she would scream anxiously.

In the second case, Tom lived in a second floor apartment during his first years of life. Soon after mastering the ability to walk, he initiated a play ritual, negotiating separation-individuation-autonomy. He repeatedly ran to the top of a flight of stairs that led to the doorway below and abruptly stopped, bursting into laughter. Each time, he was yanked back by very anxious parents and frequently slapped for "disobeying." In treatment sessions Tom described panic attacks, whether before a school exam or a track meet, that included fantasies of falling from imagined heights. When discussing these, he would frequently exclaim, "I really feel on edge!" We discussed the third adolescent in the previous chapter. Recall John, who ritualistically pulled hair from a small area above his forehead. While he did not experience thoughts or fantasies when he plucked a hair, he did experience a twinge of excitement when performing this act, and he did arch his back and thrust his stomach forward when discussing his encounters with a bearded teacher and a hairy classmate.

While each of these adolescents had available translations of aspects of his/her unrepaired disruption, the embodied representation of the disruption needed to be translated more fully into shared symbols so that each could eventually repair traumatic experiences in interactions with the therapist. How should I have helped these adolescents translate these embodied schemas into shared symbols? Should I have verbally pointed out to Sally that she was gripping the arms of her chair once again as she talked about her experience with another school exam? Should I have engaged Tom in discussing further what he meant by "I really feel on edge"? And should I have brought to John's attention that he arched his back and thrust his stomach forward whenever he talked about his teacher and his classmate?

I have maintained throughout that verbal comments are not likely to be effective in translating embodied schemas. This position is supported by two formulations. In his discussion of the cognitive unconscious Piaget (1973) proposed that the unconscious is furnished with "action schemas" expressing what an individual can do and not what he/she thinks (says). Almost fifty years earlier Freud (1916) conceptualized parapraxes, or what he called "bungled actions," such as slips of the tongue or taking out the wrong key to unlock one's door, as determined by unconscious meanings. These formulations by Piaget and Freud emphasize that embodied schemas, although underground and nonsymbolic, speak only the language of action.

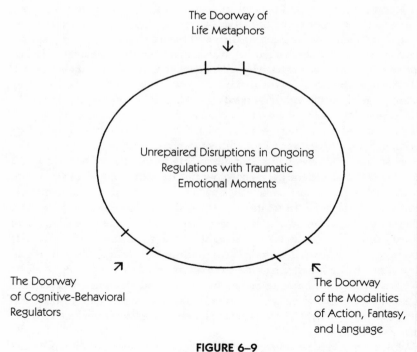

FIGURE 6–9

A Paradigm for Integrative Psychotherapy with Children and Adolescents:
Three Doorways through Which a Therapist Could Enter

When the three models are integrated, including the importance of translating embodied schemas into the language of action symbols, interrelated guidelines emerge for conducting child psychotherapy, which are detailed in the next chapter.

1. Special attention should be given to translating embodied representations of unrepaired traumatic disruptions into shared symbols.
2. To facilitate a child's translating embodied schemas it is necessary to render more flexible one or more of the domains involved in constructing symbols: life metaphors, cognitive orientation, and modalities of expression.
3. Change in maladaptive life metaphors, cognitive orientations, and inflexible modalities is brought about as child and therapist engage in persistent, repetitive, interactive rituals and enactments.

Each of the models, then, provides a doorway through which a therapist could enter to facilitate change in a child's functioning and to relieve a child's suffering. As diagrammed in Figure 6–9, a therapist could enter the doorway leading to a child's life metaphors or the doorway leading to a child's cognitive orientation or the doorway leading to a child's modalities of expression. But through which doorway should a therapist enter first? Or should the therapist enter two doorways at the same time, and if so, why and when? And once a therapist enters a doorway, what does he/she do? These questions and others are addressed in the next chapter and illustrated with clinical cases in the chapters that follow.

7
Guidelines for Integrative Psychotherapy with Children and Adolescents: A Developmental-Dialectical Approach

CONTENTS

In this chapter we tour the third floor of the proposed "developmental house" (Chapter 5, Table 5–1) and consider guidelines for conducting integrative psychotherapy with children and adolescents. The reader should be familiar with the developmental-dialectical model, and issues that derive from it, discussed previously.

GOAL OF TREATMENT

The goal of treatment is to assist a child in reorganizing maladaptive life metaphors, cognitive orientations, and modes of expression, rendering each domain more differentiated and flexible. If this goal is accomplished, a child's cognitive orientation adaptively coordinates the calls for action from life metaphors and environments, and his/her modes of expression respond flexibly and assimilate and accommodate to opportunities and limitations presented by changing situations and relationships. Empowered by these tools, a child is equipped to continue a growth-fostering developmental course during day-to-day encounters with family members, peers, and teachers.

This goal is in accord with those proposed by both cognitive-behavioral and psychodynamic therapists, for example, Coppolillo's (1987) enhancing a child's self-regulation; Brems's (1993) strengthening a child's overall psychological and emotional adjustment so that she/he reenters a healthy point in her/his developmental trajectory; Strupp's (1986a) changing a person's cognition, feelings, and behavior; Kazdin and colleagues' (1990a) decreasing distress symptoms and maladaptive behaviors, and/or improving adaptive prosocial functioning; and Kendall and Braswell's (1985) teaching thinking processes. But the goals of cognitive-behavioral and psychodynamic therapies are elaborated by the goal proposed here, which operationalizes cognition, emotions, behaviors, change, and prosocial functioning in particular ways. In addition, the proposed goal leads to concepts and techniques that differ from those of cognitive-behavioral and psychodynamic therapies, yet integrates aspects of each. We observed that mainstream cognitive-behavioral therapies attempt to change behaviors directly, more or less ignoring their meanings, while psychodynamic therapies attempt to change the meanings of behaviors, more or less ignoring the behaviors themselves. The techniques outlined below view behaviors and their meanings as two sides of the same coin and attempt to change both simultaneously. With a foundation in the first two years of life, the technique attempts to facilitate change by engaging a child in repeated interactive dialectical cycles of self- and mutual regulation.

ASSESSMENT: SELECTING DOORWAYS TO ENTER

A therapist needs data to decide which of the model's doorways to enter first: the one leading to life metaphors, cognition, or modes of expression (see Figure 6–9, Chapter 6). Traditionally, to plan treatment, therapists have relied on data provided by a variety of assessment methods: intake interviews with child and family members; cognitive, intellectual, and projective tests; and questionnaires (e.g., Brems 1993, Coonerty 1993, Coppolillo 1987, Matson and Ollendick 1988). Typically, however, data from interviews are given the most emphasis. Brems (1993) proposed a four-hour intake session with child and family, preferably taking place on a single day: "[The treatment plan] is based largely upon information derived from intake interviews . . ." (p. 97).

While I agree with the importance of intake interviews and the need to consider the ways in which various adults define a child's problem (Coonerty 1993, Spiegel 1989), I believe interview data have limited value unless they are related to data from diagnostic tests. During an initial meeting, parent, teacher, and school psychologist each peers through a particular metaphor and provides information about how he/she construes a child. Mother's main concern about 8-year-old Laura was that she experienced "weird" fears (e.g., without any obvious precipitating event, Laura would not take a shower because she believed large bugs might come out of the drain). On the other hand, father was concerned about the discrepancy between Laura's obvious high intelligence and her lack of motivation toward schoolwork. The teacher believed Laura had an "auditory discrimination problem" because she frequently did not follow instructions. The school psychologist wondered if Laura was "borderline psychotic or atypical" because during a classroom observation she seemed tuned out and sometimes talked to herself. Similarly, during an initial meeting, a child presents what he/she construes as the reason for seeing the therapist. When Laura was asked why she thought her parents asked her to come for a meeting, she replied that it was probably because she and her younger sister frequently argued. As we learn later, diagnostic test data were crucial in addressing each of these "presenting problems" and in selecting a doorway the therapist would enter first.

From these introductory remarks I discuss issues, emphasized by the developmental-dialectical model, that should be considered when conducting an assessment before beginning treatment.

Intake Interview with Parents

In addition to determining how parents define and contribute to a child's current problems because of the importance assigned to the first three years of life by our developmental-dialectical model, I recommend that a therapist devote some of the interview to exploring whether, during the child's first years, disruptions and heightened emotional moments occurred in ongoing regulations, and whether and how these disruptions were repaired. These disruptions might give clues to embodied meanings the child constructed that have remained unnamed yet active, influencing the child's maladaptive behaviors. In many instances parents have "forgotten" events that occurred in the child's first years that might have significance, or they tend not to attach significance to these events in terms of the child's current difficulties. More frequently, parents spontaneously mention stressful events that occurred within the past year or so. When asked whether anything upsetting happened in the family or neighborhood during the first three years of the child's life, one set of parents recalled a break-in that occurred when the referred child (now 14) was 3 years old. The family returned from a vacation and found items strewn about. During the next several months (the parents could not agree as to how long) the child refused to go out to play and cried when left with a sitter. At these times father occasionally became angry, as mother recalled, which father reluctantly acknowledged. Both parents noted with relief that the child "soon got over it."

In another case, when a child was 2 years old a hurricane disrupted electrical power for days so that in the evenings mother (a single parent) moved about the apartment aided by a flashlight. In the months that followed, this child had difficulty going to bed, and mother handled the dilemma by having the child sleep with her. In still another case, the parents of an adolescent girl, referred because of poor school performance and occasional "defiant behavior," recalled that her maternal grandmother, afflicted with cancer, moved in with the family when the adolescent was a toddler. The grandmother was located in a bedroom, which was equipped with an oxygen tank, next to the adolescent's bedroom. After a bout that lasted six months, the grandmother died in that bedroom when the adolescent was 30 months old. This event, needless to say, affected the emotional climate of the entire family. Significantly, when asked in her intake interview what upset her a lot, the adolescent shared a concern that proved to relate to a relevant embodied meaning. "When people breathe heavily, like when their nose is blocked with a cold, it really makes me irritated and nervous." Months later this adolescent revealed in treatment a "vague" memory of grandmother breathing heavily and the oxygen tank hissing in the next room.

I also recommend that a therapist explore whether a child showed any behaviors from 24 to 36 months to suggest that the foundation of a pathological cognitive orientation was being formed (e.g., "Do you remember how Sally played during that time? How she handled toys and material?"). Here a therapist is on the alert for observations that suggest the child was beginning to show cognitive rigidity by excessively "patterning" or "dramatizing" stimulation and not combining both cognitive styles. The adolescent discussed above spent a great deal of time lining up dolls and "arranging" their garments. "She did not seem to pretend doing anything very much." The child who endured several nights without lights seemed to become lost in dramatizing. "As I remember, he could sit on the floor for hours, moving his toy trucks and making these little noises. It was great, I could get my ironing done." Similarly, guided by our model, a therapist should explore whether a child showed expressions of a derailed action mode. For example, before the grandmother died, the parents of the adolescent found animal figures and dolls with heads twisted off, which puzzled them because she would line them up so neatly during play. After grandmother died, the adolescent dropped various items in the toilet bowl, and on a few occasions, when cuts were observed on the ears and tail of the family's dog, she explained that she had given the dog "haircuts."

Intake Interview with Child

I recommend that whenever possible the child should be seen first so that the therapist can form her/his own initial impressions without being influenced by the parents' views. In addition, by seeing the child first, the therapist has a "live experience" to refer to when listening to the parents' concerns. I also recommend that a therapist not conduct an intake interview with the intention of getting the child to talk about his/her concerns in a straightforward manner (for a similar position see Spiegel 1989). In the previous chapter I described behaviors children displayed during the initial contact that eliminated the possibility of asking them to discuss the difficulties they were experiencing (e.g., the boy who, when greeted, had his jacket pulled over his head). If a child is open to a discussion, the therapist could ask what he/she sees as the problem, more to learn how the child's view relates to views described by others. Recall Laura, who responded that her parents brought her for an appointment because she and her sister argued, a view that differed from those of parents, teacher, and school psychologist.

　　With a younger child a therapist could use the technique of play interview, a favorite among psychodynamic therapists. Excellent discussions of this method are available (Conn 1993, Schaefer and Cangelosi 1993). Inviting a child to select dolls and play any game he/she wishes, the therapist asks questions based upon what the child has enacted with the dolls (e.g., "How does she feel?" "Does anything happen during the night?" "Why was she kidnapped?" "So the boy went upstairs with his brother. Whom did he want to go first?"). But the vivid examples Conn described, for example, make clear that a play interview is productive when a child has developed the capacity to construct and enact elaborate fantasies while moving dolls through limited space. If a child has this capacity, a therapist learns a great deal about the metaphors that are a source of the child's strengths and difficulties. In my experience, however, a number of children in need of treatment do not have the cognitive capacity to symbolize or the verbal facility to share linguistic meanings through what dolls are thinking, doing, and saying. Moreover, I have found the method to be relatively unproductive with inner-city children, who usually have not made use of dolls or toys to express meanings. Last, play and verbal interviews usually provide limited information about a child's cognitive orientation and preferred modes of expression, domains that can be effectively evaluated with psychological tests.

For these reasons and others discussed in Chapter 10, I devote most of the time to administering psychological tests and only about 15–20 minutes to administering the "Life Stressor Interview." This simple method is designed to help a child describe, either directly or metaphorically, any disruptions and traumatic emotional moments he/she has experienced. The child's reports are viewed as conscious, verbalized expressions of disruptions that are then related to unconscious expressions elicited by projective tests. A child is asked, "Has anything happened that upset you a lot?" The child's responses are scored in terms of the type of stressor reported (e.g., physical aggression, physical disability/illness of a loved one, a storm); the agent and recipient of the stressor (e.g., parent, sib, animal, landscape); whether the child witnessed the stressor or learned of it from others; whether the stressor is ongoing; whether the stressor occurred in the home, neighborhood, or elsewhere in the country; when the stressor occurred; and whether the disruption was repaired (e.g., "A building caught fire down the block; the ambulance came right away").

Psychological Testing

I view psychological tests as indispensable "X-ray machines" that provide "pictures" of psychological functioning not readily observable when one interacts with a child during an interview. But which test methods should a therapist use? From the view of the developmental-dialectical model, methods should assess a child's developmental status rather than focus on selecting a diagnostic category, a position that agrees with some (e.g., Coppolillo 1987, Spiegel 1989) but disagrees with others (e.g., Brems 1993). In addition, our model prescribes that test methods evaluate the developmental status of three domains: life metaphors, cognitive orientations, and modes of expression and their interrelations. Test methods developed specifically to assess these domains are discussed in Chapter 10. Here I consider how traditional psychological test methods could be used to gather the required data.

Assessing Life Metaphors

A child's representations of past negotiations with life metaphors should be evaluated at three levels: embodied schemas/action, fantasy, and language. The therapist then determines whether life metaphors represented at one level are linked to, or segregated from, representations at other levels.

To assess body-based representations, I have developed the Action Test of Body Image and the Touch Association Test (Chapter 10). With the former, the child assumes various body postures and describes what each body experience brings to mind. With the latter, the child feels ambiguous clay objects placed under a cloth and describes what each brings to mind. With each procedure, then, body perceptions are the stimuli. In addition to such methods, discussions are available of various forms of nonverbal behavior, which could guide a therapist in observing what a child is saying when his/her body speaks (e.g., Scherer and Ekman 1982, Rosenthal et al. 1979, Weitz 1979). Projective tests (e.g., Rorschach's inkblot test, Michigan pictures tests, Children's Apperception Test, Robert's Apperception Test) (Siegel 1987) are effective in eliciting representations of life metaphors in the fantasy mode. And the Continuous Word Association Test (see Chapters 6 and10; Santostefano 1978) and sentence completion tests are effective in eliciting representations of life metaphors expressed in the language mode. With the latter the examiner speaks aloud part of a sentence, and the child completes the sentence in whatever way he/she chooses (e.g., "When I was a baby I . . ." "I would be really happy if . . ." "My mother and I . . ." "I like my father but . . ."). The Life Stressor Interview described above also provides information that a child produces at a conscious, verbal level about heightened traumatic disruptions he/she has experienced whether at home, in the community, or when watching TV.

Assessing Cognitive Orientations

Published normed tests (Santostefano 1988a) are available to assess a child's cognitive orientation, as well as unpublished methods described in Chapter 10. If these procedures are not available, observing how a child responds to traditional psychological tests frequently provides useful information. In general, a child's cognitive efficiency and level of anxiety/stress is compared when he/she is dealing with structured test items that require information to be experienced as it is versus unstructured test items that require information to be imagined as it might be. If a child's performance reflects marked differences, he/she is very likely functioning with an inflexible cognitive orientation.

Observations that Suggest a Pathological, Outer Cognitive Orientation

When dealing with structured procedures such as the Digit Span, Arithmetic, and Information subtests of the Wechsler Intelligence Scales, or drawing geometric designs of the Bender-Gestalt Test, the child is related to the examiner, shows little anxiety/stress, and performs efficiently with a sense of pleasure and industry; for example, drawings of geometric designs are nearly photocopies of the standards, and digits are repeated forward and backward as if they had been tape-recorded. In contrast, when dealing with unstructured items, such as describing what an inkblot could be or telling a story about a picture, the child is detached from the examiner (e.g., slumps in the chair, engages in little eye contact), shows signs of anxiety/stress and fatigue (e.g., "This is boring," "This is hard," yawns), and takes more time to respond. In addition, images constructed in response to inkblots, while sometimes suggesting symbolic meanings, tend to be global in organization and/ or conventional (e.g., "a bat") or descriptive ("It's just an inkblot").

Observations that Suggest a Pathological, Inner Cognitive Orientation

When dealing with structured procedures, the child seems detached (e.g., frequently tunes out and needs to be refocused), expresses anxiety/stress and fatigue (e.g., interrupts several times to get a drink of water, rests his/her head on the tabletop), takes more time to respond, and performs less efficiently. Repeating digits results in a significantly lower score than arranging pictures in the Picture Arrangement Subtest; with the latter the child spontaneously tells a story about each item. Similarly, when copying geometric designs, for example, the child may spontaneously embellish, animate, or associate to the stimuli; for example, while drawing Bender-Gestalt Test Design A, "These are two spaceships crashing in space." In contrast, when dealing with unstructured items the child is more affiliated, shows pleasure and involvement, responds with less hesitation, and performs more adequately. Further, when constructing images and fantasies, the child may take "liberties," freely going beyond test stimuli. For example, to Card I of the Rorschach test, an 8-year-old child responded, "This person in the middle has his arms up, the king is on one side telling him 'climb up,' and the queen is on the other side telling him 'don't climb up'; all the people [tiny specks surrounding the main inkblot] are cheering; they don't know what he'll do; the wind is blowing smoke all over."

Observations that Suggest Pathological Shifts in Cognitive Orientation

When dealing with both structured and unstructured tests, a child rapidly alternates between moments of high and low efficiency, shifting from the cognitive orientation required by the task at hand to its opposite. For example, a child abruptly stops copying a geometric design (which requires an outer cognitive orientation, experiencing information as it is) to discuss a movie about "ghostbusters." While responding to a Rorschach inkblot, the child abruptly stops and slowly passes his finger over pencil marks on the tabletop or asks about a picture hanging on the wall. Usually there is no apparent connection between the meaning of an external detail from which the child's cognition jumps into some fantasy or between the meaning of a fantasy from which the child's cognition jumps into some external detail. In addition, the child usually experiences moments of high anxiety/stress with both structured and unstructured test items and rapid shifts in mood from pleasure to boredom/fatigue. At the same time, the child shifts the quality of the relationship back and forth between alliance and opposition.

Assessing Modes of Expression

The previous chapter described procedures designed to assess behavioral expressions in action, fantasy, and language as well as whether a child prefers one or another mode. In addition to using these procedures, a therapist could observe whether, when dealing with traditional psychological tests, a child flexibly engages the mode required by a test procedure or regularly shifts to its opposite. For example, while dealing with thematic pictures, a child begins constructing a story and then interrupts to enact some part of it. Or when dealing with the Rorschach test, the child says, "It's a fly!" and slaps the card with her hand. Such behaviors suggest that the child is action-oriented and has difficulty with sustained expression in the fantasy mode. As another example, while responding to a questionnaire or interview, a child frequently slips into a fantasy using materials in the playroom and/or describes a TV program or movie. Such behavior suggests this child is fantasy-oriented and has difficulty with sustained expression in the language mode. Moreover, some children as young as 8 years of age show a tendency to prefer the language mode and to experience difficulty expressing themselves in fantasy or action behaviors. For example, while responding to the Rorschach test, a child frequently interrupts to "talk about" his/her teacher, a school assignment, a trip the family took last week, a younger sib who is a pest, and so on. While these "spontaneous" discussions appear "rich" in content and grist for the therapeutic mill, especially if the therapist is verbally oriented, they suggest a rigid use of language and a tendency to avoid other modes of expression.

Assessing the Relations among Life Metaphors, Cognitive Orientations, and Modes of Expression: Three Broad Treatment Plans

Whether a child's life metaphors, cognitive orientation, and modes of expression are interrelated or segregated indicates one of three broad treatment plans. The initial task is to evaluate whether the child shows evidence that body-based action meanings have been translated and extended into the levels of fantasy and language. For example, consider a child who, when assuming various body postures, describes seeing a tree trunk that had been broken by lightning, a physically handicapped person in a wheelchair, and a squirrel that had been flattened by a car. Yet when constructing images in response to inkblots, or stories in response to pictures, the meaning of the body-self as deformed and injured does not appear. And this meaning is conspicuously absent from conscious self-statements elicited by the Sentence Completion Test; for example, *When I think about my body* "I think it's the greatest." In this case the body-based meaning is "unnamed," underground yet active. Treatment with this child would include the goal of translating this embodied meaning into fantasy and language symbols that are shared with the therapist and therefore available for negotiation and revision.

The second task is to evaluate whether one or another of a child's life metaphors impacts his/her cognitive orientation and modes of expression in ways that interfere with adaptation. In the previous chapter we discussed a study of boys undergoing surgery for hernia repair. With some boys the meaning of this experience was associated with cognition turning flexibly toward an inner orientation so that anxiety about imagined bodily injury (castration) was expressed and worked through in fantasy. Moreover, these boys adjusted best postoperatively. Here the meaning of the surgery did not interfere with cognitive flexibility. On the other hand, with other boys cognition turned less toward an inner orientation so that imagined bodily injury was not worked through in fantasy. In these cases the meaning of surgery resulted in cognitive rigidity, and postoperative adjustment did not go well. The issue, then, is to evaluate, as much as data permit, whether cognition and modes of expression have become rigid in the service of managing the disrupting influence of a pathological meaning (life metaphor). These data help a therapist decide which meanings should be integrated within tasks designed to structure interactions that promote flexibility in cognition and modes of expression.

After these steps are taken, one of the following broad treatment plans is selected:

1. If a child shows evidence that his/her cognitive orientation and modes of expression are excessively rigid, treatment would first emphasize structured interactions designed to reorganize a child's cognitive orientation and modes of expression, and then emphasize unstructured interactions that translate embodied meanings into shared symbols and revise life metaphors.
2. If a child shows evidence of a flexible cognitive orientation but rigidity in modes of expression, treatment initially would emphasize structured interactions that differentiate and integrate action, fantasy, and language expressions, and then emphasize unstructured interactions that translate embodied meanings into shared symbols and reorganize life metaphors.
3. If a child shows evidence of stage-appropriate flexibility in cognitive orientation and modes of expression, treatment would emphasize, from the start, unstructured interactions that translate embodied meanings into shared symbols and reorganize life metaphors.

I discuss guidelines for structured and unstructured interactions after considering how change is facilitated in a child's cognitive orientation, modes of expression, and life metaphors.

FACILITATING CHANGE

The view a therapist holds of how behavior is changed exerts a major influence on the techniques she/he uses to facilitate change. We should therefore consider change from the view of our developmental-dialectical model. I have proposed that the processes that take place between child and therapist are fundamentally the same as those that take place between infant/child and his/her caregivers. This proposal was nested within a particular view of change: initially the organization of some behavior is relatively global and with development becomes more differentiated and integrated. This view was used in Model II to conceptualize levels of cognitive-behavioral regulators and in Model III to conceptualize levels of behavioral expression. Each of these models viewed change as occurring within a level as well as from one level to another. To elaborate this view, and to set the stage for treatment guidelines, I rely upon two early volumes (Watzlawick et al. 1974; Wohwil 1973) and a more recent publication (Overton, in press,b) that I believe are particularly relevant for child psychotherapy.

Broadly stated, change is an inherent characteristic of behavior. As Robert Burns put it, "Look abroad thro' Nature's range. Nature's mighty law is change" (Wohwill 1973, p. xiii). While change occurs over time (whether short or long term), an increase in chronological age is *not* the "cause" of change. Wohwill cogently argued, in the language of researchers, that age is not an "independent variable" but is a part of the "dependent variable." With age, or time, as part of the dependent variable, a therapist traces the relationship between the duration of a particular set of interactions between child and therapist on the one hand and changes that occur in some dimension of a child's behavior (e.g., inhibition of movement, cognitive or physical impulsivity) on the other.

If we apply these notions to our model, we could represent a child who comes to a therapist as a rushing river of life metaphors, cognitive regulators, and expressions in action, fantasy, and language. By interacting with a child in mutual regulations, a therapist attempts to change the course of this river in much the same way as does a caregiver. But if we take a closer look at our model, with its levels of functioning, we recognize that this representation of a child needs to be elaborated. A more accurate image would portray a child as bringing a hierarchy of lakes (levels) connected by a river: from global lakes with smooth coastlines to differentiated lakes with many complex inlets. The model of life metaphors would be represented by a river connecting a hierarchy of numerous lakes (e.g., attaching to and loving others, reciprocating, asserting). The model of cognitive regulators would be represented by a river connecting a hierarchy of five lakes, regulating body tempos, scanning, articulating relevant and irrelevant information, conserving images of past information and comparing them with present perceptions, and categorizing and conceptualizing. The model of modalities would be represented by a river connecting a hierarchy of three lakes: action, fantasy, and language. With this image of each model, the question of which doorway a therapist should enter becomes elaborated. Where do therapist and child embark on a therapeutic journey, or canoe trip, in an effort to facilitate change? Do they explore one or another lake or do they canoe the river connecting them? To address this question we need to consider the processes of change that take place when canoeing a lake versus a river.

Change within a Level of Functioning: First-order Change

Imagine a level of inflexible functioning to be like a lake that is stagnant and constricted by weeds. To facilitate change in this lake, that is, to make a level of functioning more flexible (whether a life metaphor, a cognitive orientation, or a behavioral modality), a therapist interacts with a child *within the child's maladaptive mode* in ways that promote flexibility. Here therapist and child explore a particular lake and clear it of weeds. Borrowing a term used by Watzlawick and colleagues (1974), I refer to this process as "first-order change," which occurs within a level or modality of functioning and primarily involves facilitating change in self-regulation.

Change in the Connection between One Level of Functioning and Another: Second-order Change

Now imagine a river that is dammed up, constricted by rocks and debris at some point along its course. Because the river's flow is impeded, one lake, or level of functioning, is insufficiently connected with others. To facilitate change the therapist connects (integrates) one level of functioning with another by removing debris that impedes the river's flow. For example, a therapist's interactions would connect reciprocating behaviors with oppositional behaviors, or regulating body tempo with articulating relevant information, or action expressions with fantasy expressions. In these interactions a therapist approaches the child *from outside the child's habitual, maladaptive mode*, and therefore "bumps into" the level or mode typically used by the child. I refer to this process as "second-order change," which emphasizes negotiating mutual regulation. The concept of the arrow of time, discussed in previous chapters, applies here (see Overton 1994).

Relation between First-order and Second-order Change

To address the relation between first-order and second-order change, I leave the image of rivers and lakes and elaborate an image of a car and driver used by Watzlawick and colleagues (1974). Imagine a car with a standard (stick) shift, gas pedal, and driver. The performance of the driver and car can be changed in two ways. With one, while the driver is, let us say, in first gear, he/she learns to regulate the gas pedal with increasing differentiation, flexibly depressing and lifting the gas pedal, quickly and slowly, in many different increments and in harmony with speeds required by traffic, road conditions, stop signs, and so forth. The critical point is that these various foot movements and speeds are taking place within the range that belongs to first gear. In learning movements required to operate in first gear, the driver is functioning within a level and involved in the processes of first-order change and self-regulation. Applied to our developmental models, changing how the gas pedal is depressed involves three particular "movements" within cognition and modes of expression that coordinate the calls for action from a child's life metaphors with those of surrounding circumstances: differentiation, delay, and indirectness.

But what if a desired speed falls outside the range of first gear? What if, for example, instead of operating the vehicle on a rarely traveled, narrow dirt road, the vehicle is operated on a superhighway with heavy traffic? Because of constant changes in the flow of traffic, the driver must now shift back and forth among gears and sometimes stop or perhaps go in reverse. The critical point here is that each gear has its own range of foot movements coordinated with surrounding circumstances. In learning to change from first to third gear, the driver is responding to a major change in expectations outside himself/herself and is involved in the processes of second-order change and mutual regulation.

Applying this image to one of our developmental models, we could imagine that expressing meanings in the action mode could be, let us say, like driving in first gear. Consider a 10–year-old boy who is confronted in the playground by a bully standing in his way. In response, the boy pushes the bully to one side. Later he races him to the top of a mount—interactions representing different degrees of directness and delay or different foot movements within first gear or action mode. Then the bell rings, bringing recess to a close. When in the classroom, this boy is surrounded by a very different set of expectations, which bump into the action mode and require the ability to shift to another. Accordingly, he shifts gears to the fantasy mode. Now glaring at the bully seated at the other end of the room, he fantasizes pounding him in a fist fight and then fantasizes beating him in a 100-yard dash at the school Olympics—fantasized interactions representing different degrees of directness and delay, or different foot movements, within second gear or fantasy mode.

At any phase of treatment it is important that a therapist pay close attention to whether the child requires the processes of first-order or second-order change. If attention is not paid to differences between these two processes, the therapist might interact in a way that the child experiences as an "assault" and evoke behaviors from the child that do not promote the desired change. Recall a moment of psychotherapy reported by Coppolillo (1987; see Chapter 4) involving a boy who had "little inclination to explore the significance of anything he said" (p. 215). The boy began to play solitaire with a deck of cards he had brought with him, behavior the therapist interpreted verbally. In response the boy angrily mumbled, "No solitaire. Just sit here and talk to this old, shithead, son-of-a-bitch" (p. 215). From the view of our present discussion, by giving linguistic meaning to the solitaire game, the therapist approached the boy from outside his preferred mode, requiring him to engage in second-order change and lift the meaning of playing solitaire from the level of action to the level of language. The child's reaction strongly suggested he was not yet ready for second-order change. In contrast, to facilitate first-order change in the meaning of the solitaire game, a therapist could sit at the far end of the room and involve himself in a game of solitaire, "speaking" to the child within his mode, and preparing him for second-order change. Heard and Linehan's (1994) notion of "accepting" and "extending" strategies of change is related.

Resistance to Change

We have discussed that, beginning with Freud's first publications, psychodynamic psychotherapy has given a central position to the issue of resistance to change, an issue that has since been considered from cognitive and behavioral as well as psychodynamic viewpoints (e.g., Wachtel 1982). Recall that Freud observed that in order to avoid remembering and discussing earlier ways in which he/she interacted with others, a patient experienced and transferred these modes of relating onto the therapist during treatment sessions. In other words, a person resisted changing modes of relating by "doing" instead of "remembering and discussing." But our developmental-dialectical model, emphasizing that children frequently bring a rigid mode of functioning that is the opposite of another, requires that we elaborate this view of resistance. If a 12-year-old is rigidly action-oriented and avoids fantasizing, or an 8-year-old rigidly engages in discussions and avoids taking action, are they resisting change because they don't want to remember something?

The notion of the "interdependence of opposites" adds to an understanding of resistance. This concept includes the mind's tendency to draw boundaries and experience opposites (Chapter 2) and dialectics (Chapters 4 and 5) and proposes that the identity of some behavior (e.g., a belief, action, fantasy) is defined and preserved by its opposite. For example, the meaning of good is preserved by the meaning of evil, the meaning of an action by the meaning of a fantasy, and a verbalized belief by an action expressing that belief. Carl Jung's (1953) view of the interdependence of opposites as a fundamental psychological mechanism sets the stage for my use of this concept.

> Each psychological extreme secretly contains its own opposite or stands in some sort of intermediate and essential relation to it . . . there is no hallowed custom that cannot on occasion turn into its opposite and the more extreme a position is, the more easily may we expect . . . a conversion of something into its opposite. [p. 375]

To illustrate how the notion of opposites as resistance applies to our models, recall 15-year-old Tom who sat still, preoccupied himself with the creases of his trousers and the position of a box of tissues, and seemed unable to share with the therapist meanings and feelings he was experiencing. His cognition sharply divided experiences in terms of things as they are and as he imagined them to be, and rigidly focused on the former. This rigid outer cognitive orientation was preserved by its opposite, namely, avoiding things as he imagined them to be. Tom's "resistance" to discussing personal concerns and fantasies, then, was not so much the outcome of refusing to "remember" but due primarily to his employing a mode of cognitive functioning that avoided its opposite, that may at one time have coped successfully with disruptions and traumatic emotions, but that then became habitual, operating independent of contexts. To help Tom, techniques are needed that dissolve the interdependence of extreme, opposite cognitive orientations by developing his capacity to integrate meanings/emotions with external stimulation (i.e., symbolize) without being overwhelmed by painful emotions.

CATALYSTS FOR CHANGE

What does a therapist do that facilitates change in how a child acts and in what a child imagines, thinks, and says? What are the catalysts that change a child's life metaphors, cognitive orientation, and modes of expression? Our model proposes three interrelated catalysts: 1) dialectical interactions between child and therapist that result in 2) enactments between child and therapist that express, revise, and repair the meanings of disruptions that occurred in the child's development; these enactments in turn result in 3) the child's idealizing and internalizing the therapist and the therapist idealizing and internalizing the child.

To bring the proposed catalysts into sharp focus, I begin by reminding the reader that the spoken word has been, and continues to be, assigned a major role as the catalyst for change both by mainstream cognitive-behavioral therapies and by psychodynamic therapies (see previous chapters). The view that words have power to change behavior was influenced by the emphasis given to verbalizing by psychodynamic therapy, which was already flourishing when behavioral and cognitive therapies emerged. Recall that Anna Freud, one of the founders of psychodynamic child therapy, took the position that games, drawings, and other activities are not valid substitutes for a child's putting into words the conflicts he/she was experiencing. At the base of this position was the assumption that by verbally describing and conceptualizing the unconscious meanings of a child's behavior, the words and concepts used produced change by lifting the meaning into conscious awareness where it could be controlled by insight and thought. Psychodynamic therapists still rely on the content of interpretations alone to account for therapeutic action (Mitchell 1994).

But even as this point of view was taking shape, some psychodynamic therapists proposed different catalysts for change (e.g., interactions between patient and therapist provided a "corrective emotional experience" and a "holding environment"). Since these early proposals, two points of view have emerged in recent years within psychodynamic therapy, each challenging the notion that what the therapist says is the main catalyst for change, and each stimulating major revisions in the very theory that initially assigned central power to verbalizing (Eagle 1984, Mitchell 1994, Stolorow and Lachmann 1980). The interpersonal viewpoint emerged, emphasizing the importance of how a patient and therapist act and interact with each other in the here and now. The developmental viewpoint emerged emphasizing the importance of distinguishing between maladaptive behaviors that derive from intrapsychic conflict and inefficient mental mechanisms of defense versus maladaptive behaviors that derive from developmental disruptions ("developmental arrests") that occur in the first years of life before intrapsychic conflicts develop (Stern 1985). This distinction is important because the emphasis of therapy with each is different. With intrapsychic conflict, techniques should change how a person regulates his/her thoughts, feelings, and actions. With developmental arrests, techniques should provide behavioral experiences that repair the effects of early disruptions on cognitive and behavioral modes of functioning.

In proposing cycles of dialectical interactions, enactments, and idealization/internalization as the catalysts for change, phenomena that derive from infant research, the developmental-dialectical model integrates the interpersonal and developmental viewpoints, bridges cognitive-behavioral and psychodynamic therapies, and integrates principles of objectivism and interpretationism (Chapter 2). This integration should become clear as I define each catalyst.

Cycles of Dialectical Interactions

The notion of cycles of dialectical interactions assumes that a person is inherently directed toward evolving relationships with others and that the process of growing with another person itself has power to heal. Dialectical interactions address the fact that child and therapist initially are different, more or less, in terms of *overt self-expressions and self-experiences*: emotional tones, preferred levels of excitation, cognitive orientations, and modes and style of expression, especially tonic experiences such as gestures, touch, postures, and tempo of body movements. When engaging in cycles of dialectical interactions, child and therapist negotiate and regulate their respective self-expressions and get to know the way the other walks and moves when excited versus when tired; how the other smells, sighs, laughs, and glances when disappointed versus when pleased, and so on. This interactive process is analogous to Stern's (1985) "core relatedness" between infant and caregiver.

As diagrammed in Figure 7–1, every interaction between child and therapist does not necessarily involve their participating in a dialectical interaction. Imagine a circle that represents differences in self-expression between child and therapist. In the beginning each is standing outside this circle, although each is engaged in some interaction—talking about a school trip, playing a game, dealing with a task the therapist has introduced (I, Figure 7–1). Sometimes, of course, the child will step into the circle to negotiate a difference or to articulate a characteristic of the therapist, and the therapist does not; sometimes the therapist steps into the circle and the child does not (II, Figure 7–1). As child and therapist participate in repeated interactions, whether in free play/discussions or structured tasks, at one point

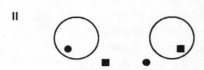

Dialectical Circle
● = Child   ■ = Therapist

I

Interactions: Discussions of a school trip; playing a game; dealing with a task.

II

Interactions: Child or therapist step into the dialectical circle to negotiate some differ- ence in overt self-expressions; the other does not step in.

III

Dialectical Interactions: Child and therapist step into the circle to negotiate and regulate differences in overt self-expressions; e.g., preferred level of stimulation, emotional tone, bodily movements. Child and therapist "contour" their self-expressions.

IV

Enactments: Child and therapist step into the circle to share a subjective experience and/or influence a subjective experience of the other; constellations of actions, images, words, emotions communicate and contribute a meaning to their intersubjective world.

Dialectical interactions and enactments require empathy and selective attunement.

V

Idealization/Internalization: Child and therapist each idealizes and internalizes behaviors and meanings of the other devoted to solving the dilemmas they share.

FIGURE 7–1
Catalysts for Change

or another each eventually steps into the circle with the intention of negotiating one or another of their differences and "getting to know" and regulating some attribute of the other's overt self-expressions (III, Figure 7–1). In this process child and therapist contribute to "contouring" the overt self-expressions each displays to the other, a term Stern (1985) used to conceptualize infant–caregiver interactions. The critical point is that as child and therapist step into the circle and increasingly articulate, recognize, and regulate each other's self-expressions, a relational foundation is established upon which they eventually coauthor meanings they share, a process that involves enactments, the next catalyst we consider.

Enactments

Enactments are constellations of actions/gestures, touch, fantasies, words, thoughts, and emotions that are intended to communicate and introduce a particular meaning into the intersubjective world child and therapist are constructing (IV, Figure 7–1). While the focus of dialectical interactions is on child and therapist attempting to know, regulate, and negotiate each other's overt self-expressions, the focus of enactments is on child and therapist *sharing subjective experiences* (meanings) and attempting to influence the subjective experiences of the other. In this process they are also negotiating whether each can share subjective experiences with the other, and if so which ones. The process of enactments parallels Stern's (1985) "intersubjective relatedness."

Enactments signal that child and therapist know or understand something about their shared subjective world. Conversely, knowing and understanding inherently leads to the desire to take action and enact what is known or understood (Gold 1994, Smith and Franklin 1979). When a child and/or therapist enact, he/she (1) steps into the dialectical circle; (2) assumes the other is also in the circle; (3) constructs and expresses some meaning to communicate and share, related to one or another life metaphor they are negotiating; and (4) expects the other to understand the communication and to respond in a synchronous way.

From this definition I note other characteristics of enactments as used here. When repeated over time, whether or not enactments are embedded in verbal discourse they construct and communicate the meanings of events and interactions that take place between child and therapist, and gradually change/revise these meanings (Messer and Winokur 1984, Shirk 1988). Enactments are not necessarily equal to what is conceptualized as discourse and play by psychodynamic, behavioral, and relational approaches to therapy (Brems 1993). A child may be engaged in a discussion or some form of play with dolls, toys, or games and not necessarily intend to construct and share some meaning that serves negotiating a developmental issue with the therapist. And enactments may take place during brief moments. Recall Coppolillo's patient who stepped into the circle and enacted a game of solitaire, sharing some meaning. The therapist stepped into the circle and expressed his understanding of this shared symbol in the form of a verbal interpretation that apparently was not synchronous with the meaning being shared since the boy expressed frustration. And recall Spiegel's patient who, after hearing the therapist ask whether he had soiled himself in school, stepped into the circle by placing a piece of clay at the end of his nose, enacting a meaning within their intersubjective world.

Enactments are also gradually elaborated and ritualized over several sessions, as illustrated by the treatment of a child we consider in more detail below. For several sessions this child enacted flipping a hand puppet he called "Mr. Fall" across the room. Each time the therapist stepped into the circle, he responded by tying one end of a string around the puppet and the other around a doorknob in order to prevent Mr. Fall from hitting the wall and being injured. Later, when the child stepped into the circle and repeatedly spit on and bit the therapist, the therapist stepped into the circle in response to each enactment and tied one end of a string around his forehead and the other around the child's to prevent him from "falling" as did Mr. Fall. With this enactment the therapist used a meaning (symbolized by string) that child and therapist had already coauthored and shared.

Relating Dialectical Interactions and Enactments: Empathy and Selective Attunement

As these vignettes illustrate, enactments as well as cycles of dialectical interactions require the therapist to be empathic, understanding, and selectively attuned. Empathy goes beyond a feeling of caring (Brems 1993) and requires the therapist to understand how a child is feeling, thinking, and experiencing at the moment given the issue being negotiated and the experiences and meanings child and therapist have shared thus far. The capacity to be empathic in these terms enables a therapist to discover himself/herself within a child's subjective world. Dialectical interactions and enactments also require what Stern (1985) described as "selective attunement" between caregiver and infant, "one of the most potent ways that a parent can shape the development of a child's subjective and interpersonal life" (p. 207). During treatment sessions a child displays a wide range of activity, emotions, and meanings accompanied by little or considerable enthusiasm. Faced with this continuous flow of behavior, the therapist must choose what to attune to, and respond to, from among the almost infinite opportunities available. If a therapist has empathically discovered himself/herself within a child's subjective world, and is in tune with the intersubjective, symbolic world constructed thus far, the therapist is likely to initiate and/or participate in enactments with the child that, more often than not, serve the treatment process and change. To engage in successful dialectical interactions and enactments, then, a therapist must shift back and forth from being a participant to being an observer, from introspection to empathy, from intuition to problem solving, and from becoming more involved to becoming more detached (Greenson 1977). The therapist must continually oscillate between these positions and also blend them together. Guided by empathy and selective attunement, the therapist observes what is going on, why the interaction is occurring, and decides what to enact next in the service of promoting change.

As conceptualized, cycles of dialectical interactions and enactments are "the very stuff of treatment," as Mitchell (1994) put it. Although Freud viewed taking action and thinking/remembering as inversely related, our model views dialectical interactions and enactments as constellations of actions, fantasies, words, thoughts, and emotions that continually interpenetrate each other and substitute for each other. Cycles of dialectical interactions and enactments, whether as part of free play or structured tasks, are processes that continue simultaneously throughout treatment, regulating overt self-expressions and subjective experiences, and reorganizing life metaphors, cognitive orientations, and modes of expression.

Idealization and Internalization

When dialectical interactions and enactments are accompanied by appropriate empathy and selective attunement, they result in the child's idealizing and internalizing the therapist and the therapist's idealizing and internalizing the child (V, Figure 7–1). Recall that infant research provides considerable support for the view that during the first two years of life enactments between infant and caregiver become internalized within the infant's mind as organized expectations or schemas. One expression of internalization/idealization is observed when, in the absence of a caregiver, an infant imitates some characteristic of a caregiver. This process continues beyond the third year as a child internalizes interactions with others as well as caregivers, whose attributes also become idealized. These attributes serve as symbolic standards against which a child evaluates his/her behaviors and define what the child wants to be rather than what a child should do. If representations of an idealized adult are not met, a child typically experiences a sense of guilt and fear of losing the adult's love. Internalized, idealized standards, then, play a role in self-regulation and in the development of restraining and delaying behaviors that do not satisfy these standards. Whether child and therapist engage in cycles of enactments while dealing with structured tasks or when involved in free play/discussions, the child gradually idealizes and internalizes attributes of the therapist, attributes the child takes on as his/her own.

The importance of the therapist's idealizing and internalizing the child usually is not given attention, or at least I have not run across discussions of this topic by others. It follows from the developmental-dialectical model that if a therapist steps into the dialectical circle, and gradually discovers himself/herself within the child's subjective world, over the course of many enactments a therapist experiences, as does a caregiver, excitement, fatigue, boredom, pleasure, pride, irritation, and anger. Within these experiences a therapist, like a caregiver, should idealize and internalize the child. It may seem hard to believe that a therapist finds himself/herself imitating some verbal expression or gesture the child typically uses or becoming very interested in a child's favorite athletic team or the like as well as experiencing a surge of "therapeutic love" whenever the child makes some gain within or outside the treatment situation. Lear's (1990) discussion of the power of love in the process of therapy and Orlinsky and Howard's (1987) discussion of the "special attachment" that develops between patient and therapist are relevant to this issue, although presented in the domain of adult psychotherapy.

GUIDELINES FOR INTEGRATING TWO SUBJECTIVE CULTURES: IN THE BEGINNING, CHILD AND THERAPIST ARE FOREIGN TO EACH OTHER

The preceding discussion of catalysts for change emphasizes an issue we should discuss further before considering the process of therapy. Before stepping into a dialectical circle, child and therapist are essentially foreign to each other, bringing different subjective cultures. This issue relates to the growing interest in therapists' becoming sensitive to cultural differences (e.g., American Psychological Association 1990, Division of Child, Youth, and Family Services 1994, Division of Clinical Psychology 1990, Fischer 1995, Franklin et al. 1993).

Johnson's (1993) lucid discussion of therapy and cultural differences frames my view. He noted, "It is virtually inevitable that the child therapist will work with a client who has a social, ethnic, or cultural background different from her or his own . . . gaining skills and knowledge necessary to deal with a socially, ethnically, or culturally diverse child clientele is as important to a trainee's education as gaining basic skills and knowledge of child therapy itself" (p. 68). Because child and therapist come from different cultural and ethnic backgrounds, various issues arise; for example, the name each expects the other to use; the understanding each has of the nonverbal communications of the other; the potential for a child to experience a therapist in terms of stereotypes he/she holds of the therapist's race and cultural and ethnic background; and similarly the potential for a therapist to experience a child in terms of stereotypes he/she holds. "Countertransference can be based on previous experiences with members of another ethnic or cultural group or from public media representations of that culture . . . [therefore] the therapy may become focused not on a child's presenting issues, but rather on the problems a therapist has projected on the family" (Johnson 1993, p. 91).

The issues raised by Johnson and others concerning sensitivity to cultural diversity, when viewed through our model, take on a wider significance. Metaphorically speaking, in the beginning infant and caregiver, as well as child and therapist, are *always* of "different cultures," whether or not they are of the same race and ethnic background; in the case of infant and caregiver, from the first day they engage in a dialectical process within which they gradually forge their intersubjective culture. In the first months, then, from the infant's point of view the caregiver is a "foreigner," and from the caregiver's point of view the infant is a "foreigner." Similarly, in the first months of treatment child and therapist are foreign to each other.

In addition to this similarity there is an important difference. An infant and caregiver begin at the beginning. While a caregiver has already constructed a subjective world that he/she carries into a dialectical circle, the infant has not. In contrast, a child who enters therapy and the therapist have already constructed a subjective world that has been and is being shared with others (e.g., parents, sibs, spouse, children, peers, teachers, professional colleagues). Given that child and therapist come together with well-established subjective worlds, a number of issues arise in their relationship as they begin interacting and negotiating. Accepting those articulated by Johnson, which emerge from race, ethnic, and cultural differences, I focus on others that emerge from the developmental-dialectical model: (1) modes of self-expression (e.g., gestures, preferred levels of excitation, emotional tones) and life metaphors each has adequately and incompletely negotiated; (2) cognitive orientations each maintains; and (3) modes each prefers for expressing meanings—action, fantasy, and language. These differences require formal attention because they influence the success with which child and therapist construct a shared world and engage in ongoing regulations and enactments that promote change.

Child and Therapist Negotiate Developmental Issues to Construct a Shared, Intersubjective Culture

If child and therapist come with differences in these characteristics, and if these characteristics exert an influence on the success with which treatment will promote change, what can a therapist do to negotiate this paradox? I recommend that, as opportunities present themselves, a therapist engage a child in negotiating one or another of the issues articulated by Sander's model of mother–infant negotiations (Chapter 5). Some children may require many negotiations with one of these issues, others a few negotiations with several issues. Some issues may need to be negotiated only a few times, and others repeatedly throughout treatment. Negotiating these issues operationalizes the catalysts for change described earlier.

Cycles of Dialectical Interactions: Negotiating Initial Adaptation and Reciprocal Exchange

When negotiating initial adaptation and reciprocal exchanges, child and therapist are discovering and contouring each other's overt self-expressions. In terms of initial adaptation, the therapist is alert to observing a child's unique postures, gestures, rhythms of activity, and preferences for pace and level of stimulation, especially involving sound, touch, and temperature, and to understand whether and how these characteristics match his/her own. Negotiating initial adaptation depends upon the therapist's skill in exercising selective attunement and the balance a therapist maintains between his/her empathy and perceptions of the child as an individual apart from her/his projections. One child commented that the playroom was "screaming bright"; the therapist lowered the illumination without saying a word. Another child wrapped her arms around herself; the therapist raised the thermostat and obtained the child's jacket, even though for the therapist it was relatively warm. And recall the 10-year-old boy who arrived for an initial appointment with a jacket pulled over his head, obscuring his face. He entered the playroom slowly, hooded by his jacket, and stood a few feet from the doorway. Noticing the boy's body rhythm and preference for interpersonal stimulation, the therapist said nothing, left the door open, and walked to the far end of the room, moving much more slowly than her usual vigorous pace. There she stood looking out of a window, careful to keep her full face obscured.

When negotiating reciprocal exchange, the therapist is alert for opportunities to engage the child in active-passive exchanges, especially involving emotions and body rhythms that match the child's. A 6-year-old girl sang "oooh" with pleasure, in rhythm with her repeatedly raising and lowering the lid of a music box, each time triggering the melody. The therapist joined in, expressing the singsong "oooh" each time the lid was raised. Another child sat outside under a large hew. He reached up and slowly pulled down a branch while lowering his torso, simultaneously singing a long "aaaaah." Then he released the branch, and when it snapped back into position, he sat up straight and completed his "song" with "choo!" The therapist joined in, rhythmically bowing and singing "aaah-choo!" Another child typically walked behind the therapist. Eventually noticing this, the therapist adjusted her tempo and was careful to walk alongside the child.

Enactments: Negotiating Early Directed Activity, Focalizing, and Self-Assertion

When negotiating early directed activity, a child becomes more active in directing his/her own behavior and that of the therapist, indicating a particular experience is anticipated and another is to be avoided. The therapist is now required to be passive, modifying the active response involved in negotiating the previous two issues even though the meaning of the directed behavior is not yet clear. One child insisted that she and the therapist sit on the floor instead of at a table, and the therapist accommodated. Another child ignored the therapist for most of two sessions, "flying" a helicopter throughout the playroom, occasionally mumbling to imaginary characters. The therapist said and did nothing except sit and watch the child, expressing some interest with facial expressions whenever the child turned to look at the therapist. And recall the adolescent who returned the therapist's greeting with a long stare, grunting that she would not go in an office to talk, but would go outside. Saying only, "Let's go outside," the therapist accommodated, resulting in developments discussed later.

In terms of negotiating focalizing, as a child experiences a therapist assuming a passive role in response to her/his directions, her/his "requests" become more explicitly concerned with establishing that the therapist is unconditionally available, receptive to sharing a subjective experience, and capable of providing safety and protection when the unknown/unfamiliar is explored. In this process a child frequently refers to his/her body or representations of the body-self. While busying herself drawing pictures, a child repeatedly broke the point of her pencil and then glanced at the therapist, who sharpened the pencil each time. Upon entering the playroom, another child stopped and "examined" her knee, rubbing her fingers over several minor scratches. The therapist showed concern and applied a Band-Aid. When a child began to jump from the top of a climber to the floor, the therapist placed a mat in the area. And when a child began crawling under bushes, enacting danger, the therapist also crawled under, aiming a flashlight in many directions, enacting caution. By negotiating a therapist's unconditional availability, a child establishes whether each can share subjective experiences and meanings with the other and which ones can and cannot be shared.

If a child adequately establishes that the therapist is unconditionally available, the child attempts to negotiate self-assertion both on materials and the person of the therapist. Negotiating self-assertion and aggressive expressions is probably the most difficult task a therapist faces if he/she views these behaviors as "fighting," a view that conflicts with the intention of helping the child. But if viewed in a different way, the task might become easier. When engaging in assertive behaviors, the child is developing "interactive tools" *designed to determine whether the therapist is "up to battling" not the child but the child's difficulties.* The child's expressions of assertion/aggression, and the therapist's ability to survive them, play an important role in helping the child experience the therapist as someone who can be used in the struggle to overcome difficulties (Safran 1993).

This position is different from the view of most who propose that self-assertive behaviors should be controlled by "rules and regulations." Reisman (1973) believed it was "absurd" if a therapist allowed a child to act on his person (e.g., to be tied in a game of cowboys). Brems (1993) noted, "When aggression is threatened or just beginning, the child needs to be reminded of the physical safety rules . . . a contingency must be set up. The child must be informed of what will occur if she or he chooses to continue to escalate the behavior" (p. 226). Prohibiting behaviors, and requiring a child to accommodate to pre-formed rules, shifts the relationship from a climate of negotiating to one in which a therapist becomes a "probation officer" and a child the "offender." From our view, the therapist should be as resourceful as possible in inventing and experimenting with various ways in which the child's expressions of self-assertion and aggression can be permitted in some displaced form rather than blocked by some rule. And the therapist should find ways of participating in the expression.

Tom, a 10-year-old, had already participated with the therapist in negotiations of reciprocating and directing activity. In this particular session, as he entered the playroom he pushed the therapist to one side, angrily kicked a wastebasket, and defiantly stated, "This is fucking boring." Then he picked up boxing gloves and invited the therapist to "take me on." The therapist, not comfortable with

.boxing, challenged Tom to "take me on" with something else that was not boring. Tom wandered about for a moment, picked up two puppets, and smashed them against each other (very likely an action symbol of child and therapist in battle). This activity quickly escalated as Tom slammed the puppets against toys and shelves. Expressing amazement over Tom's "karate chops," the therapist invited him "to chop these wooden cutouts just like karate fighters do." The invitation worked; Tom grinned and agreed. The therapist placed eight large, wooden, colored cutouts in a row, commented that the cutouts were enemies to be "demolished," and suggested that each be given a name. Tom readily obliged (e.g., "Geek," "Grink," "Retard," "X"—the therapist's first name). The therapist challenged Tom to stand with his back to the cutouts, listen for the cutout named by the therapist, and then turn as quickly as possible and chop it. Tom enthusiastically chopped away as the therapist timed and recorded how many seconds Tom required to turn, scan the row of cutouts, and chop the one named. Then the therapist suggested that Tom call out a name and the therapist would chop the cutout while Tom timed him. Intense competition developed between them, with the therapist displaying the same vigor and anger as did Tom.

In this vignette the therapist negotiated that aggression is permitted ("I can take it") within a form and level of vigor that was fitted to his style. Of course, therapists vary in terms of the degree and form of assertion/aggression with which they feel at ease. It is as important for the child to "know" this about the therapist, as it is for the therapist to "know" this about the child. One child may ask the therapist to engage in a boxing match, while another, without any physical gestures, may quietly yet persistently change the rules of a formboard game so that the child always wins. Another child may spit on the therapist or hurl a wooden cube at the wall. Negotiating each expression of assertion/aggression enables a child to establish that the therapist has the knowledge and strength to combat the child's difficulties. The therapist facilitates this process by inventing alternative, displaced forms of aggression within the child's preferred mode. This suggestion agrees with Heard and Linehan's (1994) use of "extending techniques" with borderline adults that derive from the martial art of aikido; that is, the therapist extends the patient's behavior, rather than blocking it, so that the movement continues in a deflected direction.

Outcome of Successful Dialectical Interactions and Enactments: Constructing Shared Symbols and Interactive Embodied Images

As child and therapist engage in negotiating each of the issues discussed above, participating in cycles of dialectical interactions and enactments, they simultaneously construct symbols representing the uniqueness of their relationship and shared experiences: gestures, actions, images, fantasies, emotional tones, and invented and conventional language expressions. In addition, following the proposal that all representations initially are embodied, negotiations with each issue result in child and therapist constructing "interactive embodied images" that are gradually elaborated through experiences they share in future sessions. These symbols become the "language" of child and therapist, which solidifies their relationship; enables each to understand, idealize, and internalize the other; and enables them eventually to enact solutions to the child's pathological life metaphors, cognitive orientations, and modes of expression.

Throughout this process the therapist has opportunities to evaluate a child's style of symbol formation and help him/her cultivate the capacity to construct symbols that communicate more readily to others. The therapist is careful not to prematurely force a symbol the child constructs into the therapist's network of meanings. When Spiegel's patient placed clay on the end of his nose, he seemed to locate this symbolic enactment within his network, understanding the gesture to mean, "A long nose equals Pinocchio which equals not telling the truth." A child I discuss below repeatedly toppled items from shelves to the floor. Initially I understood these enactments as expressing the meaning of aggression but soon learned they symbolized body instability and the absence of being grounded. The therapist, then, should participate as much as possible within the process of first-order change, helping the child clarify the meaning of some newly constructed symbol before responding.

TYPICAL QUESTIONS ABOUT CHILD PSYCHOTHERAPY: RULES AND LIMITS VERSUS NEGOTIATION

The preceding view, that child and therapist should step into a dialectical circle and negotiate various issues in order to activate catalysts for change and integrate their respective, subjective cultures, relates to questions typically raised about child psychotherapy. Who decides where therapy should take place? How involved should a therapist get when interacting with a child? If a therapist becomes too involved, what about the transference? Who decides how long a treatment session should last? And who decides what to do if a child requests a gift, food, some item to take home, or some information about the therapist's personal life? When addressing these and related questions decades ago, authors presented the view that the therapist makes these decisions, establishes rules, and sets limits. Hammer and Kaplan (1967), for example, devoted special attention to setting rules and limits; for example, a child should not be permitted to act on the person or clothing of the therapist; a child should be informed of the time limit of sessions; and a child should not be permitted to leave the treatment room except to go to the bathroom or to get a drink of water. "It should be obvious that nothing therapeutic can be accomplished if the therapist is chasing the child around the block or through hallways of the clinic . . ." (p. 5). And if the child is reluctant to leave the treatment room when time is up, these same authors recommended that the child may need to be carried out. Similarly, Reisman (1973) emphasized the need for the therapist to set limits and cautioned against the therapist allowing the child to act on her/his person in play.

The notion that the therapist should make decisions and set limits appears to have been sustained over the years and prevails at the present time even when child psychotherapy is discussed from interpersonal and developmental viewpoints. Spiegel (1989) devoted a chapter to "limit setting," which I recommend to readers. Tracing the history of permissiveness in child psychotherapy, he pointed out that child therapists began "to recognize that complete freedom in the playroom was not always in the best interest of treatment" (p. 114). While presenting an excellent discussion of how a therapist could provide a child with alternative ways of expressing feelings, Spiegel proposed the guiding principle that ". . . to maintain and enhance self-esteem requires limiting behaviors and not feelings" (p. 116). From this position he recommended, for example, that a child should not be allowed to take a toy home or to bring a peer or sib or other guest into the playroom, and the therapist should try to explore the reasons for the request; the therapist should avoid offering food, and if she/he does, a limited quantity (e.g., "three cookies") should be set out; if a child tries to end a treatment session, the therapist should try to learn the reason why; and the therapist should not become too involved when interacting, as if he/she is the child's "playmate."

Brems (1993) also devoted considerable attention to the need for limits and rules. "Physical and psychological safety are best ascertained through the creation of limits . . . and rules" (p. 15); for example, a therapist could give a child a gift if the reason for giving it is not embedded in the therapist's countertransference; if a child places some item in his/her pocket, direct, gentle confrontation is necessary, and the child should be asked to return it. If the child asks a question about the therapist's personal life (e.g., "Do you have kids?"), the "hidden" meaning should be considered before answering, and when in doubt the therapist should refrain from self-disclosure; or the therapist could say, "Yes, and I have enough love and caring for them and all the children I work with" (p. 251).

While I agree with a number of points these and other authors make, these discussions of limits are not sufficiently cast within a dialectical framework. If a child asks to have a sib enter the treatment room, or remarks, for example, "You look tired today. How come?" or asks for food, or wants to leave the treatment room, the child has stepped into a dialectical circle, introducing an enactment and meaning. If the therapist prohibits and/or attempts to explore the child's reasons for such requests, the therapist does not step into the circle but bumps into the child's emerging meaning (second-order change), losing an opportunity to participate in an enactment that could contribute to integrating their unique, subjective cultures. In general, I recommend that, whenever possible, the therapist step into the circle. Questions should be answered, food and gifts should be given, and a child should be allowed to keep an item in his/her pocket. Then the therapist observes the gestures, actions, and emotions a child displays moments after, and especially during the next session, to learn what meaning the child is introducing into their intersubjective culture.

To illustrate this recommendation I turn to rules and limits typically proposed about the setting in which therapy should take place and the material that should be used. Of all the issues addressed with limits, the place of treatment and materials have perhaps received the most attention.

Space and Materials for Therapy: Is the Playroom a "Sacred Temple"? Are Toys the "Holy Grail"?

Typically, the view is presented that psychotherapy with children and adolescents must take place in a treatment room and make use of carefully selected toys and materials. As presented, this view conjures up an image that the playroom is some kind of "sacred temple" and toys the "holy grail." Reisman (1973) stated that leaving the playroom for whatever reason "decreases the already limited time of the session" (p. 48). More recently, both Coppolillo (1987) and Spiegel (1989) took a similar position, emphasizing that psychotherapy with children appropriately takes place "behind closed doors" and "going outside the playroom raises ethical and therapeutic questions." Brems (1993) agreed that "there is little need for a child to ever leave the therapy room . . ." (p. 7). Moreover, she construed a child's leaving the playroom as an attempt to escape: "While play therapy is generally confined to the playroom, it does happen that children 'escape'" (p. 5). Reviewing opinions about how therapists should handle a child's attempts to leave the playroom (e.g., one therapist advocated blocking the door), Brems proposed a more balanced approach, recommending that the therapist find out why the child wants to leave. "Often children who ask to leave have reached a point in their session that is anxiety provoking [and they] avoid this anxiety by removing themselves from the stimulus. This is an unrealistic approach to life in which no one can always escape difficult situations. Therapy can . . . help the child verbalize her or his feelings and deal with them constructively rather than through avoidance" (p. 250). The inference that the child is trying to escape from the playroom, and that such behaviors are "unrealistic," is based upon how the therapist, not the child, construes what the playroom means. Moreover, requiring a child to verbalize his/her reasons for leaving may fit the therapist but not the child, who may be "speaking" in a nonverbal language.

Brems (1993) also discussed strategies the therapist could use to minimize a child's attempts to escape. If a child asks to go to the bathroom, the therapist gives permission to the first request, but in subsequent sessions reminds the child to use the bathroom before entering the playroom. A water cooler could be located in the playroom to prevent the child from leaving to get a drink. The playroom and bathroom could be located so that the child does not cross through the waiting room and make contact with parents, which "may interfere with therapy." And windows could be equipped with blinds "to screen out distractions."

Our developmental-dialectical model presents a view that does not construe the playroom as the only geography of treatment or focus on ways of preventing a child from "escaping," physically by leaving the playroom or cognitively by looking out a window. If we accept the position that child and therapist need to step into a dialectical circle to integrate their respective, subjective worlds, then they should create any number of "geographies" that symbolize the evolving, unique, intersubjective culture they are creating and within which they continually transact to promote change. Following this view, my colleagues and I have conducted therapy with children and adolescents shifting from one geography to another during the course of treatment. When treating children in the inner city, geographies included the school's gym, hallways, supply rooms, playground, nearby streets, and stores. When treating children in the suburbs, geographies included playrooms, therapist's office, secretary's office, hallways, cellar of the building, nearby streets and stores, and a "therapeutic garden" we constructed as a laboratory to explore a child's use of nature in resolving difficulties. We pay close attention to the issues being negotiated when a child spontaneously moves, for example, from the school building to the streets, from the playroom to a hallway, or from the playroom to the therapeutic garden. We have learned, for example, that when a child shifts from the geography of a playroom to the outdoors, this shift frequently facilitates a child's (1) expressing embodied meanings and translating them into symbolic forms; (2) engaging a cognitive orientation different from the pathological orientation within which he/she typically functions; and (3) engaging a mode of expression different from the mode he/she typically uses.

I mention a few clinical examples here and reserve more detailed discussions for later chapters. A 5-year-old, very hyperactive and impulsive girl, plagued by rapid shifts in cognitive orientation, initially engaged the therapist throughout the building (therapist's office, playroom, hallways on the first and second floors, stairway, waiting room, conference room, secretary's office). Assimilating experiences provided by the therapist during these journeys, she gradually limited her interactions and negotiations to the first floor and later to the playroom. A 7-year-old adopted boy, whose functioning had been compromised by traumatic experiences he endured in an orphanage, engaged the therapist in constructing and living in a "village" within which they enacted a common theme: the village and persons of child and therapist were repeatedly invaded in a variety of ways by "bad" people, and child and therapist invented various strategies to fend them off. This child first constructed the village in the therapist's office, using three large plastic containers, four pillows, and an old bedsheet draped over an easel. In sessions that followed, these same items were used to construct the same village in the hallway just outside the therapist's office, then in the playroom, then outdoors immediately out-side a doorway that leads from the playroom to the therapeutic garden, and then in a cave area some thirty yards from the playroom door.

The hyperactive girl used space to negotiate a change from a cognitive orien-tation and mode of expression that lacked organization and delay—frantically fly-ing throughout diffuse, large geographies—to an orientation and mode of expres-sion consisting of organization and delay that could operate within the microspace of a playroom. The adopted boy used space to negotiate a change from coping with embodied fears within the microspace of the therapist's office to coping with the same fears in the geography of "the larger world."

The last example illustrates the proposal that a child often uses the outdoors to experience an embodied meaning rather than to escape from therapy. During about ten sessions, Ellen (mentioned in Chapter 1), who initially refused to go to the office, complained almost continuously about female teachers, who were char-acterized as insensitive and ungiving. Then her mother became the target of these fixed opinions and feelings. At this point she asked if she could go outside in our therapeutic garden, which she had used in her first meeting. The therapist agreed. Upon entering the garden, Ellen climbed to the top of a mount. At first she sat and chatted, and the therapist sat nearby. Then she stretched out in a prone posi-tion, continuing her conversation. Suddenly she stopped, acknowledging that she had just experienced a "very embarrassing feeling." The therapist encouraged her to share it. The adolescent reciprocated, sharing that for a moment she felt she was lying on the belly of a pregnant woman. "It feels fantastic. I can't describe it." This bodily experience was followed, with considerable turmoil, by associations to "vague memories": "My mother lost a baby," "She went away," "The house was dark and empty." The therapist had learned about this tragedy from the parents during the intake interview months earlier. When Ellen was 24 months old, mother gave birth, but the infant tragically died a few days later. Mother slipped into a deep depres-sion that lasted for over a year. The bodily experience of lying belly-down on the mount seemed to enable Sally to experience an embodied meaning (lying on a preg-nant belly). From this embodied experience she gradually translated meanings rep-resenting her experiences during mother's depression. Eventually she could see how her daily complaints about "insensitive, ungiving teachers" were extensions of these meanings and the traumatic, unrepaired disruption she had suffered.

As for materials to be used in therapy, authors typically propose that a play-room should be equipped with care and provide detailed lists of various items that have proven productive in therapy: clay, sand, dolls, puppets, graphics, sculpting materials, toys, games, costumes (e.g., Brems 1993, Schaefer and Cangelosi 1993, Spiegel 1989). The attention given to such material could suggest that these items are the "holy grail" to successful treatment. While a therapist should become familiar with materials found to be therapeutically productive, I agree with Coppolillo's (1987) view that conventional toys should be kept to a minimum so that materials serve more as vehicles for symbolic expression rather than "dazzling or seducing" the child (p. 25). I would also add that if the playroom contains too many items that the therapist construes as having potential symbolic meaning, the therapist may engage the child with these materials, expecting to elicit the traditionally expected, symbolic behaviors, and not be alert to material the child may use to construct her/his unique meanings.

As the clinical vignettes discussed above illustrate, I recommend that in addition to a basic set of traditional toys (dolls of different races, ambulance, police car, conventional car, telephone, paper, crayons), the playroom should also contain a box of "junk" (a rope, an assortment of buttons, wooden geometric cutouts, cubes and beads of different sizes and colors, pillows, a blanket or bedsheet). Materials such as geometric cutouts have no inherent or conventional meaning and therefore enable a child to use them as vehicles to invent a wide variety of meanings (a wooden cutout could become a hamburger, a bomb, a magic circle that fends off evil aliens, an ID card). In addition, I recommend that child and therapist accumulate items that belong to their unique "intersubjective culture." For this reason I give each child and adolescent a plastic container (approximately 2 feet by 2 feet by 18 inches) in which he/she keeps materials from session to session. One child, who never used dolls or puppets, accumulated the following items in his container: a golf ball, a piece of rope about 3 feet long, a dart gun, wooden lettered blocks, a book about butterflies, a plastic spaceship, a rubber toy eagle. From session to session he used some items while ignoring others, returning to them after not using them for weeks. Gradually each item became a particular symbol that child and therapist shared in their negotiations.

Frequency, Duration, Involvement, and Conduct of Directed versus Nondirected Treatment

To this point I have recommended that a therapist step into a dialectical circle with a child to negotiate geographies in which treatment occurs, materials child and therapist use, and requests by the child for personal information, food, gifts, and visitors. I have recommended that, as much as possible, the therapist accommodate to a child's direction. In doing so, a therapist discovers himself/herself within a child's subjective experiences and contributes to the integration of their respective subjective cultures. Other issues over which therapists have disagreed deserve comment: duration of sessions and treatment, the therapist's degree of involvement, and whether or not treatment should be directed or structured (Mahoney 1993).

Frequency and Duration

A therapist's view of a child's needs and goals to be achieved influences the length of sessions and the duration of treatment. Mainstream psychodynamic therapy is usually conducted with traditional fifty-minute sessions, one or two sessions per week, for one or two years; child psychoanalysis is conducted three or four sessions per week for three years and sometimes longer. Mainstream cognitive-behavioral therapy is conducted with weekly fifty-minute sessions; the duration may be as brief as ten sessions or as long as one year.

Guided by our developmental-dialectical model, my colleagues and I have been influenced by the degree of a child's cognitive and behavioral rigidity when considering duration and frequency of sessions. We have observed that if a child comes with a severely rigid cognitive orientation and modes of expression, she/he sustains interacting with a therapist for short periods of time; the longer the session, the more the child tries to avoid stepping into the dialectical circle. Severely rigid cognitive orientations and modes of expression are likely to bump into a therapist's interventions that require flexibility and the process of second-order change. If this child is available on a daily basis (if she/he is participating in a residential or day-treatment program, or treatment is being conducted at school during the school day), and if a therapist is on site, we have found fifteen- to twenty-minute sessions conducted four to five times a week most effective. In one study (Santostefano 1978, Santostefano and Stayton 1967), two daily, fifteen-minute sessions were conducted with retarded children by their mothers, who were trained to use structured therapeutic interactions following guidelines discussed below. If a child who presents a rigid cognitive orientation and modes of expression is available less frequently, sessions should be as brief yet as frequent as practical circumstances permit.

When children are equipped with flexibility in cognitive orientation and modes of expression, readily stepping into the dialectical circle and easily joining the therapist in integrating their subjective cultures, they sometimes generate a vigorous treatment process, so much so that fifty-minute sessions for ten to twenty weeks is sufficient to revise pathological metaphors. Others may require two sessions per week for up to two years. All of this is from the therapist's point of view; what about the child's?

Here I will limit myself to a few comments about those children who introduce treatment plans that differ from those of the therapist. According to one study cited by Brems (1993), older children and adolescents are more likely to end treatment prematurely. In my experience and that of colleagues, this appears to be the case. But on occasion a younger child may also make a strong bid to stop treatment. Similarly, a child of any age may request that the frequency be changed from, for example, once a week to every other week or to once a month. If a child has successfully stepped into a dialectical circle, contributing to the construction of shared symbols, and if a therapist has negotiated to her/his best ability the child's request to stop treatment or change frequency, I recommend that the request be granted. When treatment is terminated before the therapist believes it should be, a follow-up session should be negotiated and scheduled in two, four, or six months to explore the meaning the child's request holds within the unique intersubjective world child and therapist have constructed.

Sometimes, after treatment has been conducted for the proposed length of time, a child may indicate he/she prefers to continue. Here too a therapist explores this request within their intersubjective culture and makes a decision accordingly. A child might be correct in recognizing that issues not adequately negotiated need additional attention. And sometimes a child wants to hold onto the idealized therapist, reflecting some absence in the child's environment, an issue a therapist would need to negotiate with caregivers and school personnel. Duration of treatment, of course, raises the issue of how to terminate a therapeutic relationship constructively. Excellent discussions from different theoretical viewpoints are available of the process of termination and of various forces that interfere with the proposed frequency and duration of treatment (Brems 1993, Coppolillo 1987, Spiegel 1989). What our developmental-dialectical model adds to these discussions is developed through clinical cases presented in subsequent chapters.

Involvement by the Therapist

Picasso has been quoted as saying, "One must get one's hands dirty to achieve anything" (Colby and Stoller 1988). Some child therapists, especially those using a psychodynamic approach, remain physically distant from a child, sit in a chair much like Whistler's mother, and interact primarily through verbal discourse while occasionally manipulating toys and dolls. Cognitive-behavioral therapists are more likely to become physically involved in their interactions, especially if live modeling is used (Brems 1993). As the reader may have surmised from the preceding discussion of catalysts for change, our developmental-dialectical model requires that a therapist step into a dialectical circle and "live" in it as fully as possible while trying to discover and define herself/himself within the intersubjective culture being constructed with the child. A therapist should become as "involved," physically and emotionally, as he/she is capable of and as required by a child's self-expressions, preferred levels of stimulation, and emotional tone. For one, child involvement may include crawling on the floor; for another, sitting in a chair; for another, considerable physical bodily contact such as wrestling, boxing, chasing, and being chased; for another, more subtle touching such as exchanging "high fives" or an occasional brief leaning by the child on the body of the therapist. While touch and various forms of physical contact are the foundation of experience (Barnard and Brazelton 1990), and given the suggestion that a therapist be as physically involved as required by a child, a therapist is also obligated to carefully monitor whether her/his involvement is being excessively eroticized by the child (Brems 1993) and/or is stirring up aggressive tensions the child is not yet equipped to regulate. The involvement recommended by our model, then, requires considerable practice and presents a therapist with a formidable task: enacting a wide range of physical actions, tempos, and emotional tones while remaining ever alert to whether the level of involvement is too little or too much in terms of the particular intersubjective culture child and therapist have constructed and the unique way a child is negotiating some issue.

Directed and Nondirected Treatment

The issue of directed versus nondirected treatment has sharply divided cognitive-behavioral and psychodynamic approaches. As discussed in previous chapters, the use of tasks and directed therapy is a hallmark of the former and frowned upon by the latter. Tasks the child is asked to engage in are intended to activate and promote the growth of overt behaviors and cognitions that are causes of a child's difficulties. The psychodynamic position holds that structured activity enables a child to avoid learning the unconscious meanings of her/his behavior because a child is not free to experience her/his feelings, thoughts, and behaviors and then project them onto the therapist, all of which a therapist uses to infer and interpret unconscious meanings (Coppolillo 1987).

Our developmental-dialectical model does not view directed and nondirected treatment as opposite approaches but as poles defining a continuum. If a child habitually uses an inflexible cognitive orientation and behavioral mode of functioning and is required to step into a dialectical circle, he/she repeats the same rigid behaviors he/she uses in daily living to avoid giving meaning to experiences or to avoid accommodating to and assimilating opportunities and limitations of available environments. This child lacks cognitive and behavioral tools necessary to join a therapist in cycles of dialectical interactions and enactments, negotiating issues in the service of coauthoring symbols, constructing an intersubjective culture, and revising pathological life metaphors. In short, this child is not equipped to experience and transfer behaviors onto the therapist and discover unconscious meanings. The same line of reasoning applies when, during treatment, a child temporarily assumes a severely rigid cognitive orientation and/or mode of expression to avoid meanings (whether from the environment or from her/his personal world) that would be revealed if the opposite orientation were assumed.

Whether a child's functioning is habitually or temporarily rigid, the child requires structured interactions that form a handrail, so to speak, that a child could hold while stepping into a dialectical circle and engaging in negotiating self-expressions and enactments that resolve the rigidity interfering with the dialectical process. On the other hand, when a child readily steps into a dialectical circle, participating in cycles of interactions and enactments, he/she benefits from the freedom to project motives, feelings, and issues into the relationship. Therefore, our developmental model prescribes a process that shifts back and forth from structured to unstructured interactions, providing whatever degree of direction and freedom is required to enable child and therapist "to live" within their dialectical circle and engage in enactments that promote change in behavioral modes, cognitive orientations, and meanings. This process is outlined below after we consider issues unique to the first treatment sessions.

THE FIRST TREATMENT SESSIONS: NEGOTIATING AN UNDERSTANDING OF WHY CHILD AND THERAPIST ARE MEETING

The first treatment sessions, while providing opportunities to observe a child's life metaphors, cognitive orientation, and modes of expression, should focus on constructing an understanding of why child and therapist are meeting. This understanding, in my opinion, should be conveyed as much as possible with symbolic actions and minimal verbal explanation. But this view disagrees with proposals from both psychodynamic and cognitive-behavioral approaches, which emphasize verbal explanations. For example, in Chapter 1 we noted that Coppolillo (1987) proposed that in the first session a therapist should help a child understand why he/she is participating in therapy with a comment such as, "You already told me that sometimes you have sad thoughts and scary feelings. During our meetings we will try to find out the reason why these thoughts and feelings keep coming back . . ." (p. 123). Similarly, Meichenbaum (1977) proposed that a therapist begin by saying, for example, "As I understand it, you came here because you are having trouble [Here the therapist notes the referral problem, e.g., doing schoolwork; teachers and parents think you move around too much]. I would like you to tell me more about this" (p. 250). Brems (1993) recommended that at the start of treatment a therapist inform a child of the hour and day the appointment will take place, the length of sessions, the interval between them, and that the toys in the room will always be available from session to session. "Yes, everything stays, including me. I will be here every week for you, always at the same time, always for fifty minutes . . . every Tuesday at four o'clock" (p. 228).

I believe verbal instructions such as these could limit a child from conveying in his/her language what seeing the therapist means. Instead, I propose the therapist make every effort to convey *in nonverbal terms* that she/he and the child are together to find solutions to dilemmas expressed in the here and now. *Ideally, the therapist responds to some symbolic behavior the child expresses that conveys a dilemma he/she is experiencing at the moment, whether or not the dilemma relates to the child's presenting problem.* In this approach the therapist engages the child within the child's mode and world (first-order change), whereas the verbal instructions suggested by others come from outside the child and require second-order change.

To illustrate, I return to 5-year-old Jane, mentioned in Chapter 1, who, upon being invited to the playroom, anxiously clutched mother. During the intake interview the therapist had learned that while Jane could leave mother (a single parent) to attend school, she insisted on sleeping with mother and would protest if mother left her with a sitter. It seemed clear that when greeted in the waiting room, gripped by separation anxiety, this child could not benefit from hearing, "During our meeting we will figure out why you get so afraid," or "I understand that you can't sleep in your own bed. How do you see the problem?" or "We will meet every week on Tuesday at 4 P.M. for fifty minutes."

Responding to the maladaptive metaphor the child was experiencing in vivo (separation-individuation-autonomy), the therapist left the waiting room and returned with a long rope. Giving mother a reassuring glance, the therapist tied one end of the rope around mother's waist in a playful manner, saying, "Now Mom can't get away," and handed the other end of the rope to Jane. Rope firmly in hand, Jane entered the playroom with mother in tow, cautiously exploring various items with one hand while clutching the rope with the other. Midway through the session the therapist set two chairs near the doorway to the playroom and invited mother to have a seat. Through most of the session Jane did not engage material or the therapist, but examined items, showing each to mother and sometimes sitting in the chair next to her.

In the next session, rope in hand, the therapist greeted Jane and mother. Jane immediately took the rope, playfully tied it around mother's waist, and with mother in tow entered the playroom without hesitation. Again the therapist located two chairs near the doorway, and mother sat in one. Now Jane became more involved with dolls and a playhouse, less often showing mother items. Midway through the session the therapist asked mother to sit on the other side of the threshold with the door open. Jane did not object, although she clutched the rope more tightly. In the next two sessions mother's chair was located outside the playroom and to one side of the doorway so that only a part of her body could be seen, and then so that mother was out of sight. During these sessions the therapist occasionally tugged at the rope playfully, exclaiming, "Are you still there, Mother?" Jane imitated the therapist, laughing as she tugged the rope. Gradually, Jane engaged the therapist in cycles of dialectical interaction, frequently leaving her end of the rope on the floor. Eventually she was able to enter the playroom with mother remaining in the waiting room.

This vignette illustrates how the therapist set out to "clarify" why she and the child were meeting by enacting a solution to a dilemma that the child was experiencing in the here and now as a present-day force. The enactment (rope) simultaneously addressed Jane's overt behavior (clutching mother) and its meaning (remaining attached to her as one). A minimum of words were used by the therapist, which were embedded in the metaphor the child was experiencing. Applying this view to Coppolillo's case, did his child display "scary feelings" in any way in the office that could have been engaged in an enactment? And in Michenbaum's case, did the child "move around too much" in the office, behavior that could have been engaged in some way that conveyed solutions are possible?

To illustrate this approach with an older child, I return to the adolescent girl who eventually lay belly-down on the mount. As mentioned earlier, when first approached, she refused to enter the office but offered to go outside. Ellen shuffled into the therapeutic garden, sat in an area overhung by a canopy of yews, and lit a cigarette. While smoking, she mentioned several items in a low, slow voice: she liked the outdoors, completed a survival course last year in the West, and complained about two of her teachers. The therapist made a few comments throughout this monologue; he noted that he had once been in the state where she had taken a survival course. At one point she interrupted herself, stared at the ground, pointed to ants crawling about, and mumbled, "They're looking for food." The therapist jokingly commented, "Hey, we can do something about that," excused himself, and returned with two crackers. Handing one to Ellen, and crumpling the other, he carefully located crumbs in the area where the ants were crawling. Ellen did the same while continuing her commentary. Here I bring attention to the moment the therapist seized upon to enact a solution to the dilemma that Ellen was "experiencing" in the here and now and that bore no direct connection to her presenting difficulty (getting schoolwork done): the ants were hungry and searching for food.

THE PROCESS OF PSYCHOTHERAPY WITH CHILDREN AND ADOLESCENTS FROM A DEVELOPMENTAL-DIALECTICAL PERSPECTIVE

The topics discussed thus far frame the treatment process defined by our developmental-dialectical model to address the goal stated at the start and the issues articulated in Chapter 4: surface behaviors (conscious, cognitive products and emotions) and deep behaviors (unconscious structures that organize and give meaning to experiences); and the relations among what a person does, imagines, and says. The model assumes that all children who require treatment come with maladaptive life metaphors, representing unrepaired, traumatic disruptions, and that many also bring varying degrees of rigidity in cognitive orientation and/or modes of expression they habitually use when coping with relationships and situations. When helping these children in psychotherapy, the process shifts back and forth from a nondirected to a more directed format, depending upon the degree of cognitive and behavioral rigidity that characterizes a child's functioning at the start of treatment, and whether during some phase of treatment a child's functioning becomes noticeably more rigid than is typical for her/him.

If a child enters treatment with cognitive and behavioral rigidity and is invited to participate within a nondirected relationship, she/he does not readily step into a dialectical circle with a therapist, as noted earlier, but repeats the same rigid modes of behaving that have served to avoid giving meanings to experiences or responding to the expectations of situations and relationships. This child endlessly plays formboard games, engages in numerous discussions, or manipulates the same dolls and toys in stereotyped fantasy play. Therefore, initially a therapist enters the doorways to cognition and modes of expressions, emphasizing structured interactions designed to cultivate the capacity to symbolize and express meanings flexibly. As a child's rigidity is modified, the therapist gradually provides less direction, responds to the child's symbolic expressions, and focuses on revising pathological life metaphors. (See Chapter 6, Figure 6–9.)

If a child enters treatment with stage-adequate flexibility in symbolizing and expressing meanings, a therapist initially enters the doorway to metaphors and participates in cycles of enactments designed to revise the child's maladaptive life metaphors. However, sometimes during phases of treatment a child may assume rigid modes of functioning to resist experiencing a particular metaphor or available stimulation. For example, after flexibly participating in interactions that addressed a maladaptive metaphor, one child may shift to playing formboard games for many sessions, another to endless discussions about school events, and another to playing solitaire or drawing numerous pictures while essentially ignoring the therapist. At these times the therapist introduces structured interactions to dissolve the rigidity and resistance.

In general, then, using a musical metaphor, the process proposed here requires that a therapist orchestrate and conduct the performance of three instruments, sometimes emphasizing structured interactions that promote flexibility in cognitive orientation, sometimes emphasizing structured interactions that promote flexibility in modes of expression, and sometimes emphasizing unstructured interactions that promote the revision of maladaptive life metaphors. The critical point is that throughout treatment the three instruments are always performing together. The therapist is required to exercise creativity in deciding when and how one of the instruments should be emphasized and how they should be combined. Whether treatment structures interactions or is nondirected, the process contains the same catalysts for change activated by a series of interrelated interpersonal developments between child and therapist. As the reader considers these developments, he/she should keep in mind that they are parts of a unified process.

Projective Identification: A Basic Interpersonal-Dialectical Process

How does a therapist increase the flexibility of cognition and modes of expression and facilitate the revision of life metaphors? Whether participating in unstructured or structured interactions, a therapist relies upon an interpersonal-dialectical process conceptualized as "projective identification" (Ogden 1979). In this process a child eventually projects (transfers) onto the therapist a cognitive orientation, mode of expression, embodied schema, life metaphor, or some combination thereof; manipulates the therapist to experience the dilemma the configuration creates; and observes how the therapist solves it. Over many such interactions, a child gradually idealizes, identifies with, and assimilates the ways in which the therapist copes with the dilemma. As a result, the therapist's behaviors and emotions eventually become a part of the child's functioning. This process illuminates Gill's (1984) position that the therapist should endure a patient's behaviors and emotions, and Mitchell's (1988) that the therapist discover himself/herself within the patient's

Table 7–1. Components of Process during Unstructured and Structured Interactions

I	Circular Dialectical Interactions: Ritualizing Experiences	Translate embodied schemas of body-image disruptions into symbolic forms. Child idealizes therapist's efforts to find solutions and internalizes therapist as evoked companion; displays deferred imitation.
II	Interactive Metaphor: The Need for Help	Child symbolically enacts the need for help. Therapist enacts she/he is able to provide assistance required.
III	Interactive Metaphor: Disrupted, Unrepaired Life Metaphor	Child organizes interactions representing unrepaired life metaphors, projects symbolic characters of the metaphor onto the therapist, manipulates therapist to cope with its demands. Child idealizes/internalizes therapist's solutions.
IV	Interactive Metaphor: New Editions of Disrupted Life Metaphors	Child introduces new editions of the disrupted life metaphor that elaborate the initial one; projects characters onto therapist, who struggles for solutions that the child idealizes/internalizes.
V	Interactive Metaphor: Core Pathological Life Metaphor	Child introduces interactions representing a developmentally basic, unrepaired disruption, with its heightened traumatic emotions, that is at the core of the child's difficulties. Child idealizes/internalizes therapist's solutions.
VI	Here-and-Now Interactions and Concerns	Child focuses interactions on here-and-now interests and concerns and displays more stage-appropriate functioning in his/her environments.

subjective world. This process also illuminates the view that, paralleling child and caregiver interactions, child and therapist promote change as they engage in repeated cycles of dialectical interactions, experience and repair disruptions in their ongoing regulations, and share heightened emotional moments.

But as Mitchell (1994) reminded us, during the process of projective identification, a therapist is not "a smooth, clean container" into which a child places her/his projections. Rather, converging with our earlier discussions, child and therapist each bring uniqueness (e.g., a preferred level of stimulation and style of expression) that influences what and how a child projects onto the therapist and how the therapist enacts solutions. When child and therapist engage in the process of projective identification, then, they define and organize different aspects of each other and of the subjective world they intend to share. As conceptualized here, projective identification is a basic interpersonal process consisting of several components, as outlined in Table 7–1.

Circular Dialectical Interactions that Ritualize Experiences, Integrate Subjective Cultures, and Translate Embodied Schemas into Symbols

Piaget pointed out that symbols and meanings do not already exist in a dark cave and become known when we shine a light on them. Rather, symbols are gradually constructed as infant and caregiver—and I include child and therapist—participate in many "circular dialectical interactions" organized as rituals (I, Table 7–1). The first symbols constructed with rituals are translations of embodied experiences. For an example of this process in normal development, the reader is reminded of the toddler and father, discussed in Chapter 6, who ritualized engaging in circular dialectical interactions involving the child's body and the father's body and shirt. The significance of circular dialectical interactions for child psychotherapy rests on the view that for every mental knot there is a corresponding embodied knot. Embodied schemas that children bring to therapy, which have been tied into a knot and require translation, typically relate to disruptions in body-image experiences that were not repaired, such as body imbalance, excessive body constriction or assertion, and body-image deformation.

As child and therapist become less foreign to each other, a child eventually repeats some constellation of actions/gestures/emotions related to an embodied schema representing a disruption. When the therapist imitates the child's behavior and/or responds by acting in a relevant way, a circular interaction is launched. The therapist now has an opportunity to join the child in experiencing and expressing the embodied schema and grappling with its dilemma. As these circular interactions are repeated, the embodied schema becomes symbolized cognitively. And, as with infant and caregiver, if the child values (idealizes) the therapist, the child begins to construct mental representations of the therapist as a "companion" (see Chapter 5) and imitates his/her behaviors, the beginnings of internalization. The need to translate embodied schemas into symbolic form is usually greatest during early phases of treatment, especially as child and therapist negotiate becoming less foreign to each other. However, at later phases, as the child begins to articulate metaphors, the child may again introduce a constellation that expresses an embodied schema linked to the metaphor under construction.

Interactive Metaphors

As child and therapist construct and ritualize a world of shared symbols, the child begins to organize interactions around a metaphor. I refer to these ritualized activities as "interactive metaphors." With each metaphor the child now projects an organized, symbolic "character" or "voice" onto the therapist and manipulates the therapist to experience and respond to its call for action. As the therapist takes on attributes of this character and struggles to solve its call for action, the child observes, idealizes, and internalizes the therapist's struggle and solution.

Typically, several metaphors emerge during this process. The first interactive metaphor a child organizes frequently expresses the need for help. Here a child is establishing whether the therapist is attuned and up to dealing with expressions of maladaptation that will follow (II, Table 7–1). If a therapist enacts successfully within this metaphor, demonstrating that he/she is unconditionally available and is capable of providing the assistance required, a child follows this experience with an interactive metaphor that expresses the first edition of a pathological life metaphor representing an unrepaired developmental disruption that contributes to the child's difficulties and suffering (III, Table 7–1). Again, a "character" or "voice" is projected onto the therapist, who is manipulated to struggle with the dilemma depicted. Here the character projected is typically symbolized as some "evil force" that does not exist within the child but in the therapist and her/his environment. Again the therapist is manipulated to assume this character and again the child observes, idealizes, and internalizes the therapist's struggle and solution. The first interactive metaphor may be followed by any number of others, each of which is either a "new edition" of the first, elaborating the previous metaphor in some way, or a representation of another pathological life metaphor that in some way is connected to the first (IV, Table 7–1).

In some cases, after enacting and revising the calls for action of several editions of a life metaphor, a child eventually organizes an interactive metaphor that expresses a "core, pathological life metaphor" representing a fundamental, unrepaired disruption that has been at the base of most of the child's difficulties (V, Table 7–1). In these cases, equipped with interactive tools provided by previous negotiations, the child's functioning "regresses" significantly to a core issue, making available the roots of her/his difficulty for therapeutic work. Ideally, the treatment process should provide a patient with opportunities to experience basic interferences in development that contribute to present problems (Gill 1984). In our case we are especially interested in a child's enacting a disrupted, basic life metaphor and the expectation that the disruption will not be repaired. Frequently, when a core, pathological life metaphor is negotiated, the therapist is not assigned the role of an evil force that the child battles. Rather, the evil force is projected "out there" as a common enemy. Child and therapist become allies battling this force, displaying strength and confidence against its dictates, and demonstrating that standards oppose it. Here too a child indicates that the therapist's strength and respect for rules are idealized and internalized.

Once a core, pathological metaphor is successfully negotiated, the child (especially older children and adolescents) sometimes shifts the content of interactions from constructing symbols and metaphors to discussions of interests and concerns in the here and now (e.g., peers, sports, school). These discussions frequently rely on the foundation of shared symbols and understanding that child and therapist have constructed. At this time the child typically displays more stage-appropriate functioning in her/his environment (VI, Table 7–1).

Several technical issues related to this process should be emphasized:

1. The therapist and various materials are available for the child to engage within a treatment room and other areas when indicated (especially the outdoors). Therefore, materials should not be present, including clothing worn by the therapist that the therapist does not want manipulated.

2. The therapist should be aware of his/her emotional/relational world in order to enter the child's and participate easily in circular dialectical interactions and enactments, whether the therapist experiences these interactions as uncomfortable, stressful, exciting, or boring. Being at ease with one's world assumes that a therapist is aware of meanings expressed by his/her body images and how these embodied meanings influence his/her thoughts, feelings, and actions. Awareness of one's body images requires time and effort to develop and is a skill that needs to be learned and practiced (Pruzinsky 1990).

3. The therapist makes a special effort to remain alert for ritualized gestures/actions/emotions expressed by the child that reveal some unique embodied meaning; for example, expressions of body disequilibrium (a child repeatedly staggers as if dizzy, or drops material to the floor); excessive or inadequate stimulation (a child repeatedly complains that the temperature is too hot or cold, always wears a jacket or coat during the sessions, or runs about outside without a jacket in spite of cold weather); interference with body assertiveness (a child insists on standing on a table to be taller than the therapist, or insists on using the therapist's pen or chair).

4. When embodied schemas are translated into symbolic forms, and when interactions and enactments are organized to express a metaphor, the symbols and metaphors themselves contribute to repairing disruptions and heightened traumatic emotional moments since symbols bring order and organization to what has been chaotic and rigid (Beebe and Lachmann 1994, Overton 1997b, Overton and Horowitz 1991).

5. With each interactive metaphor, a therapist enacts characters and solutions as much as possible, following a developmental progression from emphasizing actions to fantasies to language. Interpreting and discussing meanings the child experiences, and connecting them to relationships in the child's past and present, are reserved until the last phase of treatment and introduced only if the child's developmental stage indicates he/she would benefit from direct discussions of his/her feelings and motives. In many cases, conceptualizing a child's behavior with interpretations and explanations is not necessary since the child carries modes of functioning he/she has achieved in treatment to interactions with others at home and school and continues a course of adaptive growth in daily living. The actions a child has taken in treatment, and the interactive

metaphors the child has assimilated, constitute the child's "insight" (Wachtel 1987).

Comparing the treatment process outlined here with other conceptualizations should help clarify similarities and differences. For example, some authors (Brems 1993, Coppolillo 1987) conceptualize a process in which the child recalls events, reconstructs and reexperiences them with the therapist, and then develops solutions. Explanations and interpretations by the therapist play an important role as interventions. Rather than viewing process as a sequence from recalling to reexperiencing events to solving problems, the conceptualization proposed here emphasizes that with every circular interaction and enactment child and therapist, from the start of treatment to its completion, are integrating past and present in symbolic forms.

Guidelines for Structuring Interactions

The methods outlined here to structure interactions are intended to help a child step into a dialectical circle so she/he can participate in circular dialectical interactions and enactments. It is important to note that these methods attempt to reorganize *how* a child's cognition and modes construct and express meanings and focus less on promoting particular meanings as such. The significance of the behaviors required by the tasks a therapist introduces, then, is in the meanings of the behaviors, not their contingencies (Shirk 1988).

Guided by the concept of the interdependence of opposites (see above), the tasks I recommend for structuring interactions begin by accommodating to the child's rigid cognitive orientation or preferred behavioral mode, promoting first-order change, and then gradually requiring the child to employ the opposite orientation or mode. At this point, tasks "bump into" a child's habitual, cognitive, or behavioral mode of functioning and attempt to promote second-order change. As the child's cognitive orientation and modes of expression become more flexible, a therapist gradually relinquishes giving direction and allows the child to guide their interactions. Now equipped with tools to symbolize and to stand within a dialectical circle, the child invents interactive metaphors, expressing and repairing disrupted life metaphors. As future clinical cases illustrate, some children require the use of tasks during most of treatment, others only for intermittent phases.

Methods to Structure Enactments and Interactive Metaphors

To make as clear as possible the contents of graded tasks that emerge from the developmental-dialectical model, I begin by addressing how these tasks are similar to, yet different from, those used in mainstream cognitive-behavioral therapy and how they meet the objections of psychodynamic therapy.

Of the tasks typically used in cognitive-behavioral therapy, two broad types appear, at first glance, to be similar to those outlined below. With one, self-instructions are designed to change cognitive products (see Chapters 3 and 4); that is, self-statements intended to focus the child on a task, or modify his/her conscious view of a situation (cognitive mediators), or to match what one says with what one does (correspondence training). In contrast, methods described here are designed to change cognitive structures; that is, unconscious processes that organize and symbolize stimulation. The structure either rigidly centers on the demands of meanings/emotions, avoiding the demands of contexts, or rigidly centers on the demands of contexts and avoids the demands of life metaphors.

With the second type, which might appear to resemble methods proposed here, some cognitive-behavioral tasks decrease or increase behaviors by reinforcing "appropriate" behaviors and ignoring "inappropriate" behaviors. With this technique, called "shaping," the desired behavior is divided into successive steps, and the child is reinforced each time a step is accomplished. For example, if a child frequently wanders about the treatment room, a therapist could give a reward each time the child remains within 10 feet of a table, then 5 feet, then remains seated for five minutes, then engages in self-instruction training (Brems 1993). In contrast, tasks proposed here to cultivate flexibility in a child's action, fantasy, and language behaviors do not include extrinsic reinforcements delivered by the therapist in response to some behavior performed by the child. Rather, the behavior in question gradually undergoes change as the child experiences "intrinsic" rewards, stemming from his/her idealizing and internalizing the behaviors of the therapist (Santostefano 1978).

One more issue distinguishes the proposed method. Typically, tasks in cognitive-behavioral therapy are designed by the therapist and administered to all children in pretty much the same way. In contrast, *tasks outlined here are coauthored, as much as possible, by child and therapist and framed within a meaning unique to the child's developmental needs.*

At this point I turn to psychodynamic therapy's opposition to the use of tasks. This position holds that the more the therapist structures interactions, the less the child is able to project characters and voices onto the therapist and engage in bringing unconscious meanings and motives to conscious awareness (e.g., Gill 1984, Messer and Winokur 1984, Spiegel 1989). From the vantage point of our model, I hold to the opposite position *for some children.* If a child's cognition is rigidly inner- or outer-oriented, and/or if a child makes inflexible use of one modality of expression that is segregated from others, the child is limited in being able to step into a dialectical circle. One child plays numerous games of checkers, another plays with a dollhouse, each child doing and saying little that hints they are projecting unconscious meanings and characters onto the therapist. Rather than enabling these children to avoid unconscious meanings, the methods proposed here help these children enter a dialectical relationship to construct and express meanings/emotions.

Table 7–2.   Guidelines for Graded Tasks to Treat Rigid Cognitive Orientations and Modes of Expression

General Guidelines for Graded Tasks

A. Simple to complex
B. Physical actions to mental actions
C. Little delay to much delay
D. No meaning (symbolic) experienced to elaborate meanings
E. No emotions aroused to emotions aroused

Treating Cognitive Orientations

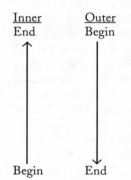

Inner	Outer
End	Begin
Begin	End

A. Engage stimulation as it is with one or more cognitive regulators (body tempo, focal attention, field articulation, leveling-sharpening, equivalence range)
B. Engage stimulation as one imagines it to be
   1. Assign usual (conventional) meanings
   2. Assign personal meanings
   3. Express meanings in a progression of nested behaviors (vehicles) (see below)
   4. Shift flexibly among meanings and behaviors (vehicles) expressing them
   5. Shift flexibly among roles (identities) enacted while pretending.

Treating Behavioral Modalities

Inflexible Mode	Begin ⟶ End
Action	Macroaction—Microaction and Fantasy—Fantasy—Language
Fantasy	Macrofantasy—Microfantasy and Action—Macroaction—Language
Language	Macrolanguage—Fantasy—Fantasy and Microaction—Macroaction

Table 7–2 diagrams guidelines for devising tasks that promote a child's capacity to construct symbols and express them flexibly using various behaviors as vehicles. Tasks that emphasize cognitive activity help a child distinguish between and coordinate stimulation from representations and from opportunities provided by material and the relationship. Tasks that emphasize modes of expression help a child cultivate alternative means and the capacity to delay. While the content of tasks may vary from child to child, the form and process of each task follow the same general considerations. As much as possible, tasks should vary along four dimensions: from simple to complex in makeup, from requiring physical actions to requiring mental actions, from requiring little delay to considerable delay, and from ignoring meanings to evaluating meanings. Within these dimensions, tasks

are constructed by integrating two sets of guidelines. One addresses a child's pathological cognitive orientation, the other a child's inflexible modes of expressing meanings. How these guidelines are combined depends upon the unique needs of a child.

Guidelines for Treating a Rigid Outer Cognitive Orientation

If a child's cognitive orientation is rigidly outer-oriented, tasks initially accommodate to this orientation and promote first-order change by requiring a child to engage stimulation as it is; for example, copy or produce stimulation. With each task the child engages the process of one or more of the cognitive regulators discussed in Chapter 6: body image-tempo regulation, focal attention, field articulation, leveling-sharpening, and equivalence range. Since these cognitive functions are viewed as hierarchically related, the notion of first- and second-order change guides which function is emphasized first by a task. For example, if a child shows rigidity in leveling-sharpening, tasks initially emphasize field articulation, the hierarchically lower cognitive function promoting first-order change. Tasks are then introduced emphasizing the leveling-sharpening process, promoting second-order change. Or if a child shows rigidity in scanning, tasks initially emphasize the process of tempo regulation (the function hierarchically lower) and then include focal attention.

Tasks gradually change in makeup, requiring the child to shift from copying to transforming stimulation, engaging it as he/she imagines it to be. At this point tasks encourage a child to experience and express emotions associated with symbols being constructed. Recall the study in which subjects were asked to examine with their hands geometric shapes placed in a container of crankcase oil and flour (representing fecal material) and to match the shapes with standards. In one sense this study characterizes the goal of structured tasks with outer-oriented children. Eventually they should freely construct symbols while balancing intense, associated emotions. During this process, the first meanings a child assigns to stimulation are typically conventional ones. The child is encouraged to invent more personal meanings and to express associated emotions. As child and therapist construct and elaborate a network of conventional and personal meanings/emotions, they enact these meanings while assuming roles of various pretend characters and voices. These enactments make use of action, fantasy, and language expressions in a sequence that is guided by the mode that the child uses in inflexible ways (see below).

Guidelines for Treating a Rigid Inner Cognitive Orientation

If a child's cognitive orientation is rigidly inner-oriented, the opposite course is followed. The child is already freely transforming information in highly personal terms. Accommodating to this orientation, the therapist initially attempts to promote first-order change, entering some aspect of the child's personal world and shifting flexibly among roles defined by the child's fantasy. These roles are enacted using various action, fantasy, and language symbols, again depending upon the mode of expression the child prefers (see below). More conventional meanings are then constructed and expressed within the child's fantasy, using a variety of vehicles. As conventional meanings are introduced, interactions gradually require stimulation to be experienced as it is, emphasizing the process of copying and producing stimulation.

Facilitating Flexibility in Cognitive Orientations

Whether treatment has focused on a child's outer or inner orientation, tasks are introduced, when indicated, that engage a child in shifting flexibly between experiencing information as it is and as it is imagined to be. Various techniques are described in upcoming chapters discussing clinical cases; here I sketch one. The therapist places two chairs side by side; a sign reading "Make Believe" is attached to the back of one, and "Real" to the back of the other. The chairs are introduced in the format of a "game." When sitting in the "make believe" chair, the child responds to stimuli presented by the therapist by "making believe" or inventing some way to use it or by making up a story about it. When sitting in the "real" chair, the child responds by "doing something real" with the stimuli. As the game unfolds, the child is challenged to shift back and forth, without warning, from one chair to the other whenever the therapist taps the chair. Therefore, the child experiences shifting back and forth from an inner to an outer orientation and from one mode of expression to another. Stimuli the child engages as real and when pretending evoke meanings the child already revealed as salient during previous tasks.

Guidelines for Treating Rigid Behavioral Modalities

The second set of guidelines addresses whether a child makes inflexible use of the action, fantasy, language mode to express meanings (Table 7–2). In defining these guidelines, I make use of several terms in case illustrations. *Macroaction* indicates that the child moves his/her body elaborately through total space provided by the area in which the activity is taking place. The actions may be accompanied by fantasy and language expressions, but these modes are subordinate to body actions. *Microaction* indicates that the child's body is more or less stationary, and the child is engaged in miniature actions manipulating materials within a few square feet of space. Microactions accompany and are dominated by fantasies. *Macrofantasy* designates an elaborate fantasy accompanied by little or no physical activity (see Knapp's [1988] distinction between "phantasy" as images that are enacted and "fantasy" as images that are not enacted). Although the fantasy is communicated with words and gestures, these modes are subordinate to and operate in the service of the fantasy. *Macrolanguage* indicates that words dominate in expressing meanings about persons and events in the past or present. The conversation may be accompanied by images and actions, but these behaviors are subordinate to, and in the service of, communicating meanings through spoken words.

In general, a therapist emphasizes a progression of behavioral expressions during treatment that follows the principle of promoting first-order change and then second-order change. We discussed in the previous chapter that when a child experiences unrepaired disruptions and heightened traumatic emotions, his/her modes of expression become segregated, and one or another mode becomes emphasized and rigid. The action mode may dominate a child's functioning to avoid experiencing meanings contained in fantasies. Or the fantasy mode may dominate to avoid expressing meanings in action. Or the language mode may dominate to avoid experiencing fantasized meanings and/or expressing these meanings in action.

To promote first-order change in the behavioral mode that rigidly dominates, interactions are structured to promote a child's ability to use alternative expressions and to delay expressions within that mode. The study discussed in Chapter 6 of action versus fantasy-oriented boys illustrated first-order change in modes of expression. When action-oriented children engaged in twisting coat hangers and breaking sticks, they subsequently showed greater delay in the action mode. When fantasy-oriented children engaged in viewing pictures depicting violence, intended to simulate therapeutic experiences, they subsequently showed greater delay in the fantasy mode. To promote second-order change, structured interactions are designed to connect each mode with the others so that meanings in one mode establish representational roots in the others.

These considerations prescribe the following guidelines. If a child typically makes inflexible use of the action mode, tasks initially accommodate to this preference, permitting meanings to be expressed in alternative macroactions. Task requirements gradually undergo change and encourage a child to express the same or related meanings with microactions accompanied by a fantasy, and then with macrofantasy accompanied by little or no action. Last, language expressions subordinating fantasy and action are encouraged. With this progression the action mode is connected to the fantasy mode, and then the action and fantasy modes are connected to language.

If a child typically makes inflexible use of the fantasy mode, tasks initially require the construction of macrofantasies, then fantasies accompanied by microactions, and then macroactions with little or no fantasy activity. With this progression tasks attempt to connect the fantasy mode to action. When this integration is achieved to some degree, the tasks begin to require language expressions. If the child typically makes inflexible use of language expressions, tasks initially emphasize expressing meanings in language followed by expressions in fantasy. Fantasy expressions are then accompanied by microactions; and last, macroactions dominate without language or fantasy playing a major role. Once the three modes are connected, the tasks encourage the flexible use of all three modes.

CLINICAL ILLUSTRATIONS OF UNSTRUCTURED
AND STRUCTURED INTERACTIONS

Previous publications (e.g., Santostefano 1978, 1995a) provided detailed descriptions and clinical illustrations of the guidelines outlined here. How these guidelines are followed to promote unstructured and structured interactions in treatment is illustrated in future chapters. To serve the present discussion, I illustrate the proposed processes with sketches of the treatment of children who presented with either flexible or exceptionally rigid cognitive orientations and modes of expression.

Clinical Illustration: Unstructured Interactions with an Aggressive Child

Harry, a 5-year-old expelled from preschool because of aggressive behavior, provides an illustration of aspects of the process characterized primarily by unstructured, nondirected interactions. During the first three sessions, Harry essentially ignored the therapist and raced about the playroom from toy to toy, manipulating each for a few seconds. Sometimes, however, he punctuated this activity by flipping an object off a shelf with a flick of the wrist and a slap of the hand while expressing anxiety, tension, and anger. On a hunch that this repetitive gesture/emotion might be related to some salient, embodied meaning, the therapist placed a geometric cutout under each of five or six toy animals and puppets arranged on shelves. In doing so, he intended the cutouts to bring some organization to Harry's chaotic activity, which the therapist guessed might relate to aggressive tensions, by nonverbally suggesting that the objects on the cutouts could be toppled. By placing cutouts under some items, the therapist attempted to include himself in Harry's world. The intervention seemed to work since Harry soon limited his toppling to objects under which a cutout had been placed. In the following sessions he elaborated this activity. After toppling a puppet or toy animal, Harry fell to the floor, arms flailing, as if he were falling through space. With this action the therapist revised his initial hunch and now assumed Harry was expressing an embodied meaning of severe body-self imbalance. Throughout, the therapist struggled to find solutions. He leaped to catch the falling object before it hit the floor, sometimes succeeding but frequently failing, and he propped pillows, chairs, wastebaskets, and so forth around Harry to provide stability and prevent him from falling.

The embodied meaning of imbalance soon became translated into the first symbolic form and extended into an interactive metaphor. Harry ritualized flipping a hand puppet he called "Mister Fall" across the room and sometimes against the wall ("He's flipping out!"). The therapist experimented with pieces of string of various lengths, tying one end to a doorknob and the other to the hand puppet, to determine the length of string that would enable "Mr. Fall" to fly nearly to the wall without hitting it and "flipping out." Then Harry introduced another interactive metaphor in which he threw himself on the floor yelling, "Help, I'm sinking!" Here, while repeating the metaphor of the body-self lacking stability, Harry now seemed to be negotiating whether the therapist was available and powerful enough to save him from sinking and "flipping out." Each time, the therapist responded by grabbing Harry and pulling him onto a "raft" (a newspaper). In later sessions, after a period of diffuse agitation, Harry began to spit at and hit the therapist without any apparent provocation, repeating behaviors that caused his expulsion from preschool, an enactment that could be conceptualized as representing his core pathological metaphor. The therapist tied one end of a long piece of string around his head and the other end around Harry's head, repeating the "action solution" he used to prevent the puppet, "Mr. Fall," from flipping out. This body/action "interpretation" proved successful. Connected by a long string, Harry and therapist continued engaging each other in a productive treatment process, as we learn in a future chapter.

During the series of circular interactions sketched above, Harry was able to translate the embodied meaning, "My body-self is not grounded," into symbolized metaphors consisting of constellations of actions, emotions, images, and words (e.g., a puppet "flipping out," Harry "sinking"). Except for the initial sessions when the therapist structured the process to some degree by locating cutouts under toy animals and puppets, Harry's cognitive orientation and modes of expression were equipped to construct these interactive metaphors.

Clinical Illustration: Structured Interactions with a Child Who Functions with a Rigid Outer Cognitive Orientation

John was described as a loner and "mopey." While managing marginally in the first grades, he seemed almost unable to learn in the third grade, which he was now repeating. At school he frequently rearranged his desk; at home he spent much time lining up, counting, and pasting stickers in a scrapbook. John was initially referred for a consultation by his therapist because during nearly a year of non-directed therapy he had maintained control over himself and the treatment process by repeatedly initiating games of checkers and tic-tac-toe. The therapist had introduced numerous interpretations in an attempt to establish trust, dissolve resistance, and help John engage the conflicts being controlled by his obsessive activity. But John clung to formboard games, especially tic-tac-toe, for which he had developed numerous strategies. Psychological test results indicated that he was not aware of representations of violence and cataclysmic happenings that influenced his functioning. For example, with Card X of the Rorschach test, he imaged a volcano exploding with people and animals being hurled in all directions. But this representation had not gained expression during his previous treatment sessions, the diagnostic play interview, or his day-to-day functioning. Therefore, the "integrative" therapist who agreed to work with John set as a goal helping him step into a dialectical circle by initially accommodating to his rigid, outer-orientation and then helping him construct symbols, shared with the therapist, that gradually integrated this inner meaning of cataclysmic violence with external stimulation.

During the first session, John initiated games of tic-tac-toe and checkers as he had done with the previous therapist. To set the stage for a task that would engage John in the process of symbolizing, the therapist suggested that, in addition to using pencil marks on a sheet of paper when playing tic-tac-toe, each player would locate geometric cutouts on a matrix the therapist had drawn on a large poster board. As with tic-tac-toe, each player was to set down a geometric cutout on one of the squares with the goal of locating three in a row. John participated with enthusiasm, expressing relief that he had "something to do" and that the therapist was not "bugging him" with questions.

In the following sessions the therapist increased the complexity of the task— still casting the activity so that information was to be managed as it is without emphasizing what one could imagine it to be. Using a larger matrix, each player must now locate six cutouts in a row. John enthusiastically accepted, challenged by the need to develop more complex strategies. The therapist increased the complexity of the task again, now emphasizing the process of field articulation. For example, during any one game, each player had to locate six stacks of two particular cutouts in a row; for example, three small red triangles set on medium white squares, two medium yellow diamonds set on large blue circles, and one medium green triangle set on a large black square. In this format, then, particular geometric shapes and colors were relevant in one game and not relevant in another. Before each game, John and therapist took turns deciding which cutouts were required to win.

As therapist and John participated in these ritualized cycles of interaction, John occasionally showed signs that he was beginning to imagine the cutouts as animals, displaying the first brief expressions of his repressed anger. When locating a particular stack of cutouts on the poster board, he sometimes growled and pushed it toward one of the therapist's cutouts as if to enact one animal growling at another. In an effort to assimilate this personal fantasy into the task, and to stimulate the process of constructing shared symbols, the therapist suggested that they "make the cutouts be something." John responded to this invitation and designated each stack of cutouts as a particular animal (e.g., a medium black diamond set on a large black square was a panther). As the game continued, John and therapist took turns designating six animals to be located in a row in order to win (e.g., three lions, two panthers, and one gorilla). As symbols were constructed and shared, John began to animate the cutouts more often. Sometimes he would have a stack of cutouts stalk or pounce upon the poster board, and sometimes one of his stacks would leap and land on one of the therapist's, enacting, for example, that a panther had attacked a giraffe. When taking his turn, the therapist imitated John, moving a stack while growling and stalking one of John's stacks.

At this point the therapist introduced still another elaboration intended to help John develop the capacity to anticipate and equilibrate sudden surges of emotional tension. With this game each player located two or three stacks of cutouts on the edge of a table (the cutouts were joined with tape), each one representing the same animals. The player then drew on a sheet of paper where the animals would fall (the pattern they would form) after they were pushed from the table to the floor. John engaged in these sessions with enthusiasm, becoming even more animated in his interactions. In addition, he began to express aggression toward the therapist, sometimes angrily disagreeing with the therapist's opinion about the match between a drawing and a pattern the cutouts formed once pushed to the floor. Then, to structure "interactions" between their animals and symbolize aggression between John and therapist, another elaboration was introduced. Taking turns, each player held three of his own animals (cutouts) and three of the other player's. With arms outstretched, the cutouts were dropped to the floor. Prior to taking a turn, each player again drew a picture of the pattern the cutouts would form, anticipating and imagining which animals would "pounce" upon which. During these enactments, John showed flashes of intense anger. On a few occasions, when the therapist's animals had pounced upon his, he abruptly hurled a cutout across the room.

At this point John's angry tensions were now more available to his subjective experience, benefiting from a more flexible cognitive orientation that symbolized cutouts as fierce animals. Relying on this achievement, the therapist introduced a more elaborate, structured fantasy. The fantasy permitted more direct expressions of fantasized aggression and provided opportunities for John to enact and control these expressions with different body tempos as well as with cognitive regulators. The therapist asked John to pretend that a bomb scare had been reported and that he was a member of a special team trained to locate and defuse bombs. John accepted the invitation with enthusiasm. Extending the previously constructed shared symbol, the therapist located stacks of cutouts (two in each stack) throughout the playroom floor and on shelves. With each trial, the therapist named the makeup of a bomb, and John searched for and located the bomb, taking it to a "defusing box" (a cardboard box) where it was dismantled. For example, if a bomb consisted of a medium yellow triangle taped to a large blue diamond, two of the stacks arrayed contained all of the designated attributes. Other stacks contained none of the attributes that made up the bomb; still others contained only one or two of the attributes (e.g., a small yellow triangle taped to a large blue diamond; in this instance the shape and color of the yellow cutout were correct but the size was incorrect). As this game unfolded, John and therapist competed searching for bombs designated by the other. If the wrong stack was touched or removed, the player lost points. If the correct stack was defused, the player was honored by the town's mayor—introduced by John.

Gradually, cutouts symbolizing a bomb became more complex (e.g., stacks consisted of three cutouts and then four), requiring John and the therapist to engage the process of field articulation at a more differentiated level when examining a stack before removing it. In addition, the therapist introduced the regulation of various body tempos. With some trials each player searched for bombs as rapidly as possible. Timed scores were recorded to determine whether the therapist or John won. In other trials they searched for bombs while each moved as if he were in a slow motion movie. Now the person who took the most time won.

John's rigid, outer cognitive orientation served to avoid its opposite and thereby prevent the construction of representations of rage contained in his personal world. When he entered treatment with the first therapist, his cognition and modes of expression were not equipped to equilibrate these meanings/emotions in interactions with the therapist and required that he control his aggressive meanings by obsessively playing tic-tac-toe. The tasks introduced by the second therapist enabled John to step into a dialectical circle, reorganize his rigid, outer cognitive orientation, construct symbols that integrated his repressed rage with available stimulation, and experience and express these meanings/emotions in ways that served the therapeutic process. The symbols constructed brought some order and control over the chaos his mind had been avoiding. Following the "bomb game," John initiated enacting other "games" of violence as the therapist shifted to a more nondirected format. In the course of this work John associated to father's temper and beatings he had received from father (acknowledged by father). He also enacted disruptions during interactions with the therapist in which he expected the therapist to become angry and "tear me apart." As these disruptions occurred, and as he experienced that they were not followed by beatings, he developed a more affiliated relationship with the therapist, as well as peers, and became more productive in school and less obsessional.

Clinical Illustration: Structured Interactions with a Child Who Functions with a Rigid Inner Cognitive Orientation

Alice's parents reported that she was always lost in fantasy and was content to spend hours in her room. At school she had no friends and sometimes displayed "peculiar" behaviors. For example, after sitting thirty minutes before a math problem, she had written only a four-letter expletive in the margin. Although she had managed the first school grades, now during the fifth grade she had steadily become more withdrawn and "odd." While her behavior suggested to school personnel that she might be psychotic, psychiatric and psychological evaluations produced no evidence supporting this impression. Alice participated in a course of psychodynamic psychotherapy for six months, two sessions weekly. Her therapist became concerned because Alice rarely engaged her, rather, sat in a corner of the playroom and manipulated items she typically brought with her, one of which was a tape recorder. The therapist tried a number of strategies to promote interactions; she located various dolls or animals on the table to initiate fantasy play; she pointed out how frightening it must be to share what was on her mind; she offered snacks. When Alice did not respond sufficiently, she was referred for consultation. Test procedures administered at this time again showed no evidence of psychotic processes, and indicated she had developed an inflexible, markedly inner cognitive orientation, and that her day-to-day functioning took place primarily within vivid, highly personal fantasies. Therefore, the "integrative" therapist began a program of structured interactions using guidelines outlined above. The following sketch focuses on those aspects of Alice's treatment that illustrate how the therapist devised tasks embedded within a metaphor Alice brought to the first session in an effort to dissolve her cognitive rigidity and enable her to flexibly engage in environmental stimulation.

Alice arrived with a large two-reel tape recorder. Removing its cover, she ignored the therapist and interacted with the recorder, fingering wires and gears. On occasion she spoke to her dog, "Cuddles," who, of course, was not present. In an effort to develop characters and voices within Alice's yet unknown personal world, following the guidelines for an inner-oriented child, the therapist began to peer into the recorder, talk with Cuddles, touch and inquire about certain parts, and engage the recorder in conversation ("What's going on in there? Who's in there?"). Alice apparently identified with and accommodated to this behavior since she began to imitate the therapist addressing the tape recorder ("Hey! Where are you going?"). Over several sessions she referred to parts of the recorder as particular places. For example, a gear at one end of the recorder was Alice's house; a gear at the other end, her school; and a red wire became the road connecting them. As Alice imposed more organized meaning to the inside of the recorder, the therapist enacted imaginary persons walking to school, walking home, and shopping in grocery stores by "walking" his fingers over pathways. Alice soon imitated the therapist. This imaginary play took place for a number of sessions with child and therapist quietly sitting and peering into the tape recorder.

With personal meanings constructed and shared, each referring to some part of the tape recorder, the therapist introduced an intervention that "bumped into" Jane's rigid use of an inner orientation and macrofantasy that arbitrarily and globally expressed the inside of a recorder as the referent for a "world." The therapist invited Alice to extend the world they had created—"So we can play it better"—by locating various objects around the recorder and over the surface of a large tabletop. To promote a more articulate use of materials in symbolizing, wooden geometric cutouts and blocks were used to designate various buildings, rods were used to designate telephone poles, streets were defined with tape, and pictures of buildings were cut out of magazines. Alice now "walked" a doll figure on streets (taped pathways) and through stores (cutouts and pictures) where items were purchased. Initially these items were symbolized by Alice in highly personal terms. For example, candy bars were sometimes represented by paper clips, sometimes by a scrap of paper. By enacting characters who entered the store (sometimes using his fingers, sometimes a doll), the therapist showed confusion over which items were what. In this way the therapist encouraged Alice to fit the attributes of items with their meanings. For example, buttons became hamburgers, pieces of string carefully cut in one-inch lengths became bananas, paper clips became candy bars, and so on. The therapist also introduced various tempos in the actions the characters performed (one doll, late for school, ran over a pathway; another doll who was taking a walk after school slowly meandered along the pathway).

In the next series of meetings the therapist extended the subjective world they had created over the entire floor of the playroom. Cutouts and blocks were stacked to represent a school building, a grocery store, home, a friend's house. When constructing these structures, and to emphasize the process of field articulation, the therapist carefully designated cutouts of different sizes and colors for each of the structures, and Alice soon joined in. The school became a stack of cutouts with a large blue circle at the bottom, a medium yellow triangle in the center, and a small red circle at the top. Once when the therapist was helping to set up their world at the start of a meeting, he inadvertently placed a large yellow triangle in the center of the school building. Alice immediately noticed the error: "The school is wrong" reflected that she was assimilating more articulate fields of relevant and irrelevant information. Also, during this phase, Alice and therapist, each holding a doll, "walked" on pathways enacting various vignettes, sometimes at different tempos. For example, Jane (a doll) walked to a friend's house (the therapist's) to play; in another vignette Alice's doll participated in a school race.

In the next phase, the therapist extended the game to the outdoors. During these sessions, Alice and therapist walked about the therapeutic garden, designating various bushes and trees as particular places and enacting a number of the same roles, which now became more elaborated. During the final phase of treatment, therapist and Alice walked to a nearby shopping area, entered stores, purchased items, talked to clerks, now dealing with information more as it is.

Clinical Illustration: Facilitating Flexibility in Cognitive Orientations and Modes of Expression

One outer-oriented child had symbolized food during previous structured interactions when required to experience stimulation as she imagined it to be. These tasks involved the process of field articulation. For example, the child had been asked to scan an array of thirty buttons and to pick up, as quickly as possible, all of the medium-sized gray ones. As similar tasks were repeated, following the guidelines noted above, the child was asked to "make believe the buttons were something else." She initially imagined them to be stones, then stars on the American flag, and then focused on buttons as pieces of candy: one type became M and M's; another, Tootsie rolls; etc. Because the metaphor of nurture seemed salient for this child, the therapist used a variety of magazine pictures for the game of real/fantasy chairs. When the child sat in the real chair, the therapist handed her a picture of individuals sitting at a table laden with food and asked her to count how many different pieces of fruit were on the table. As the child engaged in the task, the therapist tapped the "fantasy" chair, which the child quickly sat in. Now the child was asked to make up a story about what was going on in the picture. Initially struggling, the child began to develop a story; without remarking on it, the therapist tapped the "real" chair; again the child shifted seats. Now she was asked to continue counting the different types of food. Then the fantasy chair was tapped again and the child shifted, interrupting experiencing information as it is and again engaging the same information as she imagined it to be.

Materials Used to Structure Interactions

When inventing tasks to structure interactions, material should be used that initially fits the child's cognitive orientation and then the opposite orientation. As illustrated earlier, at the start of treatment (with outer-oriented children) interactions are usually structured effectively with materials that are relatively neutral in terms of representing meanings (geometric cutouts, rods, buttons, pieces of cloth and string, paper clips) and therefore provide a child with opportunities to construct symbols that contain a balance of meaning and emotion that suits his/her functioning. The items used, then, are not ends in themselves but means to an end, namely, fostering the child's cognitive ability to equilibrate the demands of emotions/meanings and of external stimulation. At the start of treatment with inner-oriented children, structuring interactions is aided by using material related to a child's unique fantasy life (a toy spider, pictures of a wounded soldier or of a baby feeding). While such items usually create stress for the outer-oriented child, whose cognition turns away from fantasies/emotions, they are welcomed by the inner-oriented child for whom geometric cutouts are stressful since his/her cognitive orientation turns away from the requirements of external reality. Last, materials are used that enable a child to experience stimulation flexibly as it is and as it could be imagined (e.g., pictures, an eggbeater).

The Use of Modeling When Structuring Interactions

When structuring interactions, the therapist is urged to make use of "live and participant modeling" (Brems 1993). This issue is stressed because in normal development before the age of 3 years (Chapter 6), cognitive regulators and flexible cognitive orientations develop within continuous nonverbal interactions between infant and caregiver. The therapist, who is inclined to conduct therapy primarily by verbalizing requirements and instructions, is encouraged to be aware of this tendency and to communicate through live and participant modeling as often as indicated.

RELATING STRUCTURED AND UNSTRUCTURED INTERACTIONS: THE IMPORTANCE OF RITUALS

Whether the treatment process is directed more by the child or therapist, change is facilitated when therapist and child step into a dialectical circle, participate in ritualized dialectical interactions and enactments, and display a wide range of emotions fitted with the child's here-and-now experiences. The reader could develop the notion, from the sketches of treatment presented, that everything a child does expresses some meaning a child intends to share, as when Harry hurried about the treatment in an open-ended process or when John played tic-tac-toe with cutouts. A child talks, moves about, and plays, displaying many behaviors not necessarily contained within the dialectical circle being constructed by child and therapist. How does a therapist know when some behavior is being introduced into their circle? If a child repeats and ritualizes some behavior, more often than not the child is stepping into the circle. Harry occasionally embedded flipping items from shelves to the floor within a flood of other behaviors. Because this brief gesture was purposefully repeated, the therapist guessed a ritual was being introduced. Support for this hunch was eventually forthcoming. By placing wooden cutouts under certain items, the therapist said, nonverbally, "I get your message," and Harry responded by toppling only dolls and puppets set on cutouts. Similarly, within many other behaviors, John repeated brief "growls" when moving cutouts on the poster board. And by imitating this behavior rather than others, the therapist said, nonverbally, "I get your message."

Some authors (e.g., Coppolillo 1987) propose that when a behavior is repeated and ritualized, this signals that it is time for a therapist to interpret the behavior. Applied to John, when he repeatedly growled while moving his cutouts, a therapist could have said, for example, "Your piece is mad at mine and wants to fight," or "I wonder if you are angry with me for some reason." While rituals signal that a meaning is being shared, from the view of our model the possible meaning of the ritual should not be expressed in words but should be expressed in the child's mode (first-order change), conveying that the meaning is acknowledged and inviting the child to elaborate the meaning further. Usually, when a therapist responds within the child's mode, and if the child assimilates (internalizes/idealizes) the therapist's response, a child elaborates its meanings and announces the next ritual with another cycle of interactions (Gold 1994).

Unifying Overt Behaviors and Their Meanings

Turning to another issue, in previous chapters we noted that in mainstream cognitive-behavioral and psychodynamic therapies intrapsychic functioning (meanings/emotions) has been split off from behavioral functioning, and words have been split off from actions (Gold 1994). If we consider the treatments sketched thus far, and those presented in future chapters, it should become clear that cycles of dialectical interactions and enactments, whether occurring during structured or unstructured treatment, connect meanings/emotions with interpersonal functioning or connect surface and deep behaviors. When the therapist tied a string around his forehead and Harry's, after Harry regressed, the deep meaning of the string as a shared symbol of control was connected to Harry's surface, interpersonal behaviors, as evidenced by the outcome: Harry calmed down and continued interacting in productive ways. And when John crawled about the playroom floor using various tempos, searching for bombs to diffuse, the deep meaning of "repressed" interpersonal violence was connected with his surface behavior as he engaged in the competition of carefully examining stacks of cutouts as bombs.

Idealizing/Internalizing the Therapist: The Most Critical Catalyst for Change

While participating in circular interactions and interactive metaphors, in structured and unstructured processes, a child gradually idealizes and internalizes behaviors the therapist used to negotiate dilemmas. I view the process of idealization/internalization as the most critical catalyst for change, the "sacred moment," rather than a therapist's verbal interpretation (see Chapter 3). Therefore, a therapist should be alert for behaviors on the part of the child that imitate attributes of the therapist, suggesting he/she is being idealized. Behavioral signs of idealization/internalization may be subtle. The child may imitate a gesture or tone of voice characteristic of the therapist. Or a child may show that a meaning expressed by the therapist has been assimilated and influences him/her. Recall that during unstructured interactions Harry idealized and internalized the symbolic meaning of a string when one end was tied to his forehead and the other to the therapist's, resulting in Harry's exercising self-regulation over his diffuse aggression. And during structured interactions, John introduced a "mayor" who honored the person who diffused a bomb, representing idealized standards of the therapist.

Behaviors the child imitates and internalizes may be more elaborate. One preadolescent girl began openly to admire various items of clothing worn by her female therapist. Then, during several sessions, she asked if she could wear the therapist's belt and earrings, a request the therapist granted. Later, requesting that she and the therapist dress alike, child and therapist devoted several minutes at the close of each session to select what they would wear for the next session.

When idealizing and internalizing attributes of the therapist, a child frequently fortifies his/her ability to engage in self-regulation while coping with stress. This is vividly illustrated by the experience of an adult patient described by Gold (1994), an example that forms a bridge to one common way children reflect this process. A woman in her mid-twenties suffered from extreme self-doubt and anxiety whenever she was faced with public speaking. She had gained insight into the developmental underpinnings of this difficulty, yet the power of this insight seemed limited since her stress when speaking in public "was still considerable." Then, in one session, she spontaneously exclaimed to the therapist, "I'm going to shrink you down to the size of a doll and take you along to my meeting this afternoon" (p. 151), developing this fantasy into a "finely articulated visual image." In subsequent sessions she reported that each time she called up this image, "her sense of anxiety and pain diminished and was replaced by a feeling of confidence, comfort and companionship" (p. 151). This patient, then, equipped with the capacity to construct vivid imagery, internalized the therapist in the form of "a doll" that she carried with her in fantasy as an idealized source of strength and companionship. The power of this internalized image apparently proved greater than verbalized insight.

While some children may have the capacity to take an image of the therapist with them as an idealized companion, more often, at various points in treatment, children ask to take some item from the playroom or the therapist's person. Some clinicians (e.g., Brems 1993) recommend that such requests "must be explored" to learn what they mean and decide how to respond. I take a different position and recommend that, within reason, the child's request should be granted without discussion. When a child requests an item, usually he/she is expressing the wish to take the therapist with him/her into other environments in the form of a transitional object, symbolizing the therapist as an idealized source of strength, much as did Gold's patient. As future cases illustrate, when a child requests an item, she/he is frequently signaling that some difficulty is to be confronted at a new level. If the therapist engages in verbal discussions, the issue is pushed into the language-conceptual mode and likely results in "explanations" or "rationalizations" unrelated to some embodied meaning that the child cannot yet express in words. Usually, the meaning of an item the child requests is revealed during future enactments between child and therapist.

I am aware that on some occasions a child may request an item that the therapist finds impossible to grant or for personal reasons is unwilling to grant. In these cases symbolic equivalents that the therapist selects from items the child has already admired could be used. One child had admired several items in the therapist's office, especially some small stone sculptures of birds. When the child asked if she could take one of the sculptures home, the therapist invited her to select a polished stone from among several that were in a basket and that the child had also already admired. If the child's request cannot be successfully negotiated, the therapist is then faced with managing and repairing a disruption of the child's attempt to internalize and idealize the therapist.

Transference

Last, I turn to the issue of transference. Usually, as discussed previously, transference refers to early maladaptive modes of functioning and expressions of feelings and beliefs that the patient assigns to the therapist, distorting who and what the "real" therapist is. As the foregoing discussion should make clear, whether treatment is structured or unstructured, transference experiences are coauthored by child and therapist. As they construct a shared culture and engage in interactive metaphors, how the therapist behaves strongly affects what the child experiences within their relationship; similarly, how the child behaves strongly influences what the therapist experiences. Each assimilates and accommodates to the other and each defines the other. While the particular metaphor a child expresses relates to some developmental issue in need of negotiation and repair, the unique form that a metaphor takes is as much a function of the therapist's subjective culture and actions as those of the child. Transference experiences, then, from the point of view of our model, are embedded in the relationship that is unique to a child and therapist. As noted in Chapter 4, I ascribe to Weimer's (1980) position that continuous cycles of dialectical interactions, in which child and therapist participate, will create new meanings they share, change the meanings of events they experienced, and change the actions each takes toward the other. In one sense, therefore, the disrupted life metaphor a child brings to treatment may be expressed in a particular form with one therapist and in a very different form with another. Similar views and comprehensive discussions of transference are available, which the interested reader is encouraged to consider (e.g., Brems 1993, Kohlenberg and Tsai 1994, Wachtel 1987).

CONCLUDING COMMENTS

In the next chapters I present treatment cases that are described in more detail, illustrating how the proposed guidelines are applied when conducting psychotherapy. These cases do not provide "cookbook recipes," each designed to treat children who qualify for one or another diagnosis. Some authors take the position that a psychodynamic, cognitive, or behavioral approach should be followed to treat a child, depending upon her/his diagnosis. Others, while receptive to each approach, take the position that "it is impossible to dictate a particular approach [for a child] nor would it be prudent to do so" (Brems 1993, p. 204). Our developmental-dialectical model does not see *DSM-IV* diagnoses, nor does it see segregated approaches to treating children: psychodynamic, cognitive, and behavioral. Our model dissolves these boundaries.

In dissolving these boundaries, the proposed model prescribes an approach to treating children, whatever their diagnoses and presenting problems, that is framed by two propositions. First, a child's knowledge and the meanings a child has constructed from experiences are embedded in what the child does, thinks, and feels. The second proposition holds that the process of constructing knowledge and meanings is always embedded in a relationship. Cognition, or the process of knowing and constructing meanings, derives from the Latin to get to know together, a notion supported by Piaget (1952) and Karl Stern (1965) as well as the infant investigators discussed in Chapter 5. Although a child inhabits a private, subjective world of meanings and knowledge, he/she always shares or has shared a part of that world with others.

Yet, for the child who is suffering and requires treatment, her/his meanings and the network of cognitive functions and modes of expression surrounding them have become rigid, limiting exchanges between her/his subjective world and that of others. When interacting with others, this child attempts to preserve this organization of meanings, cognitions, and behavioral modes, and also experiences any threat to this structure as a threat to her/his "reality." Therefore, to help these children grow, our developmental-dialectical model prescribes that a therapist shift back and forth between structured and unstructured dialectical interactions in order to promote flexibility in a child's cognitive orientation and modes of expression and so that pathological life metaphors can be revised. When engaged in this process, the therapist must continually learn who she/he is when entering the child's subjective world and discover who the child is when she/he enters the therapist's subjective world.

In selecting the cases for the next two chapters I recognize that there are a number of obstacles (Colby and Stoller 1988). It is difficult to represent how, what, and exactly when a therapist does or does not do something from session to session. It is also impossible to describe fully, for child and therapist, the constellation of tone of voice, emotions, gestures and postures, facial expressions, words and actions each is displaying during a given interaction and enactment. Along the same line, it is impossible to describe the fleeting impressions, conscious meanings, and intentions each experiences during an interaction, let alone any unconscious meanings that could exert an influence. Last, clinical cases tend to be highly selective. Those presented in the next chapters were selected to illustrate one or another aspect of the developmental-dialectical guidelines. I recognize the cases do not illustrate all of the possible ways that guidelines could be combined. While acknowledging these obstacles, I hope the treatment cases will stimulate the reader to explore and develop her/his ingenuity in using the proposed guidelines when treating children and adolescents.

8

Case Illustrations of Structured Interactions in Psychotherapy: A Developmental-Dialectical View

CONTENTS

The clinical cases discussed in this chapter provide more detailed illustrations than the previous vignettes of the guidelines for structuring a therapeutic process whenever a child's cognitive and behavioral rigidity limits the extent to which he/she can participate within a dialectical circle and enact and revise maladaptive metaphors. Although I have emphasized that typically a therapist moves back and forth between structured and unstructured dialectical interactions, for this chapter I decided to assemble cases that required primarily structured interactions. I did so for several reasons. Together the cases provide examples of some of the strategies and tasks therapists have used to structure interactions from a developmental-dialectical perspective. Other tasks are described elsewhere (Santostefano 1995a). In addition, the cases illustrate how these tasks differ from those used in traditional cognitive-behavioral therapy. Guided by the proposition that the aim of treatment is to facilitate the development of adaptive meanings that promote further growth, the tasks were coauthored by child and therapist within a metaphor unique to a child's subjective world. Moreover, although the treatment process in each case was structured, the same catalysts for change were eventually activated (cycles of dialectical interactions, enactments, and idealization/internalization) as child and therapist integrated their respective subjective cultures, grappled with the dilemmas the child projected onto the therapist, and engaged in interactive metaphors. When participating, the therapist was sometimes required to be active physically and sometimes much less so. Last, the cases illustrate that although interactions were highly structured, the process of constructing and enacting symbols and metaphors itself promoted change. The reader will notice that verbal interpretations, conceptualizations, and direct discussions of the child's difficulties played a minor role and sometimes no role at all. In each case the therapist tended to respond and "interpret" primarily through structured interactions.

As a concluding introductory remark, I would like to mention that a psychodynamic therapist will likely "see" many more meanings represented by a child's enactments than I point out. My goal is not to discuss all the possible symbolic meanings of each enactment but to illustrate that, by structuring interactions, children can be helped to engage in a dialectical process and enact metaphors that contribute to resolving their difficulties.

The first case we consider was treated by me, and therefore I have been able to include some of what I was thinking and experiencing, which guided the ways in which I structured interactions during the treatment. The other cases were treated by colleagues. Thus limited information is available about the therapist's experiences that contributed to when and how they chose to structure interactions.

JOHN: I WAS DEVASTED BY THE LOSS OF A LOVED ONE

I selected the case we are about to consider because this boy had become severely rigid in expressing himself in the action mode. Accordingly, his ability to benefit from engaging in dialectical interactions with family members and schoolmates was severely limited. When he entered treatment, he was clearly on a maladaptive, developmental course.

Ms. G telephoned me for an appointment to discuss concerns she had about her son, John, age 10. His teacher, principal, and the school psychologist had encouraged her to arrange for treatment.

Parent Intake Interview and History

Ms. G impressed me as warm, verbally articulate, and psychologically minded. She began by describing that John was "in a shell." At home he "moped and dragged himself around," and kept some distance from mother, sister, age 14, and brother, age 6. To highlight John's apathy, she emphasized that his sister and brother showed interest, energy, and a sense of pleasure typical for their ages. At school John, now in the fifth grade, showed the same apathetic behavior. There he appeared shy, expressed little enthusiasm about anything, rarely smiled, and stayed to himself when on the playground. Although he had attained high IQ scores on group intelligence tests administered at the school, his grades during the past few years had been mostly C's and D's. In addition, he took offense at his teacher's attempts to prod him to get his work done.

John began to display this withdrawn, lethargic behavior when he was 5 years old, shortly after the death of his father. The G family operated a farm. Mr. G was killed accidentally while operating a tractor that tipped over, crushing him beneath it. John and his father had become "great buddies" prior to father's death. The boy had accompanied father while he handled many of the farm chores. Moreover, father had built a special seat for John on the tractor involved in the tragedy, and they frequently rode together around the fields. John had been riding the tractor with his father during the morning prior to the accident. After lunch, John took a nap and when he woke up his father was dead. Unlike his sister, who attended the wake and funeral (his brother was only a few months old at the time), John refused to go to the wake and the cemetery.

After the funeral, John began to avoid contact with persons outside his immediate family. When company visited, he refused to go into the living room. Mother made a "periscope" so that he could see who was in the living room without his being seen. But this device, and considerable encouragement, did not help. During the year following father's death, John became increasingly quiet and isolated. Moreover, he took forever to get ready to go anywhere and always needed to be prodded.

When he was 7 years old, mother consulted a psychiatrist, who interviewed John and concluded he would very likely pull out of his apathy. Ms. G also attempted to "get John out of his shell," encouraging him to go outdoors to play. Initiating several long talks with him over a number of weeks, she pointed out that if he wanted to learn to be a boy and a man he couldn't do it by hanging around her in the house, that he should go out and have friends. "I can't be your father, you'll have to learn to get along without one, like your sister and brother are doing, and like I'm learning to get along without a husband." Following these talks, John showed some change, moving out for brief periods to play with boys living nearby.

When we reviewed John's early history, mother did not recall John's showing any difficulties. As a baby and during the preschool years, he tended to be easygoing. Mother associated this style with that of Mr. G: "That's just the way his father was, easygoing." She stressed, however, that the withdrawal and apathy that John showed since father's death was much more than this characteristic style. During the year preceding the intake interview, John joined a little league team at mother's urging and participated for a brief period of time. He did not appear to enjoy himself and played poorly, eventually dropping out. John never spontaneously asked about his father nor did he make inquiries or comments when mother brought father up for discussion.

Ms. G, along with John's teacher, considered his social withdrawal the main problem and wondered whether John's poor school performance was due to low abilities. "Maybe we're all expecting too much from him."

I explained to Ms. G that while John's current difficulties clearly suggested he was suffering and needed help, a psychological evaluation should be conducted first to gather information about how and the degree to which the tragedy John suffered impacted his intellectual and cognitive functioning and modes of expression. Information should be gathered about the meanings his mind has assigned to the way in which his father died, especially since John and father shared the tractor that killed him, and given that the loss occurred at a critical phase in John's development. Mother had some familiarity with the content and purpose of psychological testing and accepted the recommendation. I referred John to a colleague for an evaluation.

John's Psychological Evaluation

The diagnostician described John as a husky, good-looking boy with a mop of curly black hair. While he complied with all test demands, he said nothing spontaneously, sat relatively immobile, and displayed a "blank expression." On the

Wechsler Intelligence Scale, John attained a total IQ score in the superior range (135), but the examiner had provided considerable support and direction, frequently repeating instructions, refocusing John, and reassuring and coaxing him whenever he blocked or refused to tackle some item. With tests of cognitive regulators (see Chapter 6), John showed excessive rigidity when he scanned a field of information, for example, that evoked fantasies and emotions (e.g., pictures of weapons).

Results with an action test of personality (see Chapter 6) were especially revealing. John was asked to perform three actions on material in any order he chose and to describe what came to mind as he performed them. For example, he was to tear up one sheet of paper, crumple another, and cut another along a line with a pair of scissors. He performed the most indirect and delayed action first. When faced with performing an action that required more direct and immediate expressions, he became anxious and refused, or performed the action in a very constricted manner. In one instance, to crumple a sheet of paper, he slowly brought the ends together, essentially "folding" the paper. When tearing a sheet of paper, he used the thumb and forefinger of each hand and slowly produced a tear about one inch long. Significantly, he could not or would not express what came to mind when performing these actions.

With the Rorschach test, John produced images representing violence that was not visible in his day-to-day functioning and that he was struggling to keep under control. To Card II he constructed the image of two dead buffaloes that have been shot and "there are bloodstains all over"; to Card IV, the image of a monster eating a tree; to Card VIII, the image of two animals that "just killed something, tearing it apart, see—the guts are showing all over"; to Card IX, the image of "an atomic bomb blowing up"; and to Card X, the image of many bugs "caught on a spider's web and two big bugs are going after them to eat them and get all the blood out of them." These images formed a metaphor that very likely represented the death of his father, as he construed it, and contained vivid meanings and intense emotions that his rigid cognitive orientation and modes of expression were attempting to keep under control.

On the sentence completion test, John produced responses that symbolized three themes that very likely occupied his conscious thoughts. One theme concerned his need to repair his ability to move forward: *What I want more than anything is* "for my go-cart to be fixed." Another theme concerned his social isolation: *My best friend is* "my dog." The third theme concerned his fear of the dark. To those that mentioned father (*My father and I; I sure wish my father would*), John commented, "I can't stand to hear people talk about our dad."

On the basis of these data, the diagnostician viewed John as suffering from a severe inhibition, associated with the death of his father, that extended into cognition as well as the action mode. He concluded that unconsciously John construed his father's death as cataclysmic and violent (e.g., two buffaloes that had been shot with bloodstains all over), and that John's behavioral and emotional constriction was linked to the fact that the loss of father occurred at a particularly critical phase of development. Until the age of 5, John seemed to have adequately negotiated various developmental issues. As he entered a phase of development that calls for a boy to experiment with asserting against and competing with an idealized father while experiencing him as a rival for mother's affection (oedipal phase), John suddenly lost this idealized figure. John construed that he was in some way responsible for father's death, and therefore assertive and aggressive urges aroused intense anxiety. To manage this conflict, John's development relied upon an outer cognitive orientation that avoided the calls for action of metaphors. He also relied upon and evolved an action mode that remained inert at all costs, because to take action could lead to destruction. These dynamics generalized so that John eventually showed a "lack of push" in all areas, including academics, where his marginal productivity was well below his superior intellectual abilities. His characteristic body posture and style of walking (head bowed, shoulders hunched, slow, shuffling gait) were also viewed as expressions of a severely constricted body image.

The diagnostician and I discussed the results with mother, who accepted treatment beginning with one session per week. The therapist recommended that mother initiate meetings whenever John showed behaviors that concerned her, and the therapist would ask for meetings whenever mother should be alerted to developments occurring in treatment that might have relevance for John's day-to-day functioning.

John's Treatment

Given John's withdrawn, detached, and inhibited functioning at home and school since the age of 5, I elected to emphasize two short-term goals during the first months of treatment: (1) help John with structured interactions to step into a dialectical circle and join me in experiencing, negotiating, and influencing each other's self-expressions and in integrating, to some extent, our respective subjective cultures; (2) help John cultivate flexibility in the action mode so that he could express intentions, especially aggressive ones, using different degrees of directness and delay. My long-term goal was to help John participate in interactive metaphors, eventually enacting and revising core pathological metaphors that represented father's death and perhaps John as feeling responsible for it.

The diagnostician did not hold a meeting with John to discuss the results of the evaluation. We decided that John needed a number of sessions to articulate some understanding of the need for treatment, an understanding that could be constructed during the first treatment sessions. Therefore, I met John for the first time when he arrived for the initial session.

Helping John Step into a Dialectical Circle:
A Formidable Hurdle (10 sessions)

When I approached John in the waiting room, he was sitting in a corner, turned in his seat so that he nearly faced the wall. I introduced myself and asked him to come along. He got up, kept his head down, and shuffled along a couple of yards behind. Upon entering the playroom, he looked at various objects and picked up a few, only to set each back in its place. As he slowly wandered about, I did not mention his mother's concerns nor the school's. I waited for some gesture or comment on his part that suggested he was inviting me to enter a dialectical circle. One of these moments finally occurred. He picked up a football, tossed it a few feet in the air, and caught it. To test how receptive he was to stepping into a dialectical circle, I slapped my hands and held them outstretched, inviting him to throw me a pass. He did. I tossed the ball back, inviting him to play catch. For a moment I felt elated by the possibility that he might begin what could become a circular interaction. But when he caught the ball, he put it back on the shelf, clearly conveying that he was not yet ready or willing. The only interest he seemed to show was in two toy dart guns. Picking these up, he said, "What's this?" with a muted expression of anxiety and excitement, the only words he spoke spontaneously throughout the whole hour and the only communication that seemed to be directed toward me.

During the second hour, John behaved in about the same way. Ten minutes or so before the close of the hour, I proposed that he could assemble a model of his choosing, if that would interest him. Several thoughts flitted through my mind when I made this offer. I recalled his response during the evaluation to the sentence beginning *What I want more than anything is* ("for my go-cart to be fixed"). I wondered if assembling a model might give this personal meaning an opportunity to express itself in an activity. In addition, it seemed to me that while John was wandering aimlessly about the room, he was experiencing stress as he actively avoided stepping into a dialectical circle with me. By working on a model, I thought he could engage in some focused activity that would help him avoid me, yet, whenever he chose, he could engage me.

John selected the model of a car and worked with it for the next eight sessions, quietly gluing pieces together while ignoring me. Throughout these meetings I tried to set a stage that I hoped would help him eventually step into a dialectical circle. What I chose to do was influenced by the test results indicating that his action mode was rigidly held in check, avoiding direct, symbolic expressions, especially of assertion. In an attempt to promote flexibility in taking action, I initially engaged in activity that symbolized control, order, and repairing disorder, activity that I thought was attuned to John's current mode of functioning and that might facilitate first-order change.

While John quietly studied the directions for assembling the model, I busied myself clearing shelves and organizing materials in the treatment room. Our treatment room was one of several in which various therapists and children frequently left material in some degree of disarray. Initially I focused on sheets of paper strewn about on shelves. I cut a number in half with scissors and, working slowly, arranged the pieces into neat piles, commenting a few times, "This place needs to be straightened out." John occasionally glanced at me while working on his model.

In the next session I continued my "operation cleanup." I rummaged through boxes of crayons, found broken pieces, lined them up, and searched for other pieces that matched them. Working on the same table where John was assembling his model, I taped pieces of crayons together. At one point I groaned over the number of broken pieces and commented, "Anytime you want to tape some pieces together that would be cool." Several minutes passed, then John, perhaps responding to my request, complained, with a puzzled look on his face, that he could not figure out a step in the directions of his model. I leaned over, asked which step he was working on, read the directions, and manipulated the pieces, searching for the way they should be glued together. I shared the solution with John, and he glued the pieces. Moments later he spontaneously reached over and taped two pieces of crayon together. At this point I felt each of us had placed one foot in a dialectical circle.

During the following meetings, John worked on his model while I set out other tasks for myself. With each, my intention now was to help John stand in our dialectical circle for a few moments and engage in symbolic microactions representing expressions of assertion. I set a stack of paper on the table and flipped through the sheets, removing any that had crayon marks on them. Then I slowly crumpled sheets and tossed each into a wastebasket. As another task, I brought in boards, screws, and nails "that had to be screwed and nailed together." As another, I brought in a pile of junk mail and old correspondence from my office that had to be "shredded." At each meeting I again conveyed that any help would be appreciated. And I tried to be careful to move at a pace that resembled John's.

Occasionally John interrupted his work with the model and joined me for a few moments in crumpling and tossing sheets of paper, hammering nails, turning screws into wood, and tearing up old correspondence. I should comment on the form of his actions. Initially they were very constricted, as described by the diagnostician. For example, at first he took a sheet of paper, pressed it in half, walked to the wastebasket, and dropped it in. Gradually he crumpled paper with slightly more vigor (imitating me, it seemed) and tossed it into the wastebasket. At the same time, he gradually increased the number of times he indicated he needed help locating and gluing pieces of his model and interpreting some step in the instructions.

During the last two sessions of this phase, I chose to use "hammering nails" as a way to further our participating in a dialectical circle. I brought in a 2 inch by 4 inch board about 2 feet in length into which I had tapped seven nails. I invited John to compete with me to see who could drive in the nails with the *fewest* number of blows of the hammer. John accepted. As we engaged in this activity, he used slightly more vigor when pounding nails, seemed more animated, and showed more affiliation toward me. The latter is supported by an observation of his behavior in the waiting room. Previously when I entered the waiting room, I found John seated away from the doorway, looking out the window. It was necessary for me to call him by name and ask him to come along before he rose and followed. When I entered the waiting room for the sixth session, he was seated facing the doorway. Once he saw me, he got up and walked toward me without my saying a word. And while he walked to the treatment room with his characteristically slow, shuffling gait, he now walked alongside me for the first time.

At the start of the tenth session John experienced metaphorically what I understood to be his "call for help" and his view of why we were meeting. When we entered the playroom, he turned to me and commented, "I hurt my finger; I can't bend it." I expressed concern. He showed me the middle finger of his left hand, which appeared to be only slightly tender. I carefully examined his finger, touching it gingerly, "I see it; looks sore right here." John nodded, "It hurts."

"Really bad, huh?"

"Yeah, it hurts now but it really hurt when I hurt it."

I'm still examining the finger, "How did you hurt it? What happened?"

John shared he was "messing around" in the barn and jammed his finger.

Taking out the first aid kit located in the treatment room, I offered to put a Band-Aid on it. John accepted and seemed to stand close to me. I carefully bandaged his finger and commented that he could now continue working on his model better and grip the handle of the hammer better when he "takes me on" in one of our hammering contests. John grinned and agreed. His affect throughout this interaction struck me as resembling that of a preschooler who, upon displaying a minor injury, conveys that his total body-self has been wounded and needs attention.

With this interaction, symbolizing John's expression of pain and accepting me as someone who could help, I thought we had finally stepped into a dialectical circle with both feet, having discovered and negotiated each other's self-expressions, preferred levels of stimulation, and pace of interacting. These negotiations took place while we assembled the car model, crumpled and shredded paper, and turned screws and hammered nails into wood. As it turned out, my hunch proved correct. Our interaction over his "wounded finger" ushered in the first interactive metaphor expressed by John.

The First Interactive Metaphor:
I've Been Broken Into Pieces and I'm Furious (1 session)

In the next session, John introduced what I viewed as an elaboration of the meaning he expressed with his wounded finger. When he entered the treatment room, instead of taking his model out of his basket he picked up a toy dart gun from a shelf, returned to his chair, and sat about 5 feet away, facing me. He slowly waved the gun as if he were firing it in some fantasy, but he made no sounds. With his arm fully extended he took several long, steady aims at various objects, tilting his head to one side and squinting one eye. At one point, aiming at an object to one side of me, he shifted the pistol, aimed directly at my face for several seconds, and then shifted the pistol again, aiming at another object, commenting, "My tooth was loose. I went to the dentist, and he pulled it out." Again his emotional tone was that of a 4-year-old who needs comfort and attention.

"You did? Let me take a look." John opened his mouth and seemed pleased as I peered in. "Yeah, I see it back there. When did it happen?" I noticed to myself that the gum had already healed appreciably.

"Oh, I don't know. A while ago."

"What was it like? Was it hurting a lot?"

John passed his hand over his cheek. "Yeah, it was sore all over."

"You've really been banged up. You hurt your finger, and now it's your tooth."

John responded with a soft "Uh-huh" as he walked over and picked up the football and threw it at me. I caught it and passed it back. After we passed the ball back and forth several times, he suddenly hurled it at me with intensity; given the relatively short distance between us, he clearly wanted the ball to slam against my body. When I caught the ball, I grunted "Ugh!" John made no comment as he continued passing the ball.

After ten or so passes, he returned the ball to a shelf, looked over the toys, and picked up several beanbags and a rubber, he-man figure, about 5 inches tall. He stood the figure at one end of the room and from the other end hurled the beanbags at it with force. Leaving this material on the floor, he picked up three large darts (a rubber baseball with long feathers on one end and a suction cup at the other). Without hesitation, he slammed these against the wall in rapid succession. Then he stood an 8-inch plastic figure (the "Phantom of the Opera") on the table, stepped back a few feet, and hurled one of the darts at it. The figure toppled to the floor and broke into pieces. John glanced toward me, expressing, I thought, a combination of surging excitement, anxiety, and fear, and commented, "All the parts still look good."

I examined the pieces, agreed, and said, "This guy *is* all busted up; he was so mad he exploded into a million pieces." John grinned. I added, "I think we can put him back together again." For the remainder of the session we busied ourselves gluing the pieces together, successfully reconstructing the figure. At the close of the hour, John asked if he could take his model home and finish it there, and I replied, "Of course." I understood this request to symbolize that he had gradually identified with, idealized, and internalized my symbolic communications that I could repair a body-self that has been torn apart. I also understood his request to symbolize that he was now ready to engage me in dialectical interactions and no longer needed the model to avoid me.

The Second Interactive Metaphor: I Am Violent and
Harbor Murderous Wishes: Cultivating Delay and Indirectness in the
Action Mode to Displace Aggression Away from the Therapist (7 sessions)

In the next sessions, John's aggressive behaviors escalated rapidly, sometimes expressed in brief, explosive moments of fantasy play and sometimes directly at my person. He slammed together two he-man figures as they battled each other. During a brief game of catch, he hurled the ball at me, exclaiming, "I'll throw it right through your head!" On other occasions, dart gun in hand, he repeatedly shot darts randomly about the room; then, when standing only a few feet away, turned and shot a dart at my face. And as I leaned over picking up material, with John at my side, he attempted to cut my necktie with a pair of scissors. These expressions occurred, I thought, because the rigidity of his action mode, held tightly since the age of 5, was beginning to loosen too rapidly. At the same time, John had not had opportunities, since the death of his father, to develop and practice self-regulation and flexibility, expressing meanings in action with various degrees of directness and delay.

I decided to focus first on providing John with experiences cultivating flexibility and self-regulation in the action mode rather than focus on the content of his aggressive intentions. To this end I introduced two tasks. In one, I tapped three nails and three screws into a board, alternating them, and challenged John to compete with me. Each of us was to hammer a nail, then turn a screw, then hammer the next nail, and so on. Thus each of us was to shift back and forth between performing vigorous, immediate, direct actions (hammering) and indirect and delayed actions (turning a screw into wood), facilitating self-regulation and delay. As the winner required the *least* amount of time to embed the nails and screws, each of us had to aim the hammer carefully and regulate its blow and carefully regulate the turns of the screwdriver. Each of us timed the other, and we kept a log of our trials.

In the second task, I lined up ten geometric wooden cutouts of different sizes, shapes, and colors, each about 12 inches from the next. A player was to stand with his back to the array, dart gun at the ready. When the other player called out a designated target, the shooter would turn, scan the row of targets, aim, and shoot the target designated. If a player hit the correct target, he obtained two points, if he missed he lost one point, and if he hit the wrong target he lost two points.

John participated in each contest with increasing enthusiasm. His action mode slipped on only a few occasions. With the nail and screw game, he became frustrated on a few occasions and frantically pounded both nails and screws with many rapid strokes of the hammer. Once he waved the hammer at me as if to hit me on the head. With the dart gun game, on two occasions, he "playfully" shot at me instead of at the designated target, showing the same gleam in his eye that I observed earlier when he hurled a ball at me.

Enacting Interpersonal Aggression: From Dolls to the Therapist as Targets:
Cultivating Further Delay and Indirectness in the Action Mode (9 sessions)

John gradually showed increasing ability to regulate his actions when expressing aggression symbolically with wooden cutouts, nails, and screws. Relying on this gain, and looking for additional ways to direct John's aggression from my person to representations of humans, I introduced a new dart gun game that included as targets wooden figures of humans instead of geometric cutouts. The figures, each about 6 inches tall, represented a range of individuals—fireman, policeman, doctor, nurse, mother, father, children.

For three sessions we followed the format of the previous dart gun game. Each of us stood with our back to the row of wooden figures, and then turned and shot the figure named by the other player. When I was the shooter, I did not notice any particular pattern to the figures John chose as targets.

At one point John asked if "we could have a gun fight," shifting the target of aggression from dolls to our persons. I agreed. Initially, John expressed appropriate, behavioral regulation as we "battled," each of us squatting behind chairs and blasting away. On several occasions, however, John's self-regulation collapsed as he toppled chairs and frantically raced about the room in search of a "better position." On other occasions he abruptly ran up to my position, with his dart gun a few inches from my body, and shot at me.

To stem the tide, I introduced two additional structured interactions that maintained our persons as targets but that required different degrees of directness and delay. One game consisted of "pistol duels at fifteen paces." We stood back to back. When one of us gave a signal, we took fifteen steps, turned, and fired at each other. With the other, we took turns timing each other while drawing our dart guns from our belts in two ways. One contest determined who was the "fastest gun." The other determined who was best at drawing and aiming "in slow motion" and delaying squeezing the trigger.

Throughout this phase we shifted back and forth among these enactments, sometimes battling in open warfare, sometimes dueling at fifteen paces, and sometimes playing "slow motion." On two occasions, during a slow motion enactment, John lost total control when he suddenly punched me very hard in the arm. In addition, especially during the early sessions of this phase, he occasionally criticized something about the treatment room or the clothing I was wearing.

The Third Interactive Metaphor:
Die Father Die, or Did I Kill Him? (10 sessions)

John initiated one of our dart gun games, but then set his gun down to examine boxing gloves. He asked if we could "play boxing." I was not at all sure what this shift in our enactments meant. I guessed (or wished) that maybe he was now ready to express interpersonal aggression at my person in a sublimated form within the sport of boxing. Because he had shown he could shift flexibly, to some degree, among different tempos and degrees of delay and directness, I agreed but decided to represent and enact, as much as possible, symbols of regulation and structure. We taped the floor to mark the boundaries of "a boxing ring." We placed chairs in opposite corners, set a timer to beep two-minute rounds, and agreed on a three-round match. I also proposed that each of us have a "boxing name." John chose "Slaughter Sam," and I chose "Bob the Bulldozer." When this name came to me, I was not conscious of the possible connection John's mind could make between a tractor and a bulldozer. I also introduced an imaginary sports arena, announcer, and audience. After we laced our gloves, I dramatically announced the first match. "Ladies and gentlemen! In this corner, wearing blue trunks and weighing 180 pounds, from New York City, Slaughter Sam!" The crowd (John and I) cheered.

In our first match, John participated within the fantasy, bobbing, jabbing, and punching. He returned to his corner when the beeper sounded and seemed to enjoy himself. Near the close of this session, while we removed our gloves and tidied the room, he spontaneously commented that on his way home from the last appointment, as the car left the clinic's driveway, he spotted a squirrel that had been hit by a car, lying on the road. He was sure blood was coming from its mouth. He wondered if maybe he and his mother had hit it on the way to the clinic. After he left, I puzzled whether and how this association and its meaning would find its way into the treatment process.

In the next session he initiated boxing again. During these matches, unlike the previous ones, he began to swing wildly and furiously at my body and head, rather than box. Between rounds, as the announcer, I commented, "Folks, Slaughter Sam is really turning it on, but I think he's losing points." My words, spoken within our boxing metaphor, failed to stimulate John's self-regulation.

During one round, as John swung away, pounding at my arms and chest, he suddenly began to sob, crying, "Die, die, die." I put my arms around him and held him close to me. He continued sobbing for a minute or two. I did not comment, nor did John. He slumped in a chair, staring at the floor. Then he turned, took a long look at me, and whispered, "Are you hurt?" I said No, and that Bulldozer Bob was ready to get back in the ring. I thought I should repair the disruption and convey that John's "murderous onslaught" did not hurt me and that I could go on. In the last minutes of the session we boxed one more round. With tears still in his eyes, John bobbed and weaved with less vigor than he had displayed previously.

During the next session John boxed for three rounds and made no mention of the previous hour. I decided not to refer to it and waited to see what unfolded. After we completed the last round, he took off his gloves, commenting that he wanted to go outside and play basketball. We went outside to the playground adjoining the clinic. As we took turns shooting baskets, John ritualized several enactments that elaborated the meaning of the boxing episode of the previous hour when he sobbed, "Die." Taken together, these enactments represented the death of his father and John's unconscious belief that he was in some way responsible.

He called the basketball game he devised "sudden death playoff." After each player made three baskets, whoever made the next one "killed" the other player. While engaging in this game during the next seven sessions, John gradually elaborated his metaphor of death. He spotted a small insect crawling on the pavement, ran into the playroom, returned with a paper cup filled with water, and dripped water on the insect. He watched as it struggled, wondered if he "killed it," and waited until the insect crawled out of the glob of water. He repeated this "water game" a number of times, walking about looking for ants and bugs. In addition, on two occasions he bent a branch of a large yew as far back as he could, commenting, "I'll bet this hurts; I'm killing it." Then he released the branch and, when it snapped back, added, "No I didn't. I was just kidding."

The Fourth Interactive Metaphor:
I am 5 Years Old Again (9 sessions)

Our enactments shifted again when John rummaged through a small room in which the clinic maintained large equipment used by staff operating a therapeutic nursery. During the next sessions, he made use of a tricycle and wagon. He rode the tricycle around the treatment room and sometimes around the adjoining playground. He also asked me to give him rides in the wagon. As I pulled him around the playground John pretended I was a horse ("Giddy-up"). Embracing the fantasy, I tossed my head and snorted, doing my best to imitate a horse.

In one session, while riding in the wagon, John mentioned his father for the first time. "My father had a tractor. He wore a red jacket when he drove it." I was struck by this comment, so much so that I asked him several questions about his father, caught up with my eagerness to learn about other memories and to help John address father's death. As I encouraged him to tell me more, he climbed out of the wagon, clearly upset, saying it made him "sick" to talk about his father. For a few minutes I tried to provide support, commenting that I know it hurts a lot to think about his father, but I was interested in learning about him so I could help him with his sadness, anger, and confusion over losing him. However, it became clear that I had erred in asking questions. My inquiries had required John to share meanings about his father verbally and conceptually (second-order change), a process for which he was not yet prepared. John walked away, and for the rest of the session busied himself climbing a jungle gym, essentially ignoring me.

During the next sessions, John continued riding the tricycle, sometimes asking me to push him (as if he were a learner), and asked that I "play horse," pulling him in the wagon. I participated, making no further mention of his father. But John eventually referred to his father again in a very interesting symbolic way. John had been in my office frequently before each session to get his basket containing items we had been using. He must have noticed a rack of smoking pipes on a book-shelf. At the start of one session, he walked over to the pipes commenting, "My father smoked a pipe," and asked if he could "play with one." I indicated, "Of course." John took one, and with pipe in his mouth, he rode in the wagon urging the horse on, tugging at the "harness" with a little more exuberance than usual.

The Fifth Interactive Metaphor:
I'm Afraid of Losing What I Love and Can Now
Discuss My Father (17 sessions)

At the close of the last few sessions of the previous phase, John began to ritualize hiding from me. Outdoors, he crawled under a bush. In the treatment room, he crawled under a table. When I discovered him, he made various comments that conveyed what these enactments represented. "I'm not leaving." "I'm coming every day." "I'll sleep here, so I'll be here for my next appointment tomorrow." I crawled under the bush and table, sat next to him, attempted to reassure him, and made verbal interpretations (e.g., "When two guys become good friends, it's tough to say good-bye and not see each other." "It's scary to say good-bye because we can't be sure I'll be here for our next meeting"). I chose at this time not to literally con-nect the meaning of his enactments to his loss of father. In addition to these inter-pretations, to help John separate I gave him various transitional objects from my office to take home and return at our next meeting (a stone from my collection, a book). Sometimes fifteen minutes of negotiating were required before John left.

In addition, I introduced a structured interaction that I thought might help John cope with his separation anxiety and fear of loss and facilitate integrating our subjective worlds. I suggested that each of us draw a map of "where we live." John drew a map of his farm, and I of my residence. Then I suggested we draw floor plans of our houses. John readily complied and gradually included draw-ings of other structures on his farm such as sheds, a barn, a nearby pond, and the location of neighbors. As John added details, I asked various questions, as did he about my residence.

During the course of this activity he began sharing details about neighbors who live nearby, the location where he and neighborhood friends build their snow forts, the areas in which he usually takes walks. He doesn't know why, but he has become afraid of walking too far into the woods, "Like something might happen to me; like a wild animal might jump on me, or I might get shot." He also shared he had become afraid of riding the horse the family maintained, unlike his sister and brother. Of special significance, he eventually marked a spot on his map where father's tractor had tipped over. John offered that he often sits on this spot, think-ing about his father and the activities they shared, a number of which he described. I suggested he talk to his mother, brother, and sister about planting a tree there. John thought that was a good idea. We also planted a small evergreen bush in an area alongside the clinic.

We discussed his new sixth-grade teacher, a male, whom he indicated he liked very much, and his paternal grandfather, with whom he was now spending a good part of each weekend doing "odds and ends" around the farm. In this context, we discussed that while he missed his father very much, and no one could take his place, there are other men like his teacher and grandfather whom he could enjoy and learn from.

At one point John brought in the car model he had taken home at the start of treatment, which at that time was only partially constructed. It was now fully assembled, carefully painted, and covered with decals. John displayed the model with pride and offered it to me as a gift "to keep so you can remember us." I thanked him and offered him another model. He selected a battleship. I noted, "I'll bet you'll do a fantastic job putting this powerful ship together."

I understood John's giving me the model as a symbol that he had finally repaired his "go-cart" and had become "unstuck," wishes he had expressed during the evaluation. In the course of treatment he developed more flexibility in taking appropriate assertive action, worked through his repressed rage, stepped out of his shell, and eventually talked about the loss of his father. These gains, coupled with reports from mother and teacher (see below), indicated that John was on a more growth-fostering developmental path and was ready to terminate. John and I selected a date. We spent the last few meetings assembling parts of the battleship and talking about daily events. When he left, I said, "I know you'll do a good job with the rest of the battleship." With a grin, he responded, "You know it!"

Parent Conferences

At the start I extended an open invitation to Ms. G to let me know whenever she felt a conference could be of use. The following are highlights of two particular conferences. Ms. G asked for the first conference after twelve hours of treatment because John was beginning to tease his brother and sister in "quiet ways." Since the family had become accustomed to the withdrawn John, this change in behavior disrupted the family's typical rhythm of interacting. Mother understood the relationship between John's new behavior and the goals of treatment and was reassured. She recognized that the teasing was his first overt expression of assertiveness and that there would very likely be other forms as John continued working on this problem. We discussed that John needed opportunities to experiment with and express self-assertion and aggression in his day-to-day living. Should his expressions become for the family "too inappropriate," we should meet to discuss strategies. Ms. G concluded that John's teasing did not need any special disciplining.

About the time that John was riding a tricycle and I was pulling him in a wagon, mother asked for a conference to discuss her concern about John's asking her to kiss him. After father's death, John had never allowed her to cuddle or hold him. While mother joked, cuddled, and was affectionate with the other children, she had maintained an emotional distance from John. His new bid for affection made her uneasy. In a following meeting, which took place three weeks later, Ms. G gained some insight into this concern. She developed an understanding that she had tended to see John as a replica of her husband. From his early years, John looked a great deal like his father, an observation frequently expressed by relatives. Ms. G articulated intellectually (but also with some feeling) that she was anxious about expressing affection toward John because she thought it would put John in the position of "taking his father's place." As we discussed this, Ms. G understood that John had his own reasons for insulating himself from her, fearing that he had to be "the man in the house." She considered the possibility that while John felt alone, as did she, each of them could now construct a new relationship that would enable them to benefit from the affection they could express toward each other. Ms. G wondered if she should consider therapy for herself. As we explored this, she asked for and accepted a referral.

School Contact

Toward the close of treatment, I received a call from John's teacher to give me feedback about John's first weeks in the sixth grade. The teacher noted that John's academic performance was now about average, and that he was out of his shell, given his history of isolation. In the classroom John interacted with other children, and in the playground the teacher observed him playing "punchball" with other boys and enjoying himself. In addition, the teacher was struck by the fact that John has been joking a little with him, something he had been told John had never done with previous teachers. The teacher added that there were no special concerns at this point except that John was not yet showing "enough push" in completing his schoolwork. I indicated that this might be one of the last areas to respond and that his observations indicated John was gradually bringing to his everyday world a greater sense of involvement and interest and less inhibition and fear.

TEDDY: I'M TRAPPED IN A COLLAPSING CORE-SELF SO I ATTACK BEFORE ANYTHING HAPPENS

Teddy, a 9-year-old, was completing the third grade when referred for an evaluation at the school's insistence. The difficulties Teddy presented had been mounting since he started his schooling. Two weeks after he entered kindergarten his parents were informed that he was distractible and hyperactive and had difficulty coping with classroom routines. Moreover, he occasionally aggressed impulsively on materials, for instance, suddenly toppling blocks a classmate had assembled and crumpling a drawing a classmate was completing. His inattentiveness and aggressive behaviors continued into the first grade, when on two separate occasions he provoked physical fights with classmates. In the second grade his hyperactivity and impulsivity continued as well as his difficulty meeting academic demands; a program of tutoring was introduced.

During the third grade, his aggressiveness and impulsivity increased. Several episodes occurring prior to the referral prompted school personnel to insist that Teddy receive psychological treatment: Teddy had let air out of the tires of a faculty member's car in the school parking lot, and had dented the hubcaps by striking them with a large stone. When asked by the principal why he had committed this vandalism, Teddy shrugged, "I don't know," and showed no apparent anxiety or guilt. However, he did agree to contact the owner of the car and arrange to pay for damages. Teddy was also discovered by a teacher urinating on bushes alongside the school, and when a group of children at the back of the room burst out in laughter, the teacher turned to discover that Teddy was holding a ruler between his legs and moving it about as if it were a penis. Just before the referral was made, as an April fool joke, Teddy brought a jar of Vaseline to school and smeared the ointment on toilet seats.

On the basis of teacher reports, interviews with Teddy, and his performance of the Wechsler Intelligence Scale, the school psychologist diagnosed Teddy as suffering from an attention deficit disorder with hyperactivity as well as a conduct disorder, aggressive type.

Parent Intake Interview

Teddy's mother, a social worker, and father, a psychologist, were quite concerned about Teddy's poor academic performance and aggressive behavior, expressing considerable guilt over their failure as parents. Given that they were experienced mental health professionals, it is not surprising that they articulated their understanding of the origins of Teddy's difficulties. Four months after Teddy's birth, mother became seriously ill with cancer and required extensive medical treatment during the first three years of Teddy's life. When the diagnosis was first made, both parents were devastated, feeling that their newly launched marriage and the future they had anticipated with the joyful arrival of a son would be destroyed.

Mother acknowledged that once she learned of her illness, she slipped in and out of depressive moods, which she tried to battle, that lasted for more than two years. She frequently sobbed, sometimes in Teddy's presence, and "tuned out," staring out of windows for long periods of time. But she consciously struggled against her depressive moods, aware of research studies that documented how a mother's depression affected infant development. The parents decided at this time not to recruit a nanny to help with Teddy's care, believing it would be best if Teddy experienced each parent as much as possible during his first years. However, looking back at Teddy's first two years of life, the parents acknowledged, "It's all a blur," and recognized that Teddy had few sustained interactions with them until he was 4 years old.

By the time Teddy was a toddler, he preferred to engage in isolated play, rejecting mother's interactions (her illness by that time had gone into remission), and showed the first signs of impulsiveness. On one occasion, after father and Teddy constructed an elaborate structure with Tinkertoys, Teddy abruptly tore it apart. At that moment, father recalled, he experienced a surge of pleasure, rather than irritation or disapproval. From this recollection, the parents elaborated their formulations of Teddy's difficulties with regulating his aggression, relying upon insights they had constructed during their couples therapy sessions, which they had begun when Teddy was about 3 years old.

From their earliest years, each parent had been "a very good child," suppressing their anger and assertiveness and always doing exactly what parents wanted. When mother's cancer was diagnosed, instead of experiencing outrage over the fact that their new marriage and new son may have no future, the parents unwittingly permitted Teddy to be their voice of anger. From the time he began to crawl, they gave him free reign as he experimented with his own assertiveness. And they recalled deriving a sense of pleasure when he aggressed (e.g., tore up petunia plants alongside a neighbor's house).

The parents articulated another issue. Once mother's cancer was considered suppressed, they coped with their lingering depression and despair by "getting totally lost" in their professional work to fend off painful emotions. They wondered if Teddy's avoidance of schoolwork derived from his observing them constantly at their desks at home.

They concluded the interview by acknowledging that when Teddy began to experience difficulties in kindergarten, they held him "very close," believing that it was their responsibility to help Teddy overcome the effects of his first traumatic years. "We thought we should be able to fix things since we're both trained therapists." However, with Teddy's escalating antisocial behaviors during the first grade, it seemed clear that his difficulties had worsened and that they "must let Teddy go now, so he can get the help he needs from others." Apparently, the parents experienced the full impact of Teddy's difficulties when, about the time that he vandalized a teacher's car, he did something at home that disturbed them. Teddy had two hamsters. Mother had cautioned him always to make sure the cover was on the cage so that the family cat could not injure them. One evening Teddy apparently left the cover off deliberately. The next morning the hamsters were found dead, obviously mauled by the cat.

Teddy's Evaluation

Teddy was administered cognitive and personality tests by a team of two male examiners. While he engaged each in a playful manner, he regularly slipped into moments of impulsive, aggressive behavior. For instance, after completing an item of the Block Design Subtest of the Wechsler Scale, he quickly tossed the blocks into a nearby wastebasket, laughing that he was a professional basketball player. It was frequently necessary for each examiner to remind Teddy of limits and refocus him.

He obtained a Full Scale IQ of 113, falling in the bright-normal range. However, subtest scaled scores ranged from a low of 5 (Coding subtest) to a high of 15 (Information and Vocabulary subtests). When the subtests were clustered in terms of the intellectual processes involved, there was evidence of significant distractibility (Verbal Comprehension Mean = 13; Perceptual Organization Mean = 13; Freedom from Distractibility Mean = 7.3). This finding concurred with results of cognitive tests. Teddy scored at the seventh percentile with a procedure assessing the manner in which attention is focused on relevant information and withheld from irrelevant information (see Chapter 6). Lags were also observed with two other cognitive regulators: holding information in memory over time (twentieth percentile) and categorizing and conceptualizing information (twenty-fifth percentile). To illustrate the latter procedure, when asked to sort and group items that belong together for some reason, he formed groups reflecting global conceptual thinking and failed to articulate a salient feature that individual items shared. For example, he placed the following items in one group: real and toy silverware, a lock, two corks, two keys, a bicycle bell, and a piece of wood. When asked how these items belonged together, he responded, "They are things to use."

Teddy's responses to projective test stimuli indicated the extent to which he construed experiences in terms of conflict and aggression between two forces and that the anxiety associated with these metaphors was a major source of his distractibility. For example, in response to Card VI of the Rorschach test, he constructed an image of two submarines "crashing into each other." To Card X, he imaged "two armies" engaged in battle, each using a huge brick wall as a line of defense. The metaphor of cataclysmic violence was also expressed through stories constructed in response to pictures. For example, to Card 8 of the Michigan Pictures Test, he elaborated a story of lightning striking water with "a thousand volts of lighting energy," which electrocutes "the whole world." One guy who is struggling to swim to safety receives a shock and dies.

Significantly, with the Miniature Situations Test (see Chapter 6), the meanings he had produced in response to projective test stimuli did not gain expression in his associations. After each action, when asked what came to mind, he had nothing to share, saying "I can't think of anything. I'm just doing it." "I like anything with a lot of action." This performance suggested that Teddy's action mode was segregated from his fantasies and thoughts so that his actions formed an independent world, so to speak. On the few occasions when he did share, his associations concerned moments of interpersonal aggression. For instance, while sticking a dart in a dart board, he recalled sticking a dart in the arm of a friend when they were playing at his home.

One particular image Teddy constructed during the Rorschach test deserves separate attention. To Card VII, he rotated the card and described a "tunnel—It's quivering and rumbling—It's just about to fall down." Teddy became very engrossed in this image, taking pains to point to each of the black specks that border the periphery of the inkblot, which he construed as "bricks falling because the tunnel is shaking." The diagnosticians viewed this image as representing the effects exerted on the development of Teddy's body-self by the interpersonal/emotional climate he experienced during his first three years of life. At the deepest level, Teddy's core body-self lacked a sense of stability and groundedness, shaking and quivering and about to collapse.

The diagnosticians concluded that Teddy's cognition was struggling to equilibrate environmental demands and opportunities with metaphors whose calls for action prescribed aggression and anticipated destruction. As a result of this struggle, he had evolved a cognitive style that integrated several processes: one cognitive regulator remained in constant flight, shifting rapidly between stimuli of metaphors and those of environments; another maintained global images of information, avoiding salient features of environmental expectations; another conceptualized the relationships among stimuli in vague, overgeneralized terms in order to avoid their demands. In addition, the action mode had become segregated from thought and fantasy so that the latter did not serve as rehearsals for action, and so that the actions Teddy took did not provide feedback that could revise fantasies and thoughts. At the foundation of this configuration were body-image schemas Teddy had conserved from the first years of life, which derived from many unrepaired disruptions due to his mother's protracted illness and depression. These schemas represented his core, body-self as unstable, vulnerable, and at risk of collapsing. The diagnosticians understood Teddy's aggressive behaviors as stemming from this vulnerable core-self: "Attack before something happens." Moreover, his parents had not provided him with interactions that adequately negotiated self-assertion and aggression, leaving Teddy without the capacity to develop alternative means and goals of expression.

Teddy's Treatment

A female therapist provided treatment following developmental-dialectical guidelines. Treatment began during the last two months of the third grade at a frequency of two sessions per week and continued during the summer and throughout the fourth grade, ending at the start of fifth grade. Relying on the results of the diagnostic evaluation, the therapist elected to conduct treatment emphasizing structured interactions designed to reorganize Teddy's maladaptive cognitive regulators and to integrate Teddy's actions with his thoughts and fantasies. As we shall see, the therapist artfully designed a series of structured interactions that eventually helped Teddy bring his physical aggressiveness under control, resulting in his performing more effectively academically.

Phase I: Articulating and Translating Body Perceptions into Action Symbols (20 sessions)

The therapist began by asking Teddy to work on "two games" that would help his mind concentrate better with schoolwork. She elected not to mention the aggressive/antisocial episodes that had gotten him into difficulty, taking the position that she would relate to these issues when Teddy's behavior in the treatment sessions provided an opening. She explained that the games were like the tutoring he had received last year in reading and math, except that "these games will help your mind work better no matter what you are learning or doing." She then set a 4-foot by 6-foot rug in the center of the room, indicating that they would work on their games while sitting on the rug. With this detail, the therapist had in mind Teddy's Rorschach response that depicted his body-self as a quivering tunnel about to collapse. She speculated that by defining a geography she and Teddy consistently shared, the rug could become a symbol of a "solid, stable world" and help Teddy step into a dialectical circle. When the therapist sat on the rug, Teddy joined her without comment.

In one task, three "answer" buttons were placed in a cloth bag and one button (the stimulus) in another. Teddy's job was to feel the standard with his fingers and then the "answer" buttons, and select one that matched the standard, a task activating the cognitive process of field articulation involving touch perceptions. To increase the complexity of the task, over the course of these sessions the number of "answer" buttons was gradually increased to eight. In addition, the attributes of the buttons were gradually increased: various sizes, corrugated versus smooth edges, and number of holes.

For the second structured interaction, an item was placed in a cloth bag out of Teddy's view. He was asked to examine it with his hands without looking, describe its attributes, decide the category in which the item belonged, and then imagine and describe ways in which the item could be used. Last, he was to remove the object from the bag and enact the uses he had described.

As Teddy engaged each task, he quickly displayed his hyperactive, impulsive style and related to the therapist in a sarcastic, sometimes hostile tone. With the button task, for example, he initially shoved his fist in the bag, pulled out all the answer buttons, and selected one after looking them over. When attempting to select one by using touch perceptions only, if the button was incorrect, he flipped it across the room, laughing. At other times he hid the button, refusing to return it. Gradually, he took more time feeling the buttons with his fingertips, and eventually experienced some pride over the fact that he was "feeling through" six buttons and finding the correct one when at the start he had searched through only three.

In the second task he initially felt the object for only seconds and immediately labeled it without describing its attributes. In one instance, after touching a strainer, he declared, "It's a knight's helmet," and quickly placed it on his head. The categories and uses he described were dominated by the calls for action from his aggressive metaphors, representing violence toward persons, animals, and things. For example, upon feeling a nutcracker, he exclaimed, "You can flatten a mouse with it," and then paced about the room, squeezing and releasing the arms of the nutcracker. Feeling a sponge, he exclaimed, "You can wet it and throw it at someone's face," waving it in front of the therapist's face. At the close of one session, after rolling up the carpet on which they sat to work with their tasks, he spontaneously noted, "I can hit someone over the head with this," and proceeded to pound the rolled rug against a table.

On occasion, the therapist engaged Teddy in evaluating the fit between the attributes of the object at hand and his imagined use. For example, when Teddy declared that a pencil could be used to stab a pig, the therapist asked Teddy to stab the pencil into an inflated balloon and then into a ball of clay, engaging him in evaluating that it was unlikely a pencil could penetrate a pig's hide. And while the therapist agreed with Teddy that a toothbrush could clean a toilet, she scrubbed a bowl with the toothbrush, noting it would take a long time to scrub a toilet. Teddy's responses gradually suggested that he was assimilating the need to evaluate the match between attributes of an object and its imagined use. At one point he decided a 2-inch by 2-inch plastic container could hold pencils. When the therapist expressed doubt, noting the size of the container, Teddy reflected, "Well, they would have to be short ones."

Throughout this phase, Teddy elaborated his expressions of aggression. Once, spotting a fly on the window, he leaped up, seized a magazine, and smashed the fly with a tremendous blow. Looking at the stained window with glee, he commented that he had a dart gun at home that he used to "kill flies and bugs." In another instance, feeling a paper cup placed in a bag, he exclaimed, "You can punch someone with it," abruptly pulled the cup out, set it on the floor, and crushed it with a single, vicious slam of his clenched fist. On another occasion, the therapist had been sitting in a chair preparing items for their next structured interaction. When she stood up to search for an item, Teddy moved the chair away so that she nearly fell when trying to sit down. As Teddy roared with laughter, the therapist, annoyed, said, "It's OK this time, but you can't do that again." When discussing this moment with me, the therapist acknowledged that she could have provided Teddy with alternative ways of expressing aggression toward her person instead of presenting him with a prohibition. She had followed this view when Teddy crushed the fly with a magazine, inviting him to go outside to "hunt" bugs with a dart gun.

Apparently the therapist's efforts to contour her tempos and levels of stimulation with Teddy's proved successful. He eventually displayed behaviors indicating that he had stepped into a dialectical circle and was beginning to idealize the therapist. In one session he scratched his initials in the wax of a papercup, saying, "I'll keep it here for next time. Now I know it's mine." In another he brought cookies, pretzels, and soft drinks for him and the therapist to share. He arrived at another session joking that he had something hidden in his fist. When he opened it, he revealed a crystal paper weight. "This is special. I brought it for you. You can drill a hole in it and make a necklace." The therapist accepted it with pleasure and placed it on her desk. "Here we can both see it while we do our work."

In the last session of this phase, Teddy symbolically expressed a call for help. Expressing concern, he volunteered that his father had warned him not to go into a barn located on nearby property "because there's a big hole there, and I might fall in." He had gone into the barn and seen the large hole. "I heard that once a lady fell in and cracked her neck, and she died." The therapist commented that there are big holes everywhere that a person could fall into, especially now that he was starting a new grade, and she would help him figure out where the holes were so he would not fall in.

Teddy may well have been referring to "holes he had fallen into" upon starting school again after the summer recess. During music class, he burped loudly and gave a boy "the finger." On another occasion an intense argument with a classmate nearly culminated in a fist fight, and during math class he threw spitballs across the room. The therapist and parents were required to visit the school and confer with the principal. It was accepted that Teddy had just made a commitment to treatment, and while his recent behaviors were inappropriate, they were not as explicitly aggressive as those he had shown during the previous year.

Phase II: Holding Patterns of Ordered Information in Memory and Connecting Them to Fantasies (16 sessions)

At this juncture Teddy had made some gains regulating his impulsivity, articulating attributes of objects and fitting them with imagined uses, developing an alliance with the therapist, and showing a readiness to share aspects of his subjective world. The therapist decided to introduce a new, structured interaction. The task was designed to promote the growth of another cognitive regulator that the evaluation revealed was dysfunctional: holding patterns of information in memory over time. The task was also designed to help Teddy elaborate fantasies that were organized by patterns of physical stimuli. At the start of this phase the buttons game was eliminated, and the task involving feeling objects and describing imagined uses was phased out after several sessions.

Recalling that Teddy had shared that he had trouble remembering what the teacher discussed in class, the therapist explained that they could play another game that would improve his ability to remember. The therapist placed six colored, geometric cutouts on a table arranged in a 2x3 matrix and asked Teddy to study it. Then the therapist placed a cloth over the matrix, exchanged the position of two cutouts, removed the cloth, and asked Teddy if anything changed. He studied the matrix, quickly became frustrated and angry, and walked away, mumbling, "I don't want to do that stupid game." In response, the therapist pointed out that there is "a trick" to remembering the pattern. If he imagined that the pattern of cutouts "made something," it would be easier to remember it. Teddy tried again, and when asked what the new display could be, he responded "a teddy bear." "There's his red eyes and this is his yellow nose." When the cloth was removed, Teddy was able to detect the change the therapist had introduced and was quite pleased with his achievement. With this he became enthusiastic about participating in the new game.

As the sessions unfolded, the therapist increased the complexity of the matrices to be remembered by gradually increasing the number of cutouts from six to twenty-five, the sizes of the cutouts from one to three, the shapes from two to four, and the colors from two to six. Teddy was usually quick to offer an image of what the pattern reminded him of. Initially his images were relatively global, as reflected by his first "teddy bear." He construed other matrices as "a sun," "a chair," and "a ladder." As the number of cutouts increased, his images became more differentiated and animated. He construed one matrix as "space station Delta, these are the scanners," another as "a person waving flags at a car race," another as "a cheerleader holding pom-poms and jumping in the air," and another as "a man throwing a discus in Olympic games."

To encourage reciprocating, the therapist offered to study a matrix Teddy constructed. Teddy could then compare what she imagined it to be with what he had in mind. In one example, Teddy guessed the therapist imagined a truck, which was correct. In another, Teddy guessed the therapist imagined a garden hose, but the therapist had imagined a train.

Phase III: Holding Patterns of Disordered Information in Memory and Connecting Them to Fantasies (10 sessions)

As Teddy constructed more differentiated images, the therapist revised their structured interactions, now placing the cutouts in random arrays instead of in ordered rows. The task remained the same: remembering the pattern formed by the cutouts in order to detect changes. Again, the first arrays contained few cutouts (four) and gradually more (ten). Now, responding to cutouts arrayed randomly, Teddy's images increasingly represented aggressive and cataclysmic events associated with body instability. He imaged one matrix as a "smasher," another as a "roller coaster," and another as a "truck with cargo falling out of the back and things flying all around." On occasion, Teddy spontaneously volunteered more than one image for an array of cutouts, suggesting an increase in cognitive flexibility. Several of these represented a loss of body integrity and stability followed by an image of restitution. With one array he imaged an Iron Maiden. "It's a room with spikes on the wall that move in. This guy is in the Iron Maiden, and he's trying to push the walls back." Then he offered, "Or it could be two chickens with a fence around them to keep foxes away." To another array he constructed the image of "a cluster of comets crashing into each other and a black hole . . . all the things are getting sucked into it." Then, "Or it could be a big truck with headlights, windshield, flag, and wheels. Nothing could beat that."

During this phase, Teddy again displayed behaviors suggesting he was idealizing and internalizing the therapist. At one point Teddy began to hold a cutout (a large blue diamond) in his hand throughout most of the session. Sometimes he tossed it up and caught it, and sometimes he placed it under his belt. Soon he ritualized its use, placing it within the array they were working with. The therapist and Teddy referred to this cutout as "the shape of the day." On one occasion he showed the therapist a multiplication worksheet, noting with pride that he had received a grade of 100, which is "just like the shapes I remember." On another, he looked up at the skylight, commenting, "That's cool. It looks like two suns. This is a great room. It would be great to sleep here."

In the latter sessions of this phase, while studying arrays and imaging what they could represent, Teddy began to strike one cutout against another, at first tapping them lightly and then with force. Sometimes he pushed cutouts off the table onto the floor. In response, the therapist decided to incorporate action into the task, which ushered in the next phase.

Phase IV: Organizing and Translating Images of Chaos, Deprivation, and Loss into Action Symbols (32 sessions)

The therapist suggested they play their memory game in a new way, introducing an elaboration in technique that encouraged Teddy to organize and enact metaphors. Teddy selected a number of geometric cutouts from a box, stood in the center of the room, and with arms extended dropped the cutouts to the floor. Then, as with the previous task, he studied the pattern the cutouts formed, described "a picture" the pattern suggested, and attempted to detect the change introduced by the therapist. In an elaboration of this technique, Teddy made up and enacted a story based on the scene he had imagined, inviting the therapist to participate. He responded with enthusiasm. It is worth noting that Teddy began by dropping ten cutouts and gradually increased the number to twenty.

The images and stories Teddy constructed and enacted over the course of these sessions clustered around four metaphors, each of which appeared to represent an aspect of the disruptions he experienced during the first three or four years of his life: cataclysmic events, intense need for nurture, body-self instability, and loss. Eventually Teddy represented and addressed his mother's cancer directly. During this phase, he authored and enacted more than 100 fantasies rooted in the organizations the cutouts formed. Space does not permit me to describe each one, nor to trace the sequence of metaphors during one session or from session to session. However, in general, Teddy's interactive metaphors represented cataclysmic events, followed by a need for nurture. The emphasis shifted again to the body-self as unstable and then to loss, which was accompanied by resistance. With each interactive metaphor, I describe the image Teddy constructed when examining a pattern of cutouts he had dropped to the floor, the story he constructed stimulated by the image, and aspects of the enactment that appear noteworthy. I have omitted reporting whether or not Teddy was successful in detecting changes the therapist introduced into a pattern of cutouts after Teddy told his story and before enacting it.

Interactive Metaphors Representing Cataclysmic Events

Examining one pattern, Teddy imaged, "These are houses, streetlights, shopping bags, flying all over, a roof is flying off a house," and narrated the following: "A quiet village and the moon is shining. A lady was going into her house carrying shopping bags. She sees a spiral coming at her. It's a tornado. She tried to get into the house, but the tornado went through a crack in the basement. Her grocery bags were thrown all over." While telling this story, Teddy "absentmindedly" performed a symbolic action. He took two plastic objects with metal pieces on the inside and pulled and pried at the metal until it came off.

To another pattern, he imaged, "A nuclear weapon, with generators and control panel," and narrated, "The Russians have decided to have a nuclear war. Then the scanner beeps, and the American pushes the fire button. It blows up over the ocean, so nothing gets hurt except the fish. It aims right at the station, and a guy yells, 'Get out of here. Everything is all over the place.'"

At one point Teddy studied a pattern of cutouts and imaged "a research center. There's the entrance." In contrast to his typical spontaneous performance, this time he did not begin a narrative, but remained silent, seemingly lost in thought. When the therapist asked him to share what he was thinking, Teddy, obviously irritated, blurted, "The entire place blows up! That's my story!" Then he looked at his watch and noted the time (nearly 4:00 P.M.). The therapist recalled to herself that father worked in a "research center" before meeting with clients in his office at home but decided not to connect Teddy's image with father's place of employment. Instead, she commented, "Somebody must be furious if the whole place blows up," and, referring to previous enactments, "Like that lady in the tornado." "We ought to find out what the tornado is mad about." Over several sessions the therapist reflected her interest in learning why so many tornadoes and nuclear explosions were occurring. Gradually, the emphasis of Teddy's metaphors shifted to the need for nurture.

Interactive Metaphors Representing Deprivation and the Need for Nurture

Studying a pattern of cutouts, Teddy imaged, "A glass filled with wine and fruit and bubbles coming down the side," then narrated, "It's a feast. There's a horn of plenty on the table. It's New Year's Eve, and someone is raising a glass to make a toast." Teddy made several popping sounds with his mouth to mimic corks being pulled from bottles. He also took a paper cup, handed another to the therapist, and pretended to drink, "Happy New Year!" Sometime later, a buzzer from Teddy's wristwatch sounded. He explained that he had set it to go off at 4 P.M. Again the therapist elected not to comment, although she noticed that Teddy had become more focused on that time of day in recent sessions.

With another pattern, Teddy imaged, "A sundae with ice cream and a cherry on the top. The bottom stem part of the glass snapped, and the ice cream is spilling out." His story included, "It's this kid's birthday party, and he's eating ice cream in a restaurant with his friends. He says, 'What's that?' When he whirls around, his elbow knocks the ice cream over, and it spills onto the floor. He's really embarrassed. His friends go to the owners for a mop to clean it up."

When enacting this narrative, Teddy took the part of the birthday kid and assigned the therapist the role of the friend. The therapist began to mop up the ice cream when Teddy offered that he would clean it up. The therapist tossed the mop to Teddy who "mushed" the mop around, making a big mess. The manager shouted to them to get out, and they departed.

Another image included "a deer, his tongue is hanging out because he's hungry." To this image, Teddy narrated, "The deer was walking in a forest, and he meets another deer and says, 'Where's the nearest place to get a hamburger?' The other deer is surprised but answers, 'I think there's a hamburger stand over there.' The deer goes to the stand and orders a hamburger. The man gives him one, and the deer knocks over the bottles of catsup and relish. He walks away with the hamburger. The man shouts, 'You have to pay for that!' The deer goes back to his friend and says, 'These are mighty good hamburgers.' His friend goes to get a hamburger too. But the man at the stand says, 'No way, deer don't pay for hamburgers.'"

When enacting this episode, Teddy assigned himself the role of the deer and the therapist the role of the other deer and the man. Teddy was most vigorous when enacting knocking over the bottles of catsup and relish.

Glancing at another array of cutouts on the floor, Teddy began to spin in his chair, describing the image of a boy at a ski lodge. Then he told the following story, "The boy sees a sign, 'Eat Your Weight and Get Free Pizza.' If you eat 75 pounds, you get 75 pounds of free pizza to take home." While pretending he was gorging himself with pizza, Teddy commented, "I weigh 75 pounds."

Interactive Metaphors Representing Loss and the Emergence of Resistance

Teddy imaged "a dog, these are his feet, body, spiky tail, and head. It's a German shepherd," and narrated "I had a German shepherd. His name was Tut. He used to go chasing after our cat. The cat would go shooting off into the woods, and Tut chased after her. The cat left us [*long pause*]. I don't know why." As he turned to enact this scene, he paused, withdrew, and commented that he did not "feel like playing this one."

When the next set of cutouts was dropped to the floor, Teddy took an uncharacteristically long pause, imaged "a turtle," very likely representing a protective shell that he had wrapped around himself. "There's his head, feet, and tail." After looking at the display for a minute or two, he complained that he was not in the mood for a story. The therapist responded that they could skip the story and playacting and invited Teddy to decide what he wanted to do. Teddy moved about the room, occasionally staring out the window.

In the next session the resistance became more explicit. In response to an array of cutouts, he constructed the image of a sailboat, but again indicated that he did not want to tell a story. "Why do we have to do stories?" Soon Teddy provided a clue, suggesting that the metaphor about the cat that failed to return, preceded by others concerning the need for nurture, had resulted in a wave of resistance. After Teddy declined to tell a story, he took the cutouts that he had imaged as a sailboat and stacked them, saying, "It's a double cheeseburger." Laughing, he playacted biting into it and pretended that he lost a tooth because the hamburger "was too big to bite." He looked at his watch, then took the therapist's pencil and pulled the eraser off. Then he pressed the point of the pencil against the table until it broke off. The therapist commented, "The pencil lost its eraser and point, and the kid lost his tooth trying to eat the big hamburger. Everything seems to be getting lost. That's hard to take." Teddy did not respond but took a long look at the therapist.

In the next sessions Teddy constructed several interactive metaphors that represented nearly literally the threat of mother being lost, but also included a positive solution. These interactions resolved Teddy's resistance and resulted in a shift away from the metaphor of loss. Of note, Teddy looked at his watch more often. In one session, when his watch beeped again at 4 P.M., he shared its meaning. "My father is home now in his office. He sees clients beginning at 4." In the following weeks, Teddy's watch beeped regularly at 4 P.M., and each time he commented, "My father is home now." The therapist made no comment and viewed these enactments as symbolically reassuring Teddy of his father's availability, as Teddy gave more explicit expression to loss.

As one example, Teddy imaged, "A man is leaning against a pole near the water. He can see his reflection in the water." Then he narrated, "The man's wife is very sick, or she's going away, and he is very depressed about it. After looking in the water for a while, he goes to a bar. Then he drinks quite a lot. He gets in the car. He's in an accident, and an ambulance takes him to the hospital. His wife visits him and asks him what happened. He tells her he was depressed that she is going away. She says, 'Don't worry, I'm not going away. Let's go home.'" In this enactment Teddy played the role of both the husband and the wife. The hour came to a close, and Teddy picked up the box of cutouts to put them away. As he walked over to the cupboard, the box "slipped" out of his hands, and about fifty cutouts scattered over the floor. Without comment, Teddy assisted the therapist in picking them up. This "slip" of the action mode seemed to add to the meaning of the metaphor concerning the wife who was "going away"—that the world fell apart. In the next sessions the content of Teddy's metaphors shifted toward expressing the body-self as unstable and not grounded.

Interactive Metaphors Representing the Body-Self as
Unstable and Not Grounded

Teddy imaged, "Acrobats, guys, these are arms and hands, here's the ground, one acrobat is bending over, and the other guy is climbing on the top of him." His story continued, "A ringmaster at a circus is announcing that everyone come and watch the great acrobats. But this is embarrassing. One guy climbs to the top and starts to wobble. The bottom guy collapses and they all lose their balance." When enacting this story, Teddy chose to be the acrobats and assigned the therapist the role of ringmaster and audience. He was very active, hurling himself about the room when falling.

To another pattern, Teddy imaged that "a guy made of steel is on a balance beam," and narrated, "A kid is playing with a toy of a guy made out of steel. The guy is called 'the balancer.' The kid puts the toy on a shelf, but he doesn't put it up there carefully enough. The toy falls off, and a dog comes along and chews it up." Assigning himself the role of the dog, Teddy growled ferociously at the therapist, who was assigned the role of the balancer that toppled to the floor.

In addition to images and enactments of imbalance, others represented loss of control. For example, Teddy imaged "a scooter with handlebars, wheels, and a thing you step on," and narrated, "This guy went off a jump on his scooter, and he falls off, but the scooter keeps going down the road. It's totally out of control and crashes and gets stuck in the rocks." When enacting this scene, Teddy moved across the floor, pushing his right leg as if he were on a scooter, then gleefully tumbling to the floor. He assigned no role to the therapist.

In the session following the scooter episode, Teddy introduced for the first time his concerns about his health and mother's. Upon entering the playroom, he engaged the therapist in a discussion of his "bad cold" (his physical appearance did not suggest he had a cold). Then he commented, "You know AIDS is the new plague," and anxiously discussed at length a TV program he had seen about AIDS. He concluded by reassuring himself, "I'm not worried about getting it because I'm just a kid." Again he changed the direction of their conversation. "My mom is on a macrobiotic diet." While describing mother's diet in detail, he did not mention her cancer. Again, as if to manage his anxiety he commented, "Do you know I haven't been absent from school one day this year or last year?"

At this point the therapist took out the box of cutouts. Teddy complained, "This game is boring. Can't we start doing something else?" The therapist interpreted, "Something is going on inside of you that is saying, 'Wait, hold back.'" Responding with a quiet, "I don't know," Teddy took a number of cutouts from the box. The metaphors Teddy constructed subsequently gave some hint as to why he was holding back. Because these metaphors followed his comments about AIDS and his mother's diet, they could be viewed as representing some of the ways his mind had construed the impact of mother's illness.

Teddy tossed ten cutouts to the floor, studied the pattern, and said, "It's a train. Here's the wheels and the body and a smokestack," and immediately began constructing a story. "There's a rumor that Abe Lincoln's ghost train still rides." Then he paused, looked at the pattern of cutouts for several minutes and mumbled, "It's just a normal train, and there isn't much to say about it. . . . I'm having trouble thinking of a story." The therapist reassured him that it was not necessary to tell a story for every pattern, and that perhaps a story would occur to him while he examined the next array.

Teddy dropped another set of cutouts, examined the array—"It's the inside of a plane"—and immediately began his story. "This plane was flying along and then hit some turbulence. The money cart and the drink cart rolled around and crashed. The plane is going up and down. Now the food comes out and crashes. Two guys fall down, and there's food all over the place. One guy gets a pie in his face. He yells at the stewardess. She says, 'I can't help it.' The stewardess mops up the mess. Now the plane is out of the turbulence, and they are safe." The therapist thought to herself that Teddy and father hit turbulence when mother became ill, and they were the two figures whose supply of nurture was spilled; but she made no comment.

After enacting the plane episode by rocking and swinging in his chair, Teddy tossed another set of cutouts. "This looks like a statue of a skier balancing on a triangular stand. It's the middle of the night. A cat is walking around the house and jumps up on the piano keys and makes noise. This kid wakes up and goes downstairs and sees the cat. He chases the cat. The cat jumps on a shelf and knocks the skier statue over. It breaks on the floor. The kid throws it in the garbage. When the kid wakes up, he takes the statue out of the garbage, and his father fixes it for him. But it's not as good as it was, but it's okay."

Before the next session, the therapist received a phone call. The day after the previous session, Teddy was discovered by a teacher urinating on a bush alongside the school building, something he had not done since the start of treatment. The principal notified the parents that if the behavior occurred again, Teddy would be suspended. The therapist told the principal and parents that Teddy's behavior was best understood in terms of developments taking place in therapy—that he had made reference to his mother's illness for the first time and was expressing representations of disruptions her illness caused.

When Teddy arrived for the next session, he made no mention of the incident at school and immediately engaged in the structured task. After tossing a set of cutouts, he imaged "a military base with radar and canons" and told a story of a new bomb being tested in the desert. The bomb exploded and "made a hole in the ground almost to the center of the earth." The camp was destroyed, lava covered the earth, and everyone is "scared to death." The earth gets "very cold" after the lava cools. "Only a few people live to tell the tale, namely, me."

This metaphor (fantasy) seemed to summarize how the previous enactments represented the ways in which Teddy's mind construed mother's illness and depression and the many disruptions and heightened traumatic emotional moments that resulted. Teddy's world was torn asunder at its core. He was terrified, surrounded by a cold emotional environment, but he survived. At this point the theme of his metaphors shifted to socializing his aggression.

Phase V: Conquering Urges that Prescribe Unsocialized Aggression (22 sessions)

The content and form of Teddy's narratives took a turn. In the weeks that followed he spontaneously constructed a series of images, each one a continuation and elaboration of the last. As Teddy dropped each set of shapes, imaged a scene, told a story, and enacted, the sequence of activity he produced was very much like the continuous flow of fantasy play one observes in a nondirected format. Because he produced more then forty images and narratives, for convenience I summarize the characters and plots, which, as it turns out, concerned "evil" trying to capture and control "good."

A "Bully" constantly pursued a Boy on foot and with various vehicles. They battled on land, sea, and in the air. During these pursuits, the Bully invented and used a number of weapons (tank, tranquilizing gun, special suit of armor, jet plane). In each episode the Boy struggled to escape from being captured. The Bully "works out in a gym to lose weight so he can run faster and catch the kid." But the Boy took karate lessons so he can defend himself. Soon the police joined in battling the Bully, who has done a number of "bad things like break a church window."

On occasion, Teddy spontaneously represented his conflict between good and evil in enactments with the therapist. In one instance, as he left an appointment, he squatted behind a railing of a stairwell. Laughing, with his face pressed against the "bars," he exclaimed, "I'm in jail! Let me out of here!" On another occasion, after Teddy had constructed one of his stories, the therapist asked, "What part should I play?" Teddy replied, "I'll be the bully," a role he had usually assigned himself. Then pausing, "No, I'll get in trouble a lot. You be the bully. I'll be the kid." Eventually, Teddy also assigned himself the role of the police.

At one point, the Boy, assisted by the police, captured a tank the Bully had invented. The Boy aimed all of the missiles, grenades, and tranquilizing bullets at the Bully and subdued him. The Bully was finally captured and placed in a "coffin." For this achievement the Boy was awarded " the first Nobel prize for getting rid of the bully." Teddy added, "When the kid gets older, he writes a book about how he got out of being caught by the bully. It sold many copies."

From a psychodynamic view, the boy represented the executive functions of the ego battling the influences of aggressive urges (the bully) that are attempting to capture him. And the police represented rules (superego). That Teddy was resolving his conflict between good and evil forces and gaining control over his aggressive urges is illustrated by one of the interactive metaphors he authored after the bully was conquered. He imaged one array of cutouts as representing a man who "makes a mistake" repairing an engine in a factory. When the engine is turned on, it explodes. The man "apologizes to everyone" and helps rebuild the engine. After enacting this story, Teddy spontaneously offered, "A few years ago, I made a stupid mistake." He shared that he had thrown rocks at the windows of a garage located in his neighborhood. A few sessions later, he also shared that "a kid in school is selling firecrackers," and expressed the view, "That's stupid; he's definitely going to get in trouble."

Phase VI: I Become a New Person and Can Discuss My Mother's Cancer (15 sessions)

After the bully was conquered, Teddy's metaphors shifted again, now representing that his "personality" was being constructed anew. As one example, he imaged "a house, chimney, windows, and a wide front door," and narrated, "There's a new master plan to make a house like it's never been made before. It has solar energy, built-in computers, and a generator in the basement that will work for years and years . . . outside it looks like a normal house, but inside it's a house of the future." In another instance he imaged "a new riding machine for kids called 'The Hopper,'" and narrated that "kids could go as high as they want with this machine." In another session he imaged "a guy balancing on a chair on the top of a mountain" and narrated that this person "set a world record for balancing twenty-four hours . . . he gets a trophy." And in another he imaged "a machine that changes weather."

Then in one session, Teddy spontaneously drew attention directly to his mother's cancer for the first time, reflecting the gains he had made negotiating his body-self instability, need for nurture, and loss. He requested, "Let's make it a real challenge for me today. Let's drop twenty shapes." In previous sessions he had been dropping twelve. "And you can change four things instead of two." The therapist had been exchanging the position of two cutouts after Teddy developed his narratives. The therapist commented that twenty cutouts to remember and four changes to detect were indeed a challenge.

Teddy dropped the cutouts to the floor, studied the array, and imaged a wide variety of food items. Then he narrated, "A guy starts to eat dinner, but all at once the food gets up and scrambles away. The meat goes to the cat. The potatoes go to the dog, and the mice get the rest." Before the therapist introduced changes in the array, Teddy spontaneously commented, "My mother has cancer, but she eats natural food. Natural food keeps you healthy," and continued with another discussion of organic foods. Rather than engaging Teddy in a direct discussion of mother's cancer, the therapist decided to wait for further information from images he might construct. The therapist said only, "I'd like to learn more about cancer and organic food," and asked Teddy if he wanted to drop another set of cutouts. He did, and imaged "a car going downhill backwards," narrating, "A car backs out of the driveway. There's no brake fluid . . . the car rolls down a hill backwards . . . the car is getting near train tracks . . . a train is coming . . . but the last car of the train goes by just as the car crosses the tracks . . . the train just nicks the car." The therapist noticed that Teddy bit his fingernails while telling this story, behavior that was not typical for him. Teddy spontaneously elaborated his story. "So this won't happen again the police spread cigarette butts on the road that have special power to slow down cars. And they stop AIDS too." Parenthetically, Teddy's mother had smoked prior to her illness. In the sessions that followed, Teddy engaged the therapist in detailed discussions of macrobiotic foods and cancer, emphasizing that "you can't catch cancer like you can the AIDS virus."

At this point, with the school year ending, Teddy focused on the summer camp he would be attending. The school had reported to parents that Teddy had shown more enthusiasm with academics, and for the next year had been moved to the highest reading group. They also noted that he had not displayed any aggressive behaviors during the past months.

Phase VII: I Have Learned To Fly (8 sessions)

Treatment resumed in the fall when Teddy entered the fifth grade. In the first session, while he greeted the therapist warmly, he announced that he would like to stop meeting. The therapist negotiated that they meet a few times "to see how things are going" and invited Teddy to decide when he wanted to stop. Teddy chose a date that allowed eight sessions before termination. Because he actively engaged the therapist in various discussions, she did not introduce the structured interactions. Teddy described experiences at summer camp and with his new teachers and school subjects. He especially liked science. In a recent class, watching a National Geographic's film, he learned that baby owls, although they have not yet learned to fly, sometimes fly after their mothers. "So they fall a thousand feet. But they are OK." He elaborated that in the past he has dreamed that he is falling, but now when he has this dream, " I put my feet out and land okay." The film also showed "monkey experiments" that "made me sad to see what they do to them." A baby monkey had been placed with "a fake mother" (a terrycloth doll), "and when he wanted to get some milk he couldn't." Other discussions focused on current behaviors, reflecting the gains he had made regulating and socializing his aggression and his new interest in responding to rules. For example, he and his friends built fires in the backyard, but they obtained permission from parents. They were careful to dig a hole first and build the fire away from trees and grass.

During these conversations, the therapist made several connections between Teddy's discussions and the interactive metaphors they had shared; for example, when Teddy's mother was ill with cancer, his food walked away, and like the monkey, he could not get the milk he needed; because his mother was too sick, he felt like he was falling, but he is like the man who won a trophy for balancing on a mountaintop for twenty-four hours, and he can land on his feet if he falls; and that he and his friends were not like the bully who tried to capture the kid and make him do bad things, but were careful where they built fires. During the last two sessions, Teddy occupied himself with building towers with Cuisenaire rods, showing considerable patience and expressing pride when the towers remained upright. The therapist commented, "They don't fall because you've built a good foundation under them," and "Because you can build such good towers now, you're right, we don't have to meet anymore." In the last session, Teddy announced with excitement that his parents had given him two new gerbils, and that he was going to take saxophone lessons. He asked the therapist if he could have the large blue diamond cutout he had often held during his structured interactions as "a souvenir." The therapist was pleased to give it to him.

LAURA: LOST IN THE DEEPEST REACHES OF INNER SPACE

Laura was 7½ years old and in second grade when referred by her parents at the urging of school personnel. From the start of the school year she had been tuned out, struggled to complete her work, and constantly needed to be refocused, behavior she had shown during the first grade. She was essentially a nonreader in spite of considerable assistance provided by a teacher's aide. In addition, she had not developed friendships with peers and tended to remain withdrawn in the playground and hallways with one exception: as second grade got under way, she was observed frequently interacting with kindergartners. Because of her inadequate academic performance, she was assigned to a special needs class where, during the past month, she had been spending the entire day. Because she seemed "dreamy" and lost in her private world, the special education staff wondered about the possibility of a latent psychosis.

Parent Intake Interview

Mother, a computer programmer, and father, a bank teller, were particularly confused by Laura's difficulty in handling schoolwork because from her early years she showed "exceptional intellectual ability." For example, Laura's aunt (father's sister), who cared for her while both parents worked, constantly read her stories. By the time Laura was about 3 years old, she seemed to "memorize" the stories. In the evening, when parents read to Laura from the same storybooks, she spontaneously "read" the words under the pictures, apparently having memorized them. Mother added that she "tutored" Laura in math almost every night, "because math concepts and skills are basic to everything." Father joined in, recalling with pride how great Laura was with numbers and shared that he, too, helped tutor Laura in math "to exercise her brain." With obvious pride they noted that by the time Laura was 4 years old she could count to 100 and correctly perform simple addition problems using wooden blocks. When the interviewer asked about the school's view that Laura seemed "dreamy," the parents acknowledged that as a toddler, Laura sat "for hours, talking to her dolls." They viewed their tutoring her as offsetting this "spacey" quality.

The parents spontaneously introduced another issue concerning Laura's brother, who was two years younger. Shortly after his birth he developed pneumonia several times and required hospitalization. As a result, the emotional atmosphere at home was very tense. The parents could not recall how Laura responded at this time, except to note that she was "quiet and stayed to herself." When Laura turned 3 years old, she was enrolled in a preschool. Soon the parents began to hear from teachers that Laura preferred to be alone, actively avoiding interacting with other children, behaviors that were mentioned during the next school years.

Laura's Evaluation

Laura was evaluated by a team of clinical psychologists (a female and a male) who met with her individually over several weeks. Although each examiner presented different personality styles, each experienced Laura in about the same way. She moved about the examining room often, but her tempo was slow and graceful, as if she were "drifting" through space. Each examiner had to refocus her in order to complete the testing, which therefore required several weeks.

On the Wechsler Scale of Intelligence, Laura attained a Full Scale IQ of 102 (average range). However, subtest scores ranged from a low of 7 (Coding Subtest) to a high of 13 (Similarities Subtest), suggesting that she was brighter than her average IQ indicated and that her intellectual efficiency was compromised. Her performance with a reading test (fifth percentile) reflected a significant lag, coinciding with the school's view that she was essentially a nonreader.

The results of tests assessing cognitive regulators (Chapter 6) indicated moderate to significant lags and an inner cognitive orientation. The breadth and vigor of her visual scanning fell at the forty-fifth percentile when the information surveyed did not activate fantasies, but at the eighteenth percentile when surveying information that aroused fantasies/emotions associated with nurture, and at the seventh percentile when surveying information that aroused fantasies/emotions associated with aggression. Her ability to focus attention on information surrounded by distracting pictures that evoked fantasies fell at the twentieth percentile, along with her performance holding images of information in memory. These findings reflected the extent to which personal fantasies commanded her attention to the exclusion of external stimulation. In addition, with structured tasks she was more agitated and obviously stressed, reflecting an inner cognitive orientation.

The metaphors Laura constructed in response to projective tests did not support the possibility of a latent psychosis and provided some information about the fantasies that commanded most of her attention. In contrast to her anxious behavior when dealing with structured tests, Laura was more relaxed and easily produced elaborate responses that sometimes took considerable liberties, given the stimulus at hand. With one theme, Laura represented that she must aggressively compete with her younger brother for nurture. For example, to Card II of the Rorschach test she imaged two wolves "fighting with each other because they want the same thing—a candy bar . . . the birds at the top are saying stop fighting and split it up." Similarly, to Card III she imaged two "skeletons running after the same bow." Then two angels appear and "order them" to share the bow. Several of her stories to the Michigan Pictures Test elaborated the metaphor of nurture. One involved people who have "no food—they have to eat peanut butter and jelly." Another described two children who "can't find a place to have a picnic." And another depicted a girl who apologizes to her father because she hit her sister who got more to eat.

The second metaphor represented the environment as dangerous and angry and Laura as either alone, trapped, or stuck and in need of being rescued. For example, to Card IX of the Rorschach test she imaged a butterfly trying to fly away from a raging fire. Similarly, to Card X she imaged animals caught in a fire and angels trying to save them. Card V resulted in an image of two crocodiles stuck in mud. The metaphor of being in danger and anger was also elaborated by Laura's stories to the Michigan Pictures Test. Themes included a girl lost in the dark, and a girl who is alone and upset because the school assignment she worked hard to complete was "ripped up."

The test results were discussed with Laura's parents, who accepted the recommendation for treatment. The diagnosticians and therapist (a female) also met with Laura to discuss the results and recommendation. Since Laura was fantasy-oriented, they used images she had constructed to point out that the therapist would help her figure out how to "split things up" with others yet get her own needs met, and how to get unstuck and fly out of the fire so she can finish her schoolwork.

Laura's Treatment

Laura's therapist formulated a treatment plan following the developmental-dialectical guidelines. Given Laura's inner cognitive orientation, structured interactions initially would emphasize helping Laura step into a dialectical circle and construct and organize highly personal meanings that dominated her subjective world. Once this was accomplished, structured interactions would emphasize helping Laura construct more conventional symbols and meanings, extending her personal world into the environment. Last, treatment would shift to a more unstructured process, providing Laura with opportunities to revise pathological metaphors. Laura's treatment program consisted of two sessions per week. Her therapist summarized the treatment in terms of three phases.

Helping Laura Step into a Dialectical Circle (4 sessions)

When the therapist greeted Laura in the first session, Laura returned the greeting with a quiet but firm, "No talking; I'm not here to talk." Laura drifted about the playroom with the same "floating" movements she had shown during the evaluation, scanning materials but touching nothing. Looking back at this first session, the therapist acknowledged that she became too eager to help Laura step into a dialectical circle, introducing several structured tasks in the hopes that one of them would serve as a handrail. The therapist set a matrix of cutouts on a table and asked Laura to study it and then detect whether the therapist had introduced a change. With another task the therapist set two rods of different heights as targets and invited Laura to shoot darts at one of them, hoping that eventually the shorter rod would come to represent brother and the taller one Laura. But she engaged each of these tasks for only seconds and walked away.

In the next session, Laura suggested why she was reluctant to enter a dialectical circle, and how she was construing the therapist and her activities. The therapist introduced a "search and find" game that involved touch perception. Several items were placed in one small pillow case and a single item in another. Laura was asked to examine the single item ("It's all alone") and then search through the "family bag" to find "someone from the same family it could belong to." Items Laura examined as standards included a cloth napkin, latex glove, and piece of steel wool, and she found the related family member of each without too much difficulty.

At one point the therapist located a spoon in the "alone bag." Laura rummaged through the "family bag." When she could not find an item related to the spoon, she anxiously asked, "If I get an answer wrong, will you give me time-outs like my teacher does . . . do you think that means I'm stupid?" With this she seemed to reveal why she was avoiding stepping into a circle.

The therapist recalled that, during a previous school conference, the teacher had shared that whenever Laura spent too much time wandering around the classroom, she was given a "time-out" (sitting at a table in the front row). The teacher acknowledged that this was a "desperate effort" to help Laura focus and get some work done. From Laura's anxious concerns about time-outs, the therapist understood that Laura was construing her as "a teacher," who held sharp judgments about right and wrong. The roots of these concerns were probably located in the extensive "tutoring" Laura experienced from her parents and aunt during her early years. With these reflections framing her thoughts, the therapist reassured Laura that she did not give time-outs and that she was searching for games that Laura might enjoy that would help them become friends.

Laura continued with the "search and find" game, sometimes taking considerable liberties in selecting a "family member," reflecting, as she had during the evaluation, a "dramatic" style of fantasizing that was not concerned with how images fit the stimuli used to represent them. At the same time she continued to express anxiety over "getting the answers right." Laura was not assigned time-outs, of course, nor was she told her answers were wrong, resulting in what apparently for her was an important corrective, emotional experience.

At one point Laura suggested they play a "drawing game." She would draw a picture and the therapist was to guess what the figure was. The therapist recognized that Laura was negotiating directing their activity and imitating the "search and find game," but now Laura was asking the therapist to search for something. In addition, to make her drawing, Laura used the wooden cutouts they had used in memory games. This ensemble suggested to the therapist that Laura was placing one foot in a dialectical circle.

Laura arranged five geometric cutouts on a sheet of paper (a circle in the center with triangles juxtaposed at four points on its circumference), traced the pattern, and colored it with Magic Markers. Laura announced with a dictatorial tone that the therapist had "only five chances to guess what the drawing is." The therapist struggled to find a solution, and mumbled that she wasn't stupid and hoped that she would not get a time-out, to which response Laura grinned. As her first guess, the therapist ventured that the pattern was "a nice pin that you wear on a blouse," and with her last, "a weathervane." With each guess, Laura announced with the same critical tone that the therapist was "wrong." The therapist expressed frustration and asked what the drawing represented. Laura shared she had drawn "a compass; it shows you which way to go." The therapist commented that she would be happy to go wherever "our compass tells us to go." At this point Laura took the green wooden circle she had placed in the center of her compass, moved it toward the therapist, and said, "This is Ms. Green, my teacher. The lines on it remind me of the wrinkles on her face." With this interaction Laura placed both feet in a dialectical circle.

Phase I: A World of Rules and Regulations that Exists in the Deepest Reaches of My Inner Space (16 sessions)

Laura stared at the green circle. Again referring to the lines formed by the grain of the plywood cutout, and as if she were looking at an inkblot, she added that she could see the different faces her teacher makes. Then she wistfully took a large red triangle from the nearby box and set it on the table, "And this is Rudolf the reindeer. He has a red nose." With the same dreamy quality she placed the following cutouts on the table, assigning each an identity: a large black square—"This is the ghost of the night"; a large yellow square—"This is the back of a person"; a large white triangle—"This is Santa's beard." Laura carefully placed the cutouts in a row. "They're going to be in a play called 'The Show of the Night.'" With the session now over, the therapist commented, "That's great! We'll continue next time." Laura responded, "No talking."

Laura's prohibition against "talking" was restated in the next several sessions. In an attempt to cultivate their relationship and express interest in Laura's subjective world, the therapist commented on occasion, "How are you today?" or "How was school today?" or "Boy, it's sure raining today." In response to any such comment, Laura stated emphatically, "No talking. There's no time for talking!" After a number of these interactions, , it occurred to the therapist that Laura's subjective world refused to include events from her routine environments. Recalling these early sessions, the therapist shared with me, "It's as if once the door closed to the treatment room, Laura became totally submerged in the reality of her fantasy. She would have nothing to do with details, however general, that were outside of this fantasy." The only conversation Laura initiated outside her fantasy concerned reassurance that she would not be required to read and that the therapist would do any reading and writing their activities required.

Having assigned identities to wooden cutouts, what did Laura do in the next session? She immediately took out the box of cutouts, noting that more "actors" were needed for the performance of "The Show of the Night." During this and the following fourteen sessions, Laura occupied herself with selecting and naming cutouts. She fantasized the cutouts as a "troupe of actors" who were to arrive for rehearsals. To the initial group of five cutouts she gradually added twenty-four before "The Show of the Night" was finally rehearsed. Examples of additions to her "theatrical troupe" included a large blue circle—"Ms. Green's sister"; a large red circle—"Ms. Goldstein"; a large yellow triangle—"a clown"; a large blue triangle—"a wave"; a large black triangle—"a mouse"; a large red diamond—"a treasure"; a large white diamond—"Ms. Spring"; and a large green square—"grass."

But Laura did more with these cutouts than name them. From the start, she assigned herself the role of teacher and the therapist the role of "teacher's assistant" and ritualized an activity. During each session she carefully lined up the cutouts to which she had already assigned an identity. As new characters were identified, each was carefully placed in line. Significantly, Laura not only remembered the name of each character but the character's place in line. The therapist acknowledged that while she prided herself on having a good memory, she had to refer to a written log to keep track of who was who, especially as the number of characters increased.

In Laura's fantasy play, these imaginary characters had to "follow rules" in order to prepare for "rehearsals" of "The Show of the Night." She constructed a complex set of rules and directed the therapist to record them in their "rule book," for example, "You must stay in line"; "You must pay attention"; "No poking when you're in line"; "If you arrive late and the rehearsal is halfway through, you will go to the back of the line"; "You can't bring your lunch"; "You can't do cartwheels"; "No cutting in line"; and "No pushing." Laura also directed the therapist to design a "record book" and a rating scale. Each time a character broke a rule, the character received a "warning" and was sent to the back of the line, and the therapist carefully logged each infraction. If a character received five warnings, the character could not take part in the play and must "wait until next year" to participate. Significantly, Laura emphasized one key rule, "No time-outs are allowed," obviously related to the many time-outs she had experienced in school.

During these sessions, Laura sat at a table, lined up and added cutouts, and fantasized one or the other breaking a rule. Laura gently manipulated cutouts speaking as the teacher ("Rudolf, you just poked the ghost, go to the back of the line") as well as one of the characters ("I didn't mean it; they were pushing me"). While occasionally addressing the therapist as her assistant, Laura, totally submerged in her fantasy, rarely made eye contact with the therapist. During each session, the therapist waited for directions to log either a new character or a transgression. Sometimes the therapist intentionally made a mistake recording one of Laura's directives and enacted emotions and thoughts Laura had expressed previously, for example, "Oh my God, I made a mistake!" "Darn it, I must be stupid!" The therapist hoped that enacting Laura's self-expressions would facilitate her experiencing the therapist as attuned. Whenever the therapist expressed these concerns, Laura made a point of reassuring her.

Finally, in the last session of this phase, Laura spread over the tabletop the twenty-four cutouts (characters) she had identified to that point in what appeared to be a random array. Then, directing the therapist to "write down the play," she told the following story. Amazingly, each time an interaction was mentioned in the story, Laura manipulated the wooden cutouts involved.

> One day a mouse comes walking in. Then a gymnastic guy came cart-wheeling in and hit the mouse. The mouse bit his toe. Then someone said, "We need a prince and a home and we must have a princess." This is the house. The king wanted to see it. But they said "No. It's our house. You go pick your own house out." The king said, "I'll kill you. Build me a perfect house." One day they said, "Here's a house." They chopped and chopped. The gymnastics guy wouldn't help. The house just wouldn't stick together. Then came the prince. When he put his hand in his pocket, he pulled out a gold key. They wanted the key, but the prince wouldn't share his gold key. Then the king says, "Let's steal the gold key. The prince always puts it on his bureau at night." The house still wasn't done. Then it was night. Then the gymnastic guy went himself, and yes he stole the key, and he went to bed with the key and slept and slept. Early in the morning, the gymnast gave the king the key. The gymnast tells his friend that he stole the key, and then he fixed the house. "Hurray, hurray," everyone yells. Then a nice lady comes. She's very pretty. She knew everything. She was so kind. She knew what everyone needed. She was nice to everyone. "Can we have your gold key?" "Yes," says the prince, "but be patient and kind. What's the matter, Blue? This is not what I expected. Let's get going and finish putting the roof on the house."

The therapist made no comment as Laura told her story and moved the pieces about. While the therapist could guess the meaning of some parts of her fantasy, as a whole the story made no sense. The therapist complimented the "characters" on their first rehearsal. She also told them that she looked forward to future rehearsals, hoping privately that as "The Show of the Night" was repeated its metaphors would become more differentiated.

Phase II: A World of Rules and Regulations that Exists in a School (13 sessions)

The very next session, Laura took out the box of cutouts as usual. But she made no mention of "The Show of the Night" as she spread them over the table. Instead, much to the therapist's surprise, Laura commented, "These are all kids in a classroom," shifting her fantasy from a theater to a classroom. Then she selected other cutouts from the box, saying, "We need new kids for the classroom." The cutouts she added included, for example, a medium green circle—"Linda is 3 years old"; a medium yellow circle—"Mary is the kindergarten teacher"; a small green diamond—"Ms. Faye is Mary's helper"; a small green circle—"Sherry, a girl in the gymnastics class"; a large red diamond now became "Phoebe, Linda's helper" (instead of " a treasure" used in the previous fantasy). Laura designated each of twenty-nine cutouts as students or teachers and again accurately recalled the character of each.

Initially Laura occupied herself with lining up the cutouts by size and alphabetically. Then, as a teacher, she administered spelling and math contests to the "students." When manipulating the cutouts in some fantasy, she displayed a nononsense, stern, tutorial style of relating. With this interactive metaphor, the therapist believed Laura was again enacting representations of the "tutoring" she had received in her early years, but these representations were more direct expressions of reality constraints than had been the rules of "The Show of the Night." With each contest, Laura grouped the "students" into teams. Significantly, she began to write for the first time. During spelling contests Laura, as the teacher, dictated words. Then she took the role of a student and printed the words on sheets of paper. She did the same during math contests.

During this "classroom fantasy," Laura initiated interesting enactments. She introduced a "spinning game," spinning each cutout (student) to determine who could spin for the longest time before falling. She also introduced a "balancing game" and set each cutout (student) on its edge to determine who would "balance the best." The therapist viewed these enactments as representing Laura's body-image negotiating control and balance as she struggled to extend her fantasy world into the environment.

There were two noteworthy developments during this phase. One concerned Laura's enacting representations of younger children competing with older children for favors, one of the metaphors she expressed on projective tests. Initially, while administering spelling and math contests, Laura, as a teacher, enacted that she was particularly annoyed at the "little ones": "You are so fussy!" "You are so picky!" "Stop whispering!" "No, you can't be first!" "Sometimes you can't have what you want!" Gradually, Laura shifted the direction of her annoyance and anger from the little cutouts to the larger ones, enacting nurture toward the "smaller children" and instructing the "larger children" to be more considerate. "Let them go first." "Don't push them."

The other development concerned enactments that indicated Laura was idealizing and identifying with the therapist. Throughout the first phase, Laura addressed the therapist as "assistant" and only when directing her to record an infraction by one of the "actors." Moreover, Laura rarely made eye contact with the therapist. In contrast, during this phase, Laura increasingly addressed the therapist using the pronoun "we," as in "We need to help those kids learn how to spell better." In addition, Laura equated her person with that of the therapist in highly valued terms. Laura turned to the therapist in one session and said, "You know, we have the gift of height," a comment she repeated several times during the sessions that followed. Laura was a tall, slender girl for her age, and the therapist was also tall and slender. Gradually, Laura drew attention to other "gifts" she and the therapist shared. "We have the gift of hair." "We have the gift of teeth." And noticing the therapist's writing as she recorded instructions for the class, Laura added, "You know, we have the gift of penmanship."

In one session Laura spontaneously decided that all of the children had done well with their spelling, math, spinning, and balancing contests and therefore were ready "to graduate." She spent three sessions carefully arranging the cutouts in rows for a "graduation picture," taking great pains to decide where each "student" would sit or stand. The therapist brought in a camera, and a number of photographs were taken of the cutouts before Laura decided she had obtained "the right one." After the graduation ceremony, Laura began to plan for the next group of students.

In one session, however, she interrupted this fantasy and introduced a new edition of her metaphor of rules. This defined a new phase because the process by which Laura constructed symbols and metaphors changed significantly (Chapter 6). The vehicles she used to construct symbols shifted from geometric wooden cutouts to flags of different nations. With this shift Laura assimilated aspects of the environment and coordinated them with the demands of her subjective world while still rehearsing the issue of rules.

Phase III: A World of Rules and Regulations that Exists in Countries (10 sessions)

Laura arrived and announced, "Let's make flags." The therapist readily agreed, not yet understanding the possible meaning of this abrupt shift in the process, and gathered cards, crayons, and an atlas containing pictures of national flags. Laura studied the pictures and busied herself drawing flags of different countries, each on 5- × 8-inch cards. Beginning with the first flag she selected to copy (Libya's), she animated each flag and country, assigning a character to it. Libya misbehaved and broke rules as did, for example, Uruguay, Nepal, and Jamaica. Canada was "on the border," sometimes good and sometimes bad. As she produced flags, she manipulated the cards as she had the cutouts, enacting various events representing infractions of rules. For example, holding the flag with both hands, she scolded Libya, "You must pay attention! Can't you ever think of other people!" At other times she moved several flags around as she fantasized a more complex event. In one instance, Libya was arrested by police and spent the night in jail, "But it didn't help."

As Laura increased the number of flags she drew (eventually nineteen), the therapist asked her if she wanted to play "the memory game" with the flags as they had done with the cutouts. The therapist thought that this activity would engage Laura in experiencing the flags as they are, in addition to as she imagined them to be. Laura accepted. For several sessions the flags were used in a memory task as well as in dramatic play. Laura studied an array of flags. The therapist covered the array and replaced one flag with another. After a delay, the cover was removed and Laura identified the change. Although Laura initially engaged the task with some enthusiasm, it was clear that she preferred to use the flags in fantasy play.

Another shift occurred in how Laura construed the therapist. In contrast to the admiring comments of the previous phase ("We have the gift of height"), Laura began to devalue the therapist. She did not like the way the therapist was dressed and made comments with a critical tone. "You look like a grown-up today. You look perfumy today." As these comments increased, Laura declared that she planned to stop treatment. In one session she announced, "I'm not coming anymore after the last day of school." And "I have my own brain, eyes, and mouth. I can make my own decisions." The therapist agreed that Laura had her own brain and could make her own decisions quite well. She also suggested that since Laura was no longer going to be in a special needs classroom next year, and would be entering a regular third grade, she should return in the fall for a few meetings to discuss how school was going. She could decide then whether or not she wanted to stop meeting. Laura agreed to return "for one meeting."

Phase IV: Negotiating Concerns about My School Environment (28 sessions)

When Laura returned in the fall, she made no mention of her previous request to stop treatment. Instead, she focused her discussions on third-grade classmates who were "nasty": "They make fun of kids." At the same time, Laura directed that they set up "a regular classroom." She asked for dolls "as big as kids really are." The therapist and Laura went shopping and purchased a 32-inch female doll, the largest they could find. Laura propped up this doll, along with many typical dolls and hand puppets, in rows to represent a classroom. Using an easel as a blackboard, Laura assigned herself the role of teacher and the therapist the role of assistant. While these assignments resembled those given previously to Laura and therapist and to wooden cutouts representing students in a classroom, now the imaginary children were dolls. In addition, instead of focusing on rules, Laura now prescribed a series of interactions typical of a school environment, which Laura and the therapist enacted using macroactions. Before each enactment Laura drew a picture of a dilemma that occurs in the playground (e.g., one girl does not want to include another in a game) or in the classroom (e.g., one girl is making faces at another). Significantly, one scene involved a girl who had difficulty spelling. Laura proposed, "I can teach you how to spell," and proceeded to do so.

Enactments of imaginary school situations were interspersed with two other activities that Laura initiated. In one she asked the therapist, "Tell me a story about someone in your class when you were in the third grade." Borrowing details Laura shared about classmates who caused her much concern, the therapist invented "Jenny" and gradually elaborated stories. Jenny was the teacher's pet, self-centered, picky, and nasty, and made fun of kids. The stories included how children coped with Jenny's behaviors. In the other activity, Laura initiated that she and the therapist play soccer outdoors, extending their relationship and intersubjective world into the environment.

Laura's transference with the therapist during this phase shifted again from the critical remarks she expressed previously to displays of idealization and identification with the therapist. Several weeks into this phase, Laura initiated a ritual at the close of each session. She prescribed the clothing she and the therapist would wear for the next session. "We have to dress the same and look alike." For example, "Next time, let's wear jeans, white sneakers, and a sweater." From prescribing what would be worn, Laura gradually engaged the therapist in negotiating what clothing they should wear, readily accommodating to suggestions by the therapist, who also accommodated to Laura's suggestions.

Laura's treatment came to a close after two semesters in the third grade. The teacher described her as much less tuned out than had been reported when she was referred for treatment at the start of the second grade. Significantly, not only was her academic performance adequate, but Laura had begun to read in the classroom "for the first time" and appeared to enjoy it.

MARY: I'M TRAPPED IN A STRAITJACKET

I selected the case we are about to consider because this adolescent came to treatment with a history of difficulty expressing herself verbally, presenting a special challenge for any treatment program. In terms of our developmental model, not only was Mary handicapped by rigid cognitive functions, but each behavioral mode (action, fantasy, and language) was constricted and barriers segregated each from the others. Thus her fantasies provided inadequate opportunities for rehearsing actions she might take, and the actions she did take failed to contribute to revising her representations.

As we shall see, the creative use the therapist made of developmental-dialectical guidelines enabled Mary, in the course of only fourteen months of once-weekly sessions, to free herself from the straitjacket that imprisoned her psychological functioning. Throughout most of the treatment, the therapist introduced a series of highly structured interactions, following a particular progression. The therapist first designed tasks to connect language expressions to body experiences, and then language expressions to fantasy experiences. Last, language and fantasy expressions were embedded within actions and enactments. With each of these experiences, Mary was required to engage in second-order change. However, the therapist was careful to select ways of bumping into each behavioral mode so as to promote Mary's alliance and identification with and idealization of what the therapist represented.

We first encountered Mary, a ninth grader, in Chapter 1, when she and her parents were observed in a fictitious situation by four child therapists and a researcher. Mary and her parents were referred by the family pediatrician who had been following her and a younger brother since their infancies. In a telephone conference, the pediatrician noted she had recommended a consultation because during a recent conference with Mary's parents, following her annual physical exam, the parents intensified concerns that they had introduced over the years: Mary's school performance was inadequate, she lacked confidence, she had few friends, she occasionally overate and slept a lot, she was frequently silent and rarely engaged her parents. The pediatrician reported father as saying that if Mary became depressed, "She will surely get into drugs and sex." But mother disagreed, pointing out that Mary's occasional overeating related to the fact that "obesity runs in my family." Reviewing her records, the pediatrician also noted that Mary had "exceptional difficulty" with bowel training at the age of 2, was frequently "silent" as a young child, and repeated the first grade. The pediatrician wondered if Mary had a "memory problem" because, in spite of studying for many hours, she typically forgot much of what she had reviewed when taking quizzes.

Parent Intake Interview

With this preliminary information in hand, the therapist, a female, met with Mary's parents, who were both employed. Father began, noting that Mary spent a great deal of time on homework but always received poor to average grades. In contrast, Mary's brother was "a grind" and obtained high grades even though, in father's opinion, Mary was brighter. Father believed Mary's academic difficulties were her main problem and "if she had only her mild problem sleeping and eating, we wouldn't be here." He believed Mary sometimes ate or slept too much because she was nervous about school.

Mother added that Mary spent weekends at her desk but never got anything done. She had difficulty getting started and could not concentrate for long periods of time. One of Mary's biggest difficulties concerned "reading and vocabulary." In spite of several tutoring programs over the past years, reading "remains a handicap." Yet when Mary cleaned the kitchen, she did "a great job, but cleans more than necessary." Mother commented that since their recent meeting with the pediatrician, Mary had been sleeping and eating less.

Father disagreed. The therapist asked about Mary's sleeping pattern, and both parents agreed that she typically went to bed by 8:30 P.M.

At this point mother introduced her "main worry," which had plagued her over the years: Mary had always been "quiet." Father interrupted, proposing that Mary was quiet because she did not want to take risks. He added that he could "manipulate" Mary's brother but not Mary. When the therapist asked what father meant by "manipulate," he clarified that when trying to suggest how something could be done, no matter what approach he used, Mary knew he wanted something done and would refuse or stall.

Since the mother had been interrupted, the therapist asked her to clarify what she meant by "quiet." At first she described that Mary talked and "processed" very slowly. Then mother recalled that Mary repeated the first grade because she was "very nonverbal." Father interrupted again to express the opinion that Mary looked like she was doing something but was probably "daydreaming about something else." He believed Mary still felt bad about repeating the first grade, and he has tried to offer different explanations, which she rejected.

To provide mother with another opportunity to clarify what she meant by quiet, the therapist asked mother to try to recall Mary's style of play during her third year and wondered if she was "quiet" then. Mother recalled that Mary played with toys quietly, and father added that Mary "used pantomime a lot because she didn't speak." Mary could speak, they noted, but usually refused to. Mother offered that Mary was enrolled in a daycare program when 2 years old because mother returned to work. The therapist asked if the parents recalled how Mary responded to this change, either as observed by daycare staff or by them when they picked her up. Mother responded, "I think she was creative in the way she built things," but then shifted to an association concerning a later time in Mary's life when she learned to ride a tricycle (an association that suggested that, without awareness, mother was avoiding what was probably a difficult time in Mary's life). Mother added that Mary always seemed to like art, and spent a good deal of time as a child drawing pictures.

Observing that mother and father became anxious when asked about Mary's first three years of life, and that they tended to shift to more recent observations, the therapist asked again about Mary's style of play, wondering if there was anything else they could recall. Father responded that throughout her childhood, Mary used "baby talk" a great deal of which was "a bone of contention between us" (referring to himself and his wife). They had sharp disagreements about how to handle Mary's baby talk; he usually yelled at Mary to "talk right," while mother tried to "build up her confidence."

At this point mother introduced Mary's problem with toilet training, which the pediatrician had already shared with the therapist. When mother went to work, Mary had not yet learned to control her bowels. Mother had attempted to train her but was unsuccessful. When placed on the potty, Mary would "sit there like a rag doll, very quiet, but she seemed mad for some reason." When mother enrolled Mary in a daycare center, her lack of bowel control was "embarrassing." Mother was reassured by daycare staff that they "deal with this often." As the months passed, Mary continued to require a diaper while at the daycare center, and mother continued to express her embarrassment to father. One day he angrily sat Mary on the toilet and "yelled at her"; from that time she began to use the toilet. It was during this phase of Mary's early life, coinciding with struggles to toilet train her, that Mary often refused to speak. Her selective mutism persisted until the age of about 6 or 7, which resulted in Mary's repeating the first grade "because she wouldn't say anything." Mary's selective mutism transitioned into "baby talk" from about the age of 7 to 12.

At the close of the intake session, the therapist attempted to integrate concerns and observations the parents had shared in an effort to revise how they construed Mary's difficulties and style of interacting, and to help them accept a recommendation for a psychological evaluation. At the time, Mary refused to deliver academically, opposed the parent's suggestions, slept and ate a lot, and avoided contact with others. In her early years she refused to deliver when on the potty, refused to converse, and when she did used baby talk, which infuriated the parents. Taken together, these behaviors suggested that from her first years, Mary had actively withheld from them and later from teachers. Both parents found the view of "actively withholding" a useful one and had not thought of Mary in quite that way. They tended to see her, especially recently, as "doing it on purpose," behaviors that reminded father of one of his sisters. The therapist also suggested that how Mary experienced toilet training, mother's going to work, and her parents' arguing over her refusal to talk may have contributed to disruptions in her reciprocating and testing self-assertion. Information from psychological tests would help evaluate how Mary construed these experiences and how her learning style had been affected.

Father readily accepted the need for an evaluation; mother expressed reluctance because of the school time Mary would miss. The therapist reassured her that every effort would be made to schedule appointments after school. The therapist arranged for a colleague to conduct the evaluation.

Mary's Intake Interview

As we learned in Chapter 1, Mary proved to be a tall, slender, attractive, neatly dressed adolescent who showed no signs of the "obesity" to which mother had referred. Mary interacted with a reserved style, speaking softly and slowly, sometimes in a whisper, and making little eye contact. When asked to discuss why she thought her parents had requested a consultation, and whether she had any concerns she would like to share, Mary noted that her main problem was poor school grades, which she knew concerned her parents. Although she had studied all weekend for a French exam, she got an F. Mary mentioned how stressed she became when called upon to respond in French. When asked if she had concerns in addition to school grades, Mary shared her conviction that most girls were better than she was in gym, and that she feels uneasy in unfamiliar situations.

Following the Life Stressor Interview (Chapter 6), the therapist asked if anything happened years ago, or more recently, that upset her a lot. Mary shared that when the Gulf War began she became afraid, wondering if the United States would become involved in a war like "the big one," and referred to many films she had watched about World War II on television. When asked if there was anything else that had happened that worried her, Mary whispered, "My mother bugs me a lot, but I'm used to it; it doesn't bother me." In response to what she might be most afraid of, she noted, "The dark," and shared that she leaves lights on at night, which helps.

Mary's Psychological Evaluation

Highlights of the psychological test results are described to set the stage for a discussion of the structured interactions the therapist devised to engage Mary in psychotherapy. With tests evaluating cognitive regulators (Chapter 6), Mary scanned information (focal attention process) and conceptualized information (equivalence range process) at stage-appropriate levels. She showed marked rigidity with two other cognitive processes, however: when required to focus attention while information was surrounded by stimuli that evoked emotions/fantasies (field articulation), and when required to look at a series of pictures of a scene and report any changes that occurred (leveling-sharpening).

These results coincided with aspects of her performance with the Wechsler Intelligence Scale. While her full-scale IQ fell in the average range, her performance varied from borderline to very superior. Significantly, given her history of "silence," her lowest scores were with the Information and Vocabulary subtests. Reflecting her cognitive constriction in the verbal domain, she did not know in which direction the sun set and thought that Chile was in Europe. Her superior performance occurred with the Block Design subtest, stimuli that do not usually activate fantasies and emotions, reflecting Mary's superior aptitude for integrating information.

In terms of her capacity to transform information (symbolize), Mary showed limitations at each of the levels evaluated, but in particular at the embodied level. When body perceptions served as stimuli (Mary felt objects placed under a cloth and described what they brought to mind), she described physical attributes, rather than constructing symbols, suggesting that embodied meanings were segregated for the most part from fantasy ("A square box," "A large glob of clay"). Two of her responses, however, hinted at representations of developmentally early disruptions. One item reminded her of a "baby's toy" and another of a "Smurf."

With the Rorschach test, her responses also indicated that personal meanings were underground for the most part. A number of responses depicted conventional meanings ("bat"; "butterfly") while other images (a turtle) suggested that a "barrier" blocked personal meanings from gaining expression (Fisher and Cleveland 1968). However, a few responses did represent the meanings that influenced her current functioning. To Card III she described "two people just bumped into each other; they're falling down," representing that interacting with others was associated with body instability and loss of equilibrium. To Card IV she imaged that "over here are two ducks carefully sticking their heads out of a hole," representing her fear and caution when entering an interpersonal world. And to Card X she constructed an image of two people arguing, followed by an image of two inchworms, again reflecting her sense of vulnerability in response to aggression and self-assertion.

Last, the diagnostician was surprised to find that in spite of Mary's marginal school performance and history of reading difficulties, she performed well on a standardized test of academic achievement. Reading and math scores fell at about the seventy-fifth percentile.

The therapist met first with Mary and then with her parents to discuss the test results and recommendation for treatment. In Mary's meeting the therapist took as much care as possible to clarify whether Mary felt she was being required to do something by the recommendation. Mary conveyed that she wanted to meet with the therapist so that she could improve her grades. At the conference held with the parents, they preferred to discuss the recommendation for treatment with their pediatrician to whom a report had been sent by the diagnostician. A few weeks later, the parents returned, noting that the pediatrician had encouraged them to accept the recommendation. Father asked about the length of time required. The therapist recommended a minimum of ten months or about forty meetings at which point she and Mary, as well as the parents, would evaluate what had been accomplished and what else might be needed, if anything, to ensure that Mary was meeting her goal of doing better academically and enjoying school. Mother noted that the pediatrician thought four months would be sufficient. The therapist explained why she believed it was likely that more time would be needed. Reviewing the test data again, she illustrated how Mary's thinking, as well as her freedom to initiate, were in a "straitjacket" and that, from the therapist's experience, it would take more than four months to free Mary.

Mary's Treatment

Because of several issues, the therapist elected to conduct treatment with highly structured interactions: Mary's history of elective mutism; her current difficulty initiating and expressing herself verbally; test data suggesting cognitive rigidity; the segregation of embodied meanings from fantasy; and representations symbolizing that interacting and asserting resulted in "collisions," loss of body stability, and emotions of fear and vulnerability. These factors argued against a therapeutic process that emphasized nondirected verbal discussions or that required Mary to initiate activities.

The broad goal the therapist articulated was to enable Mary to develop the capacity to experience flexibility, both cognitively and physically, and to be assertive within opportunities and limitations provided by situations. This goal consisted of several interrelated subgoals: cultivate cognitive flexibility; translate embodied meanings into symbols; connect and integrate action and fantasy expressions of meanings; and then connect action and fantasy with language expressions.

The therapist's account of Mary's treatment suggested five phases, each guided by a goal and each utilizing a particular form of structured interactions. Mary's therapist was exceptionally inventive in designing a sequence of structured interactions that proved very successful.

Phase I: Helping Mary Enter a Dialectical Circle (11 sessions)

During the first session, Mary seemed anxious and awkward. When asked how things went that day, she offered that while in French class her mind "went blank" even though she had reviewed the vocabulary words the previous evening. Mary offered a belief that she had expressed previously to the diagnostician. She attributed her difficulty remembering to, "I inherited my mom's brain," while her brother must have inherited father's brain. "He's quick and bright."

Rather than exploring these beliefs, the therapist chose instead to address the dilemma Mary had experienced that day, namely, "her mind went blank" during a French quiz. Reflecting how frustrating it must be to study and then forget it all, the therapist commented, "Let's do a concentration and memory game so I can get to know firsthand what happens, and so I can figure out how we can help you concentrate and remember better." Mary accepted the invitation. The therapist placed a number of geometric cutouts on the table and noted that instead of using French words, the game would use cutouts.

With this introduction, the therapist engaged Mary in experiencing the cognitive processes of field articulation and leveling-sharpening, which the evaluation had shown to be particularly rigid. One task involved a 5 by 5 matrix of cutouts of different sizes, shapes, and colors. The therapist asked Mary to look for and pick up, as quickly as possible, only one type (e.g., all of the medium green triangles), and timed her so that "we can keep track of whether concentrating gets quicker and better." After Mary completed the trial, the therapist invited her to designate a cutout, and time the therapist while she removed them. Mary grinned and enjoyed watching the therapist cope with the task.

Then the therapist introduced the second type of task. "This will help us work on remembering." The therapist arrayed a 2 by 3 matrix of cutouts of different colors, shapes, and sizes. She asked Mary to study the pattern so that she could remember the location, color, and size of each shape. After Mary studied the array for about a minute, the therapist covered it with a cloth and replaced a cutout with another that shared only some attributes (e.g., a large yellow diamond was replaced by a small yellow diamond). Removing the cloth, the therapist asked Mary if anything changed in the pattern. Mary puzzled, noted that something "seems weird," but could not specify if anything changed. The therapist pointed to the cutout that had replaced another. Mary laughed, but was clearly upset. The therapist noted that "this must be what happens in French," reassured Mary that these games would help her remember better, and then invited Mary to give the therapist a turn. Mary again enjoyed watching the therapist struggle to remember the original location of the cutouts.

From this introduction, Mary and therapist engaged in these tasks during the next sessions. The complexity of each task was gradually increased following guidelines discussed in Chapter 7. In the first task, the number of cutouts was increased, as well as the distance between them, requiring more vigorous scanning and articulating. As another example, the matrix eventually consisted of stacks (two cutouts in each stack). Now the items removed met more complex criteria, involving a more differentiated level of field articulation (e.g., "Pick up the small, yellow diamonds that sit on blue triangles"). Some stacks contained none of the designated attributes, others contained one, and a few contained all.

The complexity of the memory task was also gradually increased. The number of cutouts to be remembered was increased (from six to ten), the length of time available to study the matrix was decreased (from ninety to thirty seconds), and the delay between examining the matrix and removing the cloth was increased (from a few seconds to ninety).

As Mary engaged in these tasks, she sometimes shared details about school or home. Of special importance, she began to observe the difficulty she experienced with each task. As one instance, when asked to pick up all of the medium green triangles, she picked up a small green triangle, noticed her error, and commented, "I guess I shouldn't rush so fast." With the second task, she typically became frustrated when she could not detect the change the therapist had introduced into the matrix. "You see! This is like when I study for an exam. When I'm in the classroom, things just drift out of my mind. . . . I have no confidence; that's what my father says." These experiences suggested that Mary was becoming aware of why she and the therapist were meeting and that Mary was relating the meaning of their therapeutic activities to her difficulties in school.

In addition, she enacted an interactive metaphor that represented an explicit request for help. At the start of the eighth session, as she walked up a flight of stairs with the therapist to the office, Mary complained that her legs hurt and she felt tired. Sitting at the table to begin a task, she commented, "This really tires out your brain, doesn't it?" The therapist pointed out that indeed concentrating is tiring, just like walking up the stairs, but the tasks are making her mind stronger since she now can remember ten cutouts after waiting more than a minute, when a few weeks ago she could remember only six and only after thirty seconds had passed. Mary seemed to feel empowered by the review of her progress and continued engaging in the tasks.

Phase II: Translating Embodied Meanings into Language Symbols (8 sessions)

Since Mary had shared personal expressions and asked for help, suggesting she had entered a dialectical circle, the therapist noted she had another game that should help Mary concentrate and remember "even better." The therapist explained that the game involved remembering patterns of words instead of cutouts, but the words were connected to tactile experiences, and sometimes it helps to remember something if a person handles it. With this, she took out a box containing various objects and asked Mary to handle each object and to think of a word the object brought to mind. Mary peered into the box, removed a doll, handled it, and said, "I haven't held a doll in a long time." The therapist asked her to think of a word the doll brought to mind. Mary hesitated, seemed to struggle, and finally responded, "brother." The therapist printed the word in large letters on an index card.

As Mary manipulated various objects, sometimes she produced a word quickly, at other times, as with the doll, she pondered before producing a word. In response to this behavior, the therapist noted there was a way Mary could learn when her mind "lets go and is free," and when it is "frozen." Mary and therapist devised a five-point rating scale: "1" indicated Mary experienced her mind as "free" when a word came to mind, "5" indicated Mary experienced her mind as "frozen." Examples of her words and associated ratings while handling various objects included *a piece of cloth*—"hide: 4"; "scary: 5"; *a mousetrap*—"click: 2"; "trash: 5"; *a wooden block*—"cliff: 4"; *a toy tractor*—"farming: 1." Mary became slightly more animated as she engaged in this task, and at one point spontaneously commented, "I like this game of let your mind go."

Mary generated about fifty words and ratings, each printed on a card. The cards were then used, as were the cutouts, to form matrices that Mary scanned to search for particular words (e.g., "Find all the nouns"; "Find all the words that have to do with the outdoors"). Similarly, the cards were also used in a memory task now involving words rather than wooden cutouts.

Significantly, during these tasks Mary increasingly shared meanings from her subjective world, hinting at various metaphors that very likely interfered with her functioning. As one instance, when she removed the card on which had been printed "cliff," she associated to a trip the family had taken in the mountains of Maine, and that her mother became frightened when they stood on the edge of a cliff. And with another, when studying a matrix within which was located the word "hook," she touched the card, paused, and complained that her mother worries about her too much and constantly checks on what she is doing. She repeated a comment she had made in the first session. "I must be stupid because I inherited my mother's brain." She also demonstrated more cognitive efficiency searching for words within a matrix and remembering a configuration of words. Given these gains, the therapist introduced another change in their structured interactions intended to help Mary connect words to fantasies and elaborate the connections and their associated emotions.

Phase III: Connecting Language Symbols to Elaborated Fantasies (12 sessions)

The therapist pointed out that as Mary probably noticed, the searching and remembering games were bringing up different feelings and memories. If more of these "came out for us to share," Mary would be able to concentrate and remember words better, because these memories and feelings "were hanging onto the words." With this, the therapist spread all of the cards they had been working with over the table. Mary's job was to look over the cards, pick two of them, and then describe a memory the two words brought to mind—"Or you can even make something up." The therapist offered to write down her stories. Reflecting the gains she had made to this point, Mary engaged in this new task with interest and enthusiasm. As she scanned the cards spread over the table, she tended to pick up one and then another, usually within a few seconds. It seemed likely therefore that when selecting cards she was not yet conscious of the story she would eventually construct. The following are examples of the associations/stories Mary elaborated to each pair of words she selected.

Mary/Running. Mary described running in a race during gym; she became tired and came in last.

Skiing/Man. Once her father went skiing, slid off the run, and became tangled in the bushes.

Dog/Past. When Mary was about 7 years old, a big dog reared up and put its front paws on her shoulders. Mary screamed. She recalled focusing on his beady, black eyes and drooling mouth. Mother was nearby talking to a neighbor and lingered for a moment to finish what she was saying before coming to Mary's aid. Referring to mother's seeming lack of concern, Mary commented with noticeable irritation, "I couldn't believe it!"

Shoe/Boy. When Mary was about 9 years old, she and a friend were hiking through nearby woods. Mary slipped and her legs became wedged between two large rocks. Her friend tried to pull her feet out but couldn't. The police arrived and rescued her. Her parents were not yet home from work. She was taken to the emergency room. The doctors "squeezed" her feet, but everything was okay.

Noise/Car. Once Mary did not want to read. She thinks she was in the fifth grade. Father shook her and yelled at her.

Basketball/Bad. Last year in gym some kids teased Mary because of the funny way she dribbled a basketball. This upset her very much.

Throughout this phase, as Mary constructed associations to pairs of words, she expressed her thoughts with increasing ease and emotional spontaneity, given her initial reserved mode. In addition, between trials, she shared events that occurred since her last session, especially achievements and disappointments concerning schoolwork. Mary also displayed more explicit attempts to negotiate self-assertion. At times she occupied herself between trials by "shooting" a rubber band across the room. On several occasions she playfully warned the therapist to "be careful, I'm a good shot." In another instance, when Mary picked up a card that contained the therapist's name, Mary said, "Yucky," returned the card to the table, and grinned, "I'm just kidding." Mary announced that her parents wanted a conference "which is fine by me." She joked, "They'll probably complain that I'm telling them off" and laughed when she imagined the therapist and parents getting into an argument.

Parent Conference

The parents described an "attitude change" on Mary's part. She has stuck with playing basketball even though she showed mediocre skills relative to other girls, she was doing a better job controlling her eating binges, and she has become more spontaneous talking about day-to-day matters with them. Mother interjected that Mary seemed happy when she left each session and clearly wanted to keep her appointments.

Mother was disappointed, however, with how early Mary still went to bed. Then, glancing at father, she commented that midyear report cards were due soon, and "that's a bad time of year" because father becomes explosive over Mary's grades. Father acknowledged this with a grin and declared this time he will be much more "laid back." Engaging father for a moment, the therapist underscored why it was important that he find ways, other than angry explosions, to express his interest in Mary's school performance.

At this point they shifted the focus from Mary to their marital relationship. Mother criticized father because he frequently arrived home at 7 P.M. after he and fellow workers stopped for a drink after work. Mother felt she was on the verge of a breakdown. Then she shared a detail that had been withheld from the intake interview. Mother's gynecologist had recommended marital counseling some time ago. The parents began counseling before Mary was referred for an evaluation, and have continued since. The therapist was pleased that they had a setting in which they could examine and improve their relationship. She offered that if they and their counselor felt that their relationship with Mary would best be discussed with the therapist, she would be open to meetings with Mary's permission.

The therapist refocused the discussion. Reminding them that since they have observed Mary speaking up more freely, they should be on the alert for moments when Mary might test self-assertion and openly disagree with them. Father noted that ever since the start of Mary's treatment, he has tried to watch his tendency to lose his temper. Rather than following suit and responding with some self-statement, mother criticized father saying that he is like her boss at work, "He isn't considerate." Since time had expired, the therapist concluded by noting they have a professional setting in which to explore these issues, and by working on their relationship they should help each other as well as Mary.

Phase IV: Integrating the Modalities of Action, Fantasy, and Language (18 sessions)

In the next meeting the therapist shared with Mary that her parents were pleased that she was discussing daily events with them. Mary asked whether her parents complained about anything. To obtain associations from Mary that might be of help in treatment, the therapist selected two details. Father said he would try to control his temper, and mother thought Mary went to bed too early. Mary offered that her father was doing "really great" with his temper, and that she and he were "talking a lot." On the other hand, mother constantly "nagged" her about bedtime and "just about everything else." Mother's nagging received considerable attention in the sessions that followed.

Relying upon Mary's gains in constructing fantasies and associations and negotiating self-assertion, the therapist introduced another elaboration in their structured interactions that resembled the say-do, cognitive-behavioral technique. As before, Mary selected two cards from among many arranged on the table, and imagined a scene the words suggested. However, now she drew a picture of the scene, constructed a story about it, and then enacted the story. The therapist demonstrated by selecting two cards, "car" and "frustration," choosing these words because they suggested a metaphor representing Mary's inhibition and sense of being stuck and frustrated. The therapist drew a picture of a car stuck in a traffic jam, and narrated that the person in the car was frustrated because she was late for work. The therapist enacted the scene, sitting in a chair, pantomiming being in a traffic jam, and expressing frustration and irritation.

In the material to follow, I describe selected drawings and fantasies Mary constructed and enacted. While I have omitted a number of her productions, those included represent the sequence of meanings that emerged. My intention is to illustrate two issues. As these structured interactions unfolded, Mary gradually expressed metaphors representing her cognitive and physical inhibitions, and the intense anxiety she experienced when asserting. Eventually she constructed and enacted a metaphor that could be viewed as a "core pathological life metaphor" at the root of her difficulties.

Hold Back/Girl (Figure 8–1)

Immediately after the therapist performed her "car/frustration" story, Mary scanned the cards spread over the table and selected "hold back/girl," very likely influenced by the therapist's enactment. Mary paused, set the cards down side by side, reflected for a minute or so, drew a picture, and told the following story: a girl on one team is trying to restrain a player on the other team. The girl being restrained is furious,

FIGURE 8–1

punches the girl who is holding her, and tells her to "stop it." Of note, when enacting this scene, Mary's physical movements were quite muted. She simply stood up, formed a circle with her arms, and then sat down.

Slip Back/Sister (Figure 8–2)

"This is a picture of a girl with a big nose and a fat body. She's slipping down a hill shouting, 'Help!'" When enacting this scene, Mary stood up and, with arms stretched forward, took a couple of steps backwards. When she sat down, she spontaneously commented that her mother contacted the school to find out how Mary was doing and expressed resentment over mother "getting into my business." At this moment, the therapist privately recalled Mary's Rorschach response of two people bumping into each other and falling, wondering if the metaphor Mary enacted, and her associations, represented that interpersonal interactions result in collisions and the loss of body groundedness. However, the therapist chose to respond only to the metaphor of help. With humor, the therapist asked Mary to "do the falling part again." Mary stood up and again took a few steps backwards. The therapist, standing behind her, placed her hands on Mary's shoulders, saying, "Gotcha—you won't slip back." Mary laughed.

FIGURE 8–2

Disobey/Nervous (Figure 8–3a)

The scene Mary drew in association to "disobey/nervous," and to the subsequent pairs of words she selected, illustrate two techniques the therapist used from time to time. In one, the therapist asked Mary to take each part of a drawing and describe what the part could mean. In the other technique, the therapist cultivated Mary's ability to elaborate a fantasy and its enactments by asking Mary to select a second pair of words related in some way to the first.

After Mary drew the scene (Figure 8–3a), the therapist asked her to list "different things about the teacher, whatever in your mind the teacher is feeling, thinking, and doing." Mary listed "fed up, annoyed, snapping, angry, dumps on students." To the sun, Mary listed only "sad." To the girl, she listed "little, green pea; nervous; scared to say anything; shrunk up." Significantly, when Mary enacted this scene, she first picked up a toy gun located on a nearby shelf, and placed it to her head, laughing. Then she returned the gun, assumed an erect position as the teacher, and thrust her arm out, shaking her forefinger. Last, she enacted the girl by sitting on the floor, assuming a sad face, and curling her body into a ball.

FIGURE 8–3a

At this point, the therapist asked Mary if there were other situations that came to mind that had something to do with what she had just enacted. Mary paused and drew the next scene (Figure 8–3b). One student is turning in an assignment and the other is thinking, "Oh great, I'm dead!" because she hadn't finished the work. Mary then spontaneously associated to math class a few weeks before. The teacher was discussing a theorem and told the class that to understand it they must remember a theorem they had discussed the other day. Mary could not recall the previous theorem. She felt awful and did not get the problem correct. At this point Mary picked up the green crayon and scribbled in the teacher's face, blocking out her eyes and nose.

After Mary enacted each of the figures, the therapist asked her to draw a picture that had something to do with how she would like to express herself to the teacher in the story. Mary depicted a French class (Figure 8–3c). First she drew

FIGURE 8–3b

FIGURE 8–3c

the large figure seated at the left, commenting, "That's me. I'm as big as the teacher." Then she drew the teacher saying "very good" in French. Then she drew other students, noting that all the other kids are "midgets" and green, but two are smart (one she drew in blue, the other red). Mary added that the chair the student was sitting on is "blocking the smartest kids in class." Relying on previous drawings, enactments, and discussions, the therapist elected to give her view of what each symbol in the picture meant. The girl on the left would like to be as smart and confident as the teacher. To accomplish this, the other kids had to be less smart and confident, and the big girl has to block competition. Mary seemed to listen but said nothing. The therapist continued, commenting that together they would find ways for Mary to be as smart and big as everyone else by getting her mind and body to be free so she "can get in there and take on the competition."

The following session Mary brought in a story she had written that appeared to be a communication to the therapist, and asked the therapist to read it aloud.

The prison door slammed behind me and silence overtook my cell. It was my second day in prison, and I couldn't wait to get out. I lay awake when I heard someone knock on the wall of my cell. I walked to the bars of my cell and answered, "Yeah?" A small voice asked if I was all right. I replied, "I'm fine, just can't sleep." The voice was nice, and it comforted me to know that I wasn't alone. I had not seen my neighbor yet, but as time went on, we began to talk freely as we became the best of friends.

In the therapist's view the prison cell symbolized Mary's "psychological confinement" and the "nice voice in the next cell" the therapist as a companion who had become a "best friend." The therapist complimented Mary and commented that she was really glad the person has a good friend in the next cell, and was confident that the friend is going to help her get out of jail.

High Confidence/Fence/Fat (Figure 8–4)

At this point in treatment, to elaborate their interactions, the therapist suggested Mary select three cards instead of two to make up a story. Mary selected cards and constructed a representation that seemed to relate to the comment the therapist

FIGURE 8–4

made in response to her story. Picking up the cards "high confidence/fence/fat," Mary drew a picture, pointing out that the person on the left wants to climb over a fat fence and is sure she can make it. The other person is not sure she can. This scene appeared to be a direct representation of Mary's conflict: confidence in being able to achieve is opposed by doubts the wall can be scaled.

It is interesting that Mary did not notice she had exchanged the punctuation marks at the end of each statement. While the figure on the left was declaring, "I can do it, I can," Mary wrote a question mark after this statement, which belongs to the doubt being expressed by the other figure. The statement, "Can you make it," is followed by an exclamation point, which belongs to the quote on the left. This "slip of the crayon" seemed to be a good example of Freud's "bungled actions," described in the previous chapter, that reflect psychological conflict created by two opposing metaphors. In Mary's case, though her mind is declaring she can do it, the declaration arouses anxiety and doubt (question mark); and the doubt is expressed with emphasis (exclamation point).

Mary invited the therapist to participate in enacting this fantasy. To represent the fence, they stacked several chairs, topped by a wastebasket. Interestingly, Mary first enacted the figure on the right who was in doubt, while the therapist was assigned the role of enacting the figure on the left. Then they switched roles several times, playfully attempting to scale the chairs. Mary wondered if the person "in the picture" could get around the fence in some way. After discussing this, they concluded that there were "no shortcuts," and the best thing the person could do was to prove to herself that she "really could do it."

Apparently, Mary assimilated the notion that there were no shortcuts and obstacles should be confronted. She steadily made gains in cultivating cognitive flexibility and constructing, elaborating, and expressing meanings that integrated the modes of action, fantasy, and language. Benefiting from these achievements, she eventually introduced a fantasy that seemed to represent a regression to a core pathological metaphor at the source of her difficulties with asserting.

Early Memory/Aggression/Baby (Figure 8–5)

We should consider first interactions that Mary and therapist shared during sessions prior to the representation she constructed. On occasion, Mary had expressed forms of aggression directed at the person of the therapist. She invented a game of double solitaire using the deck of cards on which were written the words they had been using for their "plays." Mary sorted the cards into four groups to represent four suits. At times she engaged the therapist in a game of double solitaire at the start or end of a session or between "plays." On one such occasion, Mary defeated the therapist, expressing anxiety over how the therapist experienced defeat. Yet interestingly, Mary reassured the therapist with a phrase she repeated often, "Don't kill yourself over it." This statement appeared to condense "Don't worry, it's okay" with "Kill yourself, you jerk," a combination of reassuring and aggressive wishes.

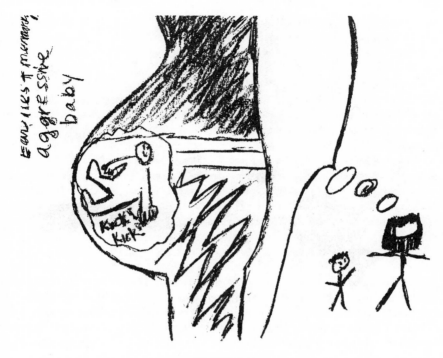

FIGURE 8–5

At the same time, Mary spontaneously expressed anger at her mother because of her lack of nurture and long-standing tendency to control every aspect of Mary's life. Mother made skimpy meals, yet scolded Mary if she ate potato chips and candy bars. And mother was forever commenting about what Mary wears, how she stands, holds her silverware during mealtimes, and so on.

Framed in this context, in one session Mary selected three cards, "early memory/ aggression/baby," and constructed the drawing shown in Figure 8–5. Mary explained that the mother is remembering and sharing with her child that when mother was pregnant, the child, while in utero, often kicked mother very hard. Enacting this scene, Mary tied a pillow around her belly and asked the therapist to punch it. They exchanged roles several times. Each time Mary played the part of the baby kicking (punching the pillow), she burst into anxious laughter mixed with glee.

Risk Taking/Special/Diving In/Father (Figures 8–6a to 8–6d)

During the next two sessions, Mary continued enacting mild forms of aggression when interacting with the therapist, always sprinkled with humor and accompanied by complaints about mother. Then she selected four cards, "risk taking/

RISK TAKING
SPECIAL
DIVINING IN
FATHER

FIGURE 8–6a

FIGURE 8–6b

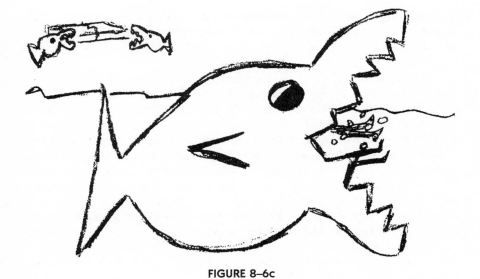

FIGURE 8–6c

FIGURE 8–6d

special/diving in/father." She puzzled for several minutes and drew the picture depicted in Figure 8–6a. Mary explained, "A daughter is swimming. Nearby is a big,
special fish who eats people. Father notices the fish and takes a risk and dives in to
save her."

Instead of enacting the scene, Mary paused for a moment and drew Figure 8–6b.
She explained, "While father is saving the girl, the raft starts to drift away. The
fish is really hungry and wants to attack the people. But the fish freezes. The fish
is really scared. The fish knows she could go for it but stops and can't decide what
to do." During the enactment, Mary initially took the role of the girl swimming.
The therapist lunged forward and put her arms around Mary's shoulders. Then,
laughing, Mary said, "I'll be the fish" and with mouth wide open moved toward
the therapist. Mary paused, sat down, and drew another picture, saying, "There's
more to this story."

She drew Figure 8–6c, noting that the fish decided "to go for it and swallow
the people." She continued drawing Figure 8–6d and pointed out that "the fish is
so undecided, she swallows the people whole and does not chomp on them. . . .
The people are kicking inside of the stomach. The fish gets a stomachache and
starts coughing."

Then Mary drew Figure 8–6e, continuing her story. "The fish coughs up the
father and daughter." The children fish, who were introduced in Figure 8–6c, but
whom Mary ignored until this point, were very confused about why their mother
coughed up the people because they were to be dinner. The baby fish were so angry
that they began "to eat her all up."

FIGURE 8–6e

Mary enacted various aspects of this metaphor; for example, she and the therapist enacted attacking and chewing up an imaginary mother fish; Mary enacted being the fish coughing up the father and daughter. Mary spent three sessions on this metaphor, during which she shared related associations but apparently was not conscious of their connection. For example, she associated to mother's skimpy meals and that she felt more identification with father since mother also nagged him.

Phase V: Discussing Concerns about the Here And Now (8 sessions)

After enacting the "fish" story, Mary shifted the process to present-day concerns. In addition, she wondered whether, with summer approaching and school soon ending, she should stop her sessions. Mary discussed her opinion that she was now more able to speak up and handle schoolwork, and that she would like to "try and see how things go on my own." Exploring Mary's wish to terminate, the therapist agreed that she had made gains, and together they set a termination date three weeks after the close of school. During these discussions, the therapist was careful to respect and accommodate to Mary's expressions of self-assertion and autonomy and to convey her confidence in Mary.

In these final sessions, Mary focused on mother's nagging ways and her anxiety about boys. When discussing mother, Mary used her deck of cards to create "stories," although it now seemed apparent she was aware of the issues she was portraying. Sometimes she expressed an issue directly, as illustrated by her drawing of a mother who is a nag even when she is driving a car ("Mom/picky" Figure 8–7). Mary pointed out that her mother constantly blows her horn and "rags

FIGURE 8–7

on" other drivers. At other times Mary used a cartoon format. The drawing depicted in Figure 8–8 was stimulated by the words "yell/animal/relaxing." Here a mother bear is using "a very relaxed voice to yell at her baby that dinner is ready." Mary did not enact these scenes. Rather, during and after drawing pictures, she engaged the therapist in discussions.

The second theme Mary emphasized during her last sessions concerned her feelings that boys are not interested in her (Figure 8–9: "sad/ignore"); her daydreams about boys, which she is sharing with girlfriends (Figure 8–10: "tall/dark/handsome"); and her hope that the therapist could help her (Figure 8–11: "Dr. A/help/boyfriend").

During the last session, Mary and therapist discussed and listed the pros and cons for continuing treatment in the fall. The reasons Mary listed that supported her continuing included how to handle her mother's nagging ways, her anxieties about boyfriends, and her tendency before exams to get sleepy and speak slowly, sometimes covering her mouth with her hand. In terms of why she thought she could discontinue treatment, Mary felt that it was time for her to "try to work things out on my own" and, as an illustration, pointed out she was going to summer lacrosse camp. Mary agreed to return for a follow-up session in the fall about one month after school began to take stock of whether or not she should continue.

yell-animal-relaxing

FIGURE 8–8

Sad - Ignore

FIGURE 8–9

FIGURE 8–10

FIGURE 8–11

The Final Session

At the start of the next school year, the therapist met with Mary and separately with her parents. Mary seemed pleased to see the therapist and talked freely about her experiences in the tenth grade. She acknowledged that she still became anxious when doing homework and when taking quizzes, but "it's nothing like last year." She had begun to "hang out" with two female classmates, and this group usually connected with boys in the hallways and at lunch. Mary decided that she would not continue weekly sessions and agreed that she would call the therapist whenever she felt she was "getting stuck again."

The parents reported that Mary was "doing well" and were pleased with her progress. She continued to be more outgoing, expressing more clearly what she was thinking and feeling. Father commented that Mary was more focused on school-work and sports than was the case the previous year. Mother noted that Mary seemed to want to be the one who "shoots the winning basket at the end of the game," referring to what mother believed was Mary's fantasy to be a "hero." The therapist engaged mother and father in a discussion of Mary's need to continue testing self-assertion and aggression, and that at times they, and mother in particular, may be irritated by this behavior given that they have been accustomed to her being passive for years. What mother saw as Mary wanting to be a "hero" related to Mary's wish to "rise up" and "be the greatest," all of which are part of self-assertion. The parents were informed that Mary elected not to continue, that the therapist believed this was an appropriate decision, and that Mary understood she could call the therapist if she was experiencing difficulties again.

9

Case Illustrations of Unstructured Interactions in Child Psychotherapy: A Developmental-Dialectical View

CONTENTS

The cases in this chapter are intended to bring attention to guidelines emphasized by the developmental-dialectical model when a child is engaged in psychotherapy that is not structured or directed (see in particular Chapters 4 and 7). At the base of these guidelines are several interrelated positions. One holds that to change how a child functions, it is necessary to change the meanings (metaphors) a child has constructed, from her/his experiences with others, that influence her/his behavior. Another holds that the meanings a child initially constructed and experienced were always holistic and contextual, consisting of organizations of sights, sounds, smells, touch and kinesthetic perceptions, images, actions, and emotions. Initially, then, the construction of meanings was rooted in sensorimotor activity that takes place at developmental levels of functioning below those of symbolic thought and language. Therefore, in the beginning, when a meaning first takes shape, it is embodied. As a meaning undergoes further differentiation and development, it becomes linked to motives, fantasies, and emotions, and in this way organizes urges and desires and guides their expression in actions, fantasies, and metaphoric language in interactions with others. Last, meanings are inherently repetitive in that they continually gain expression in evolving cycles of ritualized activity.

When applied to conducting nondirected psychotherapy with children, these interrelated positions result in broad, technical guidelines that form two sides of a coin. On one side is the guideline that as a child behaves within the treatment relationship, she/he projects onto the therapist meanings (metaphors) representing interpersonal dilemmas and unrepaired disruptions. On the other side of the coin is the guideline that the therapist should refrain from verbally interrupting (conceptualizing) these behaviors and their meanings. Rather, as much as is appropriate for a child and therapist, the therapist should initially respond to these dilemmas with embodied meanings/enactments that provide the child with holistic experiences, including sights, sounds, smells, touch and kinesthetic perceptions, images, actions, and emotions—experiences that attempt to resolve the dilemmas.

If a therapist participates with holistic enactments that communicate with the child's metaphor and draw on the intersubjective world child and therapist share, the child idealizes and internalizes the therapist's solutions. This process revises the meaning the child was experiencing and/or constructs a new meaning that is rooted in sensorimotor activity. In this way the persistent, ritualized interactions between child and therapist replicate the developmental process of metaphor construction. Having initially emphasized sensorimotor activity in her/his enactments, the therapist gradually includes and emphases differentiated fantasies and then metaphoric language that elaborate and revise the meaning further.

These interrelated guidelines are brought into focus if we compare them with a position Lewis (1977) took when proposing an integration of Piaget's theory and psychodynamic therapy. He concluded that spoken language is "the royal treatment highway," and "the great mediator between cognition and emotional development" (p. 659). The developmental-dialectical model takes a different position, proposing that the "royal treatment highway" is made up of four lanes. Verbal concepts and interpretations occupy only one; symbolic actions and fantasies, and metaphoric language, the others. I discussed in previous chapters why I believe that the lane occupying verbal concepts is the least important in promoting change. I also clarified the view that by responding with verbalized concepts and explanations, a therapist could require a child to engage in second-order change before the child is ready.

To elaborate this position, imagine that when a child is experiencing and expressing meanings in action, fantasy, or metaphoric language, the child is grading and paving the lane on the "royal treatment highway" belonging to that modality. When a therapist conceptualizes some meaning the child is expressing, the child is required to leave the lane he/she is grading and paving *before the job is complete*, and pave the lane devoted to concepts. I have proposed that a therapist should remain in the lane the child is grading and paving. If a switch in lanes is required, action, fantasy, and metaphoric language should be graded and paved before working on the lane reserved for concepts is worked on. In this way the entire width of the highway becomes available as the child journeys through childhood and adolescence.

In addition, the sequence in which these lanes are paved is important. A meaning should be experienced within each mode and expressed with as many alternative means and ends and degrees of delay as possible. This process should not be hurried or partially bypassed by a therapist insofar as the personal makeups of a child and therapist permit. To emphasize my point, I replace the metaphor of a highway with the metaphor of a plant. Imagine the leaves of a plant as a network of concepts (insights, understanding) emerging in therapy. These concepts should be connected, at a developmentally lower level, to the branches of metaphoric language. These branches in turn should be connected at a still lower level to the soil and roots of fantasy experiences, and again at a still lower level to action experiences. Without roots integrating the three modalities, insights (concepts) float detached as intellectualizations and psychologizing; fantasies are deprived of their fulfillment in environmental-related experiences; and actions become robotlike without the breadth, psychological economy, and meaning provided by metaphoric language and fantasy.

In many cases it is not necessary to provide a child with literal knowledge, or conceptual understanding, of his/her difficulties for the child to benefit from psychotherapy and undergo change. But it is necessary to provide the child with experiences that cultivate *how* the child constructs and expresses knowledge. Equipped with multiple ways of constructing and expressing knowledge, a child assumes a more growth-fostering course, benefiting from opportunities and limitations provided by family members, peers, communities, and school environments. The process of symbolizing itself has the power to promote change and resolve difficulties.

The cases we consider below are intended to illustrate these several propositions and guidelines. Notes recorded after each session were examined by me and independently by another therapist, after the treatment ended, to address several questions: What interactive metaphor is revealed in the child's play activity when examined in terms of the meaning expressed by organizations of physical actions, emotions, fantasies, and metaphoric language? What dilemma does the interactive metaphor express, and is the therapist called upon to discover solutions? Is the metaphor, with its calls for action, a factor in the child's psychological difficulties, construing self and therapist in ways that impede adequate functioning and development? As the organization of activity is repeated, does the metaphor undergo restructuring as a function of the child's idealizing and internalizing some aspect of the therapist's enactments? Does each restructuring provide the child with opportunities to redefine his/her self and the therapist in ways that advance development? When a pathological metaphor is re-formed, does it restructure to a higher developmental level with the intrinsic emergence of new coding capacities? Do these new coding capacities result in developmentally more advanced constructions of experiences that integrate modalities and more adaptive plans of action?

Last, an interactive metaphor was viewed as having been restructured if changes were observed in several domains: (1) the meaning represented by the interactions; (2) the roles assigned to child and therapist; (3) the standards and expectations represented; (4) the behavioral modes the child employed (macro- and microaction, fantasy, metaphoric language); and (5) the intensity of emotions experienced.

HARRY: MY BODY-SELF IS FALLING

We first became acquainted with Harry in Chapters 1 and 7. He was referred at the age of 4 years, 4 months after having been expelled from a preschool program because, without provocation, he spit at, bit, and hit classmates and teachers. In addition, when coping with classroom activities, his behaviors shifted between two extremes. He frantically moved about, struggling to sit and listen to the teacher read stories. On other occasions he curled up in a corner of the room, ignoring assistance from teachers, and preoccupying himself with a record player.

Intake Interview with Parents

Harry's parents reported that at home he had shown the same behaviors that led to his dismissal from preschool. On occasion he hit, bit, or spit at his parents (more often mother), his 3-year-old sister, and his grandparents. While he sometimes played with his sister, he inevitably snatched one of her toys or struck her, behaviors that led to her screaming and Harry spending a time-out in his room. The biggest current problem at home, however, concerned Harry's daily struggles with mother. He refused to get dressed in the morning and followed mother around the house demanding her complete attention. He also demanded "strange things" to eat for breakfast (e.g., potato chips), which parents tried to negotiate, frequently without success.

The parents were puzzled about other issues. Whenever Harry was left with a baby-sitter during the first three years, he showed no anxiety. Laughing, mother commented with, "I think he was glad to see us leave." Father thought this behavior reflected that Harry was "tough." Yet, in the past few months, when left with a sitter, he has experienced sudden surges of intense fear. With another concern, father sometimes took Harry to a nearby park. On several of these occasions Harry experienced a "panic attack" when he was about to move down a sliding board. Mother added that during the night Harry frequently woke up crying, and was unable to explain to them what was wrong. Father felt he could cuddle Harry and saw him as a bundle of energy that was not channeled. Mother felt she could not cuddle him and saw herself "in Harry." "I had a problem with aggression when I was a child."

In terms of Harry's early history, he crawled and walked with a vigorous style. Therefore mother thought Harry would benefit from spending time in a playpen so that he could "sit still for a while and play with his toys while I got my work done." From about 12 to 20 months Harry was placed in a playpen for several hours a day. Harry seemed to be playing with toys, but he also rocked on all fours, sometimes "chanting" while rhythmically tapping his head against the bars of the playpen. After Harry reached his second birthday he was not placed in the playpen except when he became "too frantic."

The parents could not agree on his "playing style" before the age of 3. Father thought Harry played with toy cars and animals. Mother thought Harry spent more time "just handling things" when he wasn't busy with the record player and light switches. Harry developed a fascination with light switches, turning them on and off many times in succession. They tried different ways to interrupt this activity (e.g., rewarding him with a cookie if he stopped), but their efforts failed. He also became fascinated with a record player they had given him in the hope that children's music would soothe him. Initially he would sit staring at the record turning, or would move the arm back and forth. More recently he has played records, oblivious to what was going on around him, behavior he also displayed at school and that concerned teachers.

Toilet training was a "tremendous struggle." Mother began training Harry at about 24 months, but he resisted. He wet and soiled himself during the day and while asleep until the age of 3 years when he "apparently gave up the battle." But, from the parents' point of view, Harry has defined other battlefields, such as getting dressed in the morning and asking for items to eat "when he knows we will refuse."

Guided by the developmental-dialectical model, I constructed the following preliminary hypotheses from the information provided by the parents. Several factors suggested that Harry had experienced disruptions in ongoing regulations and heightened traumatic emotions, especially involving mother. By the time he reached his second birthday, he had not evolved play rituals, with either parent, to experiment with representing things and interactions. Moreover, it seemed likely that his negotiations with three particular issues had been significantly disrupted and left incomplete: directed activity (controlling stimulation and anticipating that mother would accommodate to his direction), focalizing (establishing mother's unconditional availability), and self-assertion and testing aggression (when opposing mother she would provide alternative means). Harry had been confined to a playpen during those very months when self-assertion and testing aggression are negotiated.

The inadequate negotiation of these issues resulted in Harry's evolving inflexible rituals interacting with light switches and a record player. With these rituals he could experience directing activity and provoking responses from the environment that made interesting sights last. At the same time, in terms of self-assertion, he rigidly opposed mother's dictates, requesting foods to eat that he knew would be denied.

Teacher Conference

Harry's teacher regretted that he had been expelled and was relieved that he would receive assistance. She had experienced Harry as very intelligent and charming when he was not excessively aggressive and hyperactive. She reported that Harry had been biting and hitting children for two months prior to his dismissal and at a frequency of one to five times a day. After he hit or bit a child, he typically had a blank look on his face "as if in another world." Sometimes he curled up in a corner and, when asked what was wrong, verbalized that he was afraid he might hit someone. At other times, crying, he would express that he wanted to play but did not know how. Understandably, the children in the class avoided him whenever he attempted to engage them.

Harry's Intake Interview and Evaluation

When I first met Harry, I spent about thirty minutes experiencing him in an unstructured format. Particular qualities of his appearance and behavior immediately impressed me. A robust, good-looking boy, he was constantly on the move both physically and mentally, anxiously roaming through the entire room while throwing glances here and there. I was also impressed by his verbal facility. He constantly chatted, with pressured speech, using vocabulary that seemed to fit a 7- or 8-year-old. During these moments, as described in Chapter 1, he picked up and set down many items, hurriedly scribbled many "designs" with crayons, and threw balls of play dough against the wall. I tried to deflect this activity, inviting him to throw the balls of clay into a wastebasket "to see how many you can get in." The intervention failed to help Harry regulate his hyperactivity.

When I observed that he was becoming increasingly anxious, showing little self-regulation, I scooped a number of rubber animals and human figures from a box, set them on the table, and asked him to "show me what upsets you a lot." Harry quickly picked up a boy doll figure, sharing, "He's crying in his room; his mom put him there." Then Harry picked up an alligator doll, who told the boy, "You wait here; I'll help you." The alligator "goes downstairs" and immediately attacked the mother doll, "chewing her up." Harry repeatedly slammed the alligator doll against the mother doll, showing excitement and anger. Then the alligator crawled upstairs and told the boy, "OK, you can go down."

Harry abruptly stopped this fantasy play, returned to throwing clay balls against the wall, and then pulled on the curtain. I also tried to deflect this activity, inviting him to "tear up sheets of paper." He ignored me and continued tugging at the curtains, so much so that it was clear he was about to pull them down. I held him firmly and reassured him that I was glad the alligator helped the boy, and I wanted to help that boy get out of his room too. I did not mention his difficulties at school or his biting. As Harry calmed down, I asked him if he would come back to see me again in a few days. Harry asked if he could bring his record player. I said I would love to see it and suggested he bring a few of his favorite records.

I devoted the next several meetings to administering psychological tests that I hoped would provide data that could not be obtained by interacting with him in structured or unstructured play. Given that Harry experienced disruptions and heightened traumatic emotions from the first year of life, and recalling that he rocked in the playpen, I wondered what embodied representations he would reveal. I also wondered whether he had idealized and internalized some aspect of each parent, or of grandparents, forming the beginnings of internal standards that could serve self-regulation. And I wondered what purposes aggression served, whether cognitive regulators and orientation had been derailed, and whether he was capable of constructing symbols in the action and fantasy modes.

As it turned out, eight sessions were required to obtain what I thought were reasonably valid data. Initially, Harry ignored the first procedure I introduced (scanning a sheet of paper on which were printed various geometric shapes, and marking all of the circles and crosses). He remained seated before a record player and moved the arm on and off a record. I joined him with as much interest as I could muster and tried to locate the same spot in the middle of the record, commenting that this was like finding those circles and crosses hidden among all the other shapes. Harry imitated me, laughing with excitement, as he also tried to find the same spot on the record. After several minutes, he engaged and completed the test of visual scanning. In this way, throughout the testing, Harry shifted back and forth from the record player to a test procedure, but he frequently needed to be refocused and encouraged to continue working.

On the Wechsler Preschool and Primary Scale of Intelligence, he attained a verbal IQ of 130 (superior range), a performance IQ of 112 (bright-normal range), and full-scale IQ of 124 (superior range). His performance varied significantly from subtest to subtest, ranging from a scaled score of 17 (Information and Arithmetic subtests) and 15 (Similarities subtest) to 10 (Block Design subtest). His lower scores with performance subtests seemed to be due primarily to the impulsive way he manipulated materials. In contrast, during verbal subtests he seemed much more entrained and regulated when interacting with me.

Results from cognitive tests, described in Chapter 6, illuminated which cognitive functions were involved in Harry's inattention. Harry regulated fine-motor movements at stage expectation (fifty-fourth percentile). But the manner in which he scanned a field of information (twenty-fourth percentile) and focused attention in the face of external distractions (fourth percentile) and internal distractions (twenty-seventh percentile) showed significant compromises. Yet the manner in which he held images of information in memory and compared them to present perceptions was stage-adequate (sixtieth percentile).

These data provided information about Harry's cognitive functioning that had not been apparent from my interactions with him. Two of the cognitive functions proved to be stage-adequate. In spite of his hyperactivity, when required, he could regulate fine-motor movements and tempos, and hold patterns of information in memory over time, with efficiency expected for his age. Two other functions were compromised, however: the manner in which he scanned information and focused attention in the face of distractions. He also showed evidence of rapid shifts in cognitive orientation, which received support from observations made during personality testing.

He struggled anxiously with the Rorschach test, attempted to avoid the task, and frequently shifted his cognitive orientation from imaging what the inkblots could be to addressing stimulation in our immediate environment. As one example, he interrupted the task, looked at my wristwatch, and said, "Tomorrow, that will be *19*." The digits on my watch were *18*. "The *8* is gonna change, but the *1* won't change, right?" However, Harry did construct a number of images that defined two metaphors. One represented the need for nurture, expressed in images such as a "giant cookie" and two mothers, but the "parts aren't hooked up." The second metaphor represented Harry's body image as lacking stability, expressed in images such as a person "falling down a space in the sky," a monkey that is "falling, all the way down," and a butterfly that is trying to fly but keeps falling. Harry's Rorschach performance also provided information about the extent to which the action mode dominated his functioning and, conversely, the degree to which the process of imaging failed to subordinate action expressions. For example, when imaging the butterfly, he frantically waved the card in the air and banged it against the table, and when handed Card X, he exclaimed, "Butterflies all over!" and then repeatedly slapped the card with his hand.

With the Children's Apperception Test, which provided more structure, he showed less anxiety but also experienced difficulty constructing stories, tending to describe the picture. Story fragments he produced represented salient aspects of his subjective world. One converged with the need for nurture observed in his Rorschach images. To Card 1, after describing each "chicken," he commented, "The food is all gone." To Card 3 he commented, "This is not a good picture." I asked him why, and he responded, "Mother and father went away, and he thinks they won't come back." The other cluster of representations seemed related to his experiences in the playpen. With Card 4, a baby bear is "stuck in the crib and wants to get out—the wind comes and blows him up in the sky and the crib too." With Card 9, the bunny in the crib is crying and wants to go out and play.

Harry was also administered the Miniature Situations Test of Aggression (Chapter 6; Santostefano 1978) to obtain observations about the degree of delay and indirectness that characterized his expressions in the action mode and his capacity to construct symbols while experiencing actions. With each item he performed the most direct and immediate action first and the most indirect and delayed last. For example, he tore up a sheet of paper, then crumpled a second sheet, and last cut a third sheet in half with scissors following a line. When tearing the sheet of paper, he quickly lost self-regulation as he frantically pulled and tugged at the paper and then scattered the pieces about the room. Of particular significance, he was unable to construct any meanings or associations after having performed the actions.

Taken together, the results showed Harry to be very bright, to have adequately developed cognitive regulators for the most part, but when coordinating environmental stimulation and personal meanings, his cognition shifted rapidly, resulting in frequent slips. The frequency with which he slapped the Rorschach cards and waved them about, when the task required imaging and not action, is one illustration of these slips. In addition, the action mode dominated and showed little capacity for delay and few alternative means. In terms of the content of his subjective world, two related metaphors emerged: one represented the need for nurture and attachment; the other, the body-self as not grounded.

Influenced by these results, I decided that during our interactions in the first phase of treatment, I would emphasize the action mode and macroactions as much as possible. Because his cognition shifted rapidly back and forth from an inner to an outer orientation, I also decided that I would try to anchor his cognition for as long as possible within concrete stimuli so that he would use them as vehicles for his symbols and benefit from experiencing imaging as trial action. One short-term goal, of course, was to help Harry step into a dialectical circle and prepare him for his return to a kindergarten program in the fall.

Harry's Treatment

Harry was seen one session per week for four weeks, then two sessions per week for two months. The frequency was then increased again to three sessions per week.

Chaos: Helping Harry Step into a Dialectical Circle (2 months)

When I entered the waiting room, I found Harry under a bench, clutching a record player and two records. With some coaxing, he came out and accompanied me to the playroom. When I asked him why he had crawled under the bench, he commented with irritation, "Because I feel like it! Don't talk!" This behavior forecast the difficulty we were about to experience. During the first twelve sessions, his activity was chaotic and reflected little or no pretending as he moved restlessly, chatting almost constantly. Some of Harry's activities did not implicitly invite me to participate. As he had done during the evaluation, he sometimes sat before the record player, moving the arm back and forth on a record. He also made balls of play dough again and hurled them at the wall and sometimes at hand puppets and toy animals that he placed on a table. On occasion he placed a toy animal or puppet over another and giggled "plop, plop," clearly indicating that one figure was defecating on the other.

Other activities included me. He invited me to play different formboard games (e.g., Candyland, Uncle Wiggly) and games of "Fish" and "War" with a deck of playing cards. After initiating one of these activities, he remained involved for three or four minutes and then walked away. Sometimes when he made balls with play dough, he invited me to make various animals. As I completed my sculpture, he would seize it and tear it apart. From time to time, as he walked about in search of something to do, he swatted a puppet or toy animal from the shelf onto the floor.

Several of my attempts failed to help Harry step into a dialectical circle. On one occasion he asked if I had any milk. Seizing this request as a possible opportunity to lay the groundwork for a dialectical interaction, I eagerly replied that I could get some, left the playroom for a moment, and returned with a glass of milk. Harry responded, "Never mind. I was only thirsty. I'll get water." He went to the water cooler in the hallway, took a drink, and returned. On another occasion, noticing a Band-Aid on his hand and expressing what I thought was interest, I asked, "What happened?" He responded with irritation, "That's a secret!" and walked away.

Other attempts to help Harry step into a circle eventually proved successful. Whenever he became occupied with moving the arm of the record player back and forth, I tried to set the needle on the same spot of the record, much as I had done during the evaluation, enacting that I was very caught up with the challenge. Harry imitated me. Each time either one of us was successful in locating the same part of a song, we joined in a chorus of cheers.

With another strategy, whenever Harry toppled toy animals and puppets from shelves, I set geometric wooden cutouts under them. Looking back, I believe that in doing so I was influenced by the Rorschach images of things falling and lacking stability. I thought the cutouts might symbolize to Harry, "See, these have a ground under them, so they won't fall." But instead Harry soon limited his swats to toy animals and puppets under which I had placed a cutout, apparently experiencing the cutouts as invitations to topple the toys rather than as representing stable ground.

Although I did not understand the meaning of his swatting only those toys set on cutouts, I was pleased to find that my response resulted in a ritualized, circular interaction. Eventually, as soon as I set a cutout under a puppet, Harry walked over and toppled it. One of the hand puppets was of a boy wearing a sweater with the letter A. Harry began to focus on this puppet. If I did not place a cutout under it and did under others, he commented, "Let's get him," pointing to the puppet. With this it became clear he was beginning to include this particular puppet in some circular interaction that at the time had no meaning for me.

Similarly, whenever he lined up puppets at which he threw balls of play dough, I set cutouts under one or two of them. Harry aimed his missiles at the ones I had designated and gleefully shouted, "I got it!" when he was successful in knocking one over. Here, too, the puppet with the letter A held special meaning for Harry. Initially I had been placing cutouts at random under the puppets he had lined up. But soon, whenever I failed to place a cutout under the puppet with the letter A, Harry asked me to do so.

During the last five sessions of this phase, Harry regularly punctuated playing formboard games and card games by toppling puppets with his hand or with balls of clay. The act of toppling puppets under which I had placed a cutout became a ritual that indicated he had stepped into a dialectical circle. This ritual eventually ushered in the first interactive metaphor and marked the close of this chaotic phase.

Metaphor: My Body Is Starving and Has No Control (2 months)

Harry brought symbolic organization to his chaotic activity when in one session he referred to the puppet with the letter A as "Mr. Fall," simultaneously asking for something to eat. With this, Harry introduced a new circular interaction. While munching food, he limited his toppling to Mr. Fall. Whether Mr. Fall toppled from the shelf by a swat of his hand or from the table by a ball of play dough, Harry exclaimed with anxious laughter, "There goes Mr. Fall! He's going to get spanked. He can't stand up!"

Sensing an interactive metaphor emerging, I now rushed forward to try to catch Mr. Fall each time he plunged from a shelf. When Mr. Fall was set on the table along with other puppets, I surrounded him with toy furniture, my appointment book, and other items to prevent him from being toppled by a clay ball. Harry became very invested in my efforts, oozing with anxiety and sometimes cheering when I was successful. On occasion, whenever Mr. Fall landed on the floor, I playfully imitated the puppet and fell to the floor. Here I was guided by my initial goal to introduce metaphoric expressions in macroaction whenever possible.

Harry assimilated this action and imitated me. He began to fall to the floor, frequently while holding Mr. Fall in one hand and a cookie in the other. At these times I rushed to place various items (e.g., wastebaskets, chairs) around Harry to prevent a fall, sometimes succeeding and sometimes failing. As this interactive metaphor became ritualized, Harry sometimes stood still, obviously waiting for me to set up props around him. When my efforts were successful, I expressed victory, and when they failed, frustration. At these times my enactment and comments conveyed that it was clear Mr. Fall needed more than props to keep him from falling, and I puzzled over what else I could do. From this, Harry introduced another interactive metaphor that explicitly called for help.

Metaphor: I Need Help (1 month)

During one session, while munching a cookie, Harry fell to the floor and dramatically exclaimed, "I ate too much. Help, I'm sinking!" I carefully examined him using the toy doctor's kit. I listened to his heart with a stethoscope and tapped his knees with a neurologist's rubber hammer while Harry groaned, playing someone who was ill ("My tonsils are broken"). When repeating this metaphor he sometimes spontaneously reversed roles, assumed the role of the doctor, and asked me to lie on the floor and pretend that I was "a puppy." With stethoscope around his neck, he gently tapped my chest, listened to my heart ("What's the matter, puppy?"), and looked into my ears ("I see frogs in there"). In response I commented, for example, "A lot of things bother me, but I don't know what." To which Harry responded, "You mean your mother spanks you? The teacher yells at you?"

In one session, when Harry fell to the floor and exclaimed, "Help, I'm sinking," a newspaper happened to be nearby. I quickly spread it open and pulled Harry onto "the raft," reassuring him that "we're going to make it." For some reason this new edition of the need for help took hold, since Harry initiated this activity a number of times. During these enactments, he cuddled next to me on our "raft." I made comments that added up to, "We're going to find a lot of ways that will stop us from sinking." Following these interactive metaphors, and perhaps stimulated by my conveying that I was prepared to find solutions to "sinking," Harry introduced a new interactive metaphor that elaborated his initial representation of the body-out-of-control.

Metaphor: A Boy Flips Out Unless His Body Is Tied Down (12 months)

Harry returned to playing formboard games. When compared to his behavior with these games during earlier sessions, he now engaged in a game for a longer period of time and seemed less anxious. What was particularly conspicuous, Harry held

Mr. Fall in one hand while playing a game. I felt pleased, thinking to myself that our efforts to prevent Mr. Fall from falling had paid off. I wondered if Harry had experienced my attempts as attuned to his needs for my unconditional availability. Perhaps, having assimilated these interactions, Harry had achieved some degree of self-regulation over his hyperactivity. It seemed that Mr. Fall had now become an idealized companion who could be a source of strength for Harry. But this peaceful atmosphere was short-lived.

In one session, while playing Candyland and holding Mr. Fall in one hand, Harry flipped his wrist without warning, sending Mr. Fall sailing across the room. The first time he did this, I did not recognize its significance. But when he flipped the puppet several times, it dawned on me that another edition of the first metaphor was being authored. Significantly, now Harry began to call the puppet "Alvin," apparently following the letter A on the puppet's sweater. Once it occurred to me that Harry was shaping a new dilemma each time he flipped the puppet across the room, I got up and rushed to retrieve it.

Soon, whenever we sat before a formboard game with Harry holding Alvin, I began to keep an eye on Alvin in an attempt to anticipate his flights through space. If I noticed Harry's hand beginning to twitch, I jumped up so that I could catch the puppet in midair. Harry apparently understood what I was doing since he became involved in catching me off guard. Sometimes he jerked his wrist but did not release the puppet, and sometimes he did release it. When he released the puppet, he exclaimed, "Alvin is flipping out!" When he did not, he declared, "Alvin is OK." If I jumped up and Harry did not release the puppet, he roared with laughter: "I fooled you!" If I jumped up when Harry did release the puppet, he screamed, "You got 'em!" or "You missed 'em!" (the latter occurred most of the time). Harry repeated this enactment ten or more times a session, whether we were playing formboard games or games of War and Fish with playing cards. Of course, rushing to retrieve Alvin many times in one session frequently exhausted me.

Why Harry repeated this enactment for many sessions without revising it puzzled me. But soon he began to elaborate its meaning. Sometimes after releasing Alvin Harry announced that Alvin was "lost." In response, I crawled about the room, enacting that I was searching for Alvin, and rejoiced with Harry when I found the puppet. At other times he announced that Alvin was "flipping out," and exclaimed that Alvin had been injured when he hit the wall or floor. At these times I took the play doctor's kit and examined Alvin, pretending to give him shots and medicine, and placed Band-Aids on him.

Each time I expressed concern about Alvin's injury and wondered what we could do to prevent him from flipping out and getting hurt, I enacted several solutions. At first, repeating strategies I had used during the first phase of treatment, I leaned various items on Alvin while Harry was holding him. With some items I attempted to probe whether Harry would assimilate and elaborate some representation of me as a source of control for Alvin: for example, my appointment book, a notepad, my necktie, books. With other items I probed "in the dark," fishing for an item that Harry might latch onto in constructing a symbol of control: for example, doll figures of a father, mother, grandfather, grandmother, policeman, animals. But Harry continued flipping Alvin across the room, pushing to one side the item I had leaned on the puppet.

Then in one session I took a piece of string and tied one end around Alvin and the other around a nearby doorknob. Now when Harry flipped out, his flight was abruptly stopped by the string. Looking back, at first I thought the idea of a string had "popped" into my head. Later I realized that the string had occurred to me during one session in which I had draped my necktie around Alvin to prevent him from flipping out. Although Harry eventually sent the puppet flying, before flipping it he pulled at Alvin with one hand while holding one end of the necktie with the other, enacting for a second that Alvin was stuck and could not flip out.

Harry became fascinated with this enactment from the first time I tied the string. Initially he repeatedly threw Alvin in the air and watched the puppet's flight snap to a stop. Then he asked if we could make the string "bigger." After experimenting with a longer length, he made the same request again. It seemed clear that Harry was experimenting with the question, How long should the string be so that Alvin could fly through space and almost, but not quite, hit the wall? We cut many lengths of string, experimenting with each a number of times. Then in one session Harry interrupted this ritualized enactment and ushered in behaviors that I eventually understood represented a core pathological metaphor.

Metaphor: Bite and Stab, My Brain Is Crazy (2 months)

Harry restlessly roamed about the room, which contrasted sharply with his behaviors during previous weeks when he enthusiastically participated in experimenting with different lengths of string. If I asked him what was the matter, he would say, "Shut up! No talking!" If I took out string or a deck of playing cards, he walked away. After two sessions of this diffuse agitation, he began to attack me directly. At the start of one session, as we walked to the playroom, Harry ran ahead, entered the playroom, and slammed the door shut. I tried to communicate through the door but he would only scream, "Shut up!" When I opened the door and entered the playroom, the barrage began, "Get out!" "I hate you!" "I wish you were dead!" Sometimes I deferred and stepped out of the room, closed the door, and waited. When he would not invite me back in or respond to my comments, I reentered the room only to be greeted by another hail of insults.

In the next two sessions Harry's behavior remained pretty much the same, and all my efforts to engage him failed. Then Harry aggressed physically on my person in addition to throwing verbal insults. These physical attacks occurred when I approached him from time to time while he preoccupied himself in solo activity. But sometimes they occurred without warning. He threw toys at me, punched my arms, kicked my shins, spit at me, and tried to bite my arm. On several occasions he took a pair of scissors he was using to cut paper and lunged in an attempt to stab me.

Whenever these outbursts occurred, I tried a number of times to cultivate alternative goals at which he could direct his aggression. For example, I invited him to stab the scissors into a large ball of clay and to spit at a magazine picture of a man. But these interventions failed as Harry repeatedly attacked my person, punching, spitting, and biting. On many occasions this behavior escalated to a point that I had to restrain him by wrapping my arms around him and holding him firmly while expressing concern. Once he calmed down, I made various comments that relied upon enactments and meanings we had shared to this point. "You're flipping out just like Alvin did." "You just flipped out and you hit the wall just like Alvin did." When making these comments, I sometimes performed actions, imitating aspects of Harry's behavior, that I thought could help him assimilate the meaning I was expressing. For example, I held a pair of scissors overhead and while slowly lowering it to stab it into play dough, I enacted that I was experiencing a struggle between the wish to plunge the scissors into the play dough on the one hand and the urge to stop my arm on the other. "This is crazy!" "I can't stop my hand!" "I'm flipping out!" During his outbursts, Harry soon internalized and imitated these expressions, shouting, "My brain is crazy!" "I'm flipping out!"

Then in one session, recalling that the string had proved to be a successful symbol in preventing Alvin from flipping out, I tied one end of a long string around my forehead and the other around Harry's, reminding him how the string "helped Alvin not flip out." This enactment worked. Harry stopped his attacks. For three sessions he and I, with a string connecting our heads, sat and played games. Then Harry made a request that ushered in the next interactive metaphor.

Metaphor: The Police Station (Rules and Standards) Controls Crazy (2 months)

Harry asked me for several padlocks. I had only one, which he hung around his neck with the string we had previously tied to our heads. When he said his "police station" needed more locks, we went to a hardware store and purchased several. In the next session he used the locks to elaborate what he called the "trapping game." He located items throughout the playroom, leaning a lock on each with its key nearby. He also designated the area under a table as "the police station." Parenthetically, as Harry carefully leaned locks on various items, I recalled that previously I had leaned various items on Alvin to prevent him from flipping out. It seemed to me that this particular enactment on Harry's part assimilated a symbolic action I had used.

Harry, Alvin the puppet, and I sat under a table "in the police station." Harry asked me to "be the police station." When assuming this role, my job was to announce which item, from among those Harry had distributed throughout the room, was to be used and how. In a deep, "authoritative," voice, I announced, for example, "Harry, cut the green sheet of paper with the scissors." "Alvin, cut the play dough in half with the knife." "Harry, hit the punching bag." Once I gave a command, I walked over to the item and unlocked the lock leaning on it. Then Harry or Alvin (played by Harry) would take the item and perform the prescribed action. After the prescribed task was accomplished, the lock was secured again and leaned on the object.

As the police station, I complimented Harry and Alvin whenever they performed the prescribed action well. On several occasions, however, Harry made clear that when a lock was unlocked, his hands, or Alvin's, still "did crazy things." For example, Harry once threw a ball of clay against the wall when he had been asked by the police station to thrust a wooden stick into it. In another instance Alvin popped a balloon when the police station had requested that the balloon be bounced in the air. When this occurred, I, as the police station, repeatedly experienced frustration and puzzled what was it in Harry and Alvin that had the power to make them do crazy things even when they didn't want to. My frustration and confusion was eventually answered by Harry when he introduced another edition to his series of metaphors.

Metaphor: Mr. Bad Is Conquered (10 months)

In one session Harry decided to transform the area under the table from a police station to "a fort." We barricaded the area with chairs and wastebaskets. Harry, Alvin, and I sat in the fort peering through the chairs at a cylindrical punching bag (which had been used during the police station game). Harry had designated that the punching bag was a mean monster he called "Mr. Bad." During the enactments that followed, Harry draped my necktie around his neck, symbolizing the processes idealization and internalization. Harry authored that the punching bag (which Harry asked me to move slowly toward the fort while making menacing sounds) repeatedly attacked the fort, and attempted to capture us and take us to "monster land." With each attack, Harry fought back using different weapons. For example, he shot rubber bands at Mr. Bad with a "gun" Harry and I constructed. He rushed out of the fort and viciously whipped Mr. Bad with my belt.

In addition, Harry authored that Mr. Bad commanded one of us to "do a bad thing." Here Harry asked me to make announcements with the same deep voice I used during the police station game. For example, Mr. Bad commanded, "Harry, throw play dough against the wall." "Alvin, knock down the animals that are on the shelf." With each command Harry flexed his arms and screamed in defiance, for example, "You can't make us do that!" "Dr. S is stronger than you!" "Dr. S is president of the world!" When Alvin was ordered to perform some action, Harry screamed, "Don't do it! Hold back!" Harry brought this metaphor to a close when he crumpled newspapers around the punching bag and pretended to set fire to Mr. Bad, cheering, "Now all the monsters of the world are dead."

Metaphor: I Am Mastering My Aggression and I Can Discuss Current Problems (6 months)

After Mr. Bad was burned, Harry introduced a major change in our activity. He returned to formboard games, now engaging them for most of the session and appropriately competing with me. While we played, he occasionally introduced difficulties he was experiencing in school, where he was now attending the first grade. For example, once, while playing kickball, he kicked a classmate, for which he was sent to the principal's office. And, with considerable anxiety and shame, he reported that he had wet his pants at school (confirmed by parents). As we talked about this, he revealed that he did not use school toilets because the flushing frightened him and reminded him of thunder. Whenever he stared at the water whirling down the toilet, he was gripped with the fear that he would be sucked down into the pipe. During these discussions, Harry returned to enacting. He flushed paper cups down the toilet, exclaiming, "Help, I'm sinking!" We noted that the cup was like Mr. Fall, Alvin, and Harry, who sometimes fell and sank. As we had done with Alvin and our heads, we fastened a cup to a string that Harry held as he repeatedly flushed the toilet, confirming that the cup did not "sink away."

Harry also displayed behaviors suggesting his aggressive tensions were beginning to be experienced in terms of symbols representing ascendance and power (phallic representations) in contrast to the passive-aggressive symbols (anal representations) he used early in treatment when puppets defecated on each other and when he spit on the examiner. He brought in his record player and two records, which we played numerous times. One contained songs about a giraffe with a short neck who wanted his neck to grow longer. The other contained songs about a train that wanted to be powerful enough to climb a big hill. On occasion he also played "snake," slithering his belly over the floor. He shared that he experienced "tickly feelings" when his penis rubbed along the carpet and that at home he draped a piece of toilet paper over his penis, which also gave him "tickly feelings."

Critique

Harry's aggressive, impulsive behavior, his biting, spitting, and striking out, were rooted in an embodied metaphor constructed during the first three years of life that construed his body-self as lacking nurture and as not grounded and stable. The restructuring of this embodied metaphor required that he and I participate in a series of interactive metaphors. Once Harry stepped into a dialectical circle, he symbolically ritualized the body as not grounded and out of control by toppling the puppet Mr. Fall. When I imitated Mr. Fall with macroactions by toppling myself to the floor, Harry assimilated this enactment and toppled himself to the floor. In an effort to solve this dilemma, I surrounded Harry with furniture and the puppet with various items to prevent them from falling. Although my efforts were frequently unsuccessful, Harry identified with my commitment to finding solutions by sitting on my "raft" to avoid "sinking." Following this expression of alliance, the metaphor representing lack of groundedness and loss of control was enacted again in microactions and fantasy as the puppet, transformed into a mythical boy "Alvin," repeatedly fell through space, construed as "flipping out," Harry's first use of a linguistic metaphor elaborating the meaning of mental loss of control. Of my different attempts to prevent Alvin from flipping out, the symbol of a string tied to Alvin was assimilated by Harry.

Apparently reassured that I was capable of finding solutions to our dilemmas, from my propping up Harry with furniture to tying a string to Alvin, Harry enacted his core pathological metaphor that called for hate and violence toward others, a state of mind he construed as "going crazy." He attacked me physically as well as verbally. However, the action symbol of a string as a form of control, which Harry had already experienced as successful in helping Alvin, was now successful in helping Harry control his violence. This enactment conveyed that a "crazy mind could be controlled."

Assimilating again that solutions could be found to the dilemma of falling out of control, Harry introduced the first interactive metaphor representing standards of conduct (the police station) and control (locks), which he assigned to me as he repeatedly experienced that "bad" actions could be "trapped" and regulated when "unlocked." Although Harry could exercise control when required by another person (the therapist), he continued to experience the call for aggressive, inappropriate actions. The therapist (the police station) struggled and wondered what it was *in* Harry that continued to force him to do "bad things."

Internalizing the therapist's (police station) wish to discover this inner force, Harry authored another interactive metaphor that projected an "evil force" (Mr. Bad) that seduced Harry into doing "bad things." This force was subdued and conquered by resources Harry had idealized and internalized from the therapist. These internalized resources were symbolically expressed by Harry's wearing the therapist's necktie, using the therapist's belt to fight Mr. Bad, and construing the therapist as a powerful "president of the world."

Once Harry developed self-regulation over his aggressive impulses, his pathological metaphor dissolved. With this, his modes of expressing aggression intrinsically spiraled to a higher developmental level of coding (competition, genital excitation, fantasies, and wishes to become bigger and stronger). This developmental climb resulted in his projecting the issue of the lack of groundedness onto flushing toilets, resulting in conscious anxiety and a transient phobia that indicated that the impulses that he continued to struggle to regulate were now symbolized within his psychological makeup.

In closing, I would like to point out that over two thirds of the treatment was devoted to enactments (using wooden cutouts, strings, locks, scissors, a police station, a fort, etc.) that helped Harry develop embodied metaphors of the self as grounded and capable of self-regulation. Returning to my introduction, his biting and spitting and other behavioral problems were never literally discussed or conceptually interpreted. Rather, interpretations were provided primarily through action symbols. Harry's treatment, I propose, illustrates that the process of symbolizing in action and fantasy itself has the power to heal.

What was the relationship between this process of restructuring interactive metaphors and Harry's behaviors at school and home? During the first year and a half of treatment, he returned to and completed preschool and then kindergarten. Although he occasionally slipped, he showed steady gains in academic readiness skills and his aggressiveness decreased. No biting or spitting occurred during the last part of the kindergarten year. Moreover, because of his high intelligence and readiness, he was promoted to an accelerated first-grade program consisting of first- and second-graders, which he successfully completed at the conclusion of treatment. At home Harry had not bitten or spat at family members for months, and he was reciprocating more, no longer insisting on weird food or taking forever to get dressed.

Six weeks were devoted to negotiating termination, which Harry seemed to manage well. During the last session, he asked if he could take "his toys" with him. I asked him what he wanted to take. He selected the ball of string, Alvin the puppet, and the punching bag, and departed in a very buoyant mood.

ALBERT LIVES IN RATLAND: A VERY TROUBLED BOY

Albert, who had just completed the first grade, was referred for intensive psychotherapy at the age of 7 years. In kindergarten and during the past school year he always managed classroom demands easily and with excellence. However, from the start of his schooling, he quickly became "the biggest adjustment problem" his school had ever seen. He was impulsive, had little or no respect for rules, and stubbornly defied his teacher's requests, such as collecting papers from the children in his row. At times he was destructive and sadistic. In one instance he returned early from recess and removed two tropical fish from a tank, leaving them on a classmate's desk "as a joke." On several occasions he had stolen and hidden items from the teacher's desk. School personnel were especially disturbed by one particular behavior, which precipitated their insisting that either Albert receive treatment or enroll in a program for emotionally disturbed children. On a number of occasions while on the playground or in the bathroom, he "jokingly" tried to pull down the pants of classmates. When asked to explain himself, Albert replied he was "trying to find out what they were wearing underneath." This behavior was among others that caused Albert's parents much concern.

Parent Intake Interview

The parents consulted a senior clinician who conducted an intake interview. Albert was adopted at the age of 2 months. Details about his first two years of life were not gathered in part because the parents focused the discussion on their efforts to cope with Albert's "antisocial" and aggressive behavior, which first emerged when mother gave birth to a brother when Albert was 3 years old. In spite of their efforts to prepare Albert for the arrival of his sib, he frequently poked him and covered him with talcum powder from head to toe. When confronted, Albert protested that he was "only trying to help."

Thereafter, Albert developed a number of other problems. He had difficulty falling asleep because he was afraid of the dark. From his early years, and until the time of the intake interview, it was necessary for mother to sit at his bedside and hold his hand so that he could fall asleep. In spite of mother's efforts to comfort him, he woke up with nightmares at least three or four times a week. Albert also expressed anxiety when the family took trips because he was afraid that he would not recognize their house when they returned. And while he had been very verbal since his toddler years and tended to speak rapidly, from about the age of 4 years Albert sometimes stuttered.

Although toilet trained "very easily" at an early age, he developed a preoccupation with "anal play," which became the parent's central concern. He refused to flush the toilet, poked his fingers into the feces, and would do a "very bad job cleaning himself." "Playfully" he pinched and slapped his parents' and his brother's buttocks. At times, when his parents were standing, Albert abruptly thrust his nose and face against their buttocks, laughing. Later Albert displayed these same behaviors with neighborhood children, who complained to their parents, resulting in Albert's parents receiving numerous phone calls. With this historical backdrop, particular events during the past year were especially puzzling and disturbing for the parents. Albert's brother, now in his fourth year, complained on several occasions that Albert had tried to insert "something" in his anus. When parents confronted Albert, he replied only that he was playing. And Albert "swore like a trooper," using a variety of terms, especially those that made reference to a person's anus.

Because of Albert's preoccupation with "anal" play, the interviewer asked for more details about toilet training. Mother offered that because Albert did not clean himself well, she regularly cleaned him after he defecated. She became particularly fastidious in doing so at the time he started preschool because if she did not clean him, "He would smell, and that would be embarrassing!" Significantly, mother reported that she has continued cleaning Albert to the present. The interviewer pointed out that given Albert's age, mother's practice was overstimulating and very likely contributing to his difficulties. The interviewer proposed they discuss the matter further in future meetings to help mother cope with this practice. The interviewer recommended intensive psychotherapy and that a psychological evaluation be conducted first to obtain data that should help plan treatment.

Albert's Psychological Evaluation

When I approached Albert in the waiting room, I noticed that he had his legs on either side of mother's leg so that his genitals were pressed against her knee. As I introduced myself, he squirmed and wiggled his body against mother's leg. He looked at me with a smile and then took one of mother's hands, placing two of her fingers in his mouth. He laughed, saying he would like to "eat her up," adding, "I'm breaking her fingers." Mother seemed to be enjoying this "play." Given the physical union between Albert and mother, I was surprised to find that he separated easily when I invited him to the playroom. There, with very pressured, rapid speech, he directed a steady flow of comments at me, all centered around his brother and peers; for example, his brother had awakened him at 5 o'clock this morning; he hid the clothes Albert set out the night before and likes "to strap people and tease"; at summer camp a kid pulled down the pants of other kids to see "if they have purple underwear on."

I listened with interest and then, to determine whether he could regulate this flood of ideation, I set the first design of the Bender-Gestalt test on the table and asked him to draw it on a sheet of paper. In response, Albert subordinated his flood of thoughts and carefully copied the design and each of the others, obsessively concerned with making each as much like the stimulus as possible. During each of the following sessions, Albert talked rapidly about his brother and peers, complaining about their behaviors. Given his history, I understood these complaints as projections of his own impulses and behaviors. At the same time, he could interrupt his flow of conversation when I introduced a test. On occasion, when Albert talked rapidly about some incident, he "snorted," exhaling from his nose in a ticklike manner, or stuttered, reflecting his high anxiety.

In terms of formal test results, Albert was indeed very bright. On the Wechsler Intelligence Scale for Children, he obtained a Verbal IQ of 149 (very superior), a Performance IQ of 121 (superior), and a Full-Scale IQ of 139 (very superior). His relatively lower Performance IQ appeared to be due to his obsessive style. For example, with the Coding subtest he meticulously printed each symbol and therefore took more time, resulting in a scaled score of 11. With tests that involved assembling material (e.g., Block Design subtest) he completed each item successfully but lost time credits because he meticulously arranged the pieces. Albert's academic skill scores converged; although he had just completed the first grade, his spelling, reading, and math skills tested at the third grade level.

With tests assessing cognitive regulators (Chapter 7), he showed stage-adequate functioning when surveying information, focusing attention in the face of distraction, holding images of information in memory, and categorizing and conceptualizing. I was surprised with these results because clinically he seemed to be restless, distractible, and flooded with many thoughts. At times during these structured tests he displayed behaviors that hinted at the pressures he experienced from metaphors that he was apparently struggling to regulate. While assembling the puzzle of a horse during the Wechsler Object Assembly Test, for example, he paused for a number of seconds, passing his fingers over the hindquarter of the horse. And while grouping items that belonged together (Object Sort Test), he repeatedly poked a toy hammer into a plastic cup.

Albert produced representations coded in anal symbols more so when body perceptions served as test stimuli than inkblots and pictures. With the Action Test of Body Image (Chapter 10), when standing on a box and describing what that body experience brought to mind, Albert said, "I can see bums better." When placing his hand in a wooden box, he associated, "This is like putting a hand in somebody's pants." With the Miniature Situations Test of Aggression (Chapters 6 and 10), after vigorously tearing a sheet of paper into shreds, he clutched the fragments and laughed, "I'd like to stuff these up someone's ass."

In response to Rorschach inkblots, Albert produced a few images coded in anal symbols, some representing the anus as having power. To Card I, "Two birds; they're bumping their bums against each other," and to Card IV, a "spooky monster with a big tail . . . it shoots fire out of its tail."

When asked to tell stories in response to pictures (Michigan Pictures Test), Albert became noticeably more stressed and constricted. After struggling with the first two cards, he asked, "Does it have to do with people? Do you have any pictures with animals?" Apparently, metaphors evoked by stimuli depicting children and adults in various situation were more than his cognition and defense mechanisms could handle. In response, I administered several cards consisting of pictures of animals in various situations (Children's Apperception Test). More at ease with this task, he produced several metaphors. One hinted at his ambivalence between wanting to differentiate from mother on the one hand and "being on her team" on the other. To Card 1, he told a story of a baby chick who wants to shoot his mother. Then, shifting from imaging to action, he abruptly took a dart gun from a shelf and shot a dart at the hen in the picture. To Card 2, he described a tug of war. "The mother bear and baby bear are on the same team. They are stronger than the father bear, and they win." Other story fragments represented fear of male authority figures and envy of father's and mother's relationship. Card 3 resulted in a story of a mouse who "doesn't want to get too near the lion because the lion will pounce on him." Card 6 resulted in a story of a mother and father bear sleeping, and the baby bear "is going to sleep with a mean look on his face." Significantly, when presented Card 7, which depicts a tiger leaping at a monkey, Albert slapped the card and refused to tell a story, suggesting that his cognition and mechanisms of defense were not equipped to symbolize this direct expression of aggression.

To assess meanings at the level of metaphoric language, I administered a sentence completion test. As I expected, Albert was quite verbose. One cluster of responses concerned conscious, sadistic fantasies. For example, to the stem *The thing I can do best is*, he replied "dirty tricks," and reported that one of his friends takes pieces of toilet paper, lights them on fire, and bombs kids with them. Another cluster of responses concerned his rivalry with his brother; for example, to the stem *I like my mother but*, he responded "She won't kill my brother," and then described various ways his brother causes trouble at home. Albert's tendency to project his impulses onto others was vividly apparent when he expressed himself verbally. To the stem *At school I get along best with*, he responded "nobody," and then described "dirty tricks" one boy plays on kids like "pulling down their pants." And to the stem *I'd be really happy if*, he responded "this guy at camp would leave the kids alone," and again spontaneously described a boy who "whips the asses of kids" with a belt and "pokes them in the behind."

The test data clarified questions that could not be readily answered from Albert's history and clinical behavior. In spite of his impulsivity and conduct disorder, his intellectual and cognitive functioning were quite adequate, and his academic skills had developed well above grade level. His daily behavior made clear that when his cognition equilibrated calls for action from anal metaphors with environmental expectations, the demands of the former clearly dominated. But it was not obvious from his daily behavior which mode of expression dominated his functioning. The test data suggested that the calls for action from anal-sadistic metaphors were expressed most often in embodied schemas, actions, and unconscious fantasies and less so in conscious fantasies. The test data also indicated that although Albert possessed high verbal skills and was prone to being verbose, his metaphoric language was locked into the mechanism of projection, resulting in his perceiving his antisocial behaviors as belonging to others. Last, the data showed no evidence that standards represented by others had been idealized and internalized.

Albert's Treatment

Albert's treatment is presented to illustrate two particular aspects of the developmental-dialectical model. He certainly verbalized easily, but his verbalizations, thoughts, and beliefs, as well as those of parents and teachers, appeared to have no power in regulating his maladaptive behaviors and steering them in more socially appropriate, adaptive directions. In short, his language mode was segregated for the most part from fantasy and action. Further, while his emotional development was obviously fixated in the anal stage, his expressions of these neurotically conflicted metaphors were also fixated in the action mode. Fantasizing did not provide adequate alternative means for expressing these metaphors or he would, literally or figuratively, pull down pants and pinch buttocks in fantasy rather than in action. And his fantasies failed to provide sufficient rehearsals for expressions of these impulses or he would have authored alternative expressions in actions that were more socially acceptable.

These considerations converge on one aspect of the model. As we shall see, his severe, neurotic conflicts and anal fixations were eventually restructured and resolved as he enacted them following a particular course: first with the action mode dominating, then the fantasy mode, and last within the mode of linguistic metaphors. As a result of this progression, meanings within a mode were integrated with widespread roots with meanings in other modes. Thus, during the last phase of treatment, the meanings the therapist and Albert expressed in words eventually had power to regulate and direct Albert's behavior and enabled him to think about and steer his own thinking, emotions, and urges.

The second aspect of the model illustrated by Albert's treatment relates to the proposition that a child's capacity to delay and to develop alternative means and ends when expressing meanings and emotions is acquired as the child idealizes, identifies with, and internalizes standards symbolized by the therapist's struggles for solutions to the dilemmas the child constructed. From the psychodynamic view, Albert's disregard for rules and social expectations suggested he had developed little or no superego, and from the view of cognitive-behavioral concepts, that he was egocentric. Because of this developmental failure, I tried to introduce rules during each phase of treatment in response to the dilemmas Albert authored.

Treatment began in the summer, before Albert entered the second grade, at a frequency of two sessions per week for a period of six months. Thereafter, the frequency was increased to four sessions per week, and treatment continued for the next three years. While the length of Albert's treatment is familiar to psychodynamic therapists, especially child psychoanalysts, cognitive-behavioral therapists may wince and wonder why treatment continued for such a long period of time. I believe the behaviors Albert displayed during treatment, and the issues he eventually revealed, will answer that question.

Phase I: You Stay on Your Side. I'll Stay on Mine.
Helping Albert Step Into a Dialectical Circle (6 months)

Albert arrived for the first session carrying a box of toy matchbox cars and trucks. Eager to show them to me, he placed them in a line on the table, obsessively pointing out features of each (e.g., the doors open; the seats push back). Then Albert authored a game that expressed the initial meaning he was giving to our relationship. He instructed me to sit at one end of the table while he sat at the other. Then he rolled each matchbox car across the table. His goal was to push the car with just enough force so that it stopped before reaching my end of the table. His job, as Albert put it, was to keep the cars "inside my boundary." My job was to catch a car if it rolled off the edge of the table—and therefore outside of Albert's boundary—and roll the car back to him. He cheered each time he was successful. In addition to joining him in celebrating, I reflected, "Boy, are you working hard to keep all your stuff on your side of the boundary!" He made no comment and continued the game for the remainder of the hour.

During the next session, and for the next six months, Albert drew pictures, usually of large cannons and army tanks, and elected to play a wide range of formboard games, most of which represented battles between forces (Superman; Lost in Space; Hit the Beach). While playing these games, Albert talked constantly with rapid, pressured speech. As was the case during the evaluation, his conversations almost always concerned his brother's misbehaviors and those of classmates who broke rules, teased children, stole, and damaged property. Albert's tendency to express himself by projecting his fantasies, wishes, and behaviors onto others was formidable.

Throughout this activity, Albert oscillated between obsessiveness and impulsiveness. He carefully counted the number of squares he needed to move his game piece in order to win. Whenever he continued with a game from one session to the next, he remembered exactly where we had left off. In a bossy tone he constantly changed the rules of a game, always in favor of his position. And when a game was not going in his favor, he sometimes hurled the die across the room, and on several occasions angrily spilled the game onto the floor. At these times, showing my frustration, I invited him to punch a punching bag whenever he became furious instead of hurling things because I didn't want play material or furniture damaged. He did not accept my invitation and rarely helped me pick up.

Then, in the fifteenth session of this phase, while we were playing a game, he spontaneously commented that his friends knew some "secrets," but he does not want me to know them. Referring to the game we played with matchbox cars in the first session, I commented, "That's like those cars that have to stay on your side of the boundary." Clearly understanding my linguistic metaphor, Albert angrily retorted, "I'll tell you secrets when I'm ready, shitmouth!" With this he got up, took one of the matchbox cars from his basket, and vigorously pushed it across the table, spilling the game pieces and car onto the floor. I picked up the car and rolled it back to him, commenting, "This car is furious; it's not sure whether or not to stay on the other side of the boundary." Albert rearranged the game pieces and angrily mumbled, "Shut up! Let's play!" We continued our game in silence.

In the next session, again while playing a game, he discussed at length that yesterday his brother's friends discovered Albert's "secret hiding place" in his closet where he keeps his toys. I commented, "It sounds like it's getting harder and harder to keep your secrets in a good hiding place. Maybe you're afraid of what will happen if your hiding places are found." Albert understood my metaphor. Covering his ears, he shouted, "Shut up, shitmouth! No talking!"

Albert made no further mention of secrets during the next several sessions. However, the activities he authored gradually represented a battle between his wish to keep his "secrets" under cover and his understanding that I was interested in these secrets. He engaged me in playing "Stratego" and "Dogfight," formboard games involving warfare between opposing armies. He obsessively assigned ratings of power to each game piece, declaring that I should take the "puny red army," and he the "powerful blue army."

At one point he shifted to "Battlecry," a formboard game about the Civil War. As it turned out, our interaction with this game promoted a turning point in the treatment process. Over several sessions, as we played the game, Albert asked many questions about the Civil War. He puzzled over why two armies from the same country should fight each other, and worried that if two armies are equally strong they would "cancel each other out." During these interactions, I occasionally made comments within Albert's metaphor of the Civil War, for example, "Two armies from the same country don't have to fight each other if they agree to fight the same enemy that's against them." When I made these remarks, sometimes Albert would order me to "shut up," as in the past, but sometimes he listened without comment. During our "civil war" I noticed that Albert's stuttering increased sharply, reflecting the increase in anxiety he was experiencing as he struggled with deciding whether or not to give up our civil war and step into a dialectical circle.

Then, in the thirty-eighth session, he finally stepped in. He consolidated the game pieces of Hit the Beach, Dogfight, and Battlecry and announced that they all belonged to "our army." As we battled the enemy (Japan and Vietnam), we collaborated, strategically locating airplanes and game pieces, and planning our defenses and attacks. Significantly, during this collaborative play, Albert spontaneously described events that, for the first time, represented his preoccupation with "anal play." He reported that his friend, Tom, pulled down the trousers of Albert's brother because "he thinks asses are nice to look at." He also reported that his brother was sick but "peppy enough" to look at the panties of the housekeeper.

With Albert now standing in our dialectical circle, I asked him if he wanted to meet more often. I decided to frame the reasons for my request within his mode of projection, and referred directly to instances of anal play he had shared. I mentioned that if we met more often we would have more time to figure out the problems his brother and friend Tom were having. He listened quietly and accepted, "That's OK. Then we'll have time to build a whole fleet of ships," referring to the war we were waging against Japan, and symbolizing, I thought, his wish to break away from his anal fixation and advance developmentally.

Phase II: I Battle to Keep My Secrets
But Eventually Give In (2 months)

Albert arrived with a bag of toy plastic soldiers and divided them between us. Shifting the previous theme in which we were allies, he invented a game of war, assigning himself America and Japan to me. For the next three sessions we moved our soldiers inches at a time as we engaged in ferocious battles. At one point he mentioned "a gadget" he has, "It's like a periscope," and later elaborated that with it he can see anyone in other parts of the house. Because it has an "antenna" he can see what his friend Tom is doing "even if he is a hundred feet away." I commented that there must be a lot of things going on that he would like to see and understand.

Then he interrupted our game of armies at war and introduced a "hiding game," which he repeated for several sessions. He asked me to close my eyes while he hid his soldiers in "secret hiding places." My job was to find them. While crawling about the floor searching for soldiers, I thought I could learn more about his interest in "peeking" with his periscope. I asked on occasion, "So how is school going?" "What's happening at home?" On other occasions I linked our interactive metaphor to the fact that, because we were now meeting four times a week, he had to keep his secret places "very secret" since I had more time to find them. I also thought it would help if I drew attention to the anxiety and fear I assumed Albert was experiencing in his struggle to hide his secrets: "Maybe you're worried that I won't keep your secret places to myself"; " Maybe you're worried you might get punished when we find the secrets." I quickly learned that I had made a mistake by stepping out of Albert's interactive metaphor. His responses were familiar. "Shut your shitmouth!" "Just close your eyes while I'm hiding my soldiers." Given his reactions, I eventually gave up asking about school and home and interpreting his anxiety about secrets, and confined myself to his interactive metaphor. Crawling around the room searching for soldiers he had hidden, I enacted that I was struggling to find them and complained that it seemed impossible for me to find all of the secret places unless he helped me.

Albert rewarded me midway through this phase when he shifted our activity from finding soldiers to playing Pickup Sticks. Significantly, he did not direct us to compete. Rather, he prescribed that we work together to "untangle the sticks." At the start of one of these sessions, Albert introduced what I believe was the first interactive metaphor that called for help. When he arrived, he said, "Could you help me? My jacket zipper is stuck." Although the zipper did not appear to me to be stuck, I occupied myself freeing it, commenting, "That's why we're here, to get things unstuck."

While we played Pickup Sticks, Albert spontaneously introduced "secrets," all of which centered on his anal preoccupations. Initially he shared that he and a friend go to a dump to look for trash to burn. "It makes a nice smell." When he asked me if I liked the smell of burning trash, I understood the question to be asking, symbolically, if I could take the "smell" of what he would be producing in our future sessions. I commented, "I'll smell anything." In subsequent sessions, still playing Pickup Sticks, he reported that kids take pictures of girls in the bathroom, that his dog stepped in his own feces, that his brother's dog defecated in his brother's room, and that there was a hole in the floor of his closet that he had cut out with a knife. "It's smelly and dirty there because there are dead rats there. They're living off the mold." While sharing these "fantasies," Albert's stuttering increased.

Albert changed our activity again for three sessions. He brought in a deck of baseball cards and directed that we play "pitch" (each of us took a turn tossing a card against the wall; if a card landed on another, that player took the card). During this activity, which required that we kneel or sit on the floor, Albert at times bumped his body against mine and sniffed my face. I decided not to respond to these encounters until Albert's interactions elaborated their meaning. I thought that perhaps this was his way of "getting to know us" further.

Then in one session Albert took out the plastic soldiers he had used in the hiding game, divided them between us, and announced that each of our armies was to battle for the other's "secrets." After we set up our soldiers, I commented that my secrets were behind "this door," pointing to a large diamond in the center of a large Native American rug hanging on the wall. My intention was to facilitate expressing in macroaction our "battle for each other's secrets" by inviting us to use the total room in our symbolizing. I asked Albert where his secrets were. He set a blotter on the floor: "This is the door to my secrets." At this moment I was reminded of the "hole" in his closet floor that, as he had mentioned, contained rats. I asked, "What's behind your door?" He responded, "Rats, big rats."

With this he ushered in a phase of macroactivity and an interactive metaphor that clarified why he had struggled for so long to negotiate sharing secrets and integrating our subjective worlds. For Albert, participating in a dialectical relationship required submission and punishment.

Phase III: Giant Rat (A Bad Force) Tortures Batman (A Good Force) to Learn His Secrets (2 months)

Upon commenting that rats were behind his door, Albert immediately stretched out on the floor, saying, "Let's play I'm Batman. He's a good guy. You're a bad guy." When I asked who the bad guy was, Albert responded, "You're a giant rat. You come out of this hole [in the floor] and attack me. You're trying to get my secrets." I played the part, lunging forward and snarling as Albert rolled and twisted on the floor, groaning and enacting that he was in pain.

In each of the following sessions he began with an activity or discussion that lasted for about ten minutes (e.g., checkers, racing toy cars). Inevitably he interrupted whatever we were doing and announced, "Let's play Batman." He always directed me to attack and torture him, elaborating many methods (e.g., whip him, chop off his fingers, stretch him on a rack, boil him in oil). I enacted each attack in pantomime with as much drama as I could muster. Albert usually prescribed fifteen or more attacks in one session. Sometimes, instead of an attack, he asked me to place "a reading machine" (a tissue box) on his head. "It reads secrets." But whenever I did so, "special glands" located in his head "blocked" the reading machine.

Phase IV: The King of Ratland Battles Batman for Secrets and Control of the Universe (3 months)

At one point Albert revised the identity of the giant rat, elaborating the meaning of "bad" in our interactive metaphor. While the same issue was recycled (a battle for secrets), now the bad force was transformed into a "king," an idealized authority figure who rules the universe. With this symbol Albert represented that stepping into a dialectical circle, and sharing his subjective world, required that he submit to the sadism of an idealized authority figure. He spontaneously declared, "You're King Rat. You're in charge of infinity rats. All the rats on earth and all the rats on other planets." As Albert prescribed ways in which King Rat tortured Batman, he elaborated that each planet is ruled by a "Queen Rat" and the king rules "all the queens." In addition, Albert invented the identities of "rat monsters" who assisted the king in his battle for Batman's secrets. He carefully drew pictures of a rat monster for each letter of the alphabet, representing his anal preoccupations: the "A Monster" had an "antenna in his butt," the "B Monster" generated "gas bombs." Significantly, Albert also added that if Batman could gain control over the king, then Batman would have control over "infinity rats." With this elaboration Albert symbolized explicitly for the first time the wish to master his anal preoccupations.

With the metaphor of evil, anal forces differentiated, Albert declared that the king ordered either a "Queen Executioner" or "Rat Monster" to torture Batman. In one instance an executioner hurled Pickup Sticks as "spears" at Batman. In another, an executioner spilled "small rats" (checkers) onto Batman. Albert enacted that these rats "are climbing up my legs" and over his chest, which "feels great." With each attack, while playacting that he was being tortured, Albert made clear that he was enjoying the experience.

On two occasions Albert's enjoyment escalated to a level that led to his impulsively acting on my body. While on my hands and knees picking up checkers that had been poured on him by an "executioner," Albert suddenly got up from his prone position and leaped on my back, exclaiming with excitement, "I want to see your underwear." I commented within our metaphor that maybe King Rat's secrets had something to do with underwear. In addition, as Albert identified many rat monsters who assisted King Rat, I enacted wondering whether Batman had the strength to endure one torture after the other and continue battling.

At one point Albert abruptly interrupted the interactive metaphor of King Rat and Batman. For fourteen sessions he played catch, formboard games, and cards, while discussing his experiences at a summer day camp. During this time, I did not refer to King Rat and Batman. I did wonder to myself whether my comments about Batman's strength and ability to endure battle had pushed the metaphor underground. I waited and hoped that the metaphor would reappear in some form.

Phase V: Batman Asks King Rat to Help Him Find Energy Pills so He Can Continue Battling (1 month)

My hope was finally answered. Albert brought M & M candies to one session and offered me some. As I took a few, Albert asked, "Do you want me to put one in your bum?" Before I could respond, he returned to King Rat and Batman play, and launched a new interactive metaphor. Batman was very weak. King Rat examined him and discovered that Batman's heart "is in his bum." Batman discovered that "energy pills," and the "energy machine" that makes them, were stolen by "bad rats." As king, I was confident that he and I could find the pills and machine and asked Batman if he knew where the rats had taken them. Albert decided that rats took the pills and machine to one of the "dark tunnels underground." He elaborated that Batman had "no energy," and while King Rat had energy, he "can't see in the dark." I offered that if we combined King Rat's energy and Batman's ability to see in the dark, together we could find the energy pills and machine. With this, Batman and King Rat broke open the entrance to the tunnels (Albert lifted the blotter he had set on the floor many sessions ago) and crawled through tunnels. As we crawled around the room, I enacted—with my eyes nearly closed—that I could not see and followed Albert, who led the way. After considerable effort, we found the pills hidden in "small cracks."

With this interactive metaphor, a number of important shifts occurred in how Albert symbolized good and evil forces battling for each other's secrets. Batman, the good force, now included an anal symbol; he has a heart "in his bum." At the same time, King Rat, in addition to being the leader of evil rats, is also good and a source of strength who is capable of providing Batman (Albert) with energy and power. And of particular significance, Batman and King Rat became allies and integrated their embodied resource's "vision and strength" to continue the struggle with discovering secrets.

Phase VI: King Rat Is Assisted by the King's Highest Servant in Punishing Bad Rats Who Commit Crimes (3 months)

Apparently Albert idealized and internalized King Rat's unrelenting search for Batman's energy pills. In one session he assigned himself a new identity that more explicitly symbolized his identification with King Rat. Continuing with the revision of what King Rat represented, Albert now construed King Rat as standing for rules and regulations, symbolizing that Albert was beginning to internalize a code of conduct.

Albert initiated that the "bad rats" who had stolen energy pills must be punished. "I'm the King's Highest Servant," he proclaimed, and announced that he would search for bad rats throughout Ratland and bring them to the king for punishment. With this, Albert crawled about the room (through "tunnels"). He directed me to sit in a chair, "like a king" and hold "court hearings" to pass judgment on crimes committed by bad rats of Ratland. Once the king's highest servant "arrested" a bad rat (Albert used puppets to represent them), he presented the rat to the king for "sentencing." As one example, Albert, puppet in hand, declared that a rat not only stole energy pills but "turned on the water in school instead of the lights and flooded the place, and he called the teacher 'shithead.'" Albert immediately prescribed that the bad rat must have his head chopped off. Speaking to the puppet, he announced, "I crown you with anger," swatted the puppet across the room, stepped on it, and enacted chopping its head off. Over a number of sessions, Albert continued presenting captured rats to the king for punishment, detailing the crimes they had committed. Albert was disgusted by and uncompromising in what he called a crime. "A crime is a crime. Even stealing a stone off the streets of Ratland is a crime!"

Albert developed different characters who had committed crimes: "Grumpy," who had stolen and destroyed property, and "chewed off the clothes of rats" so "he could see them nude"; "Harry Rat Student," who was a serious behavior problem in school; "Opher," a rat scout who was a behavior problem for his scout troop; and a "Black Jet baseball team" that cheated and broke rules during games. Every rat Albert presented was beheaded no matter what crime had been committed.

Because Albert was not differentiating standards of conduct, I gradually introduced enactments symbolizing the need to distinguish among crimes and the punishments assigned to each. I enacted that King Rat had a big job deciding for Ratland which punishments fit which crimes. I also enacted that I had received many petitions from citizens of Ratland requesting the king to define different crimes and their respective punishments because everyone was confused. Initially Albert resisted this task. He responded that while King Rat was away, the Highest Servant held "an election" and "gazillion" rats voted to keep "head chopping" as the punishment for all crimes, while "only a thousand" voted for different punishments. I expressed surprise that citizen rats wanted only one punishment.

Albert eventually accommodated to my request that we make a list of different crimes and their respective punishments. He sat with me on the floor as we constructed a "rule book." The crimes Albert listed included: "If you don't bow to the king"; "If you swear"; "If you steal"; "If you take your pants off." Addressing the issue of different punishments, Albert initially defined a few: "an ax," "giant scissors," "flogging," "death." Gradually he engaged in discussions that reflected his efforts to differentiate punishments. He wondered, for example, if an executioner "ever refuses to execute"; "Does the king ever change his mind?" "What good does it do to execute a rat if you're going to die anyway? All you do is take a few years off a rat's life." In addition Albert introduced the issue of age, wondering, if a rat was "really babyish" or older, whether it made a difference how the king viewed the rat's crimes.

As King Rat, I enacted several points of view during these episodes: I agreed with the Highest Servant who wanted all of Ratland "civilized"; if we were going to civilize Ratland we should keep in mind that very young rats have a lot of feelings inside that make them do things that rules say are bad; a lot of rats are young "inside" although they are older "outside," and when rats like Grumpy and Opher learn what is inside they can find ways of doing things that are fun yet also follow rules.

Albert apparently assimilated the king's wish to help rats learn "what's inside" that gets them in trouble because he introduced the first interactive metaphor representing his anal preoccupations and fixations.

Phase VII: General Bolthead Sucks Tail Glands of Rats into His Anus:
The 1st Edition of a Core Pathological Metaphor (4 months)

Albert interrupted the construction of our "rule book" and discussions of crimes and punishment when he decided, as the king's servant, to dig a network of tunnels for the king. "Then it's easy for you to move your troops underground all over Ratland and catch bad rats." I expressed my appreciation and, referring to our discussions of "inside versus outside," I pointed out that the tunnels would help me move around "inside." While digging tunnels, Albert introduced two brief enactments that seemed to signify the gains that he had made and the wish to "reform himself." As the highest servant, he captured "Clyde," a very bad rat who, for punishment, was "chopped up in a special way. The pieces come together in a different way . . . and you can still live but in a different way." Albert also emphasized that when holding court, while the king stood for discipline, "he's fair," and carefully plans before deciding a punishment.

Albert arrived at one session with a Dust-Buster vacuum cleaner and assigned himself a new identity. He declared that he was "General Bolthead" who knows there is a "secret room" somewhere in the tunnels that he and the king have to explore. But we cannot find this room until Bolthead captures all the "bad forces." Here Albert borrowed a term I had used months ago to refer to the bad rats who had been battling the king. Bolthead crawled around the room, with the King following, through an imagined labyrinth of underground corridors. Forecasting the meaning of what was to come, on occasion Bolthead paused to smell the face and body of his comrade. "I get information about you." In one instance, he took my forefinger and exclaimed, "You play the dirtiest pranks with this!"

Then Bolthead roamed through tunnels capturing rats. After capturing a rat, he cut out the "tail and tail glands" from the rat's anus and placed them into his own. (Albert enacted this in pantomime.) Sometimes Bolthead aims his buttocks at rats walking by and "sucks up" their tail glands with his anus. "Bolthead's ass gets very nervous if he does not get any tail glands." In addition, Albert said that Bolthead had a "computer gland" in his anus to direct his many tails as well as a "special life gland" that he was afraid of losing. Other rats were envious of the many tails and tail glands Bolthead accumulated. During these enactments, Albert introduced very precious white rats who produced flatus and feces that Bolthead stored in special jars.

This interactive metaphor represented the psychologically independent life of Albert's anal fantasies and emotions. Bolthead's anxious need for tails, his "computer gland" and "life gland," and his storing precious flatus and feces in jars represented that for Albert the anus was the source of nurture, competence, and strength (indicating that oral, anal, and phallic representations were fused).

Following these enactments, Albert again shifted the focus of his metaphors. He subordinated anal representations and turned again to elaborating and assimilating ideals of conduct. While this shift could be viewed as Albert's avoiding anxieties and conflicts associated with his anal fantasies, it turned out that the next phase represented Albert's attempt to fortify himself so that he could return to and recycle his anal fixations.

Phase VIII: The Highland Police of Ratland Explore the Deepest Caves of Ratland (2 months)

Albert employed both macroactions accompanied by fantasies and fantasies accompanied by microactions to express the interactive metaphor he authored. He interrupted the metaphor of General Bolthead when he asked me to teach him how to make paper airplanes. He constructed many. For a few sessions he introduced a "contest" in which we glided paper airplanes and timed them to determine which one remained "up" in flight the longest. Perhaps because he would be attending a summer camp in several weeks, Albert created a boy's camp that included a "punishment tent" for misbehaving boys. In addition to flying airplanes, we engaged in competitive events such as soccer. In this context Albert expressed concern about how to get along with boys in camp. In response, I introduced a character, "Teddy," and pointed out that there was an "outside Teddy," who teased, broke rules, and acted tough, and an "inside Teddy," who was nervous and afraid and did not know why. Albert enacted both "inside and outside." For example, while standing with baseball bat in hand and ready to receive a pitch, outside Teddy was overly confident. Then Albert enacted inside Teddy, who was very nervous. "Like he was afraid a hand would come up from the toilet when he sat there and pull him in." I commented that these inside fears about toilets reminded me of General Bolthead and that the more Teddy learned what's going on inside of him, the better he will get along at camp.

At one point Albert asked for a jackknife and a strip of wood. He sat for a couple of sessions carving a "spear" 4 feet long. With this he introduced the metaphor of the "Highland Police of Ratland," an elite corps. As a policeman, Albert sometimes marched about the room in a military posture while I , as "the Chief of Police," led the Highland Police in many drills. Albert also crawled around the room holding a spear and flashlight, exploring tunnels and capturing rats who had stolen tail glands. He took these rats to me, as the Chief of Police, for punishment. As Albert put it, the job of the Highland Police was to explore "the deepest caves in Ratland to end the mystery."

During this phase, Albert displayed several behaviors related to the process of idealizing and identifying. In one instance he stood close to me, as the Police Chief, placed his nose close to my face, and commented, "Your shaving lotion smells good." In another he touched my necktie, commenting that I was wearing "the Highland Medal of Honor." At the close of this phase, treatment was interrupted for a month because of vacations. When we resumed treatment in the fall, Albert returned to the interactive metaphor of the Highland Police, but soon introduced the second addition of his core pathological metaphor.

Phase IX: Monsters Live in a Filthy House and Are Punished Because of Their
Anal Play: The 2nd Edition of a Core Pathological Metaphor (5 months)

Returning from vacation, Albert continued gliding airplanes and then busied himself
carving another long stick that he labeled the "Wamba Club," belonging to the
elite Highland Police of Ratland. "Savages" tried to steal the Wamba Club, and
many battles ensued between the Highland Police and savages. At one point Albert
paused and enacted a captured savage rat who had difficulty sleeping, and directed
me, as the doctor of the police force, to examine him. On another occasion Albert
spontaneously associated to Teddy, the character I had introduced in the previous
phase, and wondered if Teddy had problems sleeping. Albert also wondered whether
Teddy wanted to "shoot [his brother] in the ass to make the hole bigger." Relying
on the metaphors we had already shared, I commented over several sessions that
Teddy had "inside, savage feelings" like that and could not sleep because of these
savage feelings, and that something was blocking Teddy from using his own
"Wamba Club."

At one point Albert took a set of plastic, mythical figures from his cupboard.
I had given these to him as a birthday gift a year ago. He had not used them until
now when he introduced a second edition of his pathological metaphor, representing
more explicitly his anal, neurotic conflicts. Albert placed the plastic figures on the
floor. Over the next months he lay on the floor with the figures before him and
moved them about in a 3-foot by 3-foot area, constructing elaborate fantasies accompanied by microaction.

The figures were "dirty and wild" monsters. They spat, urinated, defecated,
and wallowed in filth. They were stupid and knew almost no language. To facilitate the fantasy I placed a sheet of construction paper on the floor and suggested
that the monsters "live in here." Albert placed the figures on the paper, calling it
"the Wild House." There the monsters rolled around in filth and "did dirty things."
Then Albert added that the monsters were owned by "a scientist" who hates people.
Again, to facilitate the fantasy, I placed a plastic container next to the Wild House
and suggested that "the scientist lives in there." I also suggested that since the scientist owned the monsters, he determined what they do.

Gradually Albert elaborated the fantasy. The scientist called out monsters from
the Wild House, one at a time, "and put his ideas in them." For the most part, the
scientist ordered a monster to go to the "village, capture people, and bring their
blood back to the Wild House." This theme was repeated many times, with Albert
moving a figure a few feet to enact the capture of someone in the village. Then he
elaborated that the monsters did not always do what the scientist ordered (they
burned buildings, they did not return with blood, they argued with each other).
Whenever I was assigned the role of the scientist, I emphasized my struggle to keep
the monsters under control and to ensure they acted out my ideas.

Albert introduced another character, "Dracula," who was "a human monster."
Dracula helped the scientist control the monsters. I placed another sheet of con-

struction paper next to the scientist's house, and alongside the Wild House, as Dracula's house. In response, Albert placed a fourth sheet alongside the Wild House and called it the "punishment chamber." Whenever a monster disobeyed the scientist, and especially whenever a monster attempted to break into Dracula's house and "make it filthy," the monster was placed in the chamber and punished. Frequently the punishment consisted of exposing the monster to intense heat to "burn the filth off."

As the scientist or Dracula, I emphasized my struggle to learn what the monsters felt and wanted so I could control them better. I also wondered if the monsters had names. With this intervention I intended to help Albert differentiate further what the monsters represented. Apparently having assimilated my suggestion, Albert assigned an identity to each. Eventually he centered on two figures, · elaborating the meaning represented by General Bolthead in earlier sessions: "Finger Monster" and "Ass Monster." When in the Wild House the Finger Monster loved to "stick his finger" in the anuses of other monsters and in his own, enjoying the latter most of all. The Ass Monster loved his buttocks, pranced about displaying them to others, and admired it in the mirror.

It is interesting to note that during this phase, while experiencing elaborate fantasies without macroactions participating, Albert sometimes became frightened, imagining that he saw the curtains move or the lights dim. Whenever this occurred, I pulled the curtains to one side or checked the light switch to demonstrate that there was nothing there. More important, I commented as the scientist that the monster he imagined behind the curtain came from his own ideas and feelings, much like the monsters who were carrying out the scientist's ideas and feelings.

As Albert continued fantasizing the monster's anal activity, whenever I was assigned the role of scientist, I asked Dracula, from time to time, if he longed to be free of this "filthy place." If assigned the role of Dracula, I wondered what I could do to be free of these filthy monsters who continually tried to break into my house and dirty it. Albert assimilated these enactments, elaborating over several sessions Dracula's attempt to escape the Wild House. Recalling our earlier play involving the Highland Police, Albert introduced a "Silver Stallion Squadron" consisting of "intelligent" soldiers who guarded "the treasury," which was filled with "silver rods." He assigned me the role of the Squadron Commander. Albert assumed the role of Dracula, who disguised himself in order to become a member of the squadron and obtain "silver rods." To qualify as a member of the squadron, Dracula was given five tasks to accomplish, which he did successfully. However, members of the squadron unmasked Dracula's disguise and inspected him, discovering that "he's clean; he doesn't have green under his fingernails." Dracula was taken to the "judge." The role of Dracula at this point was assigned to me and Albert played the judge who rejected Dracula's bid for membership because, "Even though he's clean, he is not honest, but a monster in disguise . . . a member of the squadron must first be honest."

With this episode, Albert initially enacted Dracula's wish to escape from the anal stage, represented by the Wild House, in order to become a member of the elite squadron and obtain silver rods from the treasury, symbolizing phallic competence. Significantly, Albert himself renounced Dracula's dishonesty, suggesting that Albert's superego development (the focus of the first two years of treatment) was now sufficiently organized to recognize that Albert's anal fantasies and activity required more attention. With a related issue, in forbidding Dracula membership, Albert unconsciously accepted the goal that Dracula's total reformation was necessary before he could be admitted into the "treasury."

Phase X: David Barcelona (An Ego Ideal) Helps Dracula Gain Freedom from the Wild House (4 months)

Albert elaborated the fantasy of a Silver Stallion Squadron by introducing a new character, "David Barcelona," who proved to represent an ego ideal that would help Dracula gain freedom from the Wild House. David, now the leader of the squadron, was strong, honest, and intelligent. He was not a Christian, nor a Jew, but he was "a new religion." Moreover, David was born "from both the old and new." He was born "between 11:45 P.M. of the old year and 12:15 A.M. of the new year." Here Albert provided an example of unconscious representations that contributed to the construction of ego ideals. The name David Barcelona, and the two religions that form a "new" one, appeared to integrate Albert's Jewish background and my Italian background as well as aspects of Albert's heritage and the standards he construed that I represented.

Albert gathered rulers, dart guns, and the spear and Wamba Club he had carved months ago and divided them equally between us. He assigned himself the role of David and me the role of his friend, "Tony." Shifting to macroaction, we hunted savages and monsters the scientist had created. During these forays, Albert changed the name of the Silver Stallion Squadron to the "Italian Battalion," adding to the meaning of the ego ideal that was emerging. Eventually, Albert focused on pursuing Ronald Rude, "a very bad rat." We eventually captured Ronald and placed him in a "detention center" where he was treated by a psychiatrist. At one point I asked Albert why the Italian Battalion was organized. He replied with determination: "To rid the village of dirty rats forever!"

Phase XI: Reinforced by the Italian Battalion, Albert Discussed Teddy's Anal Activity in Detail: The 3rd Edition of a Core Pathological Metaphor (5 months)

Albert shifted from macroactivity and the pursuit of bad rats to enacting two metaphors simulating power/competence and anal preoccupations. While sitting and carving swords, he elaborated anal fantasies involving a human boy. Occasional references suggested that aspects of these fantasies were autobiographical.

Albert asked to borrow my jackknife (which he had used earlier to carve spears and the Wamba Club). For the next months we carved a number of swords, each one longer and more decorative than the last, for the "Italian Battalion." Albert propped the swords in a row along the wall and became engrossed with discussing the relative power of each. While we carved swords, he asked me to tell him more about Teddy, the mythical boy I had introduced months before to symbolize someone who had "inside savage feelings" that prevented him from sleeping and obtaining his own Wamba Club. Albert asked, "What's the worst thing Teddy ever did?" When I wondered if Albert could guess, he quickly exclaimed, "His brother!" Referring to our discussion of "inside/outside," I encouraged Albert to make up stories about the things Teddy felt, was afraid of, and did. As we sat whittling swords, he narrated a number of fantasies over many weeks.

Teddy stood nude before a mirror, holding another mirror behind him, so he could look at his buttocks and "get all kinds of good feelings," a detail that replicated the activities of the "Ass Monster" in the earlier phase. Teddy placed firecrackers in his brother's anus, and made huge decorative cakes from feces and forced his brother to eat them. He assigned "stars" to the best bowel movement in terms of the length of each piece of feces.

At one point Albert introduced that Teddy was the editor of the "Ass Times," and interrupted carving swords to construct a "newspaper." He drew pictures and composed text describing "different asses," bowel movements, and a "perfect ass" that won a prize in a contest. Returning to carving swords, Albert shifted to discussions of Teddy's "Ass Club" and devoted many sessions describing what takes place at meetings. Teddy and his friends (both boys and girls) put a finger in their own anuses and those of others and powdered, pinched, and patted their buttocks (replicating the activities of the Finger Monster in the earlier phase). Gradually, Albert shifted the emphasis of the fantasy. The fathers of the children discovered them during a meeting and subjected them to severe punishments that resembled those performed by the Giant Rat at the start of the treatment (e.g., whipping the children, dipping them in hot oil, chopping off their fingers).

During Albert's "storytelling," I focused my remarks within the metaphor of Teddy and his activities. For example, I pointed out that what Teddy did, wanted to do, and imagined doing were tangled together, and that Teddy believed this tangle was so bad he deserved the most severe punishments. I also attempted to explain the distinction between moral and physical punishments, noting that sometimes Teddy felt emotionally punished (Albert offered, "That's humiliation!") and sometimes he was not satisfied until he was physically beaten. At one point during one of my comments, Albert interrupted his wood carving, fell to the floor, and pleaded that I "grab and throttle" him and swat his behind. I connected these transference reactions to our discussions of Teddy—that Albert, like Teddy, feels he should be physically punished and sometimes might "ask" for physical punishment to feel better.

In addition, I introduced the notion that Teddy was in the "ass phase." Referring to our previous enactments, I pointed out that Teddy was like the Ass and Finger Monsters stuck in the ass phase. Albert offered that, for Teddy, "his ass is the most important part of his life." I responded, "Just like General Bolthead with his tails and life glands." When Albert wanted me to tell a story, I narrated a story that all boys go through an "ass phase" where the ass is the most important part of what they feel and that this is followed by a "dink" phase (a label Albert most often used to refer to the penis). I noted that moving to the dink phase is like when Dracula wanted to escape from the Wild House, join the Silver Stallion Squadron, and own silver rods. I told him stories of boys who were afraid that "something might happen to them if they join the squadron and move into the dink phase."

Albert offered a solution, proposing that these boys could move from the ass phase to the "ass-dink" phase, an interim phase through which a boy journeyed before reaching "Penis Peak." With this, Albert pointed to the top of a large diamond woven into the Native American rug hanging on the wall. This was the same diamond figure I had used months ago as the doorway to my secrets.

Albert told stories about Teddy's attempts to climb to the top of Penis Peak. He slipped to ledges below, and frequently searched for shortcuts but found none. I pointed out that Teddy's search for shortcuts was like Dracula, who tried to find a shortcut into the squadron with his disguise. Albert wondered if Teddy was "stuck in the ass phase." I emphasized in my stories that Teddy did want to climb to the top of Penis Peak, but he was afraid that once he got there he would run into danger.

Phase XII: To Climb Penis Peak I Must Regulate My Fear of Sharks and My Excitement over Sexual Feelings (10 months)

In this phase Albert's metaphors of anal preoccupations were resolved, resulting in his emotional development spiraling to the phallic stage with the emergence of new coding capacities. These capacities included genital excitation and its associated anxieties and fear of bodily harm (castration). Midway through this phase the frequency of treatment was decreased to two sessions per week, and then to one session, in this and the next phase, as Albert showed he had become free of his anal fixations.

Albert interrupted our storytelling when he brought in reference books about sharks. Over many weeks, using these references, he wrote "chapters" and drew numerous pictures about the habits and physical anatomy of different sharks. He focused a chapter on reports of sharks injuring or killing swimmers, displaying more anxiety and stuttering. (He had not stuttered for more than a year.) Albert's effort resulted in a seventy-page manuscript that he took home with pride.

Then Albert brought in copies of *Playboy* magazine. He engaged me in devising elaborate rating scales, each consisting of several variables: "vulgar," "artistic," and "animalistic." We applied the scales to numerous photographs, discussing at length the different ratings for which each one qualified. During this activity, Albert frequently touched or clutched his crotch while expressing excitement and pleasure when reviewing and rating photographs.

Albert began to make fleeting references to his past anal behaviors and fantasies, gradually returning to them, adding details, and raising questions. The behaviors he described were the same as those he projected onto classmates at the start of treatment. For example, he shared that he would find many opportunities to observe his parents and brother when they had no clothes on, enjoying in particular looking at their buttocks, and that on many occasions he had tried to insert a crayon into the anus of the family cat. He talked about these experiences with considerable guilt and embarrassment. We made connections between his behaviors and those of General Bolthead, the Finger and Ass monsters, and Teddy. We reminded ourselves that they were stuck in the ass phase and noted that Albert was now moving past it. I offered that as was the case with Dracula, who wanted to escape the Wild House, and Teddy, who wanted to climb to Penis Peak, Albert now was also climbing to the top aided by the strength of the Italian Battalion. Using episodes Albert shared from school and sports, we also discussed that to reach the peak involved taking risks, being appropriately competitive and aggressive.

Phase XIII: Albert Enjoys Being Creative and Industrious (7 months)

Gradually he mentioned his past anal behaviors less often and occupied himself with books describing the art of origami and with constructing numerous designs, eventually producing very complex ones. Albert had also begun to take saxophone lessons. On occasion, he brought in his instrument and music and spent nearly an entire session playing for me and showing what he had learned. Whether constructing origami designs or playing the saxophone, he displayed considerable pleasure and pride in his achievements. Interspersed among these activities, Albert spontaneously discussed events at school and home typical for his age.

The parents reported that Albert was more reasonable at home and "easier to get along with," and that he had not engaged in "butt slapping" or used foul language for about a year. They also reported that in a recent school conference the teacher noted that he was "much better behaved" than had been reported in previous grades, and that for some time no one had observed the anal behaviors that had concerned the school. Albert and I chose a termination date early in this phase. In the last sessions he made frequent mention of the Italian Battalion, and I remarked that he had definitely become a member. When we concluded, he took with him his box of "monster figures," the swords and Wamba Club we had carved, and the many origami designs he had constructed.

Critique

Albert was a very verbal, bright child, capable of "sophisticated" statements. Yet he was not only resistant to comments I made early in treatment, but he made extensive use of projection, construing his anal preoccupations as belonging to other children. Albert's conscious thoughts were essentially detached from his actions and fantasies. His functioning was dominated by the action mode, and his behaviors were the outcome of calls for action from embodied meanings coded with anal symbols that had not yet been adequately translated into fantasy. Accordingly, I set out to facilitate the expression of these meanings, first emphasizing physical enactments and action symbols that then could be translated into fantasy symbols. Only when this integration was accomplished would Albert be able to discuss his anal actions and fantasies with meaningful understanding.

The progression of Albert's treatment illustrates various aspects of the developmental-dialectical model. Because of the tenacity of his projections, and the severity of his anal fixations, nine months were required before Albert stepped into a dialectical circle and indicated a readiness to explore his "secrets." However, it was clear he was not yet consciously aware of the content of what he struggled to keep from me. Once he stepped into the circle, macroactivity dominated our interactions, and I participated with as much physical vigor and emotional drama as I could muster.

For many months Albert's metaphors relied on enactments involving rats as vehicles to express a series of symbols. Initially a Giant Rat repeatedly tortured Batman, two mythical figures representing evil and good, respectively. These enactments construed evil as powerful and good as a passive victim enjoying pain. Then the Giant Rat was transformed into the "King of Ratland" in charge of the universe and infinity rats. Although still an "evil force," the king now represented the first differentiation of executive power and control. In addition, evil forces were differentiated when the king was assisted by monster rats, one for each letter of the alphabet.

Beleaguered by battling the king and his monster rats in his struggle to keep his secrets, Albert assimilated my enactments that Batman might run out of energy. For the first time he revised the symbol of King Rat to include aspects of good. When the king's strength and Batman's vision were combined, the king helped Batman obtain his energy pills. At this point the interactive metaphor that Albert constructed next suggested that a critical development had occurred within his personality organization; namely, that he was developing a superego and idealized standards. Now Albert idealized the king (therapist) not only as having strength, but as committed to civilizing bad rats. Significantly, Albert became the king's highest servant, assisting the king in punishing bad rats and in evolving a code of conduct for rats.

From this developmental achievement, the interactive metaphors Albert constructed alternated between enacting several editions of his anal fixations and fortifying himself by elaborating and strengthening ego ideals. With the first edition of his core pathological metaphor, General Bolthead collected tails and tail glands and attached them to his buttocks, symbolizing the power of the anus. This enactment was followed by Highland Rat Police who captured rats who stole tail glands. Here symbols of superego and ego ideals are represented as being critical of anal preoccupations.

Then the second edition of the core pathological metaphor appeared, but now with elaborated fantasies dominating, accompanied by microactivity. The "Ass" and "Finger" monsters, and others, lived in a Wild House and behaved according to ideas placed in their minds by a scientist who created them. With this elaboration Albert represented that a person's mind calls for some action, rather than the view he brought to treatment that one's evil behaviors belong to others. This edition of Albert's pathological metaphor was followed again by a phase during which ego ideals were elaborated further, utilizing macroactivity as the mode of expression. This elaboration proved to be crucial because the metaphor of David Barcelona, consisting of an ensemble of symbols (half-Jewish, half-Italian) and a new religion, represented an integration of the subjective worlds and ideals of the therapist and Albert. David Barcelona (Albert) and his Italian Battalion rid Ratland of bad rats forever.

When the third edition of Albert's pathological metaphor appeared, another significant development occurred. For the first time the vehicles used to represent anal preoccupation were not rats or monsters (highly personalized symbols) but a human boy, "Teddy," a symbol integrating the calls for action from the environment. While Teddy engaged in many anal activities, he longed to escape from them, as did Dracula in a previous phase, and to become free developmentally so that he could climb Penis Peak. As Teddy slipped during his climbs, and realized there were no shortcuts, Albert's next interactive metaphor introduced another major developmental advance. A new coding system emerged intrinsically, indicating that Albert had moved beyond his anal fixations. Constructing an "encyclopedia" of sharks and rating *Playboy* photographs, Albert's experiences were now coded in terms of genital excitation and anxieties (phallic stage).

Following these developments, a core aspect of the developmental-dialectical model was illustrated. With considerable effort Albert had constructed widespread roots elaborating action-embodied symbols and modes of expression that were translated into, and connected with, elaborate fantasy symbols. With this achievement Albert was able to discuss his anal activities and construct an understanding that relied on the actions and fantasies he and I had shared in numerous interactions. Now the meanings of linguistic metaphors with which we communicated had power because they derived from the action and fantasy metaphors we had coauthored and enacted.

10

Diagnosis and Clinical Research from a Developmental-Dialectical Perspective

CONTENTS

The need for a therapist to diagnose a child's difficulties before beginning treatment is self-evident. But what do we mean by diagnosis? Everyone would agree that to diagnose means to construct an understanding of a child's difficulties in a way that helps a therapist plan and conduct a treatment program. But what strategy does one use to construct this understanding? I believe most clinicians nowadays follow the strategy of objectivism. Accepting that knowledge exists independent of the observer's mental activity, the clinician gathers what she/he believes are neutral observations of a child's behaviors. Then a diagnostic category is selected from among those described in the fourth edition of the American Psychiatric Association's (1994) *Diagnostic and Statistical Manual of Mental Disorders (DSM-IV)* that best fits the "neutral" observations gathered. As one example, in her guide to child psychotherapy Brems (1993) noted that a "diagnosis is the second aspect of a thorough, all-inclusive-conceptualization" (p. 191) and proposed that a therapist achieves this conceptualization by turning to *DSM-IV* categories.

As the reader might guess from the thesis of this volume, my view of how to construct an understanding of a child's difficulties is quite different. To set the stage for my discussion, recall the difficulties presented by the children described in previous chapters and consider them in terms of *DSM-IV* categories. In Chapter 1 we considered problems Sally developed after she received a severe electric shock. Her hyperactivity and inattentiveness would qualify for a diagnosis of attention deficit hyperactivity disorder. Her fears and excessive anxiety concerning fantasies about monsters who cover a person with hot spit suggest a diagnosis of generalized anxiety disorder, and her urinating on the floor, a diagnosis of enuresis. The symptoms presented by Mary, whose treatment was discussed in Chapter 8, also suggest several diagnoses: learning disorder not otherwise specified, given her difficulties learning; expressive language disorder, given that her difficulties with expressive language interfered with her academic and social communications; obsessive-compulsive disorder, given that she spent hours ritualistically cleaning the kitchen and her room; and selective mutism, given that in her early childhood she refused to speak, and later she was often not communicative with parents, teachers, and peers.

Similarly, Harry's symptomatic behaviors described in Chapter 9 also suggest several diagnoses: pica disorder, because he insisted on eating nonnutritional substances; attention deficit hyperactivity disorder, because he did not listen when spoken to directly, avoided school tasks, was easily distracted, and often left his seat; conduct disorder, because he bit and spit at others, and toppled blocks classmates assembled; and Asperger's disorder because he engaged in repetitive, stereotypic behaviors with record players and light switches.

DSM-IV categories focus a clinician's attention on one or another aspect of a child's functioning. When looking at a child through lenses provided by categories, a clinician frequently peers through the one that brings into focus an aspect of a child's behavior that is causing the most concern in the environment. Sometimes a clinician tends to peer through a lens that has become popular. Attention deficit hyperactivity disorder at the present time has moved to the top of the bestseller list of diagnostic categories. In any case, when peering at a child through categories, a clinician's attention becomes fixed on one set of behaviors, one wedge of the orange, so to speak, while other domains of functioning are obscured.

In contrast, the developmental-dialectical model proposes that a clinician should strive as much as possible to understand the whole child and unify the wedges to form a whole orange. Recall that the viewpoint of dialectics assumes that every child is a system of relationships between, for example, cognition and emotion, cognition and interactions, fantasy and interactions, meaning and interactions, and surface (conscious) and deep (unconscious) behaviors. The model also assumes that each of these entities is in a dialectical relationship with the others, creating a difference that is continuously negotiated.

With these introductory remarks as a frame, I propose that a developmental-dialectical conceptualization of a child's difficulties is more heuristic than the one provided by *DSM-IV* categories, brings observations into focus that are potentially of greater assistance in conducting psychotherapy, and suggest new diagnostic methods (for similar positions see Coppolillo 1987, Spiegel 1989). I am aware that this proposal runs against a formidable tide. At this time *DSM-IV* is the "bible" of most therapists in all disciplines as well as of third-party payers.

But apparently this "bible" is becoming unpopular with the lay public. In addition to complaints I have heard from parents when an insurance claim requires that their children be assigned a *DSM-IV* diagnosis, objections to *DSM-IV* have also been expressed by a professional writer who is not practicing a mental health profession. In a provocative article that I recommend everyone read, titled "The Encyclopedia of Insanity: A Psychiatric Handbook Lists Madness for Everyone," Davis (1997) noted that "According to *DSM-IV* human life is a form of mental illness. We are confronted with a worldview where everything is a symptom and the predominant color is a shade of gray" (p. 62). He creatively examines many of the *DSM-IV* diagnostic categories to illustrate that apparently there is no behavior observed in everyday life that does not fall into a category. "The pages of *DSM-IV* are replete with mental illnesses that have been hitherto regarded as perfectly normal behavior" (p. 63). For example, with regard to diagnoses of children and adolescents, after reviewing the *DSM-IV* criteria for attention deficit/hyperactivity disorder, conduct disorder, oppositional defiant disorder, and disruptive disorder not otherwise specified, Davis notes, "a close reading of the text reveals that the illnesses in question consist of failure to listen when spoken to, talking back, annoying other people, claiming that someone else did it, and (among a lot of other stuff familiar to parents) failure to clean up one's room. According to *DSM-IV*, childhood and adolescence is a mental disorder" (p. 66).

To support my position that a developmental-dialectical approach is more heuristic than *DSM-IV* categories, because it does not give a name to every piece of behavior, I consider first how and why the model of nosology, as applied in psychological practice, obscures the whole person. Following this, I review selected research studies that illustrate the value of a developmental-dialectical approach to diagnosing and how this approach stimulates innovations in diagnostic methods and clinical theory that hold promise for working with children.

THE NEED TO MOVE BEYOND NOSOLOGY

It is well known that the model of nosology (or of diagnostic categories) has a long and successful history in medical science, dating back at least to the ancient Egyptians (Temkin 1965). This point of view proposes that to understand pathology it is useful, even necessary, to locate diseases in separate, independent classifications. These classifications help clinicians and researchers order the morass of phenomena presented by patients, communicate with each other about their patients, provide confidence in the decisions made about treatment, predict dispositions, and plan investigations. Given the success of the nosological model in medical science, it is not surprising that this viewpoint was gradually adopted by psychological practitioners. What are the steps the model of nosology follows when applied to psychopathology?

1. Behavioral traits and symptoms that various patients exhibit are described in as much detail as possible. These traits must be qualitatively different and relatively stable phenomena.
2. These descriptions are then clustered whenever they are observed to occur together. The traits within a cluster are used to define and label a category of pschopathology. For example, the cluster of traits that defines the *DSM-IV* category of attention deficit hyperactivity disorder includes the following: does not seem to listen; fails to finish schoolwork; easily distracted by extraneous stimuli; often runs about excessively in situations in which it is inappropriate; and acts as if "driven by a motor." The cluster of traits that defines the *DSM-IV* Category of Conduct Disorder includes the following: bullies others; deliberately destroys property; before the age of thirteen stays out at night despite parental prohibition; has run away; and is often truant from school before the age of thirteen.
3. In forming categories, an attempt is made to cluster traits that are viewed as mutually exclusive. Thus, not listening, running about excessively, and acting as if "driven by a motor," which signify an attention deficit hyper-

activity disorder, are viewed as different from ignoring parental prohibitions when staying out at night and running away, which signify a conduct disorder.

4. Once these categories are formed, individual differences tend to be subordinated so that children assigned the diagnosis of, for example, attention deficit hyperactivity disorder are viewed as similar to each other and different from children assigned the diagnosis of conduct disorder.

The model of nosology, then, permits clinicians and researchers to condense information from persons who are alike in some set of behavioral characteristics deemed important for clinical practice. The main goal is to construct concise, stable pictures of typical patients whose behavioral traits represent the mode of a category. And the purpose, as noted in *DSM-IV*, is to provide clear descriptions of diagnostic categories to enable clinicians and investigators to diagnose, communicate about, study, and treat people with various mental disorders.

While the model of nosology received some attention by behavioral scientists in the decades before the 1940s, the perspective gained particular prominence in the field of mental health when in 1952 the American Psychiatric Association published *A Diagnostic and Statistical Manual of Mental Disorders* (*DSM*), the first official manual of mental disorders to contain descriptions of diagnostic categories. In the meantime, the need for more adequate classifications dealing with psychological disorders of children and adolescents was recognized by the Group for the Advancement of Psychiatry which published its own manual of disorders in 1966. Two years later, in 1968, the American Psychiatric Association issued a second edition of its first manual (*DSM-II*) that now included a section on behavioral disorders of childhood and adolescents. A third edition (*DSM-III*) appeared in 1980 and was revised in 1987 (*DSM III-R*); the fourth edition appeared in 1994 (*DSM-IV*). With the rapid and widespread use of these manuals over four decades, it is not surprising that the most common way of thinking about psychological functioning has become either viewing behavior as pathological, and therefore qualifying for membership in a diagnostic category, or as normal and failing to fit a diagnosis.

The domain of child development research and child psychopathology soon became dominated by the perspective of nosology. This influence could be seen in handbooks of developmental psychology (Wolman 1982), in volumes devoted to the topic of child development and psychopathology (e.g., Gelfand and Peterson 1985, Gholson and Rosenthal 1984), and in life-span research (e.g., Erlenmeyer-Kimling and Miller 1986). Even journal issues devoted to developmental psychopathology (e.g., Cicchetti 1984) showed that clinicians and researchers by and large were focusing their efforts on comparing the performance of diagnostic groups in terms of some assessment.

An issue devoted to children and their development, published by the American Psychological Association, is related to my discussion. Here Kazdin (1989) offered that the diagnostic manuals published since 1952 represented a significant contribution to the field of development and psychopathology. According to Kazdin, this contribution derived from the fact that while categories of childhood disorders had been neglected in early editions of diagnostic manuals, these disorders received increasing attention in later editions. Kazdin accepted the model of nosology as a perspective useful for children, taking a position opposite from the one proposed here. Yet, significantly, he also recognized that the perspective of nosology brings obstacles to studies of development. "Several developmental considerations make investigating childhood disorders especially difficult" (p. 181). Examples Kazdin provided of these obstacles were that some behaviors such as fears and excessive activity, while usually viewed as traits of maladaptation, are relatively common in childhood, and that because children undergo rapid changes, a specific clinical problem and its diagnosis may disappear and be replaced by another. As I hope to point out later, observations such as these that conflict with the model of nosology are managed by the developmental-dialectical perspective.

As this point we might ask, was the model of nosology always accepted without criticism in behavioral science? Although gaining rapid popularity from the start, the viewpoint of diagnostic categories was in fact the subject of intense debate soon after the first diagnostic manual was published. These deliberations seem to have been lost in history, or at least appear not to have influenced the construction of subsequent manuals and the approach most clinicians apply when formulating diagnoses. Since these debates still hold significance, a brief sketch of what happened is vital to my discussion.

In 1965, three years before the second edition of *DSM* was released, the National Institutes of Mental Health (NIMH) invited professionals from various disciplines to discuss the role and methodology of classification in the mental health field (Katz et al. 1965). The invited guests did more than discuss; they vigorously debated the advantages and disadvantages of diagnostic categories, including the following: (1) Do the virtues of categorizing people outweigh the resulting loss of information about their individuality? (2) Could the mental health field advance more effectively if the characteristics of people are viewed as interacting in a complex manner rather than as fixed diagnostic entities? (3) Could more than one diagnostic category exist in a single person and if so, how many? (4) Why do some clinical conditions look relatively different at different points in time? (5) What are the limitations inherent in establishing diagnostic types on the basis of self-description, interviewing, and questionnaires? The remarks of two individuals who attended this conference relate in particular to my thesis.

Shakow's (1965) presentation addressed pitfalls unique to using diagnostic categories. He cautioned that classifying mental disorders could result in (1) reification: the danger of reifying and dealing with the abstract concept of a diagnostic category rather than actual behaviors; (2) compartmentalization: taking only a part of the picture and locating a person in a category on the basis of a few pieces of behavior; and (3) simplification: taking a simpler, more easily understood explanation for a complex phenomenon that may be difficult to grasp in all its intricacies. I drew attention to these cautions at the start of my discussion when I pointed out metaphorically that a diagnostic category conceptualizes only one wedge of an orange and fails to provide an understanding of the whole.

Shakow also questioned the principle of forming diagnoses by clustering behavioral traits that are observed to occur together and then assuming the cluster has meaning. He cited Jelinek, who as long ago as 1939 raised the same question and drew an analogy to make his point. Jelinek argued that observation would show that pencils of yellow wood have a greater incidence than pencils of any other finish or color (at least in 1939). Yet the question remained whether the color yellow is essential or even relevant to the function of pencils.

George Kelly's (1965) contribution at this conference is also relevant to my thesis. He pointed out that although the perspective of nosology may be helpful for certain practical purposes, developing categories of emotional problems "proves itself to be almost completely sterile in suggesting something new to be looked for" (p. 158). Kelly offered his own diagnosis of clinicians who use the model of nosology: "hardening of the categories," an affliction he observed among those treating and studying psychopathology (p. 158). His remedy for this affliction converges with a developmental-dialectical perspective. Kelly proposed that any behavior should be plotted along each of several basic lines of consideration that he termed "key constructs" or "universal reference axes."

In their summary remarks at this conference, Katz and Cole (1965) asked questions we might still raise today. "Are the mental disorders really made up of these particular configurations of symptoms and characteristics? And why is it that when we think of diagnosis it is difficult not to think of types?" (p. 563).

Two issues, briefly addressed in a section titled "Limitations of the Categorical Approach" (p. xxii) buried in the introduction to *DSM-IV*, relate to the deliberations of the NIMH conference that took place thirty years earlier and converge with the position I am taking. First, the clinician is reminded that *DSM-IV* is "a categorical classification which divides mental disorders into types based on criteria sets with defining features." Then, the clinician is cautioned not to assume "that each category of mental disorder is a completely discrete entity with absolute boundaries dividing it from the other mental disorders or from no mental disorder." The clinician is also cautioned not to assume that all individuals "described as having the same mental disorder are alike in all important ways." Having worked with and observed clinicians who have used *DSM* (-II, -III, -III-R, -IV), it seems to me that these precautions have not been taken into account to any noticeable degree. Once some aspect of a child's behavior has been underlined, the child is viewed as an "attention deficit disorder" or as an "anxiety disorder" or as some other disorder. And other aspects of the child's functioning, such as the meanings a child assigns to experiences, the dominant modes a child uses to express meanings, and whether and how the child's cognition coordinates the demands of environments and those of personal meanings, fade into the background or are ignored.

With the second issue raised in the introduction of *DSM-IV*, the clinician is informed that some workers have suggested that classifications should be organized following "a dimensional model rather than a categorical model" (p. xxii). Dimensional models, *DSM-IV* authors acknowledge, communicate more clinical information because, unlike a categorical model, they consider "clinical attributes that are subthreshold," that is, deep as well as surface behaviors. Kelly's proposal of thirty years ago that behaviors be plotted along several basic lines or "universal reference axes" is a dimensional model. But the committees that authored *DSM-IV* rejected dimensional models because they are "much less familiar and vivid than are the categorical names for mental disorders. Moreover there is as yet no agreement in the choice of the optimal dimensions to be used for classification purposes" (p. xxii).

It seems, then, that diagnostic categories, despite being less productive than dimensional models, remain popular because they are more "familiar." In other words, the authors of *DSM-IV* support clinicians in sticking with what they already know. And what do the authors of *DSM-IV* mean when they tell us they selected categories rather than a dimensional model because categories are more "vivid"? I suggest that in this context "vivid" relates to Shakow's cautions of 30 years ago, that diagnostic categories are reified by clinicians because they enable clinicians to deal with the abstraction of a diagnosis rather than actual behaviors and with a part of a person's functioning, providing a more easily understood explanation of complex phenomena. With diagnostic categories providing this assistance, the clinician is less anxious and therefore clings to categories instead of dialectical dimensions.

But *DSM-IV* concluded its brief comments on the limitations of the categorical approach with a statement that introduces the next topic of this chapter. " None the less, it is possible that increasing research on, and familiarity with, dimensional systems may eventually result in their greater acceptance both as a method of conveying clinical information and as a research tool" (p. xxii). From the deliberations of the 1965 NIMH conference and the precautions noted by the *DSM-IV*, I propose that a developmental-dialectical model frees us from the limitations of nosology and suggests ways of searching for new diagnostic methods that could inform treatment.

If we peer beyond nosology and through the perspective of development and dialectics, what do we see? With the developmental house depicted in Table 3–1, Chapter 3, before us, Freud and Piaget offered suggestions that serve as a bridge to the research described below. In 1916, in his introductory lectures, Freud noted, "We seek not merely to describe and to classify phenomena, but to understand them as *signs* [italics mine] or an interplay of forces of the mind, as a manifestation of purposeful intentions working concurrently or in mutual opposition. We are concerned with a *dynamic view* of mental phenomena" (Freud 1916, p. 67).

Sixty years later, Piaget (1975) expressed reservations over the fact that "psychiatry is largely based on the principle of 'syndromes'" (p. viii). He added that the use of syndromes or diagnostic categories leaves us with the "puzzling observation that some individuals remain normal in situations where others become variously disturbed" and "thus the meaning of a mental disorder can be extremely diverse" (p. viii). As an alternative to using syndromes, he proposed "an analytic approach" by which he meant that the investigator become immersed "in the 'ensemble' of elements that are involved at different levels of functioning" (p. vii). In proposing that we go beyond classifying diseases, then, Freud and Piaget suggested we look at behaviors as symbols revealing an active interplay of mental activities and constellations of behavioral elements operating at different levels (conscious and unconscious).

To gather observations of the interplay of mental activities and behaviors at different levels, patterns of results across studies are needed. As Sechrest and Smith (1994) stated, "Research findings begin to make sense only when they form part of a 'web of evidence'" (p. 15). The series of studies described below, when taken together, are intended to demonstrate how the developmental-dialectical model could serve as a guide in searching for a pattern or web of evidence that is useful in constructing a diagnostic understanding of a child's functioning in ways that serve treatment.

ACTION, FANTASY, COGNITION, AND EMOTION:
STUDIES PROBING HOW FOUR ARE ONE

To illustrate the heuristic value of the developmental- dialectical model as a research tool, the studies described here supplement those presented in previous chapters, and are intended to demonstrate the types of questions that arise and the methods designed to address them when the boundaries we discussed in Chapter 2 between real and subjective knowledge, body and mind, and cognition and emotion are dissolved. It is interesting to note that the introduction of *DSM-IV* acknowledged one of these boundaries, that between body and mind. In a section titled "The Definition of Mental Disorders," the manual noted that the "term *mental disorders* unfortunately implies a distinction . . . that is a reductionistic anachronism of mind/body dualism. A compelling literature documents there is much 'physical' in 'mental' disorders and much 'mental' in 'physical' disorders" (p. xxi).

I have proposed that when boundaries are dissolved, body, fantasy, cognition, and emotion are united by conscious and unconscious meanings a person experiences and expresses. Other investigators (e.g., Wozniak 1986) have employed the concept of meaning to these domains. The discussion by Zajonc and Markus (1984) perhaps serves best to introduce the methods I have devised for studies designed to probe the integration of body, fantasy, cognition, and emotion. Converging with Shilder (1950) and Johnson (1987) (see Chapters 2 and 5), these writers asked why enormous motor involvement is observed during mental activity, from trying to remember something to playing chess. Reviewing human and animal studies they answered the question as follows:

The motor movement can, in itself—without kinesthetic feedback and without a transformation of that feedback into cognition—serve representational functions [p. 76] . . . [motor movement] has all the critical representational properties . . . it has a fixed referent; it is symbolic in that it can substitute for that referent; it can be combined and interact with other representations. . . . we are proposing that motor responses in themselves—without cognitive mediation—can serve representational and mnestic functions. The retention of these responses is a form of memory as valid as any other. [p. 77]

But how do we assess body, fantasy, cognition, and emotion when these domains are united by meaning? Zajonc and Markus (1984) proposed that we should devise methods other than rating scales and questionnaires that create situations in which the body and action serve primarily a representational function. Here they echo a recommendation by Francis Galton (1884) who more than a hundred years ago recommended that investigators devise "traps," forecasting the use of "situational testing" (Santostefano 1968b). To illustrate what he meant, Galton described one of his attempts. After observing that friends who "have an inclination to one another [seem to] . . . incline or slope together when sitting side by side" (p. 182), he devised a pressure gage that he attached to the legs of chairs in an effort to test this hypothesis. If we look beyond Galton's particular "trap," or test method, he was advocating that assessments and stimuli should be designed to increase the likelihood of observing target behaviors that represent some combination of body (action), fantasy, cognition, and emotion all united by meaning.

I have been influenced by Galton's recommendation, and for many years have devised and explored various "situational tests" to assess the body, action, fantasy, cognition, and emotion unified by meaning (Santostefano 1960a,b, 1962a,b, 1965a,b, 1968a,b, 1977, 1978, 1985, 1995). The design of each method was influenced by the developmental-dialectical model in that the intention was to probe how meanings a person experienced when dealing with test stimuli integrated what the person did, imagined, and said.

These methods have been used in various studies, several of which I describe below. The studies were not conducted to prove or disprove hypotheses. Rather, they were intended to probe questions the developmental-dialectical model raises when boundaries are dissolved. These questions share a common denominator. Recall that patterns of bodily movements and interpersonal interactions are conceptualized as giving rise to organized meanings. In typical development these embodied meanings are eventually extended into higher levels of functioning as the modalities of fantasy and cognition differentiate and become integrated and organized as behavioral systems of experiencing and expression. Therefore each probe described below attempts to explore whether, or how, meanings in one modality are extended into another and whether the totality of the modalities is flexible or inflexible in some way.

Probe I: Are There Relationships among Embodied Meanings Constructed When the Body-Self Is a Stimulus, Fantasized Meanings Constructed When Inkblots Are Stimuli and Overt Behaviors?

Three studies involving clinical and normal populations illustrate our efforts to explore this first probe. In the first, embodied meanings expressed by a clinical population were assessed when a child's total body served as a stimulus and these meanings were related to meanings expressed when Rorschach inkblots served as stimuli. The second study evaluated embodied meanings expressed by a population of high school students. In the third study, embodied meanings expressed when touch perceptions serve as stimuli were used to predict suicidal and violent behaviors.

Study I. The Relations between Embodied and Fantasized Meanings in a Clinical Population

This study explored whether and how embodied meanings constructed when perceptions of the total body serve as stimuli (embodied meanings proximal to the body) are related to embodied meanings that are constructed cognitively when construing inkblots (meanings more distal from the body).

Subjects

The subjects consisted of 78 children and adolescents admitted to an inpatient facility (age range: 60–204 months; 38 females; 40 males).

Procedure

On admission each youth was administered the Action Test of Body Image (ATBI) (Santostefano 1992a) and the Rorschach Inkblot test.

The ATBI. With this procedure a child was asked to assume various body postures (e.g., standing on one leg with arms outstretched, leaning against a wall), to perform various body actions (e.g., encircle arms, repeatedly open and close his/her eyes), and to describe what the body experience brought to mind.

Responses were evaluated with several scales: (1) expressions of body imbalance/balance rated on a six point scale: *1* = cataclysmic loss of balance (e.g., "falling off a cliff"); *6* = differentiated forms of balance (e.g., "ballet dancing"); (2) expressions of body constriction-assertion rated on a six-point scale: *1* = active constriction/inhibition (e.g., "I'm handcuffed"); *6* = high degree of assertion (e.g., "a salmon swimming upstream"); (3) other scales rated the presence or absence of expressions of aggression (e.g., "punching a wiseguy"), fear (e.g., "seeing Freddie Krueger or some wild killer"), fatigue (e.g., "exhausted after school"), body deformed (e.g., "a cripple"), affiliation (e.g., "hanging out with my friends").

The Rorschach Inkblot Test.   In contrast to currently popular Rorschach scoring systems that focus on structural determinants of images, we have searched for ways of evaluating responses as symbolic expressions of embodied meanings. Our scales evaluated whether and how interactions between persons and things are depicted and whether a representation of an entity is whole, incomplete, or damaged. (For studies using earlier versions of these scales, see Santostefano et al. 1984, Tuber et al. 1989.) Each unit of imaged motion or interaction was rated along several lines: (1) whether the motion is completed, ongoing, or imminent (low to high numerical ratings); (2) whether the agent and recipient of motion are mythical figures, landscapes, inanimate objects, animals, or humans (low to high numerical ratings); (3) whether the motion is vigorous (two people throwing rocks—low numerical value), or attenuated/slow (someone standing still—high numerical value); (4) whether the relationship defined by an agent, recipient, and type of motion is conventional (e.g., "two people lifting a box"), or atypical (e.g., "a frog riding a motorcycle"), or mythical (e.g., "a robot grabbing this alien"). In addition, scales rated whether representations of body-self depicted humans, animals, landscape, inanimate objects, or mythical figures as complete wholes or as incomplete/disintegrated/disorganized (e.g., "a melted popsicle," "a man's head, half of it is gone").

Results

One factor analysis was conducted with only ATBI responses to explore the constructs this inpatient population defined when the body served as a stimulus. The first factor correlated age and several embodied meanings. Older children constructed more responses than did younger children representing body imbalance-balance, body constriction-assertion, and body-self as deformed.

Another factor correlated body constriction/assertion, fear, and fatigue. Children who produced embodied meanings of constriction also produced more meanings of fear and fatigue, while children who produced embodied meanings of assertion produced fewer. A third factor clustered balance/imbalance and aggression. Children who produced embodied meanings of balance also produced more embodied meanings of aggression, while children who produced embodied meanings of imbalance produced fewer. And with a fourth factor, females produced more representations of affiliation than did males.

A second factor analysis was conducted of ATBI and Rorschach scores to explore the relations between meanings constructed when the body is and is not a source of stimulation. The first factor correlated embodied meanings of constriction/assertion and the percentage of Rorschach images produced representing motion. Children who produced embodied meanings of assertion also produced more Rorschach images representing motion than did children who produced embodied meanings of constriction.

The second factor clustered embodied meanings of fatigue and types of agents performing motion represented in Rorschach images. Children who produced more embodied meanings of fatigue also constructed Rorschach images in which animals and objects were represented as agents in motion. Children who produced fewer embodied meanings of fatigue constructed Rorschach images in which humans were represented as agents in motion.

A third construct correlated embodied meanings of aggression toward others, embodied meanings of body deformation, and the intensity of motion represented in Rorschach images. Children who produced more embodied meanings representing aggression and body deformation also constructed Rorschach images that represented slow, attenuated motion. In contrast, children who produced fewer embodied meanings of aggression and body deformation constructed Rorschach images that represented vigorous, rapid motion.

Another construct defined an inverse relationship between ATBI and Rorschach representations of body deformation. Children who produced many embodied meanings of the body-self as deformed constructed fewer Rorschach images representing entities as penetrated or disintegrating. On the other hand, children who produced fewer embodied meanings of the body-self as deformed constructed more Rorschach images representing entities as penetrated or disintegrating.

Critique

While this study is intended primarily to illustrate the ATBI method as one way of probing the relation between mind and body, issues could be distilled that might stimulate future research with other clinical and nonclinical populations. This inpatient population defined embodied constructs that suggest concordance; for example, representations of body constriction correlated with embodied representations of fear and fatigue. This population also defined constructs that suggest discordance; for example, representations of body balance correlated with embodied representations of aggression toward others.

In terms of the relationship between embodied and fantasized meanings, the factors of the second analysis suggest that with this inpatient population of troubled youth, a boundary segregates embodied meanings from meanings constructed at the higher level of fantasy and cognition. When embodied meanings represented the body-self as penetrated and deformed, the same meaning was not expressed in fantasy as assessed by the Rorschach, and vice versa. In another instance, embodied representations of aggression toward others were associated with fantasized representations of slow motion in Rorschach images. Would a nonclinical population reveal the same or different relationships among embodied meanings and between embodied meanings and fantasized meanings?

Study II. Embodied Meanings Defined by a Normal Population

This study, involving high school students, relates to one part of the question that concluded the previous discussion: Would a nonclinical population reveal the same or different relationships among embodied meanings? Although the subjects of the present study were slightly older than the hospitalized children discussed above, a comparison of their embodied meanings should stimulate further research.

Subjects

The subjects consisted of 63 students who had just begun 11th grade classes in a public school serving a predominantly rural area (Mean Age = 17 years; 36 females; 26 males).

Procedure

Each student was administered the ATBI.

Results

ATBI responses were factor-analyzed to explore the embodied constructs this population defined. With the first factor, embodied representations of independence and assertion, and the body-self as safe and balanced, were intercorrelated. Children who represented dependency also expressed representations of the body-self as unsafe, imbalance, and constricted. With the second factor, representations of the body-self as valued (e.g., receiving an award) correlated with body balance and the absence of representations of aggression, while representations of the body-self as devalued correlated with representations of aggression and body imbalance. The third factor correlated representations of incompetence with body constriction and representations of competence with body assertion. The fourth factor correlated representations of fatigue and body deformation, and the fifth factor correlated representations of tension and aggression toward others.

Critique

In general, the meanings clustered within each factor appear theoretically to be concordant with each other. A comparison between these factors and those produced by the psychiatric population of the previous study reveals interesting differences. Recall that the older children of the clinical group constructed more representations of body imbalance, constriction, and deformation. Elaborating this factor, with these same children representations of body constriction correlated with representations of fear. In contrast, with the high school group the first construct correlated embodied representations of assertion, balance, safety, and independence. Moreover, in another factor, representations of constriction correlated with representations of incompetence, not fear. The clinical population also defined a factor that correlated representations of body balance with representations of aggression toward others. The picture is quite different with the high school students. Representations of aggression toward others clustered in one factor with body *imbalance* and representations of devaluation. And in another factor representations of aggression correlated with representations of tension.

A comparison of the embodied constructs defined by different clinical and nonclinical groups, as well as by age groups, should contribute valuable information about patterns of embodied meanings that should be addressed in psychotherapy.

Study III. The Relations between Embodied Meanings Experienced through Touch Perceptions and Suicidal and Violent Behavior

The third study explored meanings constructed and expressed when touch perceptions of objects (not in view) are stimuli for symbolizing and the relations between these meanings and overt action.

Subjects

207 inpatient youths (age range: 54–212 months; mean age: 154 months; females = 98; males = 101; IQ range: 81–131; mean IQ 103).

Procedure

The Touch Association Test (TAST).   Each child was administered the Touch Association Test adopted from the Twitchell 3-D Test. Six clay objects were placed one at a time under a cloth. The child examined each with both hands and described what the object could be or brings to mind: sphere, cube, cone, rectangle, coil shape, and a shape resembling a human figure. Responses were evaluated as follows:

1. *Typical score.* Responses representing things, persons, and events that fit attributes of the stimulus object in hand. Scores range from *1* (descriptions of attributes; for example, sphere, "something round and smooth") to *8* (representations of the stimulus; for example, "the Epcot Center," "a giant balloon I saw on TV that crossed the ocean"). Scores are summed

and divided by the number of typical responses, producing the Body Orientation Index. This index is conceptualized as reflecting a person's orientation when symbolizing through touch perceptions: from experiencing stimuli as they are (outer/symbolic orientation) to experiencing stimuli in terms of highly personal referents (inner/symbolic orientation). The orientation revealed in response to the humanlike figure was also included as a separate score.

2. *Atypical score.* The number of responses representing things, persons, and events that bear little or no relationship to the attributes of the stimulus object in hand (e.g., cone: "a piece of lint"; cube: "little veins").

3. *Miscellaneous scores.* Three types are defined: (1) *Action Taken.* The number of times the child takes some action with the stimulus whether or not the action is accompanied by an image (e.g., sphere: "a marble"—the child bangs the stimulus on the tabletop); (2) *See.* The number of times the child pulls the cloth away to examine the object visually; (3) *Movement.* The number of images representing movement (e.g., cone: "A rocket blasting up"). Each score is treated separately and also summed as a *Miscellaneous Total* score.

4. *Affect score.* The number of responses expressing one or another of the following emotions: aggression toward others ("a rock to hit someone on the head"), nurture ("chocolate candy"), fear ("a giant spider"), noxious texture/temperature ("cold; scratchy"), deformed/disintegrated ("a broken toy"). These scores are treated separately and also summed, resulting in a *Drive Dominated* score.

Results

Responses to the Touch Association Test were factor-analyzed to explore the constructs this population defined when touch perceptions expressed embodied meanings. The first factor correlated representations of emotions, especially concerning nurture and body orientation. Youth who produced a high number of representations of emotions, especially nurture, also displayed an inner/symbolic orientation (Body Orientation Index). In contrast, children who produced a low number of representations of emotions, especially concerning nurture, showed an outer/symbolic orientation. This inpatient population, then, defined as one body-based construct that turning into one's subjective world results in expressions of highly personalized, emotion-dominated meanings.

Two factors involved the humanlike stimulus object. Children who showed an inner/symbolic orientation when touching the humanlike figure also tended to act upon and look at the object. With the second factor, children who showed an outer/symbolic orientation when examining the humanlike figure also tended to construct more atypical meanings over all.

Two other factors concerned the phenomenon of looking at the stimulus objects when instructions asked the children to examine the objects by touch only. Children who looked at the objects produced fewer representations of fear and of something or someone deformed while children who did not look at the objects produced more of these representations. In this population, then, looking at the stimulus objects appeared to be one way of avoiding experiencing representations of fear and of body deformation. With the last factor, children who produced many representations of noxious body sensations concerning texture and temperature also produced many representations of aggression.

A second analysis probed the relations between these embodied meanings expressed through touch perceptions and overt behaviors. A number of youth in this population were admitted because they had attempted suicide or had committed acts of violence against others. A stepwise discriminant analysis explored whether body-based meanings obtained with the touch method discriminated against these children. Nonsuicide and nonviolent controls were selected from the same population if histories made clear that suicidal and violent behaviors had not played a part in their functioning.

The discriminate analysis accurately classified 70 percent of the suicidal and 69 percent of the nonsuicidal youth (Wilk's lambda = .82, X^2 (= 19.00, df = 8, p = .01, Rc = .43). A second stepwise discriminant analysis accurately classified 86 percent of the violent and 79 percent of the nonviolent youth (Wilk's lambda = .54; X^2 = 23.13, df = 8; p = .003; Rc = 68).

Different variables predicted who was violent or suicidal. Violent youth acted upon and looked at the stimulus objects and produced more responses symbolizing aggression toward others and fewer responses symbolizing noxious textures. Suicidal youth acted less upon the stimulus object and showed an inner/symbolic orientation. One variable was a predictor of both violent and suicidal youths and distinguished between them. With the humanlike stimulus object, violent youth displayed an outer/symbolic orientation, tending to describe concrete attributes of the stimulus. In contrast, suicidal youth showed an inner/symbolic orientation, tending to represent highly personal meanings.

Critique

These results illustrate that embodied meanings could also be assessed with the Touch Association Test, a method that holds promise for clinical practice and research. While the findings were obtained from an inpatient population, they raise questions that could guide future studies with nonclinical and other clinical populations. For example, these maladaptive youths produced an embodied construct that correlated an inner-oriented style of symbolizing (when touch perceptions provide stimuli) with producing emotionally charged meanings. Would nonclinical groups produce the same embodied construct? Referring to another finding, the clinical population defined a construct suggesting that looking at the stimulus object was a way of avoiding embodied representations of fear and body deformation. Would a nonclinical group of children use the same coping device of looking at stimuli, rather than experience them bodily, to avoid experiencing meanings of fear and body deformity?

Another example that could serve future research derives from combining findings of each analysis. In the factor analysis, one construct correlated producing meanings representing noxious body sensations (scratchy, rough, cold), representations of aggression toward others, and acting on stimulus objects. In the second analysis the same variables distinguished between violent and nonviolent youth in a very interesting way. While violent youth, when compared with nonviolent controls, produced more representations of aggression, and performed actions on stimulus objects, they produced fewer representations of noxious body sensations. From this ensemble of results one could speculate, relying on the developmental-dialectical model, that violent youth experienced interferences during the phases of the emergent and core selves that resulted in embodied schemes of global, noxious, and painful body/skin sensations. However, these embodied schemas were not worked through in play rituals during the phase of the subjective self, but were split off, not translated, and remained unconscious. Later in life these body/skin sensations gain expression when stimuli are touched by performing random actions when the context requires the youth to image and think. At the same time, other aspects of early disruptions have been translated, resulting in the high incidence observed of embodied meanings representing aggression.

Another finding converges with the hypothesis for future research, that aspects of embodied meanings of violent youth have been split off from higher cognitive levels because of early disruptions. In one factor, maintaining a concrete/outer orientation when symbolizing the human-stimulus object correlated with producing atypical (unrealistic) responses. Again, in the second analysis, violent youth were discriminated from nonviolent youth by their maintaining a concrete/outer orientation in response to this same stimulus. Taken together, these results suggest that meanings representing interactions with humans are avoided and/or have not been translated into higher forms.

Probe II: Is There a Relationship between Representing the Regulation of Body Tempos in Physical Space and the Regulation of Cognitive Tempos in Mental Space?

This probe explored whether embodied meanings speak through body tempos and whether this voice is metaphorically extended into cognitive tempos. One study compared the regulation of body tempos in physical space with the regulation of cognitive tempos in mental space. A second study examined whether embodied meanings are expressed through changes in body tempo that occur in response to emotionally charged meanings expressed by another person.

Study I. The Relation between Regulating Body Tempos in Three Dimensions of Physical Space and Regulating Cognitive Tempos in Fantasy

Subjects

The children who participated in this study (N = 45) were hospitalized in a psychiatric facility because of severe adjustment problems and school failure. The group consisted of 20 females and 25 males; age range: 6–15 years; mean age = 11.4 years.

Procedure

On admission each child was administered the Body-Tempo Regulation Test (BTRT), the Fruit Distraction Test (FDT), and the Rorschach Inkblot Test.

　　Body-Tempo Regulation Test (Santostefano 1978).　The child was asked to move her/his body, and representations of the body (i.e., a doll and a pencil) in three tempos: (1) regular ("Walk in your regular way"), (2) fast (" Walk as fast as you can without running"); and (3) slow ("Walk as slowly as you can without stopping").
　　The child performed each tempo in three dimensions of space: macrospace, median space, and microspace, each defining a subtest of the procedure.
　　Floor maze. Regulating body tempos in macrospace. The child walked in three tempos over an S-shaped path, 25 feet long, outlined on the floor by a carpet. Time was recorded in seconds.
　　Table maze. Regulating body tempos in median space. While seated at a table, the child moved a doll of the same gender in three tempos over an S-shaped path, 92 inches long, outlined on a board. Time was recorded in seconds.
　　Paper maze. Regulating body tempo in microspace. While seated at a table, the child moved a pencil in three tempos, drawing a line on an S-shaped path, 22 inches long, printed on a sheet of paper (8½ x 11 inches). Time was recorded in seconds.

　　Fruit Distraction Test (Santostefano 1988a).　The Fruit Distraction Test (FDT) evaluates how a child attends selectively to relevant information while subordinating external distractions and internal thoughts and fantasies, a cognitive control termed "field articulation"(see Chapter 6). Age norms are available as well as studies supporting its construct validity and reliability (Santostefano 1978, 1986, 1988a, 1995b). Initially, the child was given a practice card with colored bars (red, yellow, blue, green) and trained to name the colors as quickly as possible. Then the child was given Card II (11 x 16 inches) on which were randomly arrayed fifty colored pictures of three fruits and one vegetable arranged in ten rows, five items in each row (e.g., yellow bananas, red apples, bunches of blue grapes, heads of green lettuce). The child was asked to name the color of each fruit as quickly as possible, beginning with the fruit in the upper left-hand corner, and continuing from left to right and from the top to the bottom rows.

Card III was exactly the same as Card II except that pictures of nurture-related objects (e.g., bottle of milk, ice cream cone) were placed next to each colored fruit. The child was asked to try to ignore the pictures and name the colors again as rapidly as possible. After the child completed naming the colors, the examiner removed the card and asked the child whether he/she recalled any of the pictures surrounding the fruit. Previous research has demonstrated that performance with this card assesses a child's ability to focus attention while fantasies/emotions concerning nurture are aroused. The more peripheral items the child recalled and the more time the child required to name the colors, the more the child was distracted.

Card IV presented the same items, in the same locations, but now each was colored incorrectly (e.g., a banana was colored red, blue, or green but never yellow). The child was asked to try to ignore the colors and name, as rapidly as possible, the color of each item that should be there. Previous research has demonstrated that performance with this card measures a child's ability to focus attention while subordinating internal thoughts and distractions.

To obtain a measure of the extent to which each type of distraction resulted in the child's requiring more time to name the colors, Card II reading time and naming errors were compared with those of Card III, reflecting whether a child was distracted by stimuli arousing fantasies and emotions concerning nurture. In addition, Card II reading time and naming errors were compared with those of Card IV, reflecting whether a child was distracted by internal contradictions. As discussed in earlier chapters, previous studies (Santostefano 1986, Santostefano and Moncata 1989) supported the view that errors a child produces reflected cognitive conflict, or "slips of cognition," triggered by unconscious, conflicted meanings/fantasies/emotions aroused by test stimuli. Because of this cognitive conflict, the efficiency with which a cognitive mechanism processes information is momentarily disrupted.

Imaged Motion Scale (IMS) (see first probe).   Each Rorschach response was evaluated in terms of (1) whether motion was represented as ongoing (e.g., "a bird flying"), completed (e.g., "a bird just landed on a branch"), or imminent (e.g., "a bird; it's about to take off"); (2) whether the agents and recipients of the motion were humans, animals, inanimate objects, or mythical figures; (3) the level of vigor represented; for example, from "a maple leaf floating down" to "a rocket ship taking off."

Results

Relations among Body Tempos in Three Dimensions of Space.   The first analysis explored whether and how the three tempos a child performed within each space dimension were related, and whether and how tempos performed in one space dimension related to those performed in others. The results suggested that the children in this inpatient population were characterized by "transmissions" that contained only one "gear."

In all three space dimensions, moving fast correlated with the tempo the child used when asked to move "in your regular way" (e.g., Regular Tempo/Floor Maze x Fast Tempo/ Floor Maze: r = .90; Regular Tempo/Floor Maze x Fast Tempo/Table Maze: r = .63; Regular Tempo/Floor Maze x Fast Tempo/Paper Maze: r = .62).

Relation between Body Tempo and Cognitive Tempo.   To explore the relation between regulating body tempo in physical space and cognitive tempos in mental space, FDT time and error scores were correlated with the time a child took to perform each tempo in each space dimension. The time scores did not result in significant correlations. However, FDT Error Scores correlated significantly with Body Tempo Scores. In general, the slower the child moved, the *more* naming errors the child made on the FDT. For example, the time a child took to walk the Floor Maze as quickly as possible correlated significantly with the number of naming errors the child made when naming the colors of Card I (colored bars with no distractions) (r = .53; p = .01). Since the correlation is positive, the slower a child moved when requested to move quickly, the more naming errors the child made. As another example, the slower a child moved the doll over the Table Maze, when requested to move slowly, the more naming errors the child made when naming the colors of Card I (r = .36; p = .01).

In addition to naming errors, the number of items the child recalled after Card III was removed (i.e, the amount of attention the child paid to information designated as irrelevant) also related to a dysfunction in regulating body tempo. Moving the body *slowly* when asked to move slowly in both macrospace and median space correlated with recalling more of the peripheral figures (e.g., Slow/Floor Maze x Recalls = .54; p = .01; Slow/Table Maze x Recalls = .51; p = .01).

These results suggest that for this inpatient population delaying motion did not help cognition to equilibrate information with emotions/fantasies, suggesting an antagonistic relationship between regulating body tempos and cognitive efficiency. Rather, delaying motion was associated with cognitive imbalance which is opposite to what has been observed with nonclinical populations who show a correspondent relationship between body tempos and cognitive efficiency (Santostefano 1978).

These findings also relate to earlier discussions of research (see Chapter 4) that supports the view that errors made when performing a cognitive task could be conceptualized as "bungled cognitive actions" or "slips of cognition" that are the result of cognitive conflict a child experiences with the prospect of taking physical action.

The Relation between Body Tempos and Representing Motion in Imagery.
This aspect of the study explored whether and how regulating body tempos in physical space is related to, and extended into, the way in which motion is rep-

resented in fantasy. Time scores (regular, slow, and fast) in each space dimension (Floor, Table, Paper) were correlated with the number of Rorschach images a child produced depicting motion (units of motion), the number of agents performing the motion and recipients receiving the motion, and the level of vigor represented by the motion. Only regulating tempos in median space (Table Maze) and microspace (Paper Maze) resulted in significant correlations. In general, the slower a child moved, whether asked to move at regular, fast, or slow tempos, the more units of motion produced on the Rorschach and the more that motion was represented as performed and received by some agent (human, animal, or mythical figure) (e.g., Regular/Table Maze x Units of Motion = .58; p = .01; Slow/Table Maze x Units of Motion = .69; p = .01; Fast/Table Maze x Units of Motion = .33; p = .05).

This inpatient population, then, showed a relationship between imaging motion and delaying body tempo that is similar to that observed in nonclinical populations; namely, delaying physical motion is associated with generating more fantasies or images of motion. At the same time, as noted above, this inpatient population differed from normal subjects in showing an antagonistic relationship between cognitive slips or errors when performing a cognitive task and moving the body slowly. Instead of showing a relation between body delay and cognitive balance/efficiency, this clinical group showed that the more they delayed their body tempos, the more errors they made.

Last, the vigor of motion depicted in Rorschach images correlated only with the fast trial of the Paper Maze. In this population, children who moved the pencil quickly produced images that depicted slow motion, while children who moved the pencil slowly (after being instructed to move quickly) produced images that depicted vigorous motion. Again, with this inpatient population, moving slowly when requested to move quickly was associated with discordant functioning.

Critique

The youth in this study required hospitalization in part because they presented various difficulties with aggression, hyperactivity, and poor school performance. Their cognitive/behavioral problems seem related to the results obtained. For these children, when regulating body tempos (regular, fast, slow) in different dimensions of physical space (floor, table, paper), there is a tendency not to differentiate tempos but to move fast when requested to move regular or slow. In addition, attempts to slow down, and regulate a fast tempo, resulted in more cognitive errors or slips of cognition. This finding suggests that the antagonistic relationship among tempos at the embodied level has been extended into cognition. Further studies with other clinical and nonclinical populations should reveal other patterns of relationships among body tempos, cognitive tempos, and representations of motion in fantasy that should help clarify those patterns associated with adaptation and maladaptation.

Study II. The Relation between Regulating Body Tempos
in Microspace while Experiencing Emotions
and Fantasies Aroused by Another Person

Subjects

Teachers of a public school were asked to refer children who had not presented learning or adjustment difficulties. Parental permission was obtained for the 60 children studied: 20 (10 females; 10 males) in each of three age groups (6, 9, 12 years).

Procedure

Each child was administered three counterbalanced trials of the Spiral Test of Impulse Control and Cards II and III of the Fruit Distraction Test.

Spiral Test of Impulse Control (Santostefano 1978).   The child was given a spiral pathway (170 cm long), printed on a sheet of paper (8½ x11 inches) and asked to draw a continuous line on the pathway with a pencil from beginning to end in each of three trials: (1) "at your regular speed," (2) "as slowly as possible and without stopping," and (3) as slowly as possible without stopping and while the examiner spoke six words at 25-cm intervals. The words were father, bad, mother, blood, spanking, bullet. When introducing the trial with spoken words, the examiner explained that, "It's OK if you notice the words I say; your job is to move the pencil as slowly as you can without stopping." Time taken to complete each trial was recorded in seconds.

Fruit Distraction Test.   This test is described above in Study I. To obtain measures of shifts in cognitive tempo in the face of distracting fantasies/emotions, two cards of this test were administered: Card II (50 colored fruit) and Card III (the same 50 colored fruit surrounded by pictures of food-related objects designated as irrelevant). With each card, time and naming errors were recorded.

Results

In a preliminary analysis, to learn whether age or gender were associated with performance on the Spiral Test, time scores were entered into a two-way analysis of variance (three age levels and gender). Significant age trends were observed. Six-year-olds showed the slowest tempo with each trial (regular, slow, and slow while the examiner spoke words). The 12-year-olds showed the quickest tempo with each trial; the 9-year-olds fell between. There was no significant difference between females and males, nor in the interaction between age and gender.

In order to explore whether changes in the regulation of movement in microspace express embodied meanings, time taken to move the pencil slowly during the silent condition was subtracted, for each child, from time taken to move the pencil slowly while hearing the examiner speak emotionally evocative words. If a child's difference score was a positive value, then the child slowed down more during the slow-emotional trial than the slow-silent trial. If a child's difference score was a negative value, the child moved the pencil more quickly during the slow-emotional trial. No significant relationships were observed between these scores and age and gender. Nearly half of each age group displayed a quicker tempo when hearing evocative words, while the other half displayed a slower tempo. Therefore, the population was divided into two groups. Children who displayed quicker tempos when moving the pencil during the emotional condition versus the silent condition were assigned to the Emotional/Body Quick Group. Those who displayed a slower tempo in the emotional condition versus the silent condition were assigned to the Emotional/Body Slow Group.

To explore whether changes in regulating body tempo, which occurred when fantasy/emotions were evoked, were extended into the domain of regulating cognitive tempos, an FDT score was calculated for each child. The time a child took to name the colors of fruit without surrounding distractions (Card II) was subtracted from the time a child took to name the colors of fruit surrounded by distracting pictures of food objects (Card III). A positive value indicated that the child used a slower cognitive tempo when fantasies/emotions concerning nurture were aroused. A negative value indicated that a child used a quicker cognitive tempo when fantasy/emotions were aroused.

These FDT difference scores were entered into an analysis of variance as dependent variables with the Emotion/Body Quick and Emotional/Body Slow groups as independent variables. The Emotional/Body Quick Group used a quicker cognitive tempo when naming the colors of the fruit surrounded by pictures that evoked fantasies/emotions of nurture; the Emotional/Body Slow Group, a slower cognitive tempo. The naming errors each group made were also analyzed. The Emotional/Body Quick Group made *more* naming errors than the Emotional/Body Slow Group when coping with the card that contained the emotionally evocative pictures of food-related objects.

These results suggest that changes in body tempo employed in microspace are extended into, and are the same as, changes that occur in cognitive tempo. These results also suggest that children who quicken their body tempos in microspace when dealing with emotions/fantasies also tended to experience moments of cognitive imbalance when focusing attention in the face of distracting emotions, resulting in more errors (slips of cognition). In contrast, children who delayed their body tempos when experiencing emotions/fantasies experienced more cognitive balance and made fewer cognitive errors. This observation is opposite to that made of inpatient children (Study I), for whom moving slowly did not relate to increased cognitive efficiency.

Probe III: Is There a Relationship between Representations of Interpersonal Enactments and How Cognition Acts upon Test Stimuli Representing Interpersonal Aggression or Affiliation?

This probe used still another window to asses whether and how embodied meanings are extended into cognitive functioning. In one study a child was asked to look at the examiner through a pair of binoculars. In the other study, a child was asked to draw a picture of two persons "doing something." Behaviors observed with these simple tasks were related to how a child's cognition acted upon and remembered test stimuli representing either interpersonal aggression or affiliation.

Study I. The Relation between Action Taken with Binoculars When Interacting with Another Person and Cognitive Action Taken with Test Stimuli Representing Interpersonal Aggression and Affiliation

Subjects

Seventy-five children (35 females; 40 males; mean age = 12.5 years) admitted to a psychiatric facility participated in this study.

Procedure

On admission each child was administered the Leveling-Sharpening Shoot-Out Test, the Leveling-Sharpening Friends Test, and the Binoculars Test.

Leveling-Sharpening Shoot-Out Test (LSSOT).

Leveling-Sharpening Friends Test (LSFT) (Santostefano 1992c, 1995b).   The LSSOT and LSFT assess the manner in which a child remembers visual images of information and compares these images to perceptions of ongoing information, a cognitive control termed *leveling-sharpening* (see Chapter 6). Age norms are available as well as studies supporting reliability and construct validity (e.g., Calicchia et al. 1991, Ford-Clark 1992, Santostefano 1986, 1995, Santostefano and Rieder 1984). The LSSOT and LSFT are identical in makeup, procedure, and task requirement. With each, 63 pictures of a scene (8½ x 11 inches) are displayed in succession, 5 seconds each display. Gradually, throughout the series, twenty details are omitted accumulatively from the scene. The child was asked to report changes in the scene he/she noticed.

The LSSOT consisted of a scene of two cowboys in a shoot-out. The one being shot is located in the center of the scene, facing the viewer; he is slumping over, pistol falling from his hand, and blood spots cover his shirt. The other cowboy is located to the left of the scene, with his back to the viewer, so that one sees only his profile and the pistol he is firing. The LSFT consisted of two cowboys greeting each other. The cowboy extending a greeting is smiling and faces the viewer. The other cowboy is located to the left of the scene, with his back to the viewer, so that one sees only his profile. Studies support the proposal that the shoot-out scene arouses thoughts/fantasies/emotions concerning interpersonal aggression; the friendship scene, concerning affiliation.

Performance was evaluated with two scores: (1) *Correct Change Ratio*: the number of correct changes detected and how soon a change was perceived once it was introduced (i.e., the number of scenes displayed before a change was perceived). The greater the number of changes detected, and the sooner changes were detected, the smaller the ratio (cognitive sharpening). Numerically small ratios indicate a child holds a differentiated image in memory of the pattern of ongoing information. The fewer number of changes noticed and the greater the lag before a change was noticed, the larger the ratio (cognitive leveling). Numerically larger ratios indicate a child holds a global image in memory of the pattern of ongoing information. (2) *Incorrect Change Score*: the total number of changes reported that in fact do not occur (e.g., the sun is perceived as shifting location when it does not; bloodstains on the shirt of the cowboy are perceived as having increased, when this does not occur). These errors are interpreted as reflecting slips of cognition triggered by unconscious, conflicted meanings and emotions (Santostefano and Moncata 1989).

Binoculars Test.   The examiner provided the child with practice to clarify that looking through binoculars from one end magnified an item and "moves it close to you," while looking through the other end diminished the size of an item and "moves it far away from you." Then the examiner stood 15 feet from the child and asked the child to look at the examiner through either end of the pair of binoculars. With this procedure, we wondered whether the action of drawing the examiner close, or moving the examiner away, when peering through the binoculars, could be an expression of an embodied meaning representing interpersonal relationships, especially regarding separation-individuation.

Results

To form groups whose performance with the LSSOT and LSFT could be compared for statistical analysis, the children were divided into two age groups: Young Group, N = 36; mean age = 10.2; Old Group, N = 39; mean age = 14.9 years. In addition, some children drew the examiner near when looking through the binoculars; others moved the examiner away. Therefore, two binocular groups were formed: Near Group = 62; Far Group = 13.

In one analysis, LSSOT Correct Change and Incorrect Change Scores were entered into two-way analyses of variance, with both age and binocular groups as variables. No significant differences were observed between Young-Old and Near-Far groups. This result suggested that if an embodied meaning was represented by the action of experiencing the examiner near or far, this meaning was not related to cognitive actions taken with stimuli representing interpersonal aggression.

However, the LSFT did result in significant differences and noteworthy trends. Young subjects detected fewer correct changes and after a long lag (cognitive leveling; Correct Ratio mean = 21.33); older subjects detected more correct changes and sooner (cognitive sharpening; Correct Ratio mean = 16.68) (F = 8.88; p = .004). This finding agrees with longitudinal studies (Santostefano 1978, 1988a) showing that with age there is a progressive shift in cognitive organization from leveling to sharpening information. Further, the Near Group detected fewer correct changes and later (cognitive leveling; Correct Ratio mean = 19.62). In contrast, the Far Group detected more changes and sooner (cognitive sharpening; Correct Ratio mean = 15.49). This difference fell just short of significance (F =3.45; p =.06). The interaction between Young-Old and Near-Far did not approach significance.

In terms of incorrect changes perceived, no significant differences were observed between Young-Old and Near-Far. However, the two-way interaction fell just short of statistical significance but deserves attention. Young subjects who looked near produced *fewer* errors (mean = 0.39) than those who looked far (mean = 1.20). On the other hand, the older subjects who looked near produced *more* errors (mean = 0.26) than those who looked far (mean = .00) (F = 3.26; p = .07).

Critique

The Binocular Test appears to hold promise as a method that permits the body to speak about self–other differentiation. And the LSSOT and LSFT appear to be promising as methods that assess cognitive activity associated with interpersonal interactions representing aggression or affiliation.

This study found that children who moved the examiner away when peering through binoculars showed cognitive sharpening when dealing with a scene representing affiliation; children who drew the examiner near showed cognitive leveling. Studies of normal and clinical populations (Santostefano 1978, 1988a) support the view that cognitive sharpening indicates a differentiated, more mature developmental organization than cognitive leveling. Applied to our results, if pushing the examiner away when looking through binoculars represents self–other differentiation, this developmentally more mature stage in self-development was associated with a developmentally more mature cognitive organization when dealing with stimuli representing interpersonal affiliation. Along the same line, if drawing the examiner closer represents self–other fusion, this earlier stage of self-development was associated with a less mature cognitive organization when dealing with stimuli representing interpersonal affiliation.

The number of incorrect perceptions each group produced adds an interesting dimension. As discussed earlier, errors made with tests of cognitive control are conceptualized as reflecting cognitive conflict. In the present study, young children who pushed the examiner away when peering through binoculars produced more errors with the LSFT than did young children who drew the examiner near. It seems reasonable to propose that there is more cognitive conflict concerning affiliation in young children who pushed the examiner away than in young children who drew the examiner near. The performance of older subjects converges. Those who drew the examiner near produced more errors, suggesting cognitive conflict in these older subjects who have not successfully individuated.

Taken together, these results suggest that embodied meanings concerning relationships with others are extended into cognition, revealing themselves in cognitive actions a child takes when constructing and holding in memory images of information that represent interpersonal interactions. The heuristic value of this inference is supported by the observation that no differences were observed with the LSSOT, which contained stimuli representing interpersonal aggression. Apparently, drawing the examiner near or pushing the examiner away by manipulating binoculars is an embodied meaning that relates to affiliation and separation-individuation since differences were observed only with the LSFT. Perhaps if the child were asked either to tie the examiner's wrists with a rope or slip gloves over the examiner's hands, these expressions of embodied meanings would extend into cognition and reveal themselves in the cognitive actions a child takes with the LSSOT representing interpersonal aggression.

Study II. The Relation between Representing Interpersonal Interactions in Drawings and Action Taken with Test Stimuli Representing Interpersonal Aggression and Affiliation

To illustrate another approach to probing how meanings constructed in one domain relate to meanings constructed in another, Ford-Clark (1992) asked children to draw a picture of two persons interacting. Comparing this response to how a child managed the LSSOT and LSFT provided an opportunity to explore whether embodied meanings revealed in drawings are extended into how cognition manages stimuli representing either interpersonal aggression or affiliation.

Subjects

185 public school children, grades K to 8, participated in this study (99 females; 86 males).

Procedure

Half the children were administered the LSSOT, then the Two-Person Drawing Test, and then the LSFT. The other half were administered these procedures in the reverse order.

488 HANDBOOK OF INTEGRATIVE PSYCHOTHERAPIES

LSSOT and LSFT (see Study I above)

Two-Person Drawing Test.   The child was provided a sheet of paper (8½ x 11 inches) and a pencil, and asked to draw "two persons doing something." Drawings were scored on a 9-point scale: 1 was assigned to aggressive forms of interpersonal interacting (e.g., "two kids throwing rocks at each other"); 5 was assigned to forms of parallel activity (e.g., "two girls watching TV"), and 9 was assigned to forms of affiliative interaction (e.g., "two kids shaking hands"). On the basis of his/her drawing, each child was assigned to one of three drawing groups: Aggressive Drawing Group (Scores 1–4; N = 43), Parallel Drawing Group (Scores 5–6; N = 56), Affiliative Drawing Group (Scores 7–9; N = 74).

Results

LSSOT and LSFT Correct Ratio Scores were entered into a two-way analysis of variance with drawing groups. Our interest is addressed most directly by the interaction effect, which proved to be significant (F = 321; p =.04). Children in the Aggressive Drawing Group detected more correct changes and sooner when dealing with the scene depicting interpersonal violence (mean = 50.0; cognitive sharpening) and fewer changes after some delay, when dealing with the scene depicting affiliation (mean = 52.3; cognitive leveling). Conversely, children in the Affiliative Drawing Group showed cognitive leveling with the aggressive scene (mean = 52.1) and sharpening with the affiliative scene (mean = 49.7). The children in the Parallel Drawing Group displayed the highest degree of sharpening with both stimuli (LSSOT mean = 46.7; LSFT mean = 48.8).

In terms of incorrect changes perceived (cognitive slips), a trend was observed that, while falling short of significant, deserves mention because it converges with other studies. The Aggressive Drawing Group produced more errors (showed more cognitive conflict) when managing the affiliative scene (LSSOT mean = 0.29; LSFT mean = 0.41). The Affiliative Drawing Group produced more errors (showed more cognitive conflict) while managing the aggressive scene (LSSOT mean = 0.68; LSFT mean = 0.43). The Parallel Drawing Group produced nearly the same number of errors with each scene (LSSOT mean = 0.23; LSFT mean = 0.21).

Critique

Unlike other procedures described above, the Two-Person Drawing Test is viewed as expressing embodied meanings concerning interpersonal relations that are constructed at a cognitive level, where body perceptions and enactments play no role at all. We observed that representations of interactions depicted in a drawing were extended into, and related to, the cognitive actions a child took with two distinctly different stimuli: one depicting interpersonal violence, the other interpersonal affiliation.

Children who represented relationships in drawings as aggressive employed a developmentally higher cognitive organization when constructing images and remembering information representing interpersonal violence, and a lower organization when dealing with information representing interpersonal affiliation. Again, as with other studies reported, the errors these children made with the cognitive tasks proved to be psychologically meaningful phenomena, reflecting the degree of cognitive conflict associated with a particular meaning. These same children made more errors when dealing with information representing interpersonal affiliation, suggesting they experience cognitive conflict (imbalance) with this type of interpersonal context.

Conversely, children who represented relationships in drawings as affiliative employed a developmentally higher cognitive organization when constructing images and remembering information representing interpersonal affiliation, and a lower organization when dealing with information representing interpersonal violence. They also made more errors (showed more cognitive conflict) when managing the violent scene. These results suggest the diagnostic potential of the Two-Person Drawing Test and contribute further support to our efforts to demonstrate how meanings expressed at one level of functioning are metaphorically extended to another.

Probe IV: Relations among Embodied Meanings Children Represent, Life Stressors and Conscious Fears They Report, and Cognitive Functioning with Stimuli Arousing Different Meanings/Emotions

In previous chapters we noted that from a holistic view, a child brings an integrated system of relationships among, for example, embodied meanings, cognitions, emotions, surface (conscious) and deep (unconscious) behaviors, and the meanings assigned to experiences, and that each of these domains of functioning is dialectically related to the others. To probe this viewpoint, children were administered procedures that assess life stressors, conscious fears, meanings represented when body perceptions serve as stimuli, and cognitive functioning when dealing with stimulation that arouses meanings/emotions concerning nurture/affiliation versus interpersonal aggression. The intention was to remove boundaries that separate body from mind, cognition from emotion, and a child's subjective world from environments. In one sense, the study described in this probe brings together the issues considered by the projects previously discussed.

Subjects

The children in this study were attending an inner-city school serving a blue-collar socioeconomic population. During two successive years, all kindergarten children were evaluated, with parental consent, as part of an early detection program. In addition, children referred by teachers, and attending the first or second grade, were also evaluated. Children who presented significant learning and adjustment problems and whose test scores indicated significant lags in functioning were not included in this study. The final sample (N = 93) consisted of 80 kindergartners and 13 first and second graders: 39 females and 54 males; 37 African-Americans, 51 Latinos, 4 Caucasians, and 1 Asian. Their ages ranged from 56–115 months; mean age = 79 months; median age = 76 months; modal age = 72 months.

Procedures

Each child was individually administered the following procedures at school during the school day.

Life Stressor Interview (Santostefano 1992b).   After sufficient rapport was established, a child was asked, "Tell me whether anything happened that upset you a lot?" The examiner joined the child in discussing the events she/he described and provided assistance whenever indicated. The examiner was careful not to direct the child's thoughts in a particular direction and limited his/her comments to requests for clarification. As one example, a child responded, "My grandpa died." The examiner asked, "Is there anything else you can tell me about that?" The child responded, "He was drinking beer; his friend said get some beer in the car; when he got back, the friend shot him." As noted below, this response would receive several ratings. Some children reported more than one stressor spontaneously. If a child reported one stressor, the examiner asked only once, "Is there anything else that upset you a lot?"

The number of stressors each child reported ranged from one to eight. Two raters independently determined which of six stressors each response represented, following a scoring system developed from the responses of over 300 African-American, Latino, Caucasian, and Asian children from kindergarten through the twelfth grade (Santostefano 1992b). Raters agreed about 95 percent of the time when rating the types of stressors a child's response reflected and disagreements were negotiated. Table 10–1 lists types of stressors, examples of each, and the number of children who reported each type. The child's response noted above as an example would qualify for the rating "Shooting/Fights" ("The friend shot him") and also "Death of a Loved One" ("My grandpa died").

In forming stressor groups for statistical analyses, a child could be a member of only one group, while another child could be a member of more than one group. However, I reasoned that if children who, for example, reported shootings/fights as a stressor were compared on some variable with children who did not report this stressor, differences observed between these groups could be associated with reporting shootings/fights as an upsetting event, independent of whether some children in the stressor group reported other stressors. To gather support for this position, the types of stressors were intercorrelated and no significant correlations were

TABLE 10–1. Types of Upsetting Events (Life Stressors) Children Reported Witnessing or Learning About (N = 93)

Upsetting Events	Examples	Number of Children Reporting
Shootings/Fights	"Someone got shot next to my house. I heard the noises." "Bad guys in school beat up my friend."	52
Physical Threats/Arguments	"Some girls are mean; they push you around." "My aunt is always arguing."	51
Destruction of Property	"These kids smashed a car window." "A kid tore up everybody's papers."	18
Death of a Loved One	"My grandma died the other day a long time ago." "My father died; my mother never told me how."	33
Illness/Hospitalization of a Loved One	"My mom is in the hospital." "My dad got his stomachache; he still has it."	58
Absence of a Loved One/Disruption of a Relationship	"Grandpa's not in our family; he's in Africa." "I'm sad because my sister lives far away with my grandma."	37

observed. Coefficients ranged from a low of .02 (Shootings/Fights x Death of a Loved One) to a high of .18 (Shootings/Fights x Physical Threats/Arguments). The life stressor interview is related to the method of obtaining narratives from children after some cataclysmic event has occurred (e.g., Farver and Frosch 1996, Wigren 1994).

Fears Interview. After the Life Stressor Interview was completed, the examiner asked, "Tell me three things you are most afraid of?" The types of fears children reported and the number of reports are listed in Table 10–2. Two additional scores were calculated: one addressed whether the child explicitly depicted that she/he was afraid that some harm would befall her/him; the other score addressed whether the child feared that some harm would befall a designated other

TABLE 10–2. Types of Fears Children Reported (N = 93)

Fears	Examples	Number of Children
Aggression I	"People shooting" (stabbing)	12
Aggression II	"Getting beat up"; "Getting kidnapped"	14
Aggression III	"When people call names"; "Somebody yelling"	9
Animals/Insects	"Snakes," "Rats," "Spiders"	32
Mythical Figures/ Movies	"Ghosts," "Vampires," "Monsters in movies," "Watching scary movies"	44
General States of Fear	"The dark," "No one will take care of us if mom dies," "I'm scared to walk up the hill at the park."	42
Fear of Self Being Injured (Additional Score)	The self is explicitly depicted as the recipient of a feared action or situation; e.g., "I'm afraid of getting shot."	36
Fear of Others Being Injured (Additional Score)	A person is explicitly mentioned as the target of feared aggression (e.g., parent, sib, friend).	49
Types of Fear	The number of types of fears reported: 1–2 Types 3–4 Types	57 36

(e.g., parent, sib, friend). In addition, each child was assigned to one of two groups depending upon the number of types of fears she/he reported.

Action Test of Body Image (ATBI) (Santostefano 1992a).   Described briefly in Probe I, with this procedure the child was asked to assume various body postures (e.g., stand on one leg with arms outstretched), perform simple movements (e.g., encircle arms, open and close eyes), and describe what the body experience brought to mind. Responses were evaluated in terms of nine variables (Table 10–3).

Fruit Distraction Test (Santostefano 1988a).   This procedure was described previously in Probe II. In addition to Cards II, III, and IV, Card V was also administered in this study. With Card V, the fruit are colored correctly and located in the same sequence as Card III, but pictures of weapons (e.g., pistols, sticks of dynamite) surround the fruit instead of pictures of food items as in Card III. Pre-

TABLE 10–3. Variables and Sample Responses of the Action Test of Body Image (ATBI)

Body Image Variable	Examples of Responses
1. Imbalance/Balance (6-point scale)	*1* = "falling of a cliff" *6* = "ballet dancing"
2. Constriction/Assertion (6-point scale)	*1* = "being handcuffed" *6* = "a salmon swimming upstream"; "running the marathon"

Body-Image Meanings Scored as Expressed (1) or Not Expressed (0)

3. Positive Meanings/Emotions	"Like you just arrived safely"; "Hugging my friend"; "Quiet, peaceful because nothing is moving around me"; "Feeling free, doing what you want"
4. Dysphoric Meanings/Emotions	"Feeling awkward"; "Tired after a long day"; "When you feel tension building up"; "Like before you start crying"
5. Pain/Danger	"Pain in your legs from walking"; "Like you're facing Freddy Krueger or some monster"
6. Deformed/Inadequate	"My grandfather had a stroke"; "I saw a cripple; he had no legs"; "Everyone could lift it, I couldn't"
7. Self Value/Competence	"Getting an award"; "A strong rock"; "Throwing a shot-put"; "A telephone pole solid in the ground"; "I feel in control"
8. Aggression/Hate	"Punching someone"; "Crushing branches"; "Killing"; "I hate people who look at me"
9. Need for Nurture	"Being hugged"; "I love pizza"; "Bringing things toward me"

vious research has demonstrated that performance with Card V assesses a child's ability to focus attention while meanings/emotions concerning aggression are aroused.

With each card, the examiner recorded the time a child required to name the colors of the fruit and the number of naming errors a child made. For each analysis discussed below, a child's performances with pairs of cards were compared. Card III reading time and naming errors were compared with those of Card V. This comparison reflected whether a child was distracted more by stimuli arousing meanings/emotions concerning nurture versus aggression. Card II reading time and naming errors were compared with those of Card IV. This comparison reflected whether a child was distracted by internal (unconscious) contradictions.

Two additional types of naming errors were calculated: (1) *Sequence Error Score.* This score reflected whether a child made naming errors early (smaller numerical value) or later (larger numerical value) during the sequence of naming the colors of 50 fruits; (2) *Bursts of Errors.* This score reflected the number of times a child made two or more naming errors in succession while naming the colors of three (or fewer) consecutive fruits. I noted in Probe II that studies (e.g., Santostefano 1986, Santostefano and Moncata 1989) have supported the view that errors a child produced when naming colors of the FDT reflected cognitive conflict, or "slips of cognition," triggered by unconscious conflicted meanings/emotions aroused by test stimuli. Relative to the number of errors made, bursts of errors reflect a momentary but more severe disruption in the balance cognition maintains between information and the meanings/emotions aroused.

Leveling-Sharpening Shoot-Out Test (LSSOT) and Leveling-Sharpening Friends Test (Santostefano 1992c, 1995b). These procedures were described in Probe III. In addition to calculating the *Correct Change Ratio* and *Incorrect Change Score*, three additional scores were computed. Recall that the LSSOT consisted of two cowboys in a shoot-out. The one being shot is located in the center of the scene, facing the viewer. This figure is referred to as the "Victim." The number of changes a child perceived that occurred on the person of this figure is called the *Victim Score*. The LSFT consists of two cowboys greeting each other. The cowboy extending a greeting and smiling faces the viewer. This figure is referred to as the "Friend." The number of changes that a child perceived that occurred on the person of this figure is called the *Friend Score*. In addition, changes occurred around each figure and also in the periphery of the scene. Changes perceived in the center of the scene are reflected by the *Central Score*, and those in the periphery as the *Peripheral Score*. The third type of score calculated reflected whether correct changes were perceived early in the sequence of viewing sixty-three presentations of a scene (smaller numerical value) or later (larger numerical value). These scores are referred to as *LSF Correct Rankings* and *LSSOT Correct Rankings*.

Results

In presenting the results, I begin "inside and deep," so to speak, and use body-based representations as the point of reference to explore whether and how these unconscious meanings are extended into other domains. ATBI responses are first related to conscious fears, then to life stressors, and then to cognitive functioning. Following this, fears are related to life stressors and cognitive functioning, and then life stressors are related to cognitive functioning. I conclude by noting patterns of relationships observed to illustrate a holistic, integrative approach to assessment.

Preliminary questions should be addressed before we examine the main issues of this probe, namely, whether and how embodied meanings, fears, life stressors, and cognitive functioning are interrelated in this sample of children. These preliminary questions concern whether gender and race differences were observed.

Gender. *Life stressors.* No significant differences were observed in the total number of stressors reported by females (mean = 3.5) and males (mean = 3.7). Chi-square analyses comparing gender and each type of stressor also resulted in no significant differences.

ATBI. Only two ATBI variables resulted in significant gender differences. Females produced a higher percent of responses representing Positive Meanings/ Emotions (Mean = .15; SD = .20) than males (Mean = .09; SD = .10) (p = .05). In addition, females produced a higher percent of responses representing the Need for Nurture (Mean = .10; SD = .17) than males (Mean = .04; SD = .06) (p = .04). These relationships will be taken into account when results are discussed.

Fears. Only one Fear variable resulted in a significant gender difference. More boys (38%) than girls (19%) reported fears of aggression (X^2 = 3.7; p = .05). This relation will also be taken into account when results are discussed.

FDT/LFST/LSSOT. In terms of cognitive variables, gender was entered into a series of two-way analyses of variance with each cognitive score to determine whether gender interacted with reading time and naming errors when fruit were surrounded by distractions representing nurture versus aggression or by contradictions, and whether gender interacted with the number of changes detected in a series of pictures representing affiliation versus interpersonal aggression. No significant differences were observed.

Race. Latino and African-American children were compared since only four Caucasians and one Asian were members of the sample.

Life-stressors. A significant difference in total number of stresses was observed. African-American children reported more stressors (Mean = 4.4, SD = 2.1) than Latinos (Mean = 2.9; SD = 1.7) (F = 3.70; p < .01). However, when chi-square analyses compared race and types of stressors (children reporting a stressor versus those not reporting the stressor), no significant differences were observed.

ATBI. Only one ATBI variable resulted in a significant difference. Of their ATBI responses, African-American children produced a higher percentage representing the body-self as deformed/inadequate (Mean = .66; SD = .48) than did Latinos (Mean = .36; SD = .48) (F = 3.01; p = .003). This relationship will be considered when results are discussed.

Fears. No significant relations were observed between race and the various types of fears children reported.

FDT/LSFT/LSSOT. The race variable was also entered into separate, two-way analyses of variance with each cognitive score to determine whether race interacted with reading time and naming errors with each of the distracting conditions of the FDT and with the number of changes detected in a series of pictures representing affiliation versus interpersonal aggression. No significant differences were observed.

In summary, gender was not a possible confounding variable with two exceptions. As for race, although African-American children reported more stressors on the average than did Latino children, race was not related to types of stressors and fears reported, nor with cognitive functioning. Race was related to ATBI representations of the body-self as deformed/inadequate.

Body-Based Meanings and Conscious Fears (Table 10–4). Typically, a child is not consciously aware of the symbolic meanings revealed by her/his associations to body postures, in much the same way as when a child describes what an inkblot could be. For example, if when encircling his arms a child responded, "This is like a fish swimming hard," he/she is not aware that the meaning of body-self assertion is being expressed symbolically. On the other hand, when describing fears, a child is reporting what he/she is consciously afraid of. A comparison of ATBI and Fear responses enables us to probe whether and how these two domains are related, one embodied and unconscious, the other more cognitive and conscious.

ATBI and Fear variables were examined with a series of chi-square analyses. As shown in Table 10–4, children who represented body-based assertion reported fewer types of fears than did children who represented body-based constriction. In contrast, children who represented body balance reported more types of fears than did children who represented body imbalance. This difference leads to one speculation that requires further study. The children were young (ages 5 and 6 years) and living in an inner-city environment containing many possible stressors and dangers. The results obtained with numbers of fear types suggest that with this group, body-image representations of assertion may be accompanied by denial and little need to project anxieties onto different environmental attributes, resulting in fears. On the other hand, body representations of balance are accompanied less by denying one's anxieties, which, accordingly, are projected onto a wider range of things and events that become feared. This speculation is supported by another finding listed in Table 10–4. Children who represented body balance reported more fears of being injured by the aggressive actions of others. Is it possible that with

TABLE 10–4. Relations between Body-Based Representations and Fears

Fears		Body-Based Meanings		X^2	P
		Constriction	Assertion		
Types	1–2	53	72		
	3–4	47	28	3.3	.05
		Imbalance	Balance		
Types	1–2	74	52		
	3–4	26	48	4.8	.03
Self Being Injured	No	61	40		
	Yes	39	60	4.0	.05
		Dysphoric/Emotions			
		No	*Yes*		
Violence	No	77	55		
	Yes	23	45	4.7	.03
Mythical Figures/ Movies	No	79	58		
	Yes	21	42	4.1	.04
General States	No	61	41		
	Yes	39	59	3.2	.07
		Aggression/Hate Toward Others			
		No	*Yes*		
Mythical Figures/ Movies	No	37	60		
	Yes	63	40	4.9	.03
		Value/Competence			
		No	*Yes*		
Animals/Insects	No	78	56		
	Yes	22	44	5.0	.02
		Deformed/Inadequate			
		No	*Yes*		
Violence	No	80	60		
	Yes	20	40	3.8	.05
Self Being Injured	No	71	53		
	Yes	29	47	2.9	.08

Note: All values = percentage of children

these inner-city children a sense of body balance is accompanied by a conscious and more accurate appraisal that one could be hurt by others?

Relationships between body-based representations and types of fears were also observed. Children who expressed body-based dysphoric meanings/emotions reported more fears of violence, more fears of mythical figures/frightening movies, and more general states of fear. Children who expressed body-based representations of aggression/hate toward others reported fewer fears of mythical figures/movies. In addition, children who experienced body-based competence reported more fears of animals/insects than children who did not express competence.

This pattern of results appears concordant. Body-based representations of tension, sadness, and fatigue are fitted with fears of violence, general fear states, and the tendency to project anxieties onto mythical figures and movies. Similarly, if a child's functioning is characterized by body-based representations of aggression/hate toward others, this child is likely not to project anxieties onto mythical figures and frightening movies. Along the same line, if a child's functioning is characterized by body-based meanings of value/competence, this child is likely to project anxieties onto more displaced and distant objects such as animals/insects than onto mythical figures and frightening movies.

Last, a relation was observed between representations of the body-self as deformed/inadequate and fear of violence. Twice as many children who represented the body-self as deformed reported fears of violence than children who did not represent this sense of body-self. In addition, although falling short of significance, twice as many children who represented the body-self as deformed/inadequate also expressed the fear of being aggressed upon by others. Here we should take into account that more African-Americans are members of this group.

Body-Based Representations and Life Stressors (Table 10–5). The next set of chi-square analyses examined the relations among life stressors reported and body-based meanings (Table 10–5). First, the total number of life stressors reported was associated with ATBI representations of body pain/danger. Of the children who reported one or two stressors, fewer produced ATBI representations of body pain/danger than did children who reported three to eight stressors. Since African-American children reported more stressors, they were characterized more by embodied meanings of pain/danger.

Reporting shootings/fights and illness/hospitalization of a loved one as stressors resulted in several relationships with ATBI representations. Children who reported shootings/fights as a stressor, when compared with those who did not, produced fewer ATBI representations of the body as competent and more representations of the body as deformed/inadequate. Children who reported illness/hospitalization of a loved one as a stressor produced more body-based representations of pain/danger. Although falling short of significance, they also produced body-based representations of aggression toward others. Also falling short of sig-

TABLE 10–5. Relations between Body-Based Representations and
Life Stressors

Stressors		Body-Based Meanings Pain/Danger		X^2	P
		No	Yes		
Number of Stressors	1–2	68	40		
	3–8	32	60	6.9	.01
		Value/Competence			
		No	Yes		
Shootings/Fights	No	39	60		
	Yes	61	40	4.4	.03
		Deformed/Inadequate			
		No	Yes		
Shootings/Fights	No	59	40		
	Yes	41	60	3.2	.05
		Pain/Danger			
		No	Yes		
Illness/Hospitalization	No	63	33		
	Yes	37	67	7.3	.01
		Aggression/Hate			
		No	Yes		
Illness/Hospitalization	No	61	45		
	Yes	39	55	2.5	.10
		Constriction/Assertion			
		No	Yes		
Death of a Loved One	No	42	60		
	Yes	58	40	2.5	.09

Note: All values = percentage of children

nificance, one other finding deserves mention because it could stimulate future research. Children who reported the death of a loved one also represented the body as constricted; those who did not report this stressor represented the body as assertive. These relationships appear to be concordant except for the relation between aggression toward others and illness/hospitalization of a loved one. It is interesting to note that with this population, body representations of aggression toward others are not correlated with reporting shooting/fights as a stressor but rather with illness/hospitalization of a loved one.

Relations between Body-Based Representations and Cognitive Functioning

The Field Articulation Cognitive Control.   To explore the relations between body-based meanings and focusing attention in the face of distractions and contradictions, FDT Cards III and V and Cards II and IV were entered into a series of two-way analyses of variance. The children in each of the ATBI groups (e.g., Imbalance versus Balance, Constriction versus Assertion, Pain/Danger versus No Pain/Danger) did not differ in terms of the time they took to name the colors of the fruits on Card III (pictures of food items as distractions) versus Card V (pictures of weapons as distractions). Nor did they differ in terms of the time they required to name the colors of the fruits on Card II (no contradictions) versus Card IV (contradictory colors as internal distractions).

However, when performances with Cards III and V and Cards II and IV were combined, a number of significant differences were observed associated with body-based meanings (Table 10–6). Children who represented body balance, when compared with those who represented imbalance, named the colors more rapidly whether external or internal distractions were present. This was also the case with children who represented positive body-based meanings/emotions versus those who did not. Children who represented body value/competence were distinguished by their more efficient time scores only in the condition containing internal contradictions. These relations between body image meanings and cognitive efficiency appear to be concordant. However, one other finding at first glance appears discordant. Children who represented a need for nurture versus those who did not named the colors of the fruit more rapidly in the face of both external and internal distractions. Requiring further study, one possible speculation about this finding is that the population consisted primarily of kindergartners. Since these children were young, representing the need for nurture seemed stage-appropriate, which in turn could be related to more advanced cognitive functioning than was the case with children who repressed or were not in tune with their need for nurture. Last, children who represented body assertion made fewer naming errors when dealing with both external distractions and internal contradictions.

In addition to these general findings, the number of naming errors and bursts of errors, under conditions containing internal contradictions as distractions, resulted in several significant interactions with the presence and absence of particu-

TABLE 10–6. Relations between Body-Based Representations and FDT Time and Error Scores: Cards III+V (External Distractions) and Cards II+IV (Internal Distractions)

FDT Time Scores (Sec.)	Body-Based Meanings			
	Imbalance	Balance	F	P
III + V	93.3	78.4	3.96	.05
II + IV	101.1	94.2	4.29	.04
	No Positive Meanings/Emotions	Positive Meanings/Emotions		
III + V	93.0	76.6	3.76	.05
II + IV	110.2	91.2	6.4	.05
	No Value/Competence	Value/Competence		
II + IV	108.1	93.0	3.76	.05
	No Need/Nurture	Need/Nurture		
III + V	94.4	77.1	5.55	.02
II + IV	110.2	89.9	7.29	.01
FDT Error Scores (No.)	Constriction	Assertion		
III + V	4.5	2.7	7.08	.01
II + IV	5.7	4.1	3.73	.05

Note: All values are group means.

lar embodied meanings (Table 10–7). Children who did not represent positive meanings/emotions or the need for nurture, when compared with children who did, produced significantly more errors when naming the colors of fruits in the condition that presented contradictions as distractions. In addition to making more errors, these same children produced more errors that occurred in bursts (e.g., they made two or more errors in succession while naming the colors of three or fewer fruit). In other words, these children experienced more severe disruptions in cognitive coordination (see Chapter 7). Recall that children who did not represent embodied meanings of positive emotions and the need for nurture required more time to name the colors of the fruits (see above). In this age group and population, then, embodied meanings representing positive emotions and nurture appear to be particularly relevant to cognitive efficiency when dealing with external distractions and internal contradictions. Last, children who represented body constric-

TABLE 10–7. Relations between Body-Based Representations and Number of Cognitive Errors and Bursts of Errors under Conditions of Contradiction

| Cognitive Scores | Body Meanings | Distracting Stimuli to Manage | | | | F | |
		Neutral Card II	SD	Contradictions Card IV	SD	Body Meaning x Test Stimuli	P
FDT Number of Errors	No Positive Emotions	3.6	2.6	7.5	6.7		
	Positive Emotions	3.0	3.4	4.9	3.9	7.84	.01
	No Nurture	4.1	2.3	7.7	7.1		
	Nurture	3.2	2.8	4.9	3.7	3.86	.05
FDT Bursts of Errors	No Positive Emotions	0.57	0.89	2.06	2.91		
	Positive Emotions	0.65	1.28	1.14	1.54	4.99	.02
	No Nurture	0.71	1.25	2.38	2.79		
	Nurture	0.53	0.97	0.94	1.33	8.16	.005
	Constriction	0.36	0.73	2.2	2.9		
	Assertion	0.81	1.30	1.0	1.5	13.19	.001

Note: All values are group means.

tion produced significantly more bursts of cognitive errors when dealing with contradictions than did children who represented body assertion.

The Leveling-Sharpening Cognitive Control.   ATBI variables were entered into a series of two-way analyses of variance with LSFT and LSSOT scores to explore whether body-based meanings related to the way in which information of a friendship versus a violent scene was held in memory over time. First, body balance appeared to correlate with efficient leveling-sharpening functioning whether the information aroused fantasies/emotions of affiliation or aggression. Children who represented body balance perceived more correct changes in both scenes (LSFT + LSSOT Mean number of correct changes = 8.9), while children representing body imbalance perceived fewer correct changes (LSFT + LSSOT Mean number of correct changes = 7.5) (F= 5.51; p = .02). And children representing body balance perceived correct changes soon after they occurred (LSFT + LSSOT Mean Correct Ratio = 22.1), while children representing body imbalance perceived correct changes later (LSFT + LSSOT Mean Correct Ratio = 24.0) (F = 7.04; p = .01).

In addition, children who represented body balance perceived more changes that occurred in the center of each scene and on the persons of the Friend and Victim (Mean Central Correct Changes = 4.22) than did the children representing body imbalance (Mean Central Correct Changes = 3.25) (F = 6.47; P = .01).

Table 10–8 lists significant interactions observed between several body-image variables and leveling-sharpening when stimuli aroused meanings/emotions either of affiliation or aggression. Children who produced body-based representations of aggression toward others detected the first correct change sooner while viewing the aggressive series of pictures and later while viewing the friendship series; they also detected a greater number of changes in the aggressive scene and fewer in the friendship scene. They tended to perceive these changes in the periphery, however, therefore avoiding the Victim. In contrast, children who did not produce body-based representations of aggression toward others detected the first correct change later with the LSSOT series and sooner with the LSFT series, perceived fewer changes with the aggressive scene and more with the friendship scene, and tended to look more at the victim.

Opposite relationships occurred with children who represented the body-self as valued/competent. These children detected more changes and sooner when viewing the friendship scene compared to the violent scene than did their counterparts. In addition, they detected more correct changes that occurred on the person of the Friend than on the person of the Victim.

Body constriction/assertion also played a role in the process of remembering details. Children who produced representations of body constriction detected correct changes later with the friendship scene versus the violent scene, while children who produced representations of body assertion detected correct changes sooner with the friendship scene than with the violent scene. And children who represented body-based meanings of nurture remembered fewer details in the pe-

TABLE 10–8. Relations between Body-Based Representations and Remembering Details of a Friendly (LSFT) versus Violent (LSSOT) Scene

Cognitive Score	Body-Image Meaning	Cognitive Test Stimuli				Effect-(Fs) Body x Test Stimuli	P
		Friends	SD	Shoot-Out	SD		
	Aggression/Hate						
Card Number of First Change Detected	No	21.4	10.2	25.6	12.6		
	Yes	23.6	8.7	22.9	10.9	3.87	.05
Correct Changes	No	8.4	3.3	8.3	3.3		
	Yes	7.7	3.5	8.7	2.9	3.77	.05
Correct Peripheral Changes	No	4.8	1.6	4.4	1.7		
	Yes	4.0	1.7	4.5	1.4	5.87	.02
	Value/ Competence						
Ratio	No	23.9	4.1	22.7	4.1		
	Yes	22.5	4.7	23.0	3.6	3.55	.01
Correct Changes on Friend vs Victim	No	1.6	1.0	2.2	1.1		
	Yes	2.1	1.2	1.9	1.2	7.04	.01
Ranks of Correct Changes	Constriction	44.9	5.2	44.1	4.7		
	Assertion	41.4	7.1	43.5	3.4	4.05	.05

Cognitive Score	Body-Image Meaning	Friends	SD	Shoot-Out	SD	Effects (Fs) Body x Test Stimuli	P
	Nurture						
Peripheral Changes	No	4.6	1.6	4.2	1.6		
	Yes	4.2	1.7	4.7	1.4	4.83	.05
	Positive Emotion						
Correct Changes on	No	2.1	1.2	2.0	1.1		
Friend vs Victim	Yes	1.6	1.0	2.3	1.1	7.59	.007

Note: All values are group means.

riphery of the friendship scene (more in the center) than did children who did not represent nurture.

Another finding raises an interesting question for future research. Children who produced body-based responses representing positive meanings/emotions detected more changes that occurred on the person of the Victim. This contrasts with the observation noted earlier that children who represented body value/competence detected fewer changes on the person of the Victim. Could children who are characterized by positive embodied meanings/emotions be showing empathy or compassion by unconsciously directing their attention at and remembering more details about the Victim?

Relations between Fears and Life Stressors (Table 10–9)

The total number of life stressors a child reported was related to several fear variables. Children who reported more life stressors expressed more fears of violence and of others being injured, and more types of fears. However, they expressed fewer fears of mythical figures/movies, perhaps reflecting that they were not displacing and projecting their anxieties onto mythical events.

Children who reported illness/hospitalization of a loved one as a stressor expressed more general states of fear. Children who reported absence of a loved one as a stressor expressed more fears of violence and a wider range of fears. Children who reported the death of a loved one also expressed more types of fears and, significantly, experienced fears of being injured.

Relations between Fears and Cognitive Functioning

Field Articulation Cognitive Control.   To explore the relations between children's fears and how they focused attention in the face of distractions and contradictions, FDT scores Card III versus V and Cards II versus IV were entered into a series of two-way analyses of variance. In terms of time scores, children who expressed fears of animals/insects required the same time (80 seconds) to name the colors of the fruits to Card III (food as distractions) as did children who did not report this fear. However, they took significantly longer (Mean = 93 seconds) to name the colors of the fruits on Card V (weapons as distractions) than did children who did not report this fear (Mean = 81 seconds) (Interaction F = 4.30; P = .04). In addition, children who expressed fears of being injured in some way took longer to name the colors of both Card III and Card V (Cards III + V average = 91.7 seconds) than did children who did not express this fear (Cards III + V average = 77.1 seconds) (F = 3.54; P = .05).

The sequence of errors children made (early or later) during each of the conditions containing external distractions resulted in a pattern of concordant significant interactions with particular fears (Table 10–10). Recall that the smaller the Sequence Score, the earlier errors are made as the child names the colors of fifty

TABLE 10–9. Relations between Fears and Life Stressors

Fears		Stressors		X^2	P
		Number			
		1–2	3–8		
Violence	None	83	54		
	Yes	17	46	8.9	.002
Others Being Injured	None	67	26		
	Yes	33	74	15.5	.0001
Types	Few	73	48		
	Many	27	52	5.7	.02
Mythical Figures/Movies	None	38	59		
	Yes	62	41	3.8	.05
		Illness/Hospitalization of a Loved One			
		No	Yes		
General States	None	64	44		
	Yes	36	56	3.7	.05
		Absence of a Loved One			
		No	Yes		
Violence	None	80	56		
	Yes	20	44	6.2	.01
Types	Few	71	50		
	Many	29	50	4.1	.05
		Death of Loved One			
		No	Yes		
Types	Few	71	42		
	Many	29	58	6.4	.01
Self Being Injured	No	69	46		
	Yes	31	54	4.2	.03

Note: All values = percentage of children.

TABLE 10-10. Relations between Fears and Sequence of Cognitive Errors under Two Types of External Distractions (Nurture and Aggression)

| | | Distracting Stimuli | | | | F_s Fears x Sequence | |
		Nurture Card III Sequence	SD	Aggression Card V Sequence	SD	Errors	P
Fears							
Violence	No	23.9	13.2	22.8	14.5		
	Yes	20.2	12.1	29.6	9.4	7.65	.01
Self Being Injured	No	24.2	12.8	22.0	19.8		
	Yes	20.6	12.9	29.5	10.5	9.36	.003
Others Being Injured	No	24.9	12.2	23.7	14.0		
	Yes	20.0	12.9	26.2	12.9	5.29	.03

Note: All values are group means.

fruits; the larger the Sequence Score the later errors are made. Children who expressed fears of violence, fears of being injured by someone or some event, or fears that someone else might be aggressed upon made errors later when naming colors to Card V (weapons as distractions) versus Card III (food items as distractions). These results suggest that children who expressed fears of violence and of self or others being aggressed upon maintained particularly steady cognitive-affective balance and coordination as they focused attention while fantasies/emotions concerning aggression were aroused.

The Leveling-Sharpening Cognitive Control.   No significant interactions were observed between fears children expressed and their efficiency with remembering details of a friendly versus violent scene. However, fears of being injured by someone related to how a child remembered details contained in both scenes. Children who expressed fears of being hurt detected more changes in both scenes (LSFT + LSSOT Mean Number of Correct Changes = 9.2) than children who did not report this fear (LSFT + LSSOT Mean Number of Correct Changes = 7.9) (F= 3.89; P = .05). And these children detected changes sooner (LSFT + LSSOT Mean Ratio = 21.9) than their counterparts (LSFT + LSSOT Mean Ratio = 23.5) (F = 3.69; P = .05). In addition, children who were afraid of being injured detected more changes on the persons of the Friend and Victim (Mean Correct Changes = 2.3) than their control group (Mean Correct Changes = 1.8) (F = 4.15; P = .05). The latter observation suggests that children who are afraid of being injured or assaulted remain focused on the central figure of a situation independent of the emotional context.

Relations between Life Stressors and Cognitive Functioning

The Field Articulation Cognitive Control (Table 10–11).   A significant interaction was observed between the number of life stressors reported and the effects of distracting stimuli. Children who recorded one or two stressors required more time to name the colors of fruit surrounded by pictures of weapons than when naming the colors of fruit surrounded by pictures of food-related items. In contrast, children who reported three to eight stressors required less time to name colors of fruit surrounded by pictures of weapons than by colors of fruit surrounded by pictures of food-related objects. In short, children who reported a low number of stressors were more distracted by stimuli arousing aggressive meanings/emotions.

When children were grouped in terms of their reporting each of the life stressors, no significant interactions were observed between reading time and distracting conditions. However, an interesting result emerged when naming errors were analyzed. Children who reported Physical Threats/Arguments as a stressor produced more errors when naming colors of fruit surrounded by pictures of food-related items than when naming colors of fruit surrounded by pictures of weapons.

TABLE 10-11. Relations between Life Stressors and Distractibility Scores (FDT)

Cognitive Scores	# of Stressors	Distracting Stimuli				Fs Stressors x Test Stimuli	P
		Nurture (Card III)	SD	Aggression (Card V)	SD		
Reading Times (seconds)	(1–2)	85.3	35.5	95.2	57.7	3.68	.05
	(3–8)	81.8	29.7	81.7	31.5		
Physical Threats/Arguments							
Naming Errors	No	3.53	4.0	3.06	3.5	4.31	.05
	Yes	5.22	4.3	3.27	3.4		
Bursts of Errors	No	0.67	1.4	0.63	1.3	7.32	.01
	Yes	1.49	1.9	0.67	1.3		
		Neutral (Card II)		Contradiction (Card IV)			
Death of a Loved One							
Reading Time (seconds)	No	78.0	27.1	138.1	57.9	5.93	.05
	Yes	67.4	20.7	106.6	35.8		
Illness/Hospitalization							
Reading Time (seconds)	No	77.1	28.5	139.1	56.6	3.71	.05
	Yes	73.0	23.1	119.9	50.9		

Note: All values are group means.

Children who did not report this stressor tended to produce about the same number of errors in each condition.

Moreover, errors produced by children who reported Physical Threats/Arguments tended to occur in bursts, more so when experiencing emotions/fantasies concerning nurture than when experiencing emotions/fantasies concerning aggression. Children who did not report this stressor tended to produce about the same number of bursts of errors in each condition. This finding suggests that of all the stressors, threatening gestures, and arguments were associated with cognitive conflict when emotions/fantasies concerning nurture were aroused.

An interesting finding was also obtained when comparing Cards II (no distractions) with IV (contradictions). Death of a loved one as a stressor resulted in a significant interaction. Children who reported this stressor required less time to name the correct colors when dealing with Card IV than did children who did not report the death of a loved one. This finding converged with another result. Children who reported illness/hospitalization of a loved one as a stressor also required less time to name the colors of Card IV than did children who did not report this stressor. Death, illness, and hospitalization of a loved one share several issues, such as coping with the contradiction that a loved one who was once strong and adequate no longer is. The possible dynamics behind the finding that these stressors are associated in this age group and population with handling cognitive contradictions more successfully require further study.

The Leveling-Sharpening Cognitive Control (Table 10–12).   The interaction between test stimuli and number of stressors reported resulted in a significant difference. Recall that the larger the LS ratio the more cognitive leveling. As shown in Table 10–12, children who reported three to eight stressors tended to hold in memory global images of the shoot-out scene, detecting fewer changes and later (cognitive leveling). Children who reported one to two stressors detected more changes and sooner when dealing with the shoot-out scene (cognitive sharpening).

In terms of types of stressors, reports of shootings/fights resulted in a significant interaction with test stimuli. Children who reported shootings/fights detected fewer changes and later with the shoot-out scene (cognitive leveling) versus the friendship scene. In contrast, children who did not report this stressor detected more changes and sooner with the shoot-out scene (cognitive sharpening) than with the friendship scene.

The makeup of the LSFT and LSSOT provided another source of information about the relation between type of life stressor and test stimuli that arouse different fantasies/emotions. Children who reported shootings/fights detected fewer changes that occurred on the person of the Victim than on the person of the Friend. In contrast, children who did not report shootings/fights detected more changes on the Victim than on the Friend. This finding is elaborated by a significant interaction produced by another type of stressor. Children who reported illness/hospitalization as a stressor also perceived fewer changes on the person of the Victim

TABLE 10–12. Relations between Life Stressors and Remembering Details of a Friendly vs Violent Scene (LSFT and LSSOT)

Cognitive Scores	Stressors	Test Stimuli to Remember				Fs Stressors x Test Stimuli	P
		Friends	SD	Shoot-Out	SD		
LS Ratio	Number						
	1–2	23.9	3.8	21.9	3.5	4.48	.05
	3–8	22.7	4.6	23.7	4.0		
LS Ratio	Shootings/Fights						
	No	23.7	4.1	21.8	3.5	5.78	.05
	Yes	22.6	4.6	23.0	4.1		
Correct Changes on Friend vs Victim	No	1.5	0.9	2.3	0.8	13.18	.01
	Yes	2.2	1.1	2.0	1.3		
	Illness/Hospitalization						
Correct Changes on Friend vs Victim	No	1.6	1.0	2.3	1.1	5.20	.03
	Yes	2.0	1.2	2.1	1.1		

Note: All values are group means.

than on the person of the Friend. These results suggest that children who report shootings/fights as a stressor are similar to children who report illness/hospitalization in terms of encoding, storing, and retrieving details of ongoing information associated with the person of someone being injured, an issue that deserves further study. Does experiencing the stress of harm befalling someone result in a cognitive defense that levels information concerned with violence?

The perceptual errors children made in response to the shoot-out versus friendship scenes, although falling short of significance, suggest a trend that should also be explored in future studies. Children who reported three to eight stressors produced fewer errors (Mean = 2.0; SD = 3.2) with the aggressive scene than with the friendship scene (Mean = 2.2; SD = 3.4). In contrast, children who reported one to two stressors produced more errors with the aggressive scene (Mean = 2.8; SD = 4.0) than with the friendship scene (Mean = 1.8; SD = 3.0) (F = 2.95; P = .08). Children who reported fewer stressors, then, experienced more cognitive conflict when dealing with the violent scene; children who reported a larger number of stressors experienced more cognitive conflict with the friendship scene.

Critique

This probe set out to illustrate a holistic approach to diagnostic assessment by removing boundaries that segregate body, mind, cognition, emotion, and subjective experiences. When these boundaries were removed, various patterns emerged among the domains evaluated. To illustrate the heuristic value of these patterns, I abstracted four from the results, which are depicted in Table 10–13. These patterns take as a starting point unconscious, embodied meanings that dominated a child's representations. Children who represented the body-self as constricted, when compared to children who represented the body-self as assertive, reported many types of conscious fears and the death of a loved one as a stressor, showed bursts of cognitive conflict when dealing with information that contained contradictions, and perceived changes later in a scene depicting interpersonal affiliation (cognitive leveling) and sooner in a scene depicting interpersonal violence (cognitive sharpening).

With another ensemble of results, children who did not represent the body-self as valued and competent, when compared with children who represented body competence, did not report fears of animals and insects but did report shootings and fights as upsetting them a lot. In addition, they took more time to name the colors of fruits surrounded by distractions and embedded in contradictions. They also remembered less information contained in the scene of two cowboys greeting each other, while remembering more of the scene depicting two cowboys in a shoot-out. They also remembered more changes that occurred on the person of the Victim, while children who represented the body-self as competent remembered more changes on the person of the cowboy who was extending a greeting in the friendship scene.

TABLE 10–13. Patterns of Relationships among Body-Based Representations, Fears, Stressors, and Cognitive Functioning

	Body Constriction	Body Assertion
Fears	Many	Few
Stressors	Death of a loved one	No death of a loved one
Managing Distractions	More bursts of errors when dealing with contradictions	Fewer bursts of errors when dealing with contradictions
Remembering Information	Perceive changes later in a scene of affiliation and sooner in a scene of violence	Perceive changes sooner in a scene of affiliation and later in a scene of violence

	No Body Value/Competence	Body Value/Competence
Fears	No fears of animals/insects	Fears of animals/insects
Stressors	Shootings/fights	No shootings/fights
Managing Distractions	Slow reading time under conditions of distraction and contradiction	Faster reading time under conditions of distraction and contradiction
Remembering Information	Remember less information of a friendship scene and more of a violent scene: perceive more changes on Victim	Remember more information of a friendship scene and less information of a violent scene; perceive more changes on Friend.

	No Body Aggression/Hate	Body Aggression/Hate
Fears	Fear of mythical figures/movies	No fear of mythical figures/movies
Stressors	No illness/hospitalization of a loved one	Illness/hospitalization of a loved one
Remembering Information	Remember more information of a friendship scene and less information of a violent scene; perceive more details surrounding the Victim	Remember less information of a friendship scene and more information of a violent scene; perceive fewer details surrounding the Victim

	Body Not Deformed/Inadequate	Body Deformed/Inadequate
Fears	No fears of violence or of being injured	Fears of violence and of being injured
Stressors	No shootings/fights reported	Shootings/fights reported

With another pattern, children who represented embodied meanings of aggression and hate toward others, when compared to children who did not express this embodied meaning, did not report fears of mythical figures and frightening movies, reported illness or hospitalization of a loved one as a stressor, and remembered less information from a scene depicting affiliation and more information of a scene depicting violence. Yet they perceived fewer details on the person of the Victim.

And with another pattern, children who reported the body-self as deformed and inadequate, when compared to children who did not express this embodied meaning, reported conscious fears of violence and of being injured. They also reported shootings/fights as a life stressor.

These patterns, or ensembles of functioning, were constructed by very young inner-city children who were functioning adequately, academically and socially, at the time of the evaluation. Future studies are needed to determine patterns constructed by nonclinical children of different ages and living in rural areas and suburbs as well as the inner city. Studies are also needed to determine patterns constructed by clinical populations. These patterns should be useful in helping a therapist decide whether and how some domain of a child's functioning is discordant with other domains and whether, for example, treatment should emphasize the restructuring of cognition before emphasizing the revision of conscious fears or of embodied meanings.

Patterns could also be organized from the results of this probe, using as a starting point stressors a child reported as upsetting her/his subjective world. Table 10–14 depicts an illustration when number of stressors is used as the starting point. Children who reported more life stressors (three to eight), when compared to children who reported fewer (one to two) were distracted less by information arousing aggressive meanings/emotions, and more by information arousing meanings/emotions concerning nurture. They also remembered fewer details and experienced less cognitive conflict when dealing with information contained in a scene arousing aggressive meaning/emotions.

This pattern suggests that these children have already developed a cognitive style, or pattern of cognitive controls, that insulates them from the disrupting influences of meanings/emotions associated with interpersonal aggression. This pattern converges with other studies that show that children and adults who are functioning adequately developed a cognitive style within which the relations among several cognitive processes are supportive and correspondent. In contrast, dysfunctional individuals show a cognitive style that reflects discordant or antagonist relations among cognitive processes (Cotugno 1987, Ottenson and Holzman 1976, Santostefano 1978, 1986, Santostefano and Rieder 1984, Wapner and Demick 1991, Wertleib 1979).

I have proposed that the pattern formed by several cognitive processes could be understood as an "organismic" attempt to utilize a cognitive style that both accommodates to and serves a person's unique vulnerabilities when coping with

TABLE 10–14. Patterns of Relationships among Life Stressors and
Cognitive Functioning

Life Stressors	Few	Many
Managing Distractions	Distracted more by information arousing aggressive meanings/emotions and less by information arousing meanings/emotions of nurture	Distracted less by information arousing aggressive meanings/emotions and more by information arousing meanings/ emotions of nurture
Remembering Information	Remember more details of information arousing aggressive meanings/ emotions and fewer arousing meanings of affiliation	Remember fewer details of information arousing aggressive meanings/ emotions and more arousing meanings of affiliation
Maintaining Balance Between Cognitive and Emotion	More cognitive conflict when information arouses meanings/ emotions of aggression; less cognitive conflict when information arouses meanings/emotions of nature	Less cognitive conflict when information arouses meanings/ emotions of aggression; more cognitive conflict when information arouses meanings/ emotions of nurture.

and equilibrating the demands of external stimulation and the demands fantasies/
emotions aroused. Since the young children in this probe were functioning adequately both academically and socially, they appear to have evolved a cognitive style
that enables them to maintain successful adaptation while coping with aggressive
meanings/fantasies aroused by stimulation in their day-to-day living. Future studies
are needed to explore whether older inner-city children show the same cognitive
style consisting of correspondent relations among cognitive processes, and whether
those who have become dysfunctional show a discordant cognitive style.

Since one area evaluated in this probe involved life stressors, the results could
also be considered in terms of the literature on the effects of psychological stressors on children (Armsworth and Holaday 1993). In broadest terms, the relations
observed between stressors a child reports and her/his cognitive functioning rely
upon the proposition that stressors that produce anxiety/negative emotions are
connected to the child's unique system of symbols and representations (Janoff-
Bulman 1995). The finding in this probe, that children who reported a high num-

ber of stressors cognitively subordinated the distracting influence of aggressive-related stimuli, disagrees with one result typically cited, namely, that "traumatized children may experience intolerable, intrusive thoughts or images" (p. 50). Using test stimuli that evoked two types of "intrusive thoughts or images," this probe found that children who reported more stressors did not experience intrusive thoughts/images evoked by aggressive stimuli, while children in the low stressor group did. On the other hand, the probe also found that the children who reported more stressors were distracted more by nurture-related stimuli than were the children in the low stressor group. These results, then, emphasize that future studies of the intrusive influence of thoughts and images should assess different types of intrusive, distracting images associated with different meanings/fantasies.

The finding that the high stressor group remembered fewer details of a scene representing violence, while the low stressor group remembered more, appears at first glance to agree with reports that traumatized children show "memory impairments" (Armsworth and Holaday 1993, p. 50). However, again because test stimuli were used that evoked two types of meanings or "memory images," this probe found that the high stressor group did not show an "overall memory impairment" but showed what one could view as a "selective memory impairment." While leveling the details of a violent scene, which the low stressor group sharpened, the high stressor group also remembered (sharpened) more details of a friendship scene than did the low stressor group. Again, these results suggest that future studies of memory impairment due to stressors should consider types of images evoked by stimuli arousing different meanings and emotions.

The results this probe obtained when children were grouped in terms of whether they reported different stressors support the proposal by Pynoos and colleagues (1996) that investigators should consider conscious and unconscious fantasies/emotions evoked by various stressors and explore several forms of childhood stressors simultaneously rather than study the effects of each independently. We found that different stressors were associated with different characteristics in one or another of the cognitive processes evaluated while others were not. Two of the stressors implicated the cognitive process of field articulation (focusing attention while equilibrating emotional distractions). Children who reported death, illness, or hospitalization of a loved one were more efficient when focusing attention in the face of contradiction than were children who did not report these stressors. In contrast, the stressor of arguments/threatening gestures was associated with experiencing more cognitive conflict while focusing attention when fantasies/emotions concerning nurture were aroused. If future studies support these and other relationships, then child research has another opportunity to make a contribution to clinical practice. For example, it would be useful for a clinician to know that witnessing arguments impacts and disrupts a child's need for nurture rather than arousing fears of aggression.

Another type of stressor (shootings/fights) implicated the cognitive process of holding patterns of information in memory over time. Children who reported this stressor remembered fewer details of a shoot-out scene than did children who did not report this stressor. Moreover, in addition to "leveling" details from the entire scene, they leveled, in particular, information on the person of the Victim. In contrast, children who did not report this stressor remembered more information on the person of the Victim, as did children who reported illness/hospitalization. Since children who reported shootings/fights did not tend to report illness/hospitalization, the former group encoded fewer details than the latter group related to the Victim. This finding encourages us to explore further how different stressors, as construed by the child, impact the types of information a child avoids or approaches. This finding also lends support to the view that a cognitive function could be observed to maneuver outside awareness in ways that serve to equilibrate information and emotion so that emotions do not disrupt adaptation. It seems very likely that these children were not conscious that they were selectively encoding fewer details from the person of the cowboy being shot or, with the other task, that they were encoding and storing more information from the person of the cowboy who is waving hello.

That children who reported shootings/fights detected fewer changes with the shoot-out scene should be considered in terms of previous studies that compared LSFT and LSSOT performance of physically aggressive and nonaggressive children (Santostefano and Moncata 1989, Santostefano and Rieder 1984). In these studies, the children were older and hospitalized in psychiatric facilities frequently because of conduct disorders. Unlike our present sample, these behaviorally aggressive children consistently detected more changes that occur in a scene depicting violence than did nonaggressive youth. The findings of these studies were interpreted as follows: the demands of aggressive meanings/emotions that characterized these aggressive youth were concordant with the demands aroused by the test stimuli. Therefore, the cognitive mechanism equilibrated the two demands such that the test stimuli were readily assimilated and remembered. On the other hand, the requirements of the aggressive meanings/emotions of low aggressive children were discordant with those of the violent test scene, prescribing cognitive equilibration that leveled the stimuli, resulting in their remembering fewer details.

None of the children in the probe reported here had yet shown a significant problem with aggressive behavior. It is interesting to note that their cognitive functioning with aggression-related test stimuli is similar to that of older children, reported in previous studies, who were not behaviorally aggressive. These observations suggest another intriguing line for future study. One could follow a group of young children who report shootings/fights and observe which ones eventually develop an aggressive disorder and whether this change is related to changes in cognitive functioning.

Last, this probe brings attention to the need to devise methods to assess cognition in addition to IQ tests, questionnaires, checklists, rating scales, and projective tests that appear to be preferred in studies relating cognition to stressors (e.g., Armsworth and Holaday 1993, Lulgendorf et al. 1994, van der Kolk and Ducey

1989). This probe illustrates that to study the effects of stressors on cognition, tasks could be devised that require a discrete cognitive process to operate "in vivo," so to speak, dealing with stimulation that arouses different meanings/emotions.

CONCLUDING REMARKS

To explore the heuristic value of the developmental-dialectical model and to extend research already reported, I first constructed methods that attempted to invite the body to speak and found them to be promising. Administered to clinical and nonclinical youth, each procedure provided a different window through which one could observe how embodied meanings are metaphorically extended into higher levels, continuing to play a part in how tempos are regulated, motion is imaged, actions toward others are taken, interpersonal relationships and life stressors are represented, and cognitive organizations change when managing stimuli representing different interpersonal meanings. What are some of the implications of the model, methods, and results for diagnosing troubled youth?

When considered as an approach to diagnosis, the model and methods described here suggest a direction very different than does the prevailing model of nosology with its questionnaires and behavioral checklists. If we look beyond nosology and through the lens of the proposed developmental-dialectical model, what do we see? We do not see isolated behaviors such as failure to listen when spoken to, or fear of attending school, or running away, each unrelated to the other. Rather we see an interplay of conscious and unconscious subjective meanings and fantasies, cognitions, actions, and verbal expressions all forming a pattern and each working concurrently or in mutual opposition with the others. We see that these patterns of elements are involved at different levels of functioning. We also see that elements and changes in one part of a pattern or organization influence other parts of the organization. This observation converges with Piaget's concept of organization as a developmental invariant discussed in Chapter 4: namely, that structures of human functioning are organized to form a totality and are interrelated so that changes in one part produce changes throughout the entire organization. Last, if we look through the lens of the developmental-dialectical model we realize the need to continue searching for ways of adding to the patterns already observed so that the web of observations steadily includes as many aspects as possible of a child's cognitive, emotional, behavioral, unconscious, and conscious functioning.

Looking beyond stable classifications, then, to observe organizations of symbolic behaviors in an active interplay at different levels (conscious and unconscious) requires an integration of several developmental principles: holism, directiveness of behavior, multiple modes and levels of functioning, mobility of organizations of functioning, individual differences, and the adaptive process within which an individual and others mutually influence and accommodate to each other: all ingredients of the proposed model. When combined, these principles account for how individual differences observed at higher levels of cognitive processes are linked to individual differences observed in developmentally earlier embodied processes. This notion of "vicariousness of functioning" was elaborated by Werner and Kaplan (1963) and applied by others (e.g., Ohlmaan and Marendez 1991) to account for the links among body, cognition, and personality.

When looking beyond nosology and through the developmental-dialectical lens, then, we are reminded of the need to develop methods that permit observations of the interplay of organizations of symbols operating at several levels. To meet this need, are we limited to observations in naturalistic environments? Can the environment of a desktop provide the clinician with observations of a child's mind and body in action (White 1991)? Are there brief tasks that simulate ordinary environments in which body and mind perform purposeful acts (Neisser 1976)?

I have tried to demonstrate that tasks can be administered on a tabletop (Touch Association Test, Spiral Test, LSSOT, LSFT, Fruit Distraction Test, Two-Person Drawing Test) or within the confines of an office (Action Test of Body Image, Body-Tempo Regulation Test, and Binoculars Test) that provide observations of organizations (ensembles) of symbols operating at different levels, working either concurrently or in opposition. These methods appear to locate bodily meanings, and their emotions, within fantasy, cognition, and action and to locate fantasy, action, and cognitive processes, with their emotions, within the body, providing an approach that forges these domains into one when formulating an understanding of a child's difficulties. Although the perspective of nosology may be helpful for certain practical purposes, developing static categories of pathology, as Kelly (1968) pointed out, eventually results in "hardening of the categories" (p. 158), a common affliction among clinicians. The methods proposed here, and others stimulated by a developmental-dialectical approach, may provide a remedy for this affliction.

11
Concluding Remarks

CONTENTS

In concluding I emphasize several themes concerning psychotherapy integration that were developed throughout this volume. Fischer's (1995) discussion of "myths" that prevail in proposals for integrating approaches to psychotherapy included two points that help me frame these themes. With one he noted, "Throughout the literature authors seem to be selecting theories, or concepts and techniques from theories, for integration in a haphazard, unsystematic way using mainly their own biases or preferences as a guide" (p. 47). With the other he proposed that instead of selecting concepts and techniques haphazardly, investigators should develop ". . . a number of criteria—external to any specific theory—that a theory could or should address or around which it might be constructed . . ." (p. 46).

SELECTING A MOLD TO SHAPE PSYCHOTHERAPY INTEGRATION: I CHOSE DEVELOPMENT AND DIALECTICS

In constructing the developmental-dialectical model outlined in this volume, I did my best to avoid haphazardly selecting concepts from different theories, using my biases or preferences as a guide, and I developed a set of criteria or issues (Chapter 4) that I proposed any integrative approach to child and adolescent psychotherapy should consider and addressed these issues in a model of development from birth to adolescence (Chapter 5 and 6) that formed guidelines for conducting psychotherapy with children and adolescents (Chapter 7). Referring to our discussion of Schacht's (1984) models of integration, when formulating these issues I avoided viewing cognitive, behavioral, and psychodynamic psychotherapies as fundamentally incompatible. I also avoided translating the language of one approach into that of another. Rather, to shape a model for integrating child psychotherapies, I selected two basic, interrelated ingredients to form a mold: (a) developmental processes of change as differentiation, integration, and flexibility of functioning; and (b) dialectics as negotiation. These ingredients, I believe, remove the barrier segregating objectivism (real knowledge) and interpretationism (subjective knowledge). Once this barrier is removed, the barriers segregating body from mind and cognition from emotion collapse. When desegregation is achieved the question of what knowledge is, strategies of knowing, and metaphors that guide the construction of concepts and techniques that have divided various treatment approaches could begin to be integrated.

To illustrate this point, imagine that the "self" is represented by "Sally Self" and the "other" by two characters we will call "Otto Other" and "Emily Environment." From the developmental-dialectical perspective, when Sally Self, Otto Other, and Emily Environment step into a dialectical circle, the following takes place. From Sally's point of view, there is knowledge in her personal, subjective world and also "out there" in Otto and Emily, knowledge they hold about Sally as well as knowledge about their own worlds. Also as far as Sally is concerned, Otto's and Emily's knowledge continuously attempts to influence her knowledge of herself and how she sees them and interacts with them. In the meantime Sally's knowledge also attempts to influence the knowledge Otto and Emily hold of Sally as well as of their own worlds. The whole process is the same from the point of view of Otto Other and Emily Environment. As far as they are concerned, there is knowledge out there about them in Emily and knowledge within each of their personal, subjective worlds. They realize that they want to change the knowledge in Emily, and recognize that Emily is trying to change theirs. As Sally, Otto, and Emily continuously negotiate the paradox between their worlds, each defines and is defined by the other, and together they spiral upwards developmentally, evolving more differentiated, integrated, flexible, and adaptive modes for engaging each other. Referring again to Piaget (Chapter 2), every totality is a system of relationships and every relationship is a segment of a totality. The dialectical position blends objectivism and interpretationism in conceiving of a world out there with its knowledge, and a world within a person with its knowledge, worlds that forever engage in dialectical negotiations, each defining and influencing the other. Dialectical relationships exist not only between one person and another, but also, for example, between one cognitive function and another, between what a person does, imagines and says, and between unconscious and conscious processes.

In previous chapters, we noted that while neither mainstream cognitive-behavioral nor psychodynamic therapies fit into a developmental-dialectical mold, aspects of psychodynamic therapy, such as the importance of meaning and of unconscious processes, do. However, there are encouraging signs of change, especially in the cognitive-behavioral camp, changes which suggest the beginnings of an integration of objectivist and interpretationist images. For example, Goncalves (1995) noted that cognitive and behavioral therapies are shifting: (1) from a rationalistic toward a more constructivist philosophy; (2) from an information-processing model toward a narrative model of knowing; (3) from an emphasis on conscious processes toward an emphasis on unconscious dimensions of experience; (4) from an emphasis on strict cognitive processes toward an acknowledgment of the emotional dimension of experiences; (5) from logical, therapeutic methods to more analogic and interpersonal ones (p. 139). At the same time, psychodynamic therapies have also been shifting, giving more attention to overt behavior, interpersonal interactions, cognition, and adaptive processes in addition to unconscious meanings (e.g., Horowitz 1988, Mitchell 1988, 1994, Wachtel 1987). While the shifts occurring in both cognitive-behavioral and psychodynamic therapies converge with aspects of the integrative model I have outlined, in my view, principles of development and dialectics do not yet receive sufficient attention.

A REVIEW OF THE MODEL PROPOSED FOR INTEGRATING
CHILD PSYCHOTHERAPIES

In a lucid discussion of integrative child psychotherapy, Coonerty (1993) noted circumstances that push child therapists into eclecticism.

> In contrast to adult therapy, successful child therapy usually demands that the therapist wear many hats, skillfully changing his or her stance to meet the changing needs of the child as well as those of the various members of the child's life. At one moment, the therapist is intensely involved in play, enacting the internal struggles of the child; at the next, he or she is discussing the latest problem with a parent or fielding calls from the school psychologist or classroom teacher. In addition to the necessity of responding to the various other players in a child's life, the therapist is also thrust into the role of limit setter, educator, or mediator with the same child that he or she involves in deeply evocative, often intensely conflictual, play therapy. . . . Often, such conflicting and rapidly changing roles result in the adoption of an eclectic style, in which therapeutic interventions are chosen and changed according to the most external demand. [p. 413]

She also made a number of other points which converge with aspects of the integrative model I have presented. For example, she pointed out that rather than jump from one type of treatment to another (eclectic therapy) when following an integrative approach, a therapist " can conceive of all interventions as coming from an integrative sense of the needs of children . . ." (p. 414). Coonerty based her discussion on Wachtel's (1977, 1987) concept of cyclical psychodynamics and Gold's (1992) extension of this concept. As discussed in previous chapters, Wachtel proposed that while unconscious wishes and fantasies, representing past experiences, determine a person's difficulties, they also seek and create life circumstances in the present, and in this way difficulties persist because of constant feedback. Gold expanded this notion into a model of multiple causation that includes individual, family, and socioeconomic and political contexts, all viewed as mutually influencing each other.

From this cyclical, rather than linear, view of the development of psychopathology, intervention in any domain eventually leads to changes throughout others. "Whatever direction the therapist takes, care must be taken to ascertain how change in one area may effect other areas of functioning. For instance . . . change in a child's functioning may so threaten a systemic solution that the parents panic and end treatment" (Coonerty 1993, p. 418). As one example of this point from my practice, a child engaged in many obsessive rituals before bedtime, always insisting that mother be present. In this way, by insuring that light switches were off, doors were closed, etc., the child directed, regulated, and stabilized mother whose functioning was chaotic, as well as her own fantasies and emotions. As the child relinquished these rituals, mother became quite anxious and found herself pursuing the child. To help her deal with the interruption of the cycle she and her daughter had maintained, mother was provided with various devices with which she could organize and structure her interactions with this child and other children in the family.

Last, after reviewing various spheres in which a child gains experiences (behavioral, cognitive, interpersonal, intrapsychic), Coonerty pointed out, "whichever focus . . . [therapists] subscribe to, it is essential to child work that not only the area of dynamic conflict, but the interweaving of that conflict with cognitive, behavioral, and interpersonal development, be thoroughly understood" (pp. 420–421).

The model, techniques, and strategies proposed in this volume provide one way of addressing the several points Coonerty raised. I began by discussing how and why concepts and techniques of child psychotherapy are segregated into camps and the need to dissolve this segregation before considering a form of integration. To dissolve the segregation that currently is practiced in the field of child psychotherapy, I proposed that it is necessary first to examine some of its root causes; namely, three boundaries that psychology has maintained for decades, dividing knowledge as either real or subjective, and segregating body and mind and cognition and emotion. I then attempted to demonstrate how these boundaries, and the segregation they foster, influence the points of view, concepts, and techniques that emerged within three of the currently dominant approaches to child psychotherapy: cognitive, behavioral, and psychodynamic. From an examination of the causes of segregation, and the impact they have had on different approaches to child psychotherapy, I followed Fischer's (1995) second proposal and articulated ten criteria, or issues, that I believe should be considered in any attempt to evolve an integrative approach.

Once these issues were articulated, I was faced with the task of deciding how to conceptualize the interrelationships among them in ways that promoted integration. Pointing out the difficulties one encounters when one or another concept is used to integrate issues, Fischer (1995) noted, ". . . but when one considers the vast array of potential concepts derived from [various] theories that are available for consideration for integration, the task literally appears to be impossible. Numerous concepts only recently have been proposed as possible key concepts for integration: cognitive schemas; assimilation; balance; self conformation; levels of emotional awareness; the therapeutic alliance; self-experiencing; behavioral enactments; and many other concepts" (p. 47). In addition to the problem presented by the wide range of concepts available to integrate psychotherapies, another issue raised by Mahoney (1993) is relevant. He pointed out that in discussions and debates about integration, the words and concepts authors use "mean different things to different people" (p. 4).

In an effort to construct a model that integrated the issues listed in Chapter 4, using a language that most would understand, and rather than beginning with one or another of the delimited concepts Fischer listed, I selected a broad proposition: that processes of change and psychological growth which take place in child psychotherapy, as child and therapist interact, are the same as those that take place as infant/child and caregivers interact. Nested within this starting point was another broad proposition. Rather than emphasizing the knowledge a child should be given in psychotherapy to help him/her deal with and resolve difficulties, emphasis should be placed on changing *how* a child constructs knowledge about himself/herself and others when interacting with others.

From these propositions I set out to build a "developmental house," or model, to integrate approaches to child psychotherapy. The foundation of this house consisted of principles that integrated concepts from the developmental theories of Sigmund Freud, Jean Piaget, and Heinz Werner, because these concepts met basic criteria reviewers proposed should be met by a developmental theory. On this foundation I constructed the first floor, which considered how an infant constructs knowledge about herself/himself and others during the first two years of life, and how cognitive-behavioral modalities become organized. Here I relied upon observations and concepts of three infant investigators (Jean Piaget, Daniel Stern, Louis Sander) which I integrated using principles proposed by Beatrice Beebe and Frank Lachmann (1994). This integration placed at the center meanings (representations) an infant constructs from experiences. These initial meanings are embodied, nonverbal, and unconscious schemas, conserving and representing experiences with others and things and prescribing what an infant expects from interactions with others. After the second year of life, if an infant does not experience major, unrepaired disruptions when negotiating with others, these embodied schemas are gradually translated into symbolic forms (action symbols, fantasies, metaphoric language) shared with others. To climb from the first to the second floor, I introduced embodiment theory, which conceptualized that meanings and modalities formed during infancy are extended into and influence those that develop in childhood and beyond.

The second floor operationalized how the construction of meaning, and the organization of cognitive and behavioral modalities, are extended beyond infancy. During continuous interactions with others, the toddler/child elaborates meanings/representations, initially constructed during the first two years of life, that become organized as "life metaphors." Life metaphors concern core developmental issues such as trust, love, attachment/individuation, reciprocating, directing and accommodating to the behaviors of others, asserting, and idealizing and internalizing the standards and expectations of key persons in one's subjective world. In negotiating and developing life metaphors, a child relies upon two psychological systems that form a bridge to techniques in child psychotherapy. With one, a developmental hierarchy of evolving cognitive functions equilibrates and coordinates the demands from life metaphors with those of environments. With the other, a developmental hierarchy of evolving modalities (action, fantasy, and metaphoric language) expresses life metaphors in interactions with others, relying upon delay and multiple means and alternative ends, to cope with ever-changing environmental opportunities and limitations.

I then translated this developmental-dialectical model into guidelines for conducting integrative psychotherapy with children and adolescents, whatever their presenting problems. These guidelines did not provide a series of recipes, each defining how to conduct psychotherapy with children who are viewed as representing one or another *DSM-IV* diagnostic category (for an example see, Reinecke et al. 1996). Rather the guidelines articulated several interrelated axes that a therapist follows simultaneously when treating all children, an approach that converges with that of others (e.g., Shirk 1988, Reeve et al. 1993).

Three broad treatment plans were outlined to promote change in how any child negotiates and constructs knowledge when interacting with others. One emphasized revising a child's rigid life metaphors that construe present situations in maladaptive ways and prescribe behaviors that do not serve learning and adaptation. Another emphasized revising a child's rigid cognitive functions which fail to equilibrate information and demands from environments and the child's objective world. And the third emphasized revising rigid modalities so that what a child does, imagines, and says become interrelated.

I also considered why it is important for a therapist to distinguish between what he/she does to promote change within a level of functioning versus between levels of functioning. I articulated the main catalysts that promote change: cycles of dialectical interactions, enactments, and idealization and internalization. I emphasized techniques child and therapist could use to negotiate and construct a shared, intersubjective world, and proposed that the playroom and conventional toys should be supplemented by other places (especially the outdoors) and other materials. I articulated when and why a therapist should, much as do child and caregiver, sometimes structure her/his interactions with a child, and at other times participate in nondirected interactions. Clinical case examples of psychotherapy, emphasizing structured or unstructured interactions, were provided to illustrate the model and its guidelines.

Last I discussed why the developmental-dialectical model views nosology (diagnostic categories) as limited in providing a diagnostic understanding of a child's difficulties in a way that serves treatment. As an alternative I described several research studies that attempted to demonstrate the kinds of diagnostic questions the developmental-dialectical model raises, especially the holistic question of how functioning at one level, or in one domain, extends into and influences functioning at other levels and domains. The studies also illustrated innovative diagnostic methods that address these questions. These methods emphasized that since the foundation of a person's experiences and subjective world emerged from experiences in the first years of life, methods should assess nonverbal, embodied functioning in addition to fantasy and verbal self-report. The proposed developmental-dialectical model, the issues it raises, and the guidelines for child psychotherapy it prescribes, when taken together, assign primary significance to several domains.

THE PRIMACY OF MEANING

It wasn't too long ago that Skinner (1974) argued, "A small part of one's inner world can be felt or introspectively observed but it is *not* an *essential part* [italics mine] . . . and the role assigned to it has been overrated . . . it is impossible to estimate the havoc [that therapies about internal states and processes] have wreaked . . . [upon] efforts to describe or explain human behavior" (cited in Mahoney 1985, p. 20). Mahoney presented this quote more than a decade ago within a discussion of issues that are still very relevant, several of which converge with positions I have taken in this volume. Although he noted, "I am not writing as a representative of any particular school of thought" (p. 4), his discussion seemed to be speaking from a cognitive-behavioral view to an "imaginary audience" consisting of cognitive and behavioral therapists, given the pains he took to support the notion that meaning is primary.

At the time Skinner stated his position that a person's subjective world is not essential, psychodynamic therapists, of course, disagreed. Since the early 1900s, they had been working on the other side of the boundary, maintaining the opposite view: that a person's "internal states and processes" are more essential than her/his overt behaviors. But, as discussed in previous chapters, many cognitive and behavioral therapists have abandoned Skinner's view and embraced the position held by psychodynamic therapists, that meanings contained in a person's inner world are primary. For example, after citing Skinner, Mahoney pointed out to his cognitive and behavioral colleagues that "far from being 'vastly overrated' the inner world is probably the least understood and potentially most revealing frontier in contemporary science" (p. 20).

I could not agree more. In everyday life a child is busy, not so much acquiring knowledge but constructing meanings he/she experiences, altering these meanings, and sharing some of them with others. All meanings emerge out of interactions with others, and are co-authored with others. Therefore meanings are not evaluated in terms of whether they correspond to the "real" meaning of an event. The "real" meaning of some experience is what a person and another, present or absent, have negotiated and constructed. I have assigned meaning, and the developmental processes involved in constructing meaning, a primary role in integrating psychotherapies, and have operationalized meanings as life metaphors, representations of key developmental issues initially negotiated with others in physical interactions and embodied practices. These representations prescribe what is expected from present situations and what one should do to continue negotiations.

It is interesting to note that in the 10 years since Mahoney (1985) reminded cognitive-behavioral therapists that a person's inner world and meanings are important, a shift has been observed in cognitive and behavioral concepts and methods toward what is being called "constructive psychotherapies" (Mahoney 1995a). According to Mahoney (1995b), in the past 40 years there have been at

least three shifts in cognitive science: from information processing to connec-
tionism and most recently to constructivism. Mahoney reminded his cognitive-
behavioral audience that "fundamental to constructivism is an emphasis on the
active . . . nature of all knowing. In contrast to the relatively passive models of
the mind and brain proposed by information processing prospectives, constructivism proposes intrinsic self-organizing activity as fundamental to all knowledge
processes. Thus, the mind/brain is no longer viewed as a repository (memory bank)
of representations so much as an organic system of self-referencing activities . . ."
(p. 7). In terms of our discussion in Chapter 2, the new cognitive-behavioral
paradigm of constructivism reflects a decided shift from objectivism toward
interpretationism.

Similarly, Meichenbaum (1995), one of the cognitive-behavioral pioneers,
reviewed changes in the ruling metaphors which cognitive-behavioral therapists
have followed over the years. Initially they followed the metaphor of conditioning,
then of information processing, and more recently of "constructive narrative." The
later metaphor, he proposed, is "guiding the present development of cognitive-
behavioral therapies . . . common to [this viewpoint] is the tenet that the human
mind is a product of constructive, symbolic activity, and that reality is a product of
personal meanings that individuals create. It is not as if there is one reality and clients
distort that reality . . . rather there are multiple realities and the task for the therapist is to help clients become aware of how they create these realities and of the
consequences of such constructions" (p. 23).

These statements by Meichenbaum represent a complete turnaround from
Skinner's position of only 20 years ago, held by mainstream cognitive-behavioral
therapists, that a person's inner world is "not essential." However, although
Mahoney stated that among cognitive-behavioral therapists "constructive approaches to psychotherapy are increasingly common" (p. 8), and Meichenbaum
proposed that constructivism is now the ruling metaphor in cognitive-behavioral
therapy, this movement appears not to have reached all of the shores of cognitive-behavioral therapy (e.g., Clark and Fairburn 1997, Dobson and Craig 1996)
nor the shores of cognitive-behavioral therapy with children (Reinecke et al.
1996). At least not yet. I believe (hope) that in time it will. What I also hope is
that the contributions of the principles of dialectics and development will come
to find their way not only into cognitive-behavioral therapy but also psychodynamic therapy. While the later approach has maintained a constructivist perspective for the past century, it is still necessary, I believe, to emphasize that while
a person constructs her/his realities, as noted by constructivists, throughout development this construction takes place during dialectical exchanges with other
persons and following particular developmental principles. The developmental-
dialectical model I propose integrates processes of constructing meanings with a
child's cognitive activity and modes of expression, which leads to the next theme
I emphasize.

THE PRIMACY OF EMBEDDING COGNITION WITHIN PERSONALITY AND RELATING WHAT A CHILD DOES, IMAGINES, AND SAYS

Thompson (1981) argued that "the challenge is to help individuals develop the ability to assign meanings that will be most beneficial to them" (p. 100). And Mahoney (1985) noted that a major task facing therapists is to identify those structures and processes through which patients construe and give meaning to experiences. Along the same line, in the preface to their edited volume, Mahoney and Freeman (1985) wondered what is knowledge, how does knowledge relate to what we feel and do, and how are thoughts, feelings, and actions related. The developmental-dialectical model addressed these challenges in two ways. With one, a set of cognitive functions was operationalized that approach, avoid, and select information, and calls for action, simultaneously from existing life metaphors (meanings) and environments with which the person is negotiating. With the other, action, fantasy and language behaviors were conceptualized as modes providing vehicles for expressing these meanings. Each mode develops the capacity to flexibly express meanings in immediate or delayed and in direct or indirect forms, and the meanings expressed in one mode become connected with meanings expressed by other modes. When cognition employs a rigid orientation, either centering on the subjective world or on environmental stimulation, or when modes of expression are rigid and/or disconnected, treatment emphasizes developing flexibility in both domains, and integrating what a child means with what he/she does, imagines, and says. Promoting flexibility in meanings, cognitive functioning, and modes of expression, then, is the focus of the treatment process.

Mahoney (1985) noted that "we are committing a costly error of translation if we equate what our clients say with what they think and how they feel" (p. 21). I would add that the error of translation would be more costly if we equate what a child does with what he/she imagines, feels, and says. In the proposed model, cognition is the carburetor mixing the right amount of external stimulation (air) with internal life metaphors (fuel), and the modalities of action, fantasy, and language are the steering wheel and wheels, adaptively moving the total person through changing environments.

THE PRIMACY OF UNCONSCIOUS PROCESSES AND RELATIONS TO CONSCIOUS PROCESSES

While unconscious processes have been a cornerstone of psychodynamic therapy from its inception, Mahoney (1985) stated to his cognitive-behavioral readers, ". . . unconscious processes . . . seem to be increasingly difficult to ignore" (p. 21). He also quoted the philosopher F. A. Hayek, which I include here, because the statement conveys quite well what I mean by the primacy of unconscious processes.

It is generally taken for granted that in some sense conscious experience constitutes the highest level in the hierarchy of mental events, and that what is not conscious has remained sub-conscious because it has not yet risen to that level . . . if my conception is correct . . . [we are not aware of much that happens in our minds] not because it proceeds at too low a level but because it proceeds at too high a level. It would seem more appropriate to call such processes not sub-conscious but super-conscious, because they govern the conscious processes without appearing in them. [cited in Mahoney 1985, p. 24]

A decade after reminding cognitive-behavioral therapists that unconscious processes are difficult to ignore, Mahoney (1995b) announced, "One of the more surprising developments in cognitive therapy has been the relatively recent acknowledgment of the importance and extensive role played by unconscious processes in human experiences. The surprising aspect of this development derives from the fact that many cognitive therapists have been critical of psychoanalytic theory" (p. 10). But all cognitive-behavioral therapists have not been equally enthusiastic with the notion of an unconscious process. Mahoney noted that some cognitive and behavioral therapists have acknowledged unconscious processes "begrudgingly," admitting that "automatic thoughts" are so habitual that they occur without the individual's awareness.

Here I bring to the reader's attention that long ago Meichenbaum (1977), in his volume on cognitive-behavioral therapy, quoted the philosopher Epictetus: "Man is disturbed not by things but the view he takes of them" (p. 183). In a footnote, Meichenbaum pointed out that given the frequency with which this quote appears in volumes about cognitive and behavioral therapy, the statement has become "a sort of rallying cry" (p. 183) for these therapists. But if we are mindful of Mahoney's recent opinion that all cognitive-behavioral therapists have not been equally enthusiastic with the notion of an unconscious process, it would seem that these therapists interpret Epictetus to mean that man is not disturbed by things but by the *conscious* view he takes of them.

Mahoney goes on to discuss that an intermediate level of acknowledgment of unconscious activity by cognitive-behavioral therapists is represented by approaches that emphasize cognitive schemas. Finally, the greatest degree of acknowledgment is represented by those who have joined the movement of "constructivism," viewing "tacit" processes as central to all knowing. Although cognitive-behavioral therapists are acknowledging the significance of unconscious processes, Mahoney added, "It is important to note that not all cognitive psychotherapists are comfortable with the above-mentioned rapprochement . . ." (p. 10). His opinion is supported by the fact that the topic of unconscious processes is still absent from the indexes of recent volumes discussing advances in cognitive and behavioral therapies (Clark and Fairburn 1997, Dobson and Craig 1996), as well as from volumes focusing on cognitive-behavioral therapy with children (Reinecke et al. 1996).

In addition to noticing that interest among cognitive-behavioral therapists in unconscious processes is not widespread, Mahoney stated ". . . more important from a theoretical prospective, cognitive renditions of the unconscious have been distinctly different from those rendered by (psychoanalysis)" (p. 10). In my view recent cognitive renditions of unconscious processes, to which Mahoney referred, show the influence of objectivism which segregates subjective from real knowledge, body from mind, and cognition from emotion. For example, Muran and DiGiuseppe (1990), in discussing a cognitive formulation of metaphor use in psychotherapy, disagreed with the view that metaphor (meaning) is the language of the unconscious. They proposed that meanings are expressed either literally or metaphorically. The former is suited to expressions of "empirical truths," and the later to expressions of "intuitive truths" (p. 76). For these authors, a client should not be expected to generate her/his own meaning from a metaphor. Rather a therapist should convey the meaning to a client and then ask questions to insure the client has "understood the meaning accurately" (see pp. 79–80). This position sets a boundary separating client and therapist, with one imparting meaning to the other, and another boundary separating conscious meanings (literal) from unconscious meanings (intuitive).

In presenting an integration of the cognitive and psychodynamic unconscious within his cognitive-experiential self-theory of personality (CEST), Epstein (1994) reviewed several theories of multiple processing modes, a few of which I mention here: (a) Freud formulated the unconscious as operating in terms of principles which he termed "primary process." These principles included fulfilling wishes more or less immediately, displacing a wish or urge from one goal to another, and symbolic representation. Primary process was distinguished from secondary process, a more logical, reality-oriented, realistic mode of reasoning; (b) Paivio proposed a dual coding system distinguishing verbal from nonverbal processes, as did Werner and Kaplan; (c) Schacter and others distinguished between tacit, implicit, and explicit knowledge; (d) social psychologists proposed two forms of reasoning—a "natural," intuitive mode and an "extensional," logical mode; (e) Bruner formulated two modes of mental representation: "propositional" thought which is public, logical, theoretical, and abstract; and "narrative" thought which is storylike, imagistic, interpersonal and includes characters, settings, intentions, and emotions.

With these theories as background, Epstein (1994) proposed two systems. "How we do think, I believe, is with two minds, experiential and rational" (p. 721). He argued that "a division" according to experiential and rational modes of processing "is more integrative" than any of the other divisions that have been proposed. Processing within the mode of the experiential system includes these attributes: holistic; pleasure–pain oriented; emotionally driven; behaviors mediated by "vibes" from past experiences; encodes reality in concrete images, metaphors, and narratives; oriented toward immediate action; more crudely differentiated and integrated; and experienced passively and preconsciously. Processing within the mode of the rational system includes these attributes: "a deliberative, abstract system that operates primarily in the medium of language" (p. 715); analytic; logical; encodes reality in abstract symbols, words, and numbers; oriented toward delayed action; more highly differentiated and integrated; experienced actively and consciously; "We are in control of our thoughts" (p. 711); and requires justification via logic and evidence.

Epstein proposed that these two systems are used by persons when adapting to the world. "People have constructs about the self and the world in both systems. Those in the rational system are referred to as *beliefs* and those in the experiential system as *implicit* beliefs or, alternatively, *schemata*" (p. 715). In terms of what Epstein called "the psychodynamics" of CEST, all behavior is assumed to be the product of the joint operation of these two systems. The relative dominance of one over the other is determined by factors such as "individual differences in style of thinking and situational variables, such as the degree to which a situation is identified as one that requires formal analysis" (p. 715). He also proposed that "like psychoanalysis, CEST (also) posits two levels of information processing, each functioning according to its own principles. Also, like psychoanalysis, CEST assumes that "the unaware (experiential) level continuously influences processing at the conscious (rational) level" (p. 716). This influence is on a one-way street so to speak, and the experiential system, as with Freud's primary process, is less suited to serve adaptation. In terms of needs that motivate these systems, CEST includes Freud's pleasure principle (the need to maximize pleasure and minimize pain) and adds three other needs proposed by psychoanalysts: the need to maintain a relatively stable, coherent, conceptual system; the need for relatedness; and the need to overcome feelings of inferiority and enhance self esteem.

The view of unconscious and conscious processes held by the developmental-dialectical model proposed in this volume, while converging with aspects of Epstein's two-system model, differs in several significant ways. Rather than thinking with two minds, one experiential (driven by emotions), and the other rational (affect free), my model proposes that we think with one mind which constructs meanings that integrate and coordinate the calls for action (and associated emotions) from life metaphors with calls for action (and associated emotions) from environmental events. My model also proposes that all meanings are constructed by *both* conscious and unconscious processes, viewed as poles on a continuum, each continuously influencing the other, on a two-way street so to speak, negotiating the paradox between them, and together serving adaptation. This view of a dialectic between conscious and unconscious processes contrasts with Epstein's that unconscious and conscious processes are independent systems, each with different characteristics. However my proposal converges with Bucci's (1985). Although she conceptualized two modes of information processing, verbal and nonverbal, these modes, when combined by a "referential process," result in new cognitive structures. She also assumed that neither the verbal nor the nonverbal mode dominates and that successful adaptation and effective therapy require an integration of the two modes, a position also taken by Labouvie-Vief (1990). Last in contrast to Epstein's proposal that four fundamental needs activate the mind, the developmental-dialectical model proposes that many life metaphors, or unconscious meanings, representing a wide range of key developmental issues, are the stuff on which conscious and unconscious processes do their work and engage in dialectical exchanges.

If conscious and unconscious processes are engaged in a continuous dialectical exchange, what does my model say about how each influences the other in the process of constructing meaning? And how do unconscious meanings enter a person's conscious awareness? To set the stage for my response to these questions, I begin by reminding us that, in his discussion of the affective unconscious and the cognitive unconscious, Piaget (1973) proposed that the unconscious does not contain already formed fantasies or ideas which would come into view once we shine a light on them. Rather "the unconscious is furnished with sensorimotor or operational schemata, organized into structures, all right, but expressing what the subject can 'do' and not what he thinks . . . in just the same way, the affective unconscious is furnished with tendencies . . . with affective schemata or characteristics" (p. 257). In addition, Piaget proposed that becoming conscious consists of "a reconstruction on a higher level something that is already organized but differently on a lower level . . ." (p. 256). In relying on Piaget's formulation, I make particular use of the notions that the unconscious is furnished with "tendencies" telling what a person "can do," and that the transition from unconscious to conscious levels involves "reconstruction."

To further set the stage for my proposal, I turn next to Lear (1990), a psychoanalyst, who has made a significant contribution to our understanding of unconscious processes and on whom I rely heavily in what follows. Lear reminded us that although Freud tended to treat unconscious thoughts as fully formed and hidden, he sometimes suggested that the way repression is able to contain a thought, wish, or meaning within unconscious processes is by preventing it from developing into "a fully fledged form." In other words, Freud recognized that the transition from unconscious to conscious levels involves developmental principles. This reminder served as a spring board for Lear's thesis. Converging with Piaget's (1973) proposal that the unconscious consists of "operational" schemas expressing what a person "can do," Lear formulated that the unconscious consists of "disparate orientations to the world" (p. 93); for example, a child may feel loving and hateful toward the same person. In addition, these orientations ramify in many directions so that one unconscious meaning could become linked to another, e.g., the orientation of eliminating a sib with whom a child is competing could become linked with the orientation to recover parental love.

Life metaphors as conceptualized by our developmental-dialectical model are analogous to Piaget's "operational schemas" and Lear's "orientations." Recall that life metaphors represent past experiences, construe present situations, and prescribe what a child could do to continue negotiating some meaning/metaphor in interactions with another.

At this point I address how the dialectic between unconscious metaphors and conscious processes gradually result in an unconscious meaning becoming organized and experienced within conscious awareness. Lear elaborated Piaget's notion that becoming conscious consists of a "reconstruction" at one level of something that is already organized but differently at another. This reconstruction, Lear proposed, is a gradual process following a principle of "progressive development." Moreover, the transition from unconscious to conscious levels "does not consist of attaching a word to a thing representation" (p. 106). Rather it involves the incorporation and integration of a concept at the level of both word and thing. "The word expresses the concept, the things have been differentiated so as to instantiate the concept, and the concept and thing have been linked together" (p. 107). In this way, the organization of a structure occurs equally and simultaneously at unconscious and conscious levels of mental activity.

Applied to our model, the transition of a metaphor from unconscious to conscious levels consists of the construction of a "concept" that is defined by an organization or pattern of actions, images, emotions, and words that is shared with, and understood by, others. From this view, while representing a call for action, an unconscious metaphor is also a "candidate" for becoming a concept. The reader may notice that this notion is similar to Bucci's (1985) position, noted earlier, that verbal and nonverbal modes, when combined by a "referential process," produce new structures.

To illustrate the dialectical process that I propose takes place in treatment between conscious actions, thoughts and fantasies, and unconscious life-metaphors, I turn to clinical cases discussed in previous chapters. Recall Harry whose treatment was described in Chapter 9. He was surely aware of the difficulties he caused when biting and spitting at others, and of his daily suffering when he sometimes curled up in a corner confused by what it takes to cope with his preschool program. However, at the start of treatment, the unconscious meaning that related to this behavior was not known to him or the therapist. If one looked at Harry's overt behavior when we first met him, it seemed logical to conclude that his biting and spitting were the outcome of disruptions in his early negotiations with testing and modifying aggressive intentions. But as we learned later, this was not the case at all. The unconscious metaphor that prescribed his spitting and biting defined his body-self as not grounded, highly unbalanced, and therefore in constant jeopardy. Tracing how this unconscious metaphor was gradually reconstructed several times, until it entered his conscious intentions and thoughts, provides one illustration of the dialectic between unconscious and conscious processes as conceptualized by my model.

After a phase of chaotic behavior, Harry engaged in explicit, purposeful, ritualistic actions: he repeatedly toppled toy animals and puppets from shelves to the floor. The meaning of this action was not yet clear, although at the time I assumed this behavior was a form of aggression akin to his biting and spitting. In toppling toys, a dialectic started between a yet unknown, unconscious, sensorimotor metaphor which prescribed the action, and his conscious perception of animals, puppets, and toys located on shelves some distance from the floor. (He toppled only materials located on the top shelves.) I joined this ritualized, circular interaction by setting geometric wooden cutouts under the toys, behavior which Harry consciously perceived. My conscious understanding of placing geometric cutouts under items was that I was providing the toys with solid ground and stability. Harry's conscious understanding apparently was different since he limited his swats to those figures under which I had placed a cutout. As the dialectic continued between the unconscious "orientation" or meaning he was negotiating and his conscious perceptions of my actions and of attributes of the material on the shelves, he eventually centered on a puppet bearing the letter "A" on its sweater. His unconscious and conscious poles reconstructed the meaning being negotiated when he named this puppet "Mr. Fall" and fantasized that it would get "spanked" because "he can't stand up." At this point the unconscious metaphor was on its way, as Lear put it, toward becoming a candidate for a concept of shared meaning. Harry explicitly expressed and shared the meaning of body imbalance, a meaning forged to this point by the dialectic between unconscious and conscious processes.

I tried to prevent Mr. Fall from falling by leaning various items against him. In response, Harry enacted further what the unconscious meaning of body imbalance signified and "could do," elaborating both the unconscious meaning and the conscious processes interacting with it. Harry repeatedly fell to the floor and called for help, enacting that he was "sinking." Each time I responded by pulling him onto a raft (newspaper). Harry consciously perceived and assimilated that the newspaper as a symbol prevented him from falling and sinking.

At this point, the dialectic between the unconscious meaning of body instability and the newly formed conscious understanding of falling and sinking were pushed upwards developmentally and elaborated in a new reconstruction. Harry flipped the hand puppet, whom he now called "Alvin," across the room numerous times, declaring that Alvin was "flipping out," and expressing concern about its well being. Following Lear's formulation, at this moment, the concept of a "person flipping out" was incorporated at both the levels of conscious language and imaging and unconscious meaning and sensorimotor schemas. In contrast to Epstein's model which reserves words as a characteristic of the rational mode, the vignette we are considering illustrates that the words "Alvin" and "flipping out" became part of a structure which included falling to the floor, sinking, flying through space with no control, and being injured.

Harry eventually assimilated a solution into this organization which prevented Alvin from flipping out and being injured. Harry consciously perceived and understood that if a string is tied to Alvin and also to a door knob, the string controlled Alvin's dangerous flights through space and prevented him from flipping out. As the dialectic continued between this conscious perception and conception of a string as control, and the unconscious meaning of instability and imbalance, another reconstruction occured. When Harry regressed and bit, hit, and spit at me, the concept of a string as control proved successful in regulating his behavior and in preventing him from flipping out, a concept that had emerged from an integration of conscious and unconscious processes. When one end of the string was tied to his head and the other to mine, without elaborate explanations or verbal interpretations, Harry consciously "understood" that a string could control his imbalance as it had Alvin's. Lear pointed out that a verbal interpretation, by offering understanding and a solution, moves the process of mental development upwards, integrating unconscious and conscious processes. I have emphasized that symbolic actions or fantasies, representing an explicit meaning and/or solution, could also serve as interpretations. As with verbal interpretations, actions and images could enhance understanding, suggest solutions, and further integrate unconscious and conscious processes.

As the dialectic continued between body imbalance versus control, another reconstruction resulted in an elaboration of the "concept" of control and regulation. Harry leaned padlocks on various items and performed the action requested by the "police station" (the therapist). This organization was elaborated further when Harry authored that Mr. Bad (a punching bag) ordered him and Alvin the puppet to perform destructive actions. Harry's refusal signified that the structure of imbalance versus control had become differentiated and solidly integrated at both unconscious and conscious levels. And this structure included Harry's consciously preserving attributes of the therapist which he idealized and construed as strength and power to resist maladaptive actions.

In summary, over the course of treatment, as unconscious and conscious processes engaged in a dialectic, Harry constructed and reconstructed, in a developmental progression, a series of interrelated structures, or concepts, concerning body-self imbalance versus self-regulation/control—from items leaned against Alvin to prevent his falling, to a newspaper as a raft preventing Harry from sinking, to a string as control over flipping out and doing crazy things, to a "police station" that regulated actions, to the therapist being stronger than a bad force. Throughout this progression, unconscious meanings gradually transitioned into conscious awareness in more direct, conventional symbolic forms, e.g., from a piece of string to the therapist as a source of control and strength. Relying on these developmental achievements, which integrated unconscious and conscious processes, Harry eventually initiated verbal, conceptual discussions of conscious difficulties he experienced such as his fear that toilets would suck him down a pipe. During these discussions, he relied upon expressions of unconscious meanings connected with conscious perceptions that had been reconstructed and shared with the therapist: he held onto a string tied to a cup so that it could not be flushed down a toilet.

Another illustration of the dialectic between conscious and unconscious processes is provided by Albert's behavior during treatment (Chapter 9). He was certainly conscious of his intention to keep a distance from the therapist (I had to remain on my side of the table as he rolled a match box car across its surface). And later he was conscious of his intention to keep his army's secrets from my army. It is equally certain that during this phase he was not conscious of the content of "these secrets" which he struggled not to reveal. The dialectic between some yet unknown, unconscious meaning and the conscious intention to keep secrets was reconstructed when Albert authored battles between "a good guy, Batman," whose identity he assumed, and "a giant rat" (a role he assigned to the therapist) who continually attacked and tortured Batman in order to learn his secrets. Illustrating Lear's (1990) proposal that unconscious meanings ramify so that one becomes linked to another, later the meaning of "bad" was connected with the meaning of power, royalty, and omnipotence. The giant rat was transformed into a "king" who ruled "the universe." What this all-powerful, royal "badness" consisted of became a candidate for further conceptualizing at a more conscious level when, on occasion, Albert leaped on my back, expressing the conscious wish to see my underwear. This behavior fleetingly integrated the conscious wish with some unconscious meaning Albert was attempting to hold secret.

The metaphor revealed by his wish to see my underwear eventually became linked to another metaphor concerning crimes and punishments. Assigning himself the role of the "King's Highest Servant," Albert searched for and captured "bad rats" and presented them to King Rat for punishment. Albert also completed a "rule book," listing punishments and crimes. The list included, along with behaviors such as stealing and swearing, "if you take your pants off," revealing a further integration of conscious and unconscious processes which were soon to be more fully expressed.

Arriving with a battery-operated vacuum cleaner, Albert's unconscious metaphor now called for actions that would give full, more differentiated expression to his unconscious secret, using the consciously perceived vacuum cleaner as a vehicle. He declared that he was "General Bolthead," crawled through secret tunnels, captured rats, sucked up tails and tail glands from the anuses of rats, and attached them to his own to form a "computer gland" and a "life gland." Here we should pause to note that in contrast to the undifferentiated, "crudely integrated" complexes Epstein's model proposed were characteristic of his experiential system, Albert's unconscious was now prescribing highly differentiated, integrated, and abstract symbols which Epstein attributed to the rational system.

After constructing the concept that the anus is the source of life and power, Albert's mind produced another reconstruction which occured at an even higher level of differentiation and abstraction. Sitting on the floor, exercising considerable delay, and actively and consciously experiencing control over his thoughts (characteristics which Epstein assigned to the rational mode), Albert constructed a "wild house" in which lived "dirty monsters" who engaged in various anal activities, including sticking their fingers in each others anuses. He also constructed a "scientist's house" where a scientist lived with his assistant "Dracula," half human and half monster, both of whom attempted to control the monsters. Finally he constructed a "punishment chamber" where monsters were punished with intense heat whenever they disobeyed the Scientist's orders to perform particular sadistic acts. Soon, the scientist's assistant, an elaboration of the king's highest servant of an earlier phase of treatment, became dissatisfied with having to live in filth. Assimilating conscious perceptions of the therapist who wondered if Dracula ever longed to get out of the wild house, Albert authored that the assistant attempt an escape. He disguised himself in order to become a member of the "Silver Stallion Squadron" and obtain "Silver Rods" but was found out and refused membership. Albert declared, "Even though he's clean, he's not honest but a monster in disguise. A member of the squadron must first be honest." The conscious concept of "honesty," derived from perceptions of the therapist's enacted standards, indicated that Albert's unconscious anal orientation must first be totally reformed before Albert could be admitted into the "Treasury."

The concepts of honesty and reformation underwent another reconstruction. Albert invented "David Barcelona" who was both "a Christian and a Jew" and born "from both the old and new years," a concept that integrated particular attributes of Albert and the therapist. David Barcelona and his "Italian Battalion" eventually "rid the village of dirty rats forever." Following this, Albert's mind produced another reconstruction which, however, represented a major shift in the dialectic between conscious and unconscious processes. In this reconstruction Albert's mind made use of linguistic metaphors, centering on a mythical boy Albert's age. Albert sat and told stories about "Teddy" who engaged in various anal activities: e.g., he held a mirror so he could see his nude behind and "get all kinds of good feelings"; he formed an "Ass Club," the members of which were discovered and punished by their fathers. The notion of fathers punishing children proved to be a reconstruction of the earlier concept which included a scientist who punished dirty monsters. However, now the reconstruction involved human figures, reflecting progressive movement toward conscious awareness. Albert also constructed the "Ass Times," becoming very involved in drawing pictures of buttocks to which he assigned numerical ratings. Here I pause again to recall Epstein's model. The rational system is defined as encoding reality with words and numbers. Albert provided us with an example illustrating that numbers could be used to encode emotionally charged meanings, born out of the dialectic between unconscious and conscious processes.

Albert eventually restructured the concept he and the therapist had constructed. Much as Dracula had previously longed to escape the wild house and join the Silver Stallion Squadron, now Teddy, a human boy, was stuck in the ass phase and longed to move to the "dink phase" and climb "penis peak." At this point, the unconscious meaning of entering a new, more "up front" phallic way of representing experiences ramified and became linked with another meaning: the fear that being assertive and harboring phallic ambitions results in harm (castration). Carefully studying articles about sharks, Albert produced a 70 page manuscript which focused on reports of swimmers being attacked by sharks. He also spent considerable time evaluating *Playboy* magazine photographs using several sophisticated rating scales which he devised. Reading articles, reasoning logically, consciously appraising events, encoding reality with abstract symbols and numbers, and controlling one's thoughts are characteristic of Epstein's rational system. But in our example, these characteristics are in a dialectical exchange with unconscious meanings concerning fear of bodily harm on the one hand and, on the other, evaluating the aesthetics/vulgarity represented by photographs of female models, instead of evaluating buttocks that occupied Albert's construction of the Ass Times.

If we trace the concepts Albert constructed to this point, we see that the dialectic between conscious and unconscious processes resulted in the restructuring of an interrelated series of patterns consisting of unconscious meanings and conscious actions, perceptions, and emotions. With each construction, the pattern gradually moved closer to conscious levels. In addition, each reconstruction, representing unconscious anal urges, ramified and became linked to an unconscious meaning representing punishment: (a) keeping cars on one side of a line in a struggle to maintain segregation between conscious and unconscious processes; (b) King Rat tortures a good force, Batman, to learn his secrets; (c) King Rat rules the universe; (d) the King's Highest Servant captures bad rats who are punished according to a rule book; (e) a rat (Bolthead) sucks up tail glands and tails from other rats and attaches them to his own anus so that it becomes the most powerful; (f) a human scientist and his assistant, Dracula (who is half human and half monster), control "filthy" rats who play anal games and who are punished when they break rules; (g) Dracula attempts to escape into an honorable corp of soldiers but he must "come clean" and reveal all secrets before he can become a member; (h) David Barcelona, a concept defining a new identity, integrates consciously preserved attributes of Albert and the therapist and links these with the unconscious wish for strength and power that is "honest." David Barcelona eliminates all bad rats forever; (i) Albert tells stories about a mythical boy who "confesses" his anal activities and indulgences; (j) Albert studies references and writes a "book" about shark attacks, expressing fear of what happens if one dares to assert.

This interlocking series of reconstructions gradually transformed meanings prescribing power and pleasure in anal activity from unconscious to conscious levels. This transition in part relied upon a shift from rats and physical enactments, as vehicles for symbolic expression, to humans and verbal enactments. Only after these achievements took place did the previously unconscious meaning concerning Albert's anal fixations become a full-fledged member of Albert's conscious awareness. Albert eventually discussed literally the anal play in which he had engaged, but no longer did. Simultaneously he experienced pleasure and industry when playing the saxophone and making origami designs. With the capacity to literally and "rationally" discuss his past anal preoccupations, his emotions now coded experiences in terms of pleasure in industry and invention.

If we consider the clinical examples of Harry and Albert together, we can see that the unconscious is not a maladaptive system distorting reality, as Epstein proposed and as Freud initially formulated. Rather, unconscious and conscious processes engage in continuous dialectical interactions. Each influences the other, utilizing all of the characteristics which were listed by Epstein as related to either the experiential (unconscious) or the rational (conscious) modes: holistic and analytic; emotionally and logically oriented reasoning; behavior mediated by unconscious meanings/emotions and by conscious appraisal of events; encoding experiences in images, words, and abstract symbols; orientated toward immediate and delayed action; change slowly with the repetition of rituals and quickly with the use of thought; becoming structured in global as well as more differentiated and integrated organizations of actions, images, and words; dominated by emotion and thought; and relying on evidence from physical experiences as well as logic and propositions.

The proposed dialectic between conscious and unconscious processes is also illustrated by research studies described in Chapter 10. For example, it seems very likely that the young children who looked through binoculars in order to "push the examiner away" while aware that they were looking through binoculars, were not aware of the meaning of this microaction. Nor were they aware that when examining a series of pictures of two persons greeting each other, they failed to notice changes that took place in the scene more so than did children who looked through the binoculars so as to draw the examiner near. Along the same line, the older children in this study, who looked through the binoculars so as to draw the examiner near, were not aware that the meaning of needing a close attachment (when they should have already negotiated individuation), influenced the inefficiency they showed when looking at the same pictures of two persons greeting each other.

THE PRIMACY OF DIALECTICAL ENACTMENTS INSTEAD OF WORDS AND THE THERAPIST AS AN ACTIVE PARTICIPANT

We discussed in previous chapters that therapists from both cognitive-behavioral and psychodynamic camps have argued that rational conceptual knowing by itself does not appear to be therapeutic. Mitchell (1994), a psychoanalyst, has been a major voice disagreeing with psychodynamic therapists who rely on the content of verbal interpretation ("classical" psychoanalysis) to account for therapeutic change, and proposed that enactments and interactions ("relational" psychoanalysis) are more important. The influence exerted by Mitchell, as well as others who have emphasized a relational approach, has stirred up considerable controversy, reflected by an issue of *Psychoanalytic Psychology* (1995) devoted to debates between the two positions which the reader is encouraged to review. Along the same line, from his review of published reports by child psychoanalysts, Altman (1994) argued that, in recent years, while child psychoanalysts have been moving toward a relational theory and practice, "the lingering influence of drive theory and associated analytic technique is evident in a common tendency to ignore the impact on the patient of what the analyst does and says in the analytic interaction" (p. 383).

While cognitive-behavioral therapists initially ignored the patient–therapist relationship, they have been giving increasing attention to its importance. As one example, Safran (1990a,b) "refined" cognitive therapy in light interpersonal theory. "One's interpersonal schemas shape the perception of the interpersonal world and lead to various plans, strategies, and behaviors, which in turn shape the environment in a manner which confirms the working model. There is, thus, a self-perpetuating "cognitive-interpersonal cycle" (Safran 1990a, p. 97). An early study of the therapeutic relationship in behavior therapy (Ford 1978), observing that individual differences in therapists related to clients' perceptions of the therapeutic relationship, anticipated aspects of Safran's formulations.

A more recent study (Kazdin et al. 1989) is also related and brings attention to the power of enactments in treating children. These investigators randomly assigned children, referred because of severe antisocial behaviors, to one of three treatment conditions. One group participated in problem-solving skills training (PSST) (e.g., developing alternative solutions; taking the perspective of others). The bulk of this treatment "was devoted to enacting interpersonal situations through role play" (p. 525). Another group participated in problem-solving skills training with in vivo practice (PSST-P). In addition to receiving the identical treatment provided to participants in the PSST program, these children received "in vivo practice which consisted of therapeutically planned activities outside of the sessions" (p. 527) that involved parents and sibs. Initially the therapist provided assistance during these in vivo enactments before or after a session. Gradually the parents assisted the child, and the therapist's role during these moments "faded" (p. 527). A third group participated in relationship therapy (RT). Here the therapist used play materials to help the child talk and express feelings. Children who participated in PSST and PSST-P programs showed significantly greater reduction in antisocial behavior than children who participated in RT programs.

Safran noted that his concept of cognitive-interpersonal cycles is similar to Wachtel's (1977, 1987) cyclical psychodynamics discussed earlier. While each of these concepts bears some resemblance to the notion of cycles of dialectical enactments proposed in this volume, there is an important difference. With cycles of dialectical enactments, two persons negotiate the paradox between what each construes and expects. In Safran's concept, the person's cognition construes and constructs the environment, and in Wachtel's formulation a person construes another, and on this basis, searches for experiences with others that fit this construction. Neither of these formulations emphasizes a process in which persons negotiate the difference between what each construes and expects. Other cognitive-behavioral therapists who take the position that words spoken by the therapist and patient are not primary have proposed that "nonspecific factors" in the relationship between patient and therapist change the way a person feels, acts, and experiences herself/himself.

The developmental-dialectical model agrees that verbal conceptualizing should be subordinated especially in psychotherapy with children, and takes a step further in operationalizing what these "cognitive-interpersonal cycles" and "nonspecific relationship factors" are. Given the model's roots in the first years of life, and the pivotal role played by embodied meanings, the model takes the position that non-specific factors are in fact quite specific. They consist of child and therapist engaging in ritualized, circular, dialectical interactions and enactments. As child and therapist interact, a child negotiates the dialectic among what she/he says, imagines, and does, while the therapist negotiates the dialectic among what she/he says, imagines, and does. At the same time, child and therapist respond to, influence, and contour the other's patterns of words, fantasies, and actions, as they co-construct an intersubjective world unique to them and within which the child reorganizes her/his metaphors, cognitive functioning, and modes of expression. This dialectical process defines how change takes place both within a person and between persons, forming a bridge connecting intrapsychic interactions with interpersonal interactions. Unless words are rooted in ritualized interactions, the meanings they express float like detached balloons.

The model I propose, then, disagrees with treatment approaches that emphasize verbalizing (e.g., interpretations, self-talk, discourse) as vehicles for change, whether conducted within a cognitive-behavioral or psychodynamic framework. It seems to me Freud (1912) recognized that meanings, cognitions, and behaviors are revised more by interpersonal transactions than by verbal statements when he noted, "I dislike making use of analytic writings as an assistance to my patients. I require them to learn from personal experience, and I assure them that they will acquire wide and more valuable knowledge than the whole literature of psychoanalysis could teach them" (p. 119–120). The clinical cases discussed provide illustrations of dialectical, circular interactions and enactments, and of the therapist as an active participant rather than someone who primarily verbalizes feelings, motives, and self-instruction, whether she/he is sitting quietly at a table or crawling on all fours in a treatment room or outdoors.

THE PRIMACY OF CHANGE AS INTEGRATION AND CONSOLIDATION

The model proposed here, with its roots in development and dialectics, views change and growth as a process that assimilates and consolidates previous behaviors into emerging behaviors, rather than a process in which old behaviors are eliminated by new ones, a principle at the heart of the organismic-developmental viewpoint. Following this principle, the model also takes the position that unconscious meanings and cognitive and behavioral modalities, that are structured during infancy and the toddler years, are extended into unconscious and conscious meanings, and into cognitive and behavioral modalities that become constructed during childhood and beyond. Therefore, as a child and adolescent interact with others and negotiate developmental issues, these earlier structures continually influence the organization of structures formed throughout childhood and adolescence. In addition, since the model distinguishes between levels of functioning that are interrelated, change processes that occur within a level are distinguished from processes of change involved as a behavioral organization spirals from one level to another. Therefore, different therapeutic techniques are required to facilitate each type of change process. When applied to treatment, the focus of the proposed development-dialectical model, then, is on setting into motion processes that promote change rather than processes that attempt to achieve a predetermined end state (see also Brems 1993).

A CLOSING COMMENT

Almost a century ago Mary Cover Jones (1924) desensitized a child of his fear of rabbits by moving a caged rabbit closer and closer to the child while the child ate. Lightmer Witmer (1908) administered cognitive tasks to a child who was a poor speller. And Sigmund Freud (1909) supervised a father in using verbal and conceptual interactions with his son, interpreting unconscious meanings associated with the boy's fear of horses. Each of these early attempts to help a suffering child could be viewed as forecasting the three approaches to child psychotherapy that have emerged as dominant. The dialectical-developmental model and its therapeutic guidelines, described in this volume, represent one probe searching for a way of integrating valuable aspects of each approach in order to treat the whole child.

Modifying a leaf from Mitchell (1988), the model views unconscious, embodied meanings/metaphors as the skeletal system, representing experiences with others in the past and what one expects from others in the present. These representations are not visible to the naked eye but ever active in construing situations and prescribing what a person can do. Symbols constructed and shared by a child in interactions with others make up the child's skin near consciousness, providing a continuous flow of stimulation, and representing what the child wants and prohibits and what the environment wants and prohibits. Cognitive functions, and modalities of action, fantasy, and language, form the child's neural, vascular, and muscular networks, connecting and coordinating the requirements and performance of the skeletal system and skin. The more successful we are in developing therapeutic techniques that interrelate and coordinate a child's skin with a child's skeletal, muscular, and vascular systems, the more a child will be treated holistically and set on a growth-fostering, developmental course throughout childhood and adolescence.

In his concluding remarks to the participants at the first world congress of infant psychiatry held in Cascais, Portugal, in 1980, Erikson (1983) shared a view that to my mind captures the holistic, developmental-dialectical approach to child and adolescent therapy I presented in this volume. "As we learned to treat . . . children (and their families), we found that [therapeutic] intervention in the widest sense really means involvement in the overall dynamic of 'growing together' . . . which alone can heal" (p. 425).

References

Altman, N. (1994). A perspective on child psychoanalysis 1994: The recognition of relational theory and technique in child treatment. *Psychoanalytic Psychology* 11:383–395.

American Psychiatric Association (1994). *Diagnostic and Statistical Manual of Mental Disorders*. 4th ed.-revised. Washington, DC.

American Psychological Association (1990). Ethical principles of psychologists. *American Psychologist* 45:390–395.

Anthony, E. J. (1956). The significance of Jean Piaget for child psychiatry. *British Journal of Medical Psychology* 29:20–34.

Arieti, S. (1970). The role of cognition in the development of inner reality. In *Cognitive Studies*, vol. 1, ed. J. Hellmuth, pp. 91–110. New York: Brunner/ Mazel.

Arkowitz, H. (1984). Historical perspective on the integration of psychoanalytic therapy and behavioral therapy. In *Psychoanalytic Therapy and Behavioral Therapy: Is Integration Possible?*, ed. H. Arkowitz and S. B. Messer, pp. 1–30. New York: Plenum.

——— (1992). Integrative theories of therapy. In *History of Psychotherapy: A Century of Change*, ed. D. K. Freedkeim, pp. 261–303. Washington, DC: American Psychological Association.

Arkowitz, H., and Messer, S. B., eds. (1984). *Psychoanalytic Therapy and Behavioral Therapy: Is Integration Possible?* New York: Plenum.

Armsworth, M. W., and Holaday, M. (1993). The effects of psychological trauma on children and adolescents. *Journal of Counseling and Development* 72:49–56.

Arnkoff, D. B. (1980). Psychotherapy from the perspective of cognitive therapy. In *Psychotherapy Process: Current Issues and Future Directions*, ed. M. J. Mahoney, pp. 339–361. New York: Plenum.

Arnkoff, D. B., and Glass, C. R. (1982). Clinical cognitive constructs: examination, evaluation, and elaboration. In *Advances in Cognitive-Behavioral Research and Therapy*, vol. 1, ed. P. C. Kendall, pp. 1–34. New York: Academic Press.

Arnold, M. B. (1960). *Emotion and Personality Vol. 1. Psychological Aspects*. New York: Columbia University Press.

Baldwin, A. L. (1967). *Theories of Child Development*. New York: Wiley.

Baltes, P. B., and Schaie, K. W., eds. (1973). *Life-Span Developmental Psychology: Personality and Socialization.* New York: Academic Press.

Bandura, A. (1969). *Principles of Behavior Modification.* New York: Holt, Rinehart & Winston.

——— (1977). *Social Learning Theory.* Englewood Cliffs, NJ: Prentice Hall.

Bandura, A., and Walters, R. H. (1963). Aggression. In *Child Psychology: The Sixty-Second Yearbook of the National Society for the Study of Education*, ed. H. W. Stevenson, J. Kagan, and C. Spicker, pp. 364–415. Chicago: University of Chicago Press.

Barnard, R. E., and Brazelton, T. B., eds. (1990). *Touch: The Foundation of Experience.* Madison, CT: International Universities Press.

Barratt, B. B. (1984). *Psychic Reality and Psychoanalytic Knowing.* Hillside, NJ: Analytic Press.

Bearison, D. J., and Zimiles, H. (1986). Developmental perspectives of thought and emotion: an introduction. In *Thought and Emotion: Developmental Perspectives*, ed. D. J. Bearison and H. Zimiles, pp. 1–10. Hillsdale, NJ: Erlbaum.

Beck, A. T. (1976). *Cognitive Therapy and the Emotional Disorders.* New York: International Universities Press.

Bedrosian, R. C. (1981). The application of cognitive therapy techniques with adolescents. In *New Directions in Cognitive Therapy*, ed. G. Emery, S. D. Hoolon, and R. C. Bedrosian, pp. 68–83. New York: Gifford.

Bedrosian, R. C., and Beck, A. T. (1980). Principles of cognitive therapy. In *Psychotherapy Process: Current Issues and Future Directions*, ed. M. J. Mahoney, pp. 127–152. New York: Plenum.

Beebe, B., and Lachmann, F. M. (1994). Representation and internalization in infancy: three principles of salience. *Psychoanalytic Psychology* 11:127–165.

Benjamin, J. D. (1961). The innate and experiential in development. In *Lectures in Experimental Psychiatry*, ed. H. W. Brosin. Pittsburgh: University of Pittsburgh Press.

Billow, R. M. (1977). Metaphor: a review of the psychological literature. *Psychological Bulletin* 84:81–92.

Blaisdell, O. (1972). *Developmental changes in action aggression and in fantasy aggression.* Unpublished doctoral dissertation, Boston University.

Blake, R. R., and Ramsey, G. V., eds. (1951). *Perception: An Approach to Personality.* New York: Ronald Press.

Blatt, S. J., and Behrends, R. S. (1987). Internalization, separation-individuation, and the nature of the therapeutic action. *International Journal of Psychoanalysis* 68:279–297.

Bohart, A. C. (1993). Experiencing: the basis of psychotherapy. *Journal of Psychotherapy Integration* 3:51–67.

Boland, J., and Sandler, J. (1965). *The Hampstead Psychoanalytic Index.* New York: International Universities Press.

Bower, G. H., and Cohen, P. R. (1982). Emotional influences in memory and thinking. In *Affect and Cognition*, ed. M. S. Clark and S. T. Fiske, pp. 291–332. Hillsdale, NJ: Erlbaum.

Brems, C. (1993). *A Comprehensive Guide to Child Psychotherapy*. Boston: Allyn and Bacon.

Breuer, J., and Freud, S. (1895). Studies on hysteria. *Standard Edition* 2:1–306.

Bronfenbrenner, U. (1951). Toward an integrated theory of personality. In *Perception: An Approach to Personality*, ed. R. R. Blake and G. V. Ramsey, pp. 206–257. New York: Ronald Press.

——— (1963). Developmental theory in transition. In *Child Psychology*, ed. H. W. Stevenson, pp. 519–542. Chicago: University of Chicago Press.

Brown, F. (1958). The psychodiagnostic test battery. In *Progress in Clinical Psychology*, ed. D. Brower and L. E. Abt, pp. 60–71. New York: Grune & Stratton.

Bruner, J. (1951). Personality dynamics and the process of perceiving. In *Perception: An Approach to Personality*, ed. R. R. Blake and G. V. Ramsey, pp. 121–147. New York: Ronald Press.

——— (1986). Thought and emotion: Can Humpty Dumpty be put back together again? In *Thought and Emotion: Developmental Perspectives*, ed. D. J. Bearison and H. Zimiles, pp. 11–20. Hillsdale, NJ: Erlbaum.

——— (1990). *Acts of meaning*. Cambridge, MA: Harvard University Press.

——— (1992). Another look at the New Look I. *American Psychologist* 47:780–785.

Bucci, W. (1985). Dual coding system: a cognitive model for psychoanalytic research. *Journal of the American Psychoanalytic Association* 33:571–607.

Cacioppo, J. T., and Petty, R. E. (1981). Social psychological procedures for cognitive response assessment: the thought listing technique. In *Cognitive Assessment*, ed. T. V. Merluzzi, C. R. Glass, and M. Genest, pp. 309–342. New York: Guilford.

Calicchia, J. A., Moncata, S. J., and Santostefano, S. (1993). Cognitive control differences in violent juvenile inpatients. *Journal of Clinical Psychology* 49:731–740.

Calicchia, J. A., Santostefano, S., and Moncata, S. J. (1991). *Predicting Dangerous Juvenile Inpatients: The Ecological Validity of Cognitive Controls*. Belmont, MA: McLean Hospital and Harvard Medical School. Resources in Education (ERIC Document Reproduction Service No. ED 328813).

Camp, B. W., and Ray, R. S. (1984). Aggression. In *Cognitive Behavior Therapy with Children*, ed. A. W. Meyers and W. E. Craighead, pp. 315–350. New York: Plenum.

Campbell, S. F., ed. (1977). *Piaget Sampler: An Introduction to Jean Piaget through His Own Work*. New York: Jason Aronson.

Cangelosi, D. M. (1993). Internal and external wars: psychodynamic play therapy. In *Play Therapy in Action: A Case Book for Practitioners*, ed. T. Knottman and C. Schaefer, pp. 347–370. Northvale, NJ: Jason Aronson.

Cash, T. F., and Pruzinsky, T., eds. (1990). *Body Images: Development, Deviance and Change*. New York: Guilford.

Cicchetti, D., ed. (1984). Developmental Psychopathology [Special issue]. *Child Development* 55:(1).

Cicchetti, D., and Schneider-Rosen, K. (1984). Theoretical and empirical considerations in the investigation of the relationship between affect and cognition in atypical populations of infants. In *Emotions, Cognition and Behavior*, ed. C. E. Izard, J. Kagan, and R. B. Zajonc, pp. 366–406. Cambridge, MA: Cambridge University Press.

Clark, D. M., and Fairburn, C. G., eds. (1997). *Science and Practice of Cognitive Behavior Therapy*. New York: Oxford University Press.

Clark, M. S., and Fiske, S. T., eds. (1982). Preface. *Affect and Cognition*, pp. ix–x. Hillsdale, NJ: Erlbaum.

Cohen, L. B., and Salapatek, P., eds. (1975). *Infant Perception: From Sensation to Cognition*, vols. 1–2. New York: Academic Press.

Cohen, R., and Schleser, R. (1984). Cognitive development and clinical intervention. In *Cognitive Behavior Therapy with Children*, ed. A. W. Craighead, pp. 45–68. New York: Plenum.

Colby, K. M., and Stoller, R. J. (1988). *Cognitive Science and Psychoanalysis*. Hillside, NJ: Analytic Press.

Conn, J. H. (1993). The play-interview. In *Play Therapy Techniques*, ed. C. E. Schaefer and D. M. Cangelosi, pp. 9–44. Northvale, NJ: Jason Aronson.

Coonerty, S. (1993). Integrative child therapy. In *Comprehensive Handbook of Psychotherapy Integration*, ed. G. Stricker and J. R. Gold, pp. 413–425. New York: Plenum.

Coppolillo, H. P. (1987). *Psychodynamic Psychotherapy of Children: An Introduction to the Art and the Techniques*. Madison, CT: International Universities Press.

Corsini, R. J., and Wedding, D., eds. (1989). *Current Psychotherapies*, 4th ed. Itasca, IL: Peacock.

Cotugno, A. J. (1987). Cognitive control functioning in hyperactive and non-hyperactive children. *Journal of Learning Disabilities* 20:563–567.

Crandall, V. J. (1963). Achievement. In *Child Psychology: The Sixty-Second Yearbook of the National Society of the Study of Education*, ed. H. W. Stevenson, J. Kagan, and C. Spiker, pp. 416–459. Chicago: University of Chicago Press.

Davis, L. J. (1997). The encyclopedia of insanity: a psychiatric handbook lists a madness for everyone. *Harpers Magazine*, February.

Decarie, T. G. (1965). *Intelligence and Affectivity in Early Childhood: An Experimental Study of Jean Piaget's Object Concept and Object Relation*. New York: International Universities Press.

——— (1978). Affect development and cognition in a Piagetian context. In *The Development of Affect*, ed. M. Lewis and L. A. Rosenblum, pp. 183–230. New York: Plenum.

Dember, W. N. (1974). Motivation and the cognitive revolution. *American Psychologist* 29:161–168.

Demick, J., and Wapner, S. (1987). *A holistic, developmental approach to body expe-*

rience. Paper presented at Body Experience and Literature: An Interdisciplinary Conference, SUNY-Buffalo, Buffalo, NY, November.

DiGiuseppe, R. A. (1981). Cognitive therapy with children. In *New Directions in Cognitive Therapy*, ed. G. Emery, S. D. Hollon, and R. C. Bedrosian, pp. 50–66. New York: Guilford.

Division of Child, Youth and Family Services (1994). Multicultural issues in clinical training. *Child, Youth and Family Services Quarterly* 17:1–27.

Division of Clinical Psychology (1990). Diversity in clinical psychology: research and practice. *Clinical Psychologist* 46:42–95.

Dobson, K. S., and Craig, K. D., eds. (1996). *Advances in Cognitive-Behavioral Therapy.* Thousand Oaks, CA: Sage Publications.

Dodge, K. A. (1986). A social information processing model of social competence in children. In *Minnesota Symposium on Child Psychology*, vol. 18, ed. M. Permutter, pp. 77–125. Hillsdale, NJ: Erlbaum.

Dollard, J., and Miller, N. E. (1950). *Personality and Psychotherapy.* New York: McGraw-Hill.

Eagle, M. N. (1984). *Recent Developments in Psychoanalysis.* Cambridge, MA: Harvard University Press.

Eichler, J. (1971). *A developmental study of action, fantasy, and language aggression in latency aged boys.* Unpublished doctoral dissertation, Boston University.

Emery, G., Hollon, S. D., and Bedrosian, R. C. (1981). *New Directions in Cognitive Therapy.* New York: Guildford.

Epstein, S. (1994). Integration of the cognitive and psychodynamic unconscious. *American Psychologist* 49:709–724.

Erikson, E. (1964). Clinical observations of play disruption in young children. In *Child Psychotherapy*, ed. M. Haworth, pp. 246–276. New York: Basic Books.

Erikson, E. H. (1950). *Childhood and Society.* New York: Norton.

——— (1980). *Identity and the Life Cycle.* New York: Norton.

——— (1983). Concluding remarks: infancy and the rest of life. In *Frontiers of Infant Psychiatry*, ed. J. D. Call, E. Galenson, and R. L. Tyson, pp. 425–428. New York: Basic Books.

Erlenmeyer-Kimling, L., and Miller, N. E., eds. (1986). *Life-Span Research on the Prediction of Psychopathology.* Hillsdale, NJ: Erlbaum.

Farver, J. M., and Frosch, D. L. (1996). L.A. Stories: aggression in preschoolers' spontaneous narratives after the riots of 1992. *Child Development* 67:19–32.

Faust, J. (1993). Oh, but a heart, courage and a brain: an integrative approach to play therapy. In *Play Therapy in Action: A Case Book for Practitioners*, ed. T. Knottman and C. Schaefer, pp. 417–456. Northvale, NJ: Jason Aronson.

Feather, B. W., and Rhoads, J. M. (1972a). Psychodynamic behavior therapy: II. Clinical aspects. *Archives of General Psychiatry* 26:503–511.

——— (1972b). Psychodynamic behavior therapy: I. Theoretical aspects. *Archives of General Psychiatry* 26:496–502.

Fein, G. G., and Apsel, N. (1979). Some preliminary observations on knowing and pretending. In *Symbolic Functioning in Childhood*, ed. N. R. Smith and M. B. Franklin, pp. 87–99. Hillsdale, NJ: Erlbaum.

Feuerstein, R. (1980). *Instrumental Enrichment: An Intervention Program for Cognitive Modifiability*. Baltimore: University Park Press.

Fischer, J. (1995). Uniformity myths in eclectic and integrative psychotherapy. *Journal of Psychotherapy Integration* 5:41–56.

Fisher, S. (1990). The evolution of psychological concepts about the body. In *Body Images: Development, Deviance, and Change*, ed. T. F. Cash and T. Pruzinsky, pp. 3–20. New York: Guilford.

Fisher, S., and Cleveland, S. E. (1958). *Body Image and Personality*. New York: Dover Publications.

Flavell, J. H. (1963). *The Developmental Psychology of Jean Piaget*. New York: Van Nostrand.

Ford, J. D. (1978). Therapeutic relationships in behavior therapy: an empirical analysis. *Journal of Consulting and Clinical Psychology* 46:1302–1314.

Ford-Clark, M. E. (1992). *A developmental assessment of the cognitive principle of leveling-sharping in two interpersonal-emotional contexts: aggression and affliction*. Unpublished doctoral dissertation, Antrock University/New England Graduate School.

Franklin, A. J., Carter, R. T., and Grace, C. (1993). An integrative approach to psychotherapy with Black/African Americans: the relevance of race and culture. In *Comprehensive Handbook of Psychotherapy Integration*, ed. G. Stricker and J. R. Gold, pp. 465–482. New York: Plenum.

Franz, S. I. (1905). The reeducation of an aphasic. *Journal of Philosophy, Psychology, and Scientific Methods* 2.

Freedkeim, D. K., ed. (1992). *History of Psychotherapy: A Century of Change*. Washington, DC: American Psychological Association.

Freedman, N. (1977). Hands, words and mind: on the structuralization of body movements during discourse and the capacity for verbal representation. In *Communicative Structures and Psychic Structures*, ed. N. Freedman and S. Grand, pp. 109–132. New York: Plenum.

Freedman, R. (1990). Cognitive-behavioral perspectives in body-image change. In *Body Images: Development, Deviance, and Change*, ed. T. F. Cash and T. Pruzinsky, pp. 272–295. New York: Guilford.

Frenkl-Brunswik, E. (1951). Personality theory and perception. In *Perception: An Approach to Personality*, ed. R. R. Blake and G. V. Ramsey, pp. 356–420. New York: Ronald Press.

Freud, A. (1946). *The Ego and Mechanisms of Defense*. New York: International Universities Press.

———— (1965). *Normality and Pathology in Childhood*. New York: International Universities Press.

Freud, S. (1900). The interpretation of dreams. *Standard Edition* 4/5:1–626.

———— (1904). Freud's psycho-analytic procedure. *Standard Edition* 7:249–256.

———— (1905). On psychotherapy. *Standard Edition* 7:257–270.

———— (1912). Recommendations to physicians practicing psychoanalysis. *Standard Edition* 12:109–120.

———— (1913). On beginning the treatment (further recommendations on the technique of psychoanalysis: I). *Standard Edition* 12:121–144.

———— (1914). Remembering, repeating and working-through (further recommendations on the technique of psychoanalysis: II). *Standard Edition* 12:145–156.

———— (1915). Instincts and their vicissitudes. *Standard Edition* 14:117–140.

———— (1916). Introductory lectures on psycho-analysis. *Standard Edition* 15:15–239.

———— (1923). The ego and the id. *Standard Edition* 19:12–66.

———— (1926). Inhibition, symptoms, and anxiety. *Standard Edition* 20:87–174.

———— (1930). Civilization and its discontents. *Standard Edition* 21:64–145.

———— (1932). New introductory lectures on psycho-analysis. *Standard Edition* 22:7–182.

Furth, H. G. (1983). Symbol formation: where Freud and Piaget meet. *Human Development* 26:26–41.

Galton, F. (1884). Measurement of character. *The Fortnightly Review* 36:179–185.

Gardner, H. (1985). *The Mind's New Science: A History of the Cognitive Revolution.* New York: Basic Books.

Gardner, R. A. (1993). *Psychotherapy with Children.* Northvale, NJ: Jason Aronson.

Garfield, S. L. (1994). Eclecticism and integration in psychotherapy: developments and issues. *Clinical Psychology Science and Practice* 6:123–137.

Gaston, L., Goldfried, M. R., Greenberg, A. O., et al. (1995). The therapeutic alliance in psychodynamic, cognitive-behavioral, and experiential therapies. *Journal of Psychotherapy Integration* 5:1–26.

Gelfand, D. M., and Peterson, L. (1985). *Child Development and Psychopathology.* Beverly Hills, CA: Sage.

Gholson, B., and Rosenthal, T. L., eds. (1984). *Applications of Cognitive Developmental Theory.* New York: Academic Press.

Gill, M., ed. (1967). *The Collected Papers of David Rapaport.* New York: Basic Books.

Gill, M. M. (1984). Psychoanalysis and psychotherapy: a revision. *International Review of Psychoanalysis* 11:161–179.

Gill, M. M., and Hoffman, I. Z. (1982). A method for studying the analysis of aspects of the patient's experience of the relationship in psychoanalysis and psychotherapy. *Journal of the American Psychoanalytic Association* 30:137–167.

Gold, J. R. (1992). An integrative-systemic treatment approach to serve psychopathology of children and adolescents. *Journal of Integrative and Eclectic Psychotherapy* 2:58–63.

———— (1994). When the patient does the integrating: lessons for theory and practice. *Journal of Psychotherapy Integration* 4:133–158.

Gold, J. R., and Wachtel, P. L. (1993). Cyclical psychodynamics. In *Comprehensive Handbook of Psychotherapy Integration*, ed. G. Stricker and J. R. Gold, pp. 59–72. New York: Plenum.

Goncalves, O. (1995). Cognitive narrative psychotherapy: the hermeneutic construction of alternative meanings. In *Cognitive and Constructive Psychotherapies: Therapy, Research, and Practice*, ed. M. J. Mahoney, pp. 139–162. New York: Springer.

Gottschald, L. A., and Uliana, R. L. (1977). Further studies on the relationship of nonverbal to verbal behavior: effect of lip caressing on shame, hostility and other variables as expressed in the content of speech. In *Communicative Structures and Psychic Structures*, ed. N. Freedman and S. Grand, pp. 311–327. New York: Plenum.

Goulet, L. R., and Baltes, P. B., eds. (1970). *Life-Span Developmental Psychology: Research and Theory*. New York: Academic Press.

Grand, S. (1977). On hand movements during speech: studies of the role of self-stimulation in communication under conditions of psychopathology, sensory deficit and bilingualism. In *Communicative Structures and Psychic Structures*, ed. N. Freedman and S. Grand, pp. 199–211. New York: Plenum.

Greenson, R. (1977). That impossible profession. In *Human Dimension in Psychoanalytic Practice*, ed. K. A. Frank. New York: Grune & Stratton.

Group for the Advancement of Psychiatry, Committee on Psychiatry (1966). *Psychopathological disorders in children: theoretical considerations and a proposed classification* (Report No. 62). New York: GAP.

Gruber, H. E., Hammond, K. R., and Jessor, R., eds. (1957). *Contemporary Approaches to Cognition*. Cambridge, MA: Harvard University Press.

Guidano, V. F., and Liotti, G. (1983). *Cognitive Processes and Emotional Disorders: A Structural Approach to Psychotherapy*. New York: Guilford.

——— (1985). A constructivistic foundation for cognitive therapy. In *Cognition and Psychotherapy*, ed. M. J. Mahoney and A. Freedman, pp. 101–142. New York: Plenum.

Hammer, M., and Kaplan, A. M. (1967). *The Practice of Psychotherapy with Children*. Homewood, IL: Dorsey.

Harris, D. B. (1957). Problems in formulating a scientific concept of development. In *The Concept of Development: An Issue in the Study of Human Behavior*, ed. D. B. Harris, pp. 3–14. Minneapolis: University of Minnesota Press.

Hartmann, H. (1939). *Ego Psychology and the Problem of Adaptation*, 1st English ed. New York: International Universities Press, 1958.

Hartup, W. W. (1963). Dependence and independence. In *Child Psychology: The Sixty-Second Yearbook of the National Society of Education*, ed. H. W. Stevenson, pp. 333–363. Chicago: University of Chicago Press.

Heard, H. L., and Linehan, M. M. (1994). Dialectical behavior therapy: an integrative approach to the treatment of borderline personality disorders. *Journal of Psychotherapy Integration* 4:55–82.

Hesse, P., and Cicchetti, D. (1982). Perspectives on an integrated theory of emotional development. In *New Directions for Child Development. Vol. 16, Emo-*

tional Development, ed. D. Cicchetti and P. Hesse, pp. 57–79. San Francisco: Jossey-Bass.

Hilgard, E. R. (1951). The role of learning in perception. In *Perception: An Approach to Personality*, ed. R. R. Blake and G. V. Ramsey, pp. 95–120. New York: Ronald Press.

Hoffman, M., ed. (1984). *Foundations of Cognitive Therapy*. New York: Plenum.

Hollin, C. R. (1990). *Cognitive-Behavioral Interventions with Young Offenders*. New York: Pergamon.

Hollon, S. D., and Kriss, M. R. (1984). Cognitive factors in clinical research and practice. *Clinical Psychology Review* 4:35–76.

Holt, R. R. (1964). The emergence of cognitive psychology. *Journal of the American Psychoanalytic Association* 12:650–665.

Horowitz, M. J., ed. (1988). *Psychodynamics and Cognition*. Chicago: University of Chicago Press.

Hughes, J. N. (1988). *Cognitive Behavior Therapy with Children in Schools*. New York: Pergamon.

Izard, C. E. (1977). *Human emotions*. New York: Plenum.

——— (1978). On the ontogenesis of emotions and emotion-cognitive relationships in infancy. In *The Development of Affect*, ed. M. Lewis and L. A. Rosenblum, pp. 389–414. New York: Plenum.

——— (1982). Comments on emotions and cognition: Can there be a working relationship? In *Affect and Cognition*, ed. M. S. Clark and S. T. Fiske, pp. 229–242. Hillsdale, NJ: Erlbaum.

Izard, C. E., Kagan, J., and Zajonc, R. B. (1984). Introduction. In *Emotions, Cognition and Behaviors*, ed. C. E. Izard, J. Kagan, and R. B. Zajonc, pp. 1–14. Cambridge, MA: Cambridge University Press.

Jacobson, N. S. (1994). Behavior therapy and psychotherapy integration. *Journal of Psychotherapy Integration* 4:105–119.

Janoff-Bulman, R. (1995). Victims of violence. In *Psychotraumatology*, ed. G. S. Everly and J. M. Lating, pp. 73–86. New York: Plenum.

Johnson, M. (1987). *The Body in the Mind: The Bodily Basis of Meaning, Imagination and Reason*. Chicago: University of Chicago Press.

Johnson, M. E. (1993). A culturally sensitive approach to therapy with children. In *A Comprehensive Guide to Child Psychotherapy*, ed. C. Brems, pp. 68–73. Boston: Allyn and Bacon.

Jones, M. C. (1924). A laboratory study of fear: the case of Peter. *Pedagogical Seminary* 31:308–315.

Jung, C. G. (1952). *Symbols of Transformation*. New York: Bollingen Foundation.

Kagan, J. (1978). On emotion and its development: a working paper. In *The Development of Affect*, ed. M. Lewis and L. Rosenblum, pp. 11–41. New York: Plenum.

Kaplan, B. (1959). The study of language in psychiatry: the comparative developmental approach and its application to symbolization and language in psychopathology. In *American Handbook in Psychiatry*, Vol. 3, ed. S. Arieti. New York: Basic Books.

Katz, M. M., and Cole, J. O. (1965). Reflections on the major conference issue. In *The Role of Classification in Psychiatry and Psychopathology*, ed. M. M. Katz, J. O. Cole, and W. E. Barton, pp. 563–568. Chevy Chase, MD: U.S. Department of Health, Education and Welfare.

Katz, M. M., Cole, J. O., and Barton, W. E., eds. (1965). *The Role and Methodology of Classification in Psychiatry and Psychopathology.* Chevy Chase, MD: U.S. Department of Health, Education and Welfare.

Kay, P. (1972). Psychoanalytic theory of development in childhood and pre-adolescence. In *Handbook of Child Psychoanalysis*, ed. B. B. Wolman, pp. 53–142. New York: Van Nostrand Reinhold.

Kazdin, A. E. (1988). *Child Psychotherapy: Developing and Identifying Effective Treatments.* Elmsford, NY: Pergamon.

——— (1989). Developmental psychopathology: current research, issues and direction. *American Psychologist* 44:180–187.

Kazdin, A. E., Bass, D., Ayers, W. A., and Rodgers, A. (1990). Empirical and clinical focus of child and adolescent psychotherapy. *Journal of Consulting and Clinical Psychology* 58:729–740.

Kazdin, A. E., Bass, D., Siegel, T., and Thomas, C. (1989). Cognitive-behavioral therapy and relationship therapy in the treatment of children referred for antisocial behavior. *Journal of Consulting and Clinical Psychology* 57:522–535.

Kazdin, A. E., Siegel, T. C., and Bass, D. (1990). Drawing on clinical practice to inform research on child and adolescent psychotherapy: survey of practitioners. *Professional Psychology: Research and Practice* 21:189–198.

Kelly, G. A. (1965). The role of classification in personality theory. In *The Role and Methodology of Classification in Psychiatry and Psychopathology*, ed. M. Katz, J. O. Cole, and W. E. Barton, pp. 155–162. Chevy Chase, MD: U.S. Department of Health, Education and Welfare.

Kendall, P. C., and Braswell, L. (1985). *Cognitive-Behavioral Therapy for Impulsive Children.* New York: Guilford.

Kendall, P. C., and Hollon, S. D., eds. (1979). *Cognitive-Behavioral Interventions: Theory, Research and Procedures.* New York: Academic Press.

Kendall, P. C., and Morison, P. (1984). Integrating cognitive behavioral procedures for the treatment of socially isolated children. In *Cognitive Behavior Therapy with Children*, ed. A. W. Meyers and W. E. Craighead, pp. 261–288. New York: Plenum.

Kendall, P. C., Ronan, K. R., and Epps, J. (1991). Aggression in children/adolescents: cognitive behavioral treatment perspectives. In *The Development and Treatment of Childhood Aggression*, ed. K. Rapler and K. H. Rubin, pp. 341–360. Hillsdale, NJ: Erlbaum.

Kennedy, H. (1979). The role of insight in child analysis: a developmental viewpoint. *Journal of the American Psychoanalytic Society* 27:9–29.

Kepner, J. I. (1987). *Body Process: Working with the Body in Psychotherapy.* San Francisco: Jossey-Bass.

Klein, G. S. (1951). The personal world through perception. In *Perception: An Approach to Personality*, ed. R. R. Blake and G. V. Ramsey, pp. 328–355. New York: Ronald Press.

———— (1954). Need and regulation. In *Nebraska Symposium on Motivation*, ed. M. R. Jones. Lincoln: University of Nebraska Press.

———— (1970). *Perception, Motives, and Personality.* New York: Knopf.

———— (1976). *Psychoanalytic Theory: An Exploration of Essentials.* New York: International Universities Press.

Klein, G. S., and Schlesinger, H. J. (1949). Where is the perceiver in perceptual therapy? *Journal of Personality* 18:32–47.

Knapp, P. H. (1988). Steps toward a lexicon: discussion of "unconsciously determined defensive strategies." In *Psychodynamics and Cognition*, ed. M. J. Horowitz, pp. 95–114. Chicago: University of Chicago Press.

Knell, S. M. (1995). *Cognitive-Behavioral Play Therapy.* Northvale, NJ: Jason Aronson.

Kohlenberg, R. J., and Tsai, M. (1994). Functional analytic psychotherapy: a radical behavioral approach to treatment and integration. *Journal of Psychotherapy Integration* 4:175–201.

Kohut, H. (1977). *The Restoration of the Self.* New York: International Universities Press.

Kottman, T., and Schaefer, C., eds. (1993). *Play Therapy in Action: A Casebook for Practitioners.* Northvale, NJ: Jason Aronson.

Kramer, S., and Akhtar, S., eds. (1992). *When the Body Speaks: Psychological Meanings in Kinetic Clues.* Northvale, NJ: Jason Aronson.

Kruger, D. W. (1990). Developmental and psychodynamic perspectives on body-image change. In *Body Images: Development, Deviance and Change*, ed. T. F. Cash and T. Pruzinsky, pp. 255–271. New York: Guilford.

Kuhn, T. S. (1962). *The Structure of Scientific Revolutions.* Chicago: University of Chicago Press.

———— (1977). *The Essential Tension.* Chicago: University of Chicago Press.

Labouvie-Vief, G. (1990). Wisdom as integrated thought: historical and developmental perspectives. In *Wisdom: Its Nature, Origins, and Development*, ed. R. J. Steinberg, pp. 52–83. New York: Cambridge University Press.

Lakoff, G. (1987). *Women, Fire and Dangerous Things: What Categories Reveal about the Mind.* Chicago: University of Chicago Press.

Lazarus, A. A. (1967). In support of technical eclecticism. *Psychological Reports* 21:415–416.

———— (1976). *Multi-Modal Behavior Therapy.* New York: Springer.

———— (1981). *The Practice of Multimodal Therapy.* New York: McGraw-Hill.

———— (1995). Different types of eclecticism and integration: let's be aware of the dangers. *Journal of Psychotherapy Integration* 5:27–40.

Lear, J. (1990). *Love and Its Place in Nature: A Philosophical Interpretation of Freudian Psychoanalysis.* New York: Farrar, Straus & Giroux.

Leventhal, H. (1982). The integration of emotion and cognition: a view from perceptual-motor theory of emotion. In *Affect and Cognition*, ed. M. S. Clark and S. T. Fiske, pp. 121–156. Hillsdale, NJ: Erlbaum.

Lewis, M. (1977). Language, cognitive development, and personality. *Journal of the American Academy of Child Psychiatry* 16:646–661.

Lewis, M., and Rosenblum, L. A. (1978). Preface. In *The Development of Affect*, ed. M. Lewis and L. A. Rosenblum, pp. vii–ix. New York: Plenum.

Lichtenberg, J. D. (1983). *Psychoanalysis and Infant Research.* Hillsdale, NJ: Erlbaum.

Lindzey, G. (1952). TAT: Interpretive assumptions and related empirical evidence. *Psychological Bulletin* 49:1–25.

Lindzey, G., and Tejessy, C. (1956). TAT: Indices of aggression in relation to measures of overt and covert behaviors. *American Journal of Orthopsychiatry* 26:567–576.

London, P. (1964). *The Modes and Morals of Psychotherapy.* New York: Holt, Rinehart & Winston.

Lulgendorf, S. K., Antoni, M. H., and Kumer, M. (1994). Changes in cognitive coping strategies predict EBV-antibody titer change following a stressor. *Journal of Psychosomatic Research* 38:63–78.

Magnusson, D. (1981). *Toward a Psychology of Situations.* Hillsdale, NJ: Erlbaum.

Mahl, G. F. (1987). *Explorations in Nonverbal and Vocal Behavior.* Hillsdale, NJ: Erlbaum.

Mahler, M. (1979). *Selected Papers of Margaret S. Mahler.* New York: Jason Aronson.

Mahoney, M. J. (1974). *Cognition and Behavior Modification.* Cambridge, MA: Ballinger.

———, ed. (1980). *Psychotherapy Process: Current Issues and Future Directions.* New York: Plenum.

——— (1984). Psychoanalysis and behaviorism: the ying and yang of determinism. In *Psychoanalytic Therapy and Behavior Therapy: Is Integration Possible?*, ed. H. Arkowitz and S. B. Messer, pp. 303–334. New York: Plenum.

——— (1985). Psychotherapy and human change processes. In *Cognition and Psychotherapy*, ed. M. J. Mahoney and A. Freeman, pp. 3–48. New York: Plenum.

——— (1993). Diversity and the dynamics of development in psychotherapy integration. *Journal of Psychotherapy Integration* 3:1–13.

——— (1995a). Theoretical developments in cognitive psychotherapies. In *Cognitive and Constructive Psychotherapies. Theory, Research, and Practice*, ed. M. J. Mahoney, pp. 3–19. New York: Springer.

——— (1995b). *Cognitive and Constructive Psychotherapies: Theory, Research, and Practice.* New York: Springer.

Mandler, G. (1982). The structure of value: accounting for taste. In *Affect and Cognition*, ed. M. S. Clark and S. T. Fiske, pp. 3–36. Hillsdale, NJ: Erlbaum.

Marmor, J., and Woods, S. M., eds. (1980). *The Interface between the Psychodynamic and Behavioral Therapies*. New York: Plenum.

Masling, J. M., and Bornstein, R. F., eds. (1994). *Empirical Perspectives on Object Relations Theory*. Washington, DC: American Psychological Association.

Matson, J. L., and Ollendick, T. H. (1988). *Enhancing Children's Social Skills: Assessment and Training*. New York: Pergamon.

McCleary, R., and Lazarus, R. S. (1949). Autonomic discrimination without awareness. *Journal of Personality* 18:171–179.

McMullin, R. E. (1986). *Handbook of Cognitive Therapy Techniques*. New York: Norton.

Megargee, E. D. (1965). Relations between barrier scores and aggressive behavior. *Journal of Abnormal Psychology* 70:307–311.

Meichenbaum, D. (1977). *Cognitive-Behavior Modification: An Integrative Approach*. New York: Plenum.

—— (1995). Changing conceptions of cognitive behavior modification: retrospect and prospect. In *Cognitive and Constructive Psychotherapies: Theory, Research, and Practice*, ed. M. J. Mahoney, pp. 20–26. New York: Springer.

Melamed, B. G., Klingman, A., and Siegel, L. J. (1984). Childhood stress and anxiety: individualizing cognitive behavioral strategies in the reduction of medical and dental stress. In *Cognitive Behavior Therapy with Children*, ed. A. W. Meyers and W. E. Craighead, pp. 289–314. New York: Plenum.

Mendelsohn, E., and Silverman, L. H. (1984). The activation of unconscious fantasies in behavioral treatments. In *Psychoanalytic Therapy and Behavior Therapy: Is Integration Possible?*, ed. H. Arkowitz and S. B. Messer, pp. 255–294. New York: Plenum.

Messer, S. B., and Winokur, M. (1984). Ways of knowing and visions of reality in psychoanalytic therapy and behavior therapy. In *Psychoanalytic Therapy and Behavioral Therapy: Is Integration Possible?*, ed. H. Arkowitz and S. B. Messer, pp. 63–100. New York: Plenum.

Meyers, A. W., and Craighead, W. E. (1984). Cognitive behavior with children: a historical, conceptual and organizational overview. In *Cognitive Behavior Therapy with Children*, ed. A. W. Meyers and W. E. Craighead, pp. 1–17. New York: Plenum.

Miller, J. G. (1951). Unconscious processes and perception. In *Perception: An Approach to Personality*, ed. R. R. Blake and G. V. Ramsey, pp. 258–282. New York: Ronald Press.

Mitchell, S. A. (1988). *Relational Concepts in Psychoanalysis: An Integration*. Cambridge, MA: Harvard University Press.

—— (1994). Recent developments in psychoanalytic theorizing. *Journal of Psychotherapy Integration* 4:93–103.

Mounoud, P. (1982). Revolutionary periods in early development. In *Regressions in Mental Development*, ed. T. G. Bever, pp. 119–132. Hillsdale, NJ: Erlbaum.

Mowrer, O. H. (1960). *Learning Theory and Behavior*. New York: Wiley.

Muran, J. C., and DiGiuseppe, R. A. (1990). Towards a cognitive formulation of metaphor use in psychotherapy. *Clinical Psychology Review* 10:69–85.

Murray, H. A. (1960). Historical trends in personality research. In *Perspectives in Personality Research*, ed. H. P. David and J. C. Brenglemann, pp. 3–39. New York: Springer.

Nagel, E. (1957). Determinism and development. In *The Concept of Development: An Issue in the Study of Human Behavior*, ed. D. B. Harris. Minneapolis: University of Minnesota Press.

Nannis, E. D. (1988). A cognitive-developmental view of emotional understanding and the implications for child psychotherapy. In *Cognitive Development and Child Psychotherapy*, ed. S. R. Shirk, pp. 91–115. New York: Plenum.

Neisser, V. (1976). *Cognition and Reality: Principles and Implications of Cognitive Psychology*. San Francisco: Freeman.

Norcross, J. C., and Goldfried, M. R., eds. (1992). *Handbook of Psychotherapy Integration*. New York: Basic Books.

O'Connor, K. (1993). Child, protector, confidant: structured group ecosystemic play therapy. In *Play Therapy in Action*, ed. T. Kottman and C. Schaefer, pp. 245–280. New York: Jason Aronson.

Ogden, T. H. (1979). On projective identification. *International Journal of Psychoanalysis* 60:357–373.

Ohlmann, T., and Marendez, C. (1991). Vicarious processes involved in selection/control of frames of reference and spatial aspects of field dependence-independence. In *Field Dependence-Independence: Cognitive Style across the Life Span*, ed. S. Wapner and J. Demick, pp. 105–130. Hillsdale, NJ: Erlbaum.

Orlinsky, D. E., and Howard, K. I. (1987). A genetic model of psychotherapy. *Journal of Integrative and Eclectic Psychotherapy* 6:6–27.

Ortony, A., ed. (1979). *Metaphor and Thought*. New York: Cambridge University Press.

Ortony, A., Reynolds, R. E., and Arter, J. A. (1978). Metaphor: theoretical and empirical research. *Psychological Bulletin* 85:919–943.

Ottenson, J. P., and Holzman, P. S. (1976). Cognitive controls and psychopathology. *Journal of Abnormal Psychology* 85:125–139.

Overton, W. F. (1994). The arrow of time and the cycle of time: concepts of change, cognition, and embodiment. *Psychological Inquiry* 5:215–237.

——— (1997a, in press). Developmental psychology: philosophy, concepts and methodology. In *Theoretical Models of Human Development*, ed. R. M. Lerner, 5th ed.

——— (1997b, in press). Relational-developmental theory: a psychological perspective. In *Children, Cities and Psychological Theories: Developing Relation-*

ships, ed. D. Gorlitz, H. J. Harloff, J. Valsiner, and G. Mey. New York: de Gruyter.

Overton, W. F., and Horowitz, H. A. (1991). Developmental psychopathology: integrations and differentiations. In *Rochester Symposium on Developmental Psychopathology, Vol. 3: Models and Integration*, ed. D. Cicchetti and S. L. Toth, pp. 1–42. Rochester, NY: University of Rochester Press.

Paivio, A. (1975). Neomentalism. *Canadian Journal of Psychology* 29:263–291.

Pearson, G. H. (1968). *A Handbook of Child Psychoanalysis*. New York: Basic Books.

Piaget, J. (1952). *The Origins of Intelligence in Children*. New York: Norton.

——— (1967). *Six Psychological Studies*. New York: Random House.

——— (1973). The affective unconscious and the cognitive unconscious. *Journal of the American Psychoanalytic Association* 21:249–266.

——— (1975). Foreword. In *Explorations in Child Psychiatry*, ed. E. J. Anthony, pp. vii–ix. New York: Plenum.

——— (1977). The role of action in the development of thinking. In *Knowledge and Development*, ed. W. F. Overton and J. M. Gallagher, pp. 17–42. New York: Plenum.

——— (1981). *Intelligence and Affectivity: Their Relationship during Child Development*. Palo Alto, CA: Annual Reviews.

Pruzinsky, T. (1990). Somatopsychic approaches to psychotherapy and personal growth. In *Body Images: Development, Deviance and Change*, ed. T. F. Cash and T. Pruzinsky, pp. 296–315. New York: Guilford.

Psychoanalytic Psychology (vol. 12, no. 1) (1995). Special section: Contemporary structural psychoanalysis and relational psychoanalysis.

Pynoos, R. S., Steinberg, A. M., and Goenjian, A. (1996). Traumatic stress in childhood and adolescence: recent developments and current controversies. In *Traumatic Stress: The Effects of Overwhelming Experience on Mind, Body, and Society*, ed. B. A. van der Kolk, A. C. McFarlane, and L. Weisaeth, pp. 331–358. New York: Guilford.

Rader, G. E. (1957). The prediction of overt aggressive verbal behavior from Rorschach content. *Journal of Prospective Techniques* 5:294–306.

Rapaport, D. (1960). Psychoanalysis as a developmental psychology. In *Perspectives in Psychological Theory*, ed. B. Kaplan and S. Wapner, pp. 209–255. New York: International Universities Press.

Read, P. B. (1984). Foreword. In *Emotions, Cognition and Behavior*, ed. C. E. Izard, J. Kagan, and R. B. Zajonc, pp. ix–x. Cambridge, MA: Cambridge University Press.

Reese, H. W., and Overton, W. F. (1970). Models of development and theories of development. In *Life Span Developmental Psychology*, ed. L. R. Goulet and P. B. Baltes, pp. 116–145. New York: Academic Press.

Reeve, J., Inck, T. A., and Safran, J. (1993). Toward an integration of cognitive, interpersonal, and experiential approaches to therapy. In *Comprehensive Hand-*

book of Psychotherapy Integration, ed. G. Stricker and J. R. Gold, pp. 113–124. New York: Plenum.

Reinecke, M. A., Dattilio, F. M., and Freeman, A., eds. (1996). *Cognitive Therapy with Children and Adolescents*. New York: Guilford.

Reisman, J. M. (1973). *Principles of Psychotherapy with Children*. New York: Wiley.

Rhoads, J. M. (1984). Relationships between psychodynamic and behavioral therapies. In *Psychoanalytic Therapy and Behavioral Therapy: Is an Integration Possible?*, ed. H. Arkowitz and S. B. Meiser, pp. 195–211. New York: Plenum.

Rieder, C., and Cicchetti, D. (1989). Organizational perspective in cognitive control functioning and cognitive affective balance in maltreated children. *Developmental Psychology* 25:382–393.

Rosenthal, R., Hall, J. A., Di Matteo, M. R., et al. (1979). *Sensitivity to Nonverbal Communication: The Pons Test*. Baltimore: Johns Hopkins University Press.

Rosenwald, G. C., Mendelsohn, G. A., Fontana, A., and Portz, A. T. (1966). An action test of hypothesis concerning the anal personality. *Journal of Abnormal Psychology* 71:304–309.

Royce, J. R. (1973). The conceptual framework for a multifactor theory of individuality. In *Multivariate Analysis and Psychological Theory*, ed. J. R. Royce, pp. 305–382. New York: Academic Press.

Safran, J. D. (1990a). Towards a refinement of cognitive therapy in light of interpersonal theory: I. Theory. *Clinical Psychology Review* 10:87–105.

——— (1990b). Towards a refinement of cognitive therapy in light of interpersonal theory: II. Practice. *Clinical Psychology Review* 10:107–121.

——— (1993). The therapeutic alliance rupture as a transtheoretical phenomenon: definitional and conceptual issues. *Journal of Psychotherapy Integration* 3:33–49.

Sander, L. W. (1962). Issues in early mother–child interaction. *Journal of the American Academy of Child Psychiatry* 3:141–166.

——— (1964). Adaptive relationships in early mother–child interaction. *Journal of the American Academy of Child Psychiatry* 3:231–264.

——— (1969). Regulation and organization in the early infant–caretaker system. In *Brian and Early Behavior*, ed. R. Robinson. London: Academic Press.

——— (1975). Infant and caretaking environment: investigation and conceptualization of adaptive behavior in a system of increasing complexity. In *Explorations in Child Psychiatry*, ed. E. J. Anthony, pp. 129–160. New York: Plenum.

——— (1976). Primary prevention and some aspects of temporal organization in early infant–caretaker interaction. In *Infant Psychiatry: A New Synthesis*, ed. E. Rexford, L. Sander, and T. Shapiro, pp. 156–175. New Haven, CT: Yale University Press.

——— (1987). A 25 year follow up: some reflections on personality development over the long term. *Infant Mental Health Journal* 8:210–220.

——— (1989). Investigations of the infant and its care giving environments as a biological system. In *The Course of Life* (2nd ed., ed. S. I. Greenspan and G. H. Pollack, pp. 359–391). Madison, WI: International Universities Press.

Santostefano, S. (1960a). An exploration of performance measures of personality. *Journal of Clinical Psychology* 6:373–377.

——— (1960b). Anxiety and hostility in stuttering. *Journal of Speech and Hearing Research* 3:337–347.

——— (1962a). Miniature situations test as a way of interviewing children. *Merrill-Palmer Quarterly of Behavior and Development* 8:261–269.

——— (1962b). Performance testing of personality. *Merrill-Palmer Quarterly of Behavior and Development* 8:83–97.

——— (1964a). A developmental study of the cognitive control leveling-sharpening. *Merrill-Palmer Quarterly of Behavior and Development* 10:343–360.

——— (1964b). Cognitive controls and exceptional states in children. *Journal of Clinical Psychology* 20:213–218.

——— (1965a). Construct validity of the Miniature Situations Test: I. The performance of public school, orphaned and brain-damaged children. *Journal of Clinical Psychology* 21:418–421.

——— (1965b). Relating self-report and overt behavior: the concepts of levels of modes for expressing motives. *Perceptual Motor Skills* 21:940.

——— (1967). *Training in Attention and Concentration: A Program of Cognitive Development for Children.* Philadelphia: Educational Research Associates, Inc.

——— (1968a). Miniature situations and methodological problems in parent–child interaction research. *Merrill-Palmer Quarterly of Behavior and Development* 14:285–312.

——— (1968b). Situational testing in personality assessment. In *International Encyclopedia of the Social Sciences*, ed. D. L. Sills, pp. 48–55. New York: Macmillan and Free Press.

——— (1969a). *Clinical Education and Psychoanalytic Cognitive Theory: A Structure-Oriented Approach to Assessing and Treating Cognitive Disabilities in Children.* Paper presented at the meeting of the American Association of the Advancement of Science, Chicago, December.

——— (1969b). Cognitive controls versus cognitive styles: an approach to diagnosing and treating cognitive disabilities in children. In *Seminars in Psychiatry*, pp. 291–317. Also in S. Chess and A. Thomas, eds., *Annual Progress in Child Psychiatry and Child Development.* New York: Brunner/Mazel.

——— (1970). Assessment of motives in children. *Psychological Reports* 26:639–649.

——— (1976a). On the relation between research and practice in psychiatry and psychology: the laboratory of the McLean Hospital, 1889. *McLean Hospital Journal* 1:120–129.

——— (1976b). Shepherd Ivory Franz: the father of research for clinical practice. *McLean Hospital Journal* 1:49–55.

——— (1976c). Tell me the first word that comes to mind: the free association method and the concept of levels of expressing motives. *McLean Hospital Journal* 1:174–189.

——— (1977). Action, fantasy and language: developmental levels of ego organization in communicating drives and affects. In *Communicative Structures and Psychic Structures*, ed. N. Freedman and S. Grand, pp. 331–356. New York: Plenum.

——— (1978). *A Biodevelopmental Approach to Clinical Child Psychology Cognitive Controls and Cognitive Control Therapy*. New York: Wiley.

——— (1980a). Clinical child psychology: the need for developmental principles. *New Directions for Child Development* 7:1–19.

——— (1980b). Cognition in personality and the treatment process: a psychoanalytic view. *Psychoanalytic Study of the Child* 35:41–66.

——— (1985a). *Cognitive Control Therapy with Children and Adolescents*. New York: Pergamon.

——— (1985b). Metaphor: an integration of action, fantasy, and language in development. *Imagination, Cognition and Personality* 4:127–146.

——— (1986). Cognitive controls, metaphors and contexts: an approach to cognition and emotion. In *Thought and Emotion*, ed. D. Bearison and H. Zimiles, pp. 175–210. Hillsdale, NJ: Erlbaum.

——— (1988a). *The Cognitive Control Battery*. Los Angeles: Western Psychological Services.

——— (1988b). Process and change in child therapy and development: the concept of metaphor. In *Organizing Early Experience: Imagination and Cognition in Childhood*, ed. D. Morrison, pp. 139–172. Amityville, NY: Baywood.

——— (1991a). Cognitive style as process coordinating outer space with inner self: lessons from the past. In *Field Dependence-Independence: Bio-Psycho-Social Factors across the Lifespan*, ed. S. Wapner and J. Demick, pp. 269–286. Los Angeles: Erlbaum.

——— (1991b). Coordinating outer space with inner self: reflections on developmental psychopathology. In *Constructivist Perspectives on Developmental Psychopathology and Atypical Development*, ed. D. P. Keating and H. Rosen, pp. 11–40. Hillsdale, NJ: Erlbaum.

——— (1992a). *The action test of body image: manual of instructions and scoring*. (Unpublished manuscript.)

——— (1992b). *Life stressor interview: manual of instructions and scoring*. (Unpublished manuscript.)

——— (1992c). The leveling-sharpening friends, shoot-out and trauma tests: manual of instructions and scoring. (Unpublished manuscript.)

——— (1994). The arrow of time and developmental psychopathology. *Psychological Inquiry* 5:248–253.

——— (1995a). *Integrative Psychotherapy for Children and Adolescents with ADHD* (revised ed.). Northvale, NJ: Jason Aronson.

——— (1995b). Embodied meanings, cognition and emotion: probing how three are one. In *Rochester Symposium on Developmental Psychopathology. Vol. 6. Emotion, Cognition and Representation*, ed. D. Cicchetti and S. L. Toth, pp. 59–132. Rochester, NY: University of Rochester Press.

———— (In Press). Cycles in the life of one psychotherapist. In *Becoming a Psychotherapist*, ed. J. Reppen. New York: Psychoanalytic Books.

Santostefano, S., and Baker, H. (1972). Research in child psychopathology: the contributions of developmental psychology. In *Manual of Child Psychopathology*, ed. B. B. Wolmann, pp. 1113–1153. New York: McGraw-Hill.

Santostefano, S., and Moncata, S. (1989). A psychoanalytic view of cognition within personality: cognitive dysfunction and educating troubled youth. *Residential Treatment for Children and Youth* 6:41–62.

Santostefano, S., and Rieder, C. (1984). Cognitive controls and aggression in children: the concept of cognitive-affective balance. *Journal of Consulting and Clinical Psychology* 52:46–56.

Santostefano, S., Rieder, C., and Berk, S. (1984). The structure of fantasized movement in suicidal children and adolescents. *Journal of Suicide and Life-Threatening Behavior* 14:3–16.

Santostefano, S., and Stayton, S. (1967). Training the pre-school retarded child in focal attention: a program for parents. *American Journal of Orthopsychiatry* 37:732–743.

Santostefano, S., and Wilson, S. (1968). Construct validity of the Miniature Situations Test: II. The performance of institutionalized delinquents and public school adolescents. *Journal of Clinical Psychology* 24:355–358.

Schacht, T. E. (1984). The varieties of integrative experience. In *Psychoanalytic and Behavior Therapy: Is Integration Possible?*, ed. H. Arkowitz and S. B. Messer, pp. 107–132. New York: Plenum.

Schaefer, C. E., and Cangelosi, D. M., eds. (1993). *Play Therapy Techniques*. Northvale, NJ: Jason Aronson.

Scherer, K. R., and Ekman, P., eds. (1982). *Handbook of Methods in Nonverbal Research*. New York: Cambridge University Press.

Schneider, S. F. (1990). Psychology at a crossroad. *American Psychologist* 45:521–529.

Sechrest, L., and Smith, B. (1994). Psychotherapy is the practice of psychology. *Journal of Psychotherapy Integration* 4:1–29.

Shakow, D. (1965). The role of classification in the development of science of psychopathology. In *The Role and Methodology of Classifications in Psychiatry and Psychotherapy*, ed. M. Katz, B. Cole, and W. E. Burton, pp. 116–142. Chevy Chase, MD: U.S. Department of Health, Education and Welfare.

Shapiro, E. K., and Weber, E. (1981). Preface. In *Cognitive and Affective Growth: Developmental Interaction*, ed. E. K. Shapiro and E. Weber, pp. vii–viii. Hillsdale, NJ: Erlbaum.

Shevrin, H., and Dickman, S. (1980). The psychological unconscious: a necessary assumption for all psychological theory? *American Psychologist* 35:421–434.

Shilder, P. (1950). *The Image and Appearance of the Human Body*. New York: International Universities Press, 1935.

Shirk, S. R. (1988). Casual reasoning and children's comprehension of therapeutic interpretations. In *Cognitive Development and Child Psychotherapy*, ed. S. R. Shirk, pp. 53–89. New York: Plenum.

Shontz, F. C. (1990). Body image and physical disability. In *Body Images: Developmental, Deviance and Change*, ed. T. F. Cash and T. Pruzinsky, pp. 149–169. New York: Guilford.

Siegel, M. G. (1989). *Psychological Testing from Early Childhood through Adolescence: A Developmental and Psychodynamic Approach.* Madison, CT: International Universities Press.

Silverman, M. A. (1978). The developmental profile. In *Child Analysis and Therapy*, ed. J. Glenn, pp. 107–127. New York: Jason Aronson.

Skinner, B. F. (1971). *Beyond Freedom and Dignity.* New York: Bantam Books.
——— (1974). *About Behaviorism.* New York: Knopf.

Smith, N. R. (1979). Developmental origins of structural variation in symbol formation. In *Symbolic Functioning in Children*, ed. N. R. Smith and M. B. Franklin, pp. 11–26. Hillsdale, NJ: Erlbaum.

Smith, N. R., and Franklin, M. B., eds. (1979). *Symbolic Functioning in Children.* Hillsdale, NJ: Erlbaum.

Sollod, R. N., and Wachtel, P. L. (1980). A structural and transactional approach to cognition and clinical problems. In *Psychotherapy Process: Current Issues and Future Directions*, ed. M. J. Mahoney, pp. 1–28. New York: Plenum.

Spicker, S. M., ed. (1970). *The Philosophy of the Body.* Chicago: Quadrangle.

Spiegel, S. (1989). *An Interpersonal Approach to Child Therapy: The Treatment of Children and Adolescents from an Interpersonal Point of View.* New York: Columbia University Press.

Stern, D. N. (1985). *The Interpersonal World of the Infant: A View from Psychoanalysis and Developmental Psychology.* New York: Basic Books.

Stern, K. (1965). *The Flight from Woman.* New York: Randy Press.

Stolorow, R. D., and Lachmann, F. M. (1980). *Psychoanalysis of Developmental Arrest: Theory and Treatment.* New York: International Universities Press.

Stoops, J. W. (1974). *The assessment of aggression in children: arguments for a multimodal approach.* Unpublished doctoral dissertation, Kent State University, Kent, OH.

Stricker, G. (1994). Psychotherapy, psychology and science. *Journal of Psychotherapy Integration* 4:21–38.

Stricker, G., and Gold, J. R., eds. (1993). *Comprehensive Handbook of Psychotherapy Integration.* New York: Plenum.

Strupp, H. (1973). On the basic ingredients of psychotherapy. *Journal of Counseling and Clinical Psychology* 41:1–8.
——— (1986a). The nonspecific hypotheses of therapeutic effectiveness. *American Journal of Orthopsychiatry* 56:513–520.
——— (1986b). Psychotherapy: research, practice and public policy (how to avoid dead ends). *American Psychologist* 41:120–130.

Sullivan, H. S. (1953). *The Interpersonal Theory of Psychiatry.* New York: Norton.

Temkin, O. (1965). The history of classification in the medical sciences. In *The Role and Methodology of Classification in Psychiatry and Psychopathology*, ed. M. Katz, J. O. Cole, and W. E. Marton, pp. 11–19. Chevy Chase, MD: U.S. Department of Health, Education and Welfare.

Thompson, S. C. (1981). Will it hurt less if I can control it? A complex answer to a simple question. *Psychological Bulletin* 90:89–101.

Thompson, J. K., Penner, L. A., and Altabe, M. N. (1990). Procedures, problems and progress in the assessment of body images. In *Body Images: Development, Deviance and Change*, ed. T. F. Cash and T. Pruzinsky, pp. 21–50. New York: Guilford.

Tiemersma, D. (1989). *Body Schema and Body Image*. Amsterdam/Lisse: Swets and Zeitlinger.

Tuber, S., Frank, M. A., and Santostefano, S. (1989). Children's anticipation of impending surgery. *Bulletin of the Menninger Clinic* 53:501–511.

Valenstein, A. F. (1983). Working through and resistance to change: insight and the action system. *Journal of the American Psychoanalytic Association* 31:353–373.

Verbrugge, R. R., and McCarrell, N. S. (1977). Metaphoric comprehension: studies in reminding and resembling. *Cognitive Psychology* 9:454–533.

von Bertalanffy, L. (1962). *Modern Theories of Development*. New York: Harper Torch Books. The Science Library, 1928.

Wachtel, P. L. (1977). *Psychoanalysis and Behavior Therapy: Toward an Integration*. New York: Basic Books.

———, ed. (1982). *Resistance: Psychodynamics and Behavioral Approaches*. New York: Plenum.

——— (1984). On theory, practice and the nature of integration. In *Psychoanalytic and Behavior Therapy: Is Integration Possible?*, ed. H. Arkowitz and S. B. Messer, pp. 31–52. New York: Plenum.

——— (1987). *Action and Insight*. New York: Guilford.

——— (1994). Behavior and experience: allies, not adversaries. *Journal of Psychotherapy Integration* 4:121–132.

Wapner, S., and Demick, J., eds. (1991). *Field Dependence-Independence: Cognitive Style across the Life Span*. Hillsdale, NJ: Erlbaum.

Wapner, S., and Werner, H., eds. (1965). *The Body Perfect*. New York: Random House.

Watzlawick, P., Weakland, J., and Fisch, R. (1974). *Change: Principle of Problem Formation and Problem Resolution*. New York: Norton.

Weimer, W. B. (1980). Psychotherapy and the philosophy of science. In *Psychotherapy Process: Current Issues and Future Directions*, ed. J. M. Mahoney, pp. 369–393. New York: Plenum.

Weiner, M. L. (1975). *The Cognitive Unconscious: A Piagetian Approach to Psychotherapy*. New York: International Psychological Press.

——— (1985). *Cognitive-Experiential Therapy: An Integrative Ego Psychotherapy*. New York: Brunner/Mazel.

Weisz, J. R., Suwanlert, S., Chaiyasit, W., and Walter, B. R. (1987a). Over- and under-controlled referral problems among children and adolescents from Thailand and the United States. *Journal of Consulting and Clinical Psychology* 55:719–726.

Weisz, J. R., and Weiss, B. (1993). *Effects of Psychotherapy with Children and Adolescents.* Newbury Park, CA: Sage.

Weisz, J. R., Weiss, B., Alicke, M. D., and Klotz, M. L. (1987b). Effectiveness of psychotherapy with children and adolescents. *Journal of Consulting and Clinical Psychology* 55:542–549.

Weitz, S., ed. (1979). *Nonverbal Communication: Readings and Commentary.* New York: Oxford University Press.

Wells, F. L. (1911). Some properties of the free association method. *Psychological Review* 18:1–23.

——— (1912). The association experiment. *Psychological Bulletin* 9:435–438.

——— (1914). Professor Cattell's relation to the Association method. *Columbia Contributions to Philosophy and Psychology* 22:46–59.

Werner, H. (1948). *Comparative Psychology of Mental Development.* New York: International Universities Press.

——— (1949). Introductory remarks. *Journal of Personality* 18:2–5.

——— (1957). The concept of development from a comparative and organismic point of view. In *The Concept of Development: An Issue on the Study of Human Behavior*, ed. D. B. Harris, pp. 125–148. Minneapolis: University of Minnesota Press.

——— (1964). *Comparative Psychology of Mental Development,* rev. ed. New York: International Universities Press.

Werner, H., and Kaplan, B. (1963). *Symbol Formation: An Organismic-Developmental Approach to Language and the Expression of Thought.* New York: Wiley.

Werner, H., and Wapner, S. (1949). Sensory tonic field theory of perception. *Journal of Personality* 18:88–107.

Wertlieb, D. L. (1979). *Cognitive organization, regulations of aggression and learning disorders in boys.* Unpublished doctoral dissertation, Boston University.

White, S. H. (1991). The child as agent: issues of cognitive style and personal design in human development. In *Field Dependence-Independence: Cognitive Style across the Life Span*, ed. S. Wapner and J. Demick, pp. 7–25. Hillsdale, NJ: Erlbaum.

Whitman, T., Burgio, L., and Johnson, M. B. (1984). Cognitive behavioral interventions with mentally retarded children. In *Cognitive Behavior Therapy with Children*, ed. A. W. Meyers and W. E. Craighead, pp. 193–228. New York: Plenum.

Wigren, J. (1994). Narrative completion in the treatment of trauma. *Psychotherapy* 31:415–423.

Wilber, K. (1977). *The Spectrum of Consciousness.* London: Theosophical Publishing House.

——— (1979). *No Boundary: Eastern and Western Approaches to Personal Growth.* Boston: Shambhala Publishing.

Winnicott, D. W. (1971). *Therapeutic Consultations in Child Psychiatry.* New York: Basic Books.

Witkin, H. A. (1949). The nature and importance of individual differences in perception. *Journal of Personality* 18:145–170.

Witmer, L. (1908). The treatment and care of a case of a mental and moral deficiency. *The Psychological Clinic* 2:153–179.

Witzum, E., van der Hart, O., and Friedman, B. (1988). The use of metaphors in psychotherapy. *Journal of Contemporary Psychotherapy* 18:270–290.

Wohlwil, J. F. (1973). *The Study of Behavioral Development.* New York: Academic Press.

Wolf, D., and Gardner, H. (1979). Style and sequence in early symbolic play. In *Symbolic Functioning in Childhood*, ed. N. R. Smith and M. B. Franklin, pp. 117–138. Hillsdale, NJ: Erlbaum.

Wolff, P. (1960). The developmental psychologies of Jean Piaget and psychoanalysis. *Psychological Issues* 2(5), whole issue.

Wolman, B. B. (1972). Psychoanalytic theory of infantile development. In *Handbook of Child Psychoanalysis*, ed. B. B. Wolman, pp. 3–52. New York: Van Nostrand Reinhold.

——— , ed. (1982). *Handbook of Developmental Psychology.* Englewood Cliffs, NJ: Prentice Hall.

Wozniak, R. H. (1986). Notes toward a co-constructive theory of the emotion-cognition relationship. In *Thought and Emotion: Developmental Perspectives*, ed. D. J. Bearison and H. Zimiles, pp. 39–64. Hillsdale, NJ: Erlbaum.

Zajonc, R. B., and Markus, H. (1984). Affect and cognition: the hard interface. In *Emotion, Cognition, and Behavior*, ed. C. E. Izard, J. Kagan, and R. B. Zajonc, pp. 73–102. Cambridge: Cambridge University Press.

Zajonc, R. B., Pietromonaco, P., and Bargh, J. (1982). Independence and interaction of affect and cognition. In *Affect and Cognition*, ed. M. S. Clark and S. T. Fiske, pp. 211–227. Hillsdale, NJ: Erlbaum.

Zimmerman, B. J. (1983). Social learning theory: a contextualist account of cognitive functioning. In *Recent Advances in Cognitive-Developmental Theory*, ed. C. J. Brainerd, pp. 1–50. New York: Springer-Verlag.

Index

Child–therapist relationship (*continued*)
in integrative psychotherapy, 159
projective identification in, 319–320
in psychodynamic therapy, 81, 88
in radical behaviorism, 127
response to interpretations, 141–143
Cicchetti, D., 49–50, 113–114, 241, 464
Circular reactions, 199–201, 220
Clark, D. M., 530
Clark, M. S., 60
Cleveland, S. E., 57, 393
Clinical illustrations
of structured interactions, 345–415
of unstructured interactions, 419–458
Clinical populations
cognitive orientation in, 252–258
modes of expression in, 470–477
Clinically relevant behaviors (CRBs),
136–137
Coding systems, 57, 228, 435
and psychosexual stages, 79, 439, 455
Cognition, 104–107. *See also* Modes of
expression
and body image, 57–58
development of, 164, 165, 170–171,
175–178
differentiation of, 170–171
embedded in relationship, 341–342
and emotion, 58–61, 111–121, 484–489
and life metaphors, 226–227, 229–230
and personality, 106, 157, 531
in regulation, self- and mutual, 46
relation to other modes of expression,
53, 102–111
in self- and mutual regulation, 230–258
slips of, 480, 481, 483
in therapies
cognitive-behavioral, 108–110
integrative, 110–111, 157
psychodynamic, 107–108
unconscious, 106
vs. knowledge, 40–54
Cognitive control mechanisms, 232–233,
236–239, 251
Cognitive functioning, 48, 151, 291, 425
autonomy of, 245–246
dysfunctions, 234–235
relation to body-based meanings, 500–
506, 513–519
relation to fears, 506–509, 513–519
relationship to stressors, 516–517

Cognitive mechanisms, in clinical
populations, 252–253
Cognitive mediators, 48, 127, 146
changing, 72–73, 103, 325
in cognitive-behavioral therapy, 65, 124
in social learning theory, 46–47
Cognitive orientation, 242–252, 258, 273,
303, 425
flexibility or rigidity in, 291, 295–296,
325–328
inner, 289, 379
pathological, 253–258, 288–289
psychological testing on, 288–289,
475–476
shifts in, 289, 328, 336–337, 426
Cognitive products. *See* Cognitive
structures
Cognitive regulators, 273, 327, 478
in clinical illustrations, 364–367, 379,
392, 394, 438–439
development of, 236–242, 260
field articulation, 500–503, 506–511
leveling-sharpening, 484–489,
494–495, 503–506, 509, 511–513
and stressors, 517
Cognitive slips, 494
Cognitive structures, 118, 120–121, 127,
157, 234, 239, 245, 534
Cognitive style, 111–112, 364
organismic theory of, 515–516
Cognitive tempos, and body tempos,
477–483
Cognitive therapy, 4, 65
Cognitive-behavioral therapy, 101, 283
based in objectivism, 65–77
changes in, 524, 529–530
in comparison of approaches, 22–34
developmental principles in, 146–148
emotion and cognition in, 108–110,
118–120
environment in, 129–130
meaning in, 123–125, 529–530
overlap with psychodynamic, 19–20, 76
patient-therapist relationship in, 135–
137, 138–139
role of therapist in, 17–19
tasks in, 315, 324–325
techniques in, 69–77, 118–119, 129,
147
unconscious processes in, 125–128,
130–132, 531–533

About the Author

Since 1992, Dr. Sebastiano Santostefano has been Director of The Institute for Child and Adolescent Development, Inc., a nonprofit organization established to provide programs in the community that serve children and their families who have witnessed tragedies and endured major life stressors. The Institute also provides training to mental health professionals and conducts research on the effects of life stressors on body image and cognitive and emotional development.

From 1972 to 1992 he served as Director, Department of Child and Adolescent Psychology and Psychoeducation, Hall-Mercer Children's Center of McLean Hospital, as well as Associate Professor of Psychology, Department of Psychiatry, of the Harvard Medical School. He continues to be a member of the teaching faculty of the Boston Psychoanalytic Institute.

In 1957 Dr. Santostefano received his Ph.D. degree in clinical psychology from Pennsylvania State University and in 1972 was graduated in adult and child psychoanalysis by the Boston Psychoanalytic Institute. He has held faculty positions at the University of Colorado School of Medicine, Clark University, and Boston University School of Medicine.

Besides practicing clinical psychology and psychoanalysis, Dr. Santostefano has been an active investigator in the area of cognition in personality development and adaptation. His essay, "Cognition in Personality and the Treatment Process," published by the *Psychoanalytic Study of the Child* in 1980, was awarded the Felix and Helene Deutsch prize by the Boston Psychoanalytic Society, and the Harold S. Rosenberg Memorial Prize by the San Francisco Psychoanalytic Society. In 1968 The American Rehabilitation Association selected his published report "Training in Attention and Concentration: A Program for Parents" as one of the "top twenty" research reports. Dr. Santostefano is the author of many articles and four books that focus on research, assessment, and treatment of developmental psychopathology relying on the integration of psychoanalytic, developmental, cognitive, and behavioral concepts.